Cognitive Science

Cognitive Science.

The Science of Intelligent Systems

George F. Luger

with

Peder Johnson
Carl Stern
Jean E. Newman
Ronald Yeo

University of New Mexico
Albuquerque, New Mexico

ACADEMIC PRESS

San Diego   New York   Boston   London   Sydney   Tokyo   Toronto

Illustration and Text Credits: Sections 6.2, 6.3, and 6.4 are adapted from *Artificial Intelligence and the Design of Expert Systems* by George F. Luger and William A. Stubblefield. Copyright 1989 by Benjamin Cummings Publishing Company, Inc. Used with permission.

Chapter 10 and Section 12.4 are adapted from *Artificial Intelligence: Structures and Strategies for Complex Problem Solving* by George F. Luger and William A. Stubblefield. Copyright 1993 by Benjamin Cummings Publishing Company, Inc. Used with permission.

This book is printed on acid-free paper. ∞

Academic Press, Inc.
A Division of Harcourt Brace & Company
525 B Street, Suite 1900, San Diego, California 92101-4495

United Kingdom Edition published by
Academic Press Limited
24-28 Oval Road, London NW1 7DX

Library of Congress Cataloging-in-Publication Data

Luger, George F.
    Cognitive science : the science of intelligent systems / by George F. Luger.
       p.   cm.
    Includes bibliographical references and index.
    ISBN 0-12-459570-7
    1. Cognitive science. I. title.
  BF311.L84   1994
  153--dc20
                                          94-3150
                                          CIP

PRINTED IN THE UNITED STATES OF AMERICA
94 95 96 97 98 99 BB 9 8 7 6 5 4 3 2 1

This book is dedicated to Kathleen:
per libros liberosque in liberalitatem

Contents

Preface

Intelligence surrounds us. It is more than the occurrence of artistic and creative brilliance. It is present in the moment-to-moment adaptation of systems to complex environments. It is present in the recognition of patterns of energy, in the fine adjustments of motor movements to changes in physical orientation, and even in the retrieval of old memories. Do systems that are capable of exhibiting this behavior have something in common? If they do, what is it, and how might we describe it?

Computer software is becoming evermore sophisticated. The "smart" machine has arrived. Expert or knowledge based programs assist the human in all manner of problem solving. There are systems for diagnosing meningitis, eye disease, and many other illnesses. Programs troubleshoot assemblies of electronic components and keep satellites in orbit and functioning properly. They guide robots into dangerous domains and can create a *virtual* reality. What does it mean to have intelligence in a computing device? Can computers have intentions or exhibit purpose? Can computers learn new things or understand the meaning of sentences?

Just what is the nature of intelligence? Can intelligence exist outside the human person? Can it be described by a set of abstract laws? What is consciousness and what is its relationship to intelligence? What is perception and how can abstract concepts arise from perceptual experience? What is the mind and how does it relate to the body? How can immaterial and abstract ideas affect material reality?

These and similar questions make up the subject matter of *cognitive science*. Although these questions have been asked for centuries, it is only in the last several decades that scientists from cognitive psychology, computer science, linguistics, mathematics, neural science, education, and philosophy have joined together to form the interdisciplinary field of cognitive science. The first volume of the *Journal of Cognitive Science* (Norman 1981) laid the foundations and described the earliest applications.

The goals of cognitive science are more general than those of cognitive psychology and artificial intelligence. Artificial intelligence is concerned with understanding and constructing programs that exhibit intelligent behavior, often ignoring psychological or sociological aspects of intelligence. Cognitive psychology, as a branch of empirical psychology, studies intelligence in natural systems including humans and animals, often ignoring insights from the analysis of social systems, philosophy, or computation. Cognitive science brings together insights from these diverse disciplines in an effort to formulate laws and generalizations characterizing all intelligent behavior.

The hypothesis that there will emerge a common set of generalizations regarding intelligence is the basis of the interdisciplinary character of cognitive science. The idea of a set of laws governing the many forms of intelligence brings together scientists from a broad spectrum of fields. Although the methods and contents of their individual research disciplines differ, they are all interested in understanding the principles underlying intelligence.

A significant factor motivating this interdisciplinary approach is the difficulty of addressing these issues within the boundaries of traditional subject areas. Although unified by a common goal, researchers have had to work out the development of a common methodology and language. Cognitive science has evolved into a discipline with its own distinctive set of experimental and observational techniques in conjunction with a coherent set of issues, research tools, and results. An important part of its richness and power stems from the often diametrically opposed ideas that make up its infrastructure. Thus, a primary goal in preparing this book was to develop a coherent picture that makes this presentation a unified whole.

As the author of a book in a very diverse discipline, I am dependent on the contributions of colleagues, and have acknowledged their assistance in the chapter running heads. One of these colleagues, Peder Johnson, co-designed with me the first cognitive science course at the University of New Mexico in the early 1980s. Peder presented the psychological side and I the computer science and artificial intelligence viewpoint. We were guided by the early cognitive science researchers, including Allen Newell and Herbert Simon (1963, 1972), Zenon Pylyshyn (1984), and Jerry Fodor (1975), as well as challenged by commentators such as Searle (1980), Weisenbaum (1976), and the Dreyfus brothers (1985). In the later 1980s, as the connectionist approach became more important, we expanded our presentation to include this work. We were especially influenced by the foundational research of McClelland, Rumelhart, and the PDP Research Group (1986) at UCSD.

The other authors, Jean Newman, professor of linguistics and psychology; Carl Stern, philosopher and computer scientist; and Ron Yeo, professor of psychology with specialty in neurophysiology, presented lectures as part of our cognitive science course. During the past decade our ideas, as well as the course itself, have developed and matured through interaction with colleagues and students. This book represents the result.

We have worked diligently to avoid making the book a collection of loosely related pieces in which a number of invited primary authors present their individual ideas in the context of an edited collection. Too many of these already exist; they are particularly useless for teaching a first course in cognitive science. Our goal was to create a book that tells a coherent integrated story, and thus, for the sections of which I was not an author, I played the role of editor and critic. Our aim was to make an integrated presentation of the material of a rich and diverse discipline.

The book is divided into six parts. Part I introduces the discipline of cognitive science and lays a foundation for the remainder of the book. In Chapters 1 and 2 we describe pivotal issues and offer a vocabulary for intelligence. In Chapter 3 we introduce the notion of representational schemes. In Chapter 4 we consider empirical constraints on models of intelligence. We conclude Part I with a discussion of neurophysiological constraints on intelligence.

Part II presents the explicit symbol based approach. We describe the logic and network representation languages and present weak, or search based, models for intelligence as well as strong, or knowledge intensive, approaches to representing intelligence. The Newell/Simon tradition for modeling intelligence is presented near the end of Part II.

The three chapters of Part III present models for learning. The first chapter describes explicit symbol based learning. The final two chapters present algorithms based on the neurologically and biologically inspired learning models.

Part IV presents the study of human language, undoubtedly one of the most challenging areas in cognitive science. Language brings together virtually every cognitive faculty. We describe the roles of syntax, semantics, and pragmatics in the generation and understanding of language utterances.

Part V illustrates many of the symbol based representations of the earlier chapters in PROLOG, a very high level and easy to use programming language based on the predicate logic. We strongly encourage our readers to build and test the key representational tools from this book. Part VI serves as an epilogue summarizing the key concepts from the book as well as offering conjectures for future growth in cognitive science.

All our software, including a public domain PROLOG interpreter for PC class machines, is available through *anonymous ftp* from the University of New Mexico (ftp ftp.cs.unm.edu, go to subdirectory/pub/cogsci/). A curriculum outline for both a one quarter/semester, and a full year course, along with sample examination questions, is also available through *ftp*.

We would like to point out that a number of excellent connectionist and genetic algorithm software packages for implementing the learning models of Part III are now available. We encourage readers to obtain this software for building and testing the models and algorithms discussed.

This book, supplemented by selected readings from primary authors, will provide material sufficient for a one year senior undergraduate or beginning graduate level course. A number of chapter combinations can make up a one quarter or single semester course. In this shorter version we cover Chapters 1–5 and 17 in detail. This requires about half the time allotted for the course. We then have two lectures on Chapter 6, symbol based representations, one on Chapter 7, logic, and three on GPS and the Newell/Simon tradition in Chapters 8 and 9. This leaves time for five lectures on the connectionist approach of Part III and two on issues in psycholinguistics, Part IV. We always assign a paper and a project which includes programming. We have mid-term and final examinations.

It is important that the contributions of each author be acknowledged. Thus, although most of us have reviewed all sections of the book, the names of the primary authors of each chapter are noted in the chapter's running head. We also thank a very large number of our present and past students who have read, supported, criticized, and even spell checked earlier versions of this book. They especially have made an important contribution to its evolution.

We thank Benjamin Cummings Publishing Co. for permission to use, with some modification, material with Bill Stubblefield as co-author, which originally appeared in *Artificial Intelligence: Structures and Strategies for Complex Problem Solving* (Luger & Stubblefield 1993). We acknowledge the use of materials from other sources on the copyright page.

The book was moved from various word processing media into Framemaker format by Linda Cicarella of the University of New Mexico. Linda also produced most of the figures. We are all appreciative of her effort and care. The artwork is by Thomas Barrow, internationally known artist and University of New Mexico professor of art.

May you enjoy our work. We have enjoyed creating it.

George F. Luger

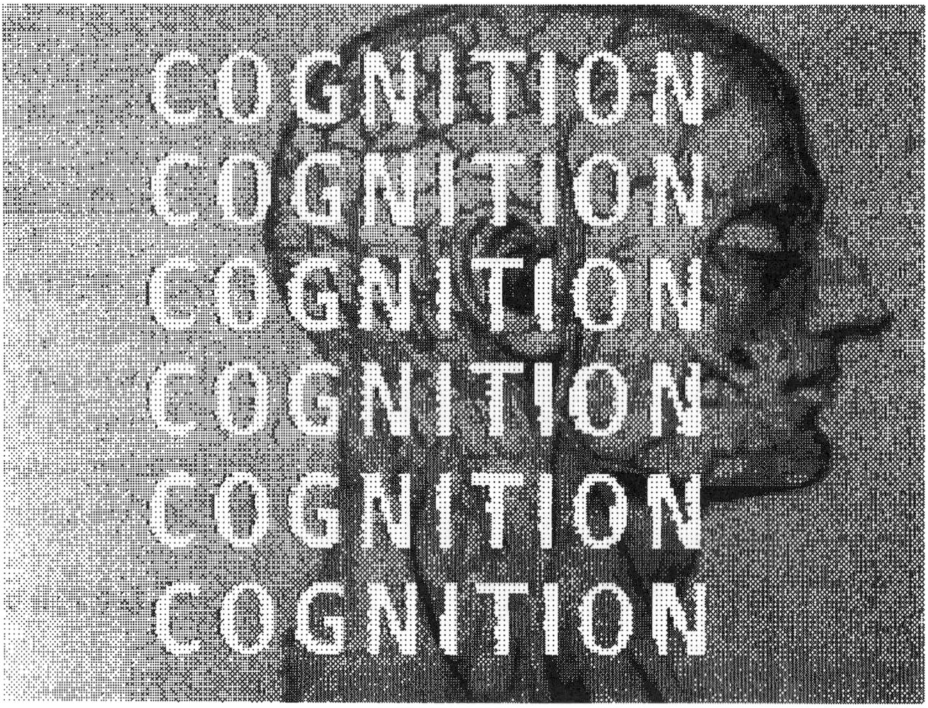

Part I

INTRODUCTION TO COGNITIVE SCIENCE

Part I lays a foundation for our book. It asks the questions that begin our investigation and establishes a vocabulary for describing intelligent systems. It introduces the issues and methods of cognitive science. It describes the synergism between the disciplines that nourish the vitality of its practice.

In Chapter 1, we discuss the notion of "intelligence as a natural category." We introduce cognitive science as the study of the general laws and relationships governing intelligent performance in humans as well as well as computers. We discuss the relevance of current measures of intelligence including IQ tests. We look back to the history of ideas, beginning with Plato and Aristotle, finding there the roots of our current concerns. Finally, we present a brief history of artificial intelligence. We introduce the Turing test and describe its use in characterizing intelligence. We end the chapter with a brief statement of the goals of cognitive science.

In Chapter 2, we begin to build a vocabulary for understanding intelligent systems. This is an important early step in the development of a science. We find it necessary to discuss a set of epistemological issues relevant to the foundations of cognitive science. In this vein we discuss folk psychology, philosophical and methodological behaviorism, and neuroscience. We conclude Chapter 2 by presenting the automated formal system, including Turing machines, universal Turing machines, and the Church-Turing thesis.

Chapter 3 presents an overview of cognitive representations. First the notion of a cognitive representation is introduced. Then explicit symbol based representation schemes are discussed. Symbol based representations are broken into the logic based, the procedure based, the network, and the structured. Sub-symbolic or connectionist representations are introduced and a brief history of their evolution offered.

Chapter 4 shows how results from cognitive psychology, neuroscience, and the cognitive science research community can offer constraints on our understanding of intelligence. We begin by discussing the ideas of necessary and sufficient models of intelligence. We then discuss the methodology that allows us to discern constraints. This empirical methodology includes the direct methods of introspection and protocol analysis. It also includes indirect methods such as Sternberg's additive-subtractive approach. Finally, we discuss potential limitations of formal equivalence, including representational indeterminacy. We conclude by reminding ourselves of the methodological issues in science, including model building and refinement.

In Chapter 5 we turn to the neurophysiological dimension of intelligence. We consider the physical structure of the human processing system in terms of neuron size, connectivity and complexity. We describe the methodology and preliminary results from research into brain activity, and see how the developmental structure and overall physical architecture of the human brain can effect behavior.

Part II of our book presents symbol based representations, while Part III gives an overview of machine learning including the connectionist approach. Part IV presents issues in language processing as a window on intelligence. Part V demonstrates how to build many of the representational and learning structures of the book in PROLOG. Part VI, our epilogue, summarizes many of the issues of the book and describes the current promises and limitations of the discipline.

Chapter 1

INTELLIGENCE AND THE ROOTS OF COGNITIVE SCIENCE

Meaning is not a thing; it involves what is meaningful to us. Nothing is meaningful in itself. Meaningfulness derives from the experience of a being of a certain sort in an environment of a certain sort...

George Lakoff (1987)

The choice of a point of view is the initial act of a culture.

Jose Ortega y Gasset (1923)

Break the pattern which connects the items of learning and you necessarily destroy all quality.

Gregory Bateson (1979)

1.0   INTRODUCTION

In Chapter 1 we provide a general introduction to cognitive science with an overview of its fundamental issues. We discuss the relation of cognitive science to its sister disciplines, cognitive psychology, philosophy, and artificial intelligence.

The first issue that we examine is whether intelligence is, as philosophers of science describe it, a *natural category*. That is, whether it is reasonable to search for a common set of properties characterizing intelligence in all its settings and forms. We elaborate this question in Section 1.1.

Section 1.2 offers some common sense descriptions of intelligence. We begin by considering IQ tests and their role in describing intelligence. We go on to early positions in psychology, such as *basic process* theory and the process/ knowledge controversy. The goal of this subsection is to present the ideas found in early psychological theories and show how they might relate to our current understanding of intelligence.

In Section 1.3 we review the development of ideas about knowledge and cognition in philosophy. We find anticipations of our thoughts on a science of intelligence in the earliest Greek writers, the Presocratics, Plato, and Aristotle. We trace their epistemological concepts and problems down through the enlightenment philosophers Descartes, Locke, and Hume. We find in Leibniz the first mathematical-computational model of cognition. Kant's attempted synthesis of rationalism and empiricism lays the foundation for the contemporary schema theory of Bartlett and Piaget. Following this historical sketch we look at a number of contemporary philosophical subdisciplines which have strongly influenced the development of cognitive science.

In Section 1.4 we introduce *artificial intelligence* (AI), that modern discipline in computer science whose focus is the automation of intelligent problem solving. We examine the ideas and tools from AI that have proved useful in developing a science of intelligence. Finally, in Section 1.5, we present the supporting research hypotheses of cognitive science, the physical symbol system of Newell and Simon, and the currently popular connectionist paradigm.

1.1   INTELLIGENCE AS A NATURAL CATEGORY

Cognitive science begins with the assumption that there is a common set of principles underlying all instances of intelligence. Although this hypothesis is the glue that provides an important part of the field's cohesiveness, it remains a global working hypothesis, continually under scientific evaluation.

In working in any scientific area one of the first questions we must ask is "a science of what?" Looking at this question a bit more abstractly we can think of nature as providing the raw phenomena which the scientist interprets. Interpretation begins with classification and classification requires categories. The categories we develop and impose on phenomena say something about the kind of science we are going to do and the success we are likely to have. We say more about this issue in our discussion of a constructivist epistemology in the next chapter. First we identify that part of nature that makes up the focus of our scientific enquiry.

Consider for a moment the decision to create a science of crystals as opposed to a science of hard objects, such as baseball bats, car bumpers, and granite. The focus on crystals may impress us as a reasonable decision, leading to further questions, on crystal structures, for example. The problem is that while it is possible to capture meaningful generalizations across crystals, we are far less certain that anything but superficial generalizations can be made about hard objects. The possibility of discovering generalizations about nature depends on how we carve it up, that is, the taxonomies we develop. Some categorizations yield insightful generalizations and laws while others do not.

When a domain of science experiences a paradigmatic shift (Kuhn 1962) the relevant categories of the field shift with the theory. Prior to the emergence of microbiology, for example, the distinction between chemistry and biology was generally accepted as valid. Prior to the advent of cognitive science there seemed little reason to bridge the fields of cognitive psychology, computer science, linguistics, and philosophy. The assumption of intelligence as a natural category provides a basis for uniting these fields. The issue is whether the phenomenon we refer to as intelligence is a valid, that is, natural, category. Cognitive scientists feel that the category "intelligent system" is potentially valid and that it is reasonable to look for generalizations that apply to all instances of "intelligent" behavior. We next examine some naive views of intelligence that have emerged from psychology, education, and folk tradition.

1.2 COMMON SENSE VIEWS OF INTELLIGENCE

Before we have a serious discussion of whether intelligence is a natural category we must reach some agreement about the definition of the category, that is, we must attempt to recognize what constitutes an intelligent action. The history of psychology is riddled with numerous attempts to provide a definition of intelligence. Indeed, it may be foolish to think that we will do any better at providing such a definition! We begin by presenting some descriptions of intelligence offered throughout the history of psychology.

It might seem that any search for a general description of intelligence is certain to be a wasted effort. This will be true if our goal is to reach a clear and final definition of intelligence. It is our hope that the discussion of different characterizations of intelligence will lead to an appreciation of why a definitive definition may in fact be impossible. More importantly, we will see that the perfect explicit definition of intelligent performance is not essential for us to proceed with the endeavor of cognitive science.

1.2.1 Intelligence Tests

A large part of the confusion regarding the concept of intelligence can be attributed to the development of IQ tests. For a first approximation of intelligence it would seem we simply should look at what it is that tests of intelligence measure! Unfortunately, there are several problems in using IQ tests as a definition of intelligence. One obvious problem is that there is little agreement among psychologists as to what an intelligence test measures. Another problem is that intelligence tests were not designed to assess the presence or measure intelligence. Rather they were designed to discriminate between those individuals who would succeed and those who would fail in a designated set of tasks, in particular, within a public education context. There is no reason to believe that the test that serves as the best discriminator or predictor will necessarily provide a good definition of intelligence.

The original reason for designing the Stanford-Binet test, one of the most widely accepted intelligence tests and a test which came to serve as model for many subsequent intelligent tests, was to predict success in school. The original Binet test (Binet & Simon 1905) was designed to identify those children who would not benefit from traditional instruction as it then existed in the French school system of the early 20th century.

The selection of test items was therefore determined by whether they were correlated with performance in a particular academic environment. It is reasonable to assume that those children who do exceedingly well in this school environment have an ample amount of this stuff we call intelligence. But it does not follow that the child who does poorly hasn't any intelligence. He or she simply doesn't have a sufficient degree of a certain kind of intelligence that is demanded by a particular school environment. One can go further and contend that academic skills are as much sociological as intellectual: understanding and using the complex school society, being able to read and communicate, and being ready to defer in the near term some of life's rewards and pleasures.

Since the creation of Binet's original test, there have been numerous developments and refinements in the construction of intelligence tests (Carroll 1982). It is now well established that their validity is quite general, extending well beyond classroom performance. But it is still the case that intelligence tests are designed to discriminate among a group of individuals by their ability to perform in some environment. Those test items that discriminate best are those for which a roughly equal percentage of the individuals pass or fail. This means that we will be selecting items that measure a relatively narrow range of abilities.

As a consequence, those abilities that the least intelligent individuals of the sample possess are not tested. An example of this is the ability to comprehend speech. Most intelligence tests, with the exception of some infant and preschool tests, do not begin to sample the lower limits of speech comprehension. Most researchers agree that the ability to comprehend speech requires an important form of intelligence.

Another problem in looking to intelligence tests as a definition for intelligence is that they are for the most part product or result oriented. That is, results are determined by whether or not the tested individual produces the "correct" answer, and not by the process by which the answer was attained. Cognitive scientists are interested in gaining an understanding of the structures and processes that underlie intelligent performance and not simply its results. The occurrence of intelligent actions is only interesting in that they signal the existence of an intelligent system. The important task is to understand what enables the system to consistently produce these responses.

1.2.2 Big G and Little s

Although we focused on the problems of using intelligence tests to define intelligence, we don't want to leave the impression that the content of these tests tells us nothing about the nature of intelligent actions. If we look at the items that make up the tests that span the developmental range from infancy to intellectual maturity we get a good representation of the activities that are important in humans' successful adaptation to their environment. By systematically analyzing these samples we can gain some insights into a number of the abilities underlying human intelligence.

This approach is seen in the work of Thurstone (1938). Thurstone questioned the notion and even the existence of a unitary general intelligence, often referred to as "big G," that was measured by tests such as the Stanford-Binet. He argued that intelligence was composed of a set of nine different and independent abilities, including verbal comprehension, spatial reasoning, and numerical processing. Thurstone felt that an individual could be gifted in one ability and at the same time be below average on others.

Taking this view to the extreme, Guilford (1956) hypothesized that there were 120 separate abilities. Over the period of a 20-year project he used factor analytic methods to isolate 98 of these hypothesized skills. If Thurstone and Guilford are correct, the task of finding some properties that are common to all intelligent systems may be difficult indeed. On the other hand, there is evidence that relatively few of these abilities play much of a role in everyday life (Ellison & Edgerton 1941). Thus, it is possible that most of what we mean by "intelligent systems" can be captured by only a few general abilities, and that a factor analytic method can point to what these abilities might be. Although this type of psychometric research can have an important impact on our conceptualizing of intelligence, we must keep in mind that these tests are always designed to discriminate among individuals and as a consequence may fail to include fundamental properties shared by intelligent systems.

1.2.3 Intelligence as Process or as Knowledge

An important distinction in our conceptualizing of intelligence is the process/ knowledge difference. From the process view we think of intelligence as involving certain basic operations or processes. Once a system is endowed with these information processing capabilities it can perform in its environment, that is, behave intelligently based on its inherent capabilities. Alternatively, the knowledge view describes intelligence in terms of acquired information. To behave intelligently one must have large amounts of knowledge about situations.

These different positions are usually argued in terms of relative degree of emphasis, since it is difficult to imagine an intelligent system with no processes or no *a priori* knowledge. Some of the more radical empiricist positions, such as that of John Locke's *Essay Concerning Human Understanding* (1690/1970), seem to assume that we begin as a *tabula rasa*, or blank slate, with no *a priori* knowledge. In a later chapter we examine this thesis in some depth, but for the moment we only need to contrast the knowledge/process positions.

The process view was emphasized in artificial intelligence in the early work of Newell and Simon (1972). These AI researchers took the position that an intelligent system only needed a few very powerful mechanisms, sometimes referred to as "weak methods." Most of the complexity of the behavior of the system was a result of the interaction between these general mechanisms and the complexity that was contained in the problem solver's environment. Simon (1981) in his book *The Sciences of the Artificial* uses as an example the complex path taken by an ant traversing uneven ground, for instance, crossing a sandy beach. Simon argues that the complexity of the ant's path is the result of a set of very simple guidance rules interacting with a rather complicated environment that the ant must traverse.

More recently, AI researchers interested in simulating human experts' skilled performance, for example, that of medical doctors dealing with patients or of geologists exploring for mineral resources, have focused on providing their programs with very extensive knowledge bases. This is referred to as "strong method" problem solving. In this vein it has been argued that a chess player is a grandmaster precisely because he or she possesses about 50,000 pieces of knowledge about chess (Chase & Simon 1973)! The assumption is that to be intelligent a system must possess a large amount of detailed knowledge of the application area of that intelligence.

It can be argued that this approach confuses knowledge with intelligence. Intelligence is the ability to acquire knowledge, and not the knowledge itself. Although it may be relevant to distinguish between intelligence and knowledge, it is also the case that it requires knowledge to acquire knowledge. For example, it has been shown that if chimpanzees are given a large number of different discrimination tasks, they begin to learn successive problems more rapidly (Harlow 1949). Psychologists refer to this process as *learning to learn*.

Much of learning is based, at least in part, on previously acquired skills. Adult humans, completely normal physiologically with all their information processing capabilities intact but raised in isolation from society and afforded limited stimulation of any type, would very likely not fit comfortably into society. They would also behave with very little of what we normally think of as intelligence.

We will see examples of approaches emphasizing one or the other of the process/knowledge views of intelligence throughout the remainder of the book. Regardless of the emphasis, it is necessary to assume some fundamental processes in all intelligent systems. The question of what these basic processes might involve is the topic of the next subsection.

1.2.4 The Basic Process Approach to Intelligence

A traditional approach in experimental psychology is to investigate the fundamental processes involved in perception, learning, and memory. Because much of this research is conducted across a spectrum of organisms, ranging from flatworms to rats, monkeys, and humans, it considers relatively primitive perception and problem solving, that is, processing that all humans and most biological systems share. In this section we consider these phenomena frequently investigated by experimental psychologists.

Reactivity.

An important factor that distinguishes rocks, trees, and flies from humans is the range of stimuli to which each system can respond. By "range of stimuli" we refer to both the quality and intensity of the stimulation. Humans have five sensory modalities which limit the types of perceived energy. Each of these sensory modalities are also limited in the ranges of energies to which they respond. Thus, most human sensitivity to sound waves is limited to the range of 40 to 20,000 Hz. Reactivity, as defined here, relates to intelligence by the fact that any system's ability to adapt to the environment is limited by its sensitivity to changes within that environment.

Discrimination and Generalization.

Almost as fundamental as reactivity is the ability to discriminate between two different stimuli. How different in frequency must two tones be for a person to discriminate one from the other? These discriminative capacities are referred to as differential thresholds. The magnitude of differential thresholds sets the limits of how finely perceptual categorizations of phenomenon may be differentiated. For example, it is estimated that humans can discriminate as many as 10 million different colors, each differing by degree of hue, lightness, or chroma!

The other side of discrimination is generalization. A very important skill of an intelligent system requires it not only to be able to detect differences, but also to perceive similarities between events that may differ in a large variety of ways. Most of the concepts and categories that make up our everyday vocabulary, for example, fruit, show the importance of generalization.

Experimental and comparative psychologists have long recognized the importance of discrimination and generalization in the evolution of intelligence. Although these processes are very basic they can also become extremely abstract. Some of the most difficult types of intelligence tests, such as the Miller analogies, require subjects to solve analogy problems. These problems may be either verbal or perceptual, see, for example, Figure 1.1.

The correct solution to analogy problems often requires the problem solver to understand situations in concrete or abstract dimensions, and sometimes even through metaphor. At the heart of these problems is the ability to generalize.

Complexity.

Biologists and general systems theoreticians have proposed that a system's ability to adapt to environmental changes is related to its organizational complexity (Lazlo 1972). Although it seems to make a lot of intuitive sense that intelligence requires some minimum level of complexity in a system, we must specify what we mean by complexity if this approach is going to help describe intelligence.

Lazlo (1972) distinguishes between a heap, which is a set of unrelated elements, and a system, which is composed of a set of interdependent parts. We change one part of a system and the whole system changes, while if we remove the old tire and the empty beer can from a pile of garbage it remains a garbage heap, minus two items. The complexity of a system (de Chardin 1959) is defined by its degree of differentiation and integration.

As a system becomes more finely differentiated, it makes distinctions that it previously did not. So the concept dog gets differentiated into breeds of dogs. Integration is seen in the relation and organization of the parts. So dogs become integrated with higher order concepts, such as pets or animals. Differentiation and integration are obviously closely related to the processes of discrimination and generalization.

In general systems theory it is often assumed that all systems, cosmological as well as biological, evolve toward increased complexity. de Chardin (1959) and Werner (1957) in particular speculate that the evolution of intelligence is marked by increased complexification. Within an individual system we can also think of complexity as related to memory or knowledge. The more sophisticated we become regarding some domain of knowledge the more finely differentiated and integrated our representations of the knowledge becomes.

In later chapters we discuss some of the effects of changes in the quantity and organization of knowledge. *Strong method* problem solvers depend on a

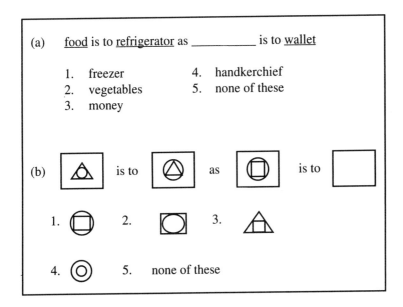

FIGURE 1.1 Examples of verbal (a) and spatial (b) analogies common to IQ tests.

large amount of knowledge for their intelligent behavior. This approach is taken in knowledge based problem solvers including medical (Buchanan & Shortliff 1984) and geological expert systems (Duda et al. 1979). Such knowledge intensive approaches are also used in computer assisted remediation of human problem solvers. Tutoring programs exist for modeling subtraction skills (Brown & vanLehn 1980), algebra problem solving (Sleeman 1982) and computer programming skills (Singley & Anderson 1989). The organization of knowledge is seen with the discussion of problem representations and search strategies in Part II of our book, in particular with the presentation of semantic nets, the production system, frames, and schemas.

Adaptation and Learning.

A view of intelligence, often referred to as the evolutionary based definition of intelligence, is that intelligence is a system's ability to adapt to changes in complex environments (Spencer 1855). The ability to adapt is usually thought to involve learning. This approach has a great deal of intuitive appeal. How well we adapt to our school environment, for example, as shown in our ability to learn, may well determine our success.

If this is true, we should easil be able to assess intelligence by observing how rapidly a system learns a task or adapts to its sociological milieu. Because of the simplicity and elegance of this notion of intelligence, it has been investigated extensively over the last several decades (Estes 1963). If the idea had worked out as originally proposed this and other books on psychology or cognitive science would be a lot shorter and easier to write! Unfortunately, as is so often the case, an idea that seems simple and straightforward upon proposal, after closer examination, begins to disintegrate. There are two major difficulties with this approach: The first problem with this definition of intelligence is that regardless of how learning is defined, i.e., what type of learning measures are used, none of them seem to correlate very highly with IQ or "test intelligence" (Estes 1963).

Of course this may be a blessing in disguise, since as we noted earlier, there is considerable doubt that IQ tests offer a very good definition of intelligence. It is clearly the case that there are more believers in the importance and validity of learning than there are believers in test intelligence. It is also difficult to imagine a viable model of an intelligent system that does not include the ability to modify itself as a consequence of its experience within its environment. For this reason, despite the problems in agreeing upon a general definition of learning, most researchers in cognitive science continue to consider learning as an essential property of all intelligent systems.

Second, learning may be no less difficult to define than intelligence. There are a very large number of different learning situations as well as measures of success in learning. Unfortunately, none of them correlate highly (Estes 1963). A person who learns very rapidly in one situation may learn more slowly on a slightly different task. Just as there are different types of intelligence, we may also have different learning abilities. One reason for this is that a number of even more basic abilities underlie differences in learning rates.

An illustration of how attentional processes are involved in learning is seen in research reported by Zeaman and House (1963). These researchers compared the learning rate of average and below average IQ children. Figure 1.2 shows that on a relatively simple two choice discrimination learning task children of both groups initially performed at chance, or .5 correct. After some number of trials and once they begin to perform above chance, they change their condition very rapidly and at an identical rate.

The important difference between the two groups is in the first segment of learning, which Zeaman and House interpreted as learning to attend to the relevant stimulus cues. When attending to irrelevant aspects of the stimulus situation, the expectation of being correct is 50% of trials. Apparently, the lower IQ children required more training before they began to attend to the relevant cues; but once they did attend, they learned as rapidly as the normal IQ children.

Estes (1963) concluded that it may be impossible to find a learning task that is not confounded by other processes. At a minimum, a learning task always involves a stimulus and a response, and this suggests that input and output

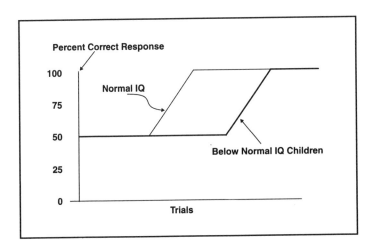

FIGURE 1.2   Percentage of correct responses as a function of training trials for normal and below normal IQ children. Adapted from Zeaman and House (1963).

systems will to some extent influence task performance. Furthermore, it may also be impossible to study pure rote learning, unaffected by previous knowledge. Although the British *associationists*, such as Hobbes and Locke, assumed that we all began as blank slates, it may be an impossible situation to recreate. In fact, most if not all learning involves some degree of transfer from other experiences. As a result, individual differences in past experiences influence how rapidly we learn specific new tasks. Finally, researchers such as Jean Lave (1988) point out that intelligence in practice is entirely different from its manifestations in the rarified environment of the psychologists' laboratories. In fact she contends that results found in the laboratory, of transfer of training, for instance, have little or no relationship to problem solving in practice, such as that required for handling pricing per quantity in a supermarket. This approach says intelligence is an artifact of skill and situation and thus not isolateable and manipulable by researchers.

1.2.5 The "Constructive" Character of Intelligence

Concepts such as intelligence and personality are what philosophers often refer to as dispositional constructs because they refer to an individual's disposition to behave in a particular manner across a variety of situations. With constructs of this nature there is a tendency for the observer to act as if the individual possesses the characteristic that is seen in his or her behavior. When we make this often unconscious inference it becomes easy to reify the construct. In other words, intelligence becomes an entity and people possess various amounts of it. In a similar fashion we often say someone has leadership, as if this were some quantifiable possession.

Once this reification is done we find ourselves looking for the locus of intelligence or leadership. Just as the soul was once said to be located in the pineal gland, we might look to find intelligence in the frontal cortex! Clearly, it is important that we avoid this reification of intelligence. But if it is not "in someone's head" then where is it? One way of thinking about this problem is to ask whether intelligence exists external to and independent of the observer.

Our first reaction to this question might be to assume that it must, for it is some property of the system we are observing. However, if we think a bit more, we begin to ask how we know when we are observing intelligent actions in another system. We might then respond that we could get a group of judges and we could show that they all agreed. This may be true if the individual being observed and the judges were all part of the same culture. But suppose that the individual were from an isolated island or from an as yet undiscovered civilization and that some of the judges were natives of the observed culture while others were part of our own. Would they still agree? What about dolphin intelligence, do we know it when we see it? And of course there is the Alpha Centurion, just arrived from a distant galaxy. Can we agree on instances of its intelligence? The Alpha Centurion may conclude that human behavior appears to exhibit no hint of intelligence!

The point we are making is that, in many important aspects, intelligence is in the eye of the beholder. Intelligence is not in the raw actions of the observed system, rather it is in the interpretations of the observer. In philosophy this is considered a phenomenological perspective. External reality exists only as it is interpreted by the observer, that is, in the semantic categories that are used to interpret the raw energy from the external world. Thus various behaviors in different situations are interpreted in terms of semantic, or what philosophers refer to as "intentional" concepts; these may sometimes be perceived as intelligent and other times as not so.

This point of view places a major constraint on defining the set of events that constitute intelligent actions. Who are the judges? For the foreseeable future we humans will also have to be the judges. Can we be trusted? Probably not, for the simple reason that we cannot transcend ourselves. We have a particular cultural, human, and biological bias that is, in principle, impossible for us to override. We are incapable of seeing intelligence in the abstract, independent of the particular perspective we have as a result of our biological and cultural history. There is an intrinsically intentional and egocentric component to what we call intelligence. There is really little that we can do about this, other than acknowledging our limitations. (We develop these epistemological issues further in Section 2.1.)

We may now ask whether there might be something unique about intelligent actions that make them particularly subjective in their interpretation. One possibility is that intelligent actions always have a purposeful component. Whether a particular action is intelligent depends on the current goals of the larger system. To judge the intelligence of an action requires that we know or are able to infer the system's goals. As we will discuss later, it may well be the case that we often don't even know what our own goals are, let alone the goals of another system!

If we accept the preceding argument, it carries with it some important implications. First, it means that we are likely to be completely blind to certain forms of intelligence. Second, and perhaps more importantly, it implies that intelligence must be described at a certain level of analysis. In other words, it requires types of concepts or categories that are intentional or semantic in nature. We return to this issue later.

1.2.6 The Representational Capability of Intelligent Systems

If a system can behave in terms of goals these future states must somehow be represented in the current functioning of the system. A major assumption in cognitive science is that intelligent systems have the ability to cognitively or mentally represent such concrete and abstract states. As a relatively simple example, the behavior of a thermostat in controlling the temperature of a room depends on its ability to represent temperatures.

We contend that humans must have the ability to represent semantic states and that their ability to behave as intelligently and abstractly as they do depends on this ability. Perhaps the most obvious manifestation of this representation of semantic states is seen in our use of language, especially to communicate information and goals.

Throughout the remainder of the book, we discuss in some detail the evidence for this representational capability, its importance in intelligent action, and how it may be modeled. For the moment we need only note that in cognitive science it is commonly assumed that representation at some level is a necessary property of all intelligent systems.

In this section we reviewed many of the features we have come to expect to be part of the phenomenon of intelligence. We also considered a number of the issues that must be addressed in creating a science of intelligence. In the next section we take more of a philosophical perspective, calling attention to important philosophical issues which help support the foundations of a science of intelligence.

1.3   PHILOSOPHY AND COGNITIVE SCIENCE

The discussion in previous sections has considered some of the conceptual issues in cognitive science which need clarification as a prelude to empirical research. The way in which a science defines its subject matter and theoretical methods determines what questions are asked and what approaches are used to search for answers. Are cognitive scientists asking the right questions? Do we know what these questions mean? Cognitive scientists seek significant data to use in selecting between competing hypotheses. We search for small, sometimes arcane pieces of data in order to find answers to large questions. We use millisecond differences in response times to lead to dramatic conclusions regarding the organization of cognitive structures. What leads from A to B is the fabric of a theory. But, how clear and well founded are the concepts with which we frame our hypotheses? Does it even make sense, for example, to ask about the organization of cognitive structures?

To adequately address these questions requires a certain degree of philosophical sophistication. Philosophers such as Pylyshyn, Dennett, Churchland, and Searle, to name but a few, have made an important contribution to the discussion of foundational issues. The prominent role played by philosophers in cognitive science is somewhat unique among the contemporary sciences. There are two main reasons for this. First, cognitive science is a young science, still struggling to build a consensus about its content and methods. Philosophers have traditionally played a significant role at this stage of development. In fact, many of the well known figures who gave their science its initial impetus called themselves *natural philosophers*. People as diverse as Galileo, Newton, Pasteur, Harvey, and Darwin all believed that the foundations of their science required the proper resolution of basic philosophical issues.

There is a second reason why philosophers play a prominent role in cognitive science. Several philosophical disciplines deal with issues which are of direct consequence to cognitive science. Many of the questions considered by philosophers in epistemology, logic, philosophy of mind, and philosophy of science, have a significant bearing on the theory and modeling of intelligent systems. We discuss the issues raised by these philosophical disciplines and their potential interest to cognitive science in Section 1.3.6.

We begin our examination of the philosophical contribution to cognitive science by tracing the evolution of certain key concepts in the Western philosophical tradition. In this thumbnail sketch we can perhaps glimpse the origins of modern discussions regarding the nature of consciousness and intentionality as well as the sources and validity of knowledge.

1.3.1 The Early History of Western Philosophy

Western philosophy originated in the eastern Mediterranean around the sixth century B.C. The Greek inhabitants of the Ionian islands were located along major trade routes, placing them in contact with a variety of cultures and civilizations, including the Babylonian, Persian, Indian, Egyptian, and Cretan. These contacts involved an exchange of ideas as well as goods. Amidst this diversity of cultural perspectives, intelligent people could no longer unquestioningly assume the correctness of their own inherited belief system. The first philosophers were thus challenged to discover a source of knowledge more solid and universal than that of mere cultural authority.

These early philosophers were strongly influenced by their observation of natural processes and astronomical events. Thales of Miletus, in about 585 B.C., is said to have successfully predicted a solar eclipse. He proposed the theory that "all is water," and that the diversity of phenomena can be explained by the variety of forms which water takes under different conditions. His followers, Anaximander and Anaximenes of Miletus, also studied astronomy, developing geometric models of remarkable clarity and precision. Like Thales, they also constructed explanations of the physical universe based on a few simple principles such as the separation of hot and cold and the condensation of air.

Pythagoras, Heraclitus, and Parmenides rejected the explanation of phenomena proposed by the Milesian school. Each of them proposed a theory which interpreted the changeable phenomena of nature as superficial or illusory. Pythagoras of Samos, about 570 B.C., saw in mathematics and music the source of ultimate revelation. He held that music and mathematics reveal the unchanging harmony of the cosmos, a mystery hidden below the surface of phenomena. Heraclitus of Ephesus, about 500 B.C., held that the flux of appearance is governed by a hidden structure or *logos*, which is only accessible to those who have trained themselves to "listen." An aspect of this structure is the unity of opposites, the law that opposites require one another and that they continually flow into and replace one another. Parmenides of Elea, about 450 B.C., argued that "being is one and unchangeable," that multiplicity and change are illusory. His student Zeno developed a set of arguments or paradoxes designed to demonstrate that the concept of motion is self-contradictory. A common thread throughout this development is the split between appearance and reality: the former characterized by diversity and change, the latter by unity and permanence.

A different response to the clash of cultures and ideas arose from the *skeptics* and *sophists*. The lesson drawn by the skeptics from the diversity of opinions was that truth is unknowable. Xenophanes of Colophon, about 575 B.C., argued that "Even if the truth were fully stated, it could not be known." That is, if the truth were ever to appear among the spectrum of diverse opinions, there would be nothing to distinguish it from other views and therefore no reason to select it.

Sextus Empiricus, a later codifier of skepticism, elaborated Xenophane's claim into an argument known as "the criteriological regress." Suppose you present a proposition which you claim to be true. I can then ask you, "By what criterion should I judge this to be true?" If you provide me with a criterion of truth, I can then ask you to provide a criterion by which I should judge your criterion of truth. If you provide me with a criterion for judging that criteria of truth, I can ask again, why should I accept it. By what criterion is it a valid criterion. And so on. You will run out of criteria before I run out of questions. Therefore, if one ever accepts a proposition as true, that acceptance can never rest on a valid epistemological foundation.

Socrates and his student Plato acknowledged the force of this skeptical argument but contested its ultimate conclusion. Socrates agreed with the skeptics that knowledge of the cosmos and the ultimate nature of things is unattainable. Wisdom, he argued, consists precisely in attaining an accurate view of our own ignorance, in a critical ability to deconstruct false beliefs in ourselves and in others. This critical, penetrating self-knowledge, he claimed, would lead to the pursuit of virtue. A deep recognition of our ignorance regarding the outcome of material goals leaves only virtue as an end worth pursuing in itself.

Plato acknowledged the problem of truth validation as defined by the skeptics, but turned it on its head. For Plato, the argument proves that learning, knowledge acquisition, in the ordinary sense, is impossible. If we did not already know that a proposition presented to us was true, we would have no reason to accept it; it could be acquired, at best, as a belief held on the authority of another.

But learning in some sense is possible. In his dialogue, the *Meno*, we are presented with the example of a student who is led through a proof of a theorem in geometry. Meno starts the discussion as a skeptic:

> And how can you inquire, Socrates, into that which you do
> not already know? What will you put forth as the subject
> of the inquiry? And if you find out what you want, how
> will you ever know that this is what you did not know?

As a result of answering a series of well-chosen questions, Meno's slave ends up learning the theorem. He has not merely memorized it; he recognizes its truth beyond doubt. Given the problem of truth validation, how is this possible?

Plato's answer is that it is only possible in the case of a certain kind of knowledge: the knowledge of formal properties or essences. With such knowledge we have, under the right conditions, the experience of a luminous self-evidence. This can only be explained, according to Plato, if learning is actually recollection: a remembering of knowledge which we already dimly possess. If this is the character of learning, then the problem of the truth validation is solved.

The theory of learning as recollection has extraordinary consequences.

When did we originally acquire the knowledge which is now recollected? Since it was not in this lifetime, it must have been in a previous existence. Furthermore, it must have been in a different kind of existence; otherwise the same problem of truth validation would have made learning impossible. On the basis of such arguments, Plato hypothesizes that each of us has a soul distinct from our body; a soul which survives from lifetime to lifetime. To explain the process of recollection we must acknowledge that this soul was at one time in direct contact with a realm of Forms or essences. Indeed, Plato argues, only these Forms or essences can be truly known and only they have true being. The realm of being known through our senses is "a shadowy world," a realm in which the Forms are only dimly reflected. Even the beauty perceived in our lover is but a shadowy reflection of the Form of beauty itself!

Plato's rejection of sense objects and his attribution of ultimate reality to Forms or essences is called *idealism*. His dismissal of sense perception and identification of mathematics and formal reasoning as the primary sources of knowledge is called *rationalism*. His identification of the soul as a separate entity, distinct from and independent of its physical embodiment, is called *dualism*. While Plato's versions of these positions may seem extreme and implausible to the modern mind, each position has repeatedly reappeared in different forms and guises throughout the history of Western thought.

1.3.2 From Aristotle to Modern Times

Aristotle was Plato's student, but rejected Plato's postulation of a world of perfect forms. Aristotle's epistemology is a blend of rationalist and empiricist elements. As an *empiricist*, Aristotle attributes to perception and observation an essential role in the acquisition of knowledge. However, Aristotle's emphasis on the role of rational methods, including mathematics and logic, in organizing and interpreting observations, distinguishes his position as a very sophisticated version of empiricism.

Aristotle argued that knowledge could not have arisen from the senses alone. Some perceptions, such as rainbows and mirages, are deceptive and misleading. If knowledge depended on perception alone, what would we do when perceptions conflict? How would we recognize which perception is veridical? This problem is similar to Xenophanes skeptical conundrum: if the truth were in fact presented, how would we recognize it? How could it be distinguished from the full spectrum of opinions?

The development of systematic knowledge, *episteme* or science, requires the contribution of reason. Aristotle proposed a scientific method: the organized gathering of observations and measurements, followed by taxonomic classification. This was then followed by the application of rational methods: categorization (interpretation) and inference (logic). Through the use of logic, particular concepts and laws are subsumed under more general ones, while their content or consequences can still be recovered through the use of deductive syllogisms.

Aristotle taught that physical objects have both a matter and a form. Thus a marble statue might have the form of some ruler. The artist gives form to the material substrate of the statue. Only the form is knowable; but the form requires matter for its embodiment. In perception, the form of the object is delivered into our sense organs; it becomes literally present in those organs.

Aristotle's empiricist compromise contains lingering residues of rationalism and dualism. Aristotle's ontology, his science of existing things, presents the notion of a chain of being, ranging in perfection from our world, the most material, least perfect, and changeable to that of the divine, or most perfect, least material, and unchangeable.

Aristotle's cosmology reflected this ontology, with earth, our human realm the imperfect center. Moving outwards the concentric spheres approach perfect existence, the quintessence or fifth sphere. In our realm the realization of form is imperfect and hindered by matter; in the highest form it is pure being: the divine thinker, thought thinking itself, form without matter.

1.3.3 Post Medieval Philosophy

Rene Descartes, the father of modern philosophy, was a mathematician, and like Plato, a rationalist. Like Plato, he also was impressed with mathematical concepts, his *clear and distinct ideas*. In fact only these clear and distinct ideas were veridical or acceptable as a basis for understanding reality.

In his *Meditations* (1637/1969), Descartes defined the modern epistemological project: to reconstruct the foundations of knowledge, starting from the *epoche*: the suspension of judgement. How do I know, Descartes asks, that our beliefs about the world are true? There is an important difference between the doubting of the Descartes' *epoche* and doubt regarding a particular belief. A particular doubt can be resolved by making further observations or bringing to bear additional evidence. General doubt calls into question the value of all evidence, both perceptual and rational. Descartes invites us to imagine a clever but evil god who deceives us at every turn. Given this possibility, is there any belief or insight about which I could not be mistaken?

Descartes asks the question: in the face of the *epoche*, what can I hold on to, what cannot be doubted? His answer is that only his own existence cannot be doubted. A consequence of this epistemological retreat, however, is that the existence of which he is aware is that of a disembodied thinking being. Only this aspect of existence is veridically presented and verified in self consciousness.

From this minimalist foundation, Descartes attempts to reconstruct knowledge and reality. His reconstruction is implausible, however, depending on a series of mathematical proofs for the existence of God. With God's existence established, Descartes appeals to the benevolence and veracity of the deity to save a portion of his former beliefs. A benevolent deity, he argues, would not allow us to be mistaken about ideas which, like those of mathematics, are perceived "clearly and distinctly." In the end, therefore, Descartes' belief in an external world is rescued, but only as reconstructed through the "clear and distinct ideas" of mathematics and analytic geometry.

For Descartes as for Plato, rationalism leads to dualism. Descartes' thinking being is disembodied, cut off from interaction with the external world. Descartes' problem then becomes to reestablish the possibility of interaction. A good part of philosophy since Descartes is focused on how to put the material and immaterial back together again!

There are three dimensions to Cartesian dualism. The first is the disengagement of mind from body. Thinking substance and extended substance are different in kind; each is governed by its own independent set of laws. This broken causal link raises the question of how a disembodied mind interacts with a body. How can the disembodied thinking substance give commands which result in physical actions? How can this thinking substance receive information about the physical world through sense organs?

The second dimension of Cartesian dualism is the disengagement of representational systems from their field of reference. The issue is whether the semantics of a representation can be defined independent of its application conditions. If the world were completely different from all our beliefs, could our symbols and concepts still have a meaning? Could we use them at all if their actual reference always diverged from their intended reference? This is a serious epistemological issue only fully addressed in the subsequent chapters of Part I.

The third dimension of Cartesian dualism is the disengagement of the cognitive subject from the community of knowers. This retreat, sometimes referred to as the *Cartesian theater*, isolates the individual from the social milieu. In this sense, the individual is seen as "watching" reality move by, understanding and criticizing as a detached observer. We believe this is mistaken; just as intelligence itself is an embodied phenomenon, so also each individual is socially rooted. Individual goals and purposes can only be understood in the context of society's evolving goals and traditions.

The human cannot retreat into the Cartesian theater without taking along assorted baggage. The very concepts with which thoughts are framed are rooted in a shared language and tradition. The individual cannot escape the intersubjective aspect of knowledge and truth: If knowledge were achieved by an isolated individual outside the milieu of shared language, culture, and symbols, how could it be validated or communicated?

Gottfried Wilhelm von Leibniz represents the *extremum* of the rationalist tradition. Like Descartes before him, Leibniz takes mathematics as the sole model and ideal of knowledge. He was the co-inventor of calculus along with Newton. Leibniz proposed a *universal characteristic*, a language of primitives from which all concepts and properties can be defined. Leibniz further proposed a mathematical calculus for constructing true propositions from this language. Interestingly enough, Roger Schank (Schank & Reiger 1974, and Section 6.2.2) takes a similar approach with the creation of conceptual dependency theory.

Like Descartes, Leibniz questions the reality of physical causality and the interaction of objects in the world. The ultimate description of the world is in terms of noninteracting monads; each monad is governed solely by its own internal laws of development. Interaction is explained and supported by the veracity and benevolence of the Creator. Once again divine intervention is required to link up an embodied world. This linkage is described by Leibniz as the principle of preestablished harmony.

1.3.4 The British Empiricists: Hobbes, Locke, and Hume

The British empiricists rejected rationalism as a theory of knowledge. They held that knowledge must be explained through an introspective but empirical psychology. They distinguish two general types of mental phenomena: direct perceptual experience, on the one hand, and thought, memory, and imagination, on the other. Each thinker, of course, uses slightly different terms for this distinction. David Hume, for example, distinguishes "impressions" and "ideas." Impressions are lively and vivid, and not subject to voluntary control. This involuntary character suggests that they may in some way reflect the effect of an external object on the subject's awareness or sensibility. Ideas, on the other hand, are less vivid and detailed and more amenable to the subject's voluntary control.

Given this distinction between impressions and ideas, how then does knowledge arise? For Hobbes, Locke, and Hume the basic explanatory mechanism is associational. Certain properties are repeatedly experienced together in our impressions. This repeated association creates a disposition in the mind to associate the corresponding ideas. The fundamental poverty of this account of knowledge is revealed in Hume's skepticism. Hume's purely descriptive account of the origin of ideas cannot, by his own admission, provide justification for belief in causality. Indeed even the use of logic and induction cannot be rationally supported in this empiricist epistemology.

The associational account of knowledge has played a significant role in modern theories of memory organization, including semantic networks and Schank's theory of memory organization packets (MOPS, see Section 6.3.4). The empiricist attempt to interpret knowledge as habitual associations based on the repetition of certain elements in experience also influenced the behaviorist tradition.

1.3.5 Immanuel Kant

A German philosopher trained in the rationalist tradition, Kant was strongly influenced by the British empiricist tradition. Reading David Hume, Kant said, awakened him from his "dogmatic slumbers." In response to Hume, Kant developed his critical philosophy: an attempted synthesis of rationalism and empiricism. Knowledge contains two components for Kant, an a priori component coming from reason and an a posteriori component arising from experience. Experience itself is "meaningful" to a subject only through the active contribution of the subject. Without a unifying form imposed on representations by the subject, the world would offer nothing more than passing sensations.

The subject's contribution begins, for Kant, at the sensory level. Space and time, Kant argues, are forms of experience which unify perceptual representations and give then meaningful relations to one another. The framework of space and time could not have been learned from experience since this framework is a condition for the possibility of experience.

At the level of judgment, according to Kant, the subject makes a second contribution. Passing images or representations are bound together and taken as diverse appearances of an identical object. Without the active synthesis of representations, the experience of objects would not be possible. The synthesis which transforms passing sensations into appearances of an object gives mental life its intentional character. It makes representations more than mere affections of the mind; it allows them to refer to an object outside the mind. This is a difficult concept, which we will try to illustrate with an example:

> Suppose a person is walking toward me, approaching from a distance. I experience a series of images growing increasingly large, with new features gradually coming into view. First perhaps I recognize the age and gender of this person. Then, when they are close enough, I see their hair and eye color. Finally I recognize this person, an occasional acquaintance.

What is required to turn this series of images into an experience of a person with whom I am acquainted? Kant believes what is required is that they all be taken as images of the same, reidentifiable object, an object which I perhaps experienced yesterday and could potentially re-experience tomorrow. Note that this synthesis requires work, requires an active construction. The "same" object actually changes in appearance, due to perceptual factors such as distance, profile, and lighting, and also changes over a longer period of time as a result of, for example, a haircut, a change in emotional state, or even aging.

Kant argues against pure empiricism and for an *a priori* component to experience. The framework of space and time, the concept of reidentifiable objects and properties, could not have been learned from experience since they are preconditions of experience. Without these unifying structures meaningful experience would not have been possible.

Understanding, according to Kant, effects the syntheses required to construct the experience of objects. Reason effects a higher level synthesis of knowledge, constructing generalizations across objects and domains, generating scientific laws and the structure of scientific theories. Reason contributes the a priori form of these syntheses, while their matter comes from experience. Both reason and understanding ultimately rely on the same a priori principles.

Kant notes that perceptual experience is already an experience of objects in space and time, without any voluntary act or conscious intervention of the subject. He explains this by arguing that the same *a priori* principles of synthesis which inform reason at the level of conscious reflection must also operate in perception at an unconscious level. He attributes this to the work of the transcendental imagination, an active faculty governed by *schemata*, that is, by patterns which determine how perceptual elements are brought together and organized.

Kant's concept of an active subject whose schemata organize experience has had an important influence on 20th century thought. Philosophers including Peirce, Husserl, Heidegger, Kuhn, and others, and psychologists such as Bartlett and Piaget have been influenced by Kant's notion of an active epistemological subject. They agree with Kant that experience is constructed in accordance with certain organizing forms or schemata, and that this constructive activity takes place below the level of conscious awareness.

These modern thinkers depart from Kant on the question of whether the form of this constructive process is fixed. For Kant, only one set of organizing forms or schemata is possible; their nature is determined by a *transcendental logic*. For modern thinkers, alternative schemata are possible. This pluralism shifts the epistemological status of schemata. They are no longer, as Kant believed, *a priori*. Different forms of construction can be compared, at least to some extent, with respect to their effectiveness in organizing a community's practices and interactions with the natural and social environment.

We next examine the disciplines within modern philosophy which directly influence our work in cognitive science.

1.3.6 Philosophical Disciplines

Philosophy has its own tradition of addressing the nature of mind, intelligence, and rationality. Although philosophers and cognitive scientists often use different terms to frame their questions, the content of these questions is often quite similar. We now look at four areas where contemporary philosophical discussion has contributed to the foundations of cognitive science.

Philosophy of Mind.

Philosophy of mind is concerned with the nature of mind and consciousness as well as the relationship between the mental and material realms. What is mental stuff? What is consciousness, intentionality, will? How does awareness arise? How do representations in the mind of an agent control the movements of a physical body? What is the relation between brain states and conscious representations? Philosophers since Descartes have been asking such questions.

Gilbert Ryle, in his book *The Concept of Mind*, (1949) defined one of the central concerns of twentieth century philosophy of mind. According to Ryle, one of the legacies of medieval philosophy was the persistent myth of "the ghost in the machine." Ryle argued that mentalistic explanation is viciously circular. If overt actions require an inner agent to cause them, why doesn't this inner agent also require an inner agent to cause *its* actions? Ryle's challenge to mentalistic explanation was not only an attack on folk psychology. His analysis attempted to show that many psychological as well as philosophical forms of explanation have hidden in them an implicit appeal to "the ghost in the machine." Ryle's arguments are reflected in the writings of contemporary philosophers, including Dennett and Pylyshyn, and their concern with eliminating *homunculi* from the theories of cognitive science. (See Section 2.1.)

A second major concern in twentieth century philosophy of mind is the relationship between physical and mental events. Paul Ziff (1972) vigorously defended a theory called *mind brain identity theory,* an extreme form of reductionism which holds that mental events are nothing but brain events. This theory denies the nonmaterial status of mental events such as thinking, remembering, wishing, etc. Ziff's extreme version of reductionism has been strongly contested by many subsequent philosophers. This controversy continues in cognitive science in the debate between the symbolic/intentional account, defended by Pylyshyn and Dennett, and the neurophysiological reductionism championed by Patricia and Paul Churchland. (See Section 2.3 and 2.4.)

Epistemology.

Epistemology is the study of knowledge, its sources, nature, and limitations. What is perception? How does the knower progress from perception, which is fallible, varied, and changing, to the simplicity and stability of conceptual knowledge? What is the nature of representation? What is a general concept? How do general concepts arise from specific experiences? What is the difference between formal and semantic representations? What is the content of a representation, and how do representations acquire their content? What distinguishes true from false representations? Is objective truth or validity possible, given the fact that knowledge itself is only a set of representations, reflecting the subject's process of encoding, selection, and bias?

Twentieth century epistemology has seen a considerable shift in the notions of representation and truth. At the turn of the century many philosophers, including Russell (1956), Frege (1884), Moore (1986), and Wittgenstein (1933), understood representation primarily in terms of naming or denotation. Nouns, whether proper or improper, were viewed as names of objects or sets of objects. Other types of words, including adjectives, verbs, and adverbs, were seen as significant by virtue of their role in denoting expressions. Much of the work in epistemology since the turn of the century reflects an effort to progress to a more sophisticated view of representation and language. The work of the later Wittgenstein (1953) as well as the speech act theory developed by Austin (1962) and his followers (Grice 1975, Searle 1969) call our attention to the variety of ways in which words are used and the variety of purposes which representations serve. The early pragmatist (Peirce 1958) as well as the semiotic school (Eco 1976, Seboek 1985) developed a view of representation in terms of the construction and interpretation of *signs*, where sign use and interpretation are construed as situated purposive action.

A similar shift in epistemology has occurred in the concept of truth. Early theories of truth tended toward a correspondence view: truth as the agreement of a representation or belief with its object. The problem with this view is obvious: it cannot generate an operational criterion of truth. How can we compare our representation of an object with "the thing in itself," that is, the object as it is outside any encoding scheme?

In the early part of this century the logical positivist school (Carnap 1967, Ayer 1936) attempted to address this problem by operationalizing meaning. They defined the meaning of a sentence in terms of its set of verification conditions, that is, the set of observations by which the truth of or falsity of that statement could be tested. *Verificationism* allowed positivists to declare that most statements in philosophy, ethics, and aesthetics are meaningless since they have no clear verification conditions. Later schools of philosophy, including *pragmatism*, *phenomenology*, *structuralism* and *constructivism* have rejected both the correspondence as well as the verificationist views of truth. Twentieth century philosophy has thus seen a tendency to move away from an objective or abstract notion of truth toward a more contextual concern with evidence, rationality, and warranted belief.

Both AI and cognitive science have struggled, in their brief history, with the notions of representation and truth. There has been a tendency, in both communities, to work with fairly primitive models of representation and truth. The reason perhaps has to do with the relative ease in formalizing these more primitive, denotational theories. Nonetheless we see reflected in the developments of Part II and Part IV some signs of maturation as AI and cognitive science attempt the difficult task of modeling natural language understanding and common sense reasoning.

We present our own views on representation and truth in Sections 2.1 and 3.2, arguing for a constructivist interpretation of truth. We follow Kant and Piaget in holding that knowledge acquisition must be understood in terms of the interaction of the cognitive agent with its environment. On this view, the interpretive activity of the subject plays an equal role, along with the objective environment, in determining the structure of interaction. Constructivism asserts that the refinement of an interpretive framework is usually driven not by an observation which definitively refutes that framework but rather by the tension between the pattern of interpretation and the demands of successful interaction.

Philosophical Logic.

Philosophical logic studies modes of reasoning, inference, and proof. It studies relations of evidence and truth insofar as they provide criteria for evaluating the soundness of reasoning methods. What distinguishes modes of reasoning which are reliable from those which are not? What methods of reasoning are guaranteed to be truth preserving? On what does their soundness rest? Under what conditions is it rational to use unsound methods such as induction or abduction? What are the fundamental concepts and methods required for reasoning about time and change? About possibility and necessity? About what other agents (or I myself) know and believe?

Modern logic makes extensive use of formal representations and mathematical proof procedures. Unlike purely mathematical logic however, philosophical logic has a normative and descriptive thrust. It is not interested in just any formal system with an inference procedure. It is particularly interested in those systems which describe how rational agents reason or ought to reason. It is interested in studying the reasoning and inference strategies that rational agents actually use in order to determine their warrant as well as their properties and limitations.

Of all the fields of philosophy so far discussed, logic has probably had the greatest influence on the development of cognitive science. The formal methods used in logic to model reasoning have been computationally automated and applied to a variety of modeling tasks. It was an early hope of many researchers in AI and cognitive science that the methods used in the construction of formal reasoning systems could be extended to model every aspect of intelligent performance. (For example, see the discussion of GPS in Section 8.1.) Since that time, of course, those early hopes have been tempered with a greater appreciation of the non-logical constraints and non-inferential components of intelligent performance. However the construction of formal computational models as a tool for studying intelligence is still a centerpiece of the cognitive science research programme.

In the case of logic and cognitive science the direction of influence has been largely reciprocal. Many logicians have been drawn into the rich research programs of AI and cognitive science, enticed by the challenge of modeling various aspects of knowledge based task performance. This has given rise to new formalisms in areas such as hierarchical default reasoning, evidential reasoning, belief revision and truth maintenance, auto-epistemic reasoning, multi-agent representation and planning, and many others. We discuss several of these in Chapter 7. Although many in the cognitive science community question the exaggerated emphasis placed on declarative knowledge in the neo-logicist approach, few question the usefulness of formal models as a tool for understanding intelligence.

Philosophy of Science.

Philosophy of science is the study of the theoretical methods used in the sciences. How are hypotheses formulated? How are experiments chosen or constructed? What are the methods used for data selection? What is the general method of discovery that leads from theoretical hypotheses to experiments or observations and back to hypothesis? Why are theories rejected? How does change occur within a science? What is the form of scientific explanation? To what extent does this form vary from science to science? From theory to theory? Why is rapid progress made in certain sciences and not in others?

In the early part of the twentieth century logical positivists dominated the discussion of scientific methods. Positivists argued that a scientific hypothesis is meaningful to the degree that it entails some definite set of observation sentences. The hypothesis is *true* to the extent that the sentences in that set and not their negations are actually observed. Karl Popper (1959) subsequently proposed a modification of this view which replaced the notion of *verifiability* with *falsifiability*. Popper argued that scientific laws cannot be verified since they are universally quantified and therefore entail an infinite set of observation sentences. He thus concluded that scientific theories are selected through falsification rather than verification.

Popper's *falsification hypothesis* provided a focus for the research of Thomas Kuhn. Kuhn (1962) asked the question: What causes paradigm shifts in a science? What causes one theoretical framework to replace another? Examples of paradigm shifts are that from Ptolemaic to Copernican astronomy or that from *humor* theory in medicine to the theory of *infectious agents*. Kuhn rejected Popper's contention that the mechanism for paradigm shifts in the sciences is theory falsification. While specific or low level empirical claims in a science are readily refuted by empirical evidence, a high level theoretical framework is generally immune from refutation. The reasons for this are 1) the observations with which a theory is concerned are interpreted in the context of that theory and thus inevitably preformed by the concepts of that theory, and 2) the individual predictions of a high level theory can be readily *repaired* by adding or modifying parameters that affect the application of the theory.

Although Kuhn's account of paradigm shifts in science has been both challenged and refined by various philosophers, few philosophers today still cling to the view that scientific theories are nothing but distillations of theory-neutral observation sets. Many philosophers now accept in one form or another the idea that experiments and observations are not theory-neutral but rather reflect the biases induced by selection and interpretation under a particular theory. This leaves very much open the question of how a science can strive for objective validity in its observation selection and theory formation. There are a number of debates raging in cognitive science concerning the proper methods to use, where many of the methods in question are associated with particular theoretical frameworks. Examples of this appear throughout the book, for instance the controversy between first person and third person observations of mental events (Chapter 4), the contrast between traditional symbol system approaches (Part II) and the modern connectionist approaches (Part III). Philosophers can contribute to this debate, at least in clarifying the criteria that ought to be used in the selection of methods.

Although the 18th, 19th, and early 20th centuries saw the formalization of philosophy, science, and mathematics, it wasn't until the creation of the digital computer that artificial intelligence became a viable scientific discipline. By the end of the 1940s electronic digital computers had demonstrated their potential to provide the memory and processing power required by intelligent programs. It was now possible to implement formal reasoning systems on a computer and to empirically test their sufficiency for exhibiting intelligence. We next consider the contributions of AI to the science of intelligent systems.

1.4   ARTIFICIAL INTELLIGENCE

Artificial intelligence is that branch of computer science concerned with the creation of a kind of software that might be considered to exhibit "intelligent" behavior. This behavior includes qualities such as flexibility, adaptability, and the potential to learn. Because this research involves the construction and manipulation of models, AI's tools include representations, both symbolic and connectionist, and search techniques.

There are three important aspects of this definition of AI:

1. Artificial intelligence is currently considered an important subdiscipline of computer science. It wasn't always this way, with the earliest programs in AI predating by several decades the establishment of formal education in computer science.
2. The focus of AI is on building computational structures and designing strategies to search these structures for a solution. From an AI perspective, problem solving is construed as a series of operations on the models of a domain.
3. The primary goal of the AI practitioner is to build successful software, and not necessarily to implement human intelligence!

1.4.1 A Brief History

Charles Babbage, an engineer of the early nineteenth century, was one of the originators of the science of operations research. As the designer of the first programmable mechanical computing device, he was also arguably the earliest practitioner of automated or artificial intelligence. Babbage's *difference engine* was a special purpose machine for computing the values of certain polynomial functions, and was the forerunner of his analytical engine.

The *analytical engine*, designed but not successfully built during Babbage's lifetime, was a general purpose programmable computing machine that presaged many of the architectural assumptions supporting the modern computer. The most striking feature of Babbage's work is its treatment of the pattern of an intellectual activity as an entity that may be studied, characterized, and finally implemented mechanically, without concern for the particular values that are passed through the mill of the calculating machine. This is an example of the abstraction and manipulation of form first described by Aristotle!

In fact, Aristotle's logic and inference schemes were also precursors of the automated reasoning of artificial intelligence. The idea of extending Aristotle's and later Leibniz's reasoning calculi with the creation of a formal language for thought happened in the work of the 19th and early 20th century mathematicians George Boole, Gottlob Frege, Bertrand Russell, and Alfred Tarski.

Boole's contribution was in the mathematical formalization of the laws of logic, a formalization that forms the foundation of modern computer science. While the role of Boolean algebra in the design of logic circuitry is well known, Boole's own personal goals in developing this calculus are closer to those of modern cognitive scientists. In the first chapter of his work, suitably titled *An Investigation of the Laws of Thought, on Which Are Founded the Mathematical Theories of Logic and Probabilities*, Boole described his goals as:

To investigate the fundamental laws of those operations of
the mind by which reasoning is performed: to give expression to them in the symbolical language of a Calculus, and
upon this foundation to establish the science of logic and
instruct its method....

Gottlob Frege, in his *Foundations of Arithmetic*, created a mathematical
specification language for describing the calculation process of logic. Frege's
language, now called *first-order predicate logic (FOPL)* offers a representation
for the propositions and truth value assignments that make up the basis of mathematical reasoning systems in AI. FOPL offers a set of tools for automating a theory of reasoning: a language for expressions, a theory for assumptions related to
the meaning of expressions, and a logically sound calculus for inferring new
true expressions.

Russell and Whitehead's work, the *Principia Mathematica*, followed
Frege's, with their stated goal to derive the whole of mathematics through purely
formal operations on a collection of axioms. In the *Principia*, Russell and Whitehead treat mathematics as a purely formal system. This meant that axioms and
theorems would be treated solely as strings of characters, with no "meaning"
attributed to them. Proofs would proceed solely through the application of well-
defined rules for manipulating these strings: there would be no relying on "intuition" or the "meaning" of theorems as a basis for proofs. What meaning the theorems and axioms of the system might have in relation to the world would be
independent of their logical derivations. This was the ultimate rationalist and
dualist tool!

The treatment of mathematical reasoning in purely formal and mechanical
terms provided an essential basis for its automation on computers. Indeed, early
AI researchers Newell and Simon, with their creation of the *Logic Theorist,* did
exactly that: they developed a computer program that proved many of the theorems of Russell and Whitehead's *Principia*.

The logical syntax and formalization of inference rules developed in the
Principia continue to offer a foundation for representation in artificial intelligence as well as for the development of automated reasoning programs, an
important application area of AI. As we note in the next section, when, in the late
1950s, Newell, Shaw, and Simon compared the steps and solutions of their Logic
Theorist program with the work of human subjects' solving the same problem,
many historians of science feel that cognitive science was born!

Alfred Tarski is another mathematician whose work is essential to the foundation of AI. Tarski created a theory of reference wherein the well-formed formulae of Frege could be said to refer, in a precise fashion, to the physical world. In
his paper, *The Semantic Conception of Truth and the Foundation of Semantics*,
Tarski describes a theory of reference and truth value relationships. This theory

of reference is general enough to support much current work in AI, including rule based expert reasoning systems. These reasoning systems are often intended to reflect the problem solving skills of the human expert.

1.4.2 Alan Turing and the Turing Test

One of the first papers to address the question of machine intelligence, specifically in relation to the modern digital computer, was written in 1950 by the British mathematician Alan Turing. *Computing Machinery and Intelligence* is still timely for both Turing's conjecture that intelligence is open to formal characterization as well as that it can exist independent of the human mind. In his writing Turing also responded to arguments against the possibility of automating intelligence. In discussing these issues, he notes the fundamental ambiguities in both the notions of thinking and machines.

To make these questions precise, Turing created the abstract specification for the *Turing machine* and for the *universal Turing machine*, (see Chapter 2.5). This latter offers not just a mathematical description for what is computable but also specifications for actually building a programmable computer.

To make precise the notion of intelligence in a machine, Turing proposed an imitation game, now referred to as the *Turing test*. This test measures the performance of an allegedly intelligent machine against that of a human being, arguably the best and only standard of intelligent behavior.

The Turing test places a human and a computing device in rooms apart from a second human, referred to as the interrogator, as in Figure 1.3. The interrogator is not able to see or speak directly to either of them, does not know which entity is actually the machine, and may communicate with them solely by means of a text based device such as a terminal. The interrogator is asked to distinguish between the computer and the human solely on the basis of their answers to questions asked through this device. If the interrogator is unable to reliably distinguish the machine from the human, then, Turing argues, the machine must be assumed to be intelligent.

Important features of the Turing test for AI include:

1. It gives an objective notion of intelligence, that is, the behavior of a known intelligent being in response to a particular situation. This allows determination of intelligence without questions about its "true" nature.

2. It prevents us from being sidetracked by confusing and currently unanswerable questions relating to whether the computer uses the "appropriate internal processes" or whether the computer is actually "conscious" of its decisions.

FIGURE 1.3   The Turing test. The interrogator, the person isolated in the room, asks questions attempting to determine whether a computer or another person is responding.

3. It eliminates any bias toward a living organism as the only embodiment of intelligence by forcing the interrogator, by being ignorant of the origin of questions, to focus entirely on the content to the answers of the questions.

4. As with other tests of intelligence such as the IQ test, the Turing test does not directly test the process by which answers are determined. The test is simply a direct comparison of computational results with the responses of the human, and unless more detail is systematically sought by further interrogations, the notion of the process by which answers are produced is ignored.

In the more recent history of AI, the Turing test continues to play an important role. In evaluating AI programs, especially expert systems, the designers must know when they are ready for use. The current methodology, whether it be for a program delivering medical care or for configuring computers, is to design a Turing test evaluation, where the skills of the computer are compared with similar skills of humans. In the MYCIN program at Stanford, for instance, the doctor's medical recommendations for treating meningitis infections were compared with those of the computer (Luger & Stubblefield 1993, Chap. 8). In more recent times there has also been a monetary reward offered for the computer program that comes closest to passing the Turing test, and an annual event created for this competition (Epstein 1992).

1.4.2 AI as a Research Discipline

The formal beginnings of the AI community took place at a meeting held at Dartmouth College in 1956. The intended focus of this workshop, called the *Dartmouth Summer Research Project on Artificial Intelligence*, was to bring together researchers that had created computer programs that could produce intelligent results. An informal description of "intelligent results" might be "results of a running program, that if produced by a human, would be considered intelligent," in other words, programs that for some application could pass Turing's test. The name *artificial intelligence* was chosen for this workshop. The word *artificial* was selected for its literal meaning, to make by skilled effort (from the latin verb *facere*, to make, and noun *ars, artis*, with skill).

The description found in *Computers and Thought* (Feigenbaum & Feldman 1963) of several of the invited presenters at this Dartmouth workshop offers a perspective of early work in AI. Arthur Samuel described his checker playing program, one designed using techniques such as hill climbing brought from the field of operations research (see also Chapter 9). This program, remarkable for its use of memory and simple learning on the primitive computing machines of the 1950s, was subsequently to achieve world class checker proficiency. Gelernter described his geometry theorem proving program that could automatically prove many of the theorems of high school geometry texts.

Newell, Shaw, and Simon, then researchers at Carnegie Institute of Technology, presented their work on the *Logic Theorist* program, that very important early research that proved many of the theorems in Russell and Whitehead's *Principia*. Newell and Simon also presented some very interesting research comparing the run of their computer program doing mathematical proofs with human subjects solving the same problems. This comparative research is arguably the beginning of cognitive science.

One early cognitive program called *EPAM*, for *Elementary Perceiver and Memorizer*, memorized and indexed sets of nonsense syllables. EPAM was presented by Edward Feigenbaum, one of Herbert Simon's first students. Feigenbaum was later to design the first expert systems at Stanford University's AI laboratory.

Another piece of research presented at the Dartmouth conference was Newell and Simon's *General Problem Solver (GPS)*. This program introduced the concept of *means-ends analysis*. This solution strategy indexed different problem and subproblem solution techniques (the means) to the goals (the ends) they could accomplish. The means-ends analysis controller would search the problem space for goal and subgoal reductions and then link these differences to operators for their solution. This problem solving strategy was called *general* because it was anticipated that a large percent of problem application areas would be amenable to this approach. Even though many problems were solved by GPS (Ernst

& Newell 1979), which has subsequently been termed a weak problem solving method, later work has seriously called into question its generality. We consider GPS in more detail in Section 8.1.

From its beginnings in the 1950s, the artificial intelligence community looked at a wide variety of applications. The weak method search techniques and problem solving of the 1950s and 1960s gave way to the knowledge intensive approaches of the 1970s and 1980s. But the common goal remained: to understand and build intelligent artifacts. Many of these AI techniques for modeling intelligent problem solving are described in Parts II and III.

Current work in artificial intelligence is as robust and extensive as ever. Besides delivering products, such as expert system problem solvers and robot controllers, to the commercial marketplace, the AI community has developed many important tools for the computer scientist, including very high level programming languages and object oriented design. AI continues to address a wide range of research issues. These topics include machine learning, design of vision systems, natural language understanding, and all forms of automated reasoning (Luger & Stubblefield 1993).

1.4.3 The Connectionist Contribution to Problem Solving

A very different approach from the traditional explicit symbol based representation and search of Section 1.4.2 seeks to build intelligent programs using models which are analogous to the structure of neurons in the human brain.

A schematic of a neuron, as seen in Figure 1.4, consists of a cell body which has a number of branching protrusions, called dendrites and a single branch called the axon. Dendrites receive signals from other neurons. When these combined impulses exceed a certain threshold, the neuron fires and an impulse, or spike, passes down the axon. Branches at the end of the axon form synapses with the dendrites of other neurons. The synapse is the point of contact between neurons. Synapses may be either excitatory or inhibitory. An excitatory synapse adds to the total of signals reaching the neuron, an inhibitory synapse subtracts from this total.

This description of a neuron is excessively simple, but it captures most of the features that are relevant to neural models of computation. In particular, each computational unit is a simple threshold device that receives signals from other units and passes a signal on to other units when its threshold is exceeded. Instead of using explicit symbols and operations, the knowledge of the system emerges out of the entire network of neural connections and threshold values.

There are a number of reasons why connectionist or neural architectures are appealing as mechanisms for implementing intelligence. Among these are the fact that highly parallel problem solving based on multiple neuron-like computa

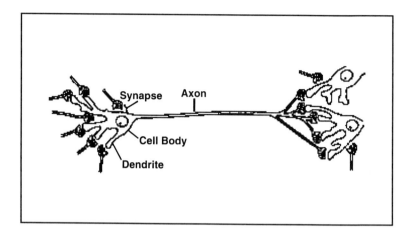

FIGURE 1.4 A simplified diagram of a neuron from Crick and Asanuma (1986).

tional units is less sensitive to noise in a system, can handle data with missing pieces of information, and degrades gracefully as information is removed, rather than simply failing as occurs in many traditional symbol systems. It is also highly parallel in its implementation, reflecting, as many researchers feel, important aspects of human information processing.

The "knowledge" of the system is distributed across multiple processors acting in parallel. Connectionist architectures provide a natural model for parallelism, since each neuron is an independent physical unit, although its connectivity to other units can be arbitrarily complex. Daniel Hillis (1985) has commented on the fact that humans get faster at a task as they acquire more knowledge while computers tend to slow down. This slow down is due to the cost of sequentially searching a knowledge base; a massively parallel architecture like the human brain would not suffer from this problem.

The earliest example of a neurally based model of computation was in work done by McCulloch and Pitts in the 1940s (McCulloch & Pitts 1943). Their networks employed an extremely simple model of neurons: each neuron had both inhibitory and excitatory inputs. It fired only if the total number of active excitatory inputs exceeded the number of inhibitory inputs and produced an output value of 1.

VonNeumann showed that by introducing redundancies into McCulloch-Pitts networks, they could continue to function reliably in spite of the malfunction of individual elements. This was an important result, in that it suggested how the human brain is able to continue functioning despite the loss of brain cells. Redundancy and the consequent robustness is an important feature of connectionist architectures.

In the 1950s, Rosenblatt proposed a neural network architecture which included adjustable thresholds on individual units and developed a procedure under which these networks could learn by systematically adjusting their weights (Rosenblatt 1962). These networks were called perceptrons and were capable of learning simple classification problems.

More modern versions of the neuron-based approach employ different hardware architectures and more flexible learning algorithms that overcome many of the problems of the earlier approaches. In fact many of the current practitioners prefer calling their work *connectionism* or *parallel distributed processing (PDP)* rather than the earlier neural-based computing. This may be seen as an explicit attempt by researchers to remove their work from the human neuron analogy. Whatever the name, the goal of the connectionist approach is to perform complex problem solving such as vision, auditory perception, and voiced-speech generation, as well as to address other important problems in learning.

Research in artificial intelligence, from both the explicit symbol based as well as from the connectionist approach, continues to influence work in cognitive science for three reasons: First, both research communities are interested in the understanding and creation of intelligent artifacts. Second, and more importantly, the cognitive science research community requires a representation and process medium to capture the invariances found in intelligent systems. A central focus of AI research has been to create such media. Finally, both approaches give the cognitive science researcher the possibility of being part of an empirical discipline: their models may be run and their results tested. The results of such experiments may be confirmation of hypotheses, but even more importantly, the possibility of model revision for further experimentation. The synergism between these two disciplines will be reflected through the topics presented in this book.

1.5 THE GOALS OF COGNITIVE SCIENCE

With all the research activity occurring in artificial intelligence, cognitive psychology, and cognitive science, there is a danger that we might lose sight of what cognitive science is all about, that is, what the specific goals of cognitive science are. Quite simply, *the goal of cognitive science* is to develop a theory of intelligent systems.

This goal is not the same as building a machine that behaves sufficiently similar to most humans so that it could pass some form of the Turing test. We could have a theory of intelligent systems and still not be able to actually build the system that would pass Turing's test. For example, like Babbage in the 19th century, we may simply lack the technical capability to physically implement certain components of the theory. It is also possible that we could have a system that would pass Turing's test, but not have a complete theory of intelligent systems. For example, the system may rely on some type of very high speed brute force search procedure that may not reflect the problem solving methods of other intelligent systems.

In the coming chapters we will be investigating specific research approaches to describe intelligent phenomena. One such approach supporting much current work in cognitive science is the *physical symbol system hypothesis*. Allen Newell and Herbert Simon (1972) hypothesized that a necessary and sufficient condition of intelligence is that system's ability to manipulate symbols. Thus, if a system doesn't have the ability to manipulate symbols, it won't have intelligence and if it does have this ability the system will also have the ability to be intelligent. As this book develops, we will see how the evolution of this idea has served as a central working hypothesis for many cognitive scientists over the past two decades. If it is valid then intelligence is indeed a natural category.

Connectionist researchers offer a different approach to describing intelligence. Effective connectionist networks constitute an existence proof, a demonstration of the possibility that the invariances of a problem solving domain may be captured in a computational system NOT containing explicit symbols to represent semantic entities. The focus of the connectionist approach is the perceptual and pattern recognition aspects of intelligence. These are often very difficult to capture in an explicit symbol based environment. It might well be the case that mature models of intelligence include a synergistic interplay of the symbol based and connectionist approaches. We will follow these two paradigms throughout the course of this book.

A complete theory of intelligence must be stated at a sufficiently abstract level to encompass the multiple forms of intelligence and not be mislead by differences in content or form. We present a vocabulary for this task in Chapter 2. A complete theory must use the language of a representation/process medium to capture the invariances found in intelligent systems. We address these issues in Chapters 2 and 3. It must furthermore distinguish between the necessary and the sufficient conditions for intelligence (Chapter 4). Finally, it must account for differences in the quantity and quality of intelligent performance.

Of course we are nowhere near having a complete theory of intelligent systems. But with the emergence of the field of cognitive science we are, for the first time, engaged in an integrated and concerted effort toward developing such a theory. This book is the story of that effort.

1.6   EPILOGUE AND REFERENCES

The roots of the science of intelligence go back to the first musings of the early Greek philosophers. The evolution of cognitive science in many ways reflects the history of western philosophical thought. Readings in philosophy, mathematics, and especially epistemology are important for understanding the questions we now ask and the research tools we necessarily employ. Donald Norman (1981) is the editor of a collection of essays by researchers that marks the start of the modern formal discipline of cognitive science.

Many writers have supported the possibility of a science of cognition. Among these are Daniel Dennett (1978, 1984), John Haugeland (1981), and Zenon Pylyshyn (1980, 1984). Allen Newell and Herbert Simon (1972) are the first modern practitioners of the discipline of cognitive science, with their comparison of human subject's solutions of logic problems with the running of their own computer program.

In the psychological tradition, there is no literature more extensive than the papers and books written on intelligence. Fortunately for those who wish to gain a better appreciation of this literature, Robert Sternberg has performed the close to impossible task of identifying the important issues and presenting them in a highly accessible and current form. His edited works, *Advances in the Psychology of Human Intelligence*, volumes I to X (1982), and *The Handbook of Intelligence* (1982) provide an excellent introduction to the history, theory, and methods of understanding intelligence.

For a look into the factor analytic approach to describing intelligence, Guilford's classic, *The Structure of Intellect* (1956) is a good source. A process or learning approach that takes an evolutionary adaptation perspective on intelligence is Jerison's (1975) book, *The Evolution of the Brain and Intelligence*.

The tools and techniques of artificial intelligence, see for example, *Artificial Intelligence: Structures and Strategies for Complex Problem Solving* (Luger & Stubblefield 1993) have offered both a representational medium as well as a computational methodology for work in cognitive science. The connectionist approach to intelligence also finds many of its roots within the artificial intelligence community. In the early days of AI much of the research was published in technical reports from various companies and universities, including Rand Corporation, Massachusetts Institute of Technology, and Carnegie Institute of Technology, that supported this research. Fortunately, Comtex Scientific Corporation has brought to market packaged sets of microfiche containing these early research reports (Comtex 1985).

The first book that collected early results of AI research, including that from the Dartmouth Summer Conference, was Feigenbaum and Feldman's *Computers and Thought*, published in 1963. Throughout the history of AI, the primary medium for presenting current topics and research in AI remains the conferences and *Proceedings of the International Joint Conference on Artificial Intelligence (IJCAI)* and of the *American Association for Artificial Intelligence (AAAI)*. We also recommend *Readings in Cognitive Science* (Collins & Smith 1988). A modern version of the Turing test, as well as the competition for best program based on the Turing test, is described in *AI Magazine*, Summer 1992.

For material complementing the approach we take in Part I of this book we recommend *Foundations of Cognitive Science*, edited by Michael Posner (1989), especially the first four papers: Herb Simon and Craig Kaplan's *Foundations of Cognitive Science*, Zenon Pylyshyn's *Computing in Cognitive Science*, Allen Newell et al.'s *Symbolic Architectures for Cognition*, and David Rumelhart's *The Architecture of Mind: A Connectionist Approach*.

Chapter 2

VOCABULARIES FOR DESCRIBING INTELLIGENCE

Think of arm chairs and reading chairs and dining-room chairs, and kitchen chairs, chairs that pass into benches, chairs that cross the boundary and become settees, dentist's chairs, thrones, opera stalls, seats of all sorts, those miraculous fungoid growths that cumber the floor of the arts and crafts exhibitions, and you will see what a lax bundle in fact is this simple straightforward term. I would undertake to defeat any definition of chair or chairishness that you gave me...

Charles Peirce (1958)

What's in a name? that which we call a rose
By any other name would smell as sweet...

William Shakespeare, *Romeo and Juliet.*

2.0 INTRODUCTION

In Chapter 1, we introduced the science of intelligent systems and began our examination of the phenomena of intelligence. To establish any science, we must first delineate carefully the focus of our investigation and create a language for describing what we find within our purview. Only then can we identify the principles or generalizations that apply. In the present chapter we discuss what Pylyshyn (1984) refers to as *the vocabulary of cognition.*

The goal of all science is to capture generalizations within the phenomena of concern. To do this for cognitive science, we must first identify a set of concepts, a vocabulary, to describe intelligence. The generalizations we seek will not simply jump out at us when we observe the phenomena. Discovering them requires that we adopt the appropriate level of analysis and type of categories; again, an appropriate vocabulary.

As scientists we ask questions of nature. These questions are framed with the vocabulary that reflects our understanding. Different questions of nature suggest answers involving a new and more sophisticated vocabulary. What is the role of quarks in the constitution of matter? How are environmental constraints related to genetic codes? What geopolitical factors determine the price of oil? What socioeconomic factors determine cycles in moral attitudes? Although a radical reductionist might argue that all these questions can ultimately be explained in terms of probabilities of particles in motion, most scientists address these different questions with different taxonomies of knowledge, that is, with different categories and vocabularies. The answers nature offers to our questions, if indeed we are within the traditions and evolution of a science, often force us to revise our understanding, along with its categories and vocabulary, for further experiment (Kuhn 1962, Newell & Simon 1976).

In Section 2.1, we discuss the influence of our conceptual framework on the process of observation. We develop the constructivist thesis that all observation involves interpretation and that interpretation is influenced by the categories or concepts into which we map or encode our perceptions. Different categories will reveal different generalizations regarding the same phenomenon.

We then consider, in Sections 2.2 through 2.4, three competing levels of explanation, a behavioral, a neural-physiological, and a mentalistic. Each of these approaches to understanding intelligence have their own advocates, as well as their individual categories and vocabularies. We present the focus of each school and criticize each approach. We conclude these sections with an argument for the necessity of using mentalistic categories to explain intelligent actions.

In Section 2.5, we present a description of the automated formal system and present a method for describing the equivalence of formal systems. This is the language computer scientists use to describe what is computable and to determine whether different systems are equivalent in their computational powers. We give examples of the *Turing machine* and the *universal Turing machine* and show how these formalisms offer a vocabulary and specifications for intelligent problem solving. We conclude Section 2.5 with some comments on decidibility, complexity, and the possibility that the computational model of intelligence might be too general. Section 2.6 points ahead to formalisms for representing intelligence: the symbolic and connectionist architectures.

2.1 "RAW PHENOMENA" AND INTERPRETATION

2.1.1 Introduction

You may remember or have seen reruns of the old television program *Dragnet*. Police detective Joe Friday, in the middle of investigating a crime, patiently reminds his anxious and overly talkative witness, "Just the facts ma'am, just the facts!" We, like Joe Friday, would like to believe that it is possible to report simply and only what is observed.

Joe Friday's epistemology, sometimes referred to as *naive realism*, assumes that perception gives direct access to an "objective" reality. Adherents of this view rest comfortably in the faith that the world is pretty much the way it appears through the senses, ignoring the role played by interpretation and judgment.

Naive realism stands in sharp contrast to an alternative epistemology, *idealism*. Idealism holds that the mind is in contact solely with its own sensations and ideas. Even sense perceptions, though possibly caused by external objects, are nonetheless nothing but sensations in the mind, and thus purely internal mental states. The belief that the sensation which the object produces in the mind resembles the object or conveys the object's properties cannot be supported. To verify this resemblance we would have to be able to get outside our mental representations and view the object "directly," an action that is clearly impossible. Therefore, the idealist argues, the world as experienced is a realm of objects as they appear in our mind, not as they are in themselves. An independent external reality, if it exists at all, is ultimately unknowable.

Between these two epistemological extremes, there is a range of intermediate positions, including *critical realism*, *pragmatism*, *constructivism*, and many others. These views reject both the naive realist assumption that reality is simply given in experience, without requiring interpretation, and the idealist argument that an external reality, if it exists, is unknowable. To illustrate how it is possible to develop a view which avoids the pitfalls of both idealism and naive realism, we describe the *constructivist* position.

Constructivists hypothesize that all perceptions are the result of interactions between external energy from the world and mental categories imposed on the world (Piaget 1954, 1970; von Glasersfeld 1978). In Piaget's terms, we *assimilate* external phenomena according to our current understanding and *accommodate* our understanding to the perceived phenomena.

Piaget uses the term *schemata* to describe our *a priori* conceptions of the external world. Its philosophical justification goes back to Kant (Section 1.3). Schemata represent the concepts or categories that we use to organize our experience of the world. For the constructivist, observation is not a passive or neutral process; rather, it is active and interpretive.

Of course, perceived information never exactly fits our preconceived *a priori* schemata. As a result of this tension, the schemata which the subject uses to organize experience are either modified or replaced. The need for accommodation in the face of unsuccessful interactions drives a process of cognitive change. In this sense the constructivist epistemology is fundamentally an account of cognitive development and evolution.

In an example from Piaget's research, children aged 7 to 9 are described at a stage of development when they are not able to "conserve volume." If this child is presented with the two containers of liquid shown in Figure 2.1 and asked which container has more of the liquid, she responds that the taller one has more. This response is made even though a measure of volume as length times width times height would have considerably more liquid in the shorter container.

As the child matures and her conception of volume becomes more sophisticated, usually at age 10 or 11, she answers the question correctly. Piaget does not contend that the child now possesses a conscious abstract specification of volume, such as length times width times height; this will only come later, at ages 12 to 14 with the "formal operations" stage of mental development. Rather, the child recognizes the correct answer to the volume problem as a reflection of a more sophisticated mental representation for the concept.

This new mental processing occurs as part of her normal problem solving, and usually at a subconscious level. This accommodation is driven by pragmatic consequences: the immature schema is no longer capable of encoding the phenomena in a sufficiently useful fashion. The constructivist view contends that the child has acquired this new more mature view of volume as a result of her continued interaction with and use of her surroundings. Her societal embodiment gives her experiences that demand maturity as well as expressions to describe them. An even more sophisticated representation will be required to cope with measures of the volumes and masses of objects at accelerations approaching that of light; but as part of a social community she will be afforded the opportunity to develop these tools, should their need arise.

Another example of this constructive process in interpretation is presented in Figure 2.2. Most observers see, quite simply, the words "the cat on the mat ate the rat." However, the "H" and the "A" are exactly the same ambiguous character. The context disambiguates the situation and the observer constructs a useful interpretation.

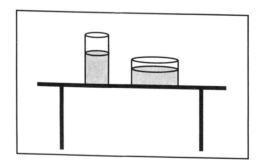

FIGURE 2.1   A Piagetian task requiring volume conservation. The 7- to 9-year-old child, when asked which container holds more liquid, selects the taller glass. A more mature schema will later see volume as a function of all three dimensions.

There is a *felicity principle*, see Chapter 12, in effect also, as the reader expects the character string to make sense. A random rearrangement of these characters would not be so perceived!

A constructivist approach is also helpful in understanding theory formation and revision in science (Kuhn 1962, Popper 1959, Quine 1953). In science as in ordinary life there is no direct access to reality. How we interpret reality depends on the set of categories through which we "see" it. An important difference between scientific and unscientific interpretations is that with science we struggle to make the presuppositions of the interpretation process explicit; everyday, unscientific interpretation occurs implicitly and with little awareness of how we come to some particular conclusion.

The only method for understanding reality and communicating our understanding to others is to use vocabulary and categories that work until the time we find something that works better. We don't have to be "true" in some ultimate objective sense; our interpretations must only be sufficient. Nature operates as a selective filter, a hidden hand eliminating those models or systems that don't measure up and leaving all the remaining models as viable for another day. The models we use are simply those that have continued to work.

Eventually every useful model breaks down and is disconfirmed; then it evolves into a more sophisticated representation that accounts for the anomalies encountered by the earlier model. Again, in von Glasersfeld's words, disconfirmation of a model with revision to a more useful representation is the peak knowledge experience. In this evolutionary sense there is also a close and interesting analogy between the evolution of scientific models and that of the human species itself. In other words, if we are not wrong periodically, with the ability to revise and expand our expectations, we become extinct!

It is quite natural to ask the source or material for our revised and enhanced expectations of phenomena. The evolutionary constructivist approach presented to this point might seem to describe the intelligent human as an isolated agent grappling with the complexities of an alien world. Nothing could be further from the truth. As responsible individuals we are embedded in the context of a complex sociological milieu. Our goals and methods are dictated not just by a code of genetic information, but perhaps more by a code acquired from our sociological context. Our science, our schools, our religions, and our families all contribute to what we are and the directions we are taking. We construct our meaning from these contexts and traditions.

THE CAT ON THE MAT ATE THE RAT.

FIGURE 2.2 The constructive process in interpretation. The ambiguous character is interpreted according to context.

As mature agents we continue our explorations by finding and responsibly affirming invariants in our environment. We acknowledge the breakdown of our understandings, find the pieces for a reconstituted viewpoint within our sociological context, and once again take responsibility for a revised understanding.

The implication of a constructivist epistemology is that the interpretation of any situation, including that reflecting intelligence, is in terms of the concepts or categories imposed by the observer on reality. We proposed earlier that the goal of cognitive science is to capture generalizations within the phenomena of intelligence. The generalizations about intelligence that emerge will necessarily reflect the categories used to interpret intelligent actions. We revisit these ideas in Section 3.1.1 when we propose an epistemological support for representations. The primary question of the remainder of this chapter is to establish a vocabulary and categories that can be used to best capture the invariants within intelligent phenomena.

2.1.2 Vocabularies for Cognition

We must first agree on what we mean by "an intelligent action." We contend that most instances of intelligence share some common properties. Specifically, an intelligent action is an action taken in a situation and that has some observable consequences on the environment. Whether the action was intelligent or not depends on the nature of the consequences relative to some goal or purpose.

We contend that intelligent actions in some general sense involve input-output relations that are judged more or less intelligent relative to some presumed goal or desired effect of the action on the environment. We recognize that it will be impossible to offer a definition of intelligent actions that is both all encompassing and precise. We have no illusions in this regard: our goal is to capture the gist of what we mean by intelligent actions.

Given this working definition, we next discuss several viewpoints or categorizations that have attempted to capture the generalizations of intelligent input-output relations. Most of these positions have evolved from earlier psychological attempts at describing intelligence. We will criticize each of them from our current constructivist approach to understanding.

2.1.3 Folk Psychology

Why do students take notes in class? Some might reply that it helps them remember, it helps studying for exams, or it makes it easier to pay attention to lectures. All of these explanations entail a number of beliefs about learning, remembering, and performing on exams.

More generally, explanations given to questions of this nature typically involve resorting to a variety of beliefs, desires, perceptions, fears, and expectations. Questions of this sort seem to demand a certain class of explanation. If someone began to explain the taking of class notes in terms of the electro-chemical state of various neurons in the brain we would suspect that person was either some type of Doctor Demento or simply misunderstood the question.

The practice of explaining human behaviors in terms of mentalistic concepts has gone on for centuries. It is *folk psychology*. While it may strike most of us as a natural and perfectly acceptable explanation of human behavior, it does not sit well with many philosophers, psychologists, and neural scientists. Folk psychology may be okay for ordinary folk, but not for the scientist. Why? Because folk psychology assumes a causal relationship between mental and physical events. This causal relationship is difficult to reconcile with the existence of purely physical laws which already completely determine the physical realm. This problem, first discussed by Descartes (1637), is called the *mind-body* problem.

There are a number of difficulties in understanding the causal relationship between mental and physical events, between an agent's thoughts and desires and her physical actions. How can mental events cause physical events when physical event are completely determined by physical causality? If mental events can in fact have a causal efficacy, what guarantees that they will not violate physical laws? How can we attribute causality to intentions when the presence of a goal may or may not result in an action? Even if we could somehow know that an agent will act on her goal, is it possible to predict when or in what manner that action will occur?

If indeed these belief states cause us to engage in concrete actions, for example to take notes, we need a set of bridge laws to cross from the mental to the physical. Descartes, in addressing this issue, posited a *res cogitans*, a "thinking substance," that complemented his mechanistic physical world, the *res extensa*. Descartes, as noted in Section 1.3, was unable to describe how these two substances interacted, except through the support of a benign deity. Creating these bridge laws, or explaining why such laws are unnecessary, remains an important open question for both psychologists and philosophers.

In the following sections we consider three broad classes of categories proposed to explain the action of intelligent systems. Perhaps the simplest and most direct approach to this problem is the one proposed by the *behaviorist* school in psychology, especially Watson (1930) and Skinner (1953). For behaviorists the appropriate level of analysis is the *stimulus-response (S - R)* relations that we "directly" observe (Section 2.2).

The second approach we present (Section 2.3) is to assume that some physical properties of the organism mediates the S - R relations. In its most general form this class of variables refers to physical states of the entire organism, such as the brain, glands, or whatever. We describe this model as the *S - Organism - R* approach. Most scientists in this group assume that the brain or nervous system is the most important factor mediating S - R relationships, so we refer to them as looking for *S - Brain - R* relationships.

The third approach we consider is based on the idea that intelligent behavior in a situation depends on how the situation is semantically or intentionally, interpreted by the system. This approach can be represented as *S - Mind - R* and is what cognitive scientists refer to as the *representational* or *constructivist* approach (Section 2.4).

2.2   BEHAVIORISM: S - R RELATIONS

The behaviorist thesis states that the vocabulary of folk psychology is simply a set of abstractions from specific relations that are observed in people's reactions to various situations. The essential point is that all relevant generalizations regarding the actions of intelligent systems can be captured at the level of the stimulus - response relationships. There are two forms of this argument that differ in the assumptions that are made regarding consciousness and other mental states. These are the *philosophical* and *methodological behaviorist* positions.

2.2.1   Philosophical and Methodological Behaviorism

Philosophical behaviorism is closely tied to the *logical positivist* school in philosophy that began in the 1920s and reached its peak in the 1930s. It involved a number of impressive minds, including Ayer (1936), Carnap (1967), Russell (1956), and Wittgenstein (1933). One of their goals was to show that it was possible to reduce any mental concept to a set of relationships between observable events: the stimuli and resulting behaviors. In effect, mental concepts are dispositions to behave in some particular manner and, in theory, it should be possible to specify the set of potential behaviors. For example, the mental state of pain can be captured by referring to various behaviors, such as saying "ouch," withdrawing, and suffering tissue damage.

Not surprisingly, the philosophical behaviorists very quickly ran into a major problem. Their lists of observable descriptions for a specific mental state became endlessly long with numerous conditionals and qualifiers. The obvious problem was that how a person behaved in a given situation depended on a potentially infinite number of factors pertaining to how the situation was perceived, the context of the situation, and various internal mental and physical states.

The methodological behaviorists initially believed that it would be possible to capture all of these factors with a more comprehensive specification of the observable events surrounding the behavior. It eventually became evident, however, that their approach was intractable. This herculean effort concluded with one of its main proponents, Wittgenstein (1953), recanting his earlier work and arguing that such a reduction is, in principle, impossible.

Methodological behaviorism is the more familiar psychological position of people like Watson (1930) and Skinner (1953). Unlike philosophical behaviorism, the methodological did not attempt to reduce mental states to behaviors, but simply dismissed mental states as epiphenomenal. That is, mental states may exist in some form, but they play no causal role in behavior. Thus, there is no need to attempt a behaviorally based definition of these various mental states. The approach of the methodological behaviorist was to include only concepts that were operationally defined in terms of the observable. If this reduction couldn't be made, then the concept should not become a part of the scientific vocabulary of psychology. Thus, most of the concepts of folk psychology were simply excluded from the vocabulary of the methodological behaviorist.

2.2.2 Critique of Methodological Behaviorism: Stimulus Definition

For the methodological behaviorists to be successful in capturing all the relevant generalizations regarding intelligent actions in terms of relationships between directly observable stimuli and responses, it is necessary that they provide an objective definition of both these stimuli and their responses. The problem they encountered in defining the stimulus was that the effective stimulus was not necessarily the stimulus as physically described.

An obvious example of this is when selective attention influences the perception of the external (nominal) stimulus. In most, even mildly complex situations, we only attend to a relatively small proportion of the energy changes that are available to our receptor systems. A general and profound problem is that we more or less automatically impose preconceived categories on our perceptions of situations. As discussed earlier, our perceptions of events are constrained or filtered by our expectations. Describing the "objective" parameters of the external stimulus is simply imposing the experimenter's categories of description, and these may or may not coincide with another observer's, or indeed the human subject's perception of the stimulus itself.

It is important to ask how the stimulus is perceived by the subject of an experiment. The problem here is illustrated by some research designed to determine whether behavior is under the control of absolute or relational properties of a stimulus (Lawrence & DeRivera 1954, Johnson & Bailey 1966). In these experiments, groups of rats or children of various ages were first trained on a brightness discrimination task. The stimuli were six cards in which the top halves differed in levels of brightness and the bottom half was at the mid-range, as in Figure 6.3. The experimenters used seven gray levels, *1* to *7*, on the cards. The bottom half of each card had the middle level gray, 4.

The subjects were trained to approach cards 1, 2, and 3, where the top half was lighter than the bottom, and to avoid cards 5, 6, and 7, where the top half was darker than the bottom half. The task could be learned either on the basis of the absolute brightness of the top half or on the basis of the relationship between the top and bottom half.

To determine how subjects had learned, the cards were inverted. Thus, if the subjects now approached cards 5, 6, and 7, they were apparently responding on the basis of the relational cues. However, if subjects continued to approach cards 1, 2, and 3, they were responding on the basis of the absolute brightness of what now was now the bottom half of the card. Finally, if subjects simply responded on the basis of the top half, shade number 4, they would respond at chance.

The results of these experiments indicated that both rats and children responded predominantly on the basis of the relational cues. However, Johnson and Bailey (1966) showed that this varied as a function of the salience of the relational cues. These studies point out the difficulty in defining the functional stimulus, the basis of the subject's response, without performing some type of transfer test, such as inverting the cards. The functional stimulus cannot be defined by just describing the physical characteristics of the stimulus.

Pylyshyn (1984) discusses the problems associated with the behavioral definition of the stimulus as the *stimulus independence* problem. If we attempt to describe behavior in terms of physical properties of a situation we will soon come to the conclusion that most human behavior is random. Given the same physical stimulus, a different response may occur on the next occasion it is presented. Furthermore, when presented with a different physical stimulus the same response may occur. It also appears to be the case that we often respond to properties of the environment that are not physically specifiable. Properties such as being beautiful, being a chair, or being an English sentence are not readily reducible to physical properties or stimuli.

We also know that much of human behavior is systematic and predictable if the situation is described in the terms by which the subject is likely to view it. The physical properties of an event may set some broad constraints on how it will be perceived. More importantly, we need to know the set of mental categories the subject uses to constrain understanding in order to predict how she will map these physical properties into the current mental state, that is, how the perceived situation fits into the current expectations and goals of the subject.

2.2.3 Critique of Methodological Behaviorism: Definition of Behavior

In reading behaviorist accounts of their experiments it is easy to believe that they were actually describing behavior as it was directly observed. After all, one can

Training:

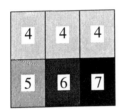

Positive Stimuli   Negative Stimuli

Testing:

FIGURE 2.3   A behaviorist conditioning experiment to evaluate what is learned in a gray level comparison task. The numbers, 1, ..., 7, on the cards indicate the lighter to darker gray levels for that half of the card. The cards are inverted for testing what is learned.

objectively observe a rat pressing a bar. However, when we look beyond the surface of these "behavioral" descriptions, we see that they were not actual accounts of the topography of a response. Rather, they were what some have called achievement descriptions of behavior. A bar press is an achievement, regardless of how it is accomplished, be it with the animal's left paw, the nose, the tail, or by sitting on it. The point is that behaviorists, like most folks, describe behavior in terms of what it accomplishes.

Describing behavior in terms of goals, of course, is just common sense. Any radio sports announcer knows that the effective communication of human actions in a sporting event is in terms of successes and failures of implied goals. To provide the listener with a topographical description of vectors, moments of inertia, and velocities of players and the ball would not attract many big-time sponsors.

A simple experiment illustrates very clearly the nature of the problem. Imagine the situation in which a shock pad is located below a subject's index finger. One second before the shock is delivered to the pad a tone sounds. What does the subject learn? If you are a hard-core behaviorist you describe in detail the upward motion of the finger. Is this a valid description of "the behavior" we all observed?

To test this description we now place the shock pad above the finger and again sound the tone. What we observe is the finger "avoiding the shock." This is an achievement based description for the behavior in that it includes an intention or goal. The goal is not directly observed. It is an inference, based on a number of implicit assumptions regarding human action. More generally, it is a description of behavior based on a certain implicit model that most of us share regarding pain and how to avoid it. A cognitive scientist might take this argument one step further and contend that *avoidance conditioning* implies *intentionality*.

Response definition is also at issue in the rat discrimination experiment presented in Section 2.2.2 and illustrated by Figure 2.3. The results of the first experiment could have been interpreted in (at least) two ways: the rats learned absolute brightness values, or they learned a top/bottom relationship. The fact is that any results can have multiple interpretations requiring further experiments, *ad infinitum*, to clarify their *meaning*.

In summary, it is impossible to capture the relevant generalizations regarding intelligent actions in terms of stimuli and responses alone. The full accounting cannot be made with the physical properties of the stimuli and responses but must include mental categories: the stimulus, as perceived, and the behavior, or response, as intended.

2.3 NEUROSCIENCE: S - BRAIN - R

The neuroscience approach shares a common goal with that of the behaviorist in that both groups desire to eliminate the mentalistic concepts of folk psychology. However, neuroscientists part company with behaviorists in the neuroscience acknowledgment that predicting human behavior requires knowing more than the physical state of the environment: they also need to know the state of the system. In this regard neuroscientists agree with folk psychologists. However, the neuroscientist is not at all happy with the use of mental categories, contending that all mental concepts are ultimately reducible to physical states of the system; in particular, to states of the brain.

2.3.1 Type-Identity and Token-Identity Accounts

Type-identity theory asserts that there are relationships between types of mental states and types of brain states, such that mental states can be reduced to, or replaced by, brain states. Taken in its strongest sense it suggests that a specific class or type of brain state implies a specific class or type of mental state, as well as the reverse. Thus, if A is a class of brain states and B is a class of mental states,

$$brain\_state\_A\ (X) <==> mental\_state\_B\ (Y).$$

The obvious implication of this assertion is that the type-type relationships we see in folk psychology between types of mental states and types of behavior can be replaced with relationships between types of brain states and the same types of behavior. All the generalizations that are captured in folk psychology are thus theoretically captured with brain states. And in the bargain we no longer have a mind-body problem!

To most of us this sounds like a great idea. It also seems to make sense because we believe that all this mental stuff actually takes place in the brain. Even most folk psychologists would agree that the mental states of humans are realized or instantiated somehow in the person's central nervous system. That being the case, type-identity theory begins to appear quite plausible.

The critical error in this reasoning is the confusion between token-identity and type-identity. *Token-identity* says that for each mental episode there is some underlying brain episode. Again, this simply says that human mental activity requires brain activity. No brain activity, no mental activity. To believe otherwise is to require the presence of some vitalistic or nonmaterial reality.

However, the acceptance of a theory of token-identity does not imply the validity of type-identity. Type-identity assumes a relationship between categories of thought and categories of brain states. Each mental and brain type can be thought of as comprising an indeterminate number of tokens. It is only by moving from the specific token to the general and abstract type that we gain the power we need to capture generalizations. There is no generality when we speak only of token-token relationships. For this reason the notion of token identity offers an insufficient basis for a theory of intelligent actions. A viable theory, if it is to have any generality, must state relations between types.

2.3.2 Problems with Type-Identity: Functional Types

In our everyday communication we often use concepts that can only be defined in terms of some function that they achieve (Bruner et al. 1956). Many of these functional categories comprise objects or events that have no physical properties in common. Consider the concept of a clock as a device that is capable of keeping time. This functional type can be realized as a digital-electrical watch, a mechanical spring driven clock, a pendulum clock, a sun dial, or an hour glass. These different physical devices only have one property in common, they are capable of keeping time. Since they have no physical properties in common, we are unable to reduce the concept clock to one or more physical primitives that all these devices share.

Mental states also often have the same functional characteristics as the concept clock. The "fear of failure" does not entail any specific physical actions. It relates to an end state, rather than to a means. And even when we disagree about the desired end state, we can capture some relevant generalities in distinguishing between individuals who share a high fear of failure and those who do not.

One can argue that even though there are no common behavioral components to functional mental states, there may still be a common internal physical state. If we look hard enough we will eventually find that whenever any individual experiences a high fear of failure he or she will also share some common physical state. But why must this be if we just agreed that there are concepts that only share a function and share nothing physically? It seems more a statement based on a commitment to physical reductionism than a belief founded on empirical evidence or logical necessity.

2.3.3 The Alpha Centurion Problem

Suppose you are backpacking in the Gila wilderness of New Mexico and suddenly a most unfamiliar large flying object lands close to you. Out walks this entity that looks something like a human male. He introduces himself as Joe, from a distant galaxy, and asks if you mind sharing one of those "cold ones" you have stored cooling in the creek.

Joe then proceeds to have a delightful conversation with you. He shares some extremely witty and amusing stories, provides some provocative insights regarding world peace and ways of solving our pollution problems. All around, one hell of a guy; someone with whom you can really communicate!

Just at the time when the two of you are really laughing it up, a sudden gust of wind blows over a large dead pine tree, which unfortunately lands right smack on poor Joe. Well, much to your surprise Joe turns into a pool of purple fluid. That's it: skin like material and purple fluid!

On the one hand you feel terrible losing this new interesting friend, but on the other hand, being a dedicated cognitive scientist, you are excited about the implications that this experience has for type-identity theory. Joe was clearly an intelligent system and yet he seemed to share none of the neurophysical properties of biological systems found on earth. It appears that mental states can be realized in completely different physical mediums.

Of course, Joe's story is truly relevant to type-identity theory only if it is in principle possible. Many cognitive scientists will say that Joe is already instantiated in some computing systems, others will say that with our present understanding we can't quite achieve this yet, and still others will answer, "impossible!" If you agree, as most cognitive scientists would like to believe, that it is possible for a system to behave in a manner that seems best described in terms of mental states, but that has nothing resembling a nervous systems as we know it, then the generalities that encompasses earthlings and Joe are at the functional-semantic level, and not at the physical level.

We can also generalize the previous argument. There exists a wide range of possible physical instantiations of the same mental or semantic state. This can be illustrated very easily with a computing system that can be seen as having a semantic level, a syntactical level, and a physical or mechanistic level. A given semantic state, for instance, for a chess playing program to capture a rook in the process of attempting to win, can be realized with a variety of syntactical states and an even larger number of physical or electrical states. Because of this one-to-many mapping from the semantic to the physical levels there may be little hope of capturing at the physical level the generalizations that exist at the semantic level.

2.3.4 A Problem: The Propositional Content of Mental States

Most of our thoughts may be represented propositionally. That is, they express an assertion as to the state of the world that, at least in principle, can be tested as either true or false. Brain states on the other hand do not have a propositional content. In this regard thoughts and brain states are different and one cannot replace the other. The type-identity theorist will argue that propositional content is not the crucial point; rather, what is important is that the propositional thought corresponds in a reliable manner to a specific state of the brain.

What this argument concedes is that knowing only brain states, without knowing the propositional translation, would not be of great interest to many. The point is that even if we were to find type-type relationships, we would have to have a folk or cognitive psychology to provide the definitions or make semantic sense of the mental types.

A version of this argument states that for language to make the distinctions and generalizations that it does, it must have a syntax. That is, there must be a structure of rules constraining the way in which the parts of speech are combined in order to give language its power. If there is some validity to this view, then it may be argued that brain states must also have something like a syntax which constrains how they are structured and combined. Until someone provides at least a hint as to what this would be, the whole idea of a taxonomy of brain states is an empty dream. These points are examined in detail by Pylyshyn (1984).

2.3.5 Summary of Problems for Type-Identity Theory

The complexity of the anatomy and physiology of the human brain is staggering. Consider the number of neurons, the degree of interconnectivity among neurons, the dynamic nature of the interactive parallel processing, the nature of the types of transitional dependencies between states over time, and the continuous influence of external changes in contextual factors. (We discuss neural constraints and the architecture of the brain in Chapter 5.) How do we begin to look for a "brain state" among this incredible complexity? Some believe this is an impossible task. We believe it is more a matter of the level of difficulty and complexity for which we simply do not yet have a viable methodology.

Most of the arguments against type-identity theory would disappear with a single study providing empirical evidence of a type-type relationship. So we ask, what are the current findings in cognitive neuroscience that pertain to this issue? Do we have evidence of relating brain and mental types?

There is considerable evidence demonstrating a relationship between neural and mental functioning. Patients with lesions in particular areas of the brain are likely to show particular types of cognitive deficits. Evoked potentials, indicative of mass actions in neural functioning, can discriminate between semantically meaningful and meaningless statements.

These are but a few of the kinds of research findings reported in the cognitive neuroscience literature, and developed further in Chapter 5. These results are an important and integral part of the cognitive science effort, but do NOT demonstrate relationships between brain states and a specific semantic state. The relationships that are found are of a far more general nature. In all likelihood most cognitive neuroscientists are little concerned with a test of type-identity theory. They take the view that we are so far from attaining this level of specificity between mind and brain that it simply does not influence their research.

At the same time many researchers take the attitude proposed by Patricia Churchland (1986) that some type of limited type-identity may be possible within a given individual or within a group of individuals for a constrained class of mental states. These researchers don't see this limited success as eliminating the need for mentalistic or semantic concepts. In fact, the *eliminative materialist* approach (Stitch 1983) concludes that the problem in these situations is with the semantic or mental type. Rather than espousing the semantic types of the cognitive or folk psychologist, they suggest we create new more constrained types that will fit within the limited understanding and identifiable analyses of the neurophysiologist. We address these issues further in Chapter 5.

2.4   REPRESENTATIONAL THEORY

2.4.1   Introduction

We have spent considerable time discussing the behavioral and neuroscience approaches to intelligent actions. We have done this for two reasons: First, to present two of the most important and commonly used vocabularies for describing intelligence, and second, to comment on these approaches in such a way as to highlight an alternative vocabulary, that of representation and intention. Before we turn to a discussion of this cognitive science approach to describing intelligence we pause and remind ourselves of several other important philosophical issues.

Our research endeavor is to capture generalizations regarding the functioning of intelligent systems. If we want to build systems or models that function at the level of humans in complex environments, these systems must function at a level of knowledge, meaning, and intention. That is, we must capture the semantic consistencies of the system's functioning. We know that any model we build will have to be realized as a physical-material entity, so our first question was whether its functioning could be characterized totally with descriptions based on the physical level alone.

On the basis of our discussions of the problems with behavioral and brain reductions it would appear that this would, at best, be difficult. We contend that we must understand the system's functioning at an intentional level. Only then can we think about the problems involved in its physical instantiation. Another way of saying this is that our intelligent machines can only be as good as our models of intentional actions.

The third proposed vocabulary for intelligent systems is that of *representational theory* (Fodor 1983). This theory, an essential component of the cognitive science approach, adopts the meaning and intentional (desire/belief) concepts of folk psychology and embeds them in a global theoretical perspective. Throughout the course of this book we will see many examples of representational theory that do not always agree on all points. In the present context we refer to representational theory in its most general sense, with the intention of including all those philosophers, cognitive psychologists, and cognitive scientists who agree that in order to capture the relevant generalizations of intelligent systems, we must include intentional or semantic concepts.

At this time we introduce a relatively restricted and simplified view of representational theory. To attempt anything more sophisticated would require that we jump ahead to discussions of the cognitive and computational representation in Chapters 3 and 4. These topics make up an integral part of a full understanding of the representational approach as it is presented in cognitive science.

All intelligent systems have the capability of representing the external world. It is the task for cognitive science to model these cognitive representational systems. A major problem remains: to describe how these representational systems actually represent the world. Although there is a great deal of disagreement about the specific structures and processes, that is, the functional architecture of intelligent systems (Palmer 1978, Luger & Stubblefield 1993), there is general agreement by most cognitive scientists that they must have the capability to represent knowledge and intentional states. For humans, it is generally assumed that the representational states have a semantic character and for our less verbal animal friends, the representations may not be strictly semantic, but they are of an intentional or belief/desire character (Gee, where did I bury that bone?).

Of course, in using the mental categories of folk psychology, representational theory runs into the mind-body problem described earlier. In concluding this introduction, we discuss how representational theory has dealt with the mind-body issue.

2.4.2 Representational Theory: Definitions

An important criticism of folk psychology is that its concepts are vacuous and without meaning. The behaviorists in particular are quick to point out that if a concept does not have observable implications it carries no meaning content. What does it mean, for instance, to be in an anxious state if this state has no observable implications? An important part of representational theory is the adoption of a functional approach to definitions of mental states. Mental states are defined in terms of a set of relationships with inputs, outputs, and other mental states.

We can imagine a type of network graph with nodes (involving stimuli, behaviors, and mental states) and links that describe the relationships among the nodes. The inclusion of relationships with other mental states in the definition of mental states is a critical difference between representational theory and the behaviorist approach to defining concepts. What representational theorists want to claim is that by including other mental states in the definition, they avoid the infinite lists of qualifiers that buried the behaviorist attempt at reducing all definitions to the observable. Moreover, we contend that in adopting this approach to defining mental states, we have made cognitive science an autonomous science in that it cannot be reduced to any other science.

While this idea of defining mental concepts within a network of inputs, outputs, and other mental concepts was carefully developed and supported by some empirical work (Jessor & Hammond 1957), it is not without its critics from within the cognitive science community (Block 1978). In later chapters we consider some of the problems introduced by this functional approach to defining mental states.

2.4.3 The Status of Mental Representations: The Intentional Stance

Daniel Dennett (1987) introduced the idea of a class of systems whose functioning can best be described in terms of their beliefs and desires. He refers to this class as *intentional* systems. Dennett is quick to note that we only move to this level of description when a physical level explanation fails. For example, we could explain the functioning of a thermostat in terms of its belief about the preferred temperature of a room, but this is unnecessary because we can capture all the relevant generalizations regarding the thermostat's functioning at a physical level without appealing to a mental or intentional level.

It is Dennett's contention that some systems, for instance humans and properly programmed computers, can only be completely explained by ascribing intentional states. In attempting to drive home this point, Dennett proposes the following thought experiment. Assume we were attempting to predict the next move of a competent chess playing computer and had our choice of three types of descriptive information. We could know the electrical state of all the components of the computer, we could be given the program that runs the chess playing computer, or, finally, we could know the best moves for this particular state of the chess game. Dennett argues that it would be very nearly impossible to accurately predict the moves of the computer on the basis of physical or programming information because these computing systems have become too complex. We would do best, he contends, by selecting an intelligent chess move for the game situation.

Having multiple levels for describing phenomena is an important part of any science. The language of the physicist, for example, includes Einstein's and Newton's laws, molecular or atomic relationships, as well as subatomic particles and indeterminacy. Within each science different phenomena are best understood at certain explanatory levels. A bat hitting a baseball is described fairly clearly with Newton's laws. The particle accelerator needs Einstein; subatomic interactions require quantum mechanics. It is not as though the principles of quantum mechanics weren't operative when a baseball player hits the ball, it's just that Newton's force, acceleration, and gravity offer a more coherent physical description. And for the sports fan the intentional descriptions including hits, outs, runs, and wining offer more coherent explanatory constructs.

Thus, the intentional stance says that we can best capture generalizations of intelligent systems, and this may include some properly programmed computers, with intentional accounts. An interesting aspect of Dennett's intentional stance is that it makes no assumptions regarding the causal role of representational states. Dennett argues that intentionality sometimes offers the best explanation for a system's behavior.

When we ask if the computer is "really an intentional system," Dennett would reply that he doesn't know the answer to this any more than he knows whether a person is "truly an intentional system." How do we know that anyone does what they do because they have a certain belief? All we observe is a correlation between evidence of the belief and certain actions. In fact, there is no clear method with which we could demonstrate that some belief caused a person to behave in some particular manner.

Dennett's intentional stance simply side steps the mind-body problem by claiming that representational models are only descriptive or predictive models of behavior and that they do not necessarily entail any causal relationships between mental states and physical states. We address this issue briefly in the next section and return to it again in Chapter 17, when we consider the philosopher John Searle's claim that computers can never be intentional systems (Searle 1980, 1992).

2.4.4 The Symbol Instantiation Hypothesis

Representational theory seems to be left with one obvious problem. Dennett argues for the utility of intentional accounts, but leaves us hanging as to what actually causes the consistencies we see in behavior. It is difficult to see how mental states can produce physical events given that physical events are determined by physical laws. It is at this point that representational theory's marriage with computation spares it the fate of folk psychology.

In the next section, we develop more fully the ideas supporting and vocabulary of computational theory; for the moment we think of computational theory as the implementation of a cognitive or intention based model in a computer program and run on a computing device. When cognitive scientist researchers do this we say that the semantic model is instantiated in terms of a symbol system, the computer code, which in turn is instantiated on the physical computing device. This is the *symbol instantiation hypothesis*, the conjecture that semantic states can be realized in terms of a symbol system, which in the case of a computer program can be realized in a particular physical system.

It is important to recognize the difference between instantiation and reduction. The instantiation hypothesis is not suggesting that mental states can be reduced to physical states, that is, it is not implying a type-type relationship; rather it simply says that a semantic type can be realized by some symbol token, which can be realized by some physical token. There are a potentially infinite number of ways that any particular mental state can be realized by a symbol state, and similarly a potentially infinite number of ways a symbol state can be realized in the physical state of a computer.

What the instantiation hypothesis and computational theory does for representational theory is to provide a means by which transitions between semantic states can be mechanistically or physically realized. Does the instantiation hypothesis once and for all solve the mind-body problem for intentionally based approaches? Newell and Simon (1976) contend that symbol instantiation successfully explains how intentional states can affect the state of a physical system. As we will see in the discussion of Chapter 17, there are still a number of unresolved issues.

We now turn to the automated formal system for a vocabulary and foundation for the symbol instantiation hypothesis.

2.5 THE AUTOMATED FORMAL SYSTEM

Many researchers feel that the birth of cognitive science occurred when scientists first compared the trace of a running computer program with the steps taken by a human solving the same problem (Newell & Simon 1972). If this paradigm is to produce successful science there are two important issues that need to be clarified. First, what are the norms under which we can compare a human and a computer? Second, how can we characterize what goes on in the computer?

We began to address the first issue in the previous section. With the symbol instantiation hypothesis we offered a plausible account of how semantic states can play a causal role in intelligent systems. We suggested how the symbol instantiation hypothesis might address the mind-body problem. Chapters 3 and 4 further clarify the role of cognitive representations in intelligent systems. The second issue, the characterization of problem solving on a computer and the generality of the computational model is addressed in this section. We now present the vocabulary for the automated formal system.

2.5.1 Definitions

A *formal system* consists of a set of *tokens* and a set of *rules* for manipulating tokens. The tokens may be physical objects or symbols. Tokens are "digital" or discrete in that they may be uniquely identified, counted, and configured with other tokens. This discrete property will also allow us to compare tokens and look for equivalences in patterns of tokens. The tokens are often seen to be in patterns such as being next to each other or having some order. The set of rules for operating on token structures may add, delete, or in any well-defined fashion rearrange the patterns of tokens.

Tokens are discrete rather than analog. An analog measure is an approximation of a continuous quantity. Examples of the difference between a digital and an analog value are the difference between the acts of counting and measuring: between integers and real numbers and between buying eggs and buying milk.

Examples of tokens are the lexical elements or words of a language, the decimal digits, or board game pieces such as in checkers or chess. Examples of patterns of tokens are English sentences as grammatical strings, large numbers or arithmetic problems composed of digits, or checkers or chess pieces laid out on the board as part of a game. Examples of rules in a formal system are the grammar rules by which we can judge a sentence as well formed, the rules of arithmetic such as algorithms for addition and subtraction, or the rules for playing checkers or chess.

Semantic systems can be treated as formal systems by ignoring the meanings of the individual symbols or words. Thus English language grammar, arithmetic, and the games of checkers and chess can be treated as formal systems. It is more difficult to treat the games of billiards and basketball as formal systems because the positions and locations of players, although important, do not have a discrete representation. Many aspects of these games are formal: in billiards, the number and color of balls on the table, whether or not a ball goes into a pocket; in basketball, the numbers of players, the number of fouls on a player or a team, the scoring. The same analog - digital issue occurs also in chess and checkers. However, it doesn't matter exactly where on a square a piece is located; it only matters whether or not the piece is on the square.

An *automated formal system* includes a mechanism for applying the rules to the tokens or patterns of tokens in the formal system. Computer programs that translate from one language into another, play chess, or solve arithmetic problems are examples of automated formal systems. We dare to ask the question whether a human solving equivalent problems may be described as an automated formal system. Before we do this we need further definitions and clarifications.

First, it doesn't matter what is used as the tokens for a formal system. There is no difference in the rules or playing strategy if the chess pieces are two or four inches tall or if they are medieval characters or of modern abstract design. What is important is that the patterns of tokens be preserved. The same is true, of course, for computers. It doesn't matter whether tokens are bits in registers or power signals across vacuum tubes. It doesn't matter whether computing devices are designed from silicon, protoplasm, or tinkertoys. The invariance of the tokens, patterns of tokens, and rules applied to tokens is what is important.

A second point is that the nature of the engine that automates the system is also unimportant. Whether the action is of a computer based chess interpreter playing itself, of two grand masters playing chess, of a group of people carrying around life size chess pieces, or of a computer playing a human: the result remains an automated formal system.

Finally, we have not yet considered whether formal systems have a meaning or semantics. To this point we have just described the syntax level of the system. The digital nature of the tokens, the patterns of tokens, and the rules for manipulating them give us all we need to describe the syntax of formal systems, and as we will see shortly, to compare two automated formal systems for equivalence.

One of the most important implications of the computational approach coupled with the symbol instantiation hypothesis is the possibility of "cashing out" the various homunculi, folklore concepts, and other ghosts that inhabit many cognitive theories. With the demise of the radical behaviorist and the poverty of the purely neurophysiological positions we must produce viable cognitive representational models.

A second consequence of the computational approach is the possibility of constructing precise models of intelligent task performance. When we see a theory embodied in a code level description and executed on a computational device we are finally precise enough for science. Our experiments are questions asked of nature and their results are sufficient for revised design and further experimentation.

2.5.2 A Mechanism for Formal Systems: The Turing Machine

We make this discussion more precise by presenting some mathematical descriptions of automated formal systems. It is important to understand the purpose of this presentation. First, it is useful to introduce a vocabulary that allows us to describe computational systems. The mathematical models we present allow us to give a precise characterization of the resources and behavior of computational systems. As cognitive scientists we are committed to fashioning models of the mind, models which are formal and precise enough to support testing and prediction. This means, as we mentioned previously, cashing out the homunculi and other under specified descriptions of human performance.

Second, we need to ask in what sense can the mind be considered a computational system. More precisely, can the mind be accurately modeled by an automated formal system? To answer these questions, we need to clarify the sense in which a formal system can model another system.

Third, we must be able to establish a method for examining the power of each formal model and asking the question in what sense are they equivalent. The equivalence of Turing complete formal systems allows us then to pose a more general question: what are the limitations of computational systems in general, and to what extent is human performance significantly constrained by these limitations?

We begin our discussion of automated formal systems by considering Turing machines. A *Turing machine* consists of four components: 1) an alphabet of tokens, 2) a potentially infinite tape, 3) a read-write head connected to 4) a finite state controller. A representation for a Turing machine is presented in Figure 2.4. Note that the symbols are digital: 0, 1, and B; note also that the tape is digital, with each square containing exactly one character. The tape is infinite in that we assume there will always be a position on the tape available for the next state of the read-write head.

The control for a Turing machine is defined as a set of 5-tuples:

(state, symbol_read, symbol_written, move_head, next_state)

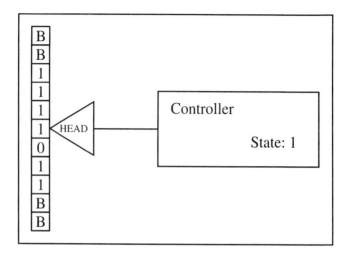

FIGURE 2.4   The organization of a Turing machine. It is assumed there will always be
a "next_state" on the tape to which the machine can move. The Turing
machine is in the first program step or control specification of Figure 2.5.
It is on the fourth step of the computation of Figure 2.6.

The symbol_read is the symbol on the tape under the read head. In
Figure 2.4 the symbol is 1. The symbol_written is the symbol written by the controller to the location on the tape under the head. The move_head is the direction
in which the tape is moved after writing. This may be any of three values, R, L,
or N for move one location right, one left, or no move. Finally, next_state is the
state the machine assumes after moving the tape. This is indicated by the number
of any of the states described previously. In our example, Figure 2.5, these states
were represented by the integers 1, .., 5 and halt.

We now use the Turing machine program presented in Figure 2.5, to solve a
problem of unary subtraction. This subtraction is simple: the number of 1s on the
right is taken away from the number of 1s on the left. If there are more 1s on the
right, the answer is 0. When there are more 1s on the left the answer is the
remainder after the removal of the number of 1s on the right. For example:

$$1111 - 11 = 11$$
$$1111 - 1 = 111$$
$$111 - 11111 = 0$$

In our implementation, presented in Figure 2.6, we take the first example
above. The - is replaced by a 0 and the left and right most 1s are delimited by Bs.
The action of the program is to scan back and forth removing one 1 from each

group each time. The step by step execution of the program is presented in Figure 2.6.

Turing machines are very tedious and extremely low level. The power that resides in the Turing model is not that of a set of specifications for building a computer but rather Turing machines provide an abstract model of what computing machines can compute. Turing machines may have any alphabet, but all that is really needed is two characters. A more complex character set can be encoded in the binary alphabet, just as with "real" computers!

It is also possible to build a *universal Turing machine*. This is a Turing machine that can read the description for any set of actions of any other Turing machine from its tape and simulate that behavior. Modern computers are like universal Turing machines in that they can read in programs and execute them.

Besides Turing machines there are a number of other mathematical models of the automated formal system. It seems that in the 1930s and 1940s, with the advent of the digital computer, a number of mathematicians created sets of abstractions to precisely specify the strengths and limitations of the computer. We will not go into any detail with these specifications, but simply list a number of them and provide references here and at the end of Chapter 2. The most important models include *production systems* (Post 1943), *partial recursive functions* (Church 1941), *McCulloch-Pitts networks* (McCulloch & Pitts 1943), and *Markov algorithms* (1954). Interestingly enough, even though all these formal models look quite different internally, they all compute exactly the same set of functions.

As we continue through the book, we use different models of computation to embody various computational theories. Post productions are more appropriate for representing rule based knowledge and encoding search strategies. Neural or connectionist networks, based on the McCulloch-Pitts model, are used to describe aspects of human perception. Each representation is designed, as we see in the beginning of Chapter 3, to encode the relevant aspects of problem situations.

And yet, despite the simplicity of the Turing machine, anything that can be computed in any formal system or computing device can also be computed on a Turing machine. This property is known as the formal equivalence of computational models, and is sometimes referred to as the Church-Turing hypothesis. Before we come to this important thesis, we must first show how two formal systems may be seen as equivalent

2.5.3 The Formal Equivalence of Systems

In this section we present two notions of the equivalence of systems. These notions each correspond to a particular sense in which one system can be said to

TURING MACHINE SPECIFICIATIONS

State	Reading	Write	Move	Next
1	1	1	R	1
1	0	0	R	1
1	B	B	L	2
2	1	B	L	3
2	0	B	N	halt
3	0	0	L	3
3	1	1	L	3
3	B	B	R	4
4	1	B	R	1
4	0	B	R	5
5	1	B	R	5
5	B	B	N	halt

FIGURE 2.5   The set of control specifications for a Turing machine to perform unary subtraction. These specifications will produce the program execution of Figure 2.6 when given the data on the tape of Figure 2.4. The state is the current state of the machine, described by one of a finite list of states. In our first example we will have six states, indicated by the integers 1,.., 5 and the word halt, as in Figure 2.5.

to model another. The first notion of equivalence is based on the mathematical notion of isomorphism: the existence of a structure preserving mapping between two systems. The second is based on the notion of equivalence in power, an equivalence which is established by showing that each system can emulate the operations of the other. This is often referred to as functional equivalence.

To give the intuition behind isomorphic equivalence, we present a simple game. There are nine poker chips on a table between two people. Each chip is marked with a unique digit 1, .., 9. The players take turns drawing a single chip. The object of the game is to be the first player with three chips that add to exactly 15. Figure 2.7 presents a win for player A, who has selected 5, 3, and finally 7. Player B selected 2 and 4. Chips 1, 6, 8, and 9 remain on the table.

TURING MACHINE EXECUTING A PROGRAM

State	Tape
1	BB<u>1</u>11011BB
1	BB1<u>1</u>1011BB
1	BB11<u>1</u>011BB
1	BB111<u>0</u>11BB
1	BB1110<u>1</u>1BB
1	BB11101<u>1</u>BB
1	BB111011<u>B</u>B
1	BB1110<u>11</u>BB
2	BB111011<u>B</u>B
3	BB11110<u>1</u>BBB
3	BB1111<u>0</u>1BBB
3	BB111<u>1</u>01BBB
3	BB11<u>1</u>101BBB
3	BB1<u>1</u>1101BBB
3	BB<u>1</u>11101BBB
3	B<u>B</u>111101BBB
4	BB<u>1</u>11101BBB
1	BBB<u>1</u>1101BBB
1	BBB1<u>1</u>101BBB
1	BBB11<u>1</u>01BBB
1	BBB111<u>0</u>1BBB
1	BBB1110<u>1</u>BBB
1	BBB11101<u>B</u>BB
2	BBB1110<u>1</u>BBB
3	BBB111<u>0</u>BBBB
3	BBB11<u>1</u>0BBBB
3	BBB1<u>1</u>10BBBB
3	BBB<u>1</u>110BBBB
3	BB<u>B</u>1110BBBB
4	BBB<u>1</u>110BBBB
1	BBBB<u>1</u>10BBBB
1	BBBB1<u>1</u>0BBBB
1	BBBB11<u>0</u>BBBB
1	BBBB110<u>B</u>BBB
2	BBBB11<u>0</u>BBBB
halt	BBBB11<u>B</u>BBBB

FIGURE 2.6 The Turing machine, configured as in Figure 2.4, using the program instructions of Figure 2.5 performing unary subtraction. The problem is stated at the top, 1111 - 11, with the answer as the last step, 11. The underlie indicates the current position of the read/write head on the tape.

	Player A	Table	Player B
Start:		1 2 3 4 5 6 7 8 9	
Turn 1:	5	1 3 4 6 7 8 9	2
Turn 2:	3	1 6 7 8 9	4
Turn 3:	7	1 6 8 9	
	Player A wins, since 5 + 3 + 7 = 15!		

FIGURE 2.7   The token selection game. Each of two players take turns selecting numbered chips from the table. The first player, A in this case, to have exactly three chips adding to 15 is the winner.

Surprisingly, this game is formally equivalent to tic-tac-toe! To see this equivalence we place each of the numbered chips in the tic-tac-toe grid of Figure 2.8. Selecting any set of three chips that add exactly to 15 is the same as getting three Xs or three 0s to be in a row in the tic-tac-toe game. Each token in each game corresponds to exactly one token in the other game. The rules correspond exactly, in that selecting a chip corresponds to a player placing a mark in the tic-tac-toe grid.

Mathematically, we say there is a *isomorphic equivalence* between two systems if and only if:

1)   There is a one-to-one correspondence between token patterns in one system and token patterns in the other.
2)   The operations on token patterns in each system can be mimicked in the other.

More precisely, suppose we have two systems, S_1 and S_2, with h a function defining a one-to-one correspondence between patterns in the two systems. Suppose, op_1 is an operator on patterns in S_1. Then there must be a corresponding operator op_2 in S_2 with the following property. Suppose P1 and P2 are corresponding patterns in S_1 and S_2, that is, h(P1) = P2. Suppose that the result of applying op_1 to P1 is Q1 and the result of applying op_2 to P2 is Q2, that is, op_1(P1) = Q1 and op_2(P2) = Q2. Then isomorphism requires that h(Q1) = Q2.

Isomorphism is the strongest form of equivalence between two systems. There is no stronger equivalence other than the identity of the two systems. Isomorphism constitutes a modeling ideal which is not often achievable. Figure 2.8 presents an isomorphic map of the token selection game and tic-tac-toe.

8	1	6
3	5	7
4	9	2

FIGURE 2.8   The marked chips from Figure 2.7 placed on the tic- tac-toe game board showing the one-to-one and onto mapping of these two games.

Functional equivalence, on the other hand, allows us to compare the power of two systems without requiring any commonality in internal structure. Two systems are functionally equivalent if and only if each can simulate the performance of the other.

Using functional equivalence we can show that there is an important set of computational models which are equivalent and maximally powerful. As a simple example, if we wanted to show that a universal Turing machine and a personal computer were equivalent we would do the following:

1) Program the PC to simulate a Turing machine.
2) Program the Turing machine to simulate the PC.

This second task would be tedious, but one method would be to store the PC program on one part of the tape and the data for the program on another part and then program the Turing machine to interpret PC assembly language. Since each automated formal system would be able to imitate the actions of the other the two computational models would be equivalent in power, even if not in efficiency, flexibility, or ease of use. In fact, due to the limited memory of the PC and the infinite tape of the Turing machine, the systems are not equivalent.

2.5.4   Formal Systems as Models for Cognitive Science

The *Church-Turing thesis* proposes that all models of computation developed to date are either equivalent or less powerful than the Turing machine. A number of these models, including the production system of Post, and McCulloch-Pitts networks were listed in the previous section. Church-Turing is a "thesis" in that it conjectures that no more powerful model of computation can be identified. Some new class of systems would be more powerful if members of that class could compute functions which no Turing machine could compute. Since no such class of models is known, the Church-Turing hypothesis conjectures that the Turing machine class of models is the most powerful model of computation possible.

There are reasons to believe that mental processes can be usefully described as the processes of a formal system. These range from the digital nature of the neuronal system to the use of representations in higher level human performance. Many of these arguments will be presented in detail in subsequent chapters.

We will use a number of different computational models from the set of Turing equivalent formal specifications when we come to describe aspects of human problem solving performance. First, we use Post's production system. There are many historical reasons for this, but most important is the research, over the past 30 years, of Allen Newell and Herbert Simon at Carnegie Mellon University. We will introduce this research, as well as show the representational congruence between aspects of human performance and the production system, in the beginning of the next chapter and again in Part II.

The second computational model we use is the McCulloch-Pitts network model, especially as it has been extended by modern connectionist research. This model is also able to compute all and only those functions computable by the class of Turing machines.

There are a number of reasons why the cognitive scientist believes that computational systems provide an invaluable tool for understanding the nature of intelligence.

First, it is possible to analyze computational systems mathematically. The mathematical model of computation allows the cognitive scientist to derive certain properties and constraints of intelligent systems. For example, the Church-Turing analysis has provided an upper bound on what is computable which no system, intelligent or otherwise, can transcend.

Second, computational models are programmable and can be tested on a computer. This means that we can empirically test theories of mind to see if they can produce the behavior intended. This allows cognitive scientists to avoid the limitations of the behaviorist tradition; be more precise than other psychological traditions, such as the Gestaltist; and perhaps even resolve the mind-body problem.

Third, the design, test, and refine approach to the science of intelligent systems fits well the evolutionary constructivist epistemology. When a computational model fails to reflect the complexities found in the world, the cognitive scientist can identify the component structures that fail and attempt appropriate refinement.

There are also a number of limitations of the Church-Turing class of formal systems. The limitation we now discuss is a form of incompleteness. The incompleteness of Turing machines was first proved by Turing, based on earlier proofs by Kurt Godel (1931) which in turn were based on conjectures first proposed by the great mathematician David Hilbert in 1900.

Incompleteness as originally formulated by Godel states that in any formal system, at least as powerful as arithmetic, there are theorems that cannot be proven either true or false using only the rules of that system. Since the class of Turing machines falls into this category, they are incomplete.

We now present an example of the incompleteness property with the *halting problem*. The halting problem is the problem of trying to decide whether or not a given Turing machine will stop executing, given a particular input. We will show that it is not possible to construct a Turing machine that can look at any Turing machine description and any input and report back whether or not that Turing machine will halt on that input. A constructive proof will show that a contradiction arises from assuming the existence of a Turing machine that can solve the halting problem.

Suppose it is possible to construct a Turing machine called halt that solves the halting problem. We embed this Turing machine in a Turing machine whose behavior is contradictory. The function paradox, written in Pascal-like pseudocode, calls halt in order to produce a paradox.

```
function paradox(input): boolean;
function halt (program, data): boolean; external;
begin
        100: if halt(paradox, paradox) then goto 100
        paradox := true;
end;
```

Does the function paradox halt when run on itself? If paradox halts, then the function halt will return true; but if halt returns true, then paradox goes into an infinite loop (at label 100) and does not halt. Conversely, if paradox does not halt, then halt returns false and paradox halts.

Thus the existence of the Turing machine halt results in a contradiction! This may seem an artificial example because of the self reference in the inner loop. Indeed, self-reference underlies many paradoxes including Godel's (1931) proof and Russell's (1956) paradoxes. However, self reference appears to be a common and perhaps necessary property of intelligent systems (Johnson-Laird 1983, Searle 1992).

Turing machines may be too general models of computation to offer descriptions for human cognition. If we say that the mind is a Turing machine, are we really offering suitable constraints on its performance? Are we really proposing anything deterministic about its essential nature? We return to these issues in subsequent chapters.

2.6   THE PROSPECT OF A SCIENCE OF INTELLIGENCE

In the first two chapters of this book we asked about the possibility of a science of intelligent systems. We spent much of this time analyzing current and historical views of intelligence. In the present chapter we set out to identify a vocabulary for describing intelligence. Our presentation showed the need for a mature epistemology to construct a foundation for a science of intelligence. We then considered and criticized the work of the behaviorist and neuroscience traditions.

In this final section of the chapter we look briefly at a controversy that has sparked heated debate within the cognitive science community. This involves two distinct research paradigms for investigating intelligent systems: the connectionist and symbol system approaches. In Chapter 3 we introduce representational schemes for each of these methodologies. It should be noted that the analysis of the automated formal system, with its discovery of an equivalence of computational paradigms and an upper bound on computability, affects both the symbol based and connectionist approaches equally.

The symbol based and connectionist approaches are sometimes regarded as competing, sometimes as complementary. The symbol based approach, which has been our primary focus up to this point, is inspired by the intentional stance. It attributes a causal role to goals, beliefs, the storage and retrieval of representations from memory, and the explicit operation on symbol structures. Newell and Simon presented the manifesto of the symbol based approach in their physical symbol system hypothesis, described in Section 2.6.1.

The connectionist approach, on the other hand, is inspired by the study of neuronal systems. Early researchers (McCulloch & Pitts 1943, Hebb 1949, Kohonen 1972) wanted to model the information processing of the human neural system. In recent years much more is known both about human information processing as well as about architectures for artificial networks that mimic that processing. Although many researchers in the area now no longer attempt to identify physiological correlates of their artificial neural systems, the neurophysiological plausibility of their computational models is still of great concern. Moreover, the level of processing in the artificial neural systems remains at the level of signal processing rather than explicit symbol manipulation.

2.6.1   The Physical Symbol System Hypothesis

The *physical symbol system hypothesis*, first proposed by Newell and Simon (1976) brings together the idea of symbol instantiation with the construction of computational models. It provides a powerful justification for the use of computational models in cognitive science. It presents a general hypothesis about the nature of intelligence, that intelligence is only to be found in systems which explicitly operate on symbolic representations. According to Newell and Simon:

> A necessary and sufficient condition for a physical system to exhibit general intelligent action is that it be a physical symbol system. *Necessary* means that any physical system that exhibits general intelligence will be an instance of a physical symbol system. *Sufficient* means that any physical symbol system can be organized further to exhibit general intelligent action.

To understand the claim which Newell and Simon are making, we need to examine what they mean by a *physical symbol system*. In Section 2.5 we presented a description of automated *formal* systems. At this level of description, we characterize systems in terms of tokens and rules for token manipulation. When a system is described as a *symbol system* we are concerned with the operation on symbols, that is representations which stand for a particular content such as an object, property, or action (Newell 1990, p. 72).

Two points are worth emphasizing. First, the physical symbol system hypothesis asserts that the use and manipulation of symbols, what folk psychology considers *mental* actions, can and must be physically embodied. Computational systems, according to Newell and Simon, give a clear example of how they *can* be embodied. Second, "general intelligence" requires not merely token manipulation, as described in the automated formal system of Section 2.5, but also requires an explicit symbolic or representational dimension.

The issue of representation is extremely complex. It must be addressed from both cognitive and computational viewpoints. We develop these representational issues in Chapter 3.

2.7 EPILOGUE AND REFERENCES

The issue of choosing a vocabulary for describing cognitive phenomena is comprehensively presented in Zenon Pylyshyn's (1984) book, *Cognition and Computation: Toward a Foundation for Cognitive Science*. The costs of choosing the intentional constructs of folk psychology as the vocabulary for cognitive science are discussed in Paul Churchland's (1984) book, *Matter and Consciousness: A Contemporary Introduction to the Philosophy of Mind*. Churchland also does an excellent delineation of the pitfalls of behavioral and neurophysiological reductions of mental types. For a more in-depth discussion of the possibility of reducing mental constructs to brain states, see Patricia Churchland's (1986) book, *Neurophilosophy: Toward a Unified Science of the Mind/Brain*.

von Glasersfeld's (1978) paper, *An Introduction to Radical Constructivism*, is a highly readable introduction to constructivism and the idea that we interact with the world in terms of the categories we impose on the world. Jean Piaget's (1954, 1970) genetic epistemology, a constant theme throughout his writings, presents large amounts of psychological data supporting the constructivist approach.

In the area of representational theory, there is extensive and rapidly growing literature, much of it from the philosophical viewpoint. A most influential researcher in this area is Jerry Fodor; his books, especially *The Language of Thought* (1975) and *Representations* (1981), provide a sophisticated approach to the issues, as well as a valuable perspective on the problems of representation. An easier introduction to these issues may be found in Flanagan (1984).

The introduction to automated formal systems, including descriptions of Turing machines, Church's lambda calculus, and Post's rewrite systems are an important part of education in computer science. The interested reader may go to the traditional texts such as Hopcroft and Ullman (1979) for more material on these topics. Roger Penrose's (1989) book, *The Emperor's New Mind*, has a very clear presentation of all these topics as well as the Church-Turing thesis, the halting problem, and undecidability.

The physical symbol system hypothesis is presented and justified by Allen Newell and Herb Simon in their 1976 Turing Award lecture, *Computer Science as Empirical Inquiry: Symbols and Search*.

Chapter 3

REPRESENTATIONAL SCHEMES

This grand book, the universe,... is written in the language of mathematics, and its characters are triangles, circles and other geometric figures without which it is humanly impossible to understand a single word of it; without these, one wanders about in a dark labyrinth...

Galileo Galilei (1638/1914)

Since no organism can cope with infinite diversity, one of the most basic functions of all organisms is the cutting up of the environment into classifications by which non-identical stimuli can be treated as equivalent...

Eleanor Rosch (1978)

3.0 INTRODUCTION

For cognitive scientists there is no topic more important, or more controversial, than the role of representation in intelligence. In Section 1.2, we saw that the use and manipulation of representations was a hallmark of intelligence. We take up this theme again in Chapter 3, and show how representation is both a medium as well as a constraint for cognition. It is a medium in that intelligence requires "capture" of information in the environment; it is a constraint in that what is not captured will not be reflected in intelligent action.

To achieve a clear understanding of mental representations we first make precise our task. Remember that our overall goal is to model intelligent systems; toward this end we need to understand how intelligent systems represent their world. Furthermore, we need to understand the knowledge they acquire from their experiences in the world. What are the critical properties of a good representational system? How do we tell a good one from a bad one? We will see that the answers to these questions are often not readily apparent. We begin our discussion with a psychological and epistemological approach to these issues.

In Sections 3.1 and 3.2 we show how a mature psychology and a well-founded epistemology are necessary for creating and understanding cognitive representational schemes. In Section 3.3 we describe features of general representational schemes, and offer several examples. We discuss common properties of representations, including the homomorphic property, naturalness, expressiveness, and efficiency. We introduce traditional representational schemes, including sample based, homomorphic, logic based, procedural, network, and structured. Full details of these systems are presented in Part II of this book. We then introduce neural or connectionist representations, with further details in Part III.

We conclude this chapter, Section 3.4, with some comments on the nature and limitations of representations. We offer preliminary discussion on how representational schemes are part of models of human intelligence, and we point to the constraint based methodology of Chapter 4 which provides us with the tools to determine the viability and validity of such models.

3.1   COGNITIVE REPRESENTATIONAL SCHEMES

An important goal for the cognitive scientist is to understand how intelligent systems capture invariances from their environment, preserve this information, and then use aspects of it to direct their actions. In an effort to accomplish this goal cognitive scientists have built up a variety of modeling tools. These tools are based on research from cognitive psychology, psycholinguistics, and artificial intelligence.

The task of this chapter is to present the research insights of these related disciplines as well as the modeling tools they have inspired. We first look at several memory studies from psychology as well as several related artificial intelligence programs.

In the Section 3.3 we present a number of data structures from computer science and artificial intelligence for modeling aspects of representation. In Chapter 4 we present various experimental methodologies for ascribing properties and structures to the representational systems of intelligent agents. In Chapter 17 we return to the role of representational modeling in cognitive science.

3.1.1 Memory Studies and Representation

It is quite natural, when beginning the study of cognitive representations, to ask what help we can get from cognitive psychology. After all, major concerns of these researchers are attention, memory, and problem solving. We also find in the artificial intelligence community several attempts to model the results of these cognitive studies. We briefly visit these research areas, in an attempt to discover constraints on cognitive representational schemes.

A representational scheme must be able to capture all types of knowledge. Several decades ago this would have been viewed as a relatively simple matter because, at that time, most psychologists saw memory and knowledge as a undifferentiated phenomena. However, beginning with Tulving and Donaldson's (1972) distinction between *episodic* and *semantic* memories, psychologists broke out remembered items into different subclasses.

Prior to Tulving and Donaldson, much of the memory research in psychology focused on the recall of lists of unrelated material. Subjects' ability to recall items on a list depended largely on their ability to retrieve the appropriate temporal and spatial cues that provided the context for the list of items. Gibson's (1940) classic paper on stimulus and response generalization was the inspiration for much of this work.

Based on Gibson's insight, Feigenbaum, in his early 1960s doctoral dissertation at Carnegie Institute of Technology built the EPAM, Elementary, Perceive and Memorizer, program. The task of EPAM was to accept and store pairs of nonsense syllables. On presentation of one element of the pair, EPAM's task was to produce the other. EPAM was an early artificial intelligence representational system. It was also a learning program, for it not only stored away response symbols but also developed a discrimination net that allowed it to sort stimuli in order to gain access to the appropriate responses in memory (Feigenbaum & Simon 1984).

Recalling memorized items often requires retrieving the context in which the information was learned, for example, a movie seen last weekend or last Christmas's dinner menu. Tulving and Donaldson referred to this autobiographical and situation-based information as part of *episodic* memory. In an important sense it helps define who a person is. Thus, a representational system that includes contextual information as a component of knowledge is important for retrieval.

Tulving and Donaldson also pointed out that there is a large part of knowledge that is not context dependent. A rose is a rose is a rose, regardless of where and when we experience it. This context-independent part of knowledge Tulving referred to as *semantic* memory. As Tulving and Donaldson (1972, p. 386) state:

> Semantic memory is the memory necessary for the use of language. It is a mental thesaurus, organized knowledge a person possesses about words and other verbal symbols, their meaning and referents, about relations among them, and about rules, formulas, and algorithms for the manipulation of these symbols, concepts, and relations.

Eight years later, Cohen and Squire (1980) proposed another distinction between what they called *declarative* and *procedural* knowledge. Procedural knowledge refers to knowledge of *how* to do things, such as ride a bicycle or swim. Declarative knowledge is generally accepted information about the world, such as that George Washington was the first president of the United States.

The declarative/procedural distinction is partially clouded by another distinction, that made between *explicit* and *implicit* knowledge or memory (Graf & Schacter 1985). Explicit or conscious memory may be accessed by measures requiring conscious recall or the recognition of past events. Implicit memory is not directly accessible to consciousness, but may be studied through indirect performance measures such as the time saved in relearning a skill. Cohen and Squire (1980) think of procedural memory as being largely implicit, whereas declarative memory is regarded as explicit.

The computer scientist and artificial intelligence practitioner often ignore any distinction between procedural and declarative knowledge. From their viewpoint, once knowledge is made explicit, it can either be used as a specification for what is true, i.e., declaratively, or as a prescription for what to do, i.e., procedurally. Examples of this include the problem solving knowledge in a production system (Chapter 9) or a network parser (Chapters 13 and 16). From the declarative view these structures contain knowledge; from the procedural, these structures can be interpreted to solve a problem. The knowledge engineering effort required in building knowledge based programs (Luger & Stubblefield 1993, Chap. 8) often requires the knowledge engineer to discover and make explicit the often implicit skills of the human expert. The same problem arises in building models of human skills for robotics or computer assisted instruction. Prolog programming offers an example of the blending of these knowledge types (Part V).

3.1.2 Structured Representational Systems

Schema based approaches to representation focus on the global structure or organization of representations in perception, memory, and reasoning. This distinguishes them from purely associationist approaches which focus solely on the proximity or conjunction of qualities or contents in experience. As we see next, these schemas have been used to explain narrow perception-based psychological phenomena such as character recognition as well as large scale phenomena such as story understanding and the interpretation of novel situations.

In Chapter 2 we noted the general line of development from Kantian schema theory to the psychological schema theories of Piaget and Bartlett. Fredrick Bartlett (1932) first referred to the structure organizing past events as a "schema;"

> A schema refers to an active organization of past reactions
> which must always be supposed to be operating in any
> well-adapted organic response.

The first major research issue we discuss is how to identify content for schemas. Researchers realized that information supporting intelligent reasoning might not be consciously available to the subject. There is little reason to believe that intelligent agents are aware of all the skills, prejudices, and other factors that go into their problem solving performance. Nonetheless, a number of psychologists have, through careful observation and scrutiny, ascribed information content to schemas simply on the grounds that such information was necessary to support the type of problem solving evidenced by the intelligent subject.

Several decades of research, much of it inspired by Allen Newell and Herbert Simon and their colleagues at Carnegie Mellon University, have taken on the task of better understanding the knowledge content of human problem solvers. Part of this research is focused on identifying and encoding exactly what human experts bring to successful problem applications. Research along this line includes Hinsley et al. (1977) who identified many of the specific skills high school students used to successfully solve algebra word problems. Jill Larkin et al. (1980) have several studies analyzing problem solving in physics. Luger (1981) identified components of problem solving knowledge that went into solving applied mathematics problems, especially distance, rate, time, and moment of inertia problems (Section 6.3).

Another important task is to characterize the differences between expert and novice problem solvers in an area. Herbert Simon and his wife Dorthea described with different sets of knowledge (production) rules the expert and novice algebra problem solver. Jill Larkin et al. (1980, 1987) and researchers at Carnegie Mellon have also considered the novice-expert differences in understanding domains of physics. Micki Chi et al. (1988a, 1988b) have looked at the nature of expertise, and compared novices and experts in physics problem solving. Young and O'Shea (1981) described children's subtraction skills. A large number of researchers model programming language skills (Singley & Anderson 1989, Anderson & Thompson 1989, Soloway et al. 1983). We return to these issues both with analysis of direct method testing in Chapter 4 and the explicit design and implementation of schema based problem solvers in Sections 7.3.2 and 16.2.

The goal of the research cited in the previous paragraphs was to understand the intelligence manifested in problem solving by building explicit knowledge structures that represented that intelligence. These structures were then interpreted by a computer to see how the results would mimic human skills in equivalent problem solving tasks. In terms we clarify in the next chapter, these models may be seen as sufficient to capture part of the phenomena of intelligence.

Some psychologists question the explicit knowledge based approach for representing complex problem solving. We see in researchers analysis of cognition and problem solving skills a swing back from explicit knowledge based models to descriptions having no explicit schematic representation of knowledge. This change in perspective is motivated in part by the influence of empirical findings, as well as by the emergence of theories that assume that only concrete specific episodic experiences are stored in memory.

On the empirical side, a number of researchers report that subjects when recalling stories (Graesser 1981) on some occasions not only remember the gist of the story, but also remember very specific detail. Most of us have had the experience while taking an exam or trying to remember some specific piece of information such as an address or phone number, of being able to remember the location of the information on a specific page of the textbook or some other particular place, but of not being able to remember the needed information itself! Some schema theorists (Graesser 1981) attempt to explain these situations by assuming that certain irregular details leave a specific *perceptual trace* in memory.

Support for a schema-like theory for pattern recognition, sometimes referred to as prototype theory, comes from a study by Posner and Keele (1968). Here subjects were first trained to classify variations of the four prototypes shown in Figure 3.1. The variations were constructed by randomly moving each of the nine dots in one of four directions, as illustrated by the variations of the triangle prototype in Figure 3.1. During training subjects were presented the variations one at a time in a random order and asked to classify each variation by pressing one of four buttons, each representing a different prototype structure. Subjects then received feedback telling them if they were correct or not on each trial. This proceeded until they had learned to classify each variation into its appropriate category.

After learning, Posner and Keele tested subjects' ability to classify stimuli not included in the training set. Two important findings were: 1) a subject's ability to classify novel forms was a function of the distance of that form from the prototype, that is, stimuli most similar to a prototype were classified most easily; and 2) subjects could classify the prototype, which they had never been trained on, as well as they classified previous experienced variations from the prototype. These findings were interpreted to indicate that subjects had created a prototype representation for each of the prototypes on the basis of the training on specific variations of the prototypes.

There are also some recent theoretical developments that question whether the ability to behave abstractly necessarily implies that we store abstractions. In this vein, Hintzman's (1986) MINERVA model only stores specific events, yet is able to learn abstract prototypes. Traditional prototype theories generally propose that we create a prototype structure to represent each of our categories, and that classification of a novel event is accomplished by comparing the event with our list of stored prototypes. The event is then classified in terms of the prototype to which it is most similar.

In Hintzman's model the only thing that is stored as a component of the representation is the individual instance that is experienced. In the learning task, only the specific variations that subjects were trained on are stored. The retrieval

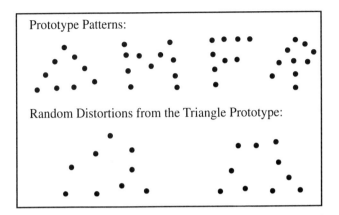

FIGURE 3.1A set of prototypes and a set of random variations from the triangle prototype. Adapted from Posner and Keele (1968).

process in the model involves a probe that is submitted to the stored data and returns an echo that is the weighted average of all stored episodes similar to the probe. Without going into technical detail on his model, Hintzman is able to simulate the findings reported by Posner and Keele (1968). Hintzman's model produced abstract classifications without assuming abstract representations.

We have just completed a survey of several psychological studies related to the structure of memory in complex problem solving. Some of the issues raised, such as whether subjects could learn general patterns in data with exposure only to specific instances, are important. This type learning is reflected in several of the connectionist architectures of Part III; specifically, perceptron classification with use of an implicit prototype (Section 11.2.2) and Kohonen network classification with an explicit prototype (Section 12.1.2). The use of knowledge in the design of explicit symbol based representations is presented of Part II and several of the learning algorithms of Chapter 10.

3.1.3 Psychological Constraints on Representation

Before discussing specific cognitive representations we must have a more concrete understanding of exactly what behaviors these models are attempting to describe. We would like to determine the capabilities of a cognitive representational system that a practical model should possess. As we shall see, these criteria are best seen as ideals to which our cognitive models aspire, but may, indeed, seldom fully attain. We introduce this section by clarifying our use of the term invariant, and then go on to describe three important properties of intelligent systems: productivity, systematicity, and compositionality. We conclude with a further list of properties that intelligence representational schemes must reflect.

To this point we have only spoken generally about patterns of data and perceived invariants in our environment. Before proceeding further, we need to clarify these issues by describing what we mean by an invariant. Eleanor Rosch (1978), as noted in the chapter introduction, states:

> Since no organism can cope with infinite diversity, one of the most basic functions of all organisms is the cutting up of the environment into classifications by which non identical stimuli can be treated as equivalent...

The term *invariant* describes two perceptually distinct things that can be seen as similar for some purpose. This is, fundamentally, an abstraction, where certain features of phenomena are seen as relevant, and others are ignored. For example, "dog" and "man" are both nouns as parts of a language specification. They are both three letter words when considered as strings of characters of some length, and they belong to different groups when species based classifications are used. The notion of an invariant in a representational scheme allows us to describe different perceptual phenomena as equivalent for some purpose.

Invariants in the environment are "captured" by representational schemes. When intelligence is observed, Fodor and Pylyshyn (1988) point out three important aspects of the use of invariants: productivity, systematicity, and compositionality. *Productivity* is the property of producing potentially infinite diversity from a finite set of elements and limited range of processes. Invariances make up the constituent pieces of representations. Within cognitive representing schemes there are syntactic combination rules for building and interpreting acceptable structures. The result of these combination rules applied to the elements of the system constitute a potentially infinite set of legal structures. Chomsky (1957, 1965) refers to this phenomenon as having a generative grammar for language structures.

We infer productivity in almost all aspects of intelligence: applying a fixed mathematics to new problems, using successful search strategies in novel situations, and above all in the generation and interpretation of language. We present productivity in some detail in the language chapters of Part IV.

Systematicity is also seen very clearly in the analysis of language and other communication. It refers to the fact that intelligence is integrated and unified. The understanding and generation of the sentences "John loves the woman" and "The woman loves John" must be intrinsically related in an intelligent language comprehension system. This systematicity arises because a) the sentences are composed of the same elements and b) the very same combination mechanisms are used in each sentence. Thus the generation and comprehension of these two sentences are fundamentally related. Classification studies from the psychological literature, for example Figure 2.5 and its analysis, also indicate systematicity within intelligent problem solving.

Compositionality is the ability to combine reasoning structures through an argument or other relational chain. An example, taken from Fodor and Pylyshyn (1988), is the argument:

> Turtles are slower than rabbits. Rabbits are slower than Ferraris. Therefore turtles are slower than Ferraris.

The conclusion, that turtles are slower than Ferraris, requires several features of representation and intelligence. First, there must be meaning associated with "slower than" wherever it appears. Second, this relationship "slower than" must be seen as *transitive*. Thus, from two contextually independent situations, related only by the fact that they share an abstract relationship, we can infer a new third situation based on those relationships.

We conclude this section with a brief list of other important cognitive aspects of representational schemes. We present this list before going into computational issues in representation. First, these schemes represent invariances: an abstraction that identifies equivalence groupings in perceived phenomena.

The idea of identifying and manipulating invariance is, of course, to represent the relevant contextual information and to specify a process that appropriately utilizes this information. The essential point is the ability to abstract and generalize: No two pieces of information will ever be identical in every respect. Even if the focal stimulus, i.e., the signal, is constant across time, the background context of noise in the environment is in a constant flux. At a minimum the system must be able to generalize across these irrelevant variations in the environment.

Second, and a somewhat more specific criterion for representations, is the ability to deal with language and other descriptive invariances; in these situations different surface structures often lead to the same semantic instantiation. While we seem to paraphrase sentences and paragraphs almost automatically, it is a nontrivial task to specify a computational representational model that can simulate this ability. Here again, the productivity, systematicity, and compositionality properties of intelligence must be reflected in representing schemes.

A third criterion is the ability to retrieve specific information from a large data set in a useful time frame. Humans seem to recognize patterns of visual and auditory information almost instantaneously. Considering the vast amounts of information that we must store, how do we retrieve a specific bit of information so rapidly?

Fourth, a representational scheme should meet the criterion of partial matching and graceful degradation. When we humans receive partial, degraded, or ambiguous information we often adjust in some manner to come to a reasonable interpretation of that ambiguous data, as for example the interpretation of the strings in Figure 2.2. It is very seldom that we completely "crash," rather we often fill in the missing pieces through semantics and context.

Fifth, and to remind ourselves how much effort remains in the understanding of representations, our models should be capable of expressing any conceptualization that we humans are able to formulate or understand. This is a most general and global criterion when we consider the possibly unlimited range of conceptualizations that we humans create and use and the limitations of a symbol system or connectionist architecture to capture these invariances. Not only must we be able to interpret novel linguistic utterances, for example, but we must also be able to interpret various pictorial and mathematical expressions.

To summarize, the first criteria we introduce to characterize representational schemes are rather broad in their implications. Not only must representations be capable of encoding a wide range of information, they must also be able to accommodate declarative, episodic, and procedural types of knowledge. Furthermore, representational schemes should be sensitive to the distinction between consciously accessible and inaccessible knowledge.

Last, and perhaps most importantly, the representational system must be capable of refinement and revision. That is, it must be capable of learning or being modifiable on the basis of new received data. As we will see, many of the early symbol based representational models were entirely static with no capability of change. The knowledge they represented was given by the designer, and no new knowledge or change resulted from subsequent processing of new data.

These important characteristics of intelligence will in later chapters be used to critique our modeling efforts. We next consider the epistemological foundations of representational schemes.

3.2   REPRESENTATIONS AND EPISTEMOLOGY

3.2.1 The Constructivist View of Representation

Throughout the history of psychology, a diversity of concepts has been employed as the units by which knowledge is represented. The behaviorists, inheriting the work of the British empiricists, adopted the correlation between stimuli and responses as this fundamental unit. They insisted that all complex knowledge could, with careful analysis, be reduced to associations (Watson 1930).

The British empiricists, including Hobbes (1651), Locke (1690), and Hume (1748), first developed this associational view of knowledge and experience. They held that perceptual experience is given as groupings or assemblages of perceptual data, such as color, size and shape. Ideas or concepts arise as a reflection of those groupings in perception. There is, on this view, no "glue" that holds concepts of objects together, except the *habit of associating* the qualities that are repeatedly grouped together in perception. Abstraction and generalization are understood here as the process of dropping from concepts those qualities that are only weakly associated with items, that is, qualities that are varying or inconstant in the perception of an object.

In contrast to the associationist view, cognitivists deny that experience consists only of assemblages of primitive qualia. Researchers, beginning with Bartlett (1932) and Piaget (1931, 1954, 1970) and continuing with more contemporary theorists such as Bransford et al. (1972), Kintsch (1974), and Hinsley et al. (1977) maintain that knowledge is stored in terms of larger, more organized units, which they called *schemas*. It is rather difficult to provide a precise definition of a schema, other than to say that it is an abstraction of past specific experiences. In principle, the abstraction can vary from something as specific as a feature of some letter, e.g., the feature "-" in the uppercase letter "A," to a structure for stories, that is, the idea that simple stories often have the same pattern involving the relation between setting, characters, a plot, and a resolution. The critical assumption for schema theorists is that knowledge consists of abstractions that cannot be reduced to associations between specific qualities or events.

Some of Bartlett's (1932) original evidence for schemas was that when his subjects were read a story and asked to recall it after a period of time, they tended to recall the gist of the story, rather then detailed verbatim information. Bartlett interpreted this to indicate that the words making up the phrases and sentences in the story were recorded by his subjects in terms of idea units that the subject imposed on the data. These idea units were the contents of schemas the subject used to comprehend the story. As a result they only remembered the main points of the story evoked, and not the specific detail.

Since Bartlett's original studies, there has accumulated a volume of literature, e.g., Bransford et al. (1972), Kintsch (1974), and Thorndyke (1977), in support of schema theory. In addition to the scientific evidence favoring the idea that we interpret and remember our experiences in terms of schemata, it also seems to make a great deal of common sense. As a result it is not surprising that schema theory and similar abstractionist views such as that of Minsky's *frames* (1975) have dominated our theorizing regarding the units of cognitive representation. In fact many researchers from the field of artificial intelligence have adopted this approach, which we address in more detail in Part II.

Let us now consider the epistemological support for a schema based theory of representation. A constructivist epistemology (Section 2.1) suggests that representational schemes arise in the process of interaction, interpretation, and adaptation with our environment. Piaget (1954), the developmental psychologist and early proponent of a constructivist epistemology, describes the stages of development children pass through in accommodating to their world. At each stage the child accommodates in a fashion that allows survival but still, at every level of development, there remains questions and unexplored relationships that will require further growth. For example, for the child in the earliest stages of development, an object that is out of sight has also ceased to exist. Similarly, in the sensori-motor stage, objects are understood to the extent that they can be seen, touched, or moved. At higher stages the child begins to relinquish this fundamental egocentrism and starts to affirm properties and relationships independent of her own existence.

From this developmental research Piaget proposed his *genetic epistemology* a constructivist approach to understanding. Piaget describes an active tension for equilibrium as an intrinsic and constitutive property of organic and mental life. Accommodation is the attempt to resolve the tension between the schema of current understanding and the interaction with actual situations. The lack of a comfortable fit of the world as it is to our current understanding of it forces a revision process. This schema revision for better understanding Piaget refers to as *accommodation*, and the continued revisions of understanding as a movement toward *equilibration*.

Revision of schemas and movement toward equilibration is not just a genetic predisposition. Nor is it totally an accommodation to the structures of society and the external world. Rather, blending both these forces, it is the embodied predisposition of the genotype to survival. Thus schema modification is not simply an *a priori* of our genetics, nor is it an *a posteriori* function of society and the world; it is a product of the synergistic interaction between our internal physical and cognitive structures and their embodiment.

There is also a hint of a compromise here between the empiricist and rationalist traditions in philosophy. As embodied, we apprehend nothing except that which first passes through the senses. As accommodating agents we survive through abstracting out and abiding by the general patterns of an external world. The tension which drives us toward equilibrium dictates that perception is mediated by our need to understand and our understanding is revised through perception.

We need not be conscious or aware of the *a priori* structures or schemata that support our accommodation with the world. In fact, as the sources of bias and prejudice both in science and society we are usually completely unaware of their content. These are constitutive of our interaction with the world and not a direct construct of our conscious mental life.

3.2.2 Toward Cognitive Representational Schemes

As just noted, our schemas for equilibration with our environment are rarely brought to a conscious level for analysis. As cognitive scientists we have developed two general methodologies for addressing the representation problem, each part of a rich tradition within our discipline: the *explicit symbol system* and the *connectionist* approaches. As we see in Section 3.3, these are but two families of differing methods that may be used in this difficult problem of identifying and capturing patterns in our environment.

First, in the explicit symbol based approach, by careful observing, measuring, and testing we can attempt to construct a system of symbols that reflects the schematization of the intelligent agent. There are multiple methodologies for accomplishing this task, most notably the direct and indirect testing methods that are described in Section 4.2. Briefly, these methods observe the subject in the context of solving a problem, and hypothesize, based on some careful analysis, parameters and constraints that can account for the activity.

The result of such analysis is the creation of an explicit symbol system that attempts to represent invariant aspects of the schema of an intelligent agent. Once the components of this symbol system are identified and assembled, they can be interpreted in the context of data from the environment. This commitment to specific invariant components that are assembled into an explicit symbol system are often referred to as the *ontology of the model*. We laid the groundwork for this approach in the previous chapter when we identified the formal properties of the physical symbol system. We continue to describe explicit representational schemes in Section 3.3.

The second method of dealing with the contents of cognitive schemata is to build a recognition system that can itself discover subsets of invariants of phenomena. One method for doing this is the subsymbolic or connectionist approach, where a network structure of distributed processors is created capable of capturing regularities of the environment and then interpreting new data in the context of these invariant patterns. Other methods for discovering patterns in our environment include genetic algorithms (Chapter 12).

Researchers take several approaches to creating the subsymbolic or connectionist architectures. First, unlike the explicit symbol system approach, specific invariances in the problem solving environment are NOT explicitly identified and directly encoded in the network. Rather they are implicitly represented in the patterns of activation and the architecture of the nodes of the net. Thus single nodes are not mapped into individual invariants, but rather the information is represented in the weights and distributed across the nodes of the network.

There are a number of different learning algorithms for connectionist networks. Some of these are teacher based, in that the network is explicitly told whether or not it has succeeded in recognizing a pattern. Then reward and/or punishment algorithms change the weights on the nodes of the network to reflect this fact. Other nets are conditioned by repeated presentation of information from the environment and come to stabilize and reflect patterns of the environment without the direct intervention of a teacher. We go into several of the different connectionist architectures and training algorithms in Part III.

Before we leave the connectionist approach to identifying invariances in perception and cognition we note that this methodology has moved a very long way from attempting to build a bottom-up model of the human neuronal system. Even though its earliest approaches to modeling human perception and performance were neurally inspired, current researchers follow the signal processing, classifier systems, or pattern recognition disciplines. This engineering tradition has its roots in operations research, and its predecessors include hill climbing algorithms, gradient descent search, cluster analysis, and other pattern recognition algorithms.

Despite the continuing evolution of connectionist networks, architectures, and algorithms away from a neurological foundation, human performance remains neurally based. Thus, investigation of cortical architecture and human biological processing is an important component of any science of cognition. We examine the neurophysiologist's techniques for identifying physical parameters and constraints in Chapter 5.

3.3   GENERAL PROPERTIES OF REPRESENTATIONAL SCHEMES

We now discuss the methods supporting particular representing schemes. First, we describe a *sample based* scheme where distinct representing points are taken as samples from a continuous environment. Second, we present an approach based on *homomorphic mappings*, where created symbols reflect invariances in the environment. Our third approach, the *procedural*, is based on the creation of descriptions of perceived qualitative relationships in the environment. These relationships are described by rules relating specified symbols.

Next, with the *production system*, we introduce a control algorithm for implementing procedures. Fifth, we introduce *network* or *association based* characterizations. Sixth, we present the *structured* or *frame/schema* representation of phenomena. Finally, we present the *connectionist* approach where patterns in data are discovered by a distributed network of nodes with trained weights. All these approaches are presented with further detail later in the book.

3.3.1 Mapping Constraints and Representations

Our goal in this section is to introduce representations with a survey of the traditional approaches to the problem employed by cognitive scientists. We begin this

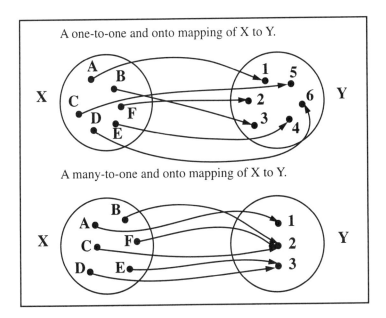

A one-to-one and onto mapping of X to Y.

A many-to-one and onto mapping of X to Y.

FIGURE 3.2   A one-to-one and onto mapping and a many-to-one and onto mapping.

section by describing a number of different types of mapping constraints. Figure 3.2 identifies the difference between a mapping that is *one-to-one* and a mapping that is *many-to-one*. An *onto* mapping exhausts all the symbols of the mapped to set; both examples of Figure 3.2 are onto. If there were elements of set Y of Figure 3.2 left over after the mapping, that is, an element of set Y with no element of X mapped to it, the mapping would be called an *into map*. We call a one-to-one onto mapping of two sets a *one-to-one correspondence* and a many-to-one onto mapping of two sets an *many-to-one correspondence*.

As shown in Section 2.5, an isomorphic map between the tokens of two systems that preserves the rules of each system is necessary to prove formal equivalence of the two systems. The symbol based cognitive representation, as we see in the following sections, identifies phenomena and maps them in a many-to-one fashion into a set of symbols that represent invariant aspects of that phenomena. The representation becomes a *model* when the manipulation rules of the representation reflect the relationships between the invariances in the phenomena. In contrast, with the connectionist approach, the mapping of information onto network nodes and the relationships between nodes is not made explicit, but is rather part of the pattern recognition process of the distributed system.

The objects within the represented world possess a large number of properties that an explicit symbol can potentially reflect. But as with most representations, only certain aspects of the represented world are selected. Therefore, it is essential that we be clear as to what precisely is being represented, what is doing the representing, as well as what properties are ignored. This is often referred to as *the ontology of a representational scheme*. The relationship between the represented property of the world and the symbols of the representing model define the *laws of correspondence* within a representational system.

Thus, in creating a model, we must specify five aspects of a representational system: 1) the represented world; 2) the representing model; 3) the aspects of the represented world that make up the invariants; 4) the symbols or symbol structures within of the representing model that are referring to these invariants; and 5) the rules of correspondences between the represented world and its model (Palmer 1978).

3.3.2 Homomorphism Based Symbol Systems

We define the *homomorphic mapping* of a representational system as a many-to-one structure preserving relationship between a set of phenomena in an environment and a set of symbols representing invariant aspects of those phenomena. Figure 3.3 presents a homomorphic mapping between words in English and their classifications as nouns, verbs, and adjectives. We assume our structure preserving map is provided by grammar rules of the representing model that reflect relationships in the represented world of English language use.

Any representational scheme will eventually breakdown when pressed to address more sophisticated situations. This breakdown is analogous to that of an intelligent agent's schema when confronted with new complexity. To address this new complexity, more invariants are identified and the homomorphic mappings of the representational system are amended. In revising the mappings of the representation of Figure 3.4, we create further homomorphic maps. This situation is seen in Figure 3.5 where more complex sentence analysis, that of an automated parser, for example, requires the distinction between proper and common nouns as well as between transitive and intransitive verbs.

Structure preserving operations or relations defined on homomorphic representations include rules describing the represented information. For instance, in our English language example we can say that a sentence is a noun phrase followed by a verb phrase and that nouns are examples of noun phrases, and verbs examples of verb phrases. We can represent these relations in a graphical mapping, as in Figure 3.5. Note that we have taken symbols, identified by the homomorphism map with certain invariant aspects of language, and then expressed relationships between these invariants with rules and a graph. We continue this approach when we introduce trees and graphs in Chapter 6 and language understanding in Part IV.

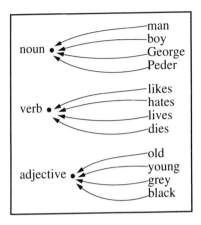

FIGURE 3.3   A homomorphic mapping of English words onto the symbols noun, verb, and adjective.

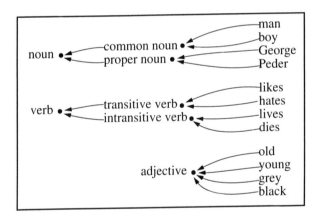

FIGURE 3.4   The homomorphic map of Figure 3.3 revised with the further homomorphic relationship of proper and common nouns, transitive and intransitive verbs.

Homomorphic representational systems are information preserving and, as such, may be called models. When we let the name *transitive verb* stand for the set of transitive verbs in the English language as in Figure 3.5, then transitive verb must preserve some information about words in that language. In the example, the representing world preserves selective information of the represented world, for example, that the verb "lives" may be used without a direct object. The mapping preserves little else, certainly nothing of the word's meaning.

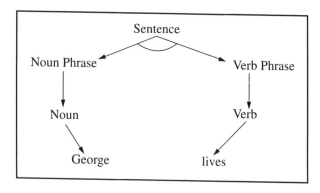

FIGURE 3.5   A parse tree representing the fact that a sentence is a noun phrase followed by a verb phrase, that a noun is an instance of a noun phrase, a verb of a verb phrase, and symbols from Figure 3.4.

3.3.3 Sample Based Representational Schemes

Consider the digitized image of Figure 3.6; it represents an image of a human cell in the *metaphase* stage, just before the cell divides. Digitization is an example of a *sample based representation*. The phenomenon represented is actually a continuum, and the representing picture a set of points, each with a different *gray level*. Newspaper pictures or television images are other examples of such representations. Samples are taken from the person or scene represented, usually at fixed though very close distances. The color or gray levels of the image represent that of the thing itself.

Size, texture, and color are all examples of properties of the phenomena that may be preserved by the sample based representational scheme. For example, in Figure 3.6, it is possible for a computer to count, compare, and contrast chromosomes. It is also possible to automatically "see" damage such as missing pieces or some mutations.

Storage for this type representation is naturally handled with a two dimensional array of picture points, where each point is a sample of the phenomenon represented. Processing of this type representation may be done by identifying edges of images, summing up gray levels for a density measure, finding and marking the centers as is done in the figure, or simply by identifying and removing isolated picture points that represent spurious data. Much of the research in computer vision develops along these lines.

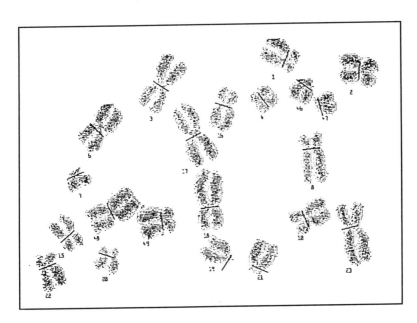

FIGURE 3.6   A sample based representation. This gray level image is of a cell in metaphase.

3.3.4 Relational or Logic Based Representations

In the previous section we described how relationships between invariants in our environment can be reflected by rules relating these invariants in our representational scheme. An example was that a sentence was a noun phrase followed by a verb phrase and a noun was a noun phrase and a verb was a verb phrase. Thus, *George lives* is an example of a sentence. The formalization of this approach to representation is called logic.

Logic based representational schemes may be described from three viewpoints. First, logic is a language. It offers a well-formed set of symbols or tokens that may be composed into sentences and used to describe aspects of the world. Logic has terms and expressions that are placed together to make structures, much like the sentences of a natural language. In this sense logic is ideal for capturing declarative and episodic information, as described by Squire (1987, 1992) in Section 3.1.1. Second, logic has a mathematics of semantic consistency (Tarski 1944) that relates logic based descriptions to entities in a possible world. Finally, mathematically sound and complete reasoning schemes may be used to conclude information about the world. We consider briefly each of these points.

First, the most commonly used logic language is the predicate calculus. This language has its beginnings in the forms first proposed by Aristotle. Even though many mathematicians since Aristotle took their turn at adding to and developing this language, it wasn't until the 20th century that logic took its present form (Chapter 7).

Second, there is a mathematical scheme by which these descriptions are precisely related to a described world. This mathematics of meaning, often referred to as a *semantics* for logic expressions, was created by Alfred Tarski (1944). A justification for this semantics is that anything deduced within the context of the logic representations can be shown to be necessarily true in the world that the logic represents.

The third aspect of the logic representation is a well understood set of reasoning rules. These rules combine descriptions of the world to create new true information about the world. If we know that "John passed the logic exam" and also know that "all students that pass the logic exam will pass the cognitive science course," then we can conclude that "John will pass the cognitive science course." What is deduced by a sound inference rule in the description language must be true in all worlds that this language describes.

The language of logic is presented in Chapter 7, where many examples of its use are given. Chapter 7 also describes some alternative logic schemes, including multi-valued, modal, and nonmonotonic logics, as well as a logic for reasoning with uncertainty.

3.3.5 Procedural Representations

Procedural schemes describe knowledge as a set of relations between symbols that represent instructions for solving a problem or accomplishing a task. Each piece of knowledge is described by a unique condition-action pair. The conditions are "pattern based" in that they are able to match situations in the environment, and when matched, produce an appropriate action or response to that situation. In this sense they are often seen to have a behaviorist flavor (Newell & Simon 1972).

The knowledge about a particular situation may be described by a large set of these condition-action procedures. Chase and Simon (1973) conjectured, for example, that the skilled behavior of a grandmaster chess player could be represented by about 50,000 pieces of procedural knowledge. When the chess player encounters a particular board position, the appropriate piece of knowledge is matched and the action, a move on the board, takes place in response to that situation.

This approach to describing knowledge is used in the rule based expert system. In the rule based program, for example, each *if...then* rule is interpreted as a procedure for solving part of a larger problem. In the MYCIN work at Stanford

(Buchanan & Shortliff 1984) the diagnostic skill of a human doctor considering a possible meningitis infection was produced in a program with about 650 condition-action procedures. In the XCON program at Digital it took several thousand rules to reproduce the skills that humans possessed in configuring computers (Bachant & McDermott 1984).

Creating a model of skilled human performance with a set of such condition-action rules has offered a valuable diagnostic tool for researchers attempting to understand and remedy human skilled performance. Brown and Burton (1978), for example, built a rule based model of children's subtraction skills. When a child would make a mistake in a subtraction exercise, the researcher (or computer) was able to compare the child's mistake to the set of rules describing the skill. An error in performance was then seen as a malformed or missing procedure and remediation was a matter of training the child with the correct rule.

This approach was used in a number of situations for diagnosis and teaching, including instruction in programming languages (Singley & Anderson 1989) and comparing novice with skilled performance in problem solving (Larkin et al. 1980, Simon & Simon 1978).

It is not sufficient to say that knowledge is just a large number of condition-action procedures. There must be an interpreter or an algorithm that organizes the use of these rules. We describe such an tool, called a *production system*, in Figure 3.7. There are three components of the production system, the *set of rules*, the *working memory*, and the pattern driven *control cycle*.

The set of rules is often referred to as the *production memory*. In this memory we find all the *if .. then ..* knowledge procedures. The working memory contains the problem solving information, such as the start, goal, and the present state of progress. The pattern driven control cycle takes the present state of the problem to the conditions of the production rules; when the condition of a rule is matched, the corresponding action takes place which serves to alter the current state of the problem solving as described in working memory. The cycle then repeats until either the goal is found or the present state of the problem solving does not match any production rule.

There are a large number of sophisticated control procedures that may be used in the production system, and several of these are demonstrated in detail in Chapter 9; for now, we offer a very simple control structure. In Figure 3.8A, a set of production rules is used to perform unary subtraction. In Figure 3.8B a different set of rules is used to sort the characters of a list. The production rules are shown and the control regime simply uses the first rule that matches. Figure 3.8 shows the state of the working memory with each cycle of the system as it performs its task.

In Figure 3.8A, unary subtraction is performed on the same problem that was used to demonstrate the Turing machine specification for computing in Section 2.5.2. Production system computing is as general purpose as is the universal

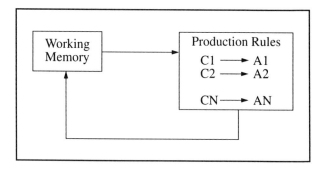

FIGURE 3.7   The set of production rules, the working memory, and the control cycle of
a production system. The system stops when the patterns of working
memory no longer match any rule.

Turing machine, that is, it can compute any computable function. A full proof of
this would require quite a detailed argument, as discussed in Section 2.5.3. However, the solution of this simple problem can begin to give a hint of what is
involved. As we will see throughout the remainder of this book, and especially in
Chapter 9, the procedure based problem solver, especially as it is represented by
the production system, plays an important role in describing human skilled performance.

There are a number of other procedure based problem solving paradigms
from AI research. Among the most prominent are *procedure tables* and *blackboards*. Procedure tables are often used in *planning*, a research area where large
plans are made up of smaller constituent actions. This might be used in the design
of a control algorithm to drive a robot. The smaller procedures are broken into
the conditions that must be met for their use, their explicit actions, and the results
to their world of performing the action. These smaller procedures are often stored
in easily accessed structures, such as *triangle tables* (Fikes et al. 1972, Luger &
Stubblefield 1993), where they can be organized in the creation of larger plans.

Blackboards are global databases where sets of procedures may work in parallel and asynchronously to solve problems. More detail on blackboard systems
is presented in Section 9.4, including discussion on the HEARSAY project
(Reddy 1976), an application of the blackboard technology for the understanding
of spoken English language sentences.

3.3.6 Network Representations

Network representations capture knowledge as a graph in which the nodes represent objects or concepts of the modeled domain and the arcs represent relations

Production Rules

1. $101 \longrightarrow 0$
2. $0B \longrightarrow B$

Iteration No.	Working Memory	Conflict Set	Rule Used
0	BB1111011BB	1	1
1	BB11101BB	1	1
2	BB110BB	2	2
3	BB11BB		halt

FIGURE 3.8A Trace of a simple production system doing unary subtraction. The problem may be compared with Figure 2.8

Production Rules

1. $BA \longrightarrow AB$
2. $CA \longrightarrow AC$
3. $CB \longrightarrow BC$

Iteration No.	Working Memory	Conflict Set	Rule Used
0	CBACA	1,2,3	1
1	CABCA	2	2
2	ACBCA	2,3	2
3	ACBAC	1.3	1
4	ACABC	2	2
5	AACBC	3	3
6	AABCC		halt

FIGURE 3.8B Trace of a production system sorting a string of characters.

or associations between objects. As noted in Section 3.2.2, this commitment of invariants of the domain to the nodes and relationships of the model is called the *ontology of the model*. Examples of network representations include *semantic networks* and *conceptual dependencies* (see Section 6.2). The mathematical support for this class of representations comes from graph theory (Section 6.1). The psychological foundation for network representational schemes comes from associationist models of meaning (Anderson & Bower 1973).

Associationist theories define the meaning of an object in terms of a structure or network of associations with other objects in a mind or knowledge base. Even though symbols denote objects in a world, this relationship is mediated by already stored pieces of knowledge. Associationist theories suggest that when we reason about an object, it is first mapped into a more complex pattern of concepts in our mind. These concepts are part of our entire knowledge of the world and are connected through appropriate relationships to other concepts. These relationships form an understanding of the properties and behaviors of objects.

For example, through experience we associate the concept snow with other concepts such as cold, white, snowman, slippery, and ice. Our understanding of snow and the truth of statements such as "snowmen are white" manifests itself through this network of associations. There is psychological evidence to support the intuition that humans also organize their knowledge hierarchically, with information kept at the highest appropriate levels of abstraction within this taxonomy.

Collins and Quillian (1969) modeled human information storage and management using a semantic network, as in Figure 3.9. The structure of this hierarchy was supported by laboratory testing of human subjects. The subjects were asked questions about different properties of birds, for example, *Is a canary a bird?*, or *Can a canary sing?*, or *Can a canary fly?*.

As obvious as the answers to these questions may seem, reaction time studies indicated that it took longer for subjects to answer *Can a canary fly?* than it did to answer *Can a canary sing?* Collins and Quillian explain this difference in response time by arguing that people store information at its most general or abstract level. And so, instead of trying to recall that canaries fly, and robins fly and swallows fly (all *fly* relations stored with the individual bird), humans remember that canaries are birds and that birds have (usually) the property of flying. Even more general properties such as eating, breathing, and moving are stored at the *animal* level, and so trying to recall whether a canary can breathe should take longer than whether a canary can fly. This is, of course, because the human must travel further up the hierarchy of memory structures to retrieve the answer.

The fastest recall was for the traits specific to the bird, for example, that a canary can sing or is yellow. Exception handling also seemed to be done at the most specific level. When subjects were asked whether an ostrich could fly, the

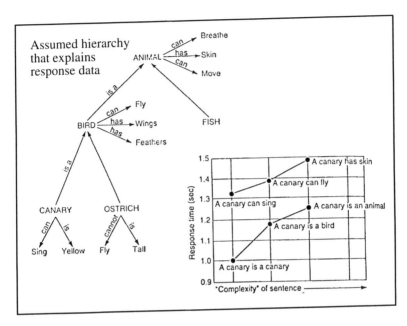

FIGURE 3.9   The semantic net developed by Collins and Quillian in their research on human associative memory. This figure is adapted from Harmon and King (1985).

negative answer was produced faster than when asked whether the ostrich could breathe. Thus the hierarchy ostrich --> bird --> animal seems NOT to be traversed to get the exception information; it is stored directly with ostrich.

The Collins and Quillian research was designed to characterize a representation and topology for information in semantic memory. Although their approach has been used to design several natural language understanding programs (Woods 1985) there is more recent research that can explain this same data with a different analysis of associations (Conrad 1972, Rosch 1978). This work states that our use and experience of world information causes some associations to be stronger and thus more easily accessed than others. For example, "robins fly" is a stronger association than "robins breathe," similarly a robin is more typically a bird than is a chicken.

There are several benefits that come from inheritance systems. They allow us to store information at the highest level of abstraction; this reduces the size of knowledge bases and helps prevent certain types of update inconsistencies. For example, if we are building a representation of birds, we can define the traits common to all birds, such as flying or having feathers, for the general class *bird* and allow particular species of bird to inherit these properties. This reduces the size of the knowledge base by requiring us to define these essential traits only once, rather than requiring their assertion for each individual in the class.

Inheritance also helps us to maintain the consistency of the knowledge base when adding new classes and individuals. Assume that we are adding the species *robin* to an existing knowledge base of birds. When we assert that *robin* is a sub-class of *songbird*, a robin automatically inherits all of the common properties of both songbirds, birds, as well as their superclasses.

Graphs, by providing a means of explicitly representing relations using arcs and nodes, have proven to be an ideal vehicle for formalizing associationist theories of knowledge. A semantic network represents knowledge as a graph, with the nodes corresponding to facts or concepts and the arcs to relations or associations between concepts. Both nodes and links are generally labeled. For example, a semantic network which defines the properties of snow appears in Figure 3.10. This network could be used (with appropriate reasoning rules) to answer a range of questions about snow, ice, and snowmen. These inferences are made by following the appropriate links of related concepts.

The term *semantic network* encompasses a family of graph based representations. Each of these differs chiefly in the names that are allowed for nodes and links and the inferences that may be performed on these structures. There is, however, a common set of assumptions and concerns shared by all network representation languages. In Chapter 6, we present more specific examples of network representations, including *semantic nets* and *conceptual dependencies*.

3.3.7 Structured Representations

Structured representation languages extend networks by allowing each node to be a complex data structure consisting of named slots with attached values. These values may be simple characters, numerics, symbolic data, pointers to other structures, or even procedures for performing tasks related to the structure. Examples of structured representations include *frames*, *scripts*, *schemas*, and *objects*. Details of these structures are presented in Chapter 6.

A structured representation such as a *frame* is intended to represent a complex situation or set of circumstances. Marvin Minsky (1975), in a now famous paper, describes a frame:

> Here is the essence of frame theory: When one encounters
> a new situation (or makes a substantial change in one's
> view of a problem) one selects from memory a structure
> called a "frame." This is a remembered framework to be
> adapted to fit reality by changing details as necessary.

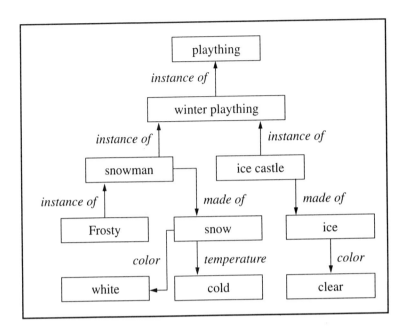

FIGURE 3.10 A semantic net representing the associations of snow, ice, and snowmen.

A frame is a data structure used to represent well-organized, stereotypical situations. We may conjecture that frame-like structures organize our knowledge of the world. We adjust to new situations by relating them to structured knowledge built from past experiences. A frame structure would be an appropriate representation for the schema information Bartlett (1932) described in Section 3.1.2, and that we used in a description of a constructivist epistemology. Thus the words *frame* and *schema* may be used almost interchangeably. Historically, it seems that most AI researchers refer to this data structure as a *frame* or *object*, while most researchers describing psychological phenomena refer to it as a *schema*.

Another method for describing a frame is as a structured semantic network. In this sense rather than capturing a situation as a large loosely structured network, aspects of each entity are gathered together under the name of that entity. A frame can include the frame name; a description, perhaps in the form of property lists; pointers to other frames; and default assumptions for that frame. The pointers to other frames can be for inheritance purposes, as was described in the network representation schemes. A frame-like version of the semantic network description of birds (Figure 3.9) may be found in the frame structure of Figure 3.11.

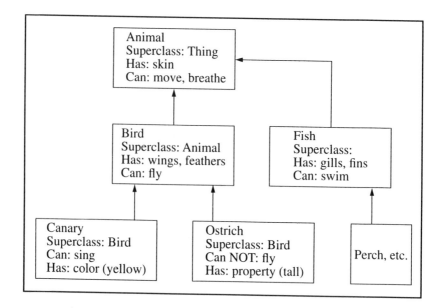

FIGURE 3.11   A frame based inheritance system for the bird hierarchy of Figure 3.9.

A number of other structured representations offer important models for problem solving. Schank and Rieger (1974) used the primitives described in his *Conceptual Dependency* theory (Chapter 6) to create *scripts*. A *script* is a structured representation that describes a stereotyped sequence of events, such as a visit to a restaurant or going to a birthday party. Scripts have much of the flavor of frames or schemas except that they are intended to represent sequences of events rather than simple situations. Scripts, adopting other tools such as *props* and *roles* from the design of a play, were used to interpret stories about restaurants or parties; examples are presented in Section 6.3.

Object-oriented design is a powerful representational tool often employed to build structured representations. Object systems with multiple inheritance, that is, where each object in the system may inherit properties from more than one parent, offer very flexible and expressive representational environments. Further details of structured representations and object-oriented languages may be found in Part II and in Luger and Stubblefield (1993).

3.3.8   Connectionist Models

All the representational schemas presented to this point in Section 3.3 are directly created and manipulated: they are what we call explicit symbol based representa-

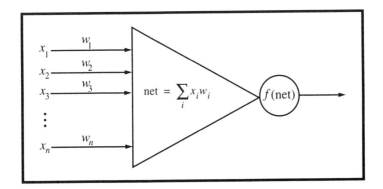

FIGURE 3.12 An artificial neuron, an input vector x_i, weights assigned to each input line, and a thresholding function f that determines the neuron's output value.

tions. In this final section we introduce an alternative representational approach, the connectionist methodology. Connectionist systems perform automated identification, collection, and classification of patterns of data, among other tasks.

The connectionist approach uses a network of nodes and links between the nodes to try to recognize both the important parameters of a solution space as well as to interpret new data in the context of this solution space. We introduced the neural or connectionist approach in the first two chapters, and offer a detailed presentation in Chapters 11 and 12.

Figure 1.4 presented a diagram of a neuron. We described this neuron as receiving input data through its dendrites. When these combined impulses exceed a certain threshold the neuron fires with an impulse or "spike" passing done its axon. This signal is then passed on to the dendrites of further neurons. We show many more examples of neuronal processing in Chapter 5.

The basis of neural networks is the artificial neuron, see Figure 3.12. An artificial neuron consists of:

- Input signals, x_i. This data may come from the environment, or the activation of other neurons. Different models vary in the allowable range of the input values; typically inputs are either discrete, from the set $\{0,1\}$ or $\{-1, 1\}$, or are real numbers.
- A set of real valued weights, w_i, used to describe connection strengths.
- An activation level. The neuron's activation level is determined by the cumulative strength of its input signals where each input signal is scaled by the connection weight w_i along that input line. The activation level is usually computed by taking the sum of the scaled input values.

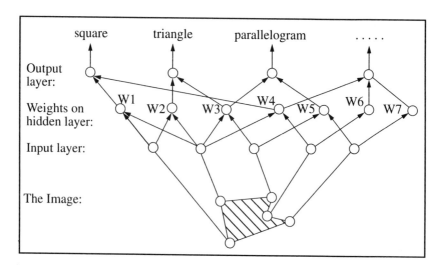

FIGURE 3.13 A three layer connectionist network. The input layer captures information from the data, the hidden layer has adjustable weights that are conditioned during training and the output layer presents the results of the network's pattern processing.

- Finally, a threshold function, f, that computes the neuron's output state by determining whether the neuron's activation level is below or above some threshold value. This produces the on/off state of the neuron.

Sets of artificial neurons are built into a network of neurons. An example backpropagation network for classification of geometric figures is presented in Figure 3.13. Once the connectionist or subsymbolic system is designed, it is trained or conditioned by example instances of that which is to be learned, in our example, the square, triangle, parallelogram figures. The inner or *hidden nodes* of the network are trained by reinforcement algorithms working over time. When the network stabilizes and has learned the training set data, it is given new situations to recognize. The prime analog of the connectionist system is the human's physical neurological makeup. As in the human, connectionist systems are parallel and asynchronous. They are able to operate without perfect information and degrade gracefully when information is fuzzy or missing, rather than, as often happens in explicit symbol systems, fail directly.

Subsymbolic or connectionist systems can emulate many of the input/output functions of explicit symbol systems, in fact, they are computationally equivalent, see Section 12.5. The critical point in connectionist networks, however, is that the causal and other relationships of the system's functioning are not represented at the symbolic rule or procedural level. Rather, the system's functioning is determined by the patterns of activation that might involve numerous computational neuron units. A symbol may be realized by some pattern of activation, but there is no simple reduction between patterns of activation and explicit symbols.

The weights of the nodes of the connectionist system are usually randomly initialized. A subset of the nodes are *input* nodes through which examples are presented to the system. These are connected to internal or *hidden nodes* that each have threshold values that determine their activation. Finally, there are *output* nodes that respond, depending on the activation of the inner nodes, to each set of input values. When this system is presented with examples, the output nodes respond. In supervised learning a training or conditioning algorithm takes the correct or erroneous response of the system and appropriately readjusts the weight values of the nodes that produced the response. There are a number of algorithms for doing this, the most common is backpropagation, Section 11.3; several others are discussed in Chapter 12.

The key point of connectionist systems is that the internal nodes, those creating the patterns of activation, may not be directly manipulated by the net designer or programmer. In fact, these hidden nodes are inaccessible, and only changed indirectly as the result of the input values and the training algorithm. Patterns of activation from the input values pass from bottom to top in Figure 3.13. The training algorithm that distributes the error of the result back across the activations of the hidden nodes moves from the top of the figure down.

There are a number of reasons why connectionist or neural architectures are appealing as mechanisms for implementing intelligence. Traditional symbol systems tend to be brittle and overly sensitive to noise rather than degrading gracefully; such programs tend to either be correct or fail completely. Human intelligence is much more flexible, it is good at interpreting noisy input, such as recognizing a face in a darkened room from an odd angle or following a single conversation at a noisy party. Even where a human may not be able to solve some problem, we generally can make a reasonable guess as to its solution rather than simply failing. Neural architectures, because they capture knowledge in a large number of fine grained units, seem to have more potential for partially matching noisy and incomplete data. Connectionist architectures are also more robust because knowledge is distributed somewhat uniformly around the network.

Connectionist architectures provide a natural model for parallelism, since each neuron is an independent physical unit, although its connectivity to other units can be arbitrarily complex. Humans get faster at a task as they acquire more knowledge while serial computers tend to slow down. This slowdown is due to the cost of sequentially searching an ever larger knowledge base. A massively parallel architecture such as the human brain does not suffer from this problem.

Connectionism has great promise and will continue to be a major focus of research in cognitive science and psychology, as well as in the traditional areas of pattern recognition and machine learning. A phenomenon as complex as intelligence requires the efforts of researchers using many different models and approaches. Connectionism can provide a lower level or *subsymbolic* description of intelligent mechanism and has already made progress toward modeling perception and associative memory. Symbolic approaches provide powerful languages for describing higher level processes as well as the organization and structure of both biological and silicon brains. We feel these different paradigms will converge on a full and unified understanding of the nature of intelligence.

It is not possible to go more deeply into connectionist architectures without more mathematical tools, including some matrix algebra and the calculus of continuous functions. Sections 11.1 and 11.2 present an historical introduction to this technology. Backpropagation, by far the most commonly used network architecture, is presented in Section 11.3.

3.4   Limitations of Representational Formalisms

We conclude Chapter 3 with a number of observations concerning representational schemes. First and most importantly, as cognitive scientists we are making models of representing systems. We use the term *representational model* to indicate that we are making models to capture the representational and processing aspects of human intelligence. Several points follow. First, the representation is always an approximation and a surrogate of the modeled phenomena. It is an approximation in that the representing system is a reflection or mapping of selected things and relationships in the environment. It is a surrogate because in our modeling we manipulate our representational system and not the environment itself.

Second, we must face the indeterminacy of representing and modeling schemes. Because each representation is a combination of information storage and inference process, it may in fact be impossible to definitively say that one model is "better" than another for a fixed situation. Finally, as introduced in Sections 3.1 and 3.2, our representational schemes are an outgrowth of our psychology and our epistemology, of our embodied attempt to work within our world.

3.4.1   Approximation and Surrogacy

We contend that approximation and surrogacy are not as fundamental a limitation as they might seem. As humans, we act totally within our created symbol systems. Language use is an excellent example. Our words approximate aspects of our environment, and our use of language assists us in surviving within that environment. One has only to read an account of such important concepts as love and responsibility to realize that our words and expressions are only pale imitations of the thing itself.

As scientists, of course, we are bound by this same limitation. We work carefully to create words and a language for describing our focus of research. Invariances within this focus are often captured by a set of equations. Philosophers of science (Popper 1959, Kuhn 1962) tell us, however, that these equation relationships are only useful if they can assist us in prediction, and perhaps later be falsified, as our ability to understand and describe the world evolves. We address these issues again in Chapter 17.

Because our representational scheme is a substitute for the thing itself, we must always know that some aspects of the thing will be omitted in the correspondence mapping. We make a commitment to what we think is important in the environment, and choose to ignore other aspects. This is an *ontological* commitment in that what we select as important in our surrogate manipulations is *de facto* important! We prune away from all concern the rest of reality. Once this choice is made we must continue to live with it.

A further point is that most of the representational schemes we now employ do not provide for revision across their use. This is a fundamental limitation of our current technology. Humans, of course, revise their ontological commitments both with the success and failure of their explorations. For humans, representational schemes are always under revision. In fact, failure to adapt can mean the quick exit of an entity or, at the very least, the judgement that it is not intelligent!

A third point of choosing a representational scheme is the allowed set of things that can be done with it. Thus, when we make a choice of a representational scheme we are also choosing a *set of sanctioned inferences*. Each choice of a representation includes a set of allowed choices or processes.

Related to the notion of sanctioned inferences is *computational efficiency*. For a model to be sufficient or viable in a situation it must not only produce results, but do this within a context under which these results can be said to be useful. An obvious example of this would be the exhaustive search of a chess game. Even though all the potential moves are clear and precise, and everything allowed in the chess context is well-understood, exhaustive search, because of its very complexity, would never produce a result that could be used. This model for a chess playing program simply wouldn't work. Any model whose time or space commitments do not reflect the situation modeled is not *viable* (Section 4.1).

3.4.2 Representational Indeterminacy

In earlier discussion, we hinted at a problem that will be taken up again in Chapter 4, that of *representational indeterminacy*. When we have, as in the Church/Turing thesis, the formal computational equivalence of multiple computing and representational paradigms, it often becomes difficult to determine which scheme may be better for representing and reasoning about a particular problem domain. In fact this is a deep problem with no easy answer.

The computational power of a representational system is only known when both the data structure and interpreting process are made explicit. This introduces the possibility that two representational systems, differing dramatically in structure and in process, may be equivalent in representing a specific situation. For instance, we saw that both the Turing machine (Figure 2.6) and production system (Figure 3.8) solved the unary subtraction problem. When testing human performance it may not in fact be possible to control both aspects of a computational design; that is, both the structure for encoding information as well as the process for interpreting that information. John Anderson (1978) refers to this problem as *representational indeterminacy*.

In Chapter 4 and Parts II and III, we turn to specific cognitive representations. We discuss models that differ radically in the data and processes that they assume. Since each representational scheme is a combination of structure and process, we will find that different representational models may be informationally equivalent and, in some contexts, impossible to separate.

3.4.3 Necessary and Sufficient Models: Looking Ahead to Chapter 4

In Chapter 4 we look carefully at the constraints used to judge a representational model of mind. We present both direct and indirect testing methods. Using these empirical tools, we discuss the possibility of moving from a viable to a valid model of mind. The sufficiency of a model of intelligent behavior can be judged by analysis of its input/output pairs. A *viable* model is "sufficient" to produce equivalent cognitive behavior. A *valid* model is much stronger: it posits a "necessary" equivalence of model and mind.

To judge a representational scheme as a necessary or valid model for intelligent performance we must show that not only is the mapping of the representational scheme "close" to the important features of the thing itself, but the relationships within the model also reflect those within the represented world. Finally, the solution steps, as well as the mistakes taken within the model, must reflect those taken in the environment itself. Both the structure used in the representation mapping as well as the process used in information management must be equivalent for the model and modeled situation. In Chapter 9 we show one attempt to accomplish this using the production system methodology. There, Newell and Simon (1972), through careful years of research and experimentation, make a case for the necessity and sufficiency of a computational interpretation of a representational scheme. Although model necessity or validity may be an important goal for the cognitive scientist, as we see in the remaining chapters, we can gain many powerful results using sufficient or viable models.

In summary then, as cognitive scientists, we must deal with representational issues as scientists in other disciplines do:

- First, it is common for different representations to be part of understanding one phenomenon. Physicists, for example, may not be entirely comfortable with both a wave and particle theory of light, but they use each to explain aspects of this phenomenon. Both models, though in current understanding incomparable, are used to advance science.
- Second, if a model and representational scheme works, then use it. Since judgement on the success of a model rests in its falsification as much as on its generalization, it is important that each scheme be pushed as far as possible. In the final analysis, the model is not the thing itself, and therefore incompatibility at some level of specification must be expected.
- Finally, representational schemes offer us a medium for communication. They provide us a language for describing aspects of our environment and they ultimately will be interpreted. Thus, the representational medium may be used by a scientist to better understand the environment, it may be interpreted by computational devices, or it may be used as a vehicle to share research insights with colleagues.

A representation is a tool for exploring our world. Its use assists understanding and promotes intervention in our environment. The quality of a representational scheme rests on its interpretative adequacy and flexibility for refinement.; this very activity demands continued model revision for further exploration.

3.5   EPILOGUE AND REFERENCES

This chapter, and especially the attempts to use formal representations to model intelligent systems, has a definite rationalist flavor. Cognitive scientists attempt, through abstraction and analysis to distill out the tokens and relationships that reflect intelligence. There is a great danger here as it can reduce a science about intelligence to a science about things. We must remember that intelligence is embodied in an agent/environment dialectic where purpose, intention, responsibility, and survival are driving forces. Without these dimensions, a model of intelligence is less than complete. Our current modeling technology only hints at how we might address these larger issues. As noted in Section 3.4, however, the power of any model is the utility it offers for furthering science.

Steve Palmer's (1978) paper, *Fundamental Aspects of Cognitive Representation* in Rosch and Lloyd's (1978) book *Cognition and Categorization*, offers an introduction to representational issues in human understanding. Over the past decade the literature on cognitive representation has grown to where it is difficult to summarize in a single paper. Despite this difficulty, there are several excellent chapters in textbooks on cognitive psychology; we recommend Solso (1991).

If one wants to take a closer look at a given detailed model of human performance, we especially recommend John Anderson's (1983b) *ACT**, as a comprehensive model of semantic memory, or Paul Rosenbloom and Allen Newell's (1987) *SOAR* research, a production system based model for perception, problem solving, memory allocation, and learning. We present the SOAR architecture in Chapters 9 and 10.

The taxonomy for representational schemes was taken in part from J. Mylopoulos and Hector Levesque's (1984) research. A presentation to the general issues of knowledge representation from the viewpoint of artificial intelligence may be found in George Luger and Bill Stubblefield's (1993) book *Artificial Intelligence: Structures and Strategies for Complex Problem Solving*. Other AI references include Allan Collins and Edward Smith's (1988) edited collection *Readings in Cognitive Science*, Ron Brachman and Hector Levesque's (1985) edited collection *Readings in Knowledge Representation*, and Michael Posner's (1989) edited *Foundations of Cognitive Science*.

A number of writers take a more philosophical approach to the issues of this chapter. We especially recommend George Lakoff's (1987) *Women, Fire, and Dangerous Things*; Eleanor Rosch's (1973; et al. 1975, 1978) writings on human categorization and prototypes; Daniel Dennett's (1991) *Consciousness Explained*; and Hilary Putnam's (1988) *Representation and Reality*.

We make a more detailed presentation of explicit symbol based representational schemes and their application in Part II of this book. In Part III we present the architectures and important uses of the connectionist approach. We build explicit representational schemes in Part V of this book, and comment on the limitations and promise of the cognitive science approach in Part VI.

Chapter 4

CONSTRAINING THE ARCHITECTURE OF MINDS

Although this may seem a paradox, all exact science is dominated by the idea of approximation...

Bertrand Russell

A necessary and sufficient condition for a physical system to exhibit general intelligent action is that it be a physical symbol system...

Allen Newell & Herbert Simon (1976)

4.0   INTRODUCTION

Most of the material in the first three chapters focused on the possibility of establishing a science of cognition. According to the physical symbol system hypothesis, introduced in Section 2.6, a necessary and sufficient condition for general intelligence in a physical entity is that it be a physical symbol system. Similarly, we asked whether a connectionist architecture was capable of describing intelligent actions. In Chapter 4 we lay out these arguments and discuss how they may be supported or refuted. In particular, we describe how empirical studies of psychological phenomena fit into cognitive science.

The physical symbol system and connectionist approaches are theories about human intelligence. Theories make assertions about classes of models and their properties. For example, the physical symbol system hypothesis asserts that physical symbol systems are necessary for and sufficient to model the entire range of intelligent human performance and that no other type of model is capable of doing so. Some connectionist theorists make similar claims about parallel distributed processing models. In this chapter we discuss properties of models.

We consider two properties of models: viability and validity. The *viability* of a cognitive model requires that it possess the ability to simulate or produce behavior similar to that of the intelligent system. Thus viability entails two criteria. First the model must be described with sufficient precision and detail so that it may be implemented computationally, and second, that when run on a machine the model can be made to simulate the behavior of the system it is intended to describe.

Our second concern, relating to a model's *validity*, addresses the far more difficult issue of equivalence. The question here is whether the assumed processes in the model are in some sense equivalent to the processes used by the system being modeled. In other words, whether intelligent systems, in fact, employ the same processes assumed by the model. A model's validity depends on the degree to which its processing is equivalent to that of the modeled intelligence.

In Section 4.1 we elaborate the notions of valid and viable models of mind. We also introduce empirical constraints whose role is to lead us toward the creation of such models. In Section 4.2 we introduce *direct methods* of examining psychological phenomena. In Section 4.3 we consider *indirect methods* of establishing models. Direct method includes the transcription and analysis of subject's verbal protocols; indirect method includes Sternberg's additive and subtractive analyses.

In Section 4.4 we present factors, including representational indeterminacy, that limit our goal of establishing strong equivalence of our models and the human processing system. In Chapter 5 we take up neurophysiological issues and their mediation of intelligent problem solving.

4.1 NECESSARY AND SUFFICIENT MODELS OF INTELLIGENCE

4.1.1 The Criterion of Sufficiency

The adequacy of models in most fields of science is evaluated by three criteria: 1) the ability to accurately predict, 2) their generality across some range of phenomena, and 3) the simplicity or elegance of the assumptions contained within the model. This final criteria is often called *Occam's razor*. In this section we introduce the idea of sufficiency, a criterion which expands and refines the prediction requirement. We first clarify the notion of sufficiency and then discuss why it turns out to be such an important issue for models of cognition.

Sufficiency is an aspect of viability. A sufficient model is one in which the various structures and processes used within the model are capable of producing the behavior the model purports to explain. Sufficiency assumes the implementation of the cognitive model in a medium which allows observation of the results of the model's functioning. One example of sufficiency would be to build a robot, or some vision based subsystem of a robot on the basis of a cognitive model and then to test whether it simulated the pattern recognition of the human visual system in the same context. Simulation in this instance would mean that the physically instantiated model produced results equivalent to those produced by the human's perceptual system.

Thus, a method of demonstrating sufficiency of a model is to build it as a computer program and then to run the program to see if it successfully simulates the function being modeled. With this approach, the model is created in terms of the possible symbol states of the computer, and then the symbol states are instantiated physically. The results of the simulation are physical actions produced by the program, such as a move in a chess game or the recognition of a visual scene. In Chapter 9, for example, Newell and Simon (1972) use knowledge encoded in a production system programming environment to mimic humans solving puzzles.

This method of computer based simulation is the essence of computational modeling in cognitive science. It has many obvious advantages over a literal physical instantiation of a model, where a designer has to build a new machine every time there is a new modeling idea. First, software modifications are usually made much more easily than hardware changes while accomplishing the same goals. Second, sufficient models tell us that the model is detailed and specific enough that it can be made to work. Third, they tell us that the cognitive constructs in the model can be physically realized. Finally, with software architectures such as the production system or a counterpropagation classifier, Section 12.1.3, we can create and retain aspects of the model that may be invariant across problem solving situations.

4.1.2 The Insufficiency Problem

In the preceding section we described how computer simulation methods can be used to meet the criterion of sufficiency. Yet there still remains a number of problems: Why is it that we as cognitive scientists are so insistent that our models of mind meet the sufficiency criterion? Is there something about cognition that motivates this concern? In this section we make the case that cognitive scientists are not the mass victims of a character disorder, but in fact have legitimate concerns regarding the sufficiency of cognitive models.

There are two reasons that make us skeptical of cognitive theories and thus eager to verify their sufficiency. The first has to do with the character of intricate biological systems interacting in complex environments. Even if we had good specific models dealing with each of the multitude of parameters influencing the system's functioning, we would have to be concerned about the unexpected outcomes resulting from the interactions of multitudes of variables. We see this in the case of aircraft design where we have good models of the high speed flow of air over surfaces, but we still must observe the performance of model aircraft in wind tunnels, and finally risk the lives of test pilots in actual flight. In other words, much of our testing is a simulation of the system's functioning in an idealized environment.

The second factor underlying our skepticism of cognitive models involves their use of *mentalistic* or *intentional* terms, such as motivations, perceptions, or beliefs. Although the assumed relations between these constructs may seem to make good intuitive sense, they are, on more critical examination, at best vague and often incomplete. For example, a good model from folk psychology might say that a person must work hard to be a good student. So when we hear that Charlie, who spends seven nights a week studying in the library, is a straight A student, we are not at all surprised. Our model predicted this outcome.

Do we really understand Charlie's behavior? Our folk model is vague, so we turn to a more objective version of this model, that found in behavioristic psychology. One of the more important models of behavior (Spence 1956) assumes that an organism's speed in making a correct response is a multiplicative function between drive or motivation and habit strength, that is, the strength of associations between a stimulus and a response.

Assuming we had objective means of quantifying drive and habit strength we might believe that we had a pretty good handle on how these variables influenced certain properties of behavior. But do we? On thinking more about this, we ask how a motivational state, such as my desire for something, interacts with my knowledge about the thing. We do not know how this might work, that is, how it can be physically implemented.

Just because a model makes intuitive sense to us does not mean the model is viable. Intentional accounts make sense to us because they are descriptions of our conscious awareness. Making intuitive sense is the primary criterion that folk accounts must meet. As Dennett (1978) points out, explaining behavior on the basis of intentional constructs usually involves "taking out a loan on intelligence." We are attempting to explain intelligent actions with a circular account using the notion of intelligent "inner" processes, that is an approach which eventually requires *homunculi*. We must eventually cash out these loans on intelligence. We can do this with computational models by instantiating our intentional constructs in terms of explicit data structures and algorithms. The beauty of computational models is that they can quickly verify whether or not it is possible to physically realize these various mental constructs in a cognitive model.

4.1.3 Beyond Sufficiency: The Problem of Equivalence

In Chapter 2 we discussed formal architectures of mind. Formal systems based on these architectures can be made into viable models of intelligent performance. However, they fall short as scientific models when we consider constraints more stringent than being able to compute a solution with no time or memory limitations. These formal architectures were intended to capture some of the abstract generalities of computational systems. For this reason they are considered by most cognitive scientists to be too general to be taken seriously as models of functional cognitive systems.

The universal Turing machine is a good example of this. It is capable of simulating any computing system and thus able to compute any computable function. This is certainly impressive and desirable if our only concern is abstract generality. But it ignores a number of constraints that functionally intelligent systems must deal with in their natural environments. The most obvious constraints are those of time and space. When the tiger charges out from the underbrush there is little time for exhaustive serial search routines over an infinite tape!

In this section we discuss the search for equivalence in terms of three general questions. First, just what exactly do we mean by equivalence? Certainly we are not looking for equivalence at the gate and bus level of sharing the same hardware/wetware. The Church-Turing hypothesis tells us that we may look for equivalence at some higher, more abstract level. What is the appropriate level for cognitive modeling? Second, assuming we know what we mean by equivalence, how do we go about achieving it? What are the methods we may use to move toward stronger equivalence?

Finally, what are the limits of the methods we employ to attain equivalence? How will we know this equivalence when we attain it? Is it even conceivable that it can be attained? If strong equivalence can't be attained, is there some type of middle ground between viability and strong equivalence worth striving for?

4.1.4 Levels of Equivalence

Before jumping into the fray and beginning a search for equivalence, it is important that we have some sense of the model we are seeking. Most cognitive scientists agree that they are looking for functional equivalence, attained by sufficient models. From this perspective two systems are considered equivalent to the extent that they function or act in a similar manner. The actual physical architecture is irrelevant as long as it is capable of simulating a particular set of actions or responses. Thus, if an essential attribute of intelligent systems is the ability to manipulate symbols, it is not important whether this function is carried out by processors on a magnetic tape, fingers on an abacus, or neurons.

Of course, to be committed to a functional equivalence leaves a great deal unspecified, given that the range of functional levels could be anything from relations between states of registers in a computer, neurons in a brain, or relations between intentional constructs. To help make some sense of this we refer to a distinction Pylyshyn makes in describing intelligent systems.

Pylyshyn (1984) divides a system into 1) its *functional architecture*, that is, the set of algorithms the system is capable of directly executing, and 2) the *representational system*, which defines the set of semantic states the system is capable of attaining. For the functional architecture, Pylyshyn contends that an algorithmic specification is the proper level of abstraction. An algorithm is more abstract than specific machine operations or computer code, but at the same time it is also objectively specifiable and mechanistically realizable. The ultimate goal would be to completely define the finite set of algorithms that make up a system's functional architecture.

As we saw in our discussion of formal architectures, some algorithms are more easily or naturally implemented in certain architectures than are others. In this regard the choice of an architecture places some constraint on the functioning of the system. For example, it may turn out that connectionist or subsymbolic architectures are more natural than programmable symbol systems for instantiating algorithms that solve visual tasks.

The importance of this issue may be seen in the fact that specific algorithms influence a system's functioning. This point was seen in some pattern recognition modeling where Fahlman (1981) noted that certain types of perceptual processes could be accomplished more efficiently if the system could compute directly the intersection between two sets of elements. Without this algorithm the system's speed was overly degraded by increases in the number of elements within the sets under consideration. Later in this chapter we discuss some of the methods that may be used to infer the algorithms employed by a system to carry out classes of intelligent actions. As we might expect, the task of figuring out which algorithms are responsible for particular classes of actions will turn out to be a fairly tricky endeavor.

Even if we assume that we can completely specify the functional architecture of a system, there is no guarantee that we will be able to predict its intelligent capabilities with any precision. This is because we have not yet specified or represented the *semantic states* the system is capable of assuming. In other words, we must also have some specification of what it is that the system knows.

Most of us would probably agree that a system's functional intelligence is to some degree dependent on its knowledge of the world. Even more specifically, it depends on its knowledge of the domain within which it is operating. For example, Chase and Simon (1973) show that chess experts have an extensive knowledge of chess, on the order of 50,000 patterns of behavior, and this knowledge is critical to performance. The training experience of a connectionist network is also critical to what it can recognize.

This suggests that in addition to constraining the functional architecture, we must also capture and represent a system's semantic knowledge. We will discuss this problem at length in later chapters that describe representation schemes. For our present purposes we want to note an important implication this may have for attaining equivalence. We must realize that we can achieve equivalent levels of functioning with a wide range of combinations of algorithms and knowledge.

The task of identifying an architecture for intelligent systems is not made easier by the fact that architectures interact with knowledge in producing a given level of performance. For example, researchers have found that children's performance on various measures of short-term memory improves between the ages of 4 and 12. Does this change in performance reflect an underlying change in the functional architecture or the acquisition of semantic knowledge? Researchers (Belmont & Butterfield 1971) reported evidence suggesting that a change in rehearsal strategies underlies the improved performance. In other words, there was no change in the functional architecture, but rather a change in knowing how to better use the given architecture. That is, as children get older they learn more sophisticated semantic pattern recognition and rehearsal strategies.

4.1.5 Baseline Constraints for Judging a System's Intelligence

We next consider the task of imposing empirical constraints on our models of intelligent systems. These constraints are founded on observation of and experimentation on functionally intelligent systems. This, for the most part, means research focused on humans performing various information processing and problem solving tasks.

This general practice of using human intelligence as the standard against which to judge the validity of models of intelligence may seem a rather egocentric and provincial perspective. Why are we so focused on human intelligence? The obvious answer is that human intelligence is the best instantiation of general intelligence that we have available. Although there are numerous other systems that carry out particular difficult tasks more efficiently and possibly more intelligently, none of them possesses the flexibility and generality of human intelligence.

While most of us are inclined to agree with the above argument, we must remember that our understanding of intelligence is limited by our perspectives in viewing it; it is difficult for us to transcend our biases. We must, for instance, entertain the possibility that at sometime in the future we will have with us computers similar to Hal in the book/movie *2001*; when this occurs, our models of intelligence and our understanding of strong equivalence will have to include Hal!

Before discussing the various methods of observation and experimentation used to discover the constraints that govern the functioning of intelligent systems, we note that many of the most important are relatively self evident. These abilities are possessed by all intelligent systems and, indeed, are often included in any definition of intelligence. They include:

- Rapid sensory processing: The ability to interpret complex information in a useful time frame.
- Learning: The ability to modify performance based on changes in the environment.
- Context sensitivity: The ability to behave differently depending on subtle contextual changes of the environment.
- Graceful degradation: The ability to perform reasonable actions in the face of partial or inconsistent information.
- Robustness: The ability to tolerate and adapt to degrees of damage to the system.

We can view these general characteristics of the human information processing system as a baseline for strong equivalence. We can say at the outset that if a system does not display these attributes, it is not strongly equivalent to human intelligence; or more usefully, the closer a model comes to these attributes, the more believable it is as a model of intelligence.

In the following sections we discuss some of the research methods used in cognitive science and cognitive psychology to constrain models of intelligence so that they are more similar to the actual functioning of intelligent systems. What this translates to in practice can be put quite simply: How do humans perform intelligent tasks?

The research procedures used to address this question are an extension of the behavioral methods used to attain simple viability. For a model to be viable it must simulate the input/output relations of the intelligent subject; for instance, in modeling chess performance it must make moves similar to those of the human chess expert. In this regard the model is constrained by the behavior of the system that it is attempting to model. The research methods described here are also behavior based, but differ in that they look at more detailed aspects of behavior and employ more analytic procedures in the hope that they will further constrain the nature of the structures and processes mediating behavior.

4.2   DIRECT METHODS

If you want to know how someone solves a problem it would seem that the obvious approach would be to ask them. This is the *direct method* approach to understanding cognitive phenomena. It has been used extensively, both in an explicit and an implicit manner, to discover the processes underlying human behavior. Wilhelm Wundt (1910), often called the founder of modern psychology, used a technique called *analytic introspection* to attempt to discover the sensations underlying human perceptions. It is interesting to note that Wundt believed the content of naive introspection failed to reveal the true sensations supporting a perception. For instance, as a naive introspectionist you might think that you are experiencing the "red" when exposed to a particular red object. Wundt wanted to go beyond this to reveal more fundamental sensations underlying these conscious experiences. Wundt believed that it required a great deal of intensive training to appropriately use analytic introspection.

For a number of reasons analytic introspection fell into disfavor. One of its problems was the assumption that introspective data were privileged. The hope was that with introspection we could look directly and objectively at the "real stuff" that was underlying our actions. More critical evaluations of introspection argued that it was in no sense special, but rather an individual's verbalizations of what she thought constituted her understanding. Moreover, it is impossible to achieve any degree of public verification of this introspection based information, since the data are by their very nature private to the subject experiencing them.

The behaviorist and logical positivist traditions, at the beginning of this century, effectively ended psychology's early experimentation with introspection. They concluded that there was no such thing as this "privileged data" and indeed, that all introspective evidence was epiphenomenal. A very positive result of this critique was that any data that were to be accepted for scientific analysis must be able to be replicated and supported within its empirical context. There is no question but that the behaviorist tradition had an important influence in moving psychology toward more "objective" methodologies.

4.2.1 Protocol Analysis: The Newell and Simon Tradition

A form of the direct method for the analysis of intelligence came back in the late 1950s, this time under the heading of *verbal report* or *protocol analysis*. Two important users of the verbal report approach were Allen Newell and Herbert Simon (1963, 1972). Their subjects are often asked to think aloud while engaged in solving a problem. The problems they presented subjects, usually logic problems or simple puzzles, involved a number of discrete steps that had observable consequences. When monitoring subject's progress toward solution, there would often occur what appeared to be sudden conceptual leaps. With the help of the verbal report, Newell and Simon hoped to begin to fill in some of the gaps observed as a subject moved toward a solution. A detailed example of this research approach, taken from the Newell and Simon work, is presented in Section 9.2.

One of the distinct advantages of Newell and Simon's use of verbal report data is that it occurred in the context of ongoing problem solving behavior. This allowed them to look for convergence between what subjects said they were doing and what they actually did. Simon has written extensively in support of this approach (Simon & Ericsson 1984, Newell & Simon 1972). In addition, by obtaining verbal protocols from a number of subjects solving the same problems, Newell and Simon were able to search across protocols looking for invariant aspects of the solution process. By doing this many of the idiosyncrasies in an individual's protocol could be filtered out.

Newell and Simon's publications using verbal protocol data had a significant impact, generating a great deal of comment both pro and con. This was followed by an increased use of verbal report data in other areas of psychology, particularly social psychology. This, in turn, prompted the publication of a widely cited paper by Nisbett and Wilson (1977) which pulled together an impressive array of evidence pointing up several serious problems with verbal report data. Nisbitt and Wilson cite cases where the reasoning of subjects about their behavior is simply incorrect.

Nisbitt and Wilson traced many of these misconceptions to socially acquired patterns of interpretation. That is, they feel that there are some generally accepted ideas about why we do things, and these models are imported into our interpretations of our own behavior, independent of what in fact is governing that behavior. In one study shoppers were stopped in a department store and asked which of two brands of nightgowns they preferred. Subjects showed a disproportionate preference for the brand that was located to their right, regardless of which brand was in the right hand location. When asked to explain the basis for their selection they typically presented a number of rationalizations, such as quality and appearance.

Of greater interest to us is the subject's awareness of his/her own cognitive processes. In one example Nisbitt and Wilson cite a classic problem-solving study done by Maier (1931) in which subjects were presented with two cords hung from the ceiling of a room strewn with a variety of objects (clamps, pliers, and so on). The subject's task was to tie the two ends of the cords together. The problem in doing this was that the cords were so far apart that it was impossible while holding the end of one cord to reach the other cord.

After the subjects had tried and failed to solve the problem for several minutes, Maier, as he wandered around the room, casually put one of the cords in motion. Usually, within 45 sec, subjects tied one of the objects to the end of the cord, set it in motion, then went to the other cord and waited for the arc of the pendulum to bring the cord within their reach. Subjects were then asked to report how they got the idea of the pendulum. This elicited a number of creative stories that typically failed to include the hint from Maier. Only after persistent probing by Maier did fewer than one-third of the subjects report the hint that, had in fact, made the difference in finding a solution.

More recent studies offer considerable evidence that subjects often learn with little explicit awareness of what they have learned (Lewicki et al. 1987, Luger & Bauer 1978, Reed & Johnson 1994) and that perceptions may be influenced by stimuli subjects have little awareness of (Marcel 1983). Most cognitive psychologists now believe that many of the mental processes that influence our behavior are not accessible to consciousness. If this is true, then we cannot expect self-report procedures to reveal all or even most of the processes underlying intelligent actions.

There are several different reactions to this skepticism regarding the reliability of verbal report data. One is to avoid using it at all cost. Another is to use verbal report data as a rich source of hypotheses that may then be evaluated with other techniques. A third reaction is to improve on the verbal report procedures. This is what was done by Simon and Ericsson (1984). In this book they investigate a number of methods for improving and assessing the reliability of verbal report procedures. For example, as subjects are reporting their thoughts while solving a problem, it is possible to monitor their eye movements. These eye movements can be used as a source of converging evidence to support the verbal data.

In concluding our discussion of the direct observation procedure, it is perhaps fair to say that while most cognitive scientists are a bit wary of basing their conclusions exclusively on verbal report data, they also recognize that it is a rich source of information that cannot be ignored. Finally, most researchers would also agree that many important processes are simply not accessible to consciousness and that these processes will have to be investigated using more indirect procedures.

4.3   INTRODUCTION TO INDIRECT METHODS

4.3.1 Sternberg's Additive-Subtractive Procedure

In this section we describe a set of procedures that were developed over the past three decades, largely in the context of the information processing approach within cognitive psychology. The overriding perspective taken by the *indirect approach* is that the adaptive processing of complex information requires the coordination of a number of independent subsystems. Therefore to understand the functioning of an intelligent system it is necessary to identify and isolate each of these many subsystems and then determine how each one functions. Essentially, it is an analytic divide and conquer approach to understanding the functioning of intelligent systems.

This analytic approach began in 1966 with the publication of a paper in *Science*, by Saul Sternberg, titled *High Speed Scanning in Human Memory*. In this paper Sternberg introduced the additive-subtractive methodology as a general approach for isolating stages of information processing. Although he used a specific task, memory scanning, to demonstrate how a stage of human information processing could be isolated, it was his intention that the method could be used with a variety of tasks to isolate different stages of processing. In essence he proposed a general paradigm that provided a window to the mind. Because of the impact this approach has had on the field we will discuss the *additive-subtractive* procedure in some detail.

4.3.2 The Subtractive Method

In the memory scan task, subjects are first presented a short list that they are to hold in memory. This list, usually between one and six items long, is called the *memory set*. When the subject is ready, a target symbol appears on a screen and it is the subject's task to respond as quickly as possible by pressing one of two buttons, "yes" or "no," to indicate whether the target is a member of the memory set. This same sequence of events occurs again and again for many trials, with the elements of the memory set continually changing both in content and in number. Because it is assumed that the items in the memory set are being held in short term memory the size of the list usually does not exceed six items.

Researchers measure, for each trial, the time elapsed between the target appearance and the response. These "reaction times" are then averaged for each of the sizes of the memory set and for "yes" (target present) and "no" (target absent) trials. Figure 4.1 presents some typical results from one of Sternberg's (1969a) studies. There are several important aspects to these results. First, let us consider the rate of change in the reaction time for the increase in the size of the memory set. This relationship is measured by the slope of the reaction time function. This aspect of the results describes the *subtractive effect*.

Notice that the slope shows a linear or a straight line increase in reaction time as the memory set size increases. For each additional item in the memory set the average reaction time increased approximately 38 msec. The *subtractive method* considers the difference in the mean reaction times between memory sets differing in size by one item; that is, the difference between set sizes of 1 and 2, of 2 and 3, and so on. The observation that this difference is a constant convinced Sternberg that each difference reflected the repetition of a uniform process, that is, the time required to scan one more item in short term memory.

It is important to realize that by looking exclusively at the slope of the function we are eliminating a great deal of noise. On any given trial a subject's reaction time includes a variety of processes, such as the time to perceive the target stimulus, the time to compare the target with items in memory, a decision regarding each comparison, a final decision, and an overt response. The time required for all of these supporting processes is measured by the intercept, that is, the point where the function describing the slope intercepts the ordinate or vertical axis. The slope isolates the additional time required when each item is added to the memory set.

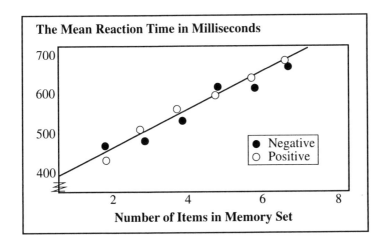

FIGURE 4.1   A reaction time graph demonstrating the subtractive method. The Y-intercept represents the constant encoding- reporting process and the constant slope represents the scan rate, about 35 msec, for the increasing memory set

We can now summarize what Sternberg was able to infer regarding the mental processes involved in scanning short term memory. First, he was able to conclude that the comparison was done in a serial rather than a parallel manner, since each additional item in the memory set resulted in a longer reaction time. If the search were done in parallel there would be a horizontal line.

Second, because the slope was linear, Sternberg was able to estimate the actual time required by this scan process. This is important because we can go on to investigate how changes in various properties of the items influence the slope. For example, Clifton and Task (1973) found that increases in the number of syllables of the names of the memory set items increased the intercept, but had no effect on the slope. This may tell us something about how the information is represented by the system. If the digits were represented in some phonological form, that is, if subjects covertly pronounced each item in the memory set as they were conducting a scan, we would expect syllable length to influence the speed of the scanning process as represented by the slope.

Finally, because the slope for positive, "yes," and negative, "no," trials was almost identical, Sternberg concluded that the serial search was exhaustive, that is, all items in the memory set were scanned on each trial. Thus, the search was not terminated once the target was scanned for a positive trial. If the search were terminated when the target was encountered in the scan, the rate of the slope for the positive trials would be approximately half that found for the negative trials, since on the average, the target would be halfway through the set of items.

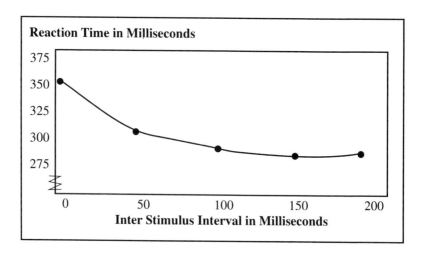

FIGURE 4.2   A reaction time experiment, after Posner and Boies (1971). Subjects are
asked to determine whether two presented pairs of stimuli were the same.

Before we turn to the additive procedure, we must again emphasize that
Sternberg's memory scan task is but a single application of a general subtractive
method. Whenever we design experiments to isolate a stage of information processing by comparing differences in reaction times, we are applying a subtractive
methodology. For example, suppose we wanted to estimate the time required to
perceive a stimulus. We might try to do this by flashing the stimulus on a screen
and measuring how long it took for the subject to name the stimulus. This measure would obviously be confounded with other stages of processing, such as the
time it takes to organize and produce a verbal response. Posner and Boies (1971)
solved this problem by having subjects respond "same" or "different" to pairs of
stimuli that were presented successively. As the temporal interval between the
two stimuli increased from 0 to 150 msec, reaction times became faster. With further increases in the interval up to 500 msec, there was no decrease in reaction
times, as may be seen in Figure 4.2.

Posner and Boies reasoned that the improvements in reaction time resulted
from subjects having time to encode the first letter before the second letter was
presented. Because there were no further improvements beyond a 150 msec interval, they concluded it required this amount of time to encode the first letter.

4.3.3 The Additive Method

Once a stage of processing is isolated by using the subtractive method, it is necessary to determine whether this stage is independent of other aspects of process-

ing. For example, if the functioning of the scan stage is dependent on the functioning of other stages, such as encoding and response selection, then there is little point in attempting to isolate the scan stage since it will change as specific aspects of the task change. In fact, the whole concept of "stages of processing" would lose much of its meaning if all stages were mutually interdependent.

Sternberg's *additive procedure* involved manipulating a second stage of processing to determine whether it influenced the isolated stage. To test the independence of the memory scanning from the encoding stage, Sternberg degraded the target stimulus to make it difficult to perceive. This had the effect of adding a constant to all reaction times regardless of memory set size; it created an intercept effect and did not effect the slope of the function. This indicated to Sternberg that the speed of the scanning operation was not influenced by the difficulty of encoding; the processes of memory scanning and encoding are additive. If the encoding stage had been influenced, there would be a slope effect in addition to the intercept effect.

Again, as with the subtractive procedure, we must look beyond the specific examples that were used to illustrate the process. We can see how, with continued research, the additive procedure may be used to investigate, on a large scale, the independence among various stages of information processing. The resulting program of research would be to isolate stages with the subtractive procedure and then assess their independence with the additive procedure.

We conclude our discussion of the additive-subtractive procedure with a good news/bad news summary. On the positive side, the advantage of this approach is that it provides a means of determining aspects of cognitive functioning that are not directly accessible. Clearly there are numerous processes that mediate between the input and the output of intelligent actions. In the case of the human, for example, it is a nontrivial matter to understand the operation of most of these processes. Moreover, as noted earlier, we cannot place all our trust in verbal report and introspection. Many, if not most, of these processes may simply not be accessible to consciousness. In this regard our success at ascertaining the processes and structures involved in intelligent actions may rest, to a large degree, on the application of additive-subtractive procedures and other similar analytic approaches.

The bad news relates to additive-subtractive procedure's history of successes. In the 25 years since its creation, the progress made in constraining the functioning of the human system has been disappointing to many of the practitioners within the field. One of the most salient problems has been the apparent paradigm specificity of the results. The parameters discovered relating to some stage of processing often seem to be specific to the particular task used to isolate the process. A related concern is that the findings are not often generalized to more realistic tasks (Neisser 1982). If we have truly isolated the operation of a basic information processing subsystem, then we should be able to use this information to better understand everyday speech and pattern recognition, speech production, reading, and problem solving. At the risk of overstating the downside, we must add that there has been some generalization across tasks and situations, but that it has been less than expected. Posner (1989) has a more optimistic assessment of the past and future uses of this methodology.

For those disenchanted with this methodology, the results are clear. There has been more than sufficient time and effort for the analytic approach to show more positive results. They argue that this microanalytic analysis is doomed in principle by the fact that each task or paradigm defines a context to which the observation will be specific. This problem can only be addressed by moving to a more global approach. Here, critics argue, we must begin with viable models of meaningful intelligent achievements, such as reading comprehension, and attempt to work within this model to refine its functioning.

The microanalytic researchers acknowledge the value of working within a global model, but contend that it is often too complex to begin to constrain assumed processes and structures in a meaningful way. The net result of this controversy is that work continues to go on at both levels. Lachman, Lachman, and Butterfield (1979), have a more in-depth discussion of this debate.

4.4   TECHNIQUES FOR ADDING CONSTRAINTS

Although the additive-subtractive approach is the most general means we have of designing experiments to indirectly infer properties of cognition, there are a number of other behavioral techniques that have been used extensively by psychologists over the past several decades. In this section we briefly describe some of the more frequently used methods.

4.4.1   Analysis of Type of Error

Piaget (1954, 1970) and Freud (1920) were two of the earliest psychologists to recognize that there is valuable information contained in the errors that humans make. The assumption behind this insight is that errors are not random. Patterns of errors and the consistency of error patterns says something about our thinking.

A very simple example of using errors to infer processes is taken from short term memory research. Using what is called the distractor procedure (Peterson & Peterson 1959) a subject is presented a few items to hold in memory and is then presented with a three digit number and told to count backwards from that number by threes until a signal is given to stop and recall the target items. The results from these experiments often show an 80% or more loss of information in less than 20 sec. When the distraction of counting backwards is omitted there is no loss of information over the same retention intervals.

As these results accumulated, psychologists such as Conrad (1964) and Wickelgren (1965) began looking more closely at the content of subject's incorrect responses and immediately saw a pattern. The incorrect guesses sounded similar to the targets. For example, if one of the target items was "rat," the errors might be "bat," "fat," or "sat."

Beyond the fact that the errors were not random, neither were they semantically similar to the target item, for example, "mouse," or "rodent," as is the case with studies of long term memory. These results suggested that the medium in which information is represented in short term memory may be some type of acoustical-phonological code, while long term memory stores information in a more abstract semantic code. Later studies have shown that a number of different codes may be employed in short term memory. For example, Baddeley et al. (1975) have shown evidence of visual codes in short-term memory. The consensus of opinion now seems to be that the codes may depend upon the demands of the experimental task.

4.4.2 Sources of Interference

We have known for some time that information processing can be disrupted by various types of competing activities. This knowledge provides the basis for a second means of constraining information processing systems. The logic underlying the source of interference technique is that if two subsystems, be they memory systems, sensory systems, output systems, or whatever, are truly distinct, then they will differ in what interferes with their functioning. For example, a number of psychologists suggest that we have both a verbal and a visual representational system, and that these two systems are relatively independent.

A clever test of this hypothesis, using the interference technique, is illustrated in an experiment by Lee Brooks (1968). Subjects in one group were given a task which Brooks reasoned was primarily visual. The task required subjects to imagine a line drawing of an uppercase block letter. The subjects would then be given a start location at one of the corners (see Figure 4.3). They are then told to move their attention around the perimeter of the letter in a clockwise direction and indicate whether each successive corner was positioned at an extreme top or bottom location by responding "yes" or "no." In the example shown in Figure 4.3, the correct responses would be yes, yes, yes, no, no, no, no, no, no, yes.

In the verbal task, subjects were presented a sentence, such as, "A bird in the hand is not in the bush." Holding the sentence in memory, subjects were asked to categorize each word successively, from the beginning to the end of the sentence, either as a noun or as a non-noun. For our example the correct responses would be no, yes, no, no, yes, no, no, no, no, yes.

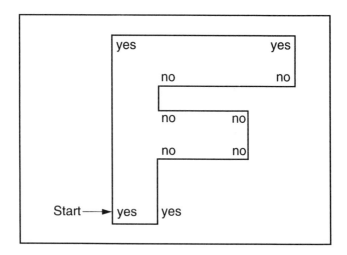

FIGURE 4.3 A visual scanning task where the subject is asked to start at the indicated
point of the block character and to tell whether or not each vertex of the
character is at an extreme top or bottom position in the full scene.

Both groups of subjects were further divided into three subgroups based on
the manner in which they indicated their responses to the task. In the "vocal"
condition subjects simply tried to vocalize the correct sequence of "yes" and
"no" utterances. In the "tapping" condition subjects indicated a "yes" or "no" by
tapping with the left or right hand. Finally, in the "pointing" condition subjects
were presented a piece of paper with a column of "Y"s and a column of "N"s,
standing for "yes" and "no," and told to indicate their response by pointing to the
appropriate letter, i.e., to the "Y" or "N." The subjects were to start at the top of
the columns and move down one row for each response. The letters in the column
were staggered, as in Figure 4.4, to force the subject to visually monitor the display.

Brooks reasoned that performance would suffer if the output task (vocal, tapping, of pointing) competed with the input task (visual or verbal scanning). His
prediction was that the pointing response was the most visual and would therefore interfere most with the visual scanning task, whereas the vocalization
response was the most verbal and would interfere most with the verbal scanning
task.

The results, summarized in Figure 4.5, are completely consistent with
Brooks' predictions. When doing the visual scanning task the pointing responses
were emitted most slowly; however, when performing the verbal scanning task
the vocal responses resulted in the slowest response rate. These results support
the idea of a separate verbal and visual processing system. More importantly for

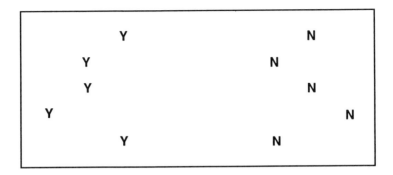

FIGURE 4.4 A typical display of response choices from Brooks (1968). Subjects began at the top pointing to the underlined with the sentence "A bird in the hand...."

our purposes, this experiment illustrates how patterns of interference between tasks can be used to infer the types of codes used in different information processing tasks.

Although certain events can disrupt processing, it is also the case that other events can be helpful. These facilitating stimuli are often referred to as *cues*. By looking at which types of cues are helpful and which are not we can often infer how the information in a given situation is processed.

4.4.3 The Type of Cue

A good example of how cueing has been used comes from the area of iconic memory. George Sperling (1960) rekindled our interest in determining how many things a person can see at once. In this research an array of stimuli, often letters of the English alphabet, are flashed very briefly, e.g., 50 msec, on a screen and subjects are asked to report as many of the letters as they can.

For more than a century it had been known that people can, on the average, only report 4.5 items. The question that Sperling asked is whether the limitation of 4.5 is actually a perceptual limit or a memory limit. It is possible that we actually see many more than four or five, but while we are reporting the first few items, the others that we saw are being lost from memory.

To circumvent the possibility of a memory limitation, Sperling developed the partial report procedure in which the complete array of stimuli are presented for 50 msec and immediately following the array a cue is presented instructing the subject to report only a subset of the array. Sperling (1960) initially used a high, medium, or low tone to cue the top, middle, or bottom row. Later Averbach and Coriel (1961) used a visual pointer as in Figure 4.6. With the visual marker it

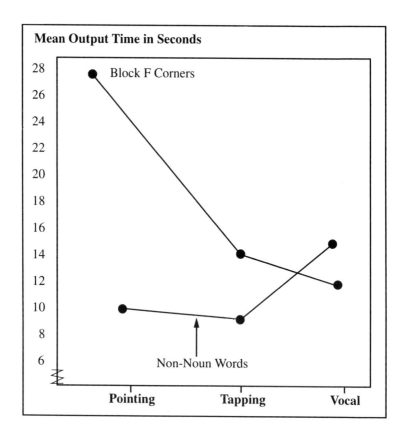

Mean Output Time in Seconds

FIGURE 4.5   The Brooks (1968) study that combines processing modes.

was only necessary for the subject to report the single letter indicated. If the subject was correct on 100% of the trials we could reason that all 16 letters were accessible, since subjects never knew on each successive trail where the marker would be pointing. Using the partial report procedure it was found that subject's proportion of correct identifications indicated they had access to approximately 12 items when a 16 item array was presented.

Our central concern is to determine what types of cues or markers facilitate performance. We already know that both a tone and a visual pointer serve as effective cues. Subsequent research has shown that any physical type of cue, such as color, size, and shape will work, but any cue that requires a semantic interpretation, such as to report the only vowel in the array, or the odd number, is completely ineffective. This pattern of findings has led researchers to speculate that information in iconic memory is being held in a visual format that is presemantic (Crowder 1976).

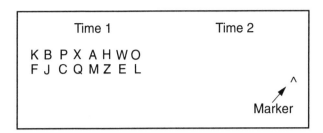

FIGURE 4.6   The subject is first presented a 2 x 8 array of letters for 50 msec. Immediately after the termination of the array, a marker appears either above or below the location of one of the letters, indicating the position for which the subject is to attempt to recall the original letter.

The above findings with iconic memory can be contrasted with studies of long term memory where the most effective retrieval cues are usually items which are semantically related to the information that is to be recalled. For example, assume subjects are given the following list of words to remember: monkey, chimp, burger, and soup. A day later they return to the experiment and are asked to recall the list either with no cues, or with the cues: primate and restaurant. Not surprisingly, the group given cues usually recalls more items.

Furthermore, cues which only look like or sound like the target items are not nearly as effective as those that are semantically related. Thus it appears that in this long term memory task the information is organized along semantic dimensions, whereas in the iconic memory task the information is stored in terms of visual-physical properties. This illustrates how the manipulation of cues can help us better understand the functioning of information processing subsystems.

4.4.4 Transfer Effects

Assume we observe an individual learning a serial list. On each trial the following words are presented in the same order: pencil-flower-chair-book-tree-dog-house-bicycle. The words are presented successively, one at a time; the subject's task is to anticipate what the next word will be. When the subject is able to make all of the correct anticipations within a single trial, we conclude that the subject has learned the list. This is all well and good, but fails to address how the list was learned or how the solution is represented.

To make the issue more concrete, let's continue with the example of the serial list learning task. One hypothesis might be that the subjects learned associations between all adjacent pairs of stimuli. This is certainly a *viable* hypothesis in that it is sufficient to account for 100% correct responses. We can test this hypothesis very simply with the following transfer experiment.

After subjects have learned the serial list they are transferred to a paired associate learning task that maintains all of the pairwise relationships, for instance, chair-book, pencil-flower, house-bicycle, that were contained in the serial list. In the paired associate task subjects are presented a single stimulus (word) and they must learn to anticipate which word is the correct response for that specific stimulus. On each successive training trial the order of the pairs is allowed to vary randomly, so while the pairwise associations are the same as in the serial list, the more global relations are not maintained.

When this experiment is conducted, we find no transfer from the serial list to the paired associate list. Thus a control group of subjects that never received training on the serial list does as well on the paired associate list as the group previously trained on the serial list. This strongly suggests that in learning the serial lists the subjects learned something other than the pairwise associations.

With transfer tests of this type we are usually unable to infer precisely what was learned. However, we are often able to determine with confidence what was NOT learned. Thus, with a series of transfer tests we begin to constrain the set of potentially viable interpretations of what was learned.

The transfer studies just described required fairly short time periods, with responses often measured in seconds or less. There are also a large number of transfer studies of longer term problem solving skills. We describe next a number of these studies without going into detail on their results. Consider the *Tower of Hanoi* problem pictured in Figure 4.7. Four rings are placed on one of three pegs. The problem solver must move all four rings, one at a time, to some target peg, here either B or C, without ever placing a larger ring on top of a smaller ring. An early definition of eternity was the time it would take to move 64 such stacked rings from one peg to another!!

Figure 4.7 also includes the state space of moves for the *Tower of Hanoi* problem. The state space and other problem solving analysis tools will be defined in Part II, when we introduce graphs; here it is sufficient to see it as a device for keeping track of all the legal moves that are possible in solving this problem.

When a problem solver's solution attempt is mapped out as paths through the state space of a problem (Hayes & Simon 1974; Reed et al. 1974; Luger 1976; Luger & Bauer 1978), a number of important questions can be asked. These include: What is the role of subproblems in problem solving? How does the subject use the symmetries of the problem? Do pauses in problem solving indicate planning ahead? How does the solution to one problem relate to solving problems of homomorphic or isomorphic structure?

Reed, Ernst, and Banerji (1974) asked some of these questions for the *missionaries and cannibals* problem and one of its isomorphs called the *jealous husbands* problem. Simon and Hayes created a number of isomorphs of the *Tower of Hanoi* and compared subject's solutions across these domains. Luger and Bauer

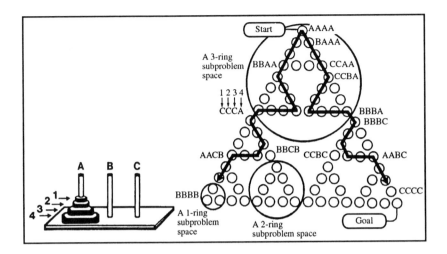

FIGURE 4.7   The four-ring Tower of Hanoi problem and its state space. The state space shows subproblem spaces and the symmetric paths of a subject. From Luger and Bauer (1978).

(1978) suggested that the richness of the problem's structure would be a factor in transfer of skills to the new domain. Lave (1988) suggested that studies such as those just mentioned, since they were isolated laboratory experiments divorced from problem solving in a practical world, had limited use.

There are many other research projects of the same type as these transference studies. Most notable are those attempting to see how subjects might use analogies to known solutions in novel situations. Glick and Holyoak (1980) tell subjects how a divided army attacking a city in small groups from many directions is able to conquer it. They then ask subjects how a cancerous tumor might be treated with radiation when the large doses required to kill the tumor can damage other organs. We consider these tests of transfer and analogy again in Part II; here it is important to see that the response of human subjects to sets of related problems can be indicative of the nature of their problem solving skills. One interesting result of this type transfer study is that subjects can show improved performance on sets of related problems without any explicit awareness of the problems relationships (Luger & Bower 1978).

4.4.5 Summary of Methods

In this section we presented a variety of empirically based methods for inferring how an intelligent system performs tasks. We began with some direct methods which rely on subject's conscious awareness of the relevant cognitive processes. We saw that there are several problems in relying exclusively on self-report (Nisbett & Wilson 1977), but that some of these problems could be minimized by adding various converging sources of information to the self-report data (Simon & Ericsson 1984). Regardless how much the direct method may be improved, it doesn't allow access to processing which occurs without awareness.

To begin to understand these subconscious processes, we were forced to turn to indirect techniques. In our discussion of indirect methods we began with the additive-subtractive procedure and then turned to several more specific techniques. It was not our intention to present an exhaustive review of all available indirect techniques, but to illustrate some of the more commonly used behavioral methods. A major part of the cognitive science effort involves the employment of these various procedures and techniques to constrain our models of intelligent systems.

4.5 THE LIMITS OF EQUIVALENCE

In this section we explore the limits of equivalence. Using all of the methods available to us to constrain our models, can we ever hope to attain a *valid* or *strongly equivalent* model of intelligence? We consider two problems that possibly stand in the way of computational models ever attaining strong equivalence. The first is based on John Searle's (1980) widely cited work, *Minds, Brains, and Programs*, where he argues that computers simply don't have the "right stuff" and will therefore never be intentional and intelligent.

The second problem, introduced first with our analysis of representational schemes in Chapter 3, finds psychological support in John Anderson's (1978) paper on *representational indeterminacy*. Here Anderson argues that it may be impossible, on the basis of behavioral data, to uniquely determine the nature of the processes and structures underlying human intelligence. We conclude this section disagreeing with Searle and Anderson. We contend that there is nothing in their arguments precluding strong equivalence as an asymptotic target for models in cognitive science. In the method of progressive approximation of truth, there is nothing that distinguishes cognitive science from the other empirical sciences.

4.5.1 Problems for Strong Equivalence: Contentless Representations

Searle (1980) believes that it is possible for computers to simulate human performance, but that they will never achieve intelligence. His pessimism stems from the fact that computational models that are physically instantiated in a computer can never be truly intentional. They may behave as if they were intentional, but in fact, they are not. This conclusion is reached on the basis of a thought experiment, the *Chinese interpreter*.

Imagine a machine to which we submit Chinese characters and that returns English translations of these character sets. Observing this machine from the outside, we might very well become impressed to the point where we are willing to conclude that the machine really understands Chinese. There is no need to speculate in this particular instance, however, because inside the machine is Searle himself, frantically shuffling cards around according to a set of rules. Searle receives an input character which to him is gobboly-gook, finds gobboly-gook on his lookup table, which in turn directs him to some English cards which he places in the output bin. Searle is the *homunculus* and can personally assure us that he doesn't understand anything at all about Chinese.

The real basis of Searle's argument is that the input-output relations manifested by the machine are not causally related to the semantic content of the representations that it manipulates. This results from the fact that the relationships between symbol states and semantic states are completely arbitrary and unconstrained, for example we might let some arbitrary x = dog. As Clark (1989) discusses this problem, the system must contain some semantic parameters that can provide meaning. Without some laws of correspondence that constrain the assignment of symbols to referents, the content of a symbol state is irrelevant to the causal function, that is, to the transitions among symbol states of the system. In Searle's view, formal and computational systems are not the "right stuff" because they are causally insensitive to content.

We make two points about Searle's contentions. First, is he correct in claiming that computational systems cannot be intentional or intelligent? We don't know whether computers will ever be generally intelligent. There are already many examples where computers show intelligence in their operations and conclusions. To deny this would be to deny that human's performing similar tasks in medicine, geology, and mathematics are intentional and intelligent. Certainly Searle's "right stuff" argument is vacuous and unconvincing. Dennett's (1987) discussion of the intentional stance shows us that the attribution of intentionality is a complex matter. Dennett demonstrates that the external behavioral characteristics of a system play an important if not definitive role in determining whether or not we believe a system is acting intentionally.

Second, if Searle is correct, does this in any way preclude the possibility of cognitive science? It certainly does not. A model is not in principle identical to the phenomenon modeled, thus, the meteorologist's model of a hurricane need not be wet, the astronomer's model of a supernova need not be hot. The cognitive scientists' models are progressive and ever closer approximations of the modeled intelligence. It is a category error to confuse one with the other. We return to these issues in Section 4.5.3.

4.5.2 Representational Indeterminacy

Earlier in this chapter we discussed several methods for inferring the nature of structures or processes that mediate human information processing. Now we must consider whether these methods have some severe limitations. We begin this discussion in the context of a specific controversy that has concerned cognitive psychologists for several decades. This issue concerns the type of representation humans use. Do we use analog representations, such as images, or can all representations be reduced to abstract propositions such as the predicate expression color(dog, black)? Or does there exists some other representational medium for intelligent activity?

Those taking the propositional position, such as Pylyshyn (1981), have argued that the question is not whether we have the conscious experience of images, but whether they play a causal role in cognitive activity. Pylyshyn's position is that we have a representational system that is more abstract than either words or images and that is not accessible to subjective experience. Pylyshyn believes that this level of abstraction is necessitated by the facility with which we go between mental words and pictures.

On the imagery side, several psychologists have conducted a number of extremely clever experiments which appear to require some type of image based code. In one experiment (Shepard & Metzler 1971), researchers presented subjects a pair of complex visual forms and asked whether they were identical.

On some attempts the forms were mirror images and not identical, but on other trials they were identical, but one of the forms had been rotated between 0 and 360 degrees from the other form. The subjects' task was to respond as rapidly as possible whether the two forms were the same or not. The results from one of Shepard's experiments, presented in Figure 4.8, shows that reaction time on "same" trials is a simple linear function of the number of degrees that one form must be rotated in order to match the other. This finding suggested to Shepard and colleagues that the algorithms employed by subjects to make the correct judgments must correspond to an analog of the literal physical rotation. In response to the findings from experiments such as Shepard's, Pylyshyn has argued that it is possible to simulate the results using a set of discrete propositional-type rules.

Who is right? John Anderson (1978), in a very influential paper, has argued compellingly that it may be impossible to discriminate between the two positions on the basis of behavioral data. The argument concerns the nature of internal representations and whether a particular input/output relationship, such as was seen in Shepard's mental rotation study, necessitates some type of analog representation.

As noted throughout Chapter 3, whenever we talk about a representational system, we imply a data structure and a process that operates on that structure.

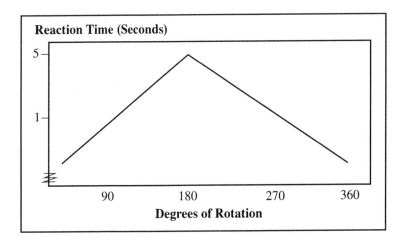

Reaction Time (Seconds)

Degrees of Rotation

FIGURE 4.8   Reaction time as a function of degrees of rotation of two similar figures. From Shephard and Metzler (1971).

Anderson's argument for representational indeterminacy is that it is logically impossible to infer the nature of the structure, that is, whether it is imagery based or propositional, if we do not know the processes that operate on the structure. For any given structure there may be an unlimited number of possible processes that interact with it to produce an unlimited number of input/output relations.

If Anderson is correct, not only is the representation indeterminate, but so is the corresponding process when we do not know the representing structure. Thus, the notion of representational indeterminacy suggests that it is only reasonable to test models of representational systems where both the structure and the process are specified. More generally, it suggests that the quest for strong equivalence, if not hopeless, will indeed be difficult.

4.5.3 A Critique of Limitations on Strong Equivalence

We have presented two problems, representations without content and representational indeterminacy, that seem to stand in our way of attaining strong equivalence. In this section we will examine whether these problems are as serious as they first appear to be. We will conclude by arguing that even though a search for strong equivalence may be doomed, abandoning strong equivalence does not mean that we abandon the idea of adding constraints to improve our models.

In regard to Searle's assertion that computational models are incapable of being intentional, there are a number of replies. One, proposed by the philosopher Daniel Dennett (1987), asks how we can know that any system is truly intentional in the sense that intentions are causing actions? If we examine the assumption that other humans are intentional, we realize that we project our own beliefs about our own behaviors onto other humans.

This projection involves two additional assumptions. First, it assumes that we know that we are indeed intentional. But we only believe this because of our introspections, and we already recognize the limitations of the introspective method. Second, it assumes that there is some set of like minds beyond our own mind that operates in a similar manner. How do we circumscribe this set? Does it include all humans regardless of age or intelligence? Does it include some non-humans such as dolphins, orangutans, and Baxter the cat? On what principled basis is this circle of intentional systems drawn? Dennett contends that he is not aware of a methodology that can tell us with certainty which systems are intentional and which are not. We can only look at patterns of behavior across a variety of situations and infer that the system behaves as if it were intentional. This attribution we refer to as Dennett's *intentional stance,* Section 2.4.3.

From the view of the intentional stance, it is possible that some properly programmed computers will appear intentional. And if this is true, then it would seem that intentionality would not necessarily be a basis for distinguishing between computational and human intelligence.

A counter argument to Dennett's intentional stance is that we should eventually be able to distinguish between a truly intentional system and an "as-if intentional" system. The argument would be along the lines that when representational content is not operating in a causal role, the system will display a type of fragility that will be apparent to the observer. This goes back to some of the general properties of intelligence mentioned earlier, including systematicity, productivity, robustness, graceful degradation, and content sensitivity. These are properties that all intelligent systems are thought to share. For most researchers, the answer is not yet final. For instance, there is a growing number of cognitive scientists who believe that content does play a causal role in connectionist systems, and that is why these networks seem to manifest some of the properties of intelligence.

Although neither of these counter arguments completely dispel all of the doubt raised by Searle, they at the very least raise questions concerning the finality of his argument and allow for the possibility that computational models can be intentional. An argument that goes against both Dennett and Searle is that neither has addressed the issues properly. With the creation of "right stuff" and "intentional stance" arguments, without specifying any further the meaning of these concepts, they have simply created further *homunculi,* and attempted to use them as explanatory constructs. We return to this discussion in Chapter 17.

Possibly a more serious obstacle for attaining strong equivalence is the question of representational indeterminacy raised by Anderson (1978). Whereas

Searle's attack focused on a specific aspect of equivalence, that is the impossibility of achieving intentionality, representational indeterminacy questions the logic of the entire methodology.

One possible approach to answering the indeterminacy problem is to turn to neurophysiological data. Perhaps with the appropriate neurophysiological information (Chapter 5), we can constrain or eliminate this indeterminacy issue. This approach might have a chance if we had *type-identity* (Section 2.3.1) in our model. Without it, there is little hope of mapping functional processes and structures, as well as representational states, onto brain states. After all, what does an image look like in the brain? Could we discriminate it from a brain state that corresponds to a proposition? Rather than trying to diminish the impact of indeterminacy by directly refuting the logic of Anderson's (1978) arguments, it makes more sense to place the problem in a larger perspective and show that it is not unique to cognitive science.

Although Anderson's arguments may rule out the possibility of strong equivalence, they do not preclude the achievement of lesser forms of equivalence. Two points follow from this: First, weaker equivalence is a perfectly acceptable goal for a science. Second, as we point out next, science has always pursued a course of progressive approximation. Philosophers of science have often recognized that models of reality are, at best, approximations of the phenomenon they model. Just as a word is a referent for an object, we must not mistake the word for the object itself.

The model, in short, never becomes the thing we are attempting to model. A meteorologist's model of hurricanes never truly captures all the aspects of the hurricane. This is true of most useful scientific models, be they models of an atom, models of the universe, or models of mind. In fact, from an information theoretic viewpoint (Chaitin 1993) it may be that no model exists simpler that the thing itself. What model, for instance, is informationally equivalent to the real number π? Acknowledging this distinction between model and the modeled phenomenon, it is apparent that most useful models will eventually be shown to be incomplete or wrong in some sense.

Although our models may never attain full and ultimate validity, they must continually move toward increased validity and generality. This, of course, is the idea behind continually adding additional constraints. We don't quit just because the constraints do not give us strong equivalence. As we satisfy more and more constraints our models gain generality. They become viable across a wider range of situations. This is science and what makes it an exciting thing to do.

When the equivalence problem is seen in this light it no longer appears to be a problem unique to computational models of mind. In fact, we might want to reconsider why it initially seemed to be such an important and special problem in cognitive science. Our guess is that rather than looking at the task of cognitive science as modeling intelligence, we took the task to be that of the creation of intelligent artifacts. This is a subtle difference in perspective. Models are in a continual process of being tested, failing, and being modified. This is as natural as the process of biological evolution or personal cognitive development. However, when a computer model can't recognize visual patterns or comprehend speech at the same level and speed as a human, we are for some reason more quick to conclude that the whole idea is misguided and wrong headed. Our guess is that this reaction is more based on social attitudes and emotional biases than on mature reasoning.

The goals of cognitive science are the same as those of any other science, namely, to develop models that will enhance prediction, control, and understanding of the phenomenon under investigation. The phenomenon in this case is extremely complex and it is quite likely that the most appropriate methodologies may not all be borrowed from other sciences. Patience and humility are the virtues of the gods!

4.5.4 Constraints and the Representational Methodology

In this chapter we discussed the notions of viability and validity as they apply to models of intelligent systems. Viability, or the criterion of sufficiency, means that we have demonstrated the model to be sufficiently defined, that it is capable of carrying out the various assumed operations within the model when these are put to code and run on a computer. We emphasized how important it is to demonstrate viability with models employing intentional concepts.

The discussion of validity or strong equivalence was organized into three subissues: 1) what do we mean by equivalence; 2) how do we achieve it; and 3) what are the limits of strong equivalence. Equivalence was defined in terms of a functional architecture or the set of algorithms available to the system and the set of representational states attainable by the system. We then discussed the various direct and indirect methods of constraining our models of cognition. Direct methods involved introspection and self-report of subjective awareness of our own thinking. Two problems with this approach were subjects' tendencies to misinterpret their mental processes in terms of social models and the argument that many important processes may not be accessible to conscious awareness.

Turning to indirect methods we began with a detailed discussion of Sternberg's additive-subtractive procedure. The subtractive procedure isolated the process and the additive procedure tested for its independence from other processes. We then discussed a number of specific techniques for determining how various information is mentally represented.

The last major section of this chapter considered whether it would be possible to attain strong equivalence by using these various procedures. Our conclusion was that while we can continue to add constraints that should make our models more general, models may never attain strong equivalence. When viewed from the perspective of models and their role in science, however, the inability to attain strong equivalence was no longer seen as a problem for cognitive science. Adding constraints and gaining generality in our models may be the best that the scientific method allows.

In summary, as cognitive scientists, we must deal with representational issues as scientists in other disciplines do:

- First, it is common for different representations/processes to be part of understanding one phenomenon. Physicists, for example, may not be entirely comfortable with both a wave and particle theory of light. Both models, though in current understanding incomparable, are used to advance science.
- Second, if a model and representational scheme works, then use it. Since judgement on the success of a model rests in its falsification as much as its generalization, it is important that each scheme be pushed as far as possible. In the final analysis, the model is not the thing itself, and incompatibility at some level of specification must be expected.
- Third, representational schemes offer a medium for communication. They offer a language for describing aspects of their environment and they ultimately will be interpreted. The interpreter of our representations can be silicone or protoplasm based or even fashioned from tinkertoys.

A final important judgement of the quality of a representational scheme rests on its interpretative adequacy and flexibility for constant refinement. A representational scheme is a tool for understanding and exploring our world. Its use assists understanding and promotes intervention in our environment, and that very activity demands model refinement for further intervention (Stern & Luger 1992).

In the next chapter we consider neurological constraints on intelligence.

4.6   EPILOGUE AND REFERENCES

In Chapter 4, we laid more groundwork for establishing cognitive science as an empirical discipline. We described and contrasted viable and valid models of mind. We also presented a variety of methods for testing these models. In Chapter 5 we consider in more detail neurophysiological constraints on intelligence.

In Chapter 4, we justified our approach as a legitimate scientific methodology. It is important to understand the nature and limitations of science and the scientific method. We recommend Karl Popper's (1959) *The Logic of Scientific Discovery* and Thomas Kuhn's (1962) *The Structure of Scientific Revolutions.*

In *Human Problem Solving*, Allen Newell and Herbert Simon (1972) go to almost exhaustive lengths in working through the empirical support for their model of mind and problem solving. Many of these issues we touch on again in Chapter 9. David Rumelhart and James McClelland (1986) in their two volume work, *Parallel Distributed Processing: Explorations in the Microstructure of Cognition*, describe evidence for the connectionist approach.

Papers by Simon and Ericsson (1984), *Protocol Analysis: Verbal Reports as Data*, and Nisbett and Wilson (1977), *Telling More than We Can Know: Verbal Reports on Mental Processes,* present detailed reviews of the problems encountered using verbal protocol data. These papers also force us to be more critical concerning the "self-evident" truths revealed to us by our consciousness. These papers have had an important effect on scientists' views of consciousness. We also recommend Daniel Dennett's (1991) *Consciousness Explained*.

Lachman, Lachman, and Butterfield's (1979) book, *Cognitive Psychology and Information Processing: An Introduction*, provides a solid overview of many reaction time procedures, including the additive-subtractive method. Michael Posner's (1978) *Chronometric Explorations of Mind* includes numerous studies employing the subtractive method to isolate stages of human information processing. Terrance Sejnowski and Patricia Churchland's *Brain and Cognition*, a contribution to Michael Posner's (1989) edited collection *Foundations of Cognitive Psychology,* lays out the neurological constraints and support for cognition.

There is an important issue of the journal *Psychological Review* (1978) that presents a debate on representational indeterminacy. The issue begins with a paper by John Anderson presenting arguments that describe the problem. Follow-up positions are presented by Zenon Pylyshyn and Fredrick Hayes-Roth; it concludes with Anderson's rejoinder. Pylyshyn's (1984) book *Computation and Cognition* presents a more lengthy discussion of the indeterminacy conjecture.

A number of writers take a critical focus on the positions we have presented. Especially important are contributions by the Dreyfus brothers (1985) in *Mind over Machine*; by John Searle (1980) in *Minds, Brains, and Programs*, where he presents his Chinese interpreter; and by Winograd and Flores (1986) book *Understanding Computers and Cognition*. The conclusion of most of these writers is that mechanistic models are simply not "the right stuff" for embodying complex cognitive activity.

Chapter 5

NATURAL INTELLIGENCE:
HUMAN BRAIN FUNCTION

The map is not the territory, the name is not the thing named...

Alfred Korzybski

The brain - is wider than the sky -
For - put them side by side -
The one the other will contain
With ease - and You - beside -

The brain is deeper than the sea -
For - hold them - blue to blue -
The one the other will absorb -
As sponges - buckets - do -

Emily Dickinson

5.0   INTRODUCTION

In preceding chapters we frequently alluded to the neurosciences both as a source of inspiration for those who attempt to design intelligent systems and as an alternative perspective to understanding the nature of cognition. In this chapter we explore more fully the workings of the human brain. A moments reflection quickly reveals the unique nature of our own "intelligent system." It is an undeniably powerful yet compact device. Although extraordinarily adept at some tasks, such as pattern recognition, it is slow and cumbersome at other tasks, such as numerical computation. It develops its own goals and pursues these with great vigor. Finally, it can study itself, slowly and gradually revealing the mysteries of its mechanisms.

The excitement about neurally inspired modeling prompts interest in real neural computation. Further, whenever we use the term *artificial intelligence* the question immediately emerges as to how it differs from *natural intelligence*. In

143

the first two sections of this chapter we discuss important aspects of human brain function to assist our understanding of the similarities and differences between artificial and natural intelligence. Our goal is not to deride any current computational model for its lack of neural realism, but to explore correspondences. Perhaps insights into brain function may help in the design of artificial intelligence and neural network systems. Perhaps development of such systems will provide insights into the manner in which the human brain solves similar problems.

There are two different types of biological constraints that must be confronted when attempting to design "realistic" intelligence systems, that is, those that operate in a fashion similar to the human brain. These are both historical and mechanistic. Historical constraints reflect the evolutionary history of our species. Natural selection has left us with a very particular type of intelligence system with some unusual characteristics. The mechanistic constraints refer to hardware, or to be more accurate, *wetware* limitations: the number of processing elements and their ability to interact. After discussing these two types of biological constraints we explore some characteristics of particular types of neural designs. Our focus here is to understand what types of neural organization are optimal for what types of problem solving.

5.1. EVOLUTIONARY CONSTRAINTS

The human mind, and hence the human brain, has been shaped by a long evolutionary history. Though little controversy emerges from evolutionary perspectives on adaptations such as bipedal locomotion or an opposable thumb, there has been a general reluctance to entertain evolutionary perspectives on the human mind. The mind and our behavior are commonly thought to be shaped only by *culture* and since cultures seem to vary so greatly, how could our minds be anything other than the product of our social environments?

But one can view the issue in another way. Culture is a product of human minds, themselves shaped by a long evolutionary history. Though certainly there are many differences in customs across different societies, there are also remarkable universal similarities, for example, in the use of oral language as a means to communicate and in judgement of physical attractiveness. Cosmides and Tooby (1992, pg. 163) write:

> Because we know that the human mind is the product of the evolutionary process, we know something vitally illuminating: that, aside from those properties acquired by chance, the mind consists of a set of adaptations, designed to solve the long-standing adaptive problems humans encountered as hunter-gatherers.

What are the problems that the human brain has had to solve? There are a great many diverse tasks that selection has allowed the brain to accomplish: recognition of familiar faces, language development, depth perception, to name but a few. Each and every one of the problem domains the brain has evolved to analyze share a single feature: they were problems in our past. *Natural selection* has no foresight; today's brains were not designed to solve tomorrow's problems or even today's problems. Human brains evolved to solve the problems encountered by human beings over the past several thousand years. They evolved to cope with the demands of what anthropologists term *hunter-gatherer societies*, that is, the type of society which was generally characteristic of our species for the past 20,000 years. Today's society is indeed radically different from hunter-gatherer societies, but the somewhat different set of problems we encounter today probably have not been around long enough to have a significant impact on the adaptive features of the human mind.

But of what relevance is all of this evolutionary mumbo-jumbo for neural mechanisms underlying intelligence? We wish to make two specific points. First, the human mind is best conceptualized as a set of relatively autonomous adaptations or skills rather than as a general problem solver. Second, the specific design features of the human brain represent convenient or simple ways to achieve a particular adaptation, not necessarily an optimal design.

5.1.1 General vs. Specific Problem Solvers

An evolutionary perspective on the nature of the human mind prompts focus on the particular problems in adaptation that have been encountered in the past. Of special relevance: were such problems best dealt with by a single, general purpose problem solver, or by a set of more specific, relatively independent neural mechanisms? Though the history of psychology has been dominated by general-purpose models (e.g., Skinner 1953, Piaget 1954, Newell & Simon 1972), contemporary efforts are more local in scale, focusing on particular processing modules (e.g., Karmiloff-Smith 1992). From an evolutionary perspective, the most important issue concerns the nature of selection processes. Symons (1992, pg. 139) provides one opinion:

> Human beings, like all other organisms, have been designed by selection to strive for specific goals, not the general goal of reproduction-maximizing: There can be no such thing as a generalized reproduction-maximizer mechanism because there is no general, universally effective way to maximize reproduction.

Stephen J. Gould (1979, pg. 386) provides another perspective on the brain:

> I don't doubt for a moment that the brain's enlargement in
> human evolution had an adaptive basis mediated by selec-
> tion. But I would be more than mildly surprised if many of
> the specific things it now can do are the product of direct
> selection "for" that particular behavior. Once you build a
> complex machine, it can perform so many unanticipated
> tasks. Build a computer "for" processing monthly checks
> at the plant, and it can also perform factor analyses on
> human skeletal measures, play Rogerian analyst, and whip
> anyone's ass (or at least tie them perpetually) in
> tic-tac-toe.

Let us consider two specific versions of this issue, the first concerning language. Is human language a manifestation of a single all-purpose learning device
or does it represent a relatively autonomous and independent intellectual capacity? Language use is of fundamental importance to our understanding of human
brain function (see Pinker and Bloom 1990, 1992, and Part IV). Several observations provide some support for the view that language may derive from a set of
neural devices relatively independent of other brain mechanisms (Pinker &
Bloom 1992, pg. 452):

> Within societies, individual humans are proficient lan-
> guage users regardless of intelligence, social status, or
> level of education. Children are fluent speakers of complex
> grammatical sentences by the age of three, without benefit
> of formal instruction. They are capable of inventing lan-
> guages that are more systematic than those they hear,
> showing resemblances to languages that they have never
> heard, and they obey subtle grammatical principles for
> which there is no evidence in their environments. Disease
> or injury can make people linguistic savants while severely
> retarded or linguistically impaired with normal intelli-
> gence. Some language disorders are genetically transmit-
> ted. Aspects of language skill can be linked to
> characteristic regions of the human brain.

A more focused (and tractable) question than that of language is whether a
single all-purpose device underlies the brain's capacity to process both depth
cues in the visual world and the ability to localize auditory stimuli in space.
Clearly, the answer to this question is "no."

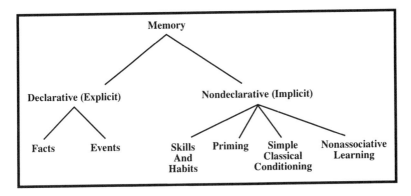

FIGURE 5.1   Classification of memory. Declarative (explicit) memory refers to conscious recollections of facts and events and depends on the integrity of medial temporal lobe cortex. Nondeclarative (implicit) memory refers to a collection of abilities and is independent of the medial temporal lobe. Nonassociative learning includes habituation and sensitization. In the case of nondeclarative memory, experience alters behavior nonconsciously, without providing access to any memory content. (From Squire and Zola-Morgan (1991).

This evolutionary perspective on the multiplicity of adaptations comprising the mind dovetails nicely with recent research in cognitive neuroscience. A major focus of cognitive neuroscience has been to identify autonomous intellectual skills in individuals with brain damage. The logic of the approach is based upon the notion of *double dissociation*. It works like this. Consider two different cognitive skills, say short term verbal memory (when you look up a phone number) versus long term verbal memory (recalling a conversation you overheard yesterday). If one can demonstrate that in one individual brain damage can produce a deficit in short term memory, but not long term memory, but that in another individual brain damage can produce a deficit in long term memory, but not short term memory, then one can conclude that these cognitive skills are separable. That is, they are not the product of the same problem solving device. A stronger inference can be made if one can consistently link a selective deficit in short term memory to one brain region (A) and a selective deficit in long term memory to another (B): region A controls short term memory and region B controls long term memory. [See Shallice (1988) for a more comprehensive treatment of the analysis of dissociations.]

Using this logic, a number of rather striking dissociations have been demonstrated. The distinction between procedural and declarative memory was introduced in Section 3.2.2. Figure 5.1 shows a more detailed view of the fractionation of memory systems. Here is a short list of other dissociations:

1. Language comprehension from language production
2. Written language from oral language
3. Manipulation of verbs versus nouns
4. Memory for verbal and non verbal information
5. Short term memory and long term memory
6. Language skills and long term memory
7. Recognition of familiar faces versus matching unfamiliar faces versus processing a facial expression

Fodor's (1983) influential analysis of modularity suggested that while modularity may characterize input and output systems, *central* or semantic systems could not possibly be modular in nature. Perhaps there remains some central or core intellectual operation distinct from sensory and motor skills, or even language, that might be considered a general problem solver. How about reason? or logic? Let us consider an influential line of investigation by Cosmides and Tooby (1992; see also Platt & Griggs 1993).

Cosmides has systematically studied a problem known as the Wason Selection task. Examples are given in Figure 5.2 (Parts a and b). The logic underlying each problem is identical, and we consider it in more detail in Section 7.1. For each situation, the correct response is *P* and *not - Q*. Despite this formal similarity, the proportion of people answering the question correctly is three times greater for Problem b than Problem a. These types of *content* effects are ubiquitous.

Cosmides has shown that all versions of this problem with high solution rates are of a specific content: types of social reasoning involving detection of *cheaters*, people who do not play by the rules, such as the underage people drinking alcohol described in Problem b. Further, Cosmides has shown that the reason for this selective application of logical inference is most likely that humans (and other primates) have evolved particular adaptations to detect cheaters, due to the general importance of social exchange throughout our evolutionary history.

Thus, reasoning skills may be domain-specific, activated only in response to particular classes of problems. Having a certain logic operation built into one neural system does not ensure its availability to other neural systems. Even in the domain of reasoning, perhaps the hallmark of the human intellect, there may be no general purpose mechanisms. Here then is one significant constraint for the attempt to develop neurally realistic intelligent systems. If one wishes to develop realistic models, focus on developing and integrating a series of specific mechanisms rather than on developing a general purpose problem solver. As we see in Parts II and III, researchers have developed a number of different problem solving architectures to address some of the diversity found in problem tasks.

a. Abstract Problem

Part of your new clerical job at the local high school is to make sure that student documents have been processed correctly. Your job is to make sure the documents conform to the following alphanumeric rule:

"If a person has a 'D' rating, then his documents must be marked code '3'."
(If   P   then   Q   )*

You suspect the secretary you replaced did not categorize the students' documents correctly. The cards below have information about the documents of four people who are enrolled at this high school. Each card represents one person. One side of a card tells a person's letter rating and the other side of the card tells that person's number code. Indicate only those card(s) you definitely need to turn over to see if the documents of any of these people violate this rule.

D	F	3	7
(P)	*(not - P)*	*(Q)*	*(not - Q)*

b. Drinking Age Problem (adapted from Griggs & Cox 1982)

In its crackdown against drunk drivers, Massachusetts law enforcement officials are revoking liquor licenses left and right. You are a bouncer in a Boston bar, and you'll lose your job unless you enforce the following law:

"If a person is drinking beer, then he must be over 20 years old."
(If   P   then   Q   )*

The cards below have information about four people sitting at a table in your bar. Each card represents one person. One side of a card tells what a person is drinking and the other side of the card tells that person's age. Indicate only those card(s) you definitely need to turn over to see if any of these people are breaking this law.

drinking beer	drinking coke	25 years old	16 years old
(P)	*(not - P)*	*(Q)*	*(not - Q)*

c. Structure of Social Contract Problems

It is your job to enforce the following law:

Rule 1 - Standard Social Contract: "If you take the benefit, then you pay the cost."
(If   P   then   Q   )*
Rule 2 - Switched Social Contract: "If you pay the cost, then you take the benefit."
(If   P   then   Q   )*

The cards below have information about four people. Each card represents one person. One side of a card tells whether a person accepted the benefit and the other side of the card tells whether that person paid the cost. Indicate only those card(s) you definitely need to turn over to see if any of these people are breaking the law.

	benefit accepted	benefit *not* accepted	cost paid	cost *not* paid
Rule 1	*(P)*	*(not - P)*	*(Q)*	*(not - Q)*
Rule 2	*(Q)*	*(not - Q)*	*(P)*	*(not - P)*

FIGURE 5.2   Examples of the Wason selection task. * The logic forms marked on the rules did not appear on problems given to subjects. From Cosmides and Tooby (1992). See Section 7.2 for further analysis of logic forms.

5.1.2 Differences in Neural Designs

There is a degree of inventiveness in the design of nonbiological intelligent systems that does not characterize the process by which brains have developed. As we examine brain designs of other mammals, and other primates in particular, we are struck by the tremendous similarity in design features. The same types of neurons are found. They are organized in similar ways. The metabolic and physiological properties are identical. Differences across species are essentially quantitative, not qualitative.

These observations support the utility of animal models of cognitive or pathological phenomena, a common research strategy in the neurosciences. But on the other hand, these observations reveal the fundamental conservatism of the evolutionary process. Once a design feature has been successful, it is unlikely to be reinvented or replaced by a different architecture attempting the same or similar purposes. For example, one of the central features of the design of the human neuron is the presence of voltage-sensitive ion channels in the neuron membrane. Such channels for sodium, potassium, and chlorine ions are necessary for the development of *action potentials*, as described in Section 5.2.2. These ion channels are seen in the earliest Metazoan organisms, predating the divergence of vertebrates from invertebrates.

Here is the central point: "Animals were not designed *de novo* by engineers, but sculpted through natural selection acting upon variations arising within their ontogenetic programs" (Arbas et al. 1991, pg. 9). Another way to phrase this is *nature is a tinkerer*. When a novel demand emerges, such as through significant climactic change, the manner in which a novel neural mechanism emerges is greatly constrained by the organism's evolutionary history and genetic heritage. New brain solutions are unlikely to be terribly original or novel. The vast majority of mutations possibly rising within the genome are not adaptive. Thus, successful change is most apt to involve fine-tuning rather than development of a completely novel neural device. Selection pressures will operate against the backdrop of available variability in skills and mechanisms seen in the population.

There are two important implications of this perspective. First, we cannot consider any given neural feature to represent an optimal design. Consider again human language, a novel behavioral competency shaped by genes conferring a particular neural architecture. The manner in which language skills are instantiated in the brain reflects the raw materials which natural selection had available, that is, the early hominid brain. Perhaps, if we were given the possibility of inventing a language system, other more efficient or capable design features could be incorporated. Though we are tempted to consider human language the signal achievement of neural evolution, its design represents a compromise, a compromise between evolutionary pressures and the raw materials available from which to fashion adaptations. Thus, despite its marvelous and unprecedented accomplishments, the human brain does not represent any optimal design or pinnacle of achievement. Its workings may provide clues as to one way to solve problems and act intelligently, but not the only way.

The second implication of this *nature is a tinkerer* perspective concerns the biological details of neural development. Alteration of a small number of design parameters may account for vast differences across species, or within the evolutionary history of the human species. For the present discussion, let us consider two such features - *replication of processing elements* and *neoteny*.

Within the hominid line there has been a very definite increase in brain size. For *Austalopithecas africanus* average brain volume was about 400 cm^3, for *Homo habilis* 659 cm^3, for *Homo erectus* 942 cm^3, and for our species, *Homo sapiens*, about 1300 cm^3. How has this difference in size been achieved? There are numerous possibilities, including the addition of new lobes to the brain, larger neuron size, etc. One of the most important differences is likely an increase in the number of *cortical columns*.

Cortical columns are organized neural ensembles in which neurons share functional properties, such as the nature of the stimulus eliciting maximal activity. They are arranged in a radial fashion, extending from deep within the cortex to the periphery. They have similar intrinsic organization. Columnar design is a characteristic of all animals who show a cortex. Further, the size of columns and the number of neurons comprising a column tend to be quite similar across species. To a certain extent columns may be considered very basic information processing devices. It appears then that increases in cortical size in part reflect a greater number of cortical columns, rather than the addition of any particular novel design feature. Having developed a workable component, evolution appears to have tinkered with the number of replications of this particular element. Had one set out to design a human brain, other novel design features may have been more efficient, but evolution had no such luxury of design.

Another design parameter which helps account for differences across species, especially within the primate line, is *neoteny*. Neoteny refers to a general retardation in the rate of development, resulting in the adult retention of physical features typically associated with juvenile forms of ancestral species. A striking and common example of human neoteny is the much greater resemblance of the human face to young, nonhuman primates (such as the chimpanzee) than to adult nonhuman primates. But the importance of neotony goes far beyond physical appearance.

Brain growth is most rapid during fetal development. By *retarding* development, or maintaining fetal development rates for long periods, brain volume is significantly increased in humans. Stephen J. Gould (1977) and others have compiled long lists of the human characteristics which can be interpreted as outcomes of a general slowing of developmental processes. Let us consider only two - *curiosity* and *plasticity*. Curiosity and play are behaviors most typical of people and of young nonhuman primates. They probably serve to facilitate acquisition of skills and knowledge of the environment. At both behavioral and neural levels, humans and many young nonhuman primates show substantial plasticity. That is, they are capable of continually modifying behavior, and of course the neural substrates of behavior, to meet current exigencies. Neoteny thus represents another rather conservative strategy by which evolution has produced the remarkable human brain. To a great extent our brains have achieved their powers by replication of elements long found to be efficient, columns, and by altering developmental rates rather than by any truly unique elements or configuration of elements.

5.2 MECHANISTIC CONSTRAINTS

In this section we focus on the "hardware," attempting to quantify and characterize the anatomy of the human brain. Brains consist of two classes of cells, *neurons* and *glia*. Different types of glial cells are found throughout the brain in approximately equal number to neurons. Some glial cells guide developing neurons to the proper location in the brain. Others help remove waste products. *Oligodendroglial* cells serve to myelinate long axons (wrap them in a sheath with only a few gaps or *nodes of Ranvier*), a process which allows axons to transmit information rapidly over long distances.

5.2.1 Gross Anatomy

The gross anatomy of the human brain is shown in Figures 5.3 and 5.4. Though space considerations preclude a detailed presentation, a few particular structures deserve mention. The two large cerebral hemispheres are each covered by the cerebral cortex, if you will, the most intelligent part of the brain. The cortex is a six-layered structure, with the outermost layer designated I and the innermost layer VI. Layers I through IV generally receive inputs from other brain centers and other parts of the cortex. Layers V and VI are often the origin of output fibers. The cortex is typically divided into lobes as shown in Figure 5.4. A *gyrus* is the individual bulge of the cortical surface (the plural is gyri). The *sulcus* is a groove or fissure (when plural, sulci). Major landmarks are the *Sylvian* (or lateral) fissure separating the temporal lobe from the rest of the cerebral hemisphere, and the *central sulcus* separating frontal and parietal lobes. Two regions within the left hemisphere crucial for language are *Broca's area*, in the inferior-frontal gyrus, and *Wernicke's area*, in the posterior portion of the superior temporal gyrus. It cannot be emphasized too strongly that different brain regions work together in a coordinated fashion, even for the most simple tasks.

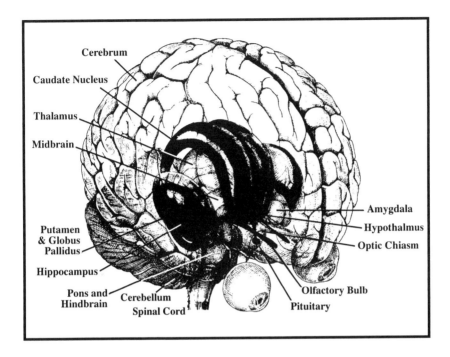

FIGURE 5.3   A view of the human brain showing internal structure. From Nauta and Feirtag (1979).

Embedded within the cerebral hemispheres are two complex, interconnected, multi-component systems known as the *basal ganglia* (including the caudate nucleus, putamen, globus pallidus) and the *limbic system* (including hippocampus, amygdala, septum). The most central functions of the basal ganglia include initiation and control of movement. The limbic system is most involved with memory and emotion.

Beneath the cerebral hemispheres are a diverse collection of brain centers collectively referred to as the *brain stem*. The *thalamus* is especially important. Many pathways between higher and lower brain centers, as well as among higher brain centers, involve connections through the thalamus. The *cerebellum*, a foliated structure at the rear of the brain, beneath the occipital lobes, is involved in motor and sensory coordination.

5.2.2 Neuronal Activity

The physiology of neurons is beyond the scope of this chapter, but some under-

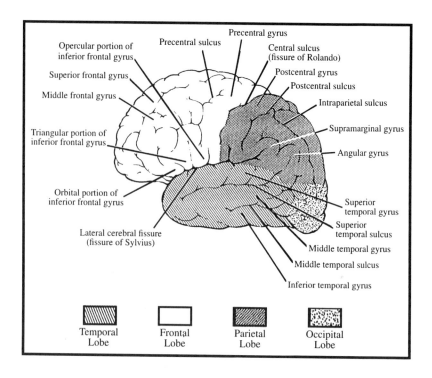

FIGURE 5.4   Lateral view of the left cerebral hemisphere. From de Groot (1991).

standing of neuronal functioning is essential if we wish to compare real and artificial neural networks. Neurons in the brain are not contiguous; they are physically separated from each other, interacting only at special junctures called
synapses. Figure 5.5 shows a variety of different neurons and Figure 5.6 provides
a detailed look at a single pyramidal cell. Differences in the shape of neurons are
related to differences in function. For the moment, let us focus on the *pyramidal
cell*, a prototypic cortical neuron. Throughout the richly branching dendrites,
approximately 4000 synapses are found. The axon of this pyramidal cell will
form synapses with a variety of other neurons. Synapses may occur between any
of the parts of neurons. While the most common synapses are likely to be *axodendritic* (i.e., from the axon of the presynaptic neuron to the dendrite of the
postsynaptic neuron), *axo-axonic* and *dendro-dendritic* synapses are also found.

Neural activity is electrical. Patterns of ion flows into and out of the neuron
determine whether a neuron is active or resting. The typical resting axon has a
relative negative charge of -70 mV as compared to the extracellular environment.
When the pyramidal cell becomes active, massive ion flows produce a reversal of
this situation, so that the axon shows a potential of -50 mV. When a given pyra-

midal is active, certain chemicals will be released from the axon terminal. These chemicals, called *neurotransmitters*, influence the postsynaptic membrane, typically by fitting into specific receptor sites rather like a key into a lock. Then, further ion flows are initiated, altering the electrical potential and thus the activity level of the postsynaptic neuron.

These postsynaptic changes in potential are of two sorts. The membrane potential for the postsynaptic neuron can be made more negative, an event termed an *inhibitory postsynaptic potential (IPSP)*, or more positive, an *excitatory postsynaptic potential (EPSP)*. EPSPs and IPSPs are constantly being generated throughout the synapses in the dendritic system of a given pyramidal

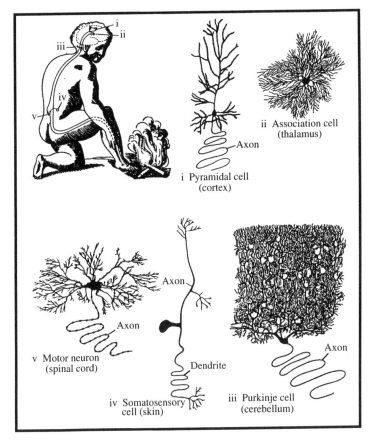

FIGURE 5.5   The nervous system is composed of neurons, or nerve cells, each of which is specialized as to function. The schematic drawings show the relative size, shape, location, and configuration of some neurons. From Kolb and Whishaw (1990).

neuron. If the net effect of all these events is sufficient to alter the membrane potential from -70 mV to approximately -50 mV, a threshold has been crossed and massive ion flows are initiated. Some ions stream into the neuron and others out. The result of these ion flows is the generation of an action potential in that pyramidal cell's axon. The difference in electrical potential travels along the length of the axon to the axon terminal, where neurotransmitters will now be released, affecting any other neurons with which this pyramidal cell has formed axodendritic synapses. An IPSP or EPSP will be generated in a postsynaptic neuron, contributing to the overall electrical potential of that neuron.

An important feature of the action potential of a pyramidal neuron is its *all or none* nature. Action potentials are of uniform magnitude. They each show the same degree of departure from the resting membrane potential. They each have the same time course. The nature of the action potential is independent of the magnitude of the electrical changes from which is it generated. That is, as long as the membrane potential changes from -70 or so to -50 mV, exceeding the threshold, an action potential is generated. Neurons may respond to strong inputs by firing more frequently, but they will not generate larger action potentials.

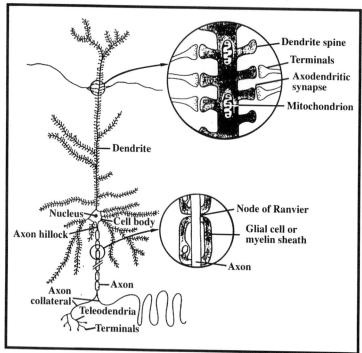

FIGURE 5.6   A typical neuron, showing some of its major physical features. From Kolb and Whishaw (1990).

At this point, we must acknowledge the diversity of forms of neural activity in the central nervous system. While the generation of action potentials is characteristic of pyramidal neurons, not all neurons work this way. In general, smaller neurons with unmyelinated (or absent) axons have *graded* potentials rather than action potentials. The magnitude of the potential changes in these neurons is proportional to the magnitude of the inputs. When we consider that neural interactions can be either inhibitory or excitatory, we conclude that small neurons may code values of +1 (active) through -1 (inhibitive). In contrast, the pyramidal neurons can code only three distinct values, +1, 0, and -1.

Another complexity of the central nervous system concerns neurotransmitter action. Not all neurotransmitters are effective only at a single synapse. While most neurotransmitters exert an influence only in receptors of the synapse where they are released, some can have more widespread influence. For example, those neurotransmitters classified as *monoamines* tend to have more diffuse effects than *amino acid neurotransmitters*, which act more rapidly and in a point-to-point fashion. Neuromodulatory peptides may have quite widespread effects on neural activity.

5.2.3 The Cellular Basis of Learning

What anatomic changes underlie learning and memory? There is probably no other topic in the neurosciences that is currently under more intensive investigation. Brains change in a great many ways, including neuronal depopulation or cell loss, dendritic growth, and myelination. These changes are occurring constantly, throughout our lifetime. But it is to the synapse that we must turn to understand the cellular basis of learning, consistent with the notion that the synapse is the most elementary information processing unit of the nervous system.

In his 1949 landmark treatise, the *Organization of Behavior*, Donald Hebb offered a profoundly simple idea that remains central to both biological and network approaches to learning. Consider a typical axodendritic synapse. Hebb proposed that if activity in the presynaptic neuron repeatedly caused the postsynaptic neuron to fire, physical changes in the synapse would occur. These changes would then make it easier for the presynaptic neuron to fire the post-synaptic neuron, increasing synaptic efficiency. A formal version of this, developed into a learning algorithm for connectionist architectures in Chapter 12, may be expressed as:

$$\Delta W_{BA} = \Sigma V_B V_A .$$

ΔW_{BA} refers to the change in the weight (or firing probability) of the synapse between neurons A and B. V_A refers to the average fire rate of neuron A and V_B to the average firing rate of neuron B. Churchland and Sejnowski (1992) describe other variations on this formula which remain consistent with Hebbs' basic proposal, and the reader is referred to their work for a more detailed discussion.

It seems quite likely that something like the *Hebbian Synapse* exists in the brain and represents at least one of the mechanisms underlying learning. Experimental analysis of such cellular changes has typically involved investigation of the phenomenon known as *longterm potentiation* (LTP). Brief, high frequency electrical stimulation of the presynaptic neuron, sufficient to fire the postsynaptic neuron, may produce longterm changes in the connectivity of the two cells. The magnitude of the postsynaptic response to normal input from the presynaptic neuron is increased. Most studies of LTP involve the hippocampus, but the phenomena can also be evoked elsewhere. The physical changes underlying LTP are not fully understood. A variety of changes may occur in both the presynaptic and postsynaptic neurons. It is also important to recall that there may be many synapses between a given presynaptic and postsynaptic neuron. Increased communication efficiency between the neurons may also involve generation of new synapses.

In what part of the brain do synaptic changes occur when we learn something new? For declarative learning the best bets involve two particular regions: hippocampus and the cerebral cortex. Most forms of new learning are abolished with bilateral destruction of the hippocampus, but knowledge accumulated a while before the brain damage is essentially unaffected (Squire 1987). This suggests a critical role for the hippocampus as a "trainer" or director of synapse modification elsewhere in the brain. Following learning a particular piece of information, the hippocampus begins to influence the most relevant parts of the cerebral cortex to alter synaptic weights. After a certain period of time (at least weeks in primates) the cortical circuitry may be sufficiently altered so as to represent the new information. The particular portion of the cortex involved is likely to be dependent on exactly what type of information is being learned. For example, visual information is likely to involve alteration of synaptic weights in the visual cortex.

5.2.4 Levels of Organization

Any attempt to relate behavior to brain function immediately confronts the problems of *level* of organization. If we wish, for example, to understand the ability to recognize familiar faces, what neural entities are most relevant? Is understanding best achieved by focus on the most elementary functional units of the brain, the synapse? Or should we focus on the integrated function of neurons comprising the right cerebral hemisphere? The neuroscientist Gordon Shepherd has provided a cogent analysis of these problems. In Figure 5.7 he provides an example of the

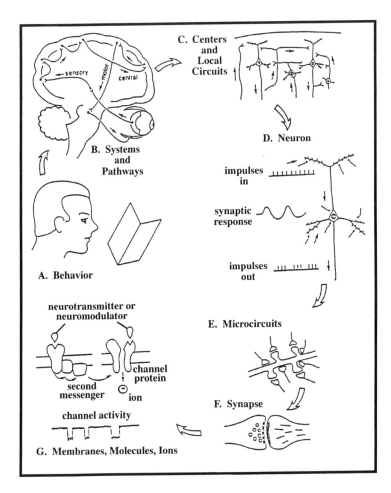

FIGURE 5.7   An analysis of neuron activity relevant to the process of reading. From Shepherd (1991).

analysis of various levels of neuron activity relevant for the process of reading.

There is no easy answer to the question of the proper level of analysis. Most neuroscientists adopt a pragmatic approach, focusing on a small set of adjacent levels which seem, at an intuitive level, most capable of illuminating a particular question. It is quite clear, however, that insights gained at a given level may provide insights into functional principles at both higher and lower levels of analysis.

When questions of neural mechanisms concern intelligence or complex problem solving, it is probably most profitable to focus on higher levels of neural integration. Understanding the physiology of the given neuron, outside the context of its typical inputs and outputs, contributes relatively little to our knowledge of higher cognitive functions. Much greater insights are likely to be achieved by understanding how populations of neurons interact. The most fruitful level of analysis, to use Shepherd's terminology, is probably *systems and pathways* and to a lesser extent *centers and local circuits*. But this is just an educated guess, a hunch. The relevance of lower levels in part depends on the extent to which properties at higher levels can be considered emergent. In our analysis at the systems and pathways level, how much constraint is engendered by principals of neural functioning at the next lowest level, that of centers and local circuits? As Shepherd (1991, pg. 29) states: "A widely accepted concept in modelling systems is that an input-output function at one level of organization can be simulated by an infinity of models based on subcomponents from lower levels."

5.2.5 Neural Realism

In Chapter 3, we noted that part of the appeal of connectionist network theories was their neural realism. There are so many types of models (see Chapters 11 and 12) varying greatly in design features, that we cannot attempt any overall summary of just how accurately they reflect brain function. In this section we shall attempt only to discuss those aspects of brain function most relevant for modelers. Cherniak (1990) has drawn attention to a prominent belief, rarely stated explicitly, that neural resources are so vast as to be "unbounded." Lack of concern for the quantitative details of neuron number, synapse size, etc, has led to the development of what Cherniak terms "impossibility engines." He cites examples of massively interconnected parallel network models which "if actually realized in nerve cells would each require a brain the size of a bathtub" (Cherniak 1990). To help avoid such situations, let us attempt to gain some understanding of quantitative neural anatomical constraints.

Cortical Resources

There are approximately 10^{10} neurons in the cerebral cortex. The cortex is a thin, convoluted sheet covering the entire cerebral hemisphere. Much of the cortex is folded in on itself, increasing total surface area. There have been numerous estimates as to the surface area of the unfolded cortical sheet. Interestingly, recent estimates vary by an order of magnitude. A commonly cited estimated is one square meter, though the volume of this cortical sheet (given an average thickness of 2 to 3 mm) would then be around 2 liters, clearly greater than the average 1.3 liters of total brain volume. The best estimate of surface area would appear to be in the range of 160,000 mm^2. It is important to note that estimates of cortical area or brain volume do not reveal directly the magnitude of neural resources. Glial cells, microvasculature, and interstitial space all contribute to total brain volume. When these volumes are taken into account, only 30 to 40% of total cortical volume reflects that contributed by individual neurons.

Connectivity

Neuron-like elements are considered the simplest elements modeled in connectionist networks, reflecting the widespread belief that the functions computed by individual neurons are quite simple. This does not appear to be the case. Both experimental studies of neuron function and anatomic studies of the number of synapses per neuron suggest that neurons are by no means simple. As noted, the most elementary unit of computation is best considered the individual synapse (Shepherd 1979). After reviewing the available anatomic studies Cherniak estimates that the volume of each cortical synapse is approximately 1 mu^3. The volume of each cortical neuron is approximately 6000 mu^3. The most common estimate of number of synapses per neuron is in the range of 10000, though a much smaller number, 4000 or so, is probably more reasonable, given overall size constraints.

From a computational perspective we need to know not only the total number of synapses, but also *fan-in* and *fan-out* parameters. Rummelhart and McClelland (1986) suggest that both fan-in and fan-out numbers are in the order of 10^3 to 10^5. However, while relatively large fan-in numbers seem to be quite characteristic of the cerebral cortex, Shepherd notes that fan-out numbers are quite a bit smaller. More realistic are estimates in the range of 10^1 or 10^2.

Moving beyond individual synapses and neurons to patterns of connections, a few features of the brain deserve specific mention, as they are typically included in network or connectionist models.

1. Cortical circuits involve different types of neurons, with distinct anatomies and computational properties. For example, some neurons function in analog fashion and others digital. Circuits may well involve a mixture of neurons of each type.
2. Connections between neurons are typically either excitatory or inhibitory. While values from -1 to +1 are found within a population of neurons, individual synapses are more constrained.
3. Some brain systems project quite widely throughout the brain and may be conceptualized as large-scale modulators. Each of these systems tends to involve a different neural transmitter: *Norepinephrine* for the *locus coeruleus*, *serotonin* for the *raphe nucleus*, *dopamine* for the *substantia nigra*, *acetylcholine* for the *nucleus basalis*, and *GABA* (gammaamino-butyric acid) for the *mammalary* region of the hypothalamus.

Also, as noted above, certain neural transmitters may exert influences
beyond a given synaptic release point.
4. Complex local circuits are quite common. For example, recurrent collateral processes may effect either excitatory or inhibitory influences.

Time

A quantitative understanding of the brain is incomplete without a sense of the
duration and speed of particular events. There are two particular ways in which
information regarding time is important. First, neural events clearly take time.
Second, coordination of neural events within a given temporal context is essential for integrating various neural systems and synchronizing neural activity with
particular sensory events. Thus, we need achieve some understanding of temporal coordination mechanisms.

An action potential at a given point in an axon lasts approximately 1 ms. In
an unmyelinated axon, the difference in electrical potential that defines the action
potential travels along the axon at a very slow speed. If we follow over time the
point within the axon at which maximal positive charge is seen, from cell body
on toward the axon terminal, this point moves at approximately 10 m per second.
Myelinated neurons are much faster. The only regions of such axons exposed to
the extracellular environment are the nodes of Ranvier. Only at these points can
the ion flows responsible for electrical potential changes occur. Instead of the
smooth and continuous progression of changes in ion flow seen along the length
of an unmyelinated axon, in the myelinated axon there is a sequence of discrete
ionic events, from node to node toward the axon terminal.

Within each node, the time course for ion flows is the same as in an unmyelinated axon (of a similar length and diameter). But between nodes, conduction is
much more rapid and is termed *electrotonic*. The potential difference jumps from
node to node (*saltatory conduction*) at the same speed at which a wire conducts
electricity, the speed of light. Thus, in a myelinated neuron the slow ionic events
occurring in each node are punctuated by extremely rapid conduction between
nodes. The overall rate of conduction of a myelinated neuron falls in between the
slow rate of unmyelinated neurons and the fast rate of electrical conduction. The
actual rate of transmission falls somewhere between 10 and 100 m per second,
depending largely upon axon diameter. The duration of effects on the post-synaptic cell may be quite variable, ranging from a millisecond to several milliseconds
to several minutes.

The manner in which neural events are synchronized in time is poorly understood. Differences in the length of neurons comprising different circuits will
serve to introduce characteristic latencies to particular computations. Most neurons in the brain are spontaneously active, even in the absence of stimulation, but
inter-spike intervals often appear random. Cortical neurons also appear to have

distinctly different patterns of spiking (or firing or bursting). Three major temporal patterns have been described, though this probably does not comprise an exhaustive list. Pyramidal cells, which are most likely excitatory, respond to a single suprathreshold input by generating a single spike. When suprathreshold input is maintained, spiking frequency gradually declines. Such neurons have been termed *regular-spiking neurons*. In terms of function, regular spiking neurons thus show attenuated activity to prolonged excitatory stimuli, maximally responding to phasic excitatory stimuli. *Fast-spiking* neurons show very rapid repetitive spiking, without attenuation to prolonged stimuli. Spike frequencies of 500 to 600 Hz may be maintained for hundreds of milliseconds. Often spike frequency is determined by the nature of inputs in such cells. Neurons with these characteristics are inhibitory, nonpyramidal cortical cells using the neurotransmitter GABA.

A third type of temporal pattern is termed *intrinsically bursting*. Bursts occur in stereotyped, clustered patterns independent of inputs, in the range of 5 to 15 Hz. Conners and Gutnick (1990) speculate that such cells may help generate the prominent cortical rhythms that can be observed on an EEG. Most intrinsically bursting cells are also pyramidal cells, though in contrast to regular-spiking cells, they tend to be seen in restricted cortical layers (IV and V, Figure 5.3).

This brief review highlights a major difference between the neuron-like elements incorporated in many connectionist models and real neurons: neurons are much more complex and much more varied in function. The uniformity of basic elements and connections among elements characteristic of most models does not faithfully reflect brain function. However, the dearth of knowledge of the systems-level interactions among neurons certainly justifies such "simplified" models. As Shepherd (1991, pg. 28) states, "with neural networks ... it is unnecessary to insist in the first instance that they are neural. They should be pursued first for their inherent interest in demonstrating systems behavior; it is then a second step to assess their relevance to the nervous system or to any other type of system."

5.3   THE NEUROPSYCHOLOGY OF EXPERTISE

In this section we attempt to understand the strengths and weaknesses of different neural designs. Our focus will be on very large collections of neurons, at the level of particular gyri, collections of gyri, and hemispheres. Such massive aggregations of neurons are levels of complexity beyond simple circuits or columns. Undoubtedly, there is a wide gap between our knowledge of the function of simple circuits and models of functional cortical areas. But we agree with the general thesis of Churchland and Sejnowski (1992) that both *bottom up* and *top down* research strategies will be necessary to achieving a comprehensive understanding of brain function.

We approach this issue from three different perspectives. First, we consider the manner in which different cortical regions accomplish different tasks. We see that there are systematic relationships between problem type and intrinsic organization. Then we examine differences in hemisphere function, reflecting the broadest biological perspective on the mind, relating the mind to two (not billions) of neural entities. Our task is to understand the origin of hemispheric differences in functioning. Finally, we approach the general issue of strengths and weaknesses of different neural designs from the perspective of individual differences. Undoubtedly, there are systematic differences between people in levels or patterns of cognitive skills. Can we uncover some basic differences in design that will help us understand these cognitive differences?

5.3.1 Parallel Computations and Mappings

Nelson and Bower (1990, pg. 403) provide a fascinating account of the similar design problems faced by parallel computers and brains. Their thesis is that "The question of how to map a computation optimally onto multiple processors (is) a fundamental issue, whether the individual processes (are) silicon chips or neurons." They described two central problems limiting the efficiency of parallel computations - *communication overhead* and *load imbalance*. The manner in which these issues are handled depends upon the nature of the particular problem to be solved. Communication overhead refers to the cost of distributing information between processors. In computers, this cost consists of both the time necessary to share information and the physical space taken up by connections between the processors. Load balance refers to the manner in which information is distributed among the variable processors. If a single processing element is especially burdened, the overall speed of parallel computation may be seriously compromised. Different types of computation require different ways to minimize problems of load imbalance and communication overhead. In practice, this amounts to different mappings of functions onto processors.

Three major types of maps are distinguished and each may be found in the brain. Figure 5.8 shows the three types of maps - *continuous maps, patchy maps*, and *scattered maps*. The upper panels (A-C) show the three ways 16 different processors may divide the job of image analysis. The lower panels (D-F) show anatomic mappings of these different types of processing.

Continuous maps are often observed in sensory and motor systems. A computationally relevant parameter is represented in a smooth and continuous manner over a portion of the cortical sheet. The familiar motor homunculus (Figure 5.9) is one example of a continuous map, revealing what has been termed *somatotopic organization*. Adjacent body features are represented in adjacent portions of the cortex. Figure 5.10 shows the continuous manner in which the visual world

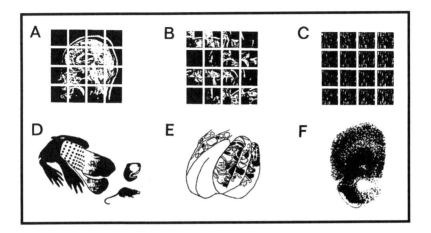

FIGURE 5.8   Parallel computer maps and brain maps. **(A-C)** Three general classes of parallel computer maps: **(A)** continuous mappings, **(B)** patchy mapping, and **(C)** scattered mapping. In each case, the pixels from a 256 ×256 MRI brain-scan image have been mapped onto a 4 ×4 array of computer processors, with each processor being assigned responsibility for one-sixteenth of the total pixels. Depending on the nature of the computation being performed, different mappings give rise to different computational efficiencies. The types of computations for which each map class is optimal are described in the text. **(D-F)** Examples of brain maps that appear to fall into these same categories: **(D)** continuous mapping of tactile inputs to somatosensory cortex of the rat, **(E)** patchy mapping of tactile inputs to cerebellar cortex in the rat, and **(F)** scattered mapping of olfactory input to piriform (olfactory) cortex of the rat, represented here by the 2-DG uptake pattern in a single section of this cortex. From Nelson and Bower (1990).

is mapped onto the *striate cortex* (occipital lobe), revealing what has been termed *retinotopic organization*. In the auditory cortex of the temporal lobe adjacent brain regions map adjacent auditory frequencies - *tonotopic organization*. These types of mappings appear to be optimal for computations in which local interactions of the problems space are most important. Comparison and analysis of adjacent portions of the visual world, for example, are more important than analysis across physically separated portions of space. Such a design might well facilitate object recognition. Three other characteristics of continuous maps are notable:

1. We tend to have multiple maps within a given modality. Thus, scattered throughout the posterior half of the brain may be as many as 10 or 12 different retinotopic mappings. These appear to represent *visual sketch pads* for different cognitive and perceptual computations.

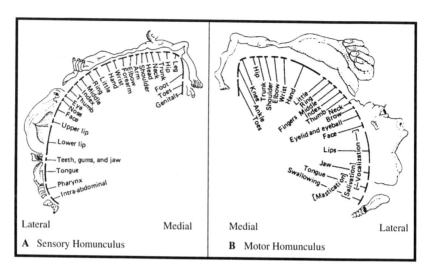

Lateral	Medial	Medial	Lateral
A Sensory Homunculus		**B** Motor Homunculus	

FIGURE 5.9   Somatic sensory and motor projections from and to the body surface and muscle are arranged in the cortex in somatotopic order. **(A)** Sensory information from the body surface is received by the postcentral gyrus of the parietal cortex. Areas of the body that are important for tactile discrimination, such as the tip of the tongue, the fingers, and the hand, have a disproportionately larger representation, reflecting their more extensive innervation. **(B)** The analogous motor map exists for the motor cortex. From Kandel and Jessel (1991).

2. The sensitivity of processing is proportionate to the size of that part of the map. Note the greater size of the hand area of the motor homunculus than for the trunk of the body. Similarly, note the proportion of the visual cortex devoted to the fovea, the central portion of the retina crucial for directed gaze. The amount of space within a particular map devoted to a given representation can be increased through relevant experience. For example, a recent study of blind people proficient in Braille revealed expansion of the sensorimotor cortical representation of the reading finger (Pasqual-Leone & Torres 1993).

3. The mappings are formed in part by patterns of inputs, such as the more dense projection of optic nerve fibers from the fovea to the occipital pole. But the mappings are also maintained dynamically. Consider the mappings of the somatosensory cortex for the hand in which each digit has its own particular piece of the total map. If the middle digit is then amputated or denervated, there is a rapid "remapping" so that the region previously responsible for the middle digit now becomes devoted to the second and fourth digits (Wall & Kaas 1985). These results suggest that

cortical maps are in a state of flux, maintained in part by dynamic competition among neurons.

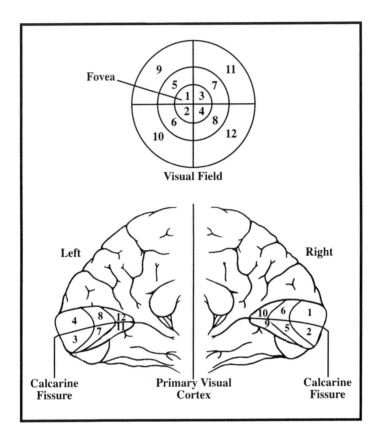

FIGURE 5.10 The primary visual cortex contains an orderly map of the visual field. In humans this cortex is located at the posterior pole of the cerebral hemisphere and lies almost exclusively on the medial surface. (In some individuals it is shifted so that part of it extends onto the lateral surface.) Each half of the visual field is represented in the contralateral hemisphere. Areas in the primary visual cortex are devoted to specific parts of the visual field, as indicated by the corresponding numbers. The upper fields are mapped below the calcarine fissure, and the lower fields above it. The striking aspect of this map is that about half of the neural mass is devoted to representation of the fovea and the region just around it. This area has the greatest visual acuity. From Mason and Kandel (1991).

Scattered mappings show no apparent spatial structure or organization. Nelson and Bower note that such mappings are often optimal for a variety of computations on a parallel computer. The class of problems for which scattered mappings represent an efficient design is characterized by "a lack of systematic structure in the pattern of interactions in the problem space ... cases in which no interactions take place or cases in which widespread interactions take place, and cases in which interaction patterns are unpredictable" (pg. 404). As shown in Figure 5.8 (Panel F) the olfactory cortex appears to have such a mapping.

Patchy maps are intermediate in nature. Within a given patch there may be smooth and continuous representations, but neighboring patches may be characterized by a different class of representations. Such maps may represent a more efficient solution to problems with both a local and nonlocal component. Nelson and Bower (1990) offer as an example the control of a robotic hand attempting to manipulate one object in an array. The necessary computations involve intensive local processing of fingertip sensors but nonlocal processing of the array of visually presented objects. A neural example of a patchy map may be the cortex of the cerebellum, in part involved in control of receptor surfaces during sensory exploration.

The anatomical organization of the language system in the left cerebral hemisphere shows a marked resemblance to patchy maps. George Ojemann (1983) and colleagues have explored the representation of sites relevant for object naming through the technique of electrical stimulation mapping. In subjects undergoing surgery for intractable epilepsy, brief electrical stimulation may be applied to different areas of the brain, creating in effect a temporary brain lesion. One can thus map sites which when stimulated impair naming, providing a map of this particular function. Particular regions (patches?) are found to be especially important to naming, but these regions are surrounded by brain tissue unrelated to naming. Ojemann has termed this type of organization as *mosaic*.

In each of these different types of mappings, the problems of communication overhead and load imbalance are solved in different ways. The correspondence across brains and parallel computers of how certain problem types are solved by particular mappings is quite impressive. These data suggest that continued investigation of shared principles of parallel computation across brains and computers may be quite fruitful.

5.3.2 Cerebral Lateralization

The single most obvious anatomic feature of the human brain is its division into two cerebral hemispheres. There is no area of investigation within the neurosciences that has attracted as much popular attention as the study of hemispheric differences in function. While we are all familiar with some of the excesses of such attention (e.g., weekend retreats for right hemisphere workshops), there is much to be gained from an understanding of this most fundamental division of the human brain. It represents a unique level of analysis of brain function, the simplest biological perspective one can adopt to the analysis of cognition.

In our attempt to understand what designs are optimal for what functions, cerebral lateralization holds the potential for unique insights. But we need to be able to answer two specific questions and the answers available now are incomplete. First, how do we best characterize the skill differences of the hemispheres? Second, what anatomic design features confer these skill differences?

One common way that skill differences have been described is as pairs of adjectives. Some of the more common adjective pairs are listed in Table 5.1.

Left	Right
verbal	nonverbal
analytic	holistic (or global or synthetic)
serial	parallel
focal	diffuse
propositional	appositional

TABLE 5.1   Adjective pairs for skill difference studies.

Although there is some validity to each of these adjective pairs, there are also considerable difficulties. Some are simply inaccurate. For example, it is clear that the verbal/nonverbal distinction fails because the right hemisphere has superior skills in some aspects of language, for example, speech prosody, and the left hemisphere may be more specialized for certain types of spatial skills, for example, representation of categorical relationships. But there is a more serious problem to this general approach to hemispheric specialization, as pointed out in an influential series of papers by Justine Sergent (1982, 1983).

These descriptive terms are only verbal labels, abstractions far removed from the neuronal ensembles they attempt to characterize. How does a neural ensemble distinguish verbal from nonverbal stimuli? Factors which affect the brain are physical - light, sound, touch, etc. What physical features distinguish verbal from nonverbal stimuli? Descriptions of different hemispheric skills need be in the physical realm, "in terms of units that are of relevance to cerebral processing" (Sergent 1982, pg. 254). Sergent offers a specific hypothesis. The hemispheres differ in their ability to process high versus low frequency stimuli. Her hypothesis was originally applied to visual processing, and though it has relevance for processing in all sensory modalities and the production of motoric sequences, let us focus on vision. High frequency stimuli are those that can be repeated frequently over a given distance. For example, a 1/8 inch wide letter "E" can be repeated 16 times over a distance of two inches. A 1 inch large letter "E" can be repeated only twice. The smaller feature has a higher spatial frequency. Sergent proposed that the left hemisphere is more efficient in processing high frequency stimuli and the right hemisphere at processing low frequency stimuli. Note that differences in hemisphere functions are expressed in terms of physical characteristics, not verbal abstractions.

Consider an early experiment of Sergent's involving presentation of letters to one hemisphere or the other using a device called a *tachistoscope*. If stimuli are presented 1.4 degrees or so to the right of central fixation, for durations of 150 msec or less, the visual information will be sent initially only to the left hemisphere. Left side presentation of similar eccentricity and duration results in stimuli being received by only the right hemisphere. Sergent showed subjects figures such as those of Figure 5.11. She asked them to depress a key if the letter "h" was present. For Panels A and B of Figure 5.11 the answer is "yes" and for Panel C it is "no." But note the difference between the two types of yes responses - in A the target feature is low frequency, i.e., the target is comprised of a collection of smaller elements, while in B the target feature is a high frequency stimulus, the individual elements themselves. Sergent discovered that the left hemisphere was relatively faster at detecting the high frequency "H" (Panel A) while the right hemisphere was relatively faster at detecting the low frequency "H" (Panel B), in support of her hypothesis.

Many studies have been carried out over the past few years to further evaluate Sergent's hypothesis. Most have been supportive, but not all (Mecacci 1993). At present, though, it remains the clearest and most elegant description of differences in hemispheric function. From this perspective it is easy to see why language comprehension, for example, involving perception of very rapid acoustic changes, would be a skill generally performed better by the left hemisphere. In contrast, perception of the emotional content of speech, involving changes in prosody over larger units of language such as sentences, would generally be performed better by the right cerebral hemisphere.

Now let us turn to a more difficult question. What anatomic differences produce such skill differentials in the cerebral hemispheres? There has been remarkably little research devoted to this question, perhaps reflecting contemporary neuroscience's preference for *basic processes* and *bottom up* modeling. There are two types of theories. The behavioral neurologist Norman Geschwind (Geschwind & Levitsky 1967) and his colleagues have championed the view that cerebral asymmetry in function reflects anatomic differences across the hemispheres in the size of particular specialized regions. Of central importance has been asymmetry in a portion of the temporal lobe known as the *planum temporale*, which is generally larger in the left hemisphere. Differences in the size particular brain centers such as this may lead one hemisphere to be relatively more

"Yes"	"Yes"		"No"
H H H H H	F	F	L L L L L L
H	F	F	L
H	F	F	L
H H H H H	F F F F		L L L L L L
H	F	F	L
H	F	F	L
H	F	F	L
A	**B**		**C**

FIGURE 5.11   Examples of stimuli used in Sergent's (1983) study of hemispheric asymmetries. See text for explanation.

skilled than another for a specific task. The left *planum temporale*, but not the right, is involved in language perception. Thus this anatomic difference may in part underlie hemispheric differences in function. Though such observations make important contributions to understanding hemispheric differences, there are significant difficulties in attempting to understand the totality of hemispheric asymmetries in terms of size differences of particular components (Witelson 1991). For the remainder of this section we focus on a different perspective on the question of hemispheric differences in anatomy, one which might more readily correspond to issues of network design.

In 1968, Josephine Semmes proposed that the right cerebral hemisphere was characterized by a more diffuse organization and the left by a more focal organization. These observations emerged from her clinical observations of patients with brain damage. Semmes suggested that the left hemisphere was comprised of more discrete, nonoverlapping processing modules, while the right was comprised of larger, more overlapping and less distinct processing modules. In accord with her hypothesis, she found that lesions outside the traditional sensorimotor cortex had a greater effect on tactile skills if the lesions were in the right hemisphere rather than the left. Other studies have provided some support for Semmes' hypothesis. For example, when multiple EEG sites are recorded from each hemisphere, there tends to be a greater degree of intercorrelation among right hemisphere sites than left hemisphere sites, suggesting greater functional coordination of diverse regions within the right hemisphere. There may also be relatively more white (myelinated) fibers in the right hemisphere (Gur et al. 1982). Since myelinated fibers are typically longer than unmyelinated fibers, this anatomic difference may allow greater integration of activity across different portions of the right hemisphere.

It is far from certain that either Sergent's theory of functional hemispheric differences or Semmes' theory of anatomic hemisphere differences is correct. But at least they suggest a specific direction. Perhaps large neural ensembles characterized by a high degree of interconnection will be optimal for problems involving low frequency stimuli. Perhaps large neural ensembles characterized by a lesser degree of interconnection would be optimal for solving problems involving high frequency stimuli. The investigation of the nature and mechanisms of hemispheric asymmetry may provide insights into what types of parallel designs are optimal for what types of problems.

5.3.3 Individual Differences

If the more focal or modular design of the left hemisphere in part underlies its greater verbal skill, those individuals with more modular organization than others may show relatively greater verbal skills. Let us examine this hypothesis in a few different ways. First, we consider sex differences. Women tend to be better than men at selected linguistic tasks, for example, verbal fluency, men at certain spatial tasks, such as mental rotation, though the skill differences are small. Are there sex differences in brain organization which might contribute to these cognitive differences?

Doreen Kimura (1983) has examined the effects of focal left hemisphere brain damage on language in adult men and women. The brain lesions were either entirely anterior to the central sulcus or entirely posterior. Striking differences were seen in the incidence of *aphasia* (language disturbance) as a function of lesion location. For men, the incidence of aphasia was equivalent after anterior lesions (40%) or posterior lesions (41%). For women, anterior lesions were much more apt to produce aphasia (62%) than were posterior lesions (11%). While these data suggest a more focal (and anterior) language system in women than in men, they offer only a very course-grained analysis of possible anatomical differences. A recent PET study (see Section 5.4 for a discussion of this imaging technique) noted sex differences consistent with Kimura's data (Azari et al. 1992).

Ojemann's (1983) electrical stimulation technique can potentially offer a more fine-grained analysis, but this technique has its own disadvantages. Only small numbers of subjects have been studied and these subjects had a pre-existing neural disorder (epilepsy) that could potentially influence the data obtained. In Ojemann's work, impaired naming ability, consequent to stimulation, was found to involve more widespread sites in males than females. Though based on quite limited data, Ojemann offers another tantalizing clue regarding the relationship of language skill to variations in anatomic localization. Study of bilingual individuals, each differing in the relative proficiency of skills in two languages, suggests "the area where naming in the least competent language was altered was substantially larger than the area in which naming the same objects in the more competent language was altered" (Ojemann 1983, pg. 194). Again, greater language skill may be linked with a more focal network.

If females have more focally organized language centers, one might expect to see different symptom patterns after left hemisphere damage. Two critical left hemisphere regions for speech are *Broca's area* and *Wernicke's area*. Damage to Broca's area results in a *nonfluent* aphasia characterized by production difficulties, short phrase length, and poor grammar. Damage to Wernicke's area produces a *fluent* aphasia, with poor comprehension and many speech errors. If these systems are more focal and discreet in women, a given brain lesion may be less apt to damage them both than would be the case for men. That is, men would perhaps be more apt to show symptoms of damage to both brain regions, resulting in what has been termed *global aphasia*. Women should show more pure syndromes. This appears to be the case, though the magnitude of the sex difference is rather small (Yeo 1989). Men do have relatively more global aphasia and women more fluent (Wernicke's) and nonfluent aphasias. Thus, sex differences in brain organization probably exist. t remains to be determined whether such differences may underlie sex differences in cognitive skills.

Analysis of age-related changes in language organization offers another perspective on the issue of concomitant variation in language skill and neural anatomic representation. Children are clearly less proficient than adults in verbal ability. Older adults clearly have more experience in producing language than younger adults. Is there any evidence for differences in neural organization of language skills as a function of age?

Table 5.2 shows the proportion of children rendered aphasic following left or right hemisphere brain damage as a function of age, as summarized from several

PERCENT SUBJECTS APHASIC

Age	Left Hemisphere Damage	Right Hemisphere Damage
5	83	26
6-16	73	2
>16	58	2

TABLE 5.2   The incidence of aphasia as a function of age and hemisphere damaged.

studies (Yeo 1989). In interpreting these data it is important to note there is little reason to believe that the size or locus of brain damage systematically varies with age. Changes in the incidence of aphasia most likely reflect individual differences in the organization of language in the brain. Two features deserve comment. First, there is a clear reduction in the frequency with which right hemisphere brain damage leads to aphasia between the first and second age groupings. Second, there is a gradual reduction in the incidence of aphasia after left hemisphere brain damage with advancing age. Let us consider these two effects separately.

The data for children of the youngest age groups suggest that there may be a shift from bilateral language representation to unilateral language representation over the early years of life. One hypothesis which helps account for this phenomenon is that the design optimal for acquisition of a symbol system may not necessarily be optimal for rapid and efficient manipulation of symbols (Goldberg & Costa 1981). There are other data consistent with this observation. Reading initially involves the right hemisphere more than the left, but this pattern shifts with advancing age. Some studies suggest that experienced musicians tend to show left hemisphere superiority for many musical functions, whereas naive musicians show a right hemisphere superiority (see Goldberg & Costa, 1981). For certain cognitive processes, shifts in cerebral lateralization may represent changes in maximal design efficiency.

Table 5.2 also shows that the incidence of individuals rendered aphasic after left hemisphere brain damage progressively declines with advancing age. Perhaps language becomes more focally organized within the left hemisphere with advancing age and skill. A given brain lesion would thus be less likely to strike language portions of the left hemisphere with advancing age, producing the declining incidence of aphasia with left hemisphere damage as shown. An increase in language skill seems to be accompanied by a progressively more focal organization. These results are consistent with Ojemann's data cited earlier. Perhaps increasing focal organization or modularity is the anatomic counterpart of an increasing cognitive automaticity. Such mappings may represent efficient neural organizations for manipulation of relatively invariant or static symbol systems (e.g., grammar, musical notation, and grapheme-phoneme relationships; see also Section 13.3).

	N	Mean Age
Fluent (Wernicke's)	423	61.8
Global	292	57.0
Nonfluent (Broca's)	547	51.9

TABLE 5.3   Mean ages of adult patients with different types of aphasia.

Similar considerations emerge from analysis within the adult age range of the changing pattern of type of aphasia with advancing age. There appears to be a relationship between type of aphasia and the age at which brain damage occurs. Table 5.3 shows this pattern, summarized from several studies (Yeo 1989). The mean age of individuals with fluent aphasia is significantly older than the mean age of individuals with a nonfluent aphasia. The age of global aphasics falls in between these two values. This same pattern is seen in patients with lesions from trauma, tumor or stroke. It thus appears that it is not the case that the lesions change with advancing age, but again, that the neural substrate of language changes with advancing age.

One hypothesis which may help account for this pattern is that certain language skills become more automatic with advancing age and additional practice and thus tend to be represented in more focal anatomic regions. With such increasing focalization, the chances that a given lesion will fall in that region will progressively decline with age. Let us consider the ways in which the grammatical and motoric aspects of language, which tend to be most impaired in a nonfluent aphasia, differ from the language comprehension or semantic deficits shown by a fluent aphasic. The rules by which we convert phonemes to motoric sequences for overt production and the rules by which we generate correct grammatical constructions do not change appreciably over one's lifetime.

In contrast, the semantic system is constantly changing with advancing experience, and at a practical level we see that vocabulary tends to increase throughout the life span. Due to their relatively unchanging nature, the skills underlying grammar and motoric language production would seem optimal for a focal or modular design characterized at a cognitive level by automaticity. The different nature of semantics would suggest that such design characteristics may not be optimal. It is not static. The pattern of age related changes seen in Table 5.3 may be plausibly attributed to a progressive shrinking of the linguistic systems underlying grammar and word production. As such systems shrink or become more focally organized, they become smaller and less likely to be damaged with a given brain lesion. Younger individuals, with relatively larger representations of these skills, would thus be more apt to show a nonfluent aphasia. This formulation is consistent with clinical data: when children suffer language problems after brain damage, it tends to be nonfluent aphasias (Brown & Jaffe 1975).

Arnold Scheibel (1990) and colleagues have analyzed dendritic branching patterns in Wernicke's and Broca's areas. Those branches of the dendrites closest to the cell body tend to be formed earliest in development, while more distal dendritic branches are formed later, through childhood and adulthood. They have noted more extensive distal proliferation of the dendritic system in Wernicke's area than in Broca's area. This observation is consistent with the notion that brain regions involved in semantic processing may be growing and developing more in later life than brain regions involved in production.

5.4   EPILOGUE AND REFERENCES

Different mappings or patterns of organization or processing elements have characteristic strengths and weaknesses. Through analysis of the organization of different brain regions performing particular computations, we can gain some insight into general principles of brain design. Further, systematic investigation of individual differences in brain organization may provide insights into the *highest* brain skills, including language. The next decade will surely witness major advances in our understanding of large collections of neurons due to the rapid progress of neuroimaging technologies and system modeling.

Neuroimaging technologies have developed extremely rapidly in recent years. Once limited to the venerable electroencephalograph, today's researchers have a variety of techniques available. The impact of these new approaches on the neurosciences is profound. We now briefly describe three new functional neuroimaging methods.

Magnetoencephalography (MEG) detects the magnetic fields generated by populations of neurons. Unlike the electrical potentials generated by these same populations, the magnetic field is not smeared by skull and scalp. Hence, greater resolution is possible, as well as the detection of subcortical events, at least in principle.

The imaging technology with the greatest impact has undoutedly been *positron emission tomography* (PET). A radioactive substance, typically O^{15}, is injected into the bloodstream. When a particular region of the brain is active, more O^{15} passes by sensitive detectors than when a region is at rest. Comparison of resting and active images can potenmtially reveal functional localization at a resolution of approximately 1 to 2 cm. For further discussion of this methodology see Stytz & Frieder (1991). For an account of the impact of the PET technology on our understanding of the neuroanatomy of language see Petersen & Fiez (1993).

Another new technique is *functional magnetic resonence imaging* (F-MRI), which has emerged from the technology of more standard structural imaging based on nuclear magnetic resonence (NMR). The alterations in blood chemistry associated with regional activation can be detected and, as with PET, compared to images of resting states to reveal potential functional localization. For a demonstration of the high resolution possible with this technique see Belliveau et al. (1991).

The interested reader may wish to pursue further some of the topics broached in this chapter. We began by considering insights into the nature of human brain function offered by evolutionary concerns. Traditional evolutionary analyses of brain anatomy or behavior (sociobiology) have recently been supplemented by evolutionary analyses of *psychological* mechanisms. Much of the recent work in evolutionary psychology is presented in *The Adapted Mind*, edited by Barkow, Cosmides, and Tooby (1992). They attempt to bring insights from evolutionary biology to bear on classic problems in psychology - from the nature of the human mind to the relationship of the individual to culture.

Neuroscience research is growing at a frightening pace. There are now more than 200 journals in the field. Keeping up with the literature is difficult even within a narrow area of specialization. One helpful guide is *Trends in Neurosciences*, a monthly journal of concise, up-to-date reviews. For a detailed review of all major aspects of neuroscience, see *Principles of Neural Science* (Kandel et al. 1992). For those who wish to gain a greater understanding of neural and synaptic function, consult *The Synaptic Organization of the Brain* by Gordon Shepherd (1979).

Much of this chapter focused on that portion of the neurosciences dealing explicitly with behavior. Kolb and Whishaw's (1990) classic text, *Fundamentals of Human Neuropsychology, 3rd ed.*, provides an overview of human brain organization and function and related research issues and methods. *The Computational Brain*, by Churchland and Sejnowski (1992), is a superb introduction to a particular approach to the neurosciences, one based on parallel distributed processing and neural nets. We develop these issues further in Chapters 11 & 12.

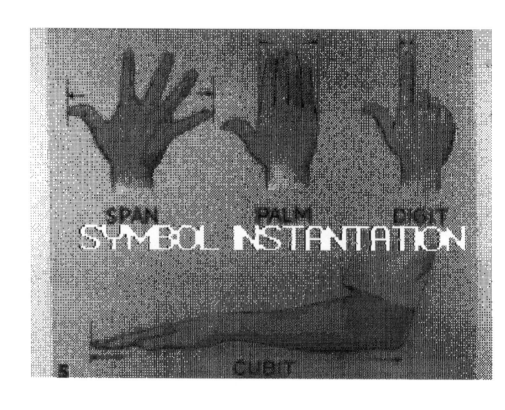

SPAN   PALM   DIGIT

SYMBOL INSTANTATION

CUBIT

5

Part II

SYMBOL BASED REPRESENTATION AND SEARCH

In Part I we introduced the possibility of a science of intelligent systems. In Chapter 1 we discussed the *foundations* of cognitive science, introducing the notion of intelligence as a "natural category." We also presented a brief history of the roots of cognitive science, philosophy, and artificial intelligence.

In Chapter 2 we examined the vocabularies for describing intelligence, including the automated formal system. Chapter 3 described a variety of issues related to the nature of representation and the role of representation in intelligent systems. Representations were classified as both symbolic and subsymbolic or connectionist. We briefly introduced each approach.

In Chapter 4 we addressed the constraint of formal models through the use of directly and indirectly obtained psychological evidence. In Chapter 5 we considered neurological methods of analysis. Throughout Part I we presented a number of studies that constrained the specifications of the formal system and, in the process, proposed a methodology of progressively refining and modifying our models. With this approach our explorations became a science: the explicit, systematic design and testing of computational models of intelligent behavior.

Part II continues our consideration of the constraints affecting automated formal systems. We pursue two important complementary issues, the design of explicit representations and the specification of search algorithms. These are important for creation of representational schemes for modeling intelligence. Part II culminates in Chapter 9, a presentation of the Newell and Simon methodology for building empirically based computational models. This research represents in many ways the keystone of the symbol based tradition, founding much of the subsequent work in this area.

The study of explicit symbol based problem solving architectures, reflects the research effort of the artificial intelligence community. Over the past 35 years, the research goal of this community has been to create data structures and search algorithms that can produce intelligent problem solving. As noted in Chapter 1, the AI goal is to produce intelligent artifacts and not necessarily to produce models that capture human intelligence. The AI community has had many important successes, particularly in the areas of expert or knowledge based systems, planning and robotics, and vision. There have also been important progress in the difficult areas of natural language understanding and learning. In support of their discipline, AI researchers have produced very high level representational schemes, including the logic, functional, and object-oriented programming languages.

And how do AI's successes relate to cognitive science? First, they offer an important collection of representational tools, as shown in Chapter 3. Second, although most AI researchers build programs without explicit use of psychological or linguistic studies or data, their results often reflect important intuitions and guesses about the nature of human intelligence. Finally, the history of cognitive science has shown how these AI tools can be adapted to the study of the science of intelligence. From the earliest cognitive modeling attempts by Newell and Simon (Sections 8.1 and 9.1) and through many efforts at understanding problems in vision, reasoning, natural language, and learning these techniques have been part of the cognitive scientist's tool kit.

We begin Chapter 6 defining trees and graphs. As examples of graphs we present semantic nets and parse trees for the analysis of English sentences. We introduce a number of important representations including conceptual dependencies, scripts, frames, schemas, and objects. The material of Chapter 6 is presented from an historical and evolutionary viewpoint.

Chapter 7 presents logic based representation schemes with the propositional and predicate calculi. Both these languages are founded in mathematics. The challenge to logic as a model for reasoning has led to the creation of logics for time and mode, as well as logics for nonmonotonic and default reasoning.

Chapter 8 presents *weak method* search mechanisms, beginning with the *general problem solver* (GPS). We introduce depth-first, breadth-first, and best-first search of trees and graphs with a number of examples.

Chapter 9 presents *strong method* or *knowledge intensive* problem solving. We examine in detail the Newell and Simon (1972) direct method analysis that first proposed a procedure based model of human problem solving. We demonstrate how procedures can be grouped together within problem solving "architectures" including the *production system* and the *blackboard*.

In Part V we use PROLOG to build and test many of the data structures and search strategies introduced in Part II.

Chapter 6

NETWORK AND STRUCTURED REPRESENTATION SCHEMES

A schema refers to an active organization of past reactions which must always be supposed to be operating in any well adapted organic response...

Frederick Bartlett (1932)

No ideas but in things.

William Carlos Williams

6.0 INTRODUCTION

In Chapter 3 we introduced the idea of representation and showed how it played an important part of human intelligence as well as offered a useful medium to model human knowledge and skill. Creating and developing the tools for knowledge representation, traditionally, is one of the chief concerns of the artificial intelligence researcher. Indeed, most of the methods and schemes of the present chapter were originally developed within the AI community.

For the cognitive scientist, beyond the arguments for representing knowledge and skill for a computational solution, there is the deeper issue of a clear and precise set of techniques and tools for modeling these skills for test, comparison, and possible extension. Representational schemes can support models of skilled activity in the full scientific sense.

We begin Chapter 6 with descriptions of trees, graphs, paths, and search spaces. Trees and graphs provide a mathematical basis for many of the representation schemes seen later in this chapter and throughout the remainder of the book. It is therefore important that we introduce graph theory first, so that we can establish a common vocabulary for describing these representational schemes. More formal definitions of the concepts needed for graph theory may be found in Luger and Stubblefield (1993).

In Section 6.2 we survey network representations, built on associational theories of meaning. These representations include *semantic networks* and *concep-*

tual dependencies. In Section 6.3 we present structured representations, including *frames, schemas,* and *scripts.* Chapter 6 ends with *object-oriented* representations, type hierarchies, inheritance, and exception handling.

6.1 A BRIEF INTRODUCTION TO GRAPH THEORY

6.1.1 Graph Theory

In Chapter 3 we introduced graphs with semantic nets (Figures 3.9, 3.10). A semantic net, as well as many of the other representations presented in Chapter 6, is an instance of a mathematical structure called a *graph*, with a mathematical system, called *graph theory* supporting its construction, manipulation, and use.

A *graph* is a set of *nodes* and *links*, sometimes called *arcs*, that connect the nodes. The nodes are usually *labeled*, in the sense that each node has a name. The links or arcs are often named by the pair of nodes they link. Sometimes, as in semantic nets, arcs are explicitly named by the relationship the two nodes have to each other. Examples of this in Figure 6.3 are the "isa" and "color" arcs.

A graph may also be *directed* in that an arc may connect or link one node to another, but not the second back to the first. This would be like "one way access" in a graph representing city streets, or "once a move is made, you can't take it back" in a game situation. We indicate that a graph is directed by putting arrowheads on the ends of the arcs to give the direction allowed. Arcs with no direction constraint indicators may be assumed to be traversed in either direction. Figure 6.1 is an example of a *directed labeled graph.*

A *path* is a sequence of steps through a graph that connects nodes by crossing the arcs between the nodes. We must restrict the path, of course, to the proper arc direction in a directed graph. Thus, in Figure 6.1 we have the path a,d,e,c,b,f. Two nodes are *connected* in the graph if there exists a path between them.

A *rooted graph* has a unique node, called the *root*, and there is a path from the root node to every other node in the graph. When we draw a rooted graph we often put the root at the top of the graph, above the other nodes. In a game graph, the root node is usually the start state of the game. A *leaf node* of the graph is a node that has no directed arcs outward to other nodes in the graph. In Figure 6.2 a is the root node and j, l, m, and n are among the leaf nodes.

The graph of Figure 6.2 is also called a *tree.* A tree is a rooted graph in which any two nodes have at most one path between them. We often use "family based" terms to describe the relationships between nodes in a graph. Thus in Figure 6.2, *parent* a has *children* b, c, and d; b, c, and d are also *siblings.* Node a is an *ancestor* of b, c, e, and f (in fact, of every node in the tree) and c, e, and f are *descendants* of node a.

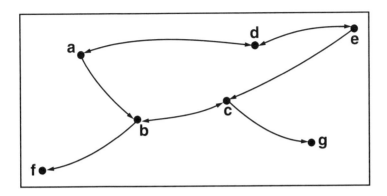

FIGURE 6.1   A labeled directed graph, including the path a,b,c,g.

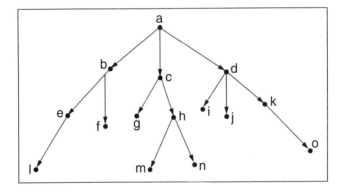

FIGURE 6.2   A rooted graph that is also a tree. The root is a; leaf nodes include e, f, g, and m.

6.1.2 Examples of Graphs: Semantic Nets and Parse Trees

Example 6.1: A Semantic Network

As we saw in Section 3.3.2, a *semantic net* is a symbol based representational scheme used to capture associations between concepts. It has been used extensively in AI programs for understanding language. Figure 6.3 presents a semantic network of a bird hierarchy. This is a labeled, directed graph, according to the previous definitions. We have "opened up" each node of the graph so it can contain its label. In this example the arcs are given explicit names, including *isa*, *covering*, and *travel*, placed next to the arcs.

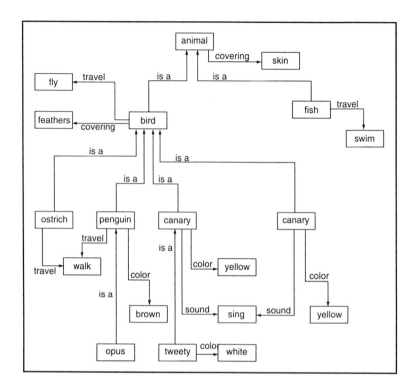

FIGURE 6.3   Portion of a semantic network describing birds and other animals.

The direction in the arcs indicates how "inheritance" will work for properties. For example, Tweety, canary, bird, feathers, is the path generated in response to the query asking whether Tweety has feathers. Inheritance, that search technique based on the fact that all property information is stored at the most general or highest node in the hierarchy, is an important search technique, as we see when we consider network and object based representations in Section 6.4.

Example 6.2: **Parse Trees**

Parse trees give us another application of graphs. English, like most languages, can be described by a set of grammar rules. These rules are used to determine when sentences in English are "well formed" or syntactically correct. Note that parse trees, while able to determine that "Green ideas sleep furiously" is syntactically correct (subject, verb, adjective modifying a noun, adverb modifying a verb, and so on), are often little help in determining whether a sentence is "meaningful." The area of meaning or semantics requires additional information, for instance, that found in a semantic net or frame system; we elaborate on these ideas in Chapters 13, 14, and 16.

We now present five simple grammar rules to describe the syntax of a subset of English sentences. After each grammar rule in English we present it in its symbolic form. The symbol <-> indicates that the symbols on each side of the arrow can replace one another. When one symbol follows another a space is between them, NP VP, to indicate that the noun phrase is followed by the verb phrase:

1. A sentence is a noun phrase followed by a verb phrase.
   S <-> NP VP
2. A noun phrase is a noun.
   NP <-> N
3. A noun phrase is an article followed by a noun.
   NP <-> ART N
4. A verb phrase is a verb.
   VP <-> V
5. A verb phrase is a verb followed by a noun phrase.
   VP <-> V NP

Next we specify a dictionary for our subset of English; this determines the sets of nouns, verbs, and articles we can use.

6. Let a and the be articles.
   ART <-> a
   ART <-> the
7. Let man and dog be nouns.
   N <-> dog
   N <-> cat
8. Let likes and bites be verbs.
   V <-> likes
   V <-> bites

Figure 6.4 represents the parse tree for this set of grammar rules and dictionary items. Note that wherever a symbol, such as NP, V, or ART, has alternate descriptions it has several possible children, called *or descendants*. Note also that when a symbol requires other symbols for its definition, such as S or VP, it generates connected children, called *and descendants*, linked as in Figure 6.4.

There are no direction restrictions on the arcs of Figure 6.4 This reflects the *is* or *may be replaced by* of <-> in the grammar rules. When S is replaced by NP VP and subsequently NP is replaced by a N, and N by a dictionary item, and so on, we are generating sentences from the grammar rules. Alternatively, when we

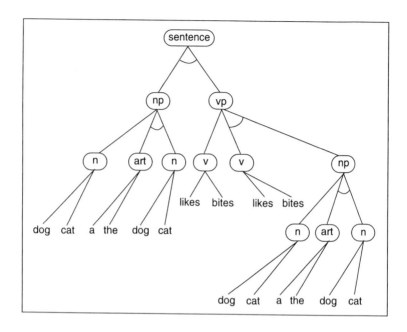

FIGURE 6.4   An and/or parse tree representing the grammar rules of Example 6.2.

take an already formed sentence such as "the cat bites the dog" and analyze its syntactic form we are said to *parse* the sentence to determine whether it is well-formed. Figure 6.5 is a parse tree for the previous sentence, and a subgraph of Figure 6.4, since every piece of the graph of Figure 6.5 is also a part of the graph of Figure 6.4.

With this example we can begin linguistic analysis of English expressions. As we enter the language chapters (Part IV) we see that sets of grammar rules and their corresponding trees are powerful tools for representing important aspects of language, for instance, its "deep structure" and the notion of tree trans-formations, or mappings, that can take a sentence in the active voice and map it into its equivalent passive voice form, or the transformation that can take a gen-eral grammar form and replace it with a particular sentence.

Of course there are multiple linguistic and psycholinguistic issues that we have not yet addressed. These include: context sensitivity of grammars, such as noun-verb agreement, the Chomsky hierarchy of grammars, control algorithms for parsing, the role of semantics, and the notion of "symbol as interpreted." These questions are addressed in subsequent chapters, especially Chapters 13, 14, and 17; the grammar-tree formalism just presented is helpful in addressing each of these topics.

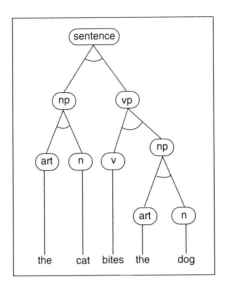

FIGURE 6.5   The and/or tree representing the parse of the sentence "the cat bites the dog." Note that Figure 6.5 is a subgraph of Figure 6.4.

6.2   NETWORK REPRESENTATIONAL SCHEMES

6.2.1   Early Work in Semantic Nets

Graphs have long been used in psychology to represent structures of concepts and associations. Seltz (1913, 1922) pioneered this work, using graphs to represent concept hierarchies and the inheritance of properties. He also developed theory of schematic anticipation which influenced AI work in frames and schemas. A number of researchers have used networks to model human memory and other intellectual performance (Anderson 1983b, Norman & Rumelhart 1975).

   Much of the research in network representations has been done in the arena of natural language understanding. Natural language understanding requires extensive knowledge. This includes an understanding of common sense, the ways in which physical objects behave, the interactions that occur between humans, and the way in which human institutions are organized. A natural language system must understand intentions, beliefs, hypothetical reasoning, plans, and goals. Because it requires such extensive knowledge, natural language understanding has always been a driving force for research in knowledge representation.

   The first computer implementations of semantic networks were developed in the early 1960s for use in machine translation programs. Masterman (1961) defined a set of 100 primitive concept types and used these to define a dictionary of 15,000 concepts. Wilks (1972) continued to build on Masterman's work in semantic network natural language systems. Other early AI workers who explored network representations include Ceccato (1961), Reitman (1965), and Simmons (1973). These approaches were not explicitly based on the analysis of human performance, although they did rely on the intuitions behind association-ist theories of meaning.

Quillian (1967) wrote an influential program which illustrates many of the features of early semantic networks. This program defined English words the same way that a dictionary does: in terms of other words. The components of the definitions are described in the same fashion. Rather than defining words in terms of formal axioms, each description leads to other descriptions in an unstructured, often circular fashion. In looking up a word, we traverse this "network" of other words until we are satisfied that we understand the original word.

Each node in Quillian's network corresponded to a word concept, with links to other word concepts that made up its definition. The knowledge was organized into *planes*, where each plane was a graph that defined a single word. Figure 6.6, taken from a paper by Quillian (1967), illustrates three planes that capture three different definitions of the word "plant:" a living organism: plant1, a place where people work, plant2; and the act of putting a seed in the ground, plant3.

The program used this knowledge base to find relationships between pairs of English words. Given two words, it would search the graphs outward from each word in a breadth-first fashion (Chapter 9.2) looking for a common concept or intersection node. The paths to this node represented a relationship between the two word concepts. For example, Figure 6.7 taken from the same paper, shows the intersection paths between the words cry and comfort.

Using this intersection path, where the numbers in the response indicate that the program has selected from among different meanings of the words, the pro-gram was able to conclude:

cry2 is among other things to make a sad sound. To comfort3 can be to make2 something less sad (Quillian 1967).

Quillian suggested that this approach to semantics might provide a natural language understanding system with the ability to:

1. Determine the meaning of a body of English text by building up collections of these intersection nodes.
2. Choose between multiple meanings of words by finding the shortest intersection path to other words in the sentence. For example, it could select a meaning for "plant" in "Tom went home to water his new plant" based on the intersection of the word concepts "water" and "plant."

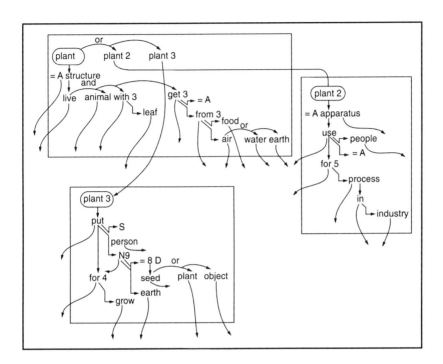

FIGURE 6.6   Three planes representing different definitions of *plant* Quillian (1967).

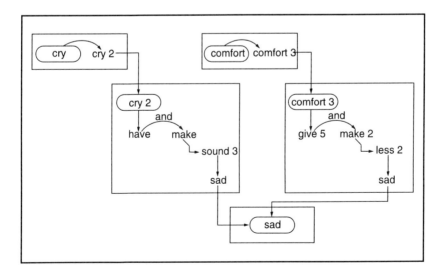

FIGURE 6.7   The intersection path between the words *cry* and *comfort* Quillian (1967).

3. Answer a flexible range of queries based on the associations between word concepts in the queries and concepts in the system.

Although this and other early work established the power of graphs to model associative meaning, it was limited by the extreme generality of the formalism. Knowledge is generally structured in terms of specific relationships such as object/property, class/subclass, and agent/verb/object. Research in network representations has often focused on the further specification of these relationships.

6.2.2 Standardizing Network Relationships

In itself, a graph notation of relationships has little advantage over predicate calculus (Chapter 7); it is just another notation for relations between objects. The power of network representations comes from the definition of links and associated inference rules which define specific relationships such as inheritance.

While Quillian's early work did establish most of the significant features of the semantic network formalism, including labeled arcs and links, hierarchical inheritance, and inferences along associational links, it proved limited in its ability to deal with the complexities of many domains. One of the main reasons for this failure was the poverty of relationships (links) that captured the deeper semantic aspects of knowledge. Most of the links in a semantic net represented extremely general associations between nodes and provided no real basis for semantic structuring. This is the same problem encountered in efforts to use pure predicate calculus (Chapter 7) to capture semantic meaning. Although the formalism is highly expressive and can represent literally any kind of knowledge, it is too unconstrained and places the full burden of constructing appropriate sets of facts and rules on the intuitions of the modeler.

Much of the work in network representations that followed Quillian's focused on defining a richer set of link labels, representing relationships that would more fully model the semantics of natural language. By implementing these semantic relationships of natural language as part of the formalism it was hoped that the represented information would achieve greater generality and consistency. Brachman (1979) states:

> The key issue here is the isolation of the primitives for semantic network languages. The primitives of a network language are those things that the interpreter is programmed in advance to understand and that are not usually represented in the network language itself.

Simmons (1973) addresses this need for standard relationships by focusing on the case structure of English verbs. In this verb oriented approach, based on work by the linguist Fillmore (1968), links define the roles played by nouns and noun phrases in the action of the sentence. Case relationships include agent, object, instrument, location, and time. A sentence is represented as a verb node, with various case links to nodes representing other participants in the action. This structure is called a *case frame*. In parsing a sentence, the program finds the verb and retrieves the case frame for that verb from its knowledge base. It then binds the values of the agent, object, and so on to the appropriate nodes in the case frame. Using this approach, the sentence "David fixed the chair with glue" might be represented by the network in Figure 6.8.

Using this technique, the representation language itself captures much of the deep structure of the natural language, such as the relationship between a verb and its subject, the agent relation, or that between a verb and its object. Knowledge of the case structure of the English language is part of the network formalism itself. When the individual sentence is parsed, these built-in relationships indicate that David is the person doing the fixing, and that glue is used to put the chair together. Note that these linguistic relationships are stored in a fashion that is independent of the actual sentence or even the language in which the sentence was expressed. Our natural language parser of Section 16.4.4 uses this method of case frames to build in semantic constraints.

Norman (1972) and Rumelhart and Norman (1973) took a similar approach in proposing network languages. A number of major research endeavors attempted to standardize link names even further (Masterman 1961, Wilks 1972,

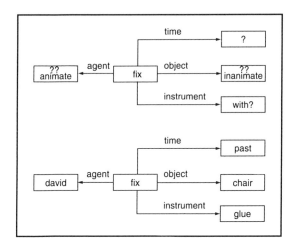

FIGURE 6.8   A case frame representation for the verb "fix," and its instantiation for the sentence "David fixed the chair with glue."

1972, Schank & Reiger 1974, Schank & Nash-Webber 1975). Each effort worked to establish a complete set of primitives that could be used to represent the deep semantic structure of natural language expressions in a uniform fashion. These were intended to assist in reasoning with language constructs and to be independent of the idiosyncrasies of individual languages or phrasing.

6.2.3 Conceptual Dependency Theory

One of the most ambitious attempts to formally model the deep semantic structure of natural language is Roger Schank's *conceptual dependency theory* (Schank & Reiger 1974). Conceptual dependency theory offers a set of four primitive concepts from which the world of meaning is built. These are equal and independent. They are:

ACTs	actions
PPs	objects (picture producers)
AAs	modifiers of actions (action aiders)
PAs	modifiers of objects (picture aiders)

For example, all actions are assumed to reduce to one or more of the primitive ACTs. These primitives, listed below, are taken as the atomic components of action, with more specific verbs being formed through their modification and combination.

ATRANS	Transfer of a relationship (give)
PTRANS	Transfer a physical location of an object (go)
PROPEL	Applying a physical force to an object (push)
MOVE	Movement of body part by owner (kick)
GRASP	Grabbing an object by an actor (grasp)
INGEST	Ingesting an object by an animal (eat)
EXPEL	Expulsion from an animals' body (cry)
MTRANS	Transfer of mental information (tell)
MBUILD	Mental making new information (decide)
CONC	Conceptualizing or thinking about an idea (think)
SPEAK	Producing sound (say)
ATTEND	Focus of sense organ (listen)

These primitives are used to define conceptual dependency relationships which describe meaning structures such as case relations or the association of objects and values. Conceptual dependency relationships are conceptual syntax rules and constitute a grammar of meaningful semantic relationships. These rela-

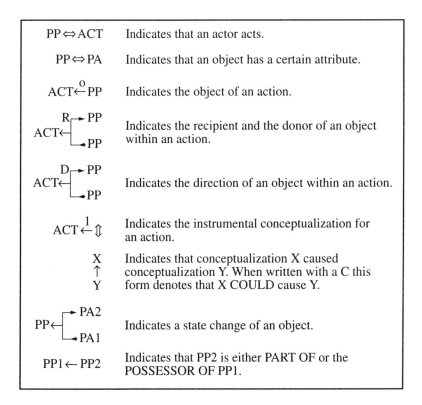

PP ⇔ ACT	Indicates that an actor acts.
PP ⇔ PA	Indicates that an object has a certain attribute.
ACT ←ᵒ PP	Indicates the object of an action.
ACT← R→PP / PP	Indicates the recipient and the donor of an object within an action.
ACT← D→PP / PP	Indicates the direction of an object within an action.
ACT ←¹ ⇕	Indicates the instrumental conceptualization for an action.
X ↑ Y	Indicates that conceptualization X caused conceptualization Y. When written with a C this form denotes that X COULD cause Y.
PP← →PA2 / PA1	Indicates a state change of an object.
PP1 ← PP2	Indicates that PP2 is either PART OF or the POSSESSOR OF PP1.

FIGURE 6.9 Some primitive conceptual dependency relationships. From Schank and Reiger (1974).

tionships can be used to construct an internal representation of an English sentence. A list of conceptual dependencies, from Schank and Reiger (1974), appears in Figure 6.9. These are intended to capture the fundamental semantic structures of natural language.

For example, the first conceptual dependency in Figure 6.9 describes the relationship between a subject and its verb; the third describes the verb-object relation. These can be combined to represent a simple transitive sentence such as "John throws the ball," as in Figure 6.10.

Finally, tense and mode information must be added to the conceptualizations. Schank supplies a list of attachments or modifiers to the relationships. A partial list of these are:

p   past
f   future

t	transition
k	continuing
t(s)	start transition
?	interrogative
t(f)	finish transition
c	conditional / negative
nil	present
delta?	timeless

These relations are the first level constructs of the theory, the simplest semantic relationships out of which more complex structures can be built. Further examples of how these conceptual dependencies can be composed to represent the meaning of simple English sentences appear in Figure 6.11.

Based on these primitives, the English sentence "Since smoking can kill you, I stopped" is represented as in Figure 6.12. In Figures 6.11 and 6.12 the symbols have the following meanings:

<--	indicates the direction of dependency
<=>	indicates the agent verb relationship
p	indicates past tense
INGEST	is a primitive act of the theory
o	object relation
D	indicates the direction of the object

Another example of the structures that can be built with conceptual dependencies is the representation of "John prevented Mary from giving a book to Bill," as in Figure 6.13. This particular example is interesting as a demonstration of how causality may be represented.

Conceptual dependency theory provides a number of important benefits. By having a formal theory of natural language semantics it reduces problems of ambiguity. Second, the representation itself directly captures much of natural language semantics.

Conceptual dependency theory attempts to provide a canonical form for the meaning of sentences. That is, all sentences that have the same meaning will be

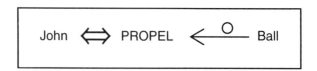

FIGURE 6.10   The conceptual dependency relationship for "John throws the ball." From Schank and Reiger (1974).

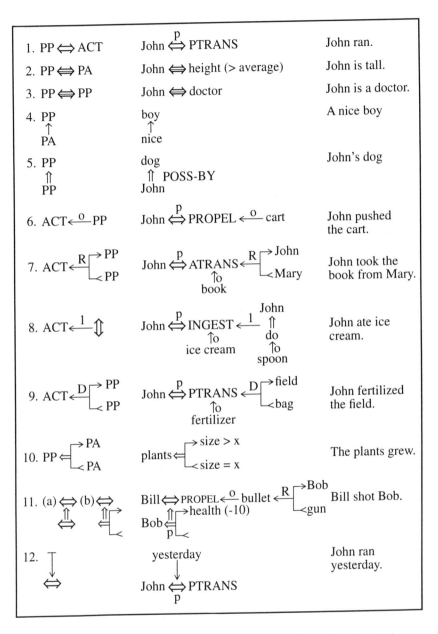

FIGURE 6.11 Some simple conceptual dependency relationships and their instantiation for simple English sentences. From Schank and Reiger (1974).

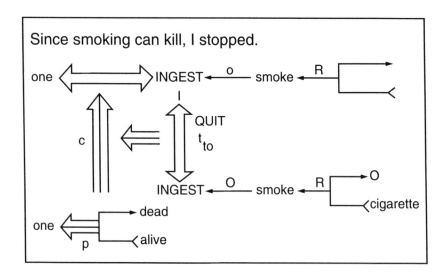

FIGURE 6.12   Schank and Reiger's (1974) conceptual dependency for the more complex sentence, "Since smoking can kill, I stopped."

represented internally by syntactically identical, not just semantically equivalent, graphs. This is an effort to simplify the inferences required for understanding or translating language. For example, we can demonstrate that two sentences mean the same thing with a simple match of conceptual dependency graphs. A representation that did not provide a canonical form might require extensive operations on differently structured graphs.

Unfortunately, it is questionable whether a program may be written to reliably reduce sentences to canonical form. As Woods (1985) and others have pointed out, reduction to a canonical form is computationally very difficult for most interesting cases. For instance, consider the complexity of representing the rather simple English sentence of Figure 6.12. Furthermore, there is no evidence that humans store their knowledge in any canonical form of semantic primitives.

Other criticisms of this point of view object to the computational price paid in reducing everything to such low level primitives; again, consider Figure 6.12. Also, the primitives used are not adequate to capture many of the more subtle concepts that are important in natural language. For example, the representation of "tall" in the second sentence of Figure 6.11 does not address the ambiguity of this term as carefully as is done in systems such as *fuzzy logic* (Zadeh 1983) or in a manner meaningful to humans. Tall has different meaning for an infant or for a professional basketball player. Tall can refer to moral character as well, "He walked tall through the difficult times." At 6'2" I feel people are tall if they are taller than I am. Perhaps some people think almost everyone is tall!

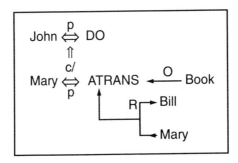

FIGURE 6.13 A conceptual dependency relation for the sentence, "John prevented Mary from giving a book to Bill." From Schank and Reiger (1974).

However, no one can say that the conceptual dependency model hasn't been fully automated and tested. More than a decade of research guided by Roger Schank focused on refining and extending this model. Two of the most important extensions of conceptual dependencies are the *scripts* and *mops* research, which are discussed in Section 6.5. Conceptual dependency theory is a fully developed model of natural language semantics with consistency of purpose and wide applicability.

6.3 STRUCTURED REPRESENTATIONS

6.3.1 Frames

With networks, we view knowledge as organized by explicit links or associations between objects. As one alternative, we can organize knowledge into more structured units that represent complex situations or objects in the represented world. These units are called *frames* or *schemas*. In a 1975 paper, Minsky describes the idea of a frame:

> Here is the essence of the frame theory: When one encounters a new situation (or makes a substantial change in one's view of a problem) one selects from memory a structure called a frame. This is a remembered framework to be adapted to fit reality by changing details as necessary.

According to Minsky, a frame may be viewed as a static data structure used to represent well-understood, stereotypical situations. Frame-like structures seem to organize our own knowledge of the world. We adjust to ever new situations by calling up information structured by past experiences. We then specially complete or revise the details of these past experiences to represent the individual differences for the new situation.

Anyone that has stayed in one or two hotel rooms has no trouble with entirely new hotels and their rooms. One expects to see a bed, a bathroom, a place to open a suitcase, a telephone, price and emergency evacuation information on the back of the door, and so on. The details of each room can be supplied when needed: for example, the color of the curtains or location and use of light switches. There is also default information supplied with the hotel room frame: no sheets, call housekeeping; need ice, look down the hall; emergency information, check the back of the entry door, and so on. We do not need to build up our understanding for each new hotel room we enter. All of the particulars that go into a description of a generic hotel room are organized into a single conceptual structure that we access when checking into a hotel.

We could represent these higher level structures directly as a semantic network by organizing it as a collection of separate networks, each of which represents some stereotypical situation. Frames, as well as object-oriented systems, provide a built-in vehicle for this organization, representing knowledge as structured objects consisting of named slots with attached values. This approach replaces the nodes of the semantic net with these more structured objects.

Figure 6.14 shows how a hotel bed might be represented using a semantic net and a frame. A **hotel bed** is a specialization of the general **bed** frame. Many of the values in both versions are default assumptions about hotel beds. These include the **size** and **firmness** relations. Specific instances of hotel beds may or may not inherit these values. The frame slot values may be factual information, pointers to other frames, or even attached procedures for performing some function.

The components of a hotel room can be described by a number of individual frames. In addition to the bed, a frame could represent a chair: expected height, 30 to 40 cm; number of legs, four (a default value); use, sitting. A further frame could represent the hotel telephone: This is a specialization of a regular phone in that billing is through the room, there is a special hotel operator (default), and a person can use the hotel phone to get meals served in the room. Figure 6.15 gives a frame representing the hotel room.

Each individual frame is a data structure that contains information relevant to stereotyped entities. The slots in the frame contain information including:

1. Frame identification information.
2. The relationship of this frame to other frames. The "hotel phone" might be a special instance of "phone," which is turn might be an instance of a "communication device."

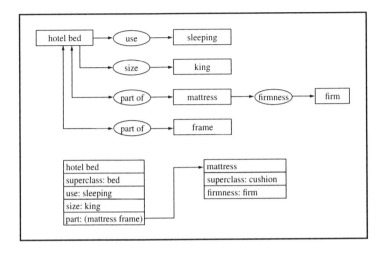

FIGURE 6.14 A semantic net and frame representation for a hotel bed.

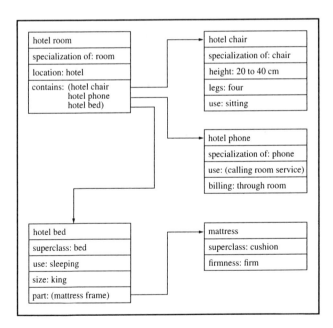

FIGURE 6.15 A portion of a frame description for a hotel room.

3. <u>Descriptions of requirements for frame match</u>. A chair, for instance has a height between 30 and 40 cm, its back higher than 60 cm, and so on. These requirements may be used to determine when new objects fit the stereotype defined by the frame.

4. <u>Procedural information on use of the structure described</u>. An important feature of frames is the ability to attach procedures or rules to a slot.

5. <u>Frame default information</u>. These are slot values which are taken to be true when no evidence to the contrary is found. For instance, chairs have four legs, telephones are push button, hotel beds are prepared by the hotel staff.

6. <u>New instance information</u>. Many frame slots may be left unspecified until given a value for a particular situation or needed for problem solving. For example, the color of the bedspread may be left unspecified in the definition of bed.

The presence, absence, or amount of detail in these six slots depends on the particular problem solving situation addressed.

Frame systems extend semantic networks in a number of important ways. Although the frame and semantic network descriptions of hotel beds in Figure 6.14 may be equivalent, the frame version makes it much clearer that we are describing a bed with its various attributes. In the network version, there is simply a collection of nodes and we depend more on our interpretation of the structure to see the hotel bed as the primary object being described.

Frame systems also make it easier to organize our knowledge hierarchically. In a network, every concept is represented by nodes and links at the same level of specification. Very often, however, we may like to think of an object as a single entity for some purposes and only consider details of its internal structure for other purposes. For example, we usually are not aware of the mechanical organization of a car until something breaks down; only then do we pull up our "car engine frame" and pursue the problem.

Frame systems support class inheritance. The slots and default values of a class frame are inherited across the class/subclass and class/member hierarchy. For instance, an hotel phone could be a subclass of a regular phone except that 1) all out of building dialing goes through the hotel switchboard for billing and 2) hotel services may be dialed directly.

Default values, assigned to selected slots, are to be used only if other information is not available. For example, assume that hotel rooms have beds and are, therefore, appropriate places to go if you want to sleep. If you don't know how to dial the hotel front desk try *zero*. Without evidence to the contrary, the phone may be assumed to be push-button. When an instance of the class frame is created, the slots are filled by querying the user, accepting the default value from the class frame, or executing an attached procedure to obtain the instance value.

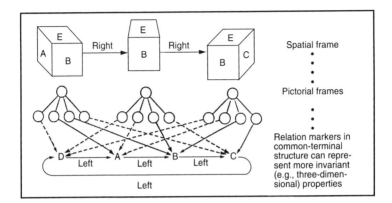

FIGURE 6.16   A spatial frame for recognizing a cube. From Minsky (1975).

As with semantic nets, slots and default values may be inherited across a class/subclass hierarchy. Of course default information can cause the data description of the problem to be nonmonotonic (Section 7.4) letting us make assumptions about default values that may be retracted later.

Minsky's own work on vision provides an example of frames and their use in default reasoning. Minsky's problem was one of recognizing that different views of an object actually represent the same object. For example, the three perspectives of the one cube of Figure 6.16 actually look quite different. Minsky (1975) proposed a frame system which recognizes these as views of a single object by inferring the hidden sides as default assumptions.

The frame system of Figure 6.16 represents four of the six faces of a cube. The broken lines indicate a particular face is out of view from that perspective. The links between the frames indicate the relations between the views represented by the frames. The nodes, of course, could be more complex if there were colors or patterns that the faces contained. Each slot in one frame can be a pointer to another entire frame. Also, since given information can fill a number of different slots, for example, face E in Figure 6.16, there need be no redundancy in the information that is stored.

Frames add to the power of semantic nets by allowing complex objects to be represented as a single structure rather than as a large network of individual nodes and links. This also provides a natural way to represent stereotypic entities, classes, inheritance, and default values. Although frames, like logical and network representations, are a powerful tool, many of the problems of understanding and building a complicated representation are solved by the model designer's skill and intuition.

6.3.2 Schemas

The terms *frame* and *schema* are almost interchangeable. Minsky first used the word *frame* to describe research at MIT in the 1975 paper cited in Section 6.3.1. Bartlett, the British psychologist, as noted in Chapter 3 used the word *schema* in 1932 to represent the information an informed human problem solver brought to a novel problem situation. In research institutions where modeling human performance is the most important focus, such as the Psychology Department of Carnegie Mellon University, *schema* seems to be the word of choice.

Hinsley, Hayes, and Simon (1977) at Carnegie Mellon, tested a group of algebra students in an attempt to determine why they were successful at solving word problems. They wished to determine what these students knew that allowed them to solve word problems never previously encountered. They ran a number of simple experiments.

First, they presented the students with a pile of index cards, each containing an algebra word problem. They asked their subjects to divide this pile into smaller piles, each pile containing a different "type" of problem. This the students did with general agreement, breaking the problems into *distance-rate-time, right triangle, work* problems, and so on.

Not only was there agreement on this classification, but students were able to make the classification with very little problem information. For instance, once hearing the words, "A boat travels ...," the typical subject would respond: "Oh, that is a river travel problem, where a boat goes one way on a river helped by the current and then against the current. It's a *distance-rate-time* problem."

The remarkable thing about this approach was that the experimenters began to understand the knowledge subjects had collected that allowed them to solve the problems. This included problem type knowledge, appropriate solution strategies and equations, and even default information such as "the river is assumed to be straight with constant current," "the boat is not slowly absorbing water," and "ignore the wind," unless, of course, the problem was given in the form of air travel with and against the winds!

The content of the knowledge schemas, supported by empirical evidence, was tightly linked to the ability to solve these classes of problems and seemed to represent what the successful algebra students took away from their classes. The Hinsley, Hayes, and Simon research did not take the next step, however, and attempt to build an explicit set of structures, perhaps with production rules, to better understand these skills.

In further work at Carnegie Mellon, Herbert and Dorthea Simon (1978) used rule sets to describe the differences between novice and expert algebra problem solvers, and Bhaskar and Simon (1977) described the support knowledge necessary to solve problems in engineering thermodynamics. These application areas were referred to as *semantically rich domains* because the successful student had

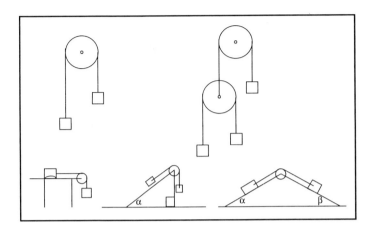

FIGURE 6.17   Five different pulley problem situations solved by experts in this problem domain. Solutions require resolution of forces with possible friction at different angles.

to possess a large amount of information about the application domain of the problems. Researchers began to fill in the details of these knowledge schemas successful subjects used in problem solving.

As an example of this use of knowledge schemas, researchers at the Artificial Intelligence Department of the University of Edinburgh (Bundy et al. 1979, Luger 1981) built schemas for describing the knowledge subjects had for successfully solving "pulley problems." These problem types, in the British education system, are taught as part of the applied mathematics or engineering curricula. In Figure 6.17 we show five different pulley problems from this application area. The students able to solve problems from this class would have the knowledge necessary to describe and relate the components of these problems. They would have learned the moment of inertia laws and friction equations for systems such as these. We present a typical problem, along with a subject's verbally reported solution, called a *protocol* (Section 9.1) in Figure 6.18.

On analyzing these solution protocols the researchers created sets of schemata that reflected the subjects understanding of the pulley problems. These were then run with the MECHO problem solver (Bundy et al. 1979) to see how the running program reflected the human subject's solution. Each schemata had three components:

1) <u>Declaration information</u> to create the needed entities of the application and to link the individual schema into a hierarchy of schemas. There was thus, for the problem of Figure 6.17, creation of a pulley, strings, lines, ends of lines, and so on. The pulley schema was linked into a

schemata hierarchy, including schemata for strings, time, and motion.

2) <u>Facts and inferences to create reasoning procedures</u> for each schema. The assertions for a string system, for example, divide the string into parts and assign a slope to each part. For the pulley it is asserted that the tension of one part of the string may be assigned to other parts if there is no friction in the pulley, and the acceleration of one part may be assigned to other parts if there is no stretch in the string.

3) <u>Default values</u> to give the schema support knowledge if no contradictory information is found in the problem statement. For instance the pulley is assumed to be frictionless and the rope not to stretch, since friction and stretch are components of the general formulae for acceleration. The pulley and rope are also assumed to have no mass.

The predicate calculus (Chapter 7) was an excellent representational medium for the facts and rule relations that made up the pulley problem schemas. The full notation in PROLOG is presented in Chapter 16 (Example 16.1). Further details of this approach to understanding problem solutions in applied mathematics may be found in (Luger 1981).

6.3.3 Scripts

We have just seen the importance of representing knowledge for applied problem solving. Another area where such knowledge representation is necessary is to create structures that will allow a computer to understand simple stories. As noted in the previous section, there is evidence that humans organize this knowledge into structures corresponding to typical situations (Bartlett 1932). If we are reading about restaurants, baseball, or politics, we resolve any ambiguities in the story in a way consistent with our knowledge of restaurants, baseball, or politics.

If the subject of a story changes abruptly, there is evidence that people pause briefly in their reading, presumably to change knowledge structures. It is hard to understand a poorly organized or structured story, possibly because we cannot easily fit it into any of our existing knowledge structures. There is also a tendency for errors in understanding when the subject of a conversation changes abruptly, presumably because we are confused over which context or schema to use in resolving pronoun references and other ambiguities.

A *script* is a structured representation describing a stereotyped sequence of events in a particular context. The script was originally designed by Schank (1977) and his research group as a means of organizing conceptual dependency structures into descriptions of typical situations. Scripts are used in natural language understanding programs to organize a knowledge base of the situations that we wish to understand. Most adults are quite comfortable in a restaurant, that

A man of 12 stone and a weight of 10 stone are connected by a light rope passing over a pulley. Find the acceleration of the man.

Protocol A

1. It's a standard pulley problem...
2. We'll draw a diagram, pulley with a light rope passing over.
3. Weight of 10 stone on one side so you draw a 10g force...
4. Don't worry about units because they are the same.
5. On the other side you've got a man, draw another block there...
6. With a force of 12g on it...
7. So you got an acceleration of the man draw it downward for convention.
8. Tension in the rope is...
9. Doesn't say the pulley is smooth so assume it is.
10. So tension T in the rope on both sides...
11. We've got the 10 gram...10 stone mass accelerating.
12. With the same acceleration as the man.
13. In the opposite direction...
14. Assuming it's an inextensible rope...
15. So resolving that and that...
16. Forces want to match on either side of the pulley.
17. We've got T - 10g times the mass of the block which is 10.
18. No-nonsense...we've got force equals mass times acceleration.
19. That's T - 10g = 10a
20. and T - 12g = -12a
21. We want to eliminate T...etc...

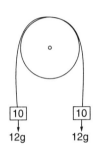

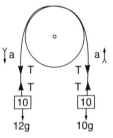

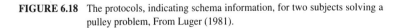

FIGURE 6.18 The protocols, indicating schema information, for two subjects solving a pulley problem, From Luger (1981).

is, they know what to expect and how to act. They are met at the entrance by the host, or by a sign indicating they should continue in, and find themselves a seat. A menu is available at the table, presented by the waitress, or they ask for it. We all understand the routines for ordering food, eating, paying, and leaving.

In fact, the restaurant script is quite different from other eating scripts such as the *fast food* model or the *formal family meal*. In the fast food model the customer enters, gets in line at the counter to order, pays for the meal before eating, waits about for a tray with the food, takes the tray and tries to find a clean table, and so on. These are two different stereotyped sequences of events and each would have a different, though related, script.

The components of a script are:

- Entry conditions: what must be true for the script to be called. This includes a restaurant that is open and a customer that is hungry.
- Results: facts that are true once the script has terminated. For example, the customer is full and poorer, the restaurant owner has more money. The fact that the customer is pleased is optional!
- Props: the "things" that make up the material support for the script. These might include tables, waitresses, and menus. This allows reasonable default assumptions about the situation. A restaurant is assumed to have tables and chairs unless stated otherwise.
- Roles: are the actions that each of the participants perform. The waitress takes orders, delivers food, and presents the bill. The customer orders, eats, and pays.
- Scenes: The script is broken into a sequence of scenes, each of which presents a time period. In the restaurant there is entering, ordering, eating, and leaving scenes.
- Tracks: the script may have different tracks. The example in Figure 6.18 is for a coffee shop which may share script components with the formal restaurant.

The elements of the script, the "pieces" of semantic meaning, are represented by Schank using conceptual dependency relationships. Placed together in a frame-like structure, they represent a sequence of meanings, or an event sequence. The restaurant script for this research is presented in Figure 6.19.

In using a script a program reads a small story about restaurants and parses it into an internal conceptual dependency representation. If the key concepts of this description match the entry conditions of the script, the program binds the people and things mentioned in the story to the roles and props mentioned in the script. The result is an expanded representation of the story contents, using the script to fill in any missing information and default assumptions. The program then answers questions about the story by referring to the script. The script supports

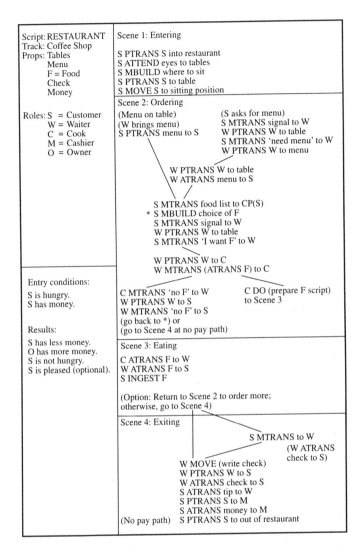

FIGURE 6.19   The restaurant script. From Schank and Abelson (1977).

reasoning with default assumptions, essential to understanding language.

Example 1:

David went to a restaurant last night. He ordered steak. When he paid he noticed he was running out of money. He hurried home since it was almost curfew.

Using a script, the computer can correctly answer questions including: Did David eat dinner last night? Did David use cash or a credit card? What could David have done to get a menu?

Example 2:

Sarah went out to dinner. She sat at a table and called a waitress who brought her a menu. She ordered scampi.

Questions that might be reasonably asked of this story include: Why did the waitress bring Sarah a menu? Was Sarah in a restaurant? Who paid? Who was the "she" that ordered the sandwich? This last question is difficult. The most recently named female is the waitress, an incorrect conclusion. Script roles help to resolve pronoun references and other ambiguities. These are deep problems, where the script with its structure of conceptual dependencies contains sufficient semantic information, in this case to determine who makes and who takes the food orders.

Scripts can also be used to interpret unexpected results or breaks in the scripted activity. Thus in Scene 2 of Figure 6.19 there is the choice point where either food is delivered to the table or it isn't. This allows the following example to be understood.

Example 3:

Kate went to a restaurant. She was shown to a table and ordered sushi from the waitress. She sat there and waited for a long time. Finally she got mad and left.

Questions that can be answered from this story, using the restaurant script, include: Who is the "she" that sat and waited? Why did she wait? Who was the "she" that got mad and left? Why did she get mad? Note that there are other questions that the script cannot answer, such as why people get upset when waiters do not come promptly.

Scripts, like frames and other structured representations, are subject to certain problems, including the "script match problem" and the "between the lines" problem. Consider Example 4, which could call either a restaurant or a concert script. The choice is critical because "bill" can refer to either the restaurant check or the playbill of the concert:

Example 4:

Peter had dinner at his favorite restaurant on the way to the concert. He was pleased by the bill because he liked Mozart.

It is often difficult to determine which of two or more potential scripts should be used. The script match problem is difficult in the sense that no algorithm exists for guaranteeing correct choices. It requires heuristic knowledge about the organization of the world into goals, beliefs and contexts; scripts only assist in the organization of that knowledge. The "between the lines" problem is equally difficult. It is not possible to know ahead of time all the possible occurrences that can be part of a script. For instance:

Example 5:

George was eating dinner at his favorite restaurant when a large piece of plaster fell from the ceiling and landed on his date...

Possible questions include: Was George eating a date salad? What did he do next? Was George's date plastered? As this example illustrates, structured representations can be inflexible. Reasoning can be locked into a single script, even though this may not be appropriate. These problems are not unique to script technology but are inherent to the problem of modeling semantic meaning. Eugene Charniak's (1972) research illustrated the amount of knowledge required to understand even simple children's stories. Consider a statement about a birthday party: "Mary was given two kites for her birthday so she took one back to the store." We must know about the tradition of giving gifts at a party. We must know what a kite is, and why Mary doesn't want two of them. We must also know about stores and their gift exchange policies.

Despite these problems, programs using scripts and other semantic representations can "understand" natural language in limited application areas. An example of this is a program which interprets messages coming over the news wire services. Using scripts for natural disasters, coups, or other stereotypic stories, programs have shown remarkable success in this limited but realistic application (Schank & Reisbeck 1981).

6.3.4 From Scripts to MOPs and Case Based Reasoning

One very important criticism of scripts is that they are too large and structured to be used as a model of human memory and learning. The restaurant script, for example, committed us to a complex structure for reasoning about restaurants. How would this relate to a script for a "fast food" chain? How would it relate to ordering pizza to be delivered? How does it relate to a dinner party or a bread line?

Psychological research (Bower et al. 1979) has shown that people often confuse events happening in similar local situations, such as happenings at the doctor's or dentist's or opthomologist's office. Learning in situations also seems to be more local than a full script might allow. For instance, how to cope in the waiting room of any medical office.

One solution to these problems is to develop a representation at a level below that of the full script, perhaps at the scene level of the script examples. These lower level structures can then be integrated into a larger and more complex context or organization. This can offer more flexibility for memory organization and learning.

Schank (1982) proposed just such a representation with *memory organization packets (MOPs)*. In fact Schank extends MOPs to include an entire theory of memory organization. A MOP is a dynamic knowledge structure that is constantly created and changed through learning and adaptation to new situations. Interactions with the world are indexed in memory by knowledge structures generalized from earlier experience. These episodes may be simultaneously indexed at a number of levels, relating information from any number of earlier knowledge structures.

The atomic unit of memory for a MOP is the *scene*. A scene is a sequence of actions occurring over a short time period in relation to a specific goal, such as within the restaurant script. Schank (1982) divides scenes into three classes, *physical*, *societal*, and *personal*. The physical scene takes place at a single simple location. The societal scene is organized by social relationships among people. Personal scenes are constructed around personal idiosyncratic goals. Organizational questions that can help us understand MOP categories are: What happened physically? What social conventions were involved? and What happened to the individual participants? Figure 6.20 offers example MOPs in each of these categories.

Events are rarely single isolated scenes; rather scenes are woven together into understood patterns, possibly directed at some goal. For instance the individual MOPs of Figure 6.20 might be brought together in the context of being in a store in order to buy dinner that will go with the evening's sporting entertainment on TV. As the reader can see, the ability to bring together novel representation structures from previously worked through scenes offers a more flexible representational structure than did scripts.

There have been a number of interesting computational models of human reasoning situations using the MOPs representational scheme. CYRUS (Kolodner 1984) was an attempt to model the reasoning of a politician Cyrus Vance. The MOPs used reflected an attempt to deconstruct Vance's knowledge, politics, and bias. Other applications of MOPs include text understanding (Lebowitz 1986), and mediation (Kolodner 1993).

A description language for generalization and learning are two of the important results of the evolving MOP paradigm. An important outgrowth of this is the representation and encoding of problem histories in *case based reasoning*. This

MOP Situation: to get dinner and watch sports on TV.
MOP CATEGORIES

PHYSICAL	SOCIETAL	PERSONAL
M-GROCERY-SHOP	M-PURCHASE	M-MAKE-DINNER
get - cart	select - purchase	heat - oven
examine - freezer	take - to - register	get - TV - dinner
select - item	exchange - for payment	cook - dinner
check - out		eat - and watch TV

FIGURE 6.20   Examples from Schank (1986) showing MOPs from the physical, societal, and personal classes.

type problem solving is based on adaptation of previous solutions to new situations. The storage of previous case information includes the situation description, ways in which the cases differ, and how each case is handled.

Case based reasoning provides a valuable tool for representation in problem solving. For instance, in order to improve game playing skills, the human expert often studies previous game openings, bidding situations, or end games. In diagnosis, human experts are often trained through the analysis of case histories or by observing human experts actively solving problems. In teaching, however, we may find the most important application of case based problem solving. Schank (1986) and his associates are using case based reasoning as a tool for instruction and training. In the context of student enquiry, these researchers propose relevant concrete situations, as well as a method for their retention and generalization, to provide what must be learned for addressing new situations.

Advantages of case based reasoning include the fact that the problem solver can access previously used potential solutions. In diagnosis, this is equivalent to saying: What did I do when I was in this situation before? The problem solver can also integrate information from diverse case histories as well as adapt old fixes to new problems.

There remain a number of difficult issues in case based reasoning research. The first is how to identify interesting cases. At one extreme, based on perceptual data, every aspect of a situation offers a measure to describe it. It is not always obvious which features of a situation should be used to index it for later use. Second, since no two situations are ever exactly alike, how can stored cases be suitably generalized to fit new situations? Third, given the multitude of experienced situations, how can these be indexed and stored for timely retrieval? Finally, how can partially matching cases, or even knowledge of previous failed cases be adapted to fit new situations?

In an attempt to answer these problems a taxonomy of top level goals, intentions, and problems, as well as a base level structure of atomic scenes, must be assumed or built. Second, stored cases must be suitably generalized so that they reflect a meaningful action sequence rather than a single special purpose intervention. Third, there must be a mechanism that allows, in an acceptable time period, the retrieval of appropriate cases. Finally, there must be a repair mechanism that can create new solutions from previous partially flawed cases. Case based reasoning is currently a very active component of artificial intelligence research.

6.4 OBJECTS, TYPE HIERARCHIES, INHERITANCE, AND EXCEPTIONS

Structured representations, such as frames, schemas and scripts, evolved from simple semantic networks, with organization and standardization added to the network structures. Another important addition found in structured representations is the ability to attach procedures as part of an object's specification. These procedures could be instructions for how to use the schema information, such as how to determine the acceleration of the system (Section 6.3.2) or how to create a graphic image for an object, as in Figure 6.16.

The first computer based implementation of frame or schema systems was in the *object-oriented* language *Smalltalk* created at Xerox PARC in the early 1970s. Smalltalk was an early interactive computer language, like Logo at MIT, designed for children's use and communication. Later object languages include C++ and CLOS (the Common LISP Object System, Steele 1989).

In an object based representation, every entity is an object. Objects have internal slots, containing descriptive information about themselves, and built-in procedures, called methods, that define their use. Objects also contain hierarchy information to describe how they are linked with individual instances and relate to other objects and classes of objects in the system. Objects can communicate with each other through their methods. We saw this approach taken for the pulley schemas in Section 6.3.2.

Inheritance across class or type hierarchies is an important feature of almost all structured and object-oriented representations. Inheritance is implemented through relations such as a type hierarchy, as well as through links including ISA,

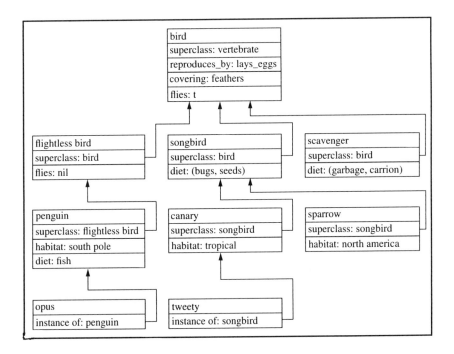

FIGURE 6.21   An inheritance representation for a bird hierarchy. From Luger and Stubblefield (1993).

AKO (A Kind Of) and SUPERC (SUPER Class). Figure 6.21 shows a frame or object based representation of knowledge about birds with directed arcs indicating the inheritance hierarchy. Individual birds with their specific differences, often called *instance values*, are the leaf nodes of the graph.

A common, although controversial, use of inheritance systems is to implement default information and exceptions. In the birds example, we have established a class, a flightless bird. If we assume that the inheritance algorithm searches the hierarchy in a bottom up order, it would encounter the flightless bird frame before the bird frame and correctly infer that Opus cannot fly.

Here we have established flying as a default value for birds, with the subclass flightless bird overriding that default value for all birds. Several authors (Brachman 1985a; Touretzky 1986) have pointed out a number of anomalies that arise in inheritance, particularly in multiple inheritance hierarchies and in the use of inheritance to implement defaults.

The network of Figure 6.21 illustrates tree inheritance. Each node has only a single parent. Tree hierarchies are relatively well-behaved since an algorithm need only search up the hierarchy until it encounters the desired property. If it reaches the top node and still has not found the desired property, it fails. There is no need for decisions in the inheritance search. The situation is complicated, however, if we allow multiple inheritance, where an entity can inherit information from more than one parent.

Multiple inheritance is supported in many knowledge representation schemes. It is an important "expressive" feature since modeled things often belong to more than one class. In the network of Figure 6.22, we have added the class cartoon character and made Opus an instance of this class as well as of the penguin class. Cartoon characters have a habitat of the funny papers. It is no longer clear whether Opus lives at the south pole or in the funnies.

This problem may be solved in several ways. Most inheritance systems allow the programmer to specify the order with which parent nodes are searched; here we could require that Opus inherit the properties of cartoon character before those of penguin. This solution is undesirable in that we must rely on knowledge of the order of search to resolve ambiguities of inheritance.

Furthermore, this would not help us if there were two conflicts and we wished to resolve one in favor of penguin and the other in favor of cartoon character. For example, we may state that penguins eat herring and cartoon characters eat hamburgers. How could we represent the fact that Opus lives in the funnies and eats fish? One solution is by defining a new class for Opus, called cartoon-penguin, that is a subclass of both penguin and cartoon character and that would resolve these conflicts explicitly, as in Figure 6.23. This solves the problem, although introduction of new classes seems artificial and can lead to further problems and to restructuring the network with later additions.

Besides the anomalies introduced by multiple inheritance, there are problems that occur when inheritance is used to implement default information and exceptions. In the network of Figure 6.21, the class flightless bird is introduced to handle exceptions to the rule that birds fly. It seems reasonable to treat class membership as a transitive relation: from the fact that penguin is a subclass of flightless bird and flightless bird is a subclass of bird, we should be able to infer that penguin is a subclass of bird.

Unfortunately, if we allow this intuitively appealing inference and add this link to the graph, we confuse the inheritance of the *flies* property. We may prohibit these inferences, but this may be no more appealing than the other remedies to multiple inheritance anomalies.

There is a deeper problem with the use of inheritance to handle defaults and exceptions: it compromises the nature of the definitions themselves (Brachman 1985a). It seems appropriate to view a frame as a definition of a class. However, if we define a penguin as a bird that doesn't fly, what is to prevent us from asserting that a block of wood is a bird that doesn't fly, doesn't have feathers, and doesn't lay eggs? This careless use of inheritance to implement exception handling illustrates the subtleties that arise in building representational structures.

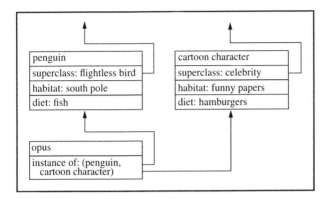

FIGURE 6.22 An ambiguous multiple inheritance representation. From Luger and Stubblefield (1993).

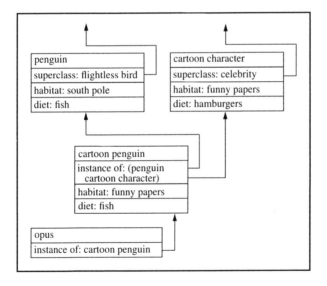

FIGURE 6.23 The introduction of a new class to resolve the ambiguity of Figure 6.22. From Luger and Stubblefield (1993).

One solution would be to restrict the representation to a form that does not allow these problems, such as tree inheritance without exception handling. This also eliminates much of the power of inheritance. Another approach is to carefully examine and refine the semantics of the representation itself. Touretzky (1986) has reformulated inheritance and has attempted to resolve many of these ambiguities. Other solutions use the predicate calculus representation with inference mechanisms such as nonmonotonic logic, truth maintenance, or belief revision. This is the material of the next chapter.

6.5   EPILOGUE AND REFERENCES

Research on representational schemes is a large and open field that lies at the heart of modern artificial intelligence as well as cognitive science. In this chapter, we examined the major issues in and techniques for representation. We encourage the reader to go to the journal and conference proceedings sources of the representational schemes presented in this chapter.

We also refer the reader to several important commentaries on the entire representational issue, in particular to Woods' (1985) important paper *What's in a Link: Foundations for Semantic Networks*, and Mylopoulos and Levesque's (1984) paper *An Overview of Knowledge Representation*.

There are a number of books that can help with the advanced study of these issues. *Readings in Knowledge Representation*, by Brachman and Levesque, is a compilation of classic articles in this area (Brachman 1985b). Many of the articles referred to in this chapter may be found there, although they were referenced in their original source. *Representation and Understanding* by Bobrow and Collins (1975) is another influential collection of articles.

Most of the representational schemes described in this chapter have their origins in the artificial intelligence research community and their main reason for existence as a medium for implementing the structures and strategies for complex problem solving on a computer, such as designing a program to understand English. We encourage the reader to go to the AI literature to examine these applications. As an introduction to these research areas we recommend the *Encyclopedia of Artificial Intelligence* edited by Stuart Shapiro (1992).

Chapter 7

LOGIC BASED REPRESENTATION
AND REASONING

The essential quality of a proof is to compel belief...

Fermat

Logic is not the end of wisdom, it is the beginning...

Spock, Star Trek VI

7.0 INTRODUCTION

In this chapter we introduce mathematical logic, identify the traditions that produced it, and see how it can be used as a representational medium and support for human reasoning and problem solving.

Aristotle, as mentioned in Section 1.3, identified the inference rule *modus ponens* as a general form for thinking, wherein when certain facts and relations are true, other facts necessarily follow. Thus "All good football players are skilled athletes" and "David is a good football player" lead necessarily to "David is a skilled athlete."

Aristotle also proposed that when the middle premise, "David is a good football player," in the example above, is weakened, perhaps by trying to quantify "good," then so is the eventual conclusion. This model of reasoning, often requiring confidence values or some measure of uncertainty, is also presented in this chapter along with some algorithms for its implementation.

Some of the modern mathematicians responsible for the *propositional* and *predicate calculus* as we present them here are George Boole, Gottlob Frege, Bertrand Russell and Alfred North Whitehead, and Alfred Tarski. Boole was one of the first mathematicians to treat logic as a formal system. Frege's analysis of the extension of concepts led to an early version of predicate calculus. Russell and Whitehead used this calculus in an attempt to establish a foundation for modern mathematics. Tarski created a set based semantic model under which the meaning of predicate expressions is defined by the set of possible worlds in which those expressions are true.

We, of course, are most interested in how this mathematical language might be used to help understand intelligent systems. First, it gives us a vocabulary for describing inference and belief. Second, it is a language for writing specifications which can be automated. Third, as seen in Chapter 3, it provides another representational scheme for modeling human knowledge and skill.

We begin this chapter (Section 7.1) by seeing how deductive inference and predicate calculus can be used as a tool to describe human reasoning. In Section 7.2 we introduce propositional calculus and in Section 7.3 predicate calculus. In Sections 7.4 and 7.5 we present alternative logics for problem solving, including nonmonotonic and abductive inferencing schemes.

7.1   LOGIC AS A MODEL FOR PROBLEM SOLVING

From the time of Aristotle philosophers have studied "the laws of thought." These have included the law of identity, the law of non-contradiction, the principle of the excluded middle, and so on. In addition, philosophers have studied various principles of reasoning and inference, including rules for deduction, induction, and abduction. Philosophical views have differed, however, regarding the nature and origin of logical principles. Some philosophers have regarded logical principles as descriptive, others as prescriptive, while many modern philosophers treat logic as a purely formal discipline.

Originally, philosophers believed that logic was a descriptive discipline. Aristotle, for example, held that logic studies the universal laws of being (as opposed to the laws of a particular science). The empiricists, particularly J.S. Mill, believed that logic was an empirical study of the "laws of thought." More recent philosophers, however, have rejected this view. Logicians such as Frege and Boole, for example, argued that logic cannot be an empirical study, since it is concerned not with how humans actually think, which is often quite erratic, but rather with how humans ought to think. Logical principles express, in other words, the rules of *valid* or *rational* thought.

Modern mathematical logicians tend to regard logical principles neither as descriptive nor prescriptive but rather as merely formal. One version of this formalist position is *conventionalism*: the view that logical principles hold by virtue of the conventions for using logical symbols. The conventionalist believes, for example, that the law of non-contradiction, which states that a proposition and its negation cannot both be true, holds solely by the conventions which define the meaning of the logical symbol not. If we define the symbol not differently the law of non-contradiction disappears and we get a different set of logical laws.

As noted in Section 1.3, logic has played two important roles in AI and cognitive science. First, the invention or discovery of efficient automated inference rules has made possible the construction of a variety of powerful tools. These tools include automated theorem provers, expert systems, planners, and even a logic based programming language -- PROLOG. Second, logical systems have provided an important medium for modeling the patterns of knowledge and reasoning used in particular types of problem solving. An automated logic system, for example, allows the cognitive scientist to give a precise specification to the knowledge content, organization, and operational structure of problem solving.

Psychologists have shown many times that humans, even humans expert in a testing area, do not always use sound mathematical reasoning methods. One of the most important of these studies, introduced in Section 5.1, was designed by Peter Wason (1966) and is discussed in Johnson-Laird and Wason (1977). In their experiment, pictured in Figure 7.1A, four cards, with **A**, **D**, **4**, and **7** showing, were placed before the subject. The subject knows that all cards have a letter on one side and a number on the other. The subject is asked which cards need to be turned over to find out whether the following rule is true or false: *If a card has a vowel on one side then it has an even number on the other side.*

Most subjects, even those trained in logic, get this task wrong! The answer, of course, is the first and last cards (The details of the logic are worked out in Example 7.2). Similar tasks confirmed, though in a slightly weakened form, these results; for example in Figure 7.1B, envelopes are placed on the table, and the subject is asked which envelopes must be turned over to check the hypothesis: *If a letter has a stamp on it then it is sealed.* Even people working in postal inspection failed this task, although they performed better than did subjects with the card task. In this type of task, knowledge of the area seems to weaken the effect. The use of logical reasoning seems dependent on the semantic knowledge and implicit skills of the problem area.

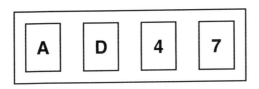

FIGURE 7.1A The four cards used in the Wason (1966) experiment.

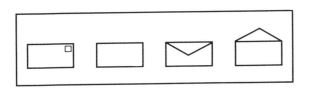

FIGURE 7.1B The envelope experiment, an isomorph of experiment of Figure 7.1A.

Staudemayer (1975) also shows that subjects' responses to logic based situations are biased by their experience. By simply changing the application context of functionally equivalent syllogisms, subjects alter their "logical" responses.

This type of finding is consistent with the distinction made between the functional architecture and the representational state of a system. The functional architecture specifies the set of algorithms available. But as Pylyshyn (1984) points out, human behavior is also influenced by representational or semantic states. This is apparently what is happening in the case of the logic problems. The subjects do not perform solely in terms of their functional architecture, that is their recognition of logical relationships. They tend to use past experiences as well as analogous situations to solve logic based problems such as these.

There are (at least) two other reasons why human intelligence does not always conform to mathematical patterns of reasoning. The first is that predicate expressions capture only declarative or propositional content. In the abstractions that form predicates, we often strip away many of the human (embodied) aspects of a description. For instance, loves(george, kate), as a predicate, does not represent much of the meaning that the human use of the words entail. Even an extension of the meaning through inference rules makes mockery of the subject:

loves (X, Y) ← isa (X, male) ∧ isa (Y, female) ∧ ....

Shakespeare's sonnets certainly do it better, but even they sound shallow when compared to love and responsibility as only we humans can know and experience. When so much of the meaning is abstracted out with this predicate naming exercise, it is not surprising that much of the meaning is lost also.

The second reason human reasoning doesn't always conform to mathematical patterns of inference is that for humans *if.. then..* statements often reflect relations of causality or evidence. The mathematician, however, sees *if.. then..* as expressing a set of possible truth values that when used in an inference are part of truth preserving operations.

For example, the English sentence "if a bird is a cardinal then it is red" may be written as the predicate expression:

For all X (cardinal (X) → red (X))

This expression may be changed, through a number of truth preserving operations, to the equivalent expression:

For all X (not (red (X)) → not (cardinal (X))).

These two expressions are logically equivalent, that is, the second is true if and only if the first is true. This *truth equivalence* overlooks the more subtle evidential relationships connoted by the original English. For example, if we were to look for physical support or evidence for the truth of these statements, the fact that this sheet of paper is not red and not a cardinal is support for the second expression. By the equivalence of expressions, these facts also support the first expression. Thus we come, by the rules of logic, to the odd conclusion that the whiteness of this paper supports the redness of cardinals.

Another simple example where the if.. then.. logical form does not capture the ordinary sense of implication is the following.

$$(2 + 2 = 6) \rightarrow (\text{Clinton is the president of the USA})$$

This implication is mathematically true because by the rules of logic a false premise implies every consequent. Nonetheless, in our normal frame of reference we regard this statement as false if not meaningless.

In pointing out the anomalies in mathematics based reasoning as a model for human thinking it is also important to recall where the mathematical system is sufficiently robust to encode human knowledge and reasoning. We now have a large number of expert systems applications in the commercial marketplace. Many of these rule based applications use the propositional and predicate calculus to encode human knowledge, as well as use mechanical reasoning to produce search and conclusions that compare favorably with the best human successes. We conclude that in these instances the representational medium, as well as its logical results, are a "sufficient" model of the equivalent human performance.

A number of researchers have addressed the discrepancies between human and mathematical reasoning. We consider some of these, especially the design of *truth maintenance systems* and *nonmonotonic logics* in Section 7.4. We present a selection of algorithms for *abductive inference* in Section 7.5. But before we see these extensions of mathematical logic, we describe propositional calculus in Section 7.2 and predicate calculus in Section 7.3. We make our presentation using a number of examples and attempt to avoid too heavy a dose of definitions. If readers would like a more precise set of specifications for these mathematical systems, they may find them in Turner (1984) or Luger and Stubblefield (1993).

7.2   THE PROPOSITIONAL CALCULUS

7.2.1   The Components of the Language

Propositional calculus and predicate calculus are, first of all, languages. That is, they offer an alphabet of symbols that may be composed into words and sentences. These sentences may then be interpreted to convey meaning about things and relationships outside themselves. There is a mathematical system that underlies the interpretation of these sentences.

We adopt the convention of using uppercase letters near the end of the alphabet to represent propositional symbols. These symbols are refer to propositions in the world. The propositions are required only to be sentences that can be verified to be true or false, such as "my car is red" or "Nixon is president." Incomplete or meaningless statements, such as "my car" or "ble is xti," are not propositions. Propositions are statements that may be verified as either true or false.

We next describe a set of connectives to link propositions together. This set of connectives include ∧ for *and* or *conjunction*; ∨ for *or* or *disjunction*; ¬ for *not* or *negation*; → for *implies* (sometimes read "if.. then.."); and ↔ for *if and only if*. More complex sentences in the propositional calculus may be formed from the propositional symbols and the connectives just described. Note that parentheses "( )" may be used to clarify the meaning of a sentence. The parentheses are called *improper symbols* of the language. They are used solely to construct sentences, including showing in an unambiguous manner which connectives relate to which symbols. As we will soon see (P ↔ Q) ∨ R is quite different from P ↔ (Q ∨ R). We refer to well-formed sentences in the propositional or predicate calculi as *WFFs* or *well-formed formulae*.

We have a straight forward method for determining whether a complex expression is a sentence of the propositional calculus: *An expression is a sentence if all its components are symbols or sentences properly joined by one of the legitimate connectives.* Consider, for example the following expression:

$$((P \vee Q) \wedge R) \leftrightarrow \neg (P \vee \neg (Q \rightarrow R))$$

It is well-formed since:

      P, Q, and R are propositions and thus sentences,

      P ∨ Q, the disjunction of two sentences is a sentence,

      (P ∨ Q) ∧ R, the conjunction of two sentences is a sentence.

      Q → R, the implication of one sentence by another is a sentence

      ¬ (Q → R), the negation of a sentence is a sentence,

      P ∨ ¬ (Q → R), the disjunction of two sentences is a sentence,

      ¬ (P ∨ ¬ (Q → R)), a negation of a sentence is a sentence,

      and finally, the association of two sentences using ↔ is a sentence.

7.2.2 A Semantics for the Propositional Calculus

So far we have given the formal specification of the syntax of the language. As a result we can tell whether any expression of propositions is well-formed. We now come to the more interesting issue of how a legitimate expression in the language may have meaning. This is referred to as the *semantics* of the language.

A proposition is a statement about the world. For example, P might denote "it is raining" or Q denote "the ground is wet," and P → Q "if it is raining then the ground is wet." Each simple proposition will either be true or false, denoted "T" or "F," given some state of the world. Furthermore, each complex sentence will be T or F depending on its simple components, that is, the T or F of its propositions and the particular connectives used. Thus the truth value of propositional sentences depends on their interpretation in some *possible world*.

More formally, given a set of propositional formulas describing some state of affairs, an interpretation is a mapping from the simple propositions, P, Q, R, ..., into a possible world where each simple proposition is assigned T or F. The T or F defines each elementary proposition as true or false in that world. The truth or falsity of the complex formulas, e.g., P ∨ ¬ (Q → R), is determined from the truth values of its simple constituent propositions by applying the rules for propositional connectives we describe in this section.

A set of propositional formulas may or may not all be true under a particular interpretation. Interpretations which make a set of formulas true are said to *satisfy* those formulas. Such a satisfying interpretation is called a *model* of those formulas. It is a model in the sense that it represents a possible state of the world in which all the formulas are true.

Note that a particular proposition might change its truth value when mapped into another possible world. We can define sets of actions in the blocks world (Example 7.1) by rules which retract certain propositions and assert new ones. The changed set of propositional formulas resulting from using such an *action rule* will thus correspond to a new state of the world. That is, because the satisfying interpretations or models for this changed set of formulas comprise a different set of possible worlds.

We next offer a simple problem where a set of proposition symbols represent blocks on a table.

Example 7.1: **A Blocks World Example**

Figure 7.2 presents a number of blocks stacked on a table and on each other. A robot arm is grasping one of the blocks. A set of propositions to represent this scene might include:

Proposition Symbols:	Propositions in English:
M	Block **a** is on the table.
N	Block **d** is on the table.
O	Block **b** is on block d.
P	Block **c** is on block a.
Q	Block **e** is on block c.
R	Block **e** is clear on top.

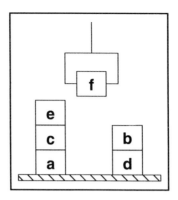

FIGURE 7.2   The blocks world used in Example 7.1.

Proposition Symbols:	**Propositions in English:**
S	Block **b** is clear on top.
T	Block **f** is held.
¬ U	Not (Hand is empty).
¬ V	Not (Block **a** is clear on top).
¬ W	Not (Block **c** is clear on top).
¬ X	Not (Block **e** is held).
etc.	

These propositions each have a mapping of "T" into the world of Figure 7.2. Note also that it is possible to construct propositions which are not true in this world, for instance, ¬M or U. Finally, this blocks world may at any period of time be described as the conjunction of all the propositions that are true at that instant. For the blocks of Figure 7.2, we have:

$$M \wedge N \wedge O \wedge P \wedge Q \wedge ..... \wedge \neg X \wedge .....$$

The truth values for complex propositional formulas can be worked out with *truth tables*. The columns on the left hand side of the truth table represent the elementary propositions and their truth values. The series of columns gives every possible combination of truth values for the elementary propositions. Columns on the right are used to represent the truth values for complex propositions. The truth value listed under a complex proposition in a certain row represents the value of that proposition when the elementary propositions have the truth values defined by the left side of the row. Thus, in Figure 7.3, P and Q are either T or F. There are four possible combinations of the truth values of P and Q. The truth value for connective ∧, with P as T and Q as F is F, the second row, T, F, F.

Figure 7.4 gives the truth tables for ∨ and →. Note that only one kind of "or" is defined here, namely *inclusive or*, which is T when either one OR BOTH disjuncts are true. *Exclusive or*, called *exor*, is F when both disjuncts are T.

The truth table for → defines the meaning of that connective. Note that the definition states that from a false premise (P is F) either a T or an F conclusion can be CORRECTLY (T) drawn. This, of course, is *the definition* for the connective → in the propositional calculus, and may or may not conform with intuitions about "implies." The reader is invited to work out an alternative mathematical scheme where → might have a different definition.

The truth value for a compound sentence is made up of the truth values of its components. Suppose we wanted to test the truth value of the expression:

$$(P \rightarrow Q) \leftrightarrow (\neg Q \rightarrow \neg P)$$

This could be determined by working through the truth table shown in Figure 7.5. The truth assignments of each piece of the expression are worked out in each successive column moving from left to right. Finally, at the far right, the truth value of the full expression is T. This is an example of logically equivalent expressions.

P	Q	P ∧ Q
T	T	T
T	F	F
F	T	F
F	F	F

FIGURE 7.3   The truth table for the conjunction of propositions P and Q.

P	Q	P → Q
T	T	T
T	F	F
F	T	T
F	F	T

FIGURE 7.4   The truth table for the inference P implies Q.

P	Q	¬ Q	¬P	¬ Q → ¬ P	P → Q	(¬Q → ¬P) ↔ (P → Q)
T	T	F	F	T	T	T
T	F	T	F	F	F	T
F	T	F	T	T	T	T
F	F	T	T	T	T	T

FIGURE 7.5   The table for analyzing the truth value of a compound sentence in terms of the truth values of its components.

7.2.3 Reasoning in the Propositional Calculus

We now describe *truth preserving inference rules* in propositional logic. These are rules which allow the derivation of new propositions from an existing set of propositions, where the new propositions are guaranteed to be true whenever the existing set of proposition is true. More precisely, an inference rule is truth preserving if it produces propositions which are satisfied by every interpretation which satisfies the original set.

One of the most commonly used inference rules is *modus ponens. Modus ponens* allows us to deduce Q from P and P → Q. We state this as

$$P ; P \rightarrow Q \therefore Q$$

We prove that *modus ponens* is truth preserving with the truth table in Figure 7.6. Note that the final column of this figure has value T for all truth values where the premises, P and P → Q are both true, in this case the top row of Ts. The proof of several other inference rules, *modus tolens, and-elimination* and *or-introduction*, is similar and left as an exercise.

$P \rightarrow Q ; \neg Q \therefore \neg P$	*modus tolens*
$P \wedge Q \therefore P$	*and-elimination*
$P \therefore P \vee Q$	*or-introduction*

Relationships such as these can be used to change propositional calculus expressions into syntactically different but *truth value* (or *logically*) equivalent expressions. These identities may then be used instead of truth tables to prove that two expressions are equivalent: We simply find a sequence of inference rules that can transform one expression into the other. Russell and Whitehead's work

P	Q	P → Q	P ∧ (P → Q)	(P ∧ (P → Q) → P)
T	T	T	T	T
T	F	F	F	T
F	T	T	F	T
F	F	T	F	T

FIGURE 7.6   The truth table proof of the validity of the inference rule modus ponens.

in the *Principia* (Whitehead & Russell 1950) did just this. Newell and Simon (1956) created an early AI program, the *Logic Theorist,* that automated this proof process. Their program was able to generate many of the proofs in the *Principia.* Newell and Simon (1963a, 1963b) also compared the protocols of humans solving logic problems with solutions produced by computer programs (Section 9.2).

Example 7.2: **The Wason Card Task.**

Let us consider again the card task of the Johnson-Laird and Wason experiment from Section 7.1. The four cards, with **A, D, 4, 7** showing as in Figure 7.1A, were presented to the subject. We can represent the two propositions:

P   The card has a vowel on one side.
Q   The card has an even number on one side.
P → Q   If the card has a vowel on one side then the card
             has an even number on one side.

There could, in fact, be more propositions added to the set of assumptions we have made here. These might include the facts that every card has two sides and that all cards in our task have a number on one side and a letter on the other. Now consider the truth table for P → Q, found in Figure 7.4.

The only values that need be checked to confirm whether P → Q is true or false are those in the T F F line of the truth table. Thus we must determine what is on the other side of the cards with the **A** and the **7** showing. The **A** must be checked to be sure that with P true Q is not false. The **7** must be checked to be sure that with Q false P is not true.

Example 7.3: **Deduction from a False Premise**

Another discussion point from Section 7.1 was the truth of the proposition:

$(2 + 2 = 6) \rightarrow$ (Clinton is the president of the USA) .

This implication will be true no matter what the year is, that is, whether Bill Clinton is actually President of the United States or not. To see this, consider again the truth table for *implies* in Figure 7.4. The third (F T T) and fourth (F F T) lines of this table each have F as the truth value of the premise, or the first column. Our premise, P, here is $(2 + 2 = 6)$. With this false premise, the final Ts in each line inform us that we can correctly conclude anything regardless of the middle T or F in each situation.

Example 7.4: The Blocks World, Continued

Consider again the blocks world of Example 7.1 and Figure 7.2. We created a set of propositional symbols to represent aspects of that world. We will now add an *action rule,* in the form of a production rule (Section 3.3.5), to let us change states in that problem solving application. Action rules differ from inference rules in that inference rules allow us to deduce additional things that must be true, given the description of a particular state of the world, whereas action rules describe a change in the state of the world. Action rules have the form:

CONDITIONS $\Rightarrow$ ACTIONS

where $\Rightarrow$ indicates a world altering transformation that can be executed anytime the conditions are true.

The first action rule for picking up block **e** is:

Pick_up **e**: $(R \wedge U) \Rightarrow add(X) \wedge add(W) \wedge add(\neg U) \wedge delete(U)$

That is, block **e** may be picked up if it is clear on top and the hand is empty. The result of this pick up is that **e** is held, the hand is not empty, and block **c** is clear on top. The operators **add** and **delete**, corresponding to the Prolog operators **assert** and **retract** (Part V), change our description of the world. Since R and U are true we can fire this action rule, resulting in a state in which X, W, and $\neg U$ are now part of our world description.

We now present a similar rule for putting block **f** down on the table. We have to create another propositional descriptor for "block **f** is on the table," call it Y. Now we have:

Put_down **f**: $true \Rightarrow add(U) \wedge add(Y)$.

More action rules can be added to *pick up, put down,* and *stack* the blocks.

We can also create rules to *reason* about states of this world. For example, suppose we have the following propositions:

O1	Block **a** is on block **b**	O2	Block **c** is on block **b**
O3	Block **d** is on block **b**	O4	Block **e** is on block **b**
O5	Block **f** is on block **b**		

The following rule allows us to infer that block **b** is clear:

$$\neg O1 \land \neg O2 \land \neg O2 \land \neg O2 \land \neg O2 \to S$$

We ask as an exercise that the inference rules for this example be extended. Meanwhile we note a number of issues:

a. Propositional calculus as a representational medium is a bit awkward in this example. Note all the different rule sets that have to be created for picking up, putting down, and stacking EACH block. This representational inflexibility is partly addressed with use of the predicate calculus.

b. Nothing has yet been said about the order for applying action rules to descriptions of the world to accomplish a task. This is considered under the topic of search, presented in Chapter 8.

c. It is seldom obvious what must be stated or omitted in any description of the world. The size, color, weight, and other aspects of the blocks were ignored in our description. Is everything ignored considered irrelevant? Perhaps stacks can only be three blocks high? Is everything not false considered to be true? Does everything not addressed by a rule such as *pick up* or *put down* remain unchanged? These are deep issues in representation and reasoning, coming under the headings of *circumscription*, *default assumptions*, the *closed world assumption*, and *non-monotonic reasoning*. They are addressed in Sections 7.4 and 7.5 and still remain major research topics in artificial intelligence.

We move now to a more powerful and *expressive* representational language, the predicate calculus, where some of the above issues are answered.

7.3   THE PREDICATE CALCULUS

7.3.1   An Introduction

The predicate calculus adds several important features to the propositional calculus. Perhaps the most important is that predicate logic gives us a finer grained vocabulary for describing the structure of the world. Recall that the most primitive referring terms in propositional logic, the propositional symbols P, Q, R, ... refer to sentences which are either true or false. Sentences in predicate logic, however, can be expressed as predicate descriptors applied to objects. For example, the fact that block **b** is clear can now be expressed as clear(b). The fact that block **e** is on block **c** can be expressed as on(e, c). This finer grain allows individual predicates to express complex relationships more easily.

For example, suppose we wished to describe the weather for each day of a particular week. In the propositional calculus we might say that P denotes the statement "it rained on tuesday," Q denotes the statement "it was sunny on wednesday," and R the statement "it rained on friday." These symbols are all atomic and unrelated in the propositional language, except that they all refer to weather during a week, but this IS NOT CAPTURED in the language's symbols.

In the predicate calculus we can radically improve on this. We first select a predicate name, called weather. We can give this predicate two arguments, first the day and second the kind of weather on that day. Our representation now is: weather(tuesday, rain), weather(wednesday, sun), weather(friday, rain). Now these descriptions are indeed related, at least by the fact that all descriptions for weather are called weather. To find the value of weather for any day we simply check the second argument where the first is the name of the day. This will also be a useful assist in designing reasoning rules for the weather.

The next powerful addition to the propositional calculus is the use of variables that stand for values from a domain of possible values. We might decide that the variable D stands for the days of the week and W for the value of the weather. By convention our variable names will begin with upper case letters. Thus Day or Weather could also have been variable names. Names of specific objects or values are called *constants*. Constants will begin with a lower case character. For example, tuesday and sun are constants.

Thus the predicate expression weather(D, W) stands for an indeterminate proposition, that the weather on day D is W, where D and W are as yet unspecified. When tuesday is substituted for D and sun for W we get the specific proposition: weather(tuesday, sun). That is, one way to turn a predicate expression into a proposition is by supplying it with constants as arguments. As we will see shortly, the truth value of the proposition weather(tuesday, sun) will be either true or false, depending on the actual values in the possible world where this predicate expression is interpreted. To have power in the propositional calculus equivalent to what variables give us in the predicate calculus we would have to exhaustively create propositions for each possible situation of weather type and day. As we saw in the blocks world Examples 7.1 and 7.4, this would be, to say the least, tedious and clumsy!

We can constrain our predicate pattern to represent sunny days by using the pattern weather(D, sun). We might also find the value of the weather on friday by constraining W with the pattern weather(friday, W) and then reasoning with this set of predicates and some inference system to find a possible correct value for W. There is no fixed convention for the form that predicates may take. They are rather intended to be flexible enough to fit the problem we wish to represent. For instance, if the weather at a particular time of day is important, we could extend our weather predicate to have three arguments: weather(D, W, T). The order of the arguments is not important as long as we pick a convention and remain consistent. Thus we could have said: weather(tuesday, 11, rain).

Another component of predicate calculus is the *function*. Function calls can be used as arguments of a predicate. Here, just as in ordinary usage, it is understood that a function applied to specific argument(s) returns a value. The description of functions is much like that of predicates. It has a name in lowercase letters and any possible number of arguments enclosed in parentheses and separated by commas. An example is the two argument function plus(X,Y). This function might be part of the expression

    cost(Name, Retail, Tax, plus (Retail, Tax))

When its arguments are constants, it may be evaluated:

    cost(car, 10000, 500, plus (10000, 500))
    cost(car, 10000, 500, 10500).

Functions need not be numerical. For example, the non-numerical function father could be used as an argument to a predicate, where the function call father(david) is later replaced by its value, perhaps george. The expression:

    parents(X, mother (X), father (X))

could be bound to constant values and then evaluated:

    parents(david, mother (david), father (david))
    parents(david, kate, george)

if these people were child, mother, and father in the given world description.

7.3.2 Predicate Calculus Syntax

The predicate calculus is a language of symbols and sentences that is meant to be interpreted. Definition of expressions begins with the alphabet of symbols and builds up complex structures from these atomic pieces. There are many conventions for creating this symbol system. We will adopt and use one that is consistent with the programming of this representation (Chapters 15 and 16). We intend to be informal in our presentation of the predicate calculus. For the reader desiring a supporting set of definitions and a bit more mathematical rigor, we recommend Luger and Stubblefield (1993) or any other presentation of mathematical logic.

There are five classes of predicate calculus symbols: *truth, constant, variable, predicate,* and *function* symbols, which we now describe:

1. *Truth symbols,* **true** and **false**, are reserved symbols,
2. *Constant symbols* are symbols with the first character lowercase,
3. *Variable symbols* are symbols beginning with an uppercase character,
4. *Predicate symbols* are symbols beginning with a lowercase character,
5. *Function Symbols* are symbols with the first character lowercase.

Note that three of these symbol types, *constants, predicates,* and *functions,* have an identical lexical form. Their full definition thus involves the different roles which they play in forming predicate calculus expressions.

Predicate calculus terms are either constant or variable symbols or function expressions. A function expression is a function symbol followed by its arguments, a list surrounded by parentheses and separated by commas. The *arity* of a function is the number of its arguments.

We have now assembled all the pieces and can go next to describe the smallest language unit in the predicate calculus, namely, the *atomic sentence*. With these units and the connectives of the language we assemble larger more complex expressions, just as we did in the propositional calculus.

A *predicate expression* is a predicate symbol followed by its arguments, a list of terms surrounded by parentheses and separated by commas. The arity of a predicate is the number of its arguments. Predicate expressions of the same name and different arities are considered different.

A *predicate expression* is an *atomic well-formed formula (WFF)*. The truth values, **true** and **false**, are well-formed formulas (WFFs). For any WFFs s and t:

1. If s is a WFF, then so is its negation, $\neg$s,
2. If s and t are WFFs, then so is their conjunction s $\wedge$ t,
3. If s and t are WFFs, then so is their disjunction s $\vee$ t,
4. If s and t are WFFs, then so is their implication s $\rightarrow$ t
5. If s and t are WFFs, then so is their equivalence s $\leftrightarrow$ t,
6. If X is a variable and s a WFF, then $\forall$X s is a WFF,
7. If X is a variable and s a WFF, then $\exists$X s is a WFF.

Statements 1 to 5 are the same as we saw in the propositional calculus. We must explain the symbols introduced in 6 and 7. Their names are the *universal* (6) and *existential* (7) *quantifiers* for variables. The *universal quantifier* indicates that the predicate expression is true for every instance of the variable. For instance, ∀ X friendly (X), indicates that all X in the domain of definition of X must have the property "friendly." The *existential quantifier* (7) indicates that there must be at least one value of the variable, across its full domain of definition, for which the predicate is true. For instance, ∃ X friendly (X), indicates that there is at least one value of X for which friendly (X) is true.

In the expression ∀X s every symbol in s is said to be within the scope of the quantifier ∀X. The same thing is true for the expression ∃X s. All the occurrences of X inside s are said to be *bound* by ∀X or ∃X. For example, in the expression

∀X (p(X) → q(X))

the occurrences of X inside the predicates p and q are both bound. A WFF is said to be *closed* when all the variables in it are within the scope of a same named quantifier, that is, when all variables are *bound*. In what follows we will only be concerned with *closed* WFFs.

The *scope* of a variable, the extent of its meaning in an expression, is always limited to the scope of the quantifier which binds it. This makes variables in predicate logic quite *local*. People with experience of low-level computer languages sometimes see variables as always *global* and accessible from anywhere in a program. The exact opposite is true in the predicate calculus. The scope of variables is restricted by the scope of the quantifiers that enclose them.

We now provide examples of the previous definitions. Suppose plus and times are functions with arity two. Let equal and foo be predicate symbols with arity two and three, respectively.

1. plus and times are examples of function symbols.
2. plus(X,Y) is an example of a function expression and a term.
3. equal is a predicate symbol.
4. equal(plus (2,3) , 5) is a predicate expression and an atomic WFF.
   (Note that the function plus(2,3) is not a sentence!)
6. foo(george, kate, plus (1,1)) is also an atomic WFF.
7. ∀X ∀Y (foo(X, Y, plus (3,4))) is an atomic WFF.
8. (foo(george, kate, plus (1,1)) → (equal (plus (3,2) , 5) ↔ true))
   is a non-atomic WFF since all its components are WFFs, appropriately joined by logic connectives.

This concludes our specification of the syntax of the predicate calculus. We now illustrate the expressiveness of predicate logic with one further example. We then describe a semantics for the predicate calculus and show how pattern matching may be used as part of reasoning with this representation.

Example 7.5: **A Biblical Genealogy**

The predicate calculus can describe a simple world. The domain is a set of family relationships in a biblical genealogy.

> mother (eve, cain)
> mother (eve, abel)
> father (adam, abel)
> father (adam, cain)
> $\forall$ X $\forall$ Y (father(X, Y) $\lor$ mother(X, Y) $\rightarrow$ parent (X, Y))
> $\forall$ X $\forall$ Y $\forall$ Z (parent(X, Y) $\land$ parent(X, Z) $\rightarrow$ sibling(Y, Z))

We have used the predicates mother and father with arity 2 to describe the parent child relationship. These atomic sentences are sometimes called *facts* describing a particular world. The two implications are *rules* relating facts. They express relationships that hold across all variable instances in the domain. In particular, the rules can relate the father and mother facts to conclude new facts such as sibling(cain, abel). We can also add to this set of specifications to describe larger and more interesting aspects of a problem domain.

7.3.3 Predicate Calculus Semantics and Inference

Before proceeding to more complex applications of predicate logic, we describe two more features: first, the mechanism by which predicate sentences can refer to a world situation, and second, the method used to deduce new information about that world. We call the first feature the definition of a *semantics*, and the second the implementation of an *inference mechanism* for the predicate calculus.

First we show how a set of closed WFFs can be mapped onto a *possible world*. Recall that such a mapping is called an *interpretation* of the set of predicate calculus expressions. This mapping is an assignment of the elements of the WFFs to the world situation such that:

1. A *domain* or set O is defined comprising the objects of this world.
2. Each constant term is assigned to an element of O.
3. Each function term is defined on m element tuples of O and is a mapping from those tuples to a unique element of O called its evaluation.
4. For each predicate p with m arguments, we define the extension of p, E_p, as follows. $E_p = \{<o_1, o_2, ..., o_m>, <...>, ...\}$ where each o_i is an element of O. $p(o_1, o_2, ..., o_m)$ is true if $<o_1, o_2, ..., o_m>$ is in E_p and false otherwise.

Observe that possible worlds are described here in terms of objects and sets or relations of objects. The meaning of a predicate in an interpretation is defined *extensionally*, that is, by the set of objects or object tuples to which the predicate correctly applies. Thus, for example, we define the meaning of the word *red* in a given world as the set of things that are red in that world. We discuss the weakness of this extensional approach to semantics in Section 17.4.

Example 7.6: The blocks World, Again

We now construct the predicate calculus version of the blocks world problem of Figure 7.2, cast earlier as a propositional calculus specification. We emphasize in Example 7.6 the expressive power of the predicate calculus and will see later (Example 7.7) a new ease in inferencing. Note that we still need quite a number of individual formulas to cast the basic facts of the blocks world.

block (a)	block (b)	block (c)
block (d)	block (e)	block (f)
holding (f)	clear (e)	clear (b)
on (d, table)	on (a, table)	on (c, a)
on (e, c)	on (b, d)	

Encoding the details of a particular state of the blocks world still requires considerable work! However, the power of the predicate calculus begins to appear as we formulate general rules. Here we state two: specifications for the hand to be empty and for a block to be clear.

$$\neg \exists Y (holding(Y) \rightarrow hand\_empty)$$
$$\forall X (\neg \exists Y (on(Y, X)) \rightarrow clear (X))$$

We now describe the semantics of the connectives and quantifiers in the predicate calculus. We do this much the same way we did for the propositional calculus. The value of each atomic WFF is either true or false. Let s and t both be WFFs. The value of ¬s is true if and only if s is false. If s and t are both true then s ∧ t is true. If either s or t is false then s ∧ t is false.

We make similar truth value assignments for the other connectives as well as for the universal and existential quantifiers of variables. For example, the value of ∀ X predicate(X) is true only if predicate(X) has a mapping of T for all substitutions for X from the domain of the variable X; otherwise, it is false.

Again, as in propositional logic, an interpretation which makes all the formulas in a set of WFFs true is said to *satisfy* that set. A *satisfying* interpretation of a set of formulas is called a *model*. It is a model in the sense that it is the description of a world in which all the WFFs are true.

Sets of formulas for which no models exist are called *unsatifiable* or *inconsistent*. For example, the formula (likes(george,wine) ∧ ¬likes(george,wine)) is inconsistent. Upon reflection it can be seen that no interpretation will make both sides of the conjunction true. On the other hand, formulas or sets of formulas which are true under all interpretations are said to be *valid*. Their truth does not depend on the particular world in which the are interpreted but on their syntactic structure alone. The following formula is true under any interpretation:

$$\forall X[((likes(X,wine) \lor likes(X,beer)) \land \neg likes(X,wine)) \rightarrow (likes(X,beer))]$$

Clearly, our presentation of predicate logic, though informal, still involves a large number of distinctions and definitions. But in the predicate calculus these are important, for only within this type of formalism is it possible to establish both a well-defined syntax as well as a mathematically clear semantics. As we see in the language chapters (Part IV) this goal is often impossible for natural languages.

Why is this mathematical basis desirable for a representational medium? First, it provides a clear, precise language to write *knowledge level specifications*. This allows us to express with precision the knowledge and skill involved in a subject's problem solving. This has been particularly important in creating production system models of cognition, as we see in Sections 3.3 and 9.2. Second, this mathematical system can be extended to include other interesting representational systems, such as that found in temporal and modal logics (Section 7.4). Finally, the predicate calculus has a mathematically based method for concluding new information about a problem area, the use of *inference rules*.

We next turn our attention to inferencing and reasoning rules. We begin by recalling the notion of *logical entailment*. A set of WFFs F *logically entails* a formula s if every interpretation that satisfies F also satisfies s. Informally, F entails s if s is true in every world in which F is true. We now describe inference rules.

1. An *inference* rule for a set of expressions is a procedure that when applied to the set of expressions produces a new predicate expression.
2. An inference procedure is *sound* if every expression produced from a set of expressions is *logically entailed* by that set of expressions.
3. An inference procedure is *complete* for a set of expressions if every expression that is logically entailed by that set of expressions can be produced using that inference procedure.

We illustrate these definitions with an example. We saw in our discussion of propositional logic that the inference procedure *modus ponens* when applied to predicate expressions p and p → q produces the new predicate q. By a separate mathematical proof (Chang & Lee 1973), we can show that q will always be true for every interpretation for which the predicates p and p → q are true. This demonstrates that *modus ponens* is a sound inference rule. There are a number of other inference rules or procedures which are sound and a smaller number which are both sound and complete. (Chang & Lee 1973)

There are two other issues related to predicate logic semantics which should be mentioned. The first is that there is no general method for determining whether an arbitrary formula in predicate calculus is valid. The difficulty in determining validity has to do with the potentially infinite number of elements in the domain of interpretation. For this reason the predicate calculus is said to be *undecidable* (see also Section 2.5.4). Second, the version of predicate logic which we have described is called *first order predicate calculus*. It is restricted in the sense that it does not allow predicates to take other *predicates* as arguments. For example, it is not possible to define a predicate in first order predicate calculus called **arity-2** which is true when applied to predicates with arity two. This restriction is relaxed in *second order* and *higher order* logics.

Example 7.7: Inference in a Blocks World

We extend Example 7.6 by adding additional action rules:

Pickup (X): ∀X (hand_empty ∧ clear (X)
            ⟹ add(holding(X)) ∧ add(¬hand_empty) ∧ delete(hand_empty))
Putdown (X): ∀X (holding (X)
            ⟹ add(hand_empty) ∧ add(on_table(X)) ∧ delete(holding(X)))
Stack(X, Y): ∀X ∀Y((holding (X) ∧ clear (Y)
            ⟹ add(stack (X, Y)) ∧ add(hand_empty) ∧ delete(clear (Y))))

After firing one of these action rules, an inference procedure allows us to reason about consequences of the changes made in the represented world and update the predicate descriptions of the blocks world, for instance, with regard to which blocks have become clear. Note that in the predicate calculus, it takes only one rule to pick up or stack any block. This is a great improvement in expressiveness over the propositional calculus as we saw it in Example 7.4.

Example 7.8: A "Structure Mapping" Example from Gentner (1983)

Suppose we want to describe reasoning through the construction of analogies. The first thing we must to is describe the source for our analogy, that domain which is already understood. To do this we describe the facts and relations that are true for this source domain. In the analogical reasoning we describe over this and subsequent examples we reason about atomic structure based on our knowledge of the solar system. To build an analogy we first make a predicate calculus representation of our knowledge of the of the solar system. We show a number of these relations in Figure 7.7A and offer next a set of predicate descriptions:

yellow(sun)   hot (sun)   massive(sun)

attracts(sun, planet1)   attracts(planet1, sun)

more_massive(sun, planet1)   revolve_around(planet1, sun)

hotter_than(sun, planet1)   attracts(Planetx, Planety)

The reader can complete this example and make a similar set of expressions for Figure 7.7B. We describe the analogical mapping in Example 7.11.

7.3.4 Pattern Matching and Example Applications

Although we have discussed the notion of an inference rule in predicate logic, we have not yet looked at any inference rules which allow us to handle quantified formulas. We first look at an example which illustrates some of the issues involved. This example dates back to Aristotle's discussion of syllogistic reasoning: "All humans are mortal. Socrates is human. Therefore Socrates is mortal." In predicate logic this can be expressed as:

1) $\forall X \ (\text{human}(X) \rightarrow \text{mortal}(X))$
2) human(socrates)
3) $\therefore$ mortal(socrates)

At first glance we might hope to use an inference rule like *modus ponens* applied to statements 1 and 2 to derive statement 3. Modus ponens *matches* a proposition p which is asserted unconditionally with the p in $p \rightarrow q$. Unfortunately this is not allowed in the example above, since human(X) occurs inside a quantifier and, moreover, does not exactly match the proposition human(socrates). However, a technique can be applied which will allow the two formulas to match.

In a universally quantified formula, $\forall X \ \Phi$, the formula Φ is asserted to hold for all elements of the domain. Clearly it will also hold for every subset or individual element of that domain. Therefore we are permitted to uniformly replace every occurrence of X in Φ with any other term in our language with the obvious

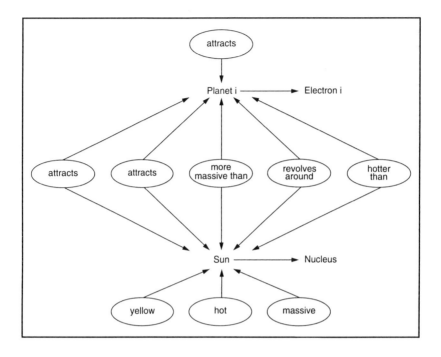

FIGURE 7.7A Relations of the solar system in Example 7.8 represented by predicate calculus. From Gentner (1983).

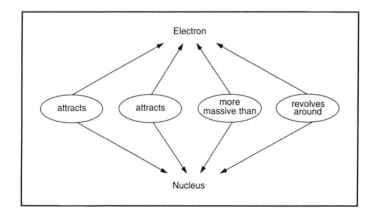

FIGURE 7.7B Relations from Rutherford's model of the atom to be used in building an analogy with Figure 7.7A. From Gentner (1983).

restrictions. In particular, we can use ∀X (human(X) → mortal(X)) to conclude human(socrates) → mortal(socrates). Since the antecedent of this result now exactly matches human(socrates), we can apply modus ponens to conclude mortal(socrates).

The technique used in this example can be generalized. We apply variable substitution to generate matching predicate expressions. We then apply truth preserving inference rules like *modus ponens*, *modus tolens*, and so on to generate new formulas.

An important effect of pattern matching is that information bearing patterns in the arguments of a predicate in one formula can be carried over into a second formula through the uniform application of a variable substitution. This substitution applies to *all* the occurrences of the variable in the second formula. For example in the argument above, the pattern mortal(socrates) does not exist in the given premises of the original argument. It is created by variable substitution and the application of *modus ponens*.

The real power of pattern matching is only seen when it is used in conjunction with functions and structures. Consider the following definitions of parent and grandparent that use as part of their definitions the functions father and mother:

∀X parent(father(X), X)   ∀X parent (mother(X), X)
∀X ∀Y ∀Z ((parent (X, Y) ∧ parent (Y, Z)) → grandparent (X, Z))

From these very simple pieces, using *modus ponens* and substitution, we can derive general patterns, such as:

∀X grandparent(father(father(X)), X)
∀X grandparent(mother(father(X)), X)

We do not present here the specific steps in this derivation. However, the important point is that the derived WFFs combine or compose patterns which were previously contained in separate formulas. This ability to compose patterns using predicate logic inference procedures is a crucial property if, as suggested in Section 3.2, *compositionality* is an essential feature of intelligent systems. We see in Part IV the pivotal role of *compositionality* in natural language as well.

Example 7.9: Pattern Based Reasoning

We illustrate pattern matching with another example. Suppose that Fred is a student, that all students pass their final exams, and that all students passing their final exams are graduating. We would like to determine whether Fred is graduating. Predicate expressions that describe this situation might be:

student (fred)
∀ X (student (X) → pass_final (X))
∀ Y (pass_final (Y) → graduate (Y)) .

We want to ask whether Fred will graduate or whether graduate(fred) is true.

The answer is obvious, but to achieve it we must match several patterns: fred must match with X and X must match with Y. This, with two uses of *modus ponens*, produces graduate (fred). Pattern matching combines predicate expressions together. The predicates must have the same name and arity, or number of terms in the parentheses separated by commas. When this fit is exact, we can:

1. Replace variables, such as X, with constants like fred when fred is in the domain of X; this is sometimes called *instantiation*.
2. Substitute a variable for any other variable, in the example, X for Y. Variables are place holders and can have any legitimate name.
3. Compose substitutions, so that the simplest set remains. Thus fred is substituted for Y.

There are additional rules such as that any function can be replaced by its evaluation. Thus, we could have student (father_of (ann)), and once we find the father_of (ann), suppose it is Fred, we can conclude student (fred). Finally, we can propagate the function through the substitutions and conclude, for example, graduate (father_of (ann)). Next, we present an example that shows how predicate expressions, pattern matching, inference or action rules, and a semantic model can all fit together in an interpretative context.

Example 7.10: **The Blocks World and Graph Search**

We now add further detail to our presentation of the blocks world description in the predicate calculus. We assume a set of descriptions similar to those of Example 7.6 and action rules similar to those of Example 7.8. With the pattern matching just described we can apply the different *pick_up*, *put_down*, and *stack* operators to produce a search space. We first present a start state and a goal state and then use action rules to produce further states in the search for the goal.

We begin with start and goal states as in Figure 7.8. We can describe the start and goal states with the following sets of predicates:

Start state: block (a) ∧ block (b) ∧ block (c) ∧ on (a, b) ∧ clear (a)
∧ clear (c) ∧ on (c, table) ∧ on (b, table) ∧ hand_empty
Goal state: block (a) ∧ block (b) ∧ block (c) ∧ on (c, b) ∧ clear (a)
∧ clear (c) ∧ on (b, table) ∧ on (c, table) ∧ hand_empty

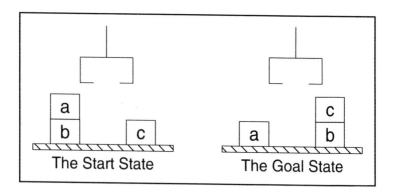

FIGURE 7.8   The start and goal states for the blocks world.

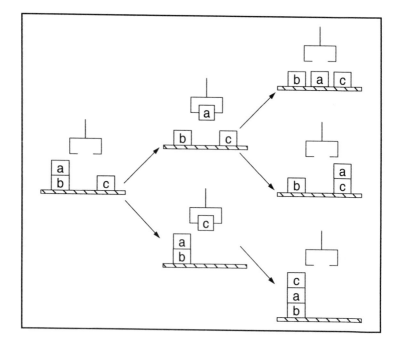

Figure 7.9   Part of the graph search produced from Example 7.9, applying the inference rules to the state descriptions.

The Pick_up, Put_down, and Stack operators, as well as the relationships
for clear and hand_empty are as in the previous examples of the block's world.
As shown in Figure 7.9, we now apply these operators to the start state to gener-

ate the search space. By traversing this space of possible states we hope to discover the goal state. In Chapter 8, we describe different search strategies that might be used to generate the search of the graph of Figure 7.9.

Example 7.11: **Analogical Reasoning, Continued (Gentner 1983)**

In Example 7.8 we created a predicate calculus description of aspects of the solar system. We then asked readers to begin a similar description of the Rutherford model of the atom. Suppose, when asked to describe an atom, a person responds, "The atom is like the solar system." Take the descriptions of the atom and those of the solar system and create a *structure mapping* to represent this analogy.

A structure mapping is a mapping between the predicate descriptions of two (or more) situations that preserves the relationships within each. Structure mappings are much like the isomorphic maps described in Section 3.2. In building analogies, we take the source of the analogy, here the solar system, and map its descriptions into a target domain, here the Rutherford atom. Once the analogy is cast with the structure mapping we take well understood relations from the source and see how they might be interpreted in the target domain. Questions that might be asked include: Which predicates are most important in building the analogy? Should we just try every possible mapping combination of the predicates? Which types of predicates can be ignored? Based on the analogy what things attract in the Rutherford atom? What relates to the sun being hot and yellow? Gentner (1983) discusses these issues and proposes mappings in Figure 7.7.

7.4 NONMONOTONIC LOGIC, TRUTH MAINTENANCE, AND ALTERNATIVE LOGICS

7.4.1 Non-monotonic Reasoning and Truth Maintenance

In the examples presented to this point we used the inference rules of the predicate calculus to conclude new facts about a problem domain. With every application of an inference rule we increased our knowledge, as represented by the set of predicate calculus formulas. The use of inference rules never caused us to reject formulas that we had deduced earlier. This property of a reasoning system, that the set of formulas is constant or increasing, is called the *monotonic* property.

Much of human reasoning is *nonmonotonic*. That is, things we learn at one time can cause us to revise and refine what we thought that we understood previously. An example comes from the inheritance hierarchy of Section 6.6. We are told about a bird named Tweety. We assume Tweety can fly. Only later do we find out Tweety has a broken wing. What we had expected with the information that Tweety was a bird was all the default assumptions that go along with the bird class. Later information revised this, and perhaps even required revision of some of our beliefs as well as conclusions we had produced with previous beliefs.

One of the weaknesses of predicate calculus as a medium for reasoning is, of course, that the forms of quantification built into the language are not very realistic. Consider the predicate expression bird(X) ∧ flies(X). Universal quantification requires something be true or false for all values of a variable; existential quantification indicates that a property is true or false for at least one value of the variable. What we actually want is quantification that a property is *usually true* for a variable X. This would correspond more closely to human reasoning.

Another example of default problem solving is reasoning about plans or actions. In the blocks world examples throughout this chapter we represented states of the world as part of a planning sequence to accomplish a task, for instance, the rearrangement of a set of blocks, as in Figure 7.8. Each state of the world was described by a set of predicates. As a stacking problem was solved, several of the predicates, those effected by the stacking rules, were changed.

What happened to those predicates not directly acted upon by the stacking rules? We assumed they remained fixed across the various states of the problem solving. In other words, we had an implicit circumscribing assumption that, nothing being stated to the contrary, the descriptors of the state of the world not addressed by our action predicates remained fixed. In a more realistic situation this may or may not be true. At the very least the world is changed by ageing, use, and the interaction of other planning systems.

The problem just described is often called the *frame problem*. The question the frame problem raises is this: when the world is represented as a set of discrete states, perhaps using predicates or objects, how is it possible to codify all information necessary to update this representation through time? How is it possible to represent what does and what does not remain invariant through causal event sequences? The fact is, this goal is not achievable, either formally or computationally. One solution to the frame problem that uses the structures of predicate logic is to build an explicit set of *frame axioms* (McCarthy & Hayes 1969). These are inference rules that are used in an application to directly deduce what parts of the world are NOT changed by actions or operators. For example, there would be a rule in our blocks world that when the arm picks up a block only that block is changed. In particular, the rule would deduce that each other block would remain as it was before the pick up operator was applied. This approach gets very cumbersome in a complex environment. Another logic based approach to the frame problem is the use of *circumscriptive* logic (McCarthy 1980).

Certainly we humans do not need this full set of logic based specifications to successfully accomplish tasks in our world. And further, when frame assumptions are violated, for example when a block is not where we last placed it, we have a set of heuristics to help us get back on track in our problem solving: look for the block near where we expect it to be or look on the floor near the table.

Another example of default reasoning is in diagnostic problem solving. We might wish to create a nutrition advisor with predicate descriptions that ask the user about tiredness, blood counts and pressure, and eating habits. There are many causes of concern in the subject besides nutritional deficiencies, however. An emotional state or situation, for example, could be causing many of the symptoms that drove the subject to the nutrition advisor. Yet, once in the context of the nutrition advisor, the assumptions that led to it may no longer be questioned. Perhaps only when the advisor indicates that there are no deficiencies, or when a particular therapy does not produce all the desired results, will the base assumptions that led to use of the advisor again be raised.

A final example of nonmonotonic reasoning is the use of the closed world assumption. When I ask my travel agent to find a direct air flight from Albuquerque to Cabo San Lucas he goes to his computer for a few minutes and then tells me that there are no direct flights. But how could he possibly reason to the fact that something doesn't exist? In this case it is simple. He looks at the flight data base, searches for flights connecting Albuquerque with Cabo San Lucas, and can't find any direct flights. He then concludes that no direct flights exist.

This is an instance of the *closed world assumption* and it is a particularly important aspect of logic based representation and problem solving. In PROLOG reasoning, for example, something is false only when its opposite cannot be proven true. The closed world assumption asserts that in a logic based model of the world if something is not provably true then it is not true. Stated from the opposite view, if items in a domain are specified by a list and an item is not mentioned on that list, we assume that it doesn't belong in the domain. This approach to reasoning, of course, is unsound and can thus lead us to further conclusions that may eventually have to be revised.

Human experts reason comfortably and successfully in each of the cases we have mentioned. Our reasoning is not sound and quite often requires revision of knowledge and beliefs about a problem. Thus the reasoning is said to be nonmonotonic, in that every new thing concluded does not increase the total of all things known: it may also cause revision of information previously thought true.

One method of implementing nonmonotonic reasoning, especially in the use of default assumptions, is to extend our logic with the operator unless. unless allows us to draw inferences based on the belief that its argument is not true. Suppose we have the following expressions:

(p unless q) → r
p
r → s

The first inference indicates that we may infer r if p is true and we do not know that q is true. Since these conditions are met, we infer r, and using r infer s.

Subsequently, if we increase our knowledge and find that q is true, r must be retracted and unless we have other ways to prove r, s must also be revised. Note that unless deals with matters of *knowledge* or *belief* rather than truth. Consequently changing the value of its argument causes us to remove all inferences that depend upon it. This extension of logic to include knowledge and belief introduces the nonmonotonicity.

The reasoning scheme just described can also be used to encode default rules (Reiter 1980). Replace (p unless q) → r with (p unless ab p) → r, where ab p represents abnormal p. This expression indicates that, unless we have an abnormal instance of p, such as a bird with a broken wing, we can infer fly(X). Thus, using bird (X) unless ab bird (X) → fly (X), if tweety is a bird then tweety can fly. We presented exception handling in object systems in Section 6.4.

One of the problems in using nonmonotonic reasoning is in effectively revising conclusions in the light of changing knowledge and belief. In our example, we used r to infer s. Retracting r removed the support for s. Unless there is an independent set of other inferences supporting s, it must also be retracted. Implementing this process is extremely complex, requiring in the worst case that we recompute all our deduced conclusions each time a belief is revised.

A *truth maintenance system* or TMS attempts to reduce this complexity by storing with each inference its justification. As supporting reasons are changed the related beliefs are revised. To perform these revisions, the TMS traces the reasons for beliefs to find the consequences of changes in the base set of assumptions. For our example, on inferring r, a truth maintenance system would also record all subsequent inferences depending on r. On changing our belief in q, and retracting r, the TMS would not have to recompute all conclusions; it would use its records to examine only the effected expressions.

Of course, in a very large deductive system this approach will prove intractable. Nonetheless with limited specifications it seems to describe quite closely what goes on in a nonmonotonic situation. Furthermore, the recording of beliefs and support predicates is important in understanding where revisions must begin when a supporting model is revised. Jon Doyle's work (1979) contains further discussion on TMSs, as well as a pseudo code model for its implementation.

Another method taken to describe nonmonotonic reasoning is to extend the first order predicate calculus itself. This direction includes the creation of *temporal* and *modal* logics and is presented in the following section.

7.4.2 Alternative Logics

There are a number of standard extensions to logic that broaden its use as a representational medium while retaining its well-defined semantics and inference strategies. Important alternatives to first order predicate calculus include:

1. *Multiple valued logics.* These extend logic by adding new truth values such as unknown to the standard values of true and false. This can, for example, provide a vehicle for distinguishing between assertions that we know to be true, those that we know to be false, and those that we simply do not know to be either true or false. Normal inference rules are extended by truth tables to offer results in multiple valued domains.
2. *Modal and epistemic logics.* These logics add predicates and reasoning operators which enable the logic to address issues of knowledge and belief as well as necessity and possibility.
3. *Temporal logics.* Temporal logics quantify expressions with regard to time, indicating that an expression is never true, always true, was true for a time in the past, or will be true in the future. Inference rules in temporal logics contain time constraints appropriate for their application.
4. *Higher order logics.* Many categories of knowledge seem to correspond to higher order logical concepts, for instance, a logic that allows us to classify types of predicates. Do we need higher order logics to deal with knowledge or can it all be done in first order logic? If higher order logics are needed, how are they best formulated? These are open issues.

In the epilogue we reference work in alternative logics in more detail. The next section introduces *abductive reasoning*, yet another extension of the predicate calculus representation, in this case adding unsound inference procedures.

7.5 ABDUCTIVE REASONING

7.5.1 Introduction

Intelligent problem solvers must often draw correct conclusions from poorly formed and uncertain evidence using unsound inference rules. This is not an impossible task. We do it successfully in almost every aspect of daily life. We deliver correct medical treatment for ambiguous symptoms. We profitably mine natural resources without a perfect guarantee of success before we start. We comprehend language statements that are often ambiguous or incomplete.

Some of the reasons for this ambiguity may be better understood by considering a predicate calculus rule for diagnosis of a car problem. Consider:

if   the engine does not turn over, and
          the lights do not come on
then   the problem is with the battery or cables.

This rule is heuristic in nature; it is possible, although less likely, that the battery and cables are fine but the car has a bad starter motor and headlights.

The rule seems to state a tight relationship such as that between cause and effect, but it does not. Failure of the engine to turn over and the lights to come on does not necessarily imply that the battery and cables are bad. What is interesting to note, however, is that the converse of the rule is a valid rule:

> if the problem is battery or cables
> then the engine does not turn over, and
> the lights do not come on.

Barring the supernatural, a car with a dead battery will not turn on its lights or turn over the starter motor! This is an example of *abductive reasoning*. Formally, abduction states that from:

$$P \rightarrow Q \text{ and } Q \text{ it is possible to infer } P.$$

Abduction is an unsound rule of inference, meaning that the conclusion is not necessarily true for every interpretation in which the premises are true. For example, if a friend says "If it rains then I will not go running at 3:00" and you do not see her on the track at 3:00, does it necessarily follow that it is raining? It is possible that she decided not to go running because of an injury or that she needed to work.

Although abduction is unsound, it is often essential to solving problems. The "correct" version of the battery rule is not particularly useful in diagnosing car troubles since its premise, the battery is bad, is the goal we are trying to determine and its conclusions are the observable symptoms with which we must work. *Modus ponens* cannot be applied and the rule must be used in an abductive fashion. This is generally true of diagnostic problem solving: Faults or diseases cause or imply symptoms, not the other way around, but diagnosis must work from the symptoms back to the cause.

When we use abductive inference or attempt to reason with missing or unreliable data, uncertainty results. To address this problem, we can attach some measure of confidence to the conclusions. For example, although battery failure does not always accompany the failure of a car's lights and starter, it almost always does, and confidence in this rule is justifiably high.

Abduction is reasoning from observable effects back to causes. Occasionally be can "deterministically" work out this effect/cause link because we have suitably constrained the situation. For example, the observation of the "smoking gun" is definitive "proof" that the gun was just fired by the person holding it. This is not a deduction, however (suppose a lit fire cracker in the gun barrel!) but it is often sufficient to get a conviction "beyond a reasonable doubt."

In this section, we discuss several ways of managing the uncertainty that results from heuristic and abductive inference rules: first, we present the Bayesian approach (Section 7.5.2), second, Stanford certainty theory (Section 7.5.3). Finally, we briefly consider Zadeh's fuzzy set theory of evidential reasoning.

7.5.2 Bayesian Probability Theory

The Bayesian approach to uncertainty is based in formal probability theory and has shown up in several areas of research, including pattern recognition, classification problems, and models for decision making. The *Prospector* expert system, built at Stanford and SRI International, and employed in mineral exploration (copper, molybdenum, and others), uses a form of the Bayesian statistical model. This problem is abductive since reasoning rules for Prospector take the form:

> if   presence of mineral X
> then   certain geological structures and
>   presence of mineral Y

The goal of the search is to find mineral X, and the only signs we have are the presence of the geological structures and mineral Y. We must determine how the presence of these data indicates that mineral X is also present.

Assuming random distribution of events, probability theory allows the calculation of more complex probabilities from previously known results. In simple probability calculations, we are able to conclude, for example, how cards might be distributed to a number of players.

Suppose that I am one person of a four person card game where all the cards are equally and randomly distributed. If I do not have the queen of spades I can conclude that each of the others players has it with probability 13/39, or 1/3, since they each have 13 of the 39 remaining cards. Similarly, I can conclude each player has the ace of hearts with probability 1/3, and that any one player has both cards at 1/3 * 1/3 or 1/9.

In the mathematical theory of probability, individual probability instances are worked out by sampling and combinations of probabilities are worked out as above, using rules such as that the probability of two events occurring is the product of their individual probabilities, given that they are independent.

One of the most important results of probability theory is Bayes' theorem (which is used by the Prospector program). Bayes' results offer a way to compute the probability of an hypothesis following from a given piece of evidence given only the probabilities with which the evidence follows from causes (hypotheses).

Suppose we want to examine the geological evidence at some location to see if it is suited to find copper. We must know in advance the probability of finding each of a set of minerals and the probability of certain evidence being present when each particular mineral is found. Then, we can use Bayes' theorem to determine the likelihood that copper will be present using the evidence we collect at the location (Duda et al. 1979).

We note that Bayes' rule does not capture cause effect relationships, that is, that the presence of mineral X *causes* certain geological structures and the presence of Y. Rather, Bayes offers a model of the *co-occurrence* of these phenomena. Bayes rule interprets signs that indicate rather than makes deductions that guarantee. Human experts in an area are quite proficient at interpreting its signs.

There are two major assumptions for the use of Bayes' theorem: First, all statistical data on the relationships of the evidence with the various hypotheses must be known. Second, and more difficult to establish, all relationships between evidence and hypotheses must be independent. This assumption of independence can be tricky when many such assumptions are needed for solving a problem.

A final issue that makes keeping the statistics of the "evidence given hypotheses" relationships virtually intractable is the need to rebuild all probability relationships when any new relationship or hypothesis about evidence is discovered. In many active research areas this is happening continuously. Bayesian reasoning requires complete probabilities if its conclusions are to be correct.

Where these assumptions are met, Bayesian approaches offer the benefit of a well-founded and statistically correct handling of uncertainty. Most problem domains do not meet these requirements, however and must rely on more heuristic approaches such as the certainty theory described in the next section.

7.5.3 A Theory for Certainty (Buchanan & Shortliff 1984)

Certainty theory, sometimes called the *Stanford certainty factor algebra*, makes some assumptions for creating confidence measures and has some equally simple rules for combining these confidences as inferences are made. The first assumption is to split confidence for a relationship from confidence against it:

Call MB (H I E) the measure of belief of an hypothesis H given evidence E.
Call MD (H I E) the measure of disbelief of hypothesis H given evidence E.

Now either:

$$1 > MB (H \mid E) > 0 \text{ while MD } (H \mid E) = 0, \text{ or}$$
$$1 > MD (H \mid E) > 0 \text{ while MB } (H \mid E) = 0.$$

The two measures constrain each other in that a given piece of evidence is either for or against a particular hypothesis. This is an important difference between certainty theory and probability theory. Once the link between measures of belief and disbelief has been broken, these may be tied together again with the certainty factor calculation CF:

$$CF (H | E) = MB (H | E) - MD (H | E).$$

Thus, as the certainty factor, CF, approaches 1 the evidence is stronger for an hypothesis; as CF approaches -1 the confidence against the hypothesis gets stronger; and a CF around 0 indicates there is little evidence either for or against the hypothesis.

When we use abductive reasoning rules, we must agree on a CF to go with each rule. This CF reflects confidence in the rule's reliability. Certainty measures may be adjusted to tune the system's performance, although slight variations in this confidence measure tend to have little effect on the overall results (Luger & Stubblefield 1993, Chap. 8).

The premises for each rule are formed of the **and** and **or** of a number of facts. When an abductive rule is used, the certainty factors that are associated with each condition of the premise are combined to produce a certainty measure for the overall premise. For P1 and P2, premises of the rule,

$$CF (P1 \text{ and } P2) = MIN (CF (P1), CF (P2)), \text{ and}$$
$$CF (P1 \text{ or } P2) = MAX (CF (P1), CF (P2)).$$

The combined CF of the premises, using the above rules, is then multiplied by the CF within the rule to get the CF for the conclusions of the rule. For example, consider the abductive rule:

$$(P1 \text{ and } P2) \text{ or } P3 \rightarrow R1 (.7) \text{ and } R2 (.3),$$

where P1, P2, P3 are premises and R1 and R2 are the results of the rule, having CFs .7 and .3 respectively. These numbers are added to the rule when it is designed and represent the expert's confidence in the conclusion if all the premises are known with complete certainty. In general, CFs of the conditions may come as the result of conclusions of other rules, or from the user, or just as a record of incomplete information. If the running program has produced P1, P2, and P3 with CFs of .7, .4, and .2, respectively, then R1 and R2 may be added to the collected case specific results with CFs .28 and .12, respectively.

Here are the calculations for this example:

$$CF (P1 (.6) \text{ and } P2 (.4)) = MIN (.6, .4) = .4$$
$$CF ((.4) \text{ or } P3 (.2)) = MAX (.4, .2) = .4.$$

The CF for R1 is .7 in the rule, so R1 is added to the set of concluded facts with the associated CF of (.7) * (.4) = .28. The CF for R2 is .3 in the rule, so R2 is added to the set of conclusions with the associated CF of (.3) * (.4) = .12.

One further measure is required: how to combine multiple CFs when two or more rules support the same result R. This is the certainty theory analog of the probability theory procedure of multiplying the probability measures to combine independent evidence. By using this rule repeatedly one can combine the results of any number of rules that are used for determining result R.

Suppose CFR1 is the present certainty factor associated with result R, and a previously unused rule produces result R again with CFR2, then the new CF of R is calculated by:

CFR1 + CFR2 - (CFR1 * CFR2) when CFR1 and CFR2 are positive,
CFR1 + CFR2 + (CFR1 * CFR2) when CFR1 and CFR2 are negative, and
CFR1 + CFR2) / (1 - MIN (|CFR1|, |CFR2|))   otherwise,
where |X| is the absolute value of X .

Besides being easy to compute, these equations have other desirable properties. First, the CFs that result from applying this rule are always between 1 and -1, as are the other CFs. Second, the result of combining contradictory CF information is to cancel each other out as would be naturally desired. Finally, the combined CF measure is a monotonically increasing or decreasing function in the manner one would expect for combining evidence.

Certainty theory has been criticized as being excessively ad hoc. Although it is defined in a formal algebra, the meaning of the certainty measures is not as rigorously founded as in formal probability theory. However, certainty theory has not attempted to produce an algebra for "correct" reasoning. Rather it is the lubrication that lets reasoning rules combine confidences. Its measures are ad hoc in the same sense that a human expert's confidence in his or her results are approximate, heuristic, and informal. In MYCIN, for example, the CFs are used with heuristic search to give a priority for goals to be attempted and a cutoff point when a goal need not be considered further. We see heuristic search in Chapter 8.

7.5.4 The Fuzzy Set Approach to Uncertainty

Because of the importance of abductive reasoning to modeling expert level problem solving and the limitations of certainty theory, work continues in this important area. In concluding this subsection, we mention briefly another approach to modeling uncertainty, Zadeh's (1983) *fuzzy set theory*.

Zadeh's main contention is that although probability theory is appropriate for measuring randomness of information, it is inappropriate for measuring the *meaning* of information. Indeed, much of the confusion surrounding the use of

English words and phrases is related to lack of clarity, its vagueness, rather than to randomness. This is a crucial point for analyzing language structures, and can also be important in creating a measure of confidence in inference rules. Thus, Zadeh proposes *possibility theory* as a measure of vagueness, just as probability theory measures randomness.

Zadeh's theory expresses lack of precision in a quantitative fashion by introducing a set membership function that can take on real values between 0 and 1. This is called a *fuzzy set* and can be described as follows: let S be a set and s a member of that set. A fuzzy subset F of S is defined by a membership function m(s) that measures the "degree" to which s belongs to F.

An example of fuzzy sets is for S to be the positive integers, and F the fuzzy subset of S called "small integers." Now various integer values can have a possibility distribution defining their "fuzzy membership" in the set of small integers:

$$m\,(1) = 1, m\,(2) = 1, m\,(3) = .9, m\,(4) = .8, ...$$
$$m\,(50) = .001, \text{ and so on.}$$

To model the statement that positive integer X is a "small integer" F creates a possibility distribution across all the positive integers (S).

Fuzzy set theory is not concerned how these possibility distributions are created, but rather with the rules for computing the combined possibilities over expressions each containing fuzzy variables. Thus it includes rules for combining possibility measures for expressions containing fuzzy variables. The laws for the "or," "and," and "not" of these expression are similar to those just presented for certainty factors. In fact, the approach taken to certainty factor algebra of Section 7.5.3 was modeled on some of the combination rules first described by Zadeh (Buchanan & Shortliff 1984).

All of the methods we have examined can be criticized for using numeric approaches to the handling of uncertain reasoning. It is unlikely that humans use any of these techniques for reasoning with uncertainty and many applications seem to require a more qualitative approach to the problem. For example, numeric approaches do not support adequate explanations of the causes of uncertainty. If we ask human experts why their conclusions are uncertain, they usually answer in terms of the qualitative relationships between features of the problem situation. In a numeric model of uncertainty, this information is replaced by numeric measures.

In Chapter 8 we describe general search algorithms for use in models of reasoning. These algorithms are appropriate for implementing many of the inferencing schemes of the present chapter. Chapter 9 presents procedure based reasoning with the production system and blackboard architectures. It also presents the Newell and Simon (1972) model for human problem solving.

7.6   EPILOGUE AND REFERENCES

The relationship between formal logic systems and human reasoning remains a fascinating topic. We recommend reading Plato's *Meno* and the last book of his *Republic*, containing his cave sequence as well as Rene Descartes' *Meditations* (1637/1969). Modern studies include Johnson-Laird and Wason (1977).

Logic based representation schemes continue to be an important research area of the artificial intelligence community, where we recommend McCarthy (1968), Hayes (1979), Weyhrauch (1980), and Moore (1982). *Logics for Artificial Intelligence* by Turner (1984) is an overview of nonstandard logics.

AI researchers have also been quite active in the recent past in attempting to understand the key issues in nonmonotonic reasoning. There are a number of approaches taken. One attempts to add supporting assumptions and related details to the axioms of the predicate calculus to bring reasoning back into a monotonic and sound inference model. John McCarthy and Patrick Hayes (1969) and McCarthy (1980) are proponents of this approach. Their articles on circumscription and common sense reasoning are classic in this area. Also important is *Readings in Uncertain Reasoning* edited by Schafer and Pearl (1990).

For more information on nonmonotonic reasoning and truth maintenance systems see Doyle (1979), Reiter (1980), deKleer (1986), and Davis (1990). We also recommend the survey of these topics in *The Encyclopedia of Artificial Intelligence*, edited by Stuart Shapiro (1992).

Chapter 8

SEARCH STRATEGIES FOR WEAK METHOD PROBLEM SOLVING

An ant, viewed as a behaving system, is quite simple. The apparent complexity of its behavior is largely a reflection of the complexity of the environment in which it finds itself.

Herbert Simon (1981)

Intelligence for a system with limited processing resources consists in making wise choices of what to do next.

Newell & Simon (1976)

8.0   INTRODUCTION TO THE ISSUES

In Chapters 6 and 7 we presented symbol based representational tools for modeling intelligent problem solving. Linked to each representational structure are search strategies appropriate to that structure. Levels of intelligence are often characterized by decisions on "what to do next." Representations describe and organize our abstractions of the problem environment, search strategies dictate what we decide to do next.

Artificial intelligence tradition has divided search into *weak* and *strong methods*. Weak methods are general, exhaustive, and "uninformed" search strategies. We will see an example of weak method problem solving with the presentation of means-ends analysis in the *general problem solver (GPS)* in Section 8.1. Syntactical differences between states are reduced by exhaustive reference to rewrite rules represented by a table of differences or "connections." Monitoring human subject's solutions in weak method problem domains (Newell and Simon 1972) is usually considered the first empirical studies in modern cognitive science. We begin our more formal description of weak methods by presenting the state space of a problem. The definition of the *state space* is built on the graph theory presented in Section 6.1. The state space gives us a context to describe general search strategies for a wide range of problems.

Breadth-first and *depth-first search* are presented in Section 8.4. These search strategies may be applied to any graph or state space. We also must clarify whether we apply these strategies in *data driven* or *goal driven* mode; this we do in Section 8.3. *Best-first search*, Section 8.5, is an heuristic based strategy for considering alternative states of a graph, and an important addition to weak problem solvers in that it provides a method to fine tune representations of human skills.

Heuristic search leads into the presentation of *strong method* problem solving, the material of Chapter 9. Strong methods stress the importance of the knowledge content within the representation. An example of strong method problem solving is the encoding of knowledge explicitly, for instance in the form of an if-then rule. Strong methods ascribe problem solving success to the amount and sophistication of the knowledge employed in problem solving. This has been an important tenet of the emergence and success of the expert systems technology. Edward Feigenbaum, an early proponent of strong methods, has stated that the power of such systems resides in the knowledge present. He contends that a simple search strategy is often sufficient for success, if it is implemented with proper amounts of knowledge.

We feel this approach is a bit simple, in that having a "lot of knowledge" offers no guarantee that we can always access the "right knowledge." Thus, we proposed the knowledge representation schemes of Chapter 6 to make knowledge representable, accessible, modifiable, and extensible; in other words, to make it useful. To model the organization of knowledge we present the production system in Chapters 3 and 9, the network and frame taxonomies in Chapter 6, and the blackboard architecture in Chapter 9. We discuss weak method search strategies used in the context of these representational schemes in this chapter.

8.1   GPS AND AN INTRODUCTION TO WEAK METHOD PROBLEM SOLVING

8.1.1   The Origins of the Cognitive Science Methodology

Early artificial intelligence research at Carnegie Institute of Technology and the Rand Corporation focused on game playing and the automated proof of mathematical theorems. This work began in the early 1950s and continued through the Dartmouth Summer Workshop in 1956. During this period, Allen Newell, Herbert Simon, and Cliff Shaw designed algorithms, with many implemented in computer programs, to play chess as well as to prove theorems from Whitehead and Russell's *Principia Mathematica* (1950).

Newell and Simon's (1956) mathematical theorem proving program was called the *Logic Theorist*. In this program three strategies, *substitution, replace-*

ment, and *detachment* (or modus ponens, Section 7.2) were used to address the hugh search space of possible paths searched for a solution. Heuristic use of these search strategies was an important component of their success. As we will see in Section 8.5, *heuristics* are search strategies that can be built into problem solving that allow the program designer to reduce the complexity of exhaustive search. This complexity is often referred to as the "combinatorial explosion." The mathematical domain of the Logic Theorist was the propositional calculus (see Section 7.2).

The original goal of the Logic Theorist research was to construct "the means to understand more about the kinds of computers, mechanisms, and programs that are necessary to handle ultra-complicated problems" (Newell 1955). This task, though often described as an early important part of research in artificial intelligence, was also of immense psychological interest. Earlier psychological work by deGroot (1965) and Bartlett (1932) had approached some of these same issues from the human perspective. Newell and Simon themselves brought to their analysis of human problem solving many ideas from current psychological theory as well as from decision making in economics.

Serious attempts to interpret the Logic Theorist program as a component in a psychological theory got under way in 1956. Slightly earlier researchers Moore and Anderson (1954) at Yale University had used problems in logic theorem proving in their research on human problem solving. This Yale research, though couched as problems in "decoding," was close enough to the problems from Russell and Whitehead to suggest using it as a basis for comparing human behavior with the Logic Theorist. In 1956, a graduate student at Carnegie Institute took tape recordings of human subjects solving the Moore and Anderson tasks.

The first "think aloud" tapes were transcribed in early 1957 (Newell and Simon 1972). The analysis of the tapes was intended to help the research team create a computer program that could parallel and thus help explain human problem solving behavior. In Figure 8.1 we present one of these first problems. Figure 8.2 is a piece of the transcript of the human subject solving the propositional calculus problem stated in Figure 8.1. As the reader can easily discern, this taking of protocols, or "think aloud" data is an instance of the direct method of capturing psychological information, discussed in Section 4.2.

The subjects for the think aloud protocol were not mathematicians. In fact the researchers were not attempting to capture the "semantic" understanding of mathematics at all. Rather, this task was seen as one of simple decoding, that is, the subjects were given one string of symbols and asked to transform that string into another, for example, to change the left hand side to the right hand side of line 1 in Figure 8.1. The subjects were also given the 12 "rewrite" or substitution rules at the top of Figure 8.1 and asked to use them to transform one expression into the other. The trace of Figure 8.2 has the flavor of symbol substitution rather than any understanding of the mathematics involved.

Objects are formed by building up expressions from letters (P, Q, R, ...) and connectives · (dot), ∨ (wedge), ⊃ (horseshoe), and ~ (tilde). Examples are P, ~Q, P ∨ Q, ~(R ⊃ S) · ~P; ~~P is equivalent to P throughout. Twelve rules exist for transforming expressions (where A, B, and C may be any expressions or subexpressions):

R 1.	A · B → B · A A ∨ B → B ∨ A	Applies to main expression only.
R 2.	A ⊃ B → ~B ⊃ ~A	Applies to main expression only.
R 3.	A · A ↔ A A ∨ A ↔ A	A and B are two main expressions.
R 4.	A · (B · C) ↔ (A · B) · C A ∨ (B ∨ C) ↔ (A ∨ B) ∨ C	A and A ⊃ B are two main expressions.
R 5.	A ∨ B ↔ ~(~A · ~B)	A ⊃ B and B ⊃ C are two main expressions.
R 6.	A ⊃ B ↔ ~A ∨ B	
R 7.	A · (B ∨ C) ↔ (A · B) ∨ (A · C) A ∨ (B · C) ↔ (A ∨ B) · (A ∨ C)	
R 8.	A · B → A A · B → B	Applies to main expression only.
R 9.	A → A ∨ X	Applies to main expression only.
R 10.	A B } → A · B	A and B are two main expressions.
R 11.	A A ⊃ B } → B	A and A ⊃ B are two main expressions.
R 12.	A ⊃ B B ⊃ C } → A ⊃ C	A ⊃ B and B ⊃ C are two main expressions.

FIGURE 8.1A Transformation rules and a proof for a logic problem. From Newell and Simon (1963b).

An example showing subject's entire course of solution on the problem:

1.	$(R \supset \sim P) \cdot (\sim R \supset Q)$	$\sim (\sim Q \cdot P)$
2.	$(\sim R \vee \sim P) \cdot (R \vee Q)$	Rule *6* applied to left and right of 1.
3.	$(\sim R \vee \sim P) \cdot (\sim R \supset Q)$	Rule *6* applied to left of 1.
4.	$R \supset \sim P$	Rule *8* applied to 1.
5.	$\sim R \vee \sim P$	Rule *6* applied to 4.
6.	$\sim R \supset Q$	Rule *8* applied to 1.
7.	$R \vee Q$	Rule *6* applied to 6.
8.	$(\sim R \vee \sim P) \cdot (R \vee Q)$	Rule *10* applied to 5. and 7.
9.	$P \supset \sim R$	Rule *2* applied to 4.
10.	$\sim Q \supset R$	Rule *2* aplied to 6.
11.	$P \supset Q$	Rule *12* applied to 6. and 9.
12.	$\sim P \vee Q$	Rule *6* applied to 11.
13.	$\sim (P \cdot \sim Q)$	Rule *5* applied to 12.
14.	$\sim (\sim Q \cdot P)$	Rule *1* applied to 13. QED.

FIGURE 8.1B   The task of symbolic logic. From Newell and Simon (1963b).

Analysis of the problem solving protocol soon made it clear that human subjects did not follow the searching techniques of the Logic Theorist at all closely. Rather, the human subjects seemed to adopt a problem solving approach that was later to be called *means-ends analysis*. This *means-ends analysis* played a major role in Newell and Simon's design of the next generation of mathematical solution procedure: the *general problem solver* or *GPS*.

8.1.2   The General Problem Solver and Means-Ends Analysis

The algorithmic methods for building the general problem solver are presented in the flow diagram of Figure 8.3 (Newell & Simon 1963a). *Means-ends analysis* is an attempt to explicitly link a set of reduction rules, the *means*, to particular goals, the *ends*. In Figure 8.3 the goal is to transform expression A into expres-

Well, looking at the left-hand side of the equation, first we want to eliminate one of the sides by using rule 8. It appears too complicated to work with first. Now - no, - no, I can't do that because I will be eliminating either the Q or the P in that total expression. I won't do that at first. Now I'm looking for a way to get rid of the horseshoe inside the two brackets that appear on the left and right sides of the equation. And I don't see it. Yeh, if you apply rule 6 to both sides of the equation, from there I'm going to see if I can apply rule 7.

Experimenter writes: 2. $(\sim R \vee \sim P) \cdot (R \vee Q)$

I can almost apply rule 7, but one R needs a tilde. So I'll have to look for another rule. I'm going to see if I can change that R to a tilde R. As a matter of fact, I should have used rule 6 on only the left-hand side of the equation. So use rule 6, but only on the left-hand side.

Experimenter writes: 3. $(\sim R \vee \sim P) \cdot (\sim R \supset Q)$

Now I'll apply rule 7 as it is expressed. Both - excuse me, excuse me, it can't be done because of the horseshoe. So - now I'm looking - scanning the rules here for a second, and seeing if I can change the R to a $\sim$ R in the second equation, but I don't see any way of doing it. (Sigh.) I'm just sort of lost for a second.

FIGURE 8.2   Part of a subject's protocol on the logic problem in Figure 8.1. From Newell and Simon (1963b).

sion B. The first step is to locate an observable difference D between A and B. This could be as simple as one expression having a letter or a connecting symbol different from that of the other expression.

A subgoal, to reduce D, is established in the second box of the first line of Figure 8.3. The method for reducing this subgoal is found in the second line of Figure 8.3, where the operator Q is identified. Actually a list of possible operators

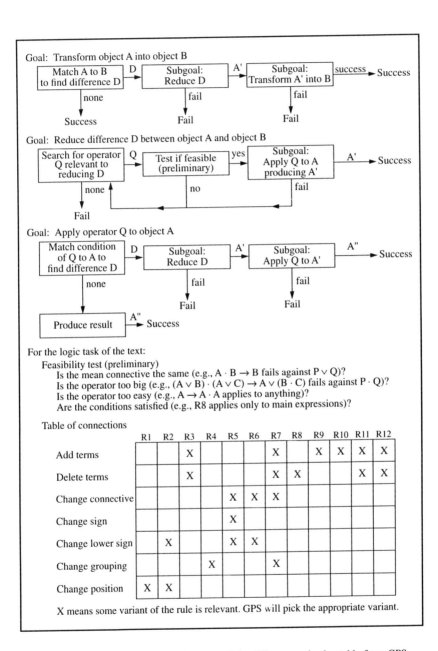

For the logic task of the text:

Feasibility test (preliminary)
Is the mean connective the same (e.g., A · B → B fails against P ∨ Q)?
Is the operator too big (e.g., (A ∨ B) · (A ∨ C) → A ∨ (B · C) fails against P · Q)?
Is the operator too easy (e.g., A → A · A applies to anything)?
Are the conditions satisfied (e.g., R8 applies only to main expressions)?

Table of connections

	R1	R2	R3	R4	R5	R6	R7	R8	R9	R10	R11	R12
Add terms			X				X		X	X	X	X
Delete terms			X				X	X			X	X
Change connective					X	X	X					
Change sign					X							
Change lower sign		X			X	X						
Change grouping				X			X					
Change position	X	X										

X means some variant of the rule is relevant. GPS will pick the appropriate variant.

FIGURE 8.3   The control flow diagram and the difference reduction table for a GPS solution for a logic problem. From Newell and Simon (1963a).

is found in the *table of connections* at the bottom of Figure 8.3. In this sense an ordered list of difference reduction rules, the means, are linked to the subgoal D, the end. If one of these rules does not work, by not passing the rule feasibility test, for instance, control reverts back to the next rule in the list. These operators are applied to the subgoal D and control is then passed back to the top to see if any further differences exist between the beginning and goal expressions of the problem.

Thus, the means-ends analysis of the GPS model of problem solving requires two components, a general procedure for comparing two symbol expressions and identifying syntactic differences and a set of difference reducing rules that can then be applied to remove those differences. This *difference reduction* model for problem solving was termed *general* in that the researchers felt that the same approach could be applied to any of a number of different problems. The "difference recognition and reduction" algorithm, the top three line flow chart of Figure 8.3, remains constant for each application, while the specific "table of connections" is changed according to the requirements of each new application area.

General methods for problem solution such as GPS have come to be called *weak method* problem solvers in AI. Ernst and Newell (1969) describe a number of different application areas where the GPS technique has been used. More recent modeling of human expertise, especially as seen in the rule based expert system, builds up the knowledge in the table of connections. Instead of emphasizing sophisticated and general difference reduction algorithms, the later approach adds more and more knowledge to the program. The knowledge intensive approach is referred to as *strong method* problem solving, and is presented in Chapter 9.

The first published attempt to draw psychological conclusions from the comparison of computer traces of a problem's solution with the protocols of human subjects was published as *Elements of a Theory of Human Problem Solving* in *Psychological Review* in 1958. This paper was organized around the idea that "an explanation of the observed behavior of the organism is provided by a program of primitive information processes that generates this behavior" (Newell & Simon 1972). The paper also examines the methodological assumptions of comparing human protocols to computer traces. Furthermore, Newell and Simon contrasted their results with current important cognitive theories of the time, including the behaviorist, gestaltist, and the neurological. This paper is the first explicit and deliberate presentation of the position later to be called *information processing psychology*.

Means-ends analysis, or difference reduction using a table of connections, is but one of the class of weak method search strategies. We continue the presentation of weak methods by introducing the state space of a problem, a formalism we can use to describe a large class of search strategies.

8.2   THE STATE SPACE OF A PROBLEM

8.2.1   A Definition

The *state space* of a problem may be used to describe search strategies. We introduced graphs and the idea of describing states of a problem solving process in Chapter 6. We augment those definitions here to create the state space. In the state space or problem space representation, nodes of a graph correspond to states in a problem's solution. Paths from the root or start state represent partial solutions of the problem. The graph also describes one or more goal states; these are often leaf nodes of the graph. A successful solution is then represented by a path from the start state to one of the goal states of the graph.

A successful solution within the state space search may also be described by a property of the solution path, for instance, to find the shortest of all paths from the start state to a goal. The state space is used to describe search strategies in games as well as solutions for expert systems and many other areas of artificial intelligence (Luger & Stubblefield 1993).

A *state space* is represented by a four-tuple [N, A, S, GD] where:

N	N is the set of nodes or states of the graph.
A	A is the set of arcs or links between nodes. These are generated by the steps or legal moves of the problem and make up the paths or partial solutions in problem solving.
S	S represents the start or root of the problem.
GD	The goal description may be either:
	i) one or more leaf nodes called goals or
	ii) a property of a solution path.

We now show two examples of the state space of a problem to make this definition more concrete. We take our first example from a game called the knight's tour and our second from the traveling salesperson problem. These are intended to be simple examples of the representation just described, as well as to let the reader be more comfortable with the state space formalism.

8.2.2   Examples of State Space Search

Example 8.1: **The Knight's Tour Problem**

In the knight's tour problem, the knight chess piece is placed alone on the 8 x 8 chessboard. When the knight is located near the center of the board it has eight moves. These moves are created by taking the present row by column position and adding all combinations of plus and minus 2 and 1 to that location. If the knight is not close to an edge of the board there are eight possible next moves, as in Figure 8.4.

There are a number of possible *knight tour* problems. We consider one of the simpler, where we start the knight at one corner and try to find a path across the board to the opposite corner. We now consider the state space created by possible knight moves. We start the knight (start state) in the position (1,1). We then apply the legal move rules to that position to get two possible next states. These are (3,2) and (2,3). All other moves would take the knight off the board. These new positions are represented by the first children in the graph of Figure 8.5. We can continue development of the graph by taking the children of (3,2) and (2,3). We see that one legitimate move is to go back to (1,1). Thus the graph representing the knight's tour will have to have arcs or links going in both directions. One can easily see how a human's attempt to solve this knight tour problem can be described by a path through the graph.

We now have examples of most of the graph definitions at the beginning of Chapter 6, as well as of the state space just presented. *Parent,* or *start* or *root* node (1,1) produces children (2,3) and (3,2), which are *siblings*. We also have *path* [(1,1), (2,3), (3,5), ...]. This is a *rooted graph,* there are *cycles,* and so on.

We have just described N, A, and S from the four-tuple [N, A, S, GD] for the state space. We may describe the *goal* of the problem to be to find a path from state (1,1) to (8,8). This meets the first criterion for a GD presented above. Alternatively we could have described the GD as finding the shortest path between (1,1) and (8,8), exemplifying the second criterion.

We will continue to use the knight's tour problem to exemplify the searches of Chapter 8. We next introduce another classic search problem, the traveling salesperson.

Example 8.2: **The Traveling Salesperson Problem**

Suppose a salesperson has to visit six cities to sell products and then return home. Each city must be visited exactly once. The cities are laid out as in the graph of Figure 8.6. The numbers on the arcs can be considered kilometer distance, airline ticket price, or any other *cost of travel* between the cities. The goal of this problem is to find the path that visits all the cities exactly once and returns home at the lowest cost, either by traveling the fewest total kilometers or spending the smallest amount of money.

We now put the material from the graph of Example 8.2 into a state space for search. For simplicity, let's assume the salesperson lives in city 1, and therefore

1,1	1,2	♞	1,4	♞	1,6	1,7	1,8
2,1	♞	2,3	2,4	2,5	♞	2,7	2,8
3,1	3,2	3,3	start ♞	3,5	3,6	3,7	3,8
4,1	♞	4,3	4,4	4,5	♞	4,7	4,8
5,1	5,2	♞	5,4	♞	5,6	5,7	5,8
6,1	6,2	6,3	6,4	6,5	6,6	6,7	6,8
7,1	7,2	7,3	7,4	7,5	7,6	7,7	7,8
8,1	8,2	8,3	8,4	8,5	8,6	8,7	8,8

FIGURE 8.4   Legal moves of the knight starting near the middle of the chessboard.

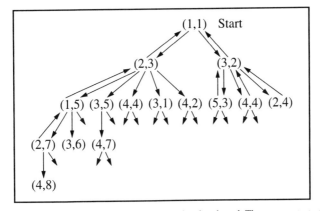

FIGURE 8.5   A graph of the knight moves on the chessboard. The moves start at (1,1).

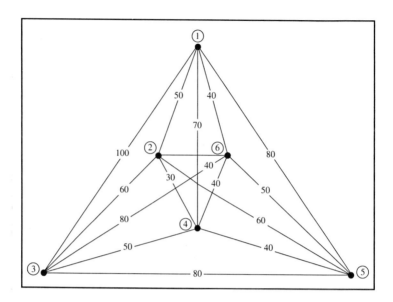

FIGURE 8.6   A graph of six cities and connection costs for the traveling salesperson
problem.

will start and end there. Thus state 1 will be the root of the graph of Figure 8.7.
All the cities the salesperson can visit from the start state, that is, any other city,
are the children of 1. Each arc is labelled by its cost. All the children of the first
generation of the root are then added to the graph. These second level arcs are
labeled by the summed cost of travel to that point. We continue until the travel
takes us back to city 1. The path crossed and summed cost are associated with the
leaf nodes in Figure 8.7. The GD for the state space search will be to find the path
from 1 back to 1 that visits all cities only once and has the smallest total cost.

Before we conclude this subsection, there are two more important points to
make. First, we discuss the complexity of a graph, and second, and consequently,
we point out the importance of heuristic techniques to search graphs. We will not
be over rigorous in our mathematical discussion of these issues. Our point is
important not just from a computational point of view, but also from the psychological. Just because a path exists doesn't mean we will ever be able to produce
it! Just because a solution is mathematically possible doesn't mean it
is computable!

Consider the graph of Figure 8.7. How many paths exist that must be examined to discover the minimal cost path? Let's again assume we start at city 1.
Since there are a total of six cities, we have five more cities to visit. Once we
have selected one of these there are four more cities left, and so on. The mathe-

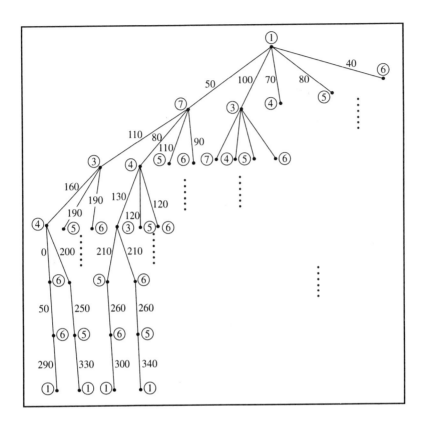

FIGURE 8.7 A search space for the traveling salesperson problem of Figure 8.6.

matical measure of the size of the graph is 5 x 4 x 3 x 2 x 1 or 5! For six cities then, when we pick one city as start and finish, we have a search of 5! or 120 paths. This isn't too bad.

But what if there were 10 cities, or 100? The mathematics we just discussed indicated that for N cities there would be (N - 1)! paths to consider. This can get to be, very rapidly, a large number. For 10 cities there are over 3.5 million paths to consider. It is left as an exercise to see what happens when there are 100 cities! At one second per city, this can never be searched!

These are not only large computations for humans, they can also quickly get impossible for computers. Too naively we say, O, the computer can do that! Not always true. Consider the game of chess. John vonNeumann estimated that the total exhaustive search space for chess was 10^{120}. This was his estimated complexity measure for exhaustive search of a chess game with all its moves and options.

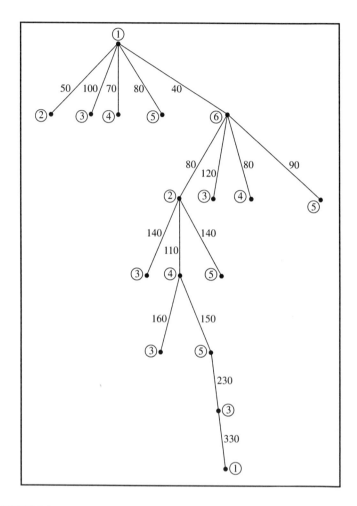

FIGURE 8.8   A graph representing the application of a heuristic, the nearest neighbor, to the traveling salesperson problem of Figure 8.6.

If this strikes you as just another large number of search states, like the national debt, say, you're wrong! It is a number we can write down, but never count. It is roughly equivalent to molecules in the universe or nanoseconds since the big bang. We can think about it, but we certainly can't search through that many potential paths for a solution. Unfortunately, we find this exponential complexity with many of the problems we want to solve!

But humans do play chess, and some humans play it quite well. We contend that they use heuristics to calculate and prune subsections of the potentially huge search space. What a heuristic search is and how it is organized is the material of Section 8.5 and Chapter 9. Here we introduce this important area by demonstrating a heuristic search for the graph of Figure 8.7. Our search path, using the *nearest neighbor* heuristic, may be found in Figure 8.8.

With the nearest neighbor heuristic we start at some city, in our example, city 1, and then go to its nearest nonvisited neighbor, in this case, city 6. Again from city 6 we go to its nearest nonvisited neighbor, here city 2. And so we continue through the graph. The power of this heuristic is that we are always only considering the children of a parent state in the graph. When we select one child from the full set of children, we eliminate continued search from all the others. But not only do we exclude all the other children, but in doing this we eliminate these children's children from the exhaustive search.

Let us briefly consider what we have done. We felt that the shortest path through all the cities had something to do with closest cities at all points in the path. This tactic, sometimes called a *greedy* heuristic, is not an unreasonable approach. In fact, this heuristic does not guarantee the shortest cost path through all the cities. Compare the solution of Figure 8.8 with those generated in 8.7. What we have done, however, is reduce the search cost from looking at (N - 1)! paths, each containing N cities, to considering only one path N cities long. The total number of cities considered is N + (N - 1) + (n - 2) + .. + 1. This is the payoff; it can get the human (or computer) the "good enough" solution in a reasonable amount of time. Simon (1981) refers to this approach of finding the "good enough" solution as *satisficing* rather than optimizing our search through a large number of situations.

Further clarification of these issues, along with the design of algorithms for building these "intelligent" search strategies, makes up the material in Section 8.5. We continue the presentation of weak search methods with an analysis of data-driven and goal-driven reasoning.

8.3   STRATEGIES FOR WEAK METHOD SEARCH

Weak method search applies a general purpose search strategy uniformly to the entire state space. These methods are usually pattern driven and exhaustive. We begin our presentation of weak methods with data-driven and goal-driven techniques.

8.3.1 Data-Driven and Goal-Driven Search

A state space may be created and searched in two directions: from the given data of a problem situation working forward toward a goal or from a goal working back to the start state. In either case the problem solver is trying to solve the problem by finding a sequence of steps through the problem space. Sometimes it is easier to start at the beginning and search forward with *data-driven reasoning*. Alternatively, the solver may start at the goal and work backwards through the problem. Working backwards through the problem is referred to as *goal-driven reasoning*.

In data-driven reasoning, sometimes called *forward chaining*, the problem solver begins with the given facts of the problem and a set of legal moves or rules for changing states. Search proceeds by applying rules of the problem domain to produce new states of the search, these are in turn used by the rules to generate further new states. This process continues until, we hope, it generates a path from the start state to the goal state which satisfies the goal condition. The description of the knight tour problem of Example 8.1, where we find a path from state (1,1) to state (8,8), is data driven. The generalization of this approach is seen in Figure 8.9.

An alternate approach is possible. Take the goal that we want to solve, see what rules or legal moves could be used to generate this goal and determine what conditions must be true to use these rules. These conditions become the new goals or subgoals for the search. Search continues, working backwards through successive subgoals, until, we hope, it works back to the start state of the problem. This process, seen in Figure 8.10, finds the chain of moves or rules leading from data to a goal, although it does so in a reverse order, working from the goal. This approach is called *goal-driven reasoning*, or *backward chaining*, and is like the simple childhood trick of trying to solve a maze puzzle by working back from the finish state of the maze to find a way out!

To summarize: data-driven reasoning takes the facts of the problem and applies the rules and legal moves to produce new facts which lead to a goal; goal-driven reasoning focuses on the goal, finds those rules that could produce the goal, and chains backwards through successive rules and subgoals to the given facts of the problem.

In the final analysis both data-driven and goal-driven problem solvers search the same state space graph. However, the order and actual number of states searched can differ (Section 8.3.2). The preferred strategy is determined by the properties of the problem itself. These include the complexity of the rules, the "shape" of the state space, and the nature and availability of the problem data. All of these may vary with different problems.

8.3.2 Examples and Comparisons of Data-Driven and Goal-Driven Search

As an example of the effect a search strategy can have on the complexity of the search, consider the problem of confirming or denying the statement: "I am a

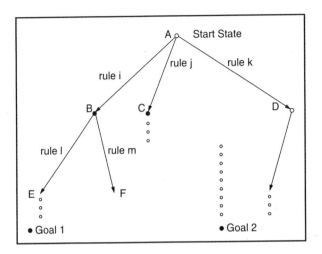

FIGURE 8.9 A graph generated by data-driven reasoning.

descendent of Paul Revere." One solution would be to find a path of direct lineage between the "I" and Revere. We can define goal driven search as starting with "I" and working back along ancestor lines to Revere. Data driven search starts with Revere and works down through his descendents to the present time.

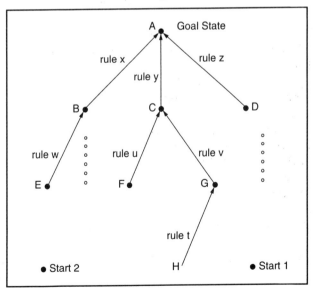

FIGURE 8.10 A graph generated by goal-driven reasoning.

Some simple assumptions let us estimate the size of the space searched in each direction. Paul Revere was born about 250 years ago. If we assume 25 years per generation, the required path will be approximately length 10. If we start from the "I," since each person has exactly two parents and each of these parents has two parents, goal directed search would examine a maximum of 2^{10} ancestors.

A search that worked forward from Paul Revere would examine more states since people tended to have more than two children, particularly in the 18th and 19th centuries. If we assume an average of three children per family, the search would examine on the order of 3^{10} nodes of the family tree. Thus, a search backwards from the "I" would examine fewer nodes. Note, however, that both directions yield an exponential complexity and will, with sufficiently high numbers, be unacceptable. We show this search space in Figure 8.11.

Example 8.3: The Logic Theorist, Revisited

The human subject solving the logic problem in the trace of Figure 8.2 is operating in data-driven mode. The subject uses a set of difference reducing rules similar to that of Figure 8.3, to change the start state, the left hand side of the problem, to the goal, the right hand side.

Example 8.4: MYCIN (Buchanan & Shortliff 1984)

In their effort to create a search algorithm that reflected how doctors analyzed patients suffering from possible meningitis infections, the MYCIN program designers built goal-driven search into a strong method problem solver . They wrote an algorithm that supposed the patient had meningitis and than searched back to determine what possible infections could cause it. They then searched back further across these potential infections until they found supporting evidence in the data of the problem, that is, in the information in the form of the patient's symptoms or laboratory results.

The search algorithm of MYCIN was designed to directly reflect the search strategies of the human experts, that is, of the doctors. This was done not just because it reflected how humans applied their medical expertise, but also so doctors would feel comfortable going through a questioning session with MYCIN. Thus MYCIN search was designed to be exhaustive and depth first (Section 8.4).

Problem solving programs reflecting human intelligence have been written using each of the data driven and goal driven approaches. The decision of which search strategy to use is often based on the structure of the problem and interviews, direct method testing (Section 4.2) of human experts solving that problem. Goal directed search is suggested if:

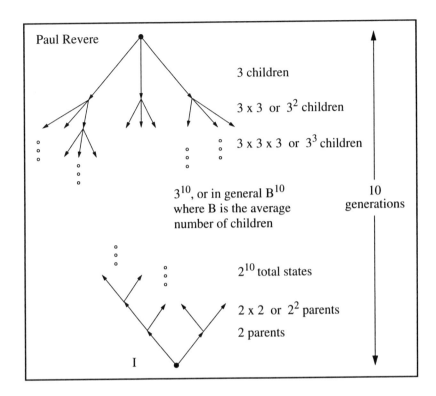

FIGURE 8.11 The search space across ten generations to determine if a person is a descendent of Paul Revere.

1. A goal or hypothesis is given in the problem statement, or may be easily formulated. In mathematics, for example, the goal may be a theorem to be proved. Many diagnostic systems, such as MYCIN (Example 8.4), consider potential diagnoses in a systematic fashion, confirming or eliminating them using goal directed reasoning.

2. There are a large number of rules that match the facts of the problem and thus produce an increasing number of conclusions or goals. Early selection of a goal can eliminate most of these branches, making goal driven search more effective in pruning the space. In logic, for example, the number of rules which conclude a given theorem is much smaller than the number of rules that can be applied to the entire set of axioms.

3. Problem data are not given, but must be acquired by the problem solver. In this case, goal directed search can help guide data acquisition. In a medical diagnosis program, for example, there are a wide range of diag-

nostic tests which can be applied. Doctors then should only order those tests which are necessary to confirm or deny a particular set of subgoals within the context of the search. Goal driven search thus uses knowledge of the desired goal to guide the search back through relevant rules.

Data-driven search, using the information and constraints found in the problem statement, is appropriate to problems in which:

1. All or most of the data are given in the initial problem statement. Interpretation problems often fit this mold since they present a collection of data and ask the system to provide an interpretation. Problems that analyze particular data, such as seismic data with PROSPECTOR (Duda et al. 1979), and that reason with this geological data to find what minerals are likely to be found at a site, fit the data-driven approach.
2. There are a large number of potential goals but only a few ways to use the facts and given information of a particular problem instance. The DENDRAL program, an expert system which finds the molecular structure of organic compounds based on their formula, mass spectrographic data, and knowledge of chemistry, is an example of this (Lindsay et al. 1980). For any organic compound, there are an enormous number of possible structures. Molecular symmetries and mass spectrographic data allow DENDRAL to eliminate all but a few of these.
3. It is difficult to form a goal or hypothesis. In a given problem consultation, for example, nothing may be initially known about the possible goals of the search.

To summarize, there is no substitute for careful analysis of experts' solutions of particular problems, considering such issues as the branching of the state space, the availability of data, and ease of determining potential goals. Above all, interviews taken from human experts solving a particular problem led to suggestions for design of search algorithms. In fact, analysis of human expertise led to the design of the search methods listed in the programs above: MYCIN, PROSPECTOR, and DENDRAL. Consulting the human expert can often elucidate not only the most efficient approach but also important heuristics (Section 8.5) that may be applicable within the problem solution process.

8.4   BREADTH-FIRST AND DEPTH-FIRST SEARCH

In addition to specifying the direction of a search as data-driven or goal-driven, a algorithm also must determine the order in which states are examined within the search space. We consider two approaches: *depth-first* and *breadth-first* search.

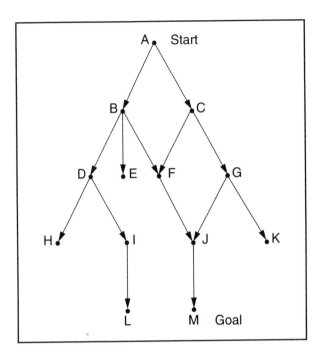

Figure 8.12   A directed graph to be searched by different search techniques.

Consider the graph represented in Figure 8.12. States are labeled (A, B, C...) so that they can be referred to in the discussion that follows. In *depth-first search*, when a state is examined, all of its children and their descendants are examined before any of the state's siblings. Thus, depth-first search goes deeper into the search space whenever this is possible. Only when no further descendants of a state can be found are its siblings considered. Depth-first search examines the states of Figure 8.12 in the order: A, B, D, H, I, L, E, F, J, M, C, G, K.

Breadth-first search, in contrast, explores the space in a level-by-level fashion. Only when there are no more states to be explored at a given level does the algorithm move on to the next deeper level. A breadth-first search of the graph of Figure 8.9 considers the states in the order: A, B, C, D, E, F, G, H, I, J, K, L, M.

8.4.1   Breadth-First Search

To keep track of the progress of the search through the graph, we use two lists, named *open* and *closed* to monitor progress through the state space. Open records all the states that have been generated but have not been examined to see where they might lead. The order with which states are removed from open determines the order of the search. Closed records states that have already been examined. We now give a pseudo code description of breadth-first search (comments follow the % sign):

procedure *breadth-first search*;

```
    begin
    Initialize: open = [Start];
    closed = [ ];
    while open < > [ ] do                     % while states remain in the search
         begin
              remove the left most state from open, call it X;
              if X is a goal then return (success);            % goal is found
              generate all children of X;
              put X on closed;                          % search with X complete
              remove children of X already on open or closed;        % loops
              put remaining descendants, in order of discovery,
                    on the right end of open
         end;
    return (fail)                                       % no states remain
    end.
```

Child states may be generated by inference rules, by legal moves of the game, or by other state transition operators. Each iteration of the procedure produces all children of the state X and adds them to open. Note that open is maintained as a *queue*, or a *first-in-first-out* data structure; that is, states are added to the right end of the list and removed from the left. This biases search toward the states that have been on open the longest, causing the search to be breadth-first. Child states that have already been discovered, that is, that already appear on either open or closed are eliminated because they can cause looping in the search path.

If the algorithm terminates because the condition of the *while* loop is no longer satisfied then the open list is empty, and breadth-first search has searched the entire graph without finding a desired goal. In this situation the search has failed. A trace of breadth-first search on the graph of Figure 8.12 appears next. Each successive number, 1, 2, 3, 4, ... at the left indicates an iteration of the *while* loop. M is the desired goal state.

1)	open = [A]	closed = [ ]
2)	open = [B, C]	closed = [A]
3)	open = [C, D, E, F]	closed = [B, A]
4)	open = [D, E, F, G]	closed = [C, B, A]
5)	open = [E, F, G, H, I]	closed = [D, C, B, A]
6)	open = [F, G, H, I]	closed = [E, D, C, B, A]
7)	open = [G, H, I, J]	closed = [F, E, D, C, B, A]
8)	open = [H, I, J, K]	closed = [G, F, E, D, C, B, A]
9)	open = [I, J, K]	closed = [H, G, F, E, D, C, B, A]
10)	open = [J, K, L]	closed = [I, H, G, F, E, D, C, B, A]

When M, the child of J, is found, return *success*, as the solution is found.

Figure 8.13 illustrates the graph of Figure 8.12 after six iterations of the while loop of breadth-first search. The states on open and closed are indicated for that iteration. States not circled have not yet been discovered by the search algorithm. Note that open records those states on the frontier of the search at any stage and closed records states already visited. Breadth-first search considers every node at each level of the graph before going any deeper into the space. Breadth-first search is therefore guaranteed to find a shortest path from the start state to each state it discovers, as well as to any goal it finds.

***Example 8.5:* Breadth-First Search of the Knight Tour Problem**

Figure 8.14 shows the states removed from open and examined in a breadth-first search of the graph of the Knight's Tour. The number to the right of each state indicates the order in which it was removed from open. Because the algorithm checks for loops in the path, all the cycles present in Figure 8.5 are removed. After five iterations of breadth-first search, open and closed are:

Open: [(4,4), (3,1), (4,2), (1,3), (2,4), (5,3), (5,1), (2,7), (3,4), (3,6)]
Closed: [(3,5), (1,5), (3,2), (2,3), (1,1)]

The reader should note that we have still not clarified how the children of a state are produced, for example, why state (2,3) comes before (3,2) in the search

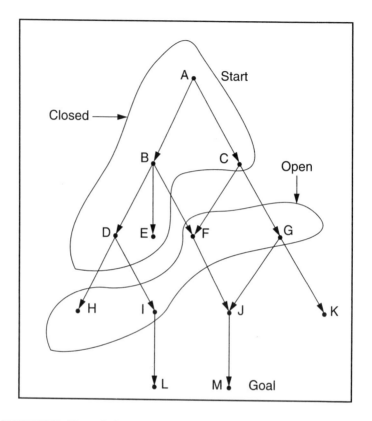

FIGURE 8.13 Figure 8.12 after six iterations of breadth-first search. The open and closed lists are indicated on the graph.

of Figure 8.14. In the examples of Section 8.4 we simply assume all children of a state are produced, without concern of the order of their production. This will also be true for depth-first search.

8.4.2 Depth-First Search

Depth-first search modifies the breadth-first search. In examining the algorithm, note that the descendent states are both added and removed from the left end of open: open is maintained as a *stack*, or *last-in-first-out* data structure. The organization of open as a stack biases search towards the most recently generated states, always forcing the search to go deeper into the graph. We next present the pseudo code for depth-first search:

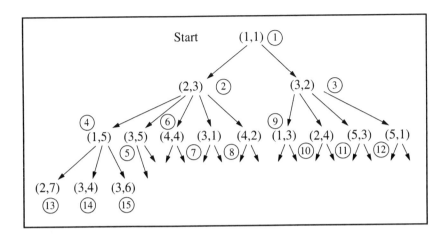

Figure 8.14   Breadth-first search of the Knight Tour problem. The numbers, 1, 2, ... 15
to the right of each state indicate the order in which it is expanded.

procedure *depth_first_search*;

```
begin
Initialize: open = [Start];
closed = [ ];
while open < > [ ] do                    % while states remain in the search
      begin
            remove the left most state from open, call it X;
            if X is a goal then return (success);        % goal is found
            generate all children of X;
            put X on closed;                   % search with X complete
            remove children of X already on open or closed;    % loops
            put remaining descendants, in order of
                  discovery, on the left end of open
      end;
      return (fail)                         % no states remain
end.
```

A trace of depth-first search on the graph of Figure 8.12 appears next. Each
successive iteration of the *while* loop is indicated by a single line numbered at the
left 1, 2, 3, 4, ... The initial states of open and closed are given on line 1. M is the
goal state.

1)   open = [A]   closed = [ ]

2)   open = [B, C]   closed = [A]

3)   open = [D, E, F, C]   closed = [B, A]

4)   open = [H, I, E, F, C]   closed = [D, B, A]

5)   open = [I, E, F, C]   closed = [H, D, B, A]

6)   open = [L, E, F, C]   closed = [I, H, D, B, A]

7)   open = [E, F, C]   closed = [L, I, H, D, B, A]

8)   open = [F, C]   closed = [E, L, I, H, D, B, A]

9)   open = [J, C]   closed = [F, E, L, I, H, D, B, A]

10) open = [M, C]   closed = [J, F, E, L, I, H, D, B, A]

11) Goal M is discovered, return success!

As with breadth-first search, the open list contains all states discovered but not yet evaluated. These states make up the current frontier of the search. Closed records states already considered. Figure 8.15 shows the graph of Figure 8.12 after the fifth iteration of the depth-first search procedure. The contents of open and closed are indicated.

Figure 8.16 gives a depth-first search of the knight's tour problem. The space is generated by the legal knight moves on the chessboard. Numbers next to the states indicate the order in which they were considered, i.e., removed from open. Note that no duplicate states are produced since they are removed by the algorithm. It is often necessary to create a depth bound on searches such as this to keep from getting lost deep in the space. The open and closed lists after five steps of the search are indicated in Figure 8.16.

8.4.3   Comparisons of Search Strategies

We now make several comments on humans selection of search techniques appropriate to the problem under consideration. As with choosing between data-driven or goal-driven reasoning for evaluating a graph, the choice of depth-first or breadth-first search depends on the specific problem being considered. The direct method of examining subjects is often sufficient for determining search strategies. As a number of researchers have noted (Simon & Simon 1978,

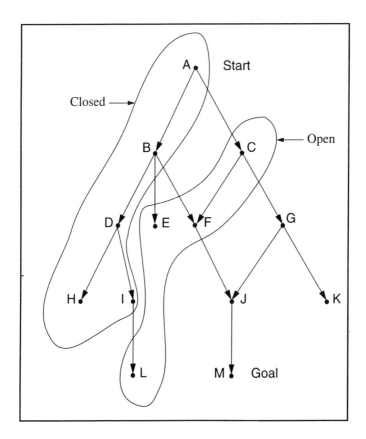

FIGURE 8.15 Figure 8.12 after five iterations of depth-first search. The open and closed lists are indicated on the graph.

Larkin et al. 1980) these search strategies can also shift as the human becomes more proficient in a problem area.

Important features humans consider in search include the importance of finding a shortest path to a goal, the branching of the state space, the available time and space resources, and the average length of paths to a goal node. In making these decisions, there are advantages and disadvantages for each approach:

Breadth-first:

Since it examines all the nodes at level n before proceeding to level n + 1, breadth-first search always finds the shortest path to any state. In a problem where it is known that a simple solution exists, breadth-first search will find it.

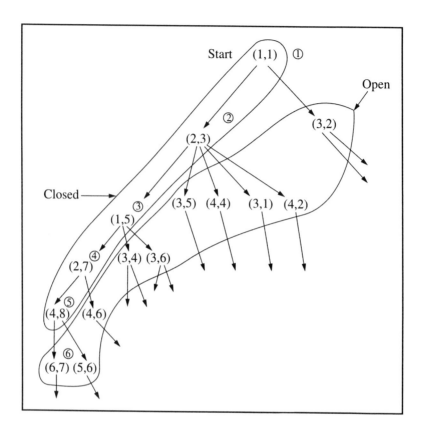

FIGURE 8.16 Depth-first search on the knight tour problem. Numbers next to the state
indicate the order in which it is expanded.

Unfortunately, if there is a bad branching factor, such as in chess where
states have a large number of children, the combinatorial explosion may prevent
the algorithm from finding a solution in a useful time period. This is partially due
to the fact that all unexpanded nodes for each level of the search must be kept on
open. If each state has an average of B children, the number of states on a given
level is B times the number of states on the previous level. This gives B^n states at
level n. Breadth-first search will have placed all of these on open when it begins
examining level n. This is prohibitive if solution paths are long.

Depth first:

Depth-first search gets quickly into a deep search space. If it is known that
the solution path will be long, depth-first search won't waste time searching a

large number of "shallow" states in the graph. On the other hand, depth-first search can get "lost" deep in a graph, missing shorter paths to a goal or becoming stuck in a very long path that does not lead to a goal.

Depth-first search is more efficient for search spaces with many branches since it does not keep all the nodes at any given level on the open list. The space usage of depth-first search for the open list is a linear function of the length of the current path. At each level, open retains the children of a single state. If a graph has an average of B children per state, it requires B * n states to go n levels deep into the space.

The best answer to the depth-first or breadth-first search issue is to examine the problem space carefully and consult with human experts solving problems in the area. In chess, as noted above, breadth-first search is simply not possible. In simpler situations breadth-first search may not only be possible, but also may be the only way to avoid losing. Most AI texts also present variants of depth-first search, such as using a depth bound, and breadth-first search, such as using pruning, that can improve on the worst case extremes of these searches.

***Example 8.6:* Subject S3 Solving a Task in Cryptarithmetic**

In Chapter 9, we introduce the cryptarithmetic problem solving task. Figures 9.2 and 9.3 present the problem behavior graph of subject S3. The search is depth-first, with a depth bound of 5 or 6. Details of this task are presented in Section 9.2.

8.5   HEURISTIC OR BEST-FIRST SEARCH

8.5.1 An Algorithm for Heuristic Search

We now introduce *heuristic* or *best-first search*. A very simple method for implementation of heuristic search is with a procedure called *hill climbing* (Pearl 1984). Hill climbing strategies expand the current node in the search and evaluate its children. The best child is selected for further expansion; neither its siblings nor its parent are retained. Search halts when it reaches a state which is better than any of its child successors.

Hill climbing is named for the strategy that might be used by a blind person attempting to climb a mountain: check the steepness of the path in all directions 1 m distant from where you now stand, then go uphill along the steepest possible gradient, and repeat this selection mechanism until you can go no further uphill. The problem with hill climbing strategies is that an unlucky starting location can lead along erroneous paths that fail to lead to a solution. Because it keeps no history, the algorithm cannot recover from these failures.

Hill climbing strategies can also become stuck at local maxima. If they reach a state which has a better evaluation than any of its children, the algorithm halts. Our more general heuristic search algorithm addresses both these shortcomings by use of the open and closed lists. In its simplest form, information as to the "goodness" of each state is retained on the open list along with that state. This goodness is measured as some property of a state, such as an estimate of how far that state is from a goal state. The "best" state is then selected from the open list each time a new state is needed to continue search.

We present pseudo code for best-first search:

procedure *best_first_search*;

```
    begin
    Initialize: open = [Start];
    closed = [ ];
    begin
        while open < > [ ] do                   % states remain to be searched
            begin
                remove next state from open, call it X;
                if X is goal then return success;
                process X, generating all its children;
                for each child of X do
                    if child is not already on open or closed:
                    then begin
                            assign a heuristic value to state;
                            add the state to open;
                        end
                    else                         % child already on open or closed
                        revise, if necessary, path information
                put X on closed;                 %we are finished with it
                re-order open by heuristic merit              % best first
            end;
        return failure;                          % open is empty
    end.
```

The use of lists in best-first search is similar to that of depth-first and breadth-first search: open is used to keep track of the current fringe of the search and closed to record states already visited. When we order the states on open by their heuristic estimate of their "closeness" to a goal, then each iteration of the search considers the most "promising" state first. Less promising states remain on open in the case that the more promising states do not lead to a solution.

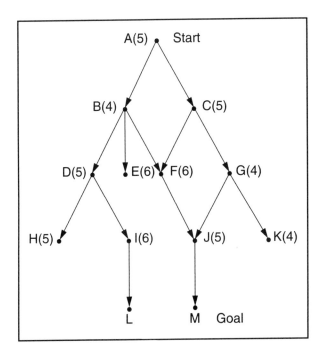

FIGURE 8.17 The graph of Figure 8.12 with heuristic cost estimate added to each state.

We consider best-first search to be a *weak method* in that the heuristic estimate may be obtained for any state on open. In the example of the knight tour problem this will be a form of the *euclidean distance* of the current state from the goal state. Similar metrics may be found for a wide range of problems. When the "goodness" of a state is reflected in a confidence measure for the knowledge used to produce that particular state, we call it a *strong method* and discuss it further in Chapter 9.

Figure 8.17 shows a hypothetical state space (Figure 8.12) with heuristic evaluations attached to all states. The purpose of this example is to demonstrate how the search moves about within the state space and to note that it may not search all of the space. The intent of best-first search is to find the goal state while looking at as few states as possible. The better the heuristic, the fewer the number of states that are processed in the course of finding the goal. This last computational advantage may be relative since there is an added cost of applying the heuristic to each new state.

At each iteration, best-first search removes the first element from the open list. If it meets the goal conditions, the algorithm returns success. If the first element on open is not a goal, the algorithm applies all matching rules or operators to generate its children. If a child state is already on open or closed, the algorithm checks to make sure that the state records the shortest of the two partial solution paths. By updating the ancestor history of nodes on open and closed when they are rediscovered, the algorithm is more likely to find the shortest path to a goal. Duplicate states are not retained. More complete details on this and related algorithms may be found in Luger and Stubblefield (1993).

Once best-first search applies a heuristic evaluation to each of the states on open, the list is sorted according to these heuristic values. This brings the "best" state to the front of open. Note that since these estimates are heuristic in nature, the next state to be examined may be from any level of the state space.

A trace of the execution of best-first search on graph of Figure 8.17 appears next. Since M is the goal, states along the path to M tend to have low heuristic values. Our heuristic is fallible: some states not on the solution path have lower heuristics than those on the path and are thus evaluated before those leading to the solution. The algorithm recovers, however, by going back to the open list and finding the correct path to the goal.

Iteration	Best	Open	Closed
1		[A5]	[ ]
2	A5	[B4, C5]	[A5]
3	B4	[D5, C5, E6, F6]	[B4, A5]
4	D5	[H5, C5, I6, E6, F6]	[D5, B4, A5]
5	H5	[C5, I6, E6, F6]	[H5, D5, B4, A5]
6	C5	[G4, I6, E6, F6]	[C5, H5, D5, B4, A5]
7	G4	[K4, J5, I6, E6, F6]	[G4, C5, H5, D5, B4, A5]
8	K4	[J5, I6, E6, F6]	[K4, C5, H5, D5, B4, A4]
9	M	return success, the solution is found!	

Figure 8.18 shows the space as it appears after the fifth iteration of the *while* loop. The states contained in open and closed are indicated. Open records the current frontier of the search and closed records states already considered. Note that the frontier of the search is highly uneven, reflecting the opportunistic nature of best-first search.

The best-first search algorithm always selects the most promising state on open for further expansion. However, since it is using a heuristic which may prove erroneous, it does not abandon all the other states, but maintains them on

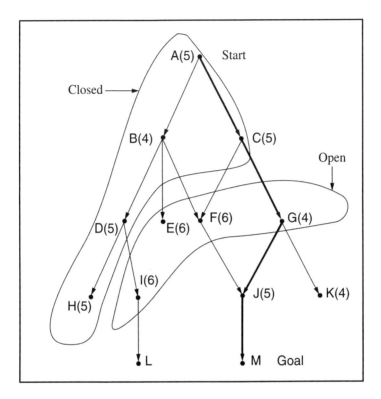

FIGURE 8.18 Best-first search applied to Figure 8.17. Open and closed are indicated after the fifth iteration of the search. The heuristic estimate is included with each state label; the solution path is bold.

open. In the event a heuristic leads the search down a path which proves incorrect, the algorithm may retrieve some previously generated next best state from open and shift its focus to another part of the space. In the example of Figure 8.18, after the children of state B and D were found by their poor heuristic value not to be thought to be leading to a solution, the search shifted its focus to state C. The children of D were kept on open in case the algorithm needed to return to them later. In best-first search the open list allows recovery from paths which fail to produce a goal.

Example 8.7: **Heuristics in the Context of the General Problem Solver**

We could reorder the difference reduction rules in the table of connections (Figure 8.3) to reflect the strategies of the human expert. This heuristic approach dictates that for each difference to be reduced, there is a priority order of the reductions attempted. This ordering information could be obtained by a direct method analysis of a subject working in the application area. Since the methods for difference reduction are related to the knowledge we have of a domain, this "prioritizing of methods" could be seen as a heuristic for strong methods. A similar approach for implementing heuristic search was used in the analysis of subjects solving applied mathematics problems (see Figure 6.18).

Human expertise is often built on an informed decision of what to do next: we do well to observe it closely. As cognitive scientists we can observe heuristics in problem solving subjects, then build these heuristics into our problem solver. As the performance diverges from our expectations, we can revise and reformulate our heuristics.

8.5.2 Applying Best-First Search

We now create a heuristic search for the knight tour problem. Our heuristic will be the calculation of the distance to the goal for each state on the open list. We use this measure to order the states on open so we always take the state closest to the goal first. This heuristic is similar to what human's might use in the knight tour problem: move the knight as directly as possible toward the goal.

A heuristic measure for states in the knight tour problem is the sum of the absolute values of their row and column distances to the goal. The difference will be calculated using absolute value so that it will always be positive. We present several states from Figure 8.19 and calculate their distance from the goal:

Present State	Goal State	Row Distance	Column Distance	Heuristic Measure
b (2,2)	(8,3)	$|2 - 8| = 6$	$|2 - 3| = 1$	7
c (3,3)	(8,3)	$|3 - 8| = 5$	$|3 - 3| = 0$	5
d (3,5)	(8,3)	$|3 - 8| = 5$	$|5 - 3| = 2$	7
e (2,6)	(8,3)	$|2 - 8| = 6$	$|6 - 3| = 3$	9

There is a problem with this heuristic, however. As the knight gets very close to the goal state, say less than three squares, the search worsens. This deterioration is due to the nature of the knight move: always two squares in one direction and one in the other. Thus being too near the goal can be bad!

This example illustrates the difficulty of devising good heuristics. Best-first search is a weak method in that we use the limited information available in a single state description to make intelligent choices. Each heuristic ignores some critical bit of information and is subject to improvement. The design of good heuristics is an empirical problem. Judgment and intuition help, but the final measure of a heuristic must be its actual performance on problem instances.

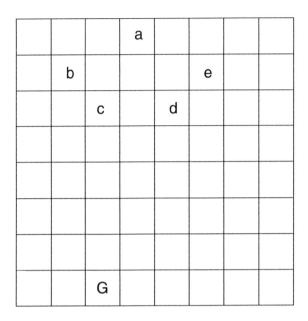

FIGURE 8.19   The chessboard for the knight tour. State a is the start, G is the goal, and b, c, d, and e are the children of the start state and on the open list.

Since heuristics are fallible it is possible that a search algorithm can be misdirected down some path which fails to lead to a goal. Even where an algorithm is not "lost," if two states have the same or nearly the same heuristic evaluations, it is generally preferable to examine the state that is nearest to the start state in the graph. This state may have a greater probability of being on the shortest path to the goal. The distance from the starting state to each state on the search path can be measured by maintaining a depth count for that state. This count is 0 for the start state and is increased by 1 for each level of the search. This count records the actual number of moves that have been used to go from the start state in the search to each descendent.

This depth measure can be added to the heuristic evaluation of each state to bias search in favor of states found shallower in the graph. We create an evaluation function, f, the sum of two components:

$$f(n) = g(n) + h(n)$$

where $g(n)$ measures actual length of the path from the start state to state n and $h(n)$ is the estimate of the distance from n to the goal. These measures are shown in Figure 8.21.

	t		a				
g	b			l	e		
m		c		d			
h			q	k			
	i		j				
r		v	p	u			
n		o					
s		G		t			

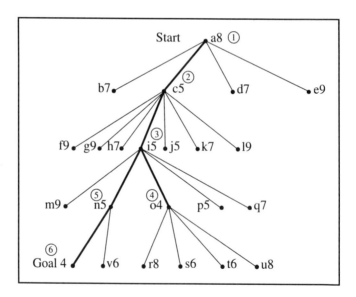

FIGURE 8.20 The continued development of the knight tour from the chessboard of
Figure 8.19 with states evaluated by best-first search. The heuristic measure, f = g + h, is next to each state label and the order in which states are
generated, 1, ..., 6, is above each state label.

The full best-first search of the knight tour graph, using f as just defined,
appears in Figure 8.20. Each state is labeled with a letter and its heuristic weight,
$f(n) = g(n) + h(n)$. The number at the top of each state indicates the order in

which it was taken off the open list. States are generated in a counterclockwise order, from 12 o'clock. Some states are not numbered since they were still on open or not yet considered when the algorithm terminates.

The successive stages of open and closed for Figure 8.20 are now presented. The number at left indicates the iteration of the best-first procedure, the number after each state the heuristic measure of that state, with a the start state:

Iteration	Open	Closed
1	[a8]	[ ]
2	[c5, b7, d7, e9]	[a8]
3	[i5, j5, h7, k7, b7, d7, f9, l9, e9]	[c5, a8]
4	[o4, n5, p5, j5, q7, h7, k7, b7, d7, m9, f9, l9, e9]	[i5, c5, a8]
5	[n5, p5, j5, s6, t6, q7, h7, k7, b7, d7, r8, u8, m9, f9, l9, e9]	[o4, i5, c5, a8]
6	[goal, p5, j5, s6, t6, v7, q7, h7, k7, b7, d7, r8, u8, m9, f9, l9, e9]	[n5, o4, i5, c5, a8]
7	Return success, the goal is found!	

In step 3 of the execution, both states i and j have an heuristic evaluation of 5. State i is examined first, producing children m, n, o, p, and q. Of these children, o, with heuristic 4, looks best. Note, however, that this is a poor choice, since it is so close to the goal. When all o's children have poor heuristic measure, the choice goes back to n, the sibling of o, which immediately produces the goal state. The full state space search of the knight tour appears in Figure 8.20. Notice the flexible, opportunistic nature of best-first search.

In effect, the g(n) component of the evaluation function gives the search more of a breadth-first flavor. This prevents it from being misled by an erroneous evaluation: if a heuristic continuously returns "good" evaluations for states along a path that continues deeper and deeper but fails to reach a goal, the g value will grow to dominate h and force search back to a shorter solution path. This guarantees that the algorithm will not become permanently lost, descending some indefinite branch.

Another view of f(n) = g(n) + h(n) is given in Figure 8.21. The g(n) is already known for state n. It is the actual cost from the start state to state n, measured in number of steps to state n. h(n) is the estimated cost of the path from state n to a goal. The f(n) is a cost estimate of the total path from a start to a goal state that contains state n.

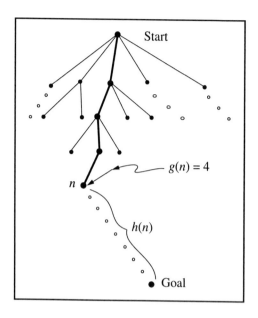

Figure 8.21   The function f for use with the best-first search algorithm. In f(n) = g(n)
+ h(n), g(n) is the distance of state n from the start and h(n) is the
estimate of the path cost from n to the goal.

The estimated cost function f is used in conjunction with the best-first search
algorithm. This evaluation function provides a general weak method formulation
of heuristic search. To summarize:

1. Inference rules or other operations on states generate the children of the
    state currently under examination. In the knight tour example, we used
    the legal moves of the knight piece and selected a simple counterclock-
    wise generation of states. This state generation order may also become
    the subject of heuristics, as we see in Chapter 9.

2. In order to prevent loops in the search space, each new state is checked
    to see if it has occurred before, that is, if it is already on either the open
    or closed lists.

3. Each state n is given an f value equal to the sum of its depth in the
    search space, g(n), plus a heuristic estimate of its distance from the
    goal, h(n). The h value guides search toward heuristically promising
    states while the g value prevents search from persisting indefinitely on a
    fruitless path.

4. States on open are sorted by their f values. By keeping all states on open
    until they are either examined or a goal is found, the algorithm can

recover from fruitless paths. At any one time, open may contain states at different levels of the state space graph, as we saw in Figures 8.18 and 8.20, allowing full flexibility in changing the focus of the search.

8.5.3 Summary and Extensions of Heuristic Search Algorithms

Best-first search is a general weak method algorithm for heuristically searching any state space graph, as were the breadth-first and depth-first algorithms presented earlier. It is equally applicable to data-driven and goal-driven searches, and can support a diversity of heuristic evaluation functions.

There are three reasons for employing an heuristic search algorithm. The first is as a method for modeling the search patterns intelligent humans employ in their problem solving. We see instances of modeling human search patterns in this chapter and in the remainder of Part II. We extend the general weak method heuristics with knowledge based heuristics in the next chapter. Knowledge based heuristics rest on the amount and quality of knowledge in the application, the ordering of the knowledge, and the shape of the representation that captures this knowledge.

The second reason for heuristic search is as a method for dealing with complex search spaces. The third is to help cope with imprecise or missing data. Handling complexity is a mark of intelligence, as is the ability to reason with imprecise or missing data. We introduced this issue with our comments on abductive inference in Section 7.5. The algorithms of Chapter 8 allow us to organize search with approximations for missing information.

There are a number of important further extensions of heuristic search. These include *admissibility*, the guarantee that an heuristic algorithm will find a minimal path solution, if it exists. We can use heuristic search to model *competitive* search, such as in two-player games or competition for resources, on a network, say. Details of these algorithms may be found in any AI textbook including Luger and Stubblefield (1993).

There are a number of other weak method search algorithms that reflect human search strategies. Among these are hierarchy search and spreading activation methods. Hierarchy search was presented with network, frame, and object representation schemes in Chapters 3 and 6. Spreading activation is presented with subsymbolic learning in Part III.

8.6 EPILOGUE AND REFERENCES

Computers and Thought by Edward Feigenbaum and Jerome Feldman (1963) is an important source for early research on the *Logic Theorist,* the *General Prob-*

lem Solver, and the first collection of problem solving protocols of subjects solving logic problems. Allen Newell and Herb Simon describe these early days of cognitive science research in *Human Problem Solving* (1972). *The Encyclopedia of Artificial Intelligence,* edited by Stuart Shapiro, (1992) is also a valuable source for these issues.

Search and weak method problem solving dominated the early years, 1955 to 1975, of research in artificial intelligence. Many of the search methods of this chapter came from that period. *Fundamentals of Computer Algorithms* by Ellis Horowitz and Sartaj Sahni (1978) describes these same algorithms from a general computer science viewpoint.

The use of graph search to model intelligent problem solving is presented in a number of AI texts: *Principles of Artificial Intelligence* by Nils Nilsson (1980), *Artificial Intelligence* by Eugene Charniak and Drew McDermott (1985), and George Luger and William Stubblefield, *Artificial Intelligence: Structures and Strategies for Complex Problem Solving* (1993). For an analysis of heuristic search methods, we especially recommend Judea Pearl's books, *Heuristics: Intelligent Search Strategies for Computer Problem Solving* (1984) and *Probabilistic Reasoning in Intelligent Systems* (1988).

Chapter 9

USING KNOWLEDGE AND STRONG METHOD PROBLEM SOLVING

Ipsa scientia potestas est.   (Knowledge is power.)

Roger Bacon

I'm sorry, Dave, I can't let you do that...

Hal, in *2001: A Space Odyssey*

9.0   INTRODUCTION TO STRONG METHODS

In Chapter 8 we made an important distinction between *weak method* or general search based techniques in problem solving and *strong method* or knowledge based problem solving. With weak methods such as the *general problem solver*, syntactic patterns were compared and modified. General methods found differences and linked these to modifying procedures. Throughout Chapter 8 we described algorithms for different general search methods. In Chapter 9 we present strong method problem solving, an approach based on using explicitly encoded pieces of knowledge or skilled behavior.

We witness human skilled performance constantly. It is seen in appliance repair when the technician knows exactly where to tap the refrigerator to see if a particular solenoid is disabled or in the library when the librarian knows exactly where and what reference information is available. Such skill is often practice based in that it is developed over many years of use and is not necessarily part of formal training. As scientists we can study these skills, often using forms of the direct observation methods of Sections 4.2 and 9.2.

Knowledge of such skill and how it is employed has important consequences for the community. First, it is important in itself, in that as cognitive scientists, we wish to understand its nature and use. Second, if we can capture this skill, we can perhaps train new experts. Finally, we can build computer based assistants to automate this skill. In all these situations we must have a medium for representing knowledge and skill. In fact, a representational medium offers a communication language for both human and machine.

Procedural representations offer a powerful tool in this regard and we explore them in Chapter 9. In Section 9.1, we give a format for procedures with the *if.. then..* notation. This allows procedures to be pattern driven and opportunistic in their application. We also note the numerous forms of procedural representation, including *demons* and *methods* in an object system.

In Section 9.2 we consider the Newell and Simon direct testing methodology in detail. These researchers, with their analysis of problem solving protocols, established the production rule as an important representational medium for capturing procedural information. We consider not just the results of this research, but the Newell and Simon justification for the comparison of human problem solving protocols with computer generated traces.

In Section 9.3, we show the *production system* as an architecture for the search algorithms of Chapter 8. In Section 9.4, with the presentation of the *blackboard*, we offer another architecture for procedural representations. These architectures are used in a number of cognitive applications, including game playing, puzzle solving, and speech recognition. In Section 9.5 we present ACT* and Soar, generalizations of the production system approach. These systems offer full *unified theories of cognition*. We conclude Chapter 9 and Part II with some general comments on the symbol based representational methodology.

9.1 KNOWLEDGE, SKILL, AND PROCEDURAL REPRESENTATION SCHEMES

There are many reasons for capturing procedural skills in the if.. then.. format. These include: 1). the pattern based description of skill, 2). the direct association of pattern to response, and 3) the ease of linking together the if.. then.. relations in reasoning.

First, knowledge and the application of skill have a strong stimulus or pattern driven component. The chess grand master responds to board positions. In fact, as Chase and Simon (1973) show, as well as earlier work by deGroot (1965), the entire understanding of chess by the expert is by patterns of positions rather than by absolute board positions. Similarly, the doctor responds to symptoms in the patient. Symptoms and patterns of pain indicate potential problems. There is no exhaustive search over all knowledge in the expert's practice of healing.

Second, in the application of skill there is a connection associating pattern to response. The situation is directly related to the remedy; there is little or no search for a response once the pattern of symptoms is identified. Even in a goal based search, when the result or action is identified, we directly link back to the supporting conditions for that action. In medicine, for example, the indication of a possible infection immediately suggests several tests for its verification (Buchanan & Shortliff 1984).

Finally, as we saw in logic based representations, it is natural to chain together sequences of if.. then.. relations to develop a larger reasoning scheme. When we use the direct method to study human subject's solving cryptarithmetic tasks in Section 9.2, we can witness this rule or procedure chaining in action. Even without carefully designed introspective studies, it seems obvious that human problem solving can be represented by chaining together pieces of skilled behavior: a situation suggesting a response which creates a new situation, suggesting a further response, and so on.

Procedural knowledge may be embedded at almost any level in an intelligent agent. We see avoidance mechanisms built in at even the subconscious level: a pattern such as the trajectory of a thrown object causes us to respond by dodging. Structured representation schemes such as frames or schemas (Section 6.3) often include specific instructions, sometimes referred to as *demons*, to guide response when certain patterns trigger them. These demons are procedures that respond when some context shifts or a pattern changes. In object based representations (Section 6.4), *methods* are procedures used to communicate with other objects in the design. In all these situations procedures are usually described and triggered by their pattern driven if.. then.. encoding.

In Section 9.2 we make detailed presentation of an experimental situation that demonstrates the nature and use of human knowledge and skill. In Section 9.2 we also describe and criticize the use of the direct methodology (Section 4.2) for analyzing human skilled performance. Second, we see the procedural nature of much of this skill and its characterization in the if.. then.. production rule format. Finally, we begin to see an architecture for the application of human skilled performance. This is, of course, the production system which we describe in further detail in Section 9.3.

9.2 FROM GPS TO THE HUMAN PROBLEM SOLVING PARADIGM

9.2.1 The Protocol and Direct Method Observation

In their book *Human Problem Solving*, Allen Newell and Herbert Simon (1972) present a clear vision of how their "information processing" model of performance evolved from their early work on the general problem solver. Their protocol-trace comparison methodology, an application of the direct method for understanding human performance presented in Section 4.2, is also presented here. A more complete rationalization of this technique may be found in Simon and Ericsson (1984).

We now consider this methodology, its justification, and some of its results. To do this we look at a problem in cryptarithmetic studied by Newell and Simon

(1972). As one would expect, these researchers were more interested in the human subject's tactics and strategies, their mistakes and shortcuts rather than whether or not each subject could solve the problem. This type of problem was taken from earlier experimental studies run by Bartlett (1932). The cryptarithmetic problem may be stated:

> Find numbers to replace the letters in the following addition problems. Each letter stands for a different number, and no single number can replace two different letters.

Problem a) below has several solutions, one of which is given. Problem b) has one solution (not related to problem a), and was one of the problems originally used by Newell and Simon.

a)	I	b)	DONALD	with D = 5
	AM		+GERALD	
	+NOT		ROBERT	
	DUM			

A solution for a) is:

$$\begin{array}{r} 3 \\ 42 \\ +867 \\ \hline 912 \end{array}$$

During the time that each human subject solved problems such as these, they worked at a table with scratch paper and a pencil. They were asked to speak their thoughts out loud so that they could be recorded. In some problem solving sessions the experimenters used other techniques, such as video recording or monitoring eye movements, to help keep track of what the human subject was doing in the process of solving the problem.

9.2.2 From Protocol Analysis to Problem Behavior Graph

The recorded words of the subject were first transcribed by the experimenters and broken into thought fragments. We see a typical example of this *protocol* in Figure 9.1. Here a subject (S3) does the first few minutes of problem solving on the DONALD + GERALD = ROBERT problem. The entire protocol had 321 such thought fragments and described the 20 min time period it required the subject to solve this problem. The protocol includes the stream of statements down the left hand side of Figure 9.1. The right hand side is the set of production rules that can account for this behavior. We will describe how the rules can be used to represent the protocol shortly.

Protocol for Subject S3 on Donald + Gerald = Robert Problem

Problem: DONALD   D = 5
           +GERALD
            ROBERT

PHRASE NUMBER	PROTOCOL	INFERRED PRODUCTIONS
B1*	Each letter has one and only one numerical value...	?: [ask E about rules]
B2	(E: One numerical value.)	
B3	There are ten different letters	
B4	and each of them has one numerical value.	
B5*	Therefore, I can, looking at the two Ds...	P1: $D \leftarrow 5 \rightarrow FC(D)$ ($\Rightarrow$ col. 1; PC [col. 1] ($\Rightarrow$ T = 0 new)
B6	each D is 5;	
B7	therefore, T is zero.	P11: $T = 0 \rightarrow TD(T, 0)$ ($\Rightarrow \prod+$)
B8*	So I think I'll start by writing that problem here.	
B9	I'll write 5, 5 is zero.	
B10	Now, do I have any other Ts?	P1: $T = 0 \rightarrow FC(T)$ ($\Rightarrow$ fail)
B11	No.	
B12	But I have another D.	P1: $D \leftarrow 5 \rightarrow FC(D)$ ($\Rightarrow$ col. 6)
B13	That means I have a 5 over the other side.	
B14	Now I have 2 As	P9: get all-letters $\rightarrow$ FL (all-letters) ($\Rightarrow$ R); get R
B15	and 2 Ls	

PHRASE NUMBER	PROTOCOL	INFERRED PRODUCTIONS
B16*	that are each...	
B17	somewhere...	
B18	and this R...	
B19	3 Rs...	
B20	2 Ls equal an R...	P2: get R → FC(R) (⟹ col. 2); PC[col. 2 for R] (⟹ R odd new)
B21	Of course I'm carrying a 1.	
B22	Which will mean that R has to be an odd number.	
B22.1		P13: PC unclear → get R; repeat PC
B23	Because the 2 Ls...	↑: PC [col. 2 for R] (⟹ R odd)
B24	any two numbers added together has to be an even number	
B25	and 1 will be an odd number.	
B26	So R can be 1,	P4: get R → GN(R) (⟹ 1 ∨ 3 ∨ 5 ∨ 7 ∨ 9)
B27	3,	
B28*	not 5,	P11: R = d → TD (R, d) (⟹ (R = 5 ☐) (D ← 5 note))
B29	7,	
B30	or 9.	
B30.1*		?:
B31	(E: What are you thinking now?)	
B32	Now G....	P2: get R → FC(R) (⟹ col. 6); PC [col. 6 for R] (⟹ G even new)
B33	Since R is going to be an odd number	

PHRASE NUMBER	PROTOCOL	INFERRED PRODUCTIONS
B34	and D is 5,	
B35*	G has to be an even number.	
B35.1		P13: PC unclear → get G; repeat PC
B36	I'm looking at the left side of this problem here where it says D + G.	↑: PC [col. 6 for G] (⟹ c6 unknown)
B37	Oh, plus possibly another number,	
B38	if I have to carry 1 from the E + 0.	
B39*	I think I'll forget about that for a minute.	?:
B40*	Possibly the best way to get to this problem is to try different possible solutions.	
B41	I'm not sure whether that would be the easiest way or not.	
B42	Well, if we assume...	P3: get R → FA(R) (⟹ col. 2); AV(L) (⟹ L ← 1);
B43	if we assume that L is, say, 1.	

*Asterisks refer to the notes that follow the protocol.

Notes to the preceding protocol:

B1	The exchange deals with the definition of the problem, hence is outside the problem space.
B5	The subject has been told that D = 5 prior to the start of the tape.
B8	We do not encode writing operations.
B16	After identifying A's and Ls, searching for more occurrences. The pattern shows for R in B18-19.
B28	"not 5" shows S3 is generating and testing at same time.
B30.1	Don't know what S3 does after GN.

B35   Shows S3 has ignored carry.

B39   Don't know what the decision is based upon; however, there
                    is no place to go as long as assignments are not made (see
                    B40).

B40   One of the few indications of development (or change) of
                    methods.

FIGURE 9.1   Part of the protocol of subject S3 on the DONALD + GERALD = ROB-
                    ERT problem. From Newell and Simon (1972).

The researchers carefully analyze the subject's and the experimenter's recorded words, and break them into the protocol fragments as seen in Figure 9.1. The asterisk (*) near the fragments indicates the researchers' added comments; these are included at the end of Figure 9.1. Creating protocols such as that of Figure 9.1 can take researchers many hours of carefully going over the recorded verbalizations and other data from the problem solving session. The protocol is next transcribed into a *problem behavior graph*.

The *problem behavior graph* is an attempt to describe the searching steps that take place during the problem solving. This graph has many of the components of graphs in general as presented in Section 6.1. The specific rules for generating the problem behavior graph include:

a)   States of knowledge are represented by nodes of the graph.

b)   The application of some operator to a state of knowledge is represented by a horizontal arrow to the right. The result of applying the operator is the node at the head of the arrow.

c)   A return to a previous state of knowledge is represented by another node below that original state and connected by a vertical line.

d)   The repeat application of the same operator is indicated by doubling the horizontal line.

In the problem behavior graph, time runs to the right and then down. Thus the graph is linearly ordered by the time of node generation. The problem behavior graph for the first 53 fragments of S3's protocol may be found in Figure 9.2. A reduced presentation of the entire problem behavior graph for S3 may be found in Figure 9.3. Note the total of 238 nodes or states of the search. Next we describe the transformation of regularities in the problem behavior graph to sets of production rules.

9.2.3   From Problem Behavior Graph to Production Rules

After mapping out the search details in the problem behavior graph, the research-ers then consider the occurrence of operators in this graph. They note that a large number of the new states of knowledge are generated by a relatively small num-ber of operators. These operators are then analyzed and described by *if.. then..* procedures. The *if* part of the procedure captures the pattern or situation that evokes the procedure. The *then* part describes the action that is taken in response to this situation.

The procedure patterns in the if.. then.. form that subject S3 used to trans-form one state of the problem into another are called *production* or *rewrite rules*. These operators are listed on the horizontal arcs joining the nodes in the problem behavior graph of Figure 9.2, as well as after the protocol fragments of Figure 9.1. We now describe briefly several of these operators:

FC(variable)	Find Column for some variable whose value you have just determined.
PC(column)	Process some Column to determine new results. PC often follows FC.
GN(variable)	GeNerate takes as input a variable and related information and returns a set of admissible values for that variable.
AV(variable)	Assigns a Value to a variable depending on infor-mation known about it.
C(expression)	Checks an expression by finding the rule that gen-erated the expression and regenerating it.

Researchers found 14 such production rules that together produced a large percentage of the new states found in the problem behavior graph of S3. A sam-ple of these inferred productions are placed opposite the sentence fragments of the protocol in the right hand column of Figure 9.1. In the next step of the research process these production rules are placed in a general production system program and run on a computer. The trace or step by step solution process of the running production system program is then compared with the steps taken by the human subjects.

We introduced the production system in Section 3.3, and show in more detail how it generates a large variety of search graphs in the next section. The produc-tion system architecture is a general computational methodology, even outside of

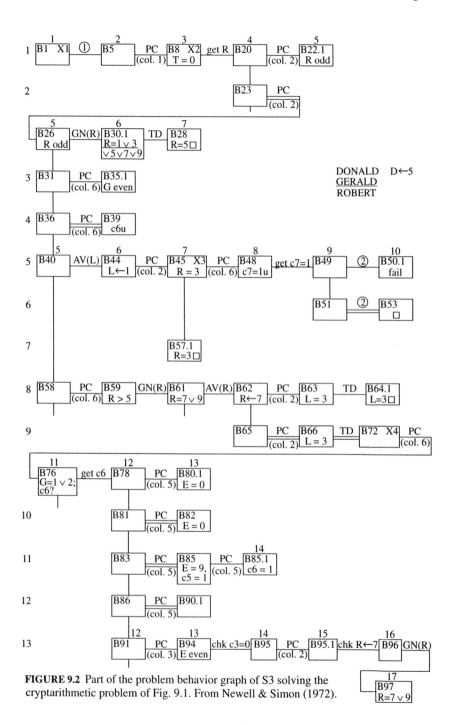

FIGURE 9.2 Part of the problem behavior graph of S3 solving the cryptarithmetic problem of Fig. 9.1. From Newell & Simon (1972).

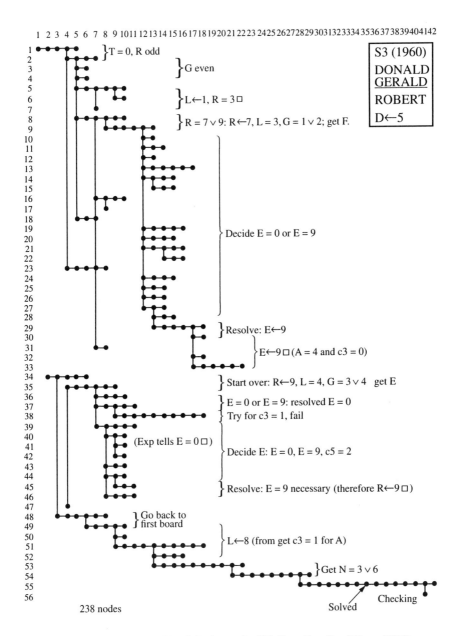

FIGURE 9.3   The full problem behavior graph of S3. From Newell and Simon (1972).

the Newell and Simon tradition. It has been used in a wide variety of applications, most importantly, the rule based expert system. We conclude this section with comments on the comparison of computer traces with the protocol for S3.

Rules are identified for the production system implementation by analysis of the operators that the subject used to change state in the problem behavior graph. The method is simple: identify commonly used rules in the behavior graph, code them as general rules, and place them in the rule set of the production system. The extreme of this approach would be to identify 238 rules, one to generate each state of the problem behavior graph.

The researchers looked for a smaller group of rules that could generate a large subset of the states. With 14 production rules they generated 267 states. The 267 states generated was a larger number than the 238 identified in the problem behavior graph. This happened as the consequence of adding in all the rules and applying them whenever their patterns matched. The 29 additional nodes were both computationally (and perhaps even psychologically) justified additions to those generated by the subject and verbalized in the think aloud protocol.

Another consequence of adding in all the rules was that some states were also generated at an inappropriate time. With the full set of 14 rules, 23 incorrect states were produced. A rough calculation of the effectiveness of this production system accounting of behavior was then (238 - 23)/ 267 or about an 80% successful characterization of S3's behavior. This 80% accounting of S3's behavior by researchers was about the same percentage as they found from the same analysis applied to other human subjects solving this cryptarithmetic problem.

Researchers could now also identify other high level strategies in S3's behavior. The behavior in the protocol was purposive and goal directed. The search strategy was depth-first (Section 8.4 and Example 8.6) and used an "enter in about six or eight steps and then back out" strategy that is sometimes called *progressive deepening.* This method for searching goes deep into a set of possibilities, in almost a "limited memory" fashion, and then backs off in a manner that seems to both make progress as well as retain the context of the search.

The ordering of the production rules also served as a technique to avoid exhaustive search. The simple heuristic that "took a partial solution, found a column that contained that constraint, and then processed that column" was used often to make progress as well as to control the search. Many of the production rules seemed to be employed in a means-ends, difference reduction manner.

We have not been very precise in describing the search and heuristic methods in the previous paragraph. Some of these methods, such as the ordering of rules, will be clear when we describe the production system search mechanism in more detail in Section 9.3. Other search methods, such as depth-first and heuristic search, were described in greater detail in Chapter 8. We finish Section 9.2 with a brief summary of the Newell and Simon approach to modeling human problem solving.

9.2.4 An Analysis of the Newell and Simon Methodology

We have just concluded the detailed analysis of a single subject, S3, with the direct observation methodology proposed by Newell and Simon in *Human Problem Solving* (1972). Let us summarize what we presented.

The problem solver's words, pencil actions, and sometimes other activity were recorded in a 15- to 30-min problem solving session. These pieces of behavior were mapped out by the researchers into a *protocol*, as in Figure 9.1. A *problem behavior graph*, representing the subject's search, was constructed from the protocol. A set of operators were then defined to account for the transformations from one state of information to the next. A set of *production rules* were proposed to account for invariances within the subject's choice of moves between states of knowledge within the problem behavior graph.

Finally, the researchers ran the production based program that represented the subject's behavior and scrutinized the details of the fit of the program's trace to the protocol. A sizeable fraction, about 80% in the case of S3, of the subject's units of behavior were accounted for by the running production system. A detailed scrutiny of discrepancies in the fit of program trace to human protocol often suggests that the remainder of the behavior is incomprehensible or random. Furthermore, many of the inadequacies of the model are due to missing data or the need for better accounts of attention and memory mechanisms.

The result of this methodology was to describe S3's arithmetic skills, search, and memory structures. This process was supported by a number of techniques:

1. The specification of the problem space, including both knowledge states and operators on these states.
2. The problem behavior graph was used for plotting S3's progress through the knowledge states of the problem space.
3. The production system allows researchers to extract invariances of behavior across nodes within the problem behavior graph.
4. The rules are ordered in the production system to build in the search heuristics of S3 (see Section 9.3.3).
5. The running production system was compared to S3's original protocol to determine the closeness of the production system characterization to S3's behavior patterns.

The five steps above operate in the context of an information processing theory of problem solving that is supported by a large number of individual experiments, many of which are presented in Newell and Simon (1972). We conclude with some general comments on the Newell and Simon methodology.

First, we note that no statistical theory of significance is employed. Perhaps the closest thing to a statistical measure, and this was applied to a single subject, was that about 80% of behavior was accounted for by the model! Newell and Simon are not looking for general effects across a population of subjects. Rather, they are attempting to account for the problem solving details of an individual subject. What Newell and Simon are saying is that this problem solving methodology can, at least in principle, be applied to any of a population of subjects working in this particular task environment. Herein lies the generality of this methodology.

Second, all subjects will not be as forthcoming as S3 was. Race, sex, or age differences can influence the subject-experimenter relationship. These issues must be carefully considered in designing an experiment. Some subjects are simply not comfortable in this "speak aloud" mode of problem solving. Other subjects will be too interested in self-justification when generating their protocol, the "see, I am pretty smart" defensiveness. All these issues are detrimental to a natural, elucidating protocol generation session. A fair number of subjects are just not suitable for this type of experimentation, and cannot be used.

Finally, researchers must guard against the incursions of folk psychology and the naive belief that "what is said is a perfect reflection of what is going on inside the subject." A large part of psychological tradition warns us about this naivete. This issue is addressed with an array of tools:

1. The protocol is a fairly detailed and cumulative piece of data. What the subject is saying at a point in time is correlated with what he or she is currently writing on the scratch paper, as well as to previous and following utterances. In some experimental situations the spoken words were also compared with the subject's eye movements. The verbal utterances are but one part of a much larger picture available to the research team.

2. Usually, several experimenters go over the protocol and other problem solving data. This is necessary to help interpret time delays, the speaking fragments, and the often almost unintelligible utterances of the subject. The creation of the sentence fragment protocol as seen in Figure 9.1 is indeed a tedious process, with multiple researchers attempting to interpret (this is certainly not just raw phenomena!!) the utterances and sentence fragments.

3. A very strong justification for this approach is the ability to in fact identify invariances, captured in the individual production rules, within the knowledge state generation process of the human subject.

4. Finally, of course, is the fact that roughly 80% of the protocol can be accounted for with the steps taken by the computer; this is true across almost all such experimental situations.

We next describe the remaining piece of this experimental methodology, the production system architecture for running the model of human skill.

9.3 THE PRODUCTION SYSTEM: A KNOWLEDGE LEVEL ACCOUNTING

9.3.1 A Definition

We introduced the production system architecture in Section 3.3. We now, after considering the analysis of skilled performance of human subjects in Section 9.2, present it in more complete detail. The abstraction that produces a rule based analysis and implementation of skilled performance is what Allen Newell (1982) calls the "knowledge level" accounting of behavior. We conclude Section 9.3 with Newell's analysis.

The production system is a model of computation that has proven particularly important in cognitive science for describing the knowledge and skilled performance of humans. A production system provides pattern directed control of a problem solving process. It consists of a set of production rules, a working memory, and a recognize-act control cycle. A schematic drawing of a production system is presented in Figure 3.7 and the solutions of two problems in Figure 3.8.

A *production system* may be defined as having three components:

1. *The set of production rules.* These are often called *productions*. A production is a condition-action pair, usually represented as an if.. then.. rule. The production defines a single chunk of problem solving knowledge or skill. The condition part of the rule is a pattern which determines when that rule may be applied to a problem instance. The action part describes the associated problem solving step.

2. *A working memory.* This structure contains start and goal descriptions and the current state of a problem solving process. The pattern representing the current state is matched against the condition part of the set of production rules. The actions of production rules are specifically designed to alter the contents of working memory in some fashion, as well as to take steps to accomplish an external task.

3. *The recognize-act cycle.* The control structure for a production system is straightforward. Working memory is initialized with the beginning problem description. The current state of the problem solving process is maintained as a set of patterns in working memory. These patterns in working memory are matched against the conditions of the production rules. This produces a subset of the productions, called the *conflict set*, whose conditions match the patterns in working memory.

The productions in the conflict set are said to be *enabled*. One of the productions in the conflict set is then selected, this choice is called *conflict resolution*, and the production is fired. That is, the action of the rule is performed, changing the contents of the working memory. After the selected production rule is fired, the control cycle repeats the matching process with the modified working memory. The process terminates when a stopping pattern is encountered or no further rule conditions are matched by the contents of working memory.

Conflict resolution chooses a rule from the conflict set for firing. Conflict resolution strategies may be simple, such as selecting the first rule whose condition matches the state of the world, or may involve complex rule selection heuristics. This is an important way in which a production system allows the addition of sophisticated control to a search algorithm. We saw examples of this with the ordering of S3's productions in Section 9.2.3.

The pure production system model has no mechanism for recovering from dead ends in the search; it simply continues until no more productions are enabled and then it halts. Most practical implementations of production systems, such as those that would purport to describe human performance, allow recovery of previous states of working memory in such situations. Our PROLOG implementation (see Part V) will use an open list (Chapter 8) to organize search as well as provide alternatives when no match or a dead end in the search path is found.

We present a number of applications of the production system solving problems in the next section. Here it is sufficient to state that production systems offer a general model of computation. They are equivalent to the class of Turing machines, by the formal equivalence arguments of Section 2.5.3. Thus the production system may be programmed to do anything that can be done on a computer. Their real strength, however, is as an architecture and model for knowledge based problem solving by humans or by computers. They have played a very important role in the design of the rule based expert system, as one would expect from a consideration of their naturalness in capturing human knowledge and expertise. The reader interested in pursuing this subject may consult the design of expert systems in Luger and Stubblefield (1993, Chap. 8).

The idea for the production system based design for computing came from writings of Post (1943), who first proposed the production rewrite rule methodology as a formal theory of computation. The main construct of this theory was a set of rewrite rules for strings, in many ways similar to the sorting rules of Figure 3.8.

An important family of production system languages comes directly out of computer language research at Carnegie Mellon. These are the *OPS* languages (OPS stands for *official production system*). Although their origins, as just noted, come from modeling human problem solving, these languages have proven highly effective for programming expert systems and other AI applications.

In the next section, we give examples of how the production system may be used to describe a variety of search strategies.

9.3.2   Examples of Production System Problem Solving

Example 9.1: **The 8-puzzle**

Figure 9.4 presents the 8-puzzle and the 15-puzzle. The 15- puzzle most of us played with as children, and perhaps even challenge our own children with now. The numbered tiles are moved into the open space one at a time creating a new open location. The 8-puzzle is a 3 by 3 subset of the 15-puzzle, using the integers 1, 2, ..., 8. A particular problem is usually described by asking the solver to transform the start state into the desired goal state. Such a situation for the 8-puzzle is presented in Figure 9.4.

The search space generated by the 8-puzzle is both complex enough to be interesting and small enough to be tractable. Thus it is frequently used to explore different search strategies, such as depth-first and breadth-first search, as well as the heuristic strategies we presented in Chapter 8. It also lends itself to human experimental situations as well as to solution using a production system. Rather than describing a large number of moves for individual tiles, for example, "move the 7 tile right" in the start state of Figure 9.4, we think of "moving the blank space." The moves of this problem may then be described by the productions of Figure 9.4.

Of course the first four of these productions are only applicable when the blank is in the center. When it is in one of the corners only two moves are possible. If a beginning state and a goal state for the 8-puzzle are now specified, it is possible to make a production system accounting of the problem's search space. Assuming that loops are prevented by keeping track of the path as well as the goal state in working memory, the space may be described by Figure 9.5. The search in Figure 9.5 is breadth-first.

Example 9.2: **The Knight's Tour**

We saw the knight tour problem extensively in Chapter 8, here we show how to implement it as a production system. This problem (see Example 8.1) requires the solver to use legal knight moves to get from the start square on the chess board to some goal state. Some descriptions of the problem require the knight to go from one corner to another, others require covering every square on the board, and still others require a set of moves to be made without landing on certain squares. We presented the eight legal moves for the knight located near the center of the chess board in Figures 8.4 and 8.5. Since the knight cannot land off the board, many fewer moves are possible near the side of the board.

We now use productions to create a knight's tour solution on the 8 x 8 chess board. Because it makes little sense to enumerate all possible moves for such a complex problem, we create a set of 8 rules to generate all legal knight moves.

The 15-puzzle and the 8-puzzle

1	2	3	4
12	13	14	5
11	■	15	6
10	9	8	7

15-puzzle

1	2	3
8	■	4
7	6	5

8-puzzle

2	8	3
1	6	4
7	■	5

Start State

1	2	3
8	■	4
7	6	5

Goal State

The production rules:

CONDITION		ACTION
blank is not on the top edge	$\Rightarrow$	move the blank up
blank is not on the right edge	$\Rightarrow$	move the blank right
blank is not on the bottom	$\Rightarrow$	move the blank down
blank is not on the left edge	$\Rightarrow$	move the blank left
goal state in working memory	$\Rightarrow$	halt

FIGURE 9.4   The 8-puzzle as a production system where the control regime is to try each production in order and not allow loops.

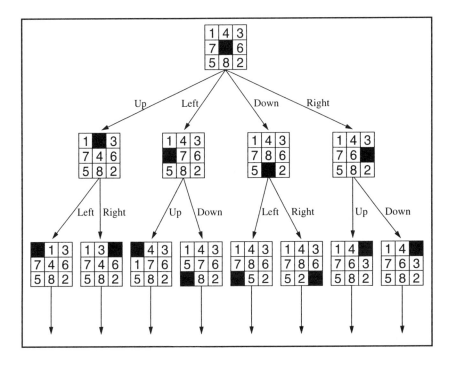

FIGURE 9.5   Part of the search space created by the production system of Figure 9.4.

These move rules correspond to the 8 possible ways a knight can move on the chessboard. If we index the board by row and column numbers, then it may be described by an 8 x 8 matrix as in Figure 8.4. We define a production rule for moving the knight down 2 squares and right 1 square:

CONDITION: Current Row <= 6 and Current Column <= 7

ACTION: New Row = Current Row + 2 and
               New Column = Current Column +1

Note that the conditions of this production rule check the patterns of the present board state to guarantee that the rule will generate a move that ends up on the board. Seven additional rules can be designed which compute the remaining possible moves. If the start of the knight's path is the square (1,1), we can describe the first steps in the knight's tour as in Figure 8.5.

In the next section we present several control procedures for the production system architecture.

9.3.3 Control of Search in Production Systems

The production system model offers a range of opportunities for adding heuristic control to a search algorithm. These include the choice of data-driven or goal-driven strategies, the structure of the rules themselves, and the choice of strategies for conflict resolution. Data-driven and goal-driven search with production systems are described next.

Control through Data-Driven or Goal-Driven Search Strategies

As presented in Section 8.3, data-driven search begins with a problem description, such as a set of logical axioms, symptoms of an illness, or a body of data that needs interpretation, and infers new knowledge from this data. Data-driven search is accomplished by directly using the production system architecture described in Section 9.3.1. Apply the rules of inference, legal moves in a game, or other state generating operations to the current description of the world and add the results, a new state of the world, to working memory. This process continues until a goal is reached or there are no more states to examine. The space searched is a graph because a state of knowledge can often be reached through more than one inference path and some combinations of rules can indeed be circular. Thus, we must apply production rules to data as well as keep track of paths. The open and closed lists and controlling algorithms of Section 8.3 offer an appropriate method for this.

This description of data-driven reasoning emphasizes its close fit with the production system model of computation. The current state of the world, data that have either been assumed to be true or deduced as true with previous use of production rules, is placed in working memory. The recognize-act cycle then passes it in front of the set of productions. When these data match the condition(s) of one of the production rules, the action of the production modifies working memory, adding new information to the current state of knowledge.

Although we have treated production systems in a data-driven fashion, they may also be used to characterize goal-driven search. Goal-driven search begins with a goal and works backwards to establish its truth. To implement this in a production system, the goal is placed in working memory and matched against the actions of the production rules. These actions are matched, just as the conditions of the productions were matched in data-driven reasoning.

All production rules whose conclusions (actions) match the goal make up the conflict set. When the action of a particular rule is matched, its conditions are added to working memory and become the new subgoals of the search. These are then matched to the actions of other production rules. This process continues until a fact is found, usually in the problem's initial description or, as is often the case in expert systems, by directly asking the user for specific information.

Search stops when the conditions of all the productions supporting the subgoals of the top level goal are found to be true.

As this discussion illustrates, the production system offers a natural characterization of both goal-driven and data-driven search. We can also employ combinations of strategies. For example, we can search in a forward direction until the number of states becomes large and then switch to a goal directed search to use possible subgoals to select among alternative states.

The danger in this situation is that when heuristic or best-first search is used, the parts of the graph actually searched may miss each other and ultimately require more search than a simpler approach. However, when the branching of a space is constant and exhaustive search is used, a combined search strategy can dramatically reduce the amount of space searched.

Control through Depth, Breadth, or Best-First Strategies

In Chapter 8, we described and presented algorithms for the implementation of these search strategies. These algorithms all relate to which production rule is selected to be used next in the problem solving. Their implementation within the production system architecture is straightforward. We present some PROLOG algorithms for building these search strategies in Chapters 15 and 16.

Control of Search through Rule Structure

The structure of rules in a production system, including the distinction between the condition and the action and the order with which conditions are tried determines how the space is searched. Two rules that were identical except for the ordering of the conditions in their premises are equivalent in their logical content. These rules, however, can be quite different psychologically and also for generating a search, since the production system implementation imposes an order on the matching and firing of rules. For this reason, the specific form of the rules determines the ease, or even the possibility, of matching a particular rule against a problem instance. We saw this with the consideration of the heuristics implicit in S3's ordering of rules in Section 9.2.

Human experts seem to encode crucial heuristics within the ordering of their rules of expertise. The order of a rule's premises also encodes important procedural information for solving the problem. It is important that this form be preserved if it is desired to build a program that solves problems with search similar to that of the human expert. When a mechanic says "if the engine won't turn over and the lights don't come on then check the battery," she is suggesting a specific sequence of things to try. This information is not captured by the logically equivalent statement: "The engine turns over or the lights come on or check the battery." The form of the rules is critical in controlling search, making the system behave logically, and making traces of rule firings reflect the skills of the human expert.

Control of Search through Conflict Resolution

While production systems, as just noted, allow heuristics to be encoded in the knowledge content of rules themselves, they offer other opportunities for heuristic control through *conflict resolution*. Although the simplest such strategy is to choose the first rule which matches the contents of working memory, a number of strategies may be applied to determine which of the enabled rules to fire:

1. *Refraction.* Refraction specifies that once a rule has fired, it may not fire again until the elements which match its conditions have been modified in working memory. This discourages looping.
2. *Recency.* The recency strategy prefers those rules whose conditions match with the patterns most recently added to working memory. This focuses the search on a single line of reasoning.
3. *Specificity.* This strategy assumes that a more specific problem solving rule is preferable to general ones. A rule is more specific than another if it has more conditions. This implies that it will match fewer potential working memory patterns.

These strategies are representative of the types of strategies that are commonly used in conflict resolution.

9.3.4 "Knowledge Level" Problem Solving

As illustrated by the preceding examples, the rule based accounting of behavior in a production system architecture offers a general framework for implementing knowledge and search. Because of its simplicity, modifiability, and flexibility in applying human problem solving knowledge, the production system has proven an important tool for the construction of cognitive models as well as AI applications such as the knowledge based expert system.

Allen Newell (1982) refers to this direct encoding of human knowledge as a *knowledge level* accounting of skill. Figure 9.6 is a schematic of how Newell sees the architecture of knowledge level problem solving. The power of this specification hierarchy is that each level of the system, although fundamentally linked to the lower levels that support it, has both descriptive and explanatory powers that are independent of those lower levels.

What the knowledge level specification means is that there is the possibility of scientific analysis for each level of the problem solving system. For example,

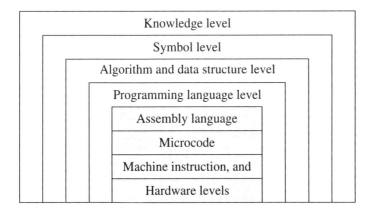

FIGURE 9.6   Levels of independent specifications in a *knowledge level account* of the architecture of intelligence. From Newell (1982).

the knowledge represented in rules is independent of the symbols selected to encode it, just as medical knowledge may be expressed in French or English. Similarly, symbol systems such as semantic nets, conceptual dependencies, or predicate logic, may be described independent of the data structures, such as property or association lists, stacks or queues used in their implementation. Again, these data structures are themselves independent of their implementation language, Lisp, PROLOG, FORTRAN, or whatever.

At the top of this hierarchy is a *knowledge level* accounting of human skilled performance. From Newell's viewpoint, knowledge may be analyzed, abstracted, encoded, and implemented in a manner independent of its supporting architecture. An existence proof of this approach is the Newell and Simon accounting of human skill we saw in Section 9.2 along with its production system encoding we saw in Section 9.3. The production system is a precise implemented model of the knowledge level theory. The Soar architecture (Section 9.4) offers an even more flexible model. We end this section with a listing of the major advantages of the production system based knowledge level account of intelligent problem solving:

1. *Separation of Knowledge and Control.* The production system is an elegant model of separation of knowledge and control. Control is provided by the recognize-act cycle of the production system loop and the problem solving knowledge is encoded in the rules themselves. The advantages of this separation for modeling cognitive behavior include ease of modifying the knowledge base without requiring a change in the code for program control and, conversely, the ability to alter the code for program control without changing the knowledge.

2. *A Natural Mapping onto State Space Search.* The components of a production system map naturally into the constructs of state space search. The successive states of working memory form the nodes of a state space graph. The production rules are the set of possible transitions between states, with conflict resolution implementing the selection of a branch in the state space. We saw this when the production system mimicked the problem behavior graph of S3 in Section 9.2, and in the search algorithms presented in Chapter 8.

3. *The Modularity of Production Rules.* An important aspect of a knowledge level account is the lack of any direct syntactic interactions between production rules. Rules may only effect the firing of other rules by changing patterns in working memory. They may not call another rule directly as if it were a subroutine, nor may they set the value of variables in other production rules. The scope or extent of the variables of these rules is limited to the individual rule.

4. *Pattern Directed Heuristic Control.* Intelligent human subjects seem to be very strongly "pattern driven" and "opportunistic" in their problem solving. Patterns drive program execution. This is accomplished by the fact that the rules in a production system may fire in any sequence and the descriptions of a problem which make up the current state of the world determine the conflict set and, consequently, the particular search path and solution generated.

5. *Transparency and Explanation.* The modularity of rules and the iterative nature of their execution make it easier to monitor execution of a production system. Since each rule corresponds to a single chunk of human problem solving skill, the rule content should provide a meaningful explanation of the system's current state and action. We saw this feature in detail when we examined the running program trace and compared it with the protocol for S3 in Section 9.2.

To summarize, in a knowledge level analysis we may view the production system as a model of human skilled performance. The production memory takes the role of the human's long term memory or permanent store of problem solving skills. The working memory represents the human's short term memory or attention. The control mechanism, matching the working memory to the set of production rules, models the current focus of attention on a subset of permanent skills. The rule firing changes the state of working memory and the process repeats.

The production system model also offers an important link between strong and weak methods for problem solving, as described in Chapters 8 and 9. The division between the knowledge and the control mechanism sets up this distinction. Focus on the control algorithm indicates a weak method approach; focus on the number and power of the rules in the knowledge base is a strong method.

9.4 THE BLACKBOARD

9.4.1 An Historical Note

The second architecture we consider for procedure based problem solving is the *blackboard*. The blackboard does not have the same wealth of empirical study supporting it as a cognitive architecture as we saw in the production system analysis of Section 9.2. It has nonetheless been used extensively as a mechanism for intelligent pattern interpretation in areas such as speech understanding (Reddy 1976) and in acoustic and visual pattern recognition. The blackboard model arose as a general problem solving architecture by abstracting features from the HEARSAY II speech understanding system (see Example 9.3).

The first reference to the term *blackboard*, can be traced back to 1962. Allen Newell was concerned with the rigidity of programs that were organized along traditional search models (Newell 1969). Newell initially proposed a new organization to synthesize complex processes by means of sequential flow of control and hierarchically organized, closed subroutines. This organization had many advantages, but still had two primary difficulties: inflexible control and restricted data accessibility.

Newell (1962) noted that the difficulties "might be alleviated by maintaining the isolation of routines, but allowing all the subroutines to make use of a common data structure." He continued, using the following figure of speech to describe such a system:

> Metaphorically we can think of a set of workers, all looking at the same blackboard: each is able to read everything that is on it, and to judge when he has something worthwhile to add to it. This conception is just that of Selfridge's Pandemonium: a set of demons, each independently looking at the total situation and shrieking in proportion to what they see that fits their natures...

Current examples of the blackboard architecture still retain this flavor; the blackboard is a central global data base operated on by a number of independent, often parallel and asynchronous knowledge sources.

9.4.2 A Definition

There are three components of the *blackboard system*: 1) the central global data base called the *blackboard*, 2) one or more independent *knowledge sources*, KSs, each operating independently on the global data base, using the data base to receive its data for processing as well as for posting the results of its work, and 3) a *control regime* for handling the interaction of the knowledge sources with the blackboard. Figure 9.7 presents a schematic of blackboard problem solving.

The blackboard control regime is often left unspecified. Its simplest form of control is to let all the knowledge sources be *event driven;* they are activated when they see data appropriate to their processing on the blackboard. When they are finished they post the results of their work back to the blackboard and then wait for more appropriate data. In this event-driven approach, the blackboard has very much a parallel and asynchronous flavor. More complex forms of control have created a second blackboard to monitor the success and assist control of the knowledge sources that are operating on the original blackboard!

We can see each knowledge source as a collected set of if.. then.. rules, a set of procedures or production rules for accomplishing part of the total problem solving task. The state of the problem solving is changed in the global blackboard whenever knowledge source takes its appropriate action. An important strength of the blackboard architecture is the modularity and independence of the rules or procedures within each knowledge source.

9.4.3 Blackboard Applications

In Figure 9.7 each knowledge source (KS) gets its data from the blackboard, processes it, and returns its results to the blackboard to be used by the other knowledge sources. Each KS is independent in that it is a separate process operating according to its own specifications and, when a multiprocessing system is used, it is independent of the other processing in the problem solving. It is an asynchronous system in that each KS begins its operation whenever it finds appropriate input data posted on the blackboard. When it finishes its processing it posts its results and awaits new input data.

Example 9.3: **Speech Understanding, from HEARSAY II**

The blackboard approach to organizing a large program was first built for the HEARSAY-II research (Balzer et al. 1980, Reddy 1976). HEARSAY-II was a speech understanding program. It was initially designed as the front end for a data base of computer science articles. The user of the library would address the computer system in spoken English with queries such as, "Are any by Feigenbaum and Feldman?" and the computer would answer the question with information from the library data base.

The blackboard architecture allowed HEARSAY to coordinate the several different knowledge sources required for this complex task. Blackboard applications are often organized along two dimensions. With HEARSAY, as in Figure

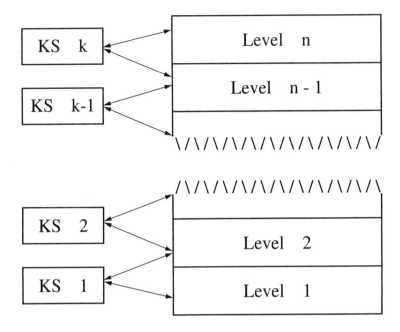

FIGURE 9.7   A schematic of the blackboard architecture: a global data base operated on by independent and asynchronous knowledge sources (KSs).

9.7, these dimensions were the time sequence in which the speech act was produced and the level of analysis of the utterance. Each level of analysis was processed by a different knowledge source. The levels of analysis of the utterance were:

KS1: The wave form of the acoustic signal.
KS2: The possible phonemes or other segments of the wave form.
KS3: The syllables that these phonemes could produce.
KS4: The possible words that could come from phoneme sets.
KS5: The possible words that could come from phonemes. KS4 and KS5 could consider words from two different parts of the data!
KS6: A KS that tried to generate possible word sequences.
KS7: A KS that put word sequences into possible phrases.

In processing spoken speech, the wave form of the spoken signal is entered at the lowest level, KS1. Knowledge sources for processing this entry are enabled and post their interpretations to the blackboard to be picked up by the appropriate process. Because of the ambiguities of spoken language, there may be multiple competing hypotheses at each level on the blackboard. The knowledge sources at the higher levels attempt to disambiguate the competing hypotheses from lower levels. When this proves impossible they ask the lower level KSs for alternative interpretations of their data.

Therefore, the analysis of HEARSAY-II should not be seen as lower levels simply producing data that the higher levels can analyze. If a KS at one level cannot make sense of the data that it receives, that KS can request that the sending KS go back to make further hypotheses about the data. Furthermore, different KSs can be working on different parts of the utterance at the same time. All the processes, as mentioned previously, are asynchronous, and being data-driven, act when they have input data, continue acting until they have finished their task, and then post their results and wait for their next task.

In HEARSAY one of the KSs is called the *scheduler*, and it handles the "consume-data post-result" communication between the KSs. This scheduler has ratings on the results of each KS's activity and thus is able to supply some direction in the problem solving. If no KS is active the scheduler determines that the task is finished and shuts down.

When the HEARSAY program had a data base of about 1000 words it worked quite well, although a bit slowly. When the number of words was further extended, the data for the knowledge sources so increased that the total system's results deteriorated. Complexity issues brought an end to this early project.

HEARSAY has been one of the few approaches by the AI community to the problem of understanding voiced speech. Speech recognition is a very complex problem also addressed by conventional research techniques. We discuss language and speech further in Part IV.

HEARSAY-III (Balzer et al. 1980, Erman et al. 1981) is a generalization of the approach taken by HEARSAY-II. The time dimension of HEARSAY-II is no longer needed but the multiple KSs for levels of analysis are retained. The blackboard for HEARSAY-III is also intended to interact with relational data base systems. Indeed, HEARSAY-III is a general programming structure, sometimes called a *shell*, for the design of any blackboard problem solving application.

One very nice addition of HEARSAY-III is to split off the scheduler KS, as described above for HEARSAY-II, and to make the scheduler a separate blackboard controller for the first, or domain blackboard. This second blackboard allows the scheduling process to be broken down, just as the domain of the problem is broken down, into separate KSs each concerned with different aspects of the solution procedure, that is, when and how to apply the domain knowledge. The second blackboard can thus compare and balance different solutions for each problem (Nii 1986, Nii & Aiello 1979).

To summarize, the key to blackboard problem solving is to separate off modules of skilled behavior, each module represented as a set of if.. then.. procedures for solving one part of the task. The global data base then collects and integrates the distributed results and prepares the next state of the processing.

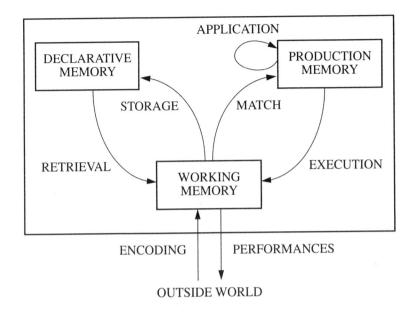

Figure 9.8   The ACT* cognitive architecture. From Anderson (1983b).

9.5 UNIFIED THEORIES OF COGNITION: ACT* & SOAR

In 1973 Allen Newell made an important challenge to cognitive psychologists. In a paper suitably entitled *You can't play 20 questions with nature and win*, he made the point that a 20 question-like focus on cognitive phenomena was not supportive of long term progress in the field. Newell saw psychology at that time as a smorgasbord of microissues and theories. Psychologists would move from dichotomy to dichotomy, worrying whether a process was serial or parallel, or whether some practice was massed or distributed. These microissues were never fully resolved, and psychology seemed an ever continuing sequence of new dichotomies. There seemed little promise of a real theory, even in the long term.

With the creation of production systems, blackboards, and other models of human skilled performance, Newell (1990) asked if there might exist the possibility of a *unified theory of cognition*. As Newell states:

> Psychology has arrived at the possibility of unified theories of cognition - theories that gain their power by positing a single system of mechanisms that operate together to produce the full range of human cognition.

There are a number of reasons for attempting to design unified theories of cognition. Among the most important: First, unification and subsumption are always goals of science. Since one system, the mind, participates in most aspects of skilled performance, it is natural to seek a unified and cohesive theory of mind. Even if the mind has parts, modules, components, or whatnot, they all merge together in the production of behavior. Second, since the mind is shaped by multiple constraints including perception, memory organization, and output processes, each with its own powers and limitations, a unified theory can offer a total picture encompassing the mutual constraints of the parts. Finally, most psychological studies focusing on a microlevel analysis create a number of theoretical constructs that support and constrain the other parts of the processing picture. A unified theory, because it proposes an architecture for the system at large, allows the psychologist to amortize or cash out most supporting constructs.

Anderson's *ACT** (1983a, 1983b) offers a first approximation of a unified theory of human cognitive architecture. ACT* specifies both the memory and processing structures supporting human performance in a wide range of tasks. Figure 9.8 offers a diagram of this architecture with a long term declarative memory in the form of a semantic net and a long term procedural memory in the form of production rules. Each production has a set of conditions based on the images, propositions, and other associations of the declarative memory and actions that create new nodes and links within the declarative memory. ACT* is activation based in that the associations in declarative memory each have a degree of activation; the working memory makes up that part of long term declarative memory that is very highly activated at any time period.

ACT* also has the ability to learn. The new nodes and associations created by productions have a high, although temporary, activation level. Each production rule itself has an associated strength which determines its likelihood of firing, given that its conditions are met. These strengths increase and decrease according to the use of the production. Finally, chains of productions can be coupled together and automatically replaced by single rules that represent their combined behavior.

Most importantly, ACT*, like Soar, has knowledge of its own structure and the way its actions and processes occur, including the parameters that monitor activation levels and the fluctuations in production strength. ACT* has been able to explain how children check geometry proofs and learn to do elementary programming. It can model language learning and a wide range of skill acquisition (Anderson 1976, 1983b; Anderson & Thompson 1989).

Soar, the most extensive current attempt at designing a unified model of cognition, was created by John Laird, Allen Newell, and Paul Rosenbloom (Newell 1990, Laird et al. 1993). Soar is an architecture for general intelligence, first produced as a computer program in 1983, with continuous modifications and extensions to the present time. Soar has the major mechanisms of a cognitive system, including a symbol system and a goal hierarchy. It uses a production system as the basis of the architecture, giving it a recognize-act flavor. It uses search spaces throughout to formulate all its tasks. It has a *chunking* mechanism as part of its architecture that allows it to learn relationships as it solves problems. It knows about (is aware of?) its own processes and knowledge structures so it can relate new knowledge structures to those things it already knows.

Rosenbloom et al. (1993) describe Soar as a four level hierarchically controlled mechanism. On the top level Soar can be described as having goals and knowledge, having sensors that provide perception and effectors providing action capabilities. This top level can be described well by Newell's own (1982) *knowledge level* specification in that it can choose actions which its knowledge says will achieve its goals. In true knowledge level accounting, this top level abstracts away from all issues of internal structure and process.

At the second or *problem space level*, Soar can be described as a set of interacting problem spaces: the graphs we saw in Section 6.1 modeling the intelligent search strategies we saw in Section 9.2. Each problem space thus represents the static and dynamic aspects of small semi-independent fragments of the internal or external world.

At the *architecture* or *symbol level* Soar has a set of four interacting processes which together implement the problem space level. These are, upwards from the lowest level, a set of independent and modular perceptual and motor units. Above these, structured as production rules, is a layer of parallel and asynchronous associations that provide the coordination and communication between the lower level modules. Above these associations is a decision layer, able to monitor and change direction based on the current strengths of the associations below. The top reflective layer is able to step back and make decisions about impasses in the decision making. This layer is also able to learn from its reflection based decisions.

At the *technology level*, Soar can be described as a large C program running on a particular hardware platform.

Soar's test bed of cognitive tasks is large and diverse. It includes covert visual attention (Weismeyer et al. 1993), intelligent tutoring (Ward 1991), modelling student learning (Conati & Lehman 1993), verbal reasoning (Polk 1992), the analysis of psycholinguistic phenomena, including natural language comprehension (Lewis 1992), as well as much lower level psychological phenomena (Rosenbloom et al. 1993). We consider again Soar's learning through chunking behavior in Section 10.4.4.

We conclude this section with some general comments on unified theories. Soar and ACT* challenge cognitive scientists and as well as psychologists to design larger more comprehensive models of intelligent performance. As we noted in introducing this section, the many forms of intelligence require mutual constraints. We must get past our current approach of a multitude of micro level relatively unrelated theories. Mind is indeed a unified whole, although a marvelously faceted, mechanism. Finally, the models that implement unified theories will not be verified or refuted at a stroke with some single study, but will be developed and modified using progressive approximation and continued refinement, as we have seen in the several decades of research on ACT* and Soar.

We describe several other unified theories of cognition, including classifier systems, in the final chapter of the book.

9.6 PART II SUMMARY: ISSUES IN KNOWLEDGE REPRESENTATION

We have now examined the major alternatives for knowledge representation, including networks and more structured representational schemes in Chapter 6, logic and inference rules in Chapter 7, and procedures or production rules in the present chapter. The results of our study have included an increased understanding of the advantages and limitations of each of these representational schemes. Nonetheless, debate continues over the relative naturalness, efficiency, and appropriateness of each approach.

A number of important problems remain in the area of knowledge representation. The first of these is the selection and granularity of atomic symbols for knowledge representation. Objects in the knowledge representational scheme constitute the domain of the representation mapping; objects in the world are the range of these mappings. The nature of the atomic elements in the representation language largely determine what can be described about the world. For example, if a "car" is the smallest atom of the representation, then we have difficulty reasoning about engines, wheels, or any of the component parts of a car.

However, if the atoms of the system correspond to these parts, than a larger structure may be required to represent "car" as a single concept. This introduces a cost in efficiency for manipulating this larger structure and a cost in expressiveness because the larger structure may obscure the fact that a car itself may be considered a single conceptual entity.

Another example of the trade-off in the choice of atomic symbols comes from work in natural language understanding. Programs which use single words as elements of meaning may have difficulty in representing complex concepts that do not have a one word denotation. There is also difficulty in distinguishing between different meanings of the same word or different words with the same meaning (see Chapter 14).

One approach to this problem, seen in Section 6.2, is to design and use semantic primitives or language independent conceptual units as the basis for representing the meaning of natural language. *Conceptual dependency theory* in

Section 6.2.3 takes this approach, and although it avoids the limitations involved in using single words as units of meaning, it involves other trade-offs, such as that many words require complex structures for their definitions. Also, by relying on a small set of primitives, many subtle distinctions, such as between *push* and *shove* or between *yell* and *scream*, are difficult to express.

When problems are described as states of knowledge about the world that are changed by a series of actions or events, these actions or events generally transform only a few components of the description. The program must be able to infer side effects and implicit changes in the world description. The problem of representing the side effects of actions is called the *frame problem*, as was seen in Section 7.4. For example, a robot that is stacking heavy boxes on the back of a truck must compensate for the lowering of the truck bed due to the increasing weight of the boxes.

Exhaustiveness is also a property of representational schemes. A representation is exhaustive if its explicit elements and relationships are sufficient to model the task at hand. Geographic maps are assumed to be exhaustive to some level of detail. A map with a missing city or river would not be well-regarded as a navigational tool. Although most knowledge representations are not exhaustive, exhaustiveness with respect to crucial objects, properties, and relationships within the modeled domain is a desirable goal. For example, the ability to assume that a representation is exhaustive may allow a problem solver to ignore possible effects of the frame problem.

Thus, if a representation is sufficiently exhaustive there will be no unspecified side effects and the frame problem effectively disappears. The difficulty of the frame problem results from the fact that it is very often impossible to build a completely exhaustive knowledge base for most domains. A representation language should assist in deciding what knowledge may safely be omitted and help deal with the consequences of this omission.

Related to exhaustiveness is the *plasticity* or *modifiability* of the representation: the addition of knowledge in response to deficiencies is the primary solution to a lack of exhaustiveness. Since most representations are not exhaustive in practice, it should be easy to modify or update them. In addition to the syntactic ease of adding knowledge, a representation should also help to guarantee the consistency of the knowledge base as new information is added or the old is deleted. Inheritance, by allowing properties of a class to be inherited by new instances, is an example of how a knowledge representational scheme may help insure consistency.

In addition to naturalness, directness, and ease of use, representational schemes may also be evaluated by their computational efficiency. Brachman and Levesque (1985) discuss the trade-off between expressiveness and efficiency. Logic, for instance, when used as a representational scheme is highly expressive as a result of its completeness. However, unconstrained logic representations pay a considerable price in computational efficiency.

A final point is that representational schemes are languages and like other human languages are valued for their expressive power, their potential for interpretation, and their use in communication. Because of these properties, they are important tools for scientific exploration.

9.7   EPILOGUE AND REFERENCES

The earliest beginnings of the Newell and Simon research tradition are found in their articles in *Computers and Thought*, edited by Edward Feigenbaum and Jerome Feldman (1963). In these papers they describe their work on the *logic theorist* as well as their early attempts to use the protocols of human problem solvers. Simon also gives a fascinating account of these early days in his autobiography, *Models of My Life* (1991).

Allen Newell and Herbert Simon's book *Human Problem Solving* (1972) is the foundation for the protocol analysis approach taken in this chapter. A rather detailed explication and justification of this approach may be found therein. The human subject's protocol, the problem behavior graph, and the production rules for subject S3 are taken from this important book. Extensive justification of the Newell and Simon direct method approach to the analysis of cognitive phenomena may be found in Simon and Ericsson (1984).

In a more recent article, in Michael Posner's edited collection, called *Foundations of Cognitive Science* (1989), Herbert Simon and Craig Kaplan give a retrospective and justification for their research methodology.

Allen Newell's (1990) *Unified Theories of Cognition* is the primary proponent of unified theories for cognitive domains. Much of this work was inspired by Newell's (1973) earlier paper *You Can't Play 20 Questions with Nature and Win*. *The Proceedings of the Fifteenth Annual Conference of the Cognitive Science Society* (Lawrence Erlbaum, publisher, 1993) contain a set of papers, part of *The Symposium in Memory of Allen Newell*, that reflect the power and diversity of the Soar approach.

The production system as a model for building artificial intelligence search strategies may be found in most AI texts, including Nils Nilsson's *Principles of Artificial Intelligence* (1980) and George Luger and William Stubblefield's (1993) *Artificial Intelligence: Structures and Strategies for Complex Problem Solving*.

Early work on blackboard models of problem solving is described by Allen Newell (1962) in *Some Problems in the Basic Organization in Problem Solving Programs*, later research is described in work on the HEARSAY project, HEARSAY-II (Reddy 1976, Erman et al. 1980). Finally, the HEARSAY-III research is described by Victor Lesser and Dan Corkill (1983), Penny Nii (1986), and by Nii and Aiello (1979).

Summary accounts of much of the material of this chapter may be found in *The Handbook of Artificial Intelligence* (Feigenbaum et al. 1989), in *The Encyclopedia of Artificial Intelligence* (Shapiro 1992), as well as in textbooks for artificial intelligence.

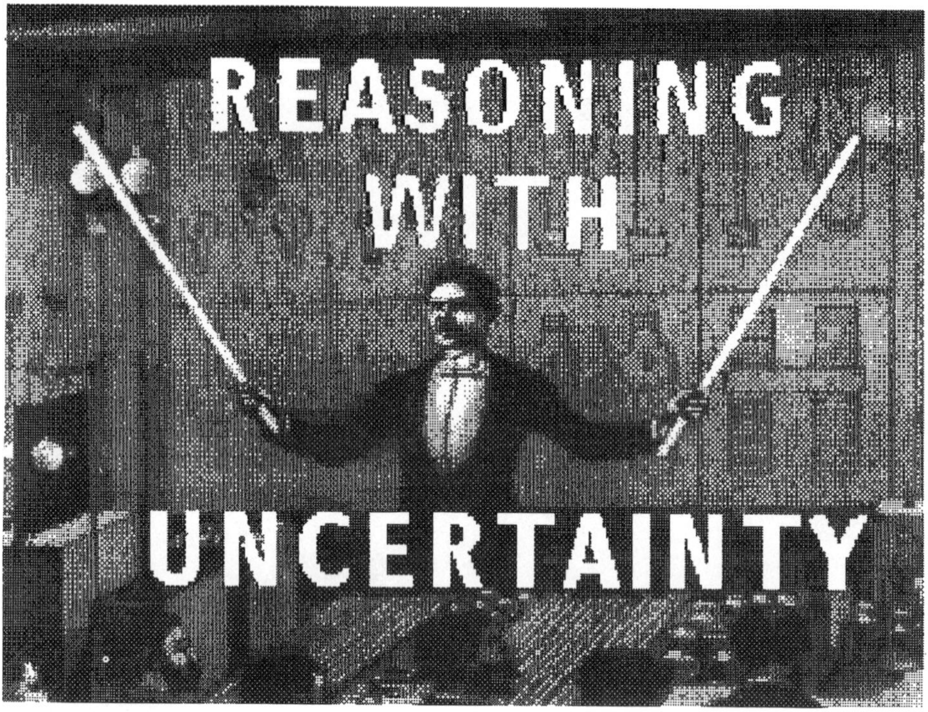
REASONING
WITH
UNCERTAINTY

Part III

MACHINE LEARNING

The next three chapters propose models for learning. The ability to learn must be part of any system that would claim to possess general intelligence. Indeed, the very notion of *intelligence as unchanging* seems contradictory. Intelligent agents must constantly adjust their knowledge and expectations in the course of their interactions with their environment, as well as through the experience of their own internal states and processes.

Herbert Simon (1983) defines learning as:

> any change in a system that allows it to perform better the
> second time on repetition of the same task or on another
> task drawn from the same population....

This definition, although brief, suggests many of the issues involved in developing programs that learn. Learning involves changes in the learner; this is obvious. However, the exact nature of those changes and the best way to represent them are far from obvious. One approach, often referred to as the *explicit symbol* approach, models learning as the acquisition of explicitly represented knowledge. Based on experience, the learner constructs or modifies expressions in a language, such as logic, and retains this knowledge for future use. The primary influence on the program's behavior is its explicitly represented knowledge.

Connectionist networks, in contrast, do not learn by acquiring sentences in a symbolic language. As an animal brain, which consists of a large number of interconnected nerve cells, neural networks are systems of interconnected, artificial neurons. The program's knowledge is stored in the organization and interaction of these neurons. Unlike symbolic learning algorithms, neural nets do not learn by adding representations to their knowledge base; they learn by modifying their overall structure of weights. We examine both explicit symbol based and connectionist approaches to learning, contrasting their strengths and limitations.

A problem, implicit in Simon's definition, is the under constrained nature of empirical learning. Learning involves generalization from experience: performance should not only improve on the "repetition of the same task," but on similar tasks in the domain. Because interesting domains tend to be large, a learner may only examine a fraction of all possible examples. From this limited experience, it must acquire knowledge that will generalize correctly to unseen instances of the domain. This is the problem of *induction*, and it is central to learning.

Solving the induction problem requires that the intelligent agent find an approximating function that fits a set of data points. These data points are located in a multidimensional space indexed by feature values, properties, and even qualitative parameters. The learned function that fits this data will be a multidimensional surface that separates and supports generalization of the learned concept. No matter how carefully the data are represented, there is always a potentially infinite number of approximating surfaces. Indeed, there is even an infinite number of characterizations of each approximating surface; brute force search in this computationally intractable domain is rarely successful in identifying solutions.

Furthermore, in most learning problems the available training data are often not sufficient to guarantee optimal generalization, no matter what algorithm the learner uses. Learning algorithms must generalize heuristically; they must select those aspects of their experience that are most likely to prove effective. Such selection criteria are known as *inductive biases*. These biases can restrict the number and type of functions considered, the number of network nodes and their connectivity, and can sometimes create a finite and tractable search space.

Finally, Simon's describes the result of learning: to "perform better the second time." As the previous paragraphs indicated, selecting the possible changes to a system that will allow it to improve is a difficult task. Learning research must address the possibility that changes may actually degrade performance. Preventing and/or detecting such problems is another task for a learning algorithm.

Despite the simplicity of Simon's definition, a number of significant issues remain to be addressed in learning. First, we must determine how learning relates to the acquisition of knowledge. Do we learn when we acquire a new fact about our environment? A new rule? Isn't it true that before a rule enhances performance we must know when and how to apply it? Do we need to generalize new information before we call it learning? Learning as the acquisition of new facts and rules is reflected in several of the symbolic approaches of Chapter 10.

Second, there is the issue whether or not the "new" knowledge is acquired by *induction* or *deduction*. Knowledge which is logically implied by what is already known falls within the deductive closure of the learner's knowledge. We can contrast this with the acquisition of new knowledge attained through induction over specific examples. This is similar to the process by which the scientist discovers genuinely new laws from experimental data.

Third, we can distinguish, with respect to the knowledge itself, whether it is empirical or linguistic. For example, the knowledge that a ball is a spherical, colored object is linguistic in that the concept and its properties are related by definition. Learning is acquiring the meaning or definition of a term rather than some new invariant property of the world. An example of empirical concept learning is acquiring the ability to identify edible mushrooms.

Finally, we need to consider the ways in which our concepts can be precise or imprecise and the consequences these distinctions have for learning. A familiar example of imprecision are concepts having degrees of membership in a category. Examples are "tall" and "short" when attributed to people. Another fuzzy term is the word "exact," in that we can always be more or less exact. There is also imprecision in value terms such as a "good" credit risk or "noisy" data.

There are also "imprecise" concepts such as "arch" or "cup." In these situations there is genuine room for disagreement between people on how the concept might apply. Furthermore, concepts, though defined clearly, can be imprecise in their use. No matter how precisely we may tie the concept "good credit risk" to a set of existing conditions our judgement can still be wrong with respect to the predictive force of the concept. Another example is the "edible mushroom." This concept is of the great interest because it captures the type of invariance many of the induction algorithms of Part III are attempting to learn.

Some of the algorithms of Part III, such as *candidate elimination* and *explanation based learning*, can only work with precise concepts, that is concepts having definitions in terms of necessary and sufficient conditions. Other algorithms, including *ID3, Cobweb*, and connectionist networks learn imprecise concepts effectively. Cobweb learns concepts that are fuzzy in their degree of set membership while other classifiers are good at handling predictive uncertainty.

Machine learning has proven to be a fruitful area of research, spawning a number of different problems and algorithms. These algorithms vary in their goals, the available training data, the learning strategies, and knowledge representation languages they employ. All of these algorithms learn by searching through a space of possible concepts to find an acceptable generalization. At the beginning of Chapter 10, we outline a framework for machine learning that emphasizes the common assumptions behind all of this work.

The algorithms presented in Sections 10.2 through 10.4, although differing in search strategies, representation languages, and the amount of prior knowledge used, all assume that the training data are classified by a teacher or some other means. The learner is told whether an instance is a positive or negative example of a target concept. A positive example is an instance that belongs to the target concept; a negative example does not. This reliance on training instances of known classification defines the task of *supervised learning*.

Section 10.5 continues the study of induction by examining *unsupervised learning*; how can an intelligent agent acquire useful knowledge in the absence of correctly classified training data? This is an important question, underlying tasks as diverse as scientific discovery, modeling human cognition, and learning by autonomous robots. *Category formation*, or *conceptual clustering*, is a fundamental problem in unsupervised learning. Given a set of objects exhibiting various properties, how may an agent divide them into useful categories? How do we know if a category is useful? What is the best way to represent those categories? In this section, we examine *CLUSTER/2* and *COBWEB*, two approaches to the problem of category formation.

Chapters 11 and 12 present neural and biology based learning architectures. These machine learning techniques identify and generalize complex patterns in data and are used quite extensively to model perception based aspects of intelligence. *Neural network* problem solving examines the way in which intelligent behavior can arise from the interactions of large numbers of small, individually simple elements. Genetic algorithms, for example, model learning as an evolutionary process operating on a population of competing, candidate solutions.

Chapter 11 introduces connectionist problem solving, giving its early history and the types of problems for which it is most often employed. Section 11.2 presents *perceptron learning* and a classification example. We also examine the *delta* rule. In Section 11.3, we present and give several examples of *backpropagation* networks. Our presentation emphasizes the evolution of artificial neural networks as they overcame the problems early systems had with learning, in particular, generalization across data points that were not linearly separable. This evolution of connectionist networks over the past 40 years also offers important insights into the present state of the discipline.

Chapter 12 presents connectionist models for *competitive* and *reinforcement* learning. Section 12.1 presents competitive models developed by Tuevo Kohonen and Robert Hecht-Nielsen. We use these architectures to model important aspects of S-R behavior. Section 12.2, picking up ideas first presented in Chapter 5, presents Hebbian models of reinforcement learning.

Sections 12.3 and 12.4 introduce the important family of *attractor* networks, sometimes called *memories*. These are often used for pattern retrieval and to create content addressable memories. In Section 12.4, with the *genetic algorithm*, we present evolutionary or biology based learning models.

Section 12.5 serves as a summary section for Part III, presenting the trends and limitations we see in the current generation of learning models. Many of the issues in the summary are fundamental to the enterprise of cognitive science and are discussed again in the final chapter, 17.

Chapter 10

EXPLICIT SYMBOL BASED LEARNING MODELS

Let us teach guessing...

George Polya

It is vain to do with more what can be done with less.... Entities should not be multiplied beyond necessity...

William of Occam

10.0   INTRODUCTION

Chapter 10 focuses primarily on explicit symbol based *inductive learning*. This includes the discovery of approximation surfaces and generalizations from sets of examples cast in a symbolic representation. *Concept learning* is a typical inductive learning problem: Given examples of some concept, say "arch," "soybean disease," or "good stock investment," infer a definition that will allow the learner to correctly recognize future instances of that concept.

Section 10.1 offers a general framework and methodology for addressing issues in machine learning. The learning problem is broken into data and goals, the selection of a representation, a set of operators, a space of possible concepts, and the specific search algorithm used. This framework is illustrated with Winston's program for learning concepts.

Sections 10.2 and 10.3 examine two algorithms used for concept induction, *version space search* and *ID3*. The algorithms of Sections 10.2 and 10.3 are data driven. They use no prior knowledge of the learning domain, but rely on large numbers of examples to define the essential properties of a general concept. Algorithms that generalize on the basis of patterns in training data are referred to as *similarity based*.

A learner may also use prior knowledge of a domain to guide learning. Humans, for example, rarely require large numbers of examples to learn effectively. Even a single example, analogy, or bit of advice can communicate a general concept. This is possible because we already know large amounts of information about our environment. Section 10.4 examines explanation-based generalization, learning by analogy, and other techniques that use prior knowledge to learn from a limited amount of training data.

The conceptual clustering algorithms discussed in Section 10.5 illustrate another variation on the induction problem: instead of a set of training instances of known categorization, these algorithms begin with a set of unclassified instances. Their task is one of discovering categorizations that may have some utility to the learner. Section 10.5 presents AM, COBWEB, and the CLUSTER/2 approaches for discovering patterns in data.

10.1   A FRAMEWORK FOR LEARNING

Learning algorithms may be characterized along five dimensions:

1.   The data and goals of the learning task.

One of the primary ways in which we characterize learning problems is according to the goals of the learner and the data it is given. The concept learning algorithms of Sections 10.2 and 10.3, for example, begin with a collection of positive, and sometimes negative, examples of a target class. The goal is to infer a general definition that will allow the learner to recognize future instances of the class.

Examples are not the only source of training data. Humans, for instance, often learn from high level advice. In teaching programming, professors generally tell their students that all loops must achieve a terminating condition. This advice, while correct, is not directly useful; it must be translated into specific rules for manipulating loop counters or logical conditions in a programming language. Analogies are another type of training data (Section 10.4.4) that must be correctly interpreted before they can be of use. If a teacher tells a student that electricity is like water, the student must infer the correct intent of the analogy: As water flows through a pipe, electricity flows through a wire. As with flowing water, we may measure the amount of electricity, amperage, and the pressure behind the flow, voltage. Unlike water, however, electricity does not make things wet or help us wash our hands. The interpretation of analogies involves finding the meaningful similarities and avoiding false or meaningless inferences.

We may also characterize a learning algorithm by the goal, or *target*, of the learner. The goal of many learning algorithms is a *concept*, or general description of a class of objects. Learning algorithms may also acquire plans, problem solving heuristics, or other forms of procedural knowledge.

The properties and quality of the training data are another dimension along which we classify learning tasks. The data may come from a teacher, from the outside environment, or it may be generated by the program itself. Data may be reliable or contain noise. It can be presented in a well-structured fashion or consist of unorganized instances. It may include both positive and negative examples or only positive examples. Data may be readily available or the program may have to construct experiments or perform some other form of data acquisition.

2. *The representation of learned knowledge.*

Machine learning programs have made use of all the representation languages discussed in this text. For example, programs that learn to classify objects may represent these concepts as expressions in predicate calculus or they may use a structured representation such as frames or objects. Plans may be described as a sequence of operations or a triangle table. Heuristics may be represented as problem solving rules.

A simple formulation of the concept learning problem represents instances of a concept as conjunctions of predicate calculus expressions with all variables bound (Chapter 7); concepts are conjunctive sentences containing variables. For example, instances of the concept ball may be represented by:

size(obj1, small) $\wedge$ color(obj1, red) $\wedge$ shape(obj1, round)
size(obj2, large) $\wedge$ color(obj2, red) $\wedge$ shape(obj2, round)

and the general concept "ball" would be defined by:

size(X, Y) $\wedge$ color(X, Z) $\wedge$ shape(X, round).

Any sentence that will match, that is can bind its variables with this general definition, represents a ball.

3. *A set of operations.*

Given a set of training instances, the learner must construct a generalization, heuristic rule or plan that satisfies its goals. This requires the ability to manipulate representations. Typical operations include generalizing or specializing symbolic expressions, adjusting the weights in a neural network, or otherwise modifying the program's representations.

In the concept learning example just introduced, a learner may generalize a concept definition by replacing constants with variables. Begin with the concept:

size(obj1, small) $\wedge$ color(obj1, red) $\wedge$ shape(obj1, round)

and replace a single constant with a variable to produce the generalization:

size(obj1, X) $\wedge$ color(obj1, red) $\wedge$ shape(obj1, round)

> size(obj1, small) ∧ color(obj1, X) ∧ shape(obj1, round)
> size(obj1, small) ∧ color(obj1, red) ∧ shape(obj1, X)
> size(X, small) ∧ color(X, red) ∧ shape(X, round)

4. *The concept space.*

The representation language, together with the operations described above, define a space of potential concept definitions. The learner must search this space to find the desired concept. The complexity of this concept space is a primary measure of the difficulty of a learning problem.

5. *Heuristic search.*

Learning programs must commit to a direction and order of search, as well as the use of available training data and heuristics to search efficiently. In our example of learning the concept "ball," a plausible algorithm may take the first example as a *candidate concept* and generalize it to include subsequent examples. For instance, on being given the training instance:

> size(obj1, small) ∧ color(obj1, red) ∧ shape(obj1, round)

the learner makes that instance a candidate concept that correctly classifies the only positive instance seen. If the algorithm is given the positive instance:

> size(obj2, large) ∧ color(obj2, red) ∧ shape(obj2, round)

the learner may generalize the candidate concept by replacing constants with variables as needed to form a concept that will match both instances. The result is a more general candidate concept that is closer to our target concept of ball.

> size(X, Y) ∧ color(X, red) ∧ shape(X, round)

Patrick Winston's work on learning concepts from good and bad examples (Winston 1975) illustrates these components. His program learns general definitions of structural concepts, such as arch, in a blocks world. This corresponds to the acquisition of linguistic knowledge as described in the Introduction to Part III. The training data are a series of positive and negative examples of the concept: examples of blocks world structures that fit in the category, along with *near misses*. These are instances that almost belong to the category but fail on one property or relation. The near misses enable the program to single out features that can be used to exclude negative instances from the target concept. Figure 10.1 shows positive examples and near misses for the concept "arch."

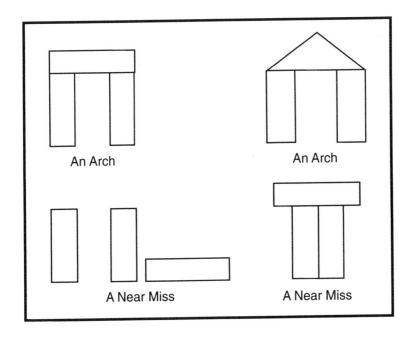

FIGURE 10.1 Examples and near misses for the concept "arch."

The program represents concepts as semantic networks (see Figure 10.2) and Section 6.2. It learns by refining a candidate description of the target concept as training instances are presented. Winston's program refines candidate descriptions through *generalization* and *specialization*. Generalization changes the graph to let it accommodate new examples of the concept. Figure 10.2a shows an arch built of three bricks and a graph that describes it.

The next training example (Figure 10.2b) is an arch with a pyramid rather than a brick on top. This example does not match the candidate description. The program matches these graphs, attempting to find a partial isomorphism between them. The graph matcher uses the node names to guide the matching process. Once it matches the graphs, it may detect differences between them. In Figure 10.2, the graphs match on all components, except that the top element in the first graph is a brick and the corresponding node of the second example is a pyramid. Part of the programs background knowledge is a generalization hierarchy of these concepts (see Figure 10.2c). The program generalizes the graph by replacing this node with the least common supertype of brick and pyramid; in this example, it is polygonal solid. The result is the concept of Figure 10.2d.

When presented with a near miss, an example that differs from the target concept in a single property, the program specializes the candidate description to

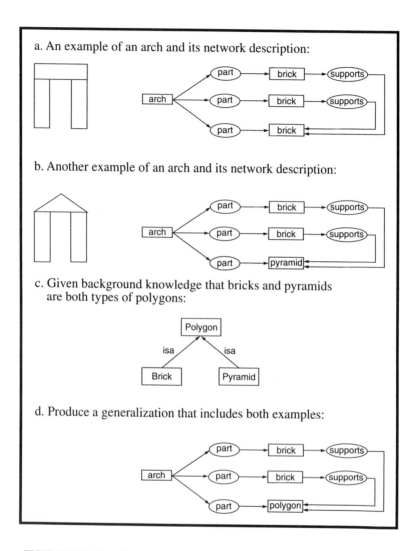

FIGURE 10.2 Generalization of descriptions to include multiple examples.

exclude the example. Figure 10.3a is a candidate description. It differs from the near miss of Figure 10.3b in the touch relations of the near-miss example. The program specializes the graph by adding must-not-touch links to exclude the near miss, as in Figure 10.3c. Note that the algorithm depends heavily upon the closeness of the negative examples to the target concept. By differing from the goal in only a single property, a near miss helps the algorithm to determine exactly how to specialize the candidate concept.

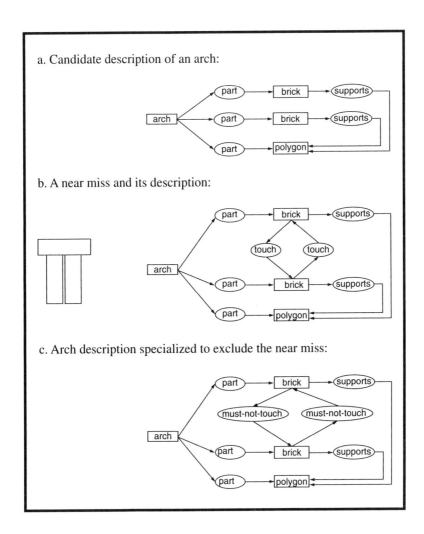

a. Candidate description of an arch:

b. A near miss and its description:

c. Arch description specialized to exclude the near miss:

FIGURE 10.3 Specialization of a description to exclude a near miss.

These operations, specializing a network by adding links and generalizing it by replacing node or link names with a more general concept, define a space of possible concept definitions. Winston's program, guided by the training data, performs a hill climbing search (Chapter 11) on this concept space. Because the program does not keep track of intermediate states of the search, its performance is highly sensitive to the order of the training examples; a bad ordering can lead the program to dead ends in the search space. Training instances must be presented to the program in an order that assists learning of the desired concept, much as a teacher organizes lessons to help a student learn. The quality and order of the training examples are also important to the program's graph matching algorithm; efficient matching requires that the graphs not be too dissimilar.

Although an early example of inductive learning, Winston's program illustrates the features and problems shared by the majority of machine learning techniques: the use of generalization and specialization operations to define a concept space, the use of data to guide search through that space, and the sensitivity of the learning algorithm to the quality of the training data. The next sections examine these problems in more detail and suggest some techniques for addressing them.

10.2 VERSION SPACE SEARCH

Version space search (Mitchell 1982) is a general and highly instructive way to approach inductive learning as search through a concept space. Version space search takes advantage of the fact that generalization operations impose an ordering on the concepts in a space and uses this ordering to guide the search. The premises of this learning task are similar to those of Winston's. We are searching for a definition of a target concept in terms of necessary and sufficient conditions where the set of predicates characterizing the search space is already given.

10.2.1 Generalization Operators and the Concept Space

Generalization and specialization are the most common operations for defining a concept space. The primary generalization operations for machine learning are:

1. Replacing constants with variables. For example,

    color(ball, red)

    generalizes to:

    color(X, red)

2. Dropping conditions from a conjunctive expression.

    shape(X, round) ∧ size(X, small) ∧ color(X, red)

    generalizes to:

    shape(X, round) ∧ color(X, red)

3. Adding a disjunct to an expression.

shape(X, round) ∧ size(X, small) ∧ color(X, red)

generalizes to:

shape(X, round) ∧ size(X, small) ∧ (color(X, red) ∨ color(X, blue))

4. Replacing a property with its parent in a class hierarchy. If we know that primary_color is a superclass of red, then

color(X, red)

generalizes to:

color(X, primary_color)

We may think of generalization in set theoretic terms: Let P and Q be the sets of sentences covered by the predicate calculus expressions p and q, respectively. Expression p is more general than q if and only if the set P contains all the elements of Q. In the above examples, the set of sentences that match color(X, red) contains the set of elements that match color(ball, red). Similarly, in Example 2, we may think of the set of round, red things as a superset of the set of small, red, round things. Note that the "more general than" relationship defines a partial ordering on the space of logical sentences. We express this using the "≥" symbol, where $p \geq q$ means that p is more general than q. This ordering is a powerful source of constraints on the search performed by a learning algorithm.

We formalize this relationship through the notion of *covering*. If concept p is more general than concept q, we say that *p covers q*. We define the covers relation: let p(x) and q(x) be descriptions that classify objects as being positive examples of a concept; that is, for an object X, p(X) → positive(X) and q(X) → positive(X). p covers q if and only if q(X) → positive(X) is a logical consequence of p(X) → positive(X). For example, the concept color(X, Y) covers color(ball, Z), which in turn covers color(ball, red). *Logical consequence* was presented in Chapter 7.

As an example, consider a domain of objects that have properties and values:

size = {large, small}
colors = {red, white, blue}
shape = {ball, brick, cube}

These objects can be represented using the predicate obj(Size, Color, Shape).

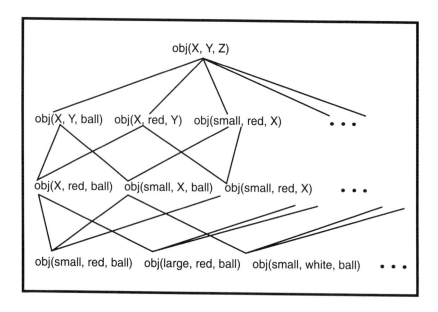

FIGURE 10.4 A version space.

The generalization operation of replacing constants with variables defines the space of Figure 10.4. We may view inductive learning as searching this space for a concept that is consistent with all the training examples.

10.2.2   The *Candidate Elimination* Algorithm

This section presents three algorithms (Mitchell 1982) for searching the concept space. These algorithms rely upon the notion of a *version space*, the set of all concept descriptions consistent with the training examples. These algorithms work by reducing the size of the version space as more examples become available. The first two algorithms reduce the version space in a specific to general direction and a general to specific direction, respectively. The third algorithm, called *candidate elimination*, combines these approaches into a bidirectional search. In this section we describe and evaluate these algorithms; Luger and Stubblefield (1993, Chap. 13) demonstrate their implementation in the PROLOG language; a simplified version may be found in Section 16.5.

These algorithms are data driven; they generalize based on regularities found in the training data. Also, in using training data of a known classification, these algorithms perform a variety of *supervised learning*.

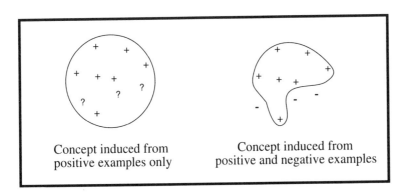

Concept induced from   Concept induced from
positive examples only   positive and negative examples

FIGURE 10.5   The role of negative examples in preventing overgeneralization.

As with Winston's program for learning structural descriptions, version space search uses both positive and negative examples of the target concept. Although it is possible to generalize from positive examples only, negative examples are important in preventing the algorithm from overgeneralizing. Not only must the learned concept be general enough to cover all positive examples, but it must also be specific enough to exclude all negative examples. In the space of Figure 10.4, one concept that would cover all sets of exclusively positive instances would be obj(X, Y, Z). This concept is too general to be interesting; it implies that all instances belong to the target concept. One way to avoid overgeneralization is to generalize as little as possible to cover positive examples; another is to use negative instances to eliminate overly general concepts. As Figure 10.5 illustrates, negative instances prevent overgeneralization by forcing the learner to specialize concepts in order to exclude negative instances. The algorithms of this section use both of these techniques.

Specific to general search maintains a set, S, of *hypotheses*, or candidate concept definitions. To avoid overgeneralization, these candidate definitions are the *maximally specific generalizations* from the training data. A concept, c, is maximally specific if it covers all positive examples, none of the negative examples, and for any other concept, c', that covers the positive examples, $c \geq c'$. Figure 10.6 applies the specific to general search to the version space of Figure 10.4.

We may also search in a *general to specific* direction. This algorithm maintains a set, G, of *maximally general concepts* that cover all of the positive and none of the negative instances. A concept, c, is maximally general if it covers none of the negative training instances, and for any other concept, c', that covers no negative training instance, $c \geq c'$. In this algorithm, negative instances lead to the specialization of candidate concepts; the algorithm uses positive instances to eliminate overly specialized concepts. Figure 10.7 applies this algorithm to the version space of Figure 10.4.

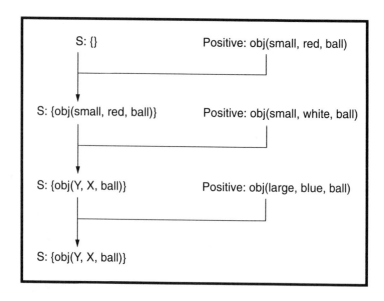

FIGURE 10.6 Specific to general search of the version space for the concept "ball."

We define specific to general search as:

```
Begin
Initialize S to the first positive training instance;
N is the set of all negative instances seen so far.
For each positive instance p:
    Begin
    For every s ∈ S, if s does not match p, replace s with its most
        specific generalizations that match p.
    Delete from S all hypotheses that are more general than
        some other hypothesis in S.
    Delete from S all hypotheses that match a previously
        observed negative instance.
    End
For every negative instance, n:
    Begin
    Delete all members of S that match n.
    Add n to N to check future hypotheses for over
        generalization.
    End
End
```

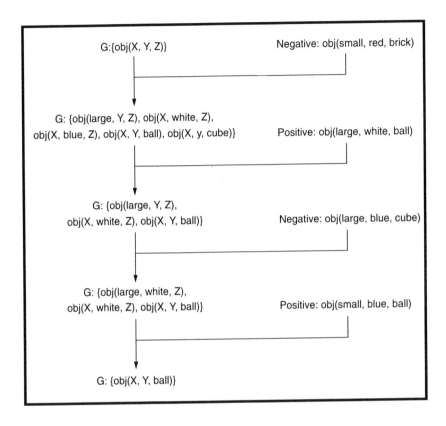

FIGURE 10.7   General to specific search of the version space for learning "ball."

We define general to specific search as:

Begin
Initialize G to contain the most general concept in the space;
P contains all positive examples seen so far.
For each negative instance, n:
  Begin
  For each g ∈ G that matches n, replace g with its most
    general specializations that do not match n.
  Delete from G all hypotheses that are more specific than
    some other hypothesis in G.
  Delete from G all hypotheses that fail to match some positive
    example in P.
  End

For each positive instance, p:
　Begin
　Delete from G all hypotheses that fail to match p.
　Add p to P.
　End
End

Figure 10.7 applies the general to specific algorithm to the version space of Figure 10.4. In this example, the algorithm uses background knowledge that size may have values {large, small}, color may have values {red, white, blue}, and shape may have values {ball, brick, cube}. This knowledge is essential if the algorithm is to specialize concepts by substituting constants for variables.

The *candidate elimination algorithm* combines these approaches into a *bi-directional search* of the version space. As we shall see, this bidirectional approach has a number of benefits for the learner. The algorithm maintains two sets of candidate concepts: G is the set of maximally general candidate concepts and S the set of maximally specific candidates. It specializes G and generalizes S until they converge on the target concept. The algorithm is defined:

Begin
Initialize G to be the most general concept in the space;
initialize S to the first positive training instance.
For each new positive instance p:
　Begin
　Delete all members of G that fail to match p.
　For every s ∈ S, if s does not match p, replace s with its most
　　　specific generalizations that match p.
　Delete from S any hypotheses that is more general than
　　　some other hypothesis in S.
　Delete from S any hypotheses that is not more specific than
　　　some hypothesis in G.
　End
For each new negative instance n:
　Begin
　Delete all members of S that match n.
　For each g ∈ G that matches n, replace g with its most
　　　general specializations that do not match n.
　Delete from G any hypotheses that is more specific than
　　　some other hypothesis in G.
　Delete from G any hypothesis that is more specific than
　　　some hypothesis in S
　End

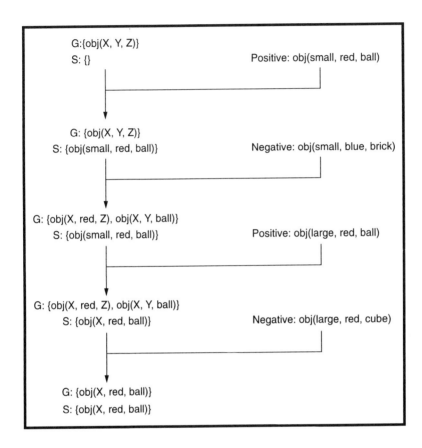

FIGURE 10.8   The candidate elimination algorithm learning the concept "red ball."

If G = S and both are singletons, the algorithm has found a single
   concept which is consistent with all the data and the
   algorithm halts.
If G and S become empty, then there is no concept that covers all
   positive instances and none of the negative instances.
End

Figure 10.8 illustrates the behavior of the candidate elimination algorithm in searching the version space of Figure 10.4. Note that the figure does not show those concepts that were produced through generalization or specialization but eliminated as overly general or specific. We leave the elaboration of this part of the algorithm as an exercise.

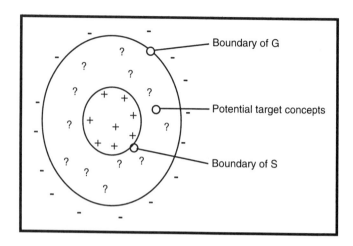

FIGURE 10.9 Converging boundaries of the G and S sets in the candidate elimination algorithm.

Combining the two directions of search into a single algorithm has several benefits. The G and S sets summarize the information in the negative and positive training instances, respectively, eliminating the need to save these instances. For example, after generalizing S to cover a positive instance, the algorithm uses G to eliminate concepts in S that do not cover any negative instances. Since G is the set of *maximally general* concepts that do not match any negative training instances, any member of S that is more general than any member of G must match some negative instance. Similarly, since S is the set of *maximally specific* generalizations that cover all positive instances, any new member of G that is more specific than a member of S must fail to cover some positive instance and may also be eliminated.

Figure 10.9 gives an abstract description of the candidate elimination algorithm. The "+" signs represent positive training instances; "-" signs indicate negative instances. The innermost circle encloses the set of known positive instances covered by the concepts in S. The outermost circle encloses the instances covered by G; any instance outside this circle is negative. The middle portion of the graphic contains the target concept, along with concepts that may be overly general or specific, the "?s." The search shrinks the outermost concept as necessary to exclude negative instances; it expands the innermost concept to include new positive instances.

Eventually, the two sets converge on the target concept. In this fashion, candidate elimination can detect when it has found a single consistent target concept. When both G and S converge to the same concept the algorithm may halt. If G and S become empty, then there is no concept that will cover all positive instances and none of the negative instances. This may occur if the training data are inconsistent with respect to the initial descriptors; in other words, if the goal concept is not expressible in the representation language. Thus, candidate elimination can only learn precise concepts; those defined by necessary and sufficient conditions.

An interesting aspect of candidate elimination is its incremental nature. An incremental learning algorithm accepts training instances one at a time, forming a usable, although possibly incomplete, generalization after each example. This contrasts with batch algorithms (ID3, Section 10.3) that require all training examples to be present before they may begin learning. Even before the candidate elimination algorithm converges on a single concept, the G and S sets provide usable constraints on that concept: If c is the goal concept, then for all $g \in$ G and $s \in$ S, $s \leq c \leq g$. Any concept that is more general than some concept in G will cover negative instances; any concept that is more specific than some concept in S will fail to cover some positive instances. This suggests that instances that have a "good fit" with the concepts bounded by G and S are at least plausible instances of the concept.

10.2.3 Human Protocols and Search through a Concept Space

A number of psychologists have asked how human subjects solve concept formation tasks such as those just seen in Section 10.2.2 The following problem solving task was first proposed by Vygotsky in the 1930s and later enhanced by Bruner and others (1956). We describe here variants of the Bruner approach. A set of possible concept instances, similar to those represented in Figure 10.10, are presented to subjects. The experimenter has in mind a conjunctive concept, say all cards with two borders and containing squares. The goal is for the subject to determine this concept.

The method the subject uses is to select one card. The experimenter then tells the subject whether or not that card is an instance of the concept. Based on the experimenter's response, the subject picks another card for consideration until the subject determines the concept under question.

The subjects used a number of strategies in their selection procedure, mostly based on confirming or eliminating parameters of the concept space. Their searches were in many aspects similar to the version space searches. For example, using a *conservative focus* strategy the subject could confirm or eliminate one parameter of the concept space at a time until the conjunctive concept was determined.

The experimenters varied the problem by offering rewards to the subjects for quick solutions. This brought on more daring strategies, such as trying to verify

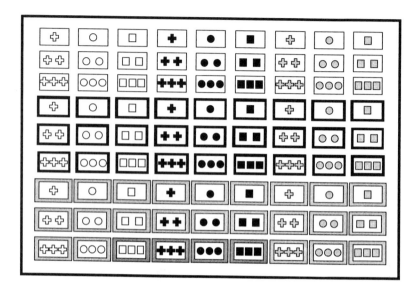

Figure 10.10   An array of instances comprising combinations of four attributes, each exhibiting three values. Plain figures are in green, grey figures in red, solid figures in black.

more than one parameter of the concept space with one card selection. These *focus gamble* strategies could produce quick results when they worked, but when they didn't the subject was in a worse situation than before making the choice. The researchers also noted the extreme search and bookkeeping problems subjects had in determining disjunctive concepts, such as the set of cards having either squares or double borders. In the next section ID3 provides a method for placing a population of instances into known concept classes.

10.3   ID3

ID3 (Quinlan 1986a), like candidate elimination, induces concepts from examples. It is particularly interesting for its representation of learned knowledge, its approach to the management of complexity, its heuristic for selecting candidate concepts, and its ability to handle noisy data. ID3 represents concepts as *decision trees*, a representation that classifies an object by testing its values for certain properties.

For example, consider the problem of estimating an individual's credit risk on the basis of such properties as credit history, current debt, collateral, and income. Table 10.1 lists a sample of individuals of known credit risks:

	Risk	Credit History	Debt	Collateral	Income
1.	high	bad	high	none	$0 to $15k
2.	high	unknown	high	none	$15k to $35k
3.	moderate	unknown	low	none	$15k to $35k
4.	high	unknown	low	none	$0 to $15k
5.	low	unknown	low	none	over $35k
6.	low	unknown	low	adequate	over $35k
7.	high	bad	low	none	$0 to $15k
8.	moderate	bad	low	adequate	over $35k
9.	low	good	low	none	over $35k
10.	low	good	high	adequate	over $35k
11.	high	good	high	none	$0 to $15k
12.	moderate	good	high	none	$15k to $35k
13.	low	good	high	none	over $35k
14.	high	bad	high	none	$15k to $35k

TABLE 10.1 Credit information for a number of individuals.

The decision tree of Figure 10.11 represents the classifications in Table 10.1 in that it can correctly classify all the objects in the table. In a decision tree, each internal node represents a test on some property, such as credit history or debt; each possible value of that property corresponds to a branch of the tree. Leaf nodes represent classifications, such as low or moderate risk. An individual of unknown type may be classified by traversing this tree: at each internal node, test the individual's value for that property and take the appropriate branch. This continues until reaching a leaf node and the object's classification.

Note that in classifying any given instance, this tree does not use all the properties present in Table 10.1. For instance, if a person has a good credit history and a low debt, we may, according to the tree, ignore their

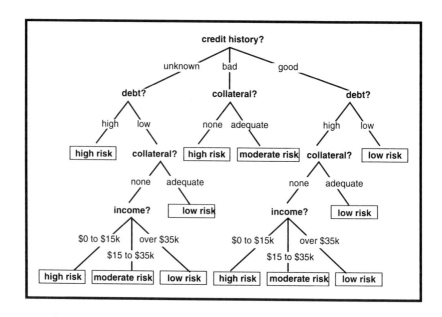

FIGURE 10.11 A decision tree for credit risk assessment.

collateral and income and classify them as a good risk. However, despite omitting certain tests, this tree correctly classifies all the examples in the table.

In general, the size of the tree necessary to classify a given set of examples varies according to the order with which properties are tested. Figure 10.12 shows a tree that is considerably simpler than that of Figure 10.11, but which also classifies the examples in Table 10.1.

Given a set of training instances, and a number of different decision trees that correctly classify them, we may ask which tree has the greatest likelihood of correctly classifying unseen instances of the population. The ID3 algorithm assumes that this is the simplest decision tree that covers all the training examples. The rationale for this assumption is the time honored heuristic of preferring simplicity and avoiding unnecessary assumptions. This principle, known as *Occam's Razor*, was first articulated by the logician, William of Occam in 1324:

> It is vain to do with more what can be done with less....
> Entities should not be multiplied beyond necessity.

A more contemporary version of Occam's razor argues that we should always accept the simplest answer that correctly fits our data. In this case, it is the smallest decision tree that correctly classifies all given examples.

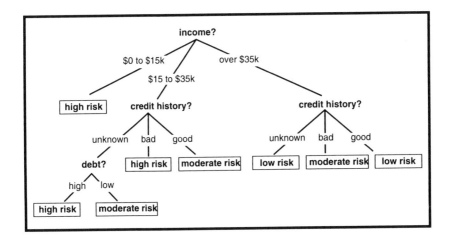

FIGURE 10.12 A simplified decision tree for credit risk assessment.

Although Occam's razor has proven itself as a general heuristic for all manner of intellectual activity, its use here has a more specific justification. If we assume that the given examples are sufficient to construct a valid generalization, then our problem becomes one of distinguishing the necessary properties from the extraneous ones. The simplest decision tree that covers all the examples should be the least likely to include unnecessary constraints. Even though this idea is intuitively appealing, it is an assumption that must be empirically tested; Section 10.3.3 presents some of these results. Before examining these, however, we present the ID3 algorithm for inducing decision trees from examples.

10.3.1   Top Down Decision Tree Induction

ID3 constructs decision trees in a top down fashion. Note that for any property, we may partition the set of training examples into disjoint subsets, where all the examples in a partition have a common value for that property. ID3 selects a property to test at the current node of the tree and uses this test to partition the set of examples. The algorithm then recursively constructs a subtree for each partition. This continues until all members of the partition are in the same class; that class becomes a leaf node of the tree. Because the order of tests is critical to constructing a simple decision tree, ID3 relies heavily on its criteria for selecting the test at the root of each subtree. To simplify our discussion, this section describes the algorithm for constructing decision trees, assuming an appropriate test selection function. In Section 10.3.2 we present the selection heuristic used by the ID3 algorithm.

The decision tree induction algorithm begins with a sample of correctly classified members of the target categories. ID3 constructs a decision tree according to the algorithm:

```
function induce_tree (example_set, Properties)
    begin
    if all entries in example_set are in the same class
        then return a leaf node labeled with that class
        else if Properties is empty
            then return leaf node with disjunction of classes in
                example_set
        else begin
            select a property, P, to test, make it the root of the
                current tree;
            delete P from Properties;
            for each value, V, of P,
                begin
                    create a branch of the tree labeled with V
                    let partition_V contain elements of
                        example_set having value V for property P;
                    call induce_tree(partition_V , Properties),
                    attach result to branch V
                end
            end
    end
```

For example, consider the way in which ID3 constructs the tree of Figure 10.12 from Table 10.1. Beginning with the full table of examples, ID3 selects income as the root property using the selection function to be described in Section 10.3.2. This partitions the example set as shown in Figure 10.13, with the elements of each partition being listed by their number in the table.

ID3 applies the induce_tree function recursively to each partition. The partition {1, 4, 7, 11} consists entirely of high risk individuals; ID3 creates a leaf node accordingly. ID3 selects the credit history property as the root of the subtree for the partition {2, 3, 12, 14}. In Figure 10.14 credit history further divides this partition into {2,3}, {14}, and {12}. Continuing to select tests and construct subtrees in this fashion, ID3 eventually produces the tree of Figure 10.12. We let the reader work through the remaining stages of this construction.

Before presenting ID3's test selection heuristic, it is worth examining the relationship between the tree construction algorithm and our view of learning as search through a concept space. We may think of the set of all possible decision trees as defining a space. Our operations for moving through this space consist of

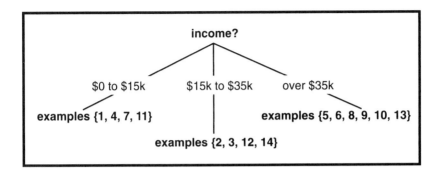

FIGURE 10.13 A partially constructed decision tree.

adding tests to a tree. ID3 implements a form of hill climbing in the space of all possible trees. It adds a subtree to the current tree and continues its search. It does not backtrack. This makes the algorithm highly efficient; it also makes it highly dependent upon the criteria for selecting properties to test.

If ID3 exhausts the property list before successfully classifying a subset of examples, that is if it creates leaf nodes with members of more than one class, this can be interpreted in one of two ways. First, the selection criteria are insufficient to classify the examples, this means that the target concept cannot be defined from the selection criteria in terms of necessary and sufficient conditions. Alternatively, we are dealing with a fuzzy concept, such as distinguishing between fruit and vegetable, or a predictive concept, such as good credit risk. In these cases we can interpret the content of leaf nodes probabilistically. For example, if 9 out of 10 members of a leaf node belong to one category, this confidence will be returned by the node.

10.3.2 Information Theoretic Test Selection

We may think of each property of an instance as contributing a certain amount of information to its classification. For example, if our goal is to determine the species of an animal, the discovery that it lays eggs, contributes a certain amount of information to that goal. ID3 measures the information gained by making each property the root of the current subtree. It then picks the property that provides the greatest information gain.

Information theory (Shannon 1948) provides a mathematical basis for measuring the information content of a message. We may think of a message as an instance in a universe of possible messages; the act of transmitting a message is the same as selecting one of these possible messages. From this point of view, it

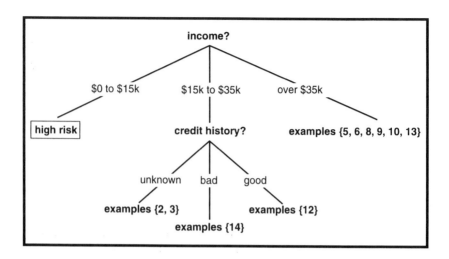

FIGURE 10.14 Another partially constructed decision tree.

is reasonable to define the information content of a message as depending upon both the size of this universe and the frequency with which each possible message occurs.

The importance of the number of possible messages is evident in an example from gambling: compare a message correctly predicting the outcome of a spin of the roulette wheel with one predicting the outcome of a toss of an honest coin. Since roulette can have more outcomes than a coin toss, a message concerning its outcome is of more value to us. Winning at roulette pays better than winning a coin toss. Consequently, we regard this message as conveying more information.

The influence of the probability of each message on the amount of information is evident in another gambling example. Assume that I have rigged a coin so that it will come up heads 3/4 of the time. Since I already know enough about the coin to wager correctly 3/4 of the time, a message telling me the outcome of a given toss is worth less to me than it would be for an honest coin.

Shannon formalized these intuitions by defining the amount of information in a message as a function of the probability of occurrence of all possible messages. Given a universe of messages, $M = \{m_1, m_2, \dots m_n\}$ and a probability, $p(m_i)$, for the occurrence of each message, the information content of a message in M is given by:

$$I(M) = \sum_{i=1}^{n} -p(m_i) \log_2 (p(m_i)).$$

The information in a message is measured in bits. For example, the information content of a message telling the outcome of the flip of an honest coin is:

$$I(\text{Coin toss}) = - p(\text{heads}) \log_2 (p(\text{heads})) - p(\text{tails}) \log_2 (p(\text{tails}))$$
$$= -1/2 \log_2 (1/2) -1/2 \log_2 (1/2)$$
$$= 1 \text{ bit}$$

However, if the coin has been rigged to come up heads 75% of the time, then the information content of a message is:

$$I(\text{Coin toss}) = - 3/4 \log_2 (3/4) - 1/4 \log_2 (1/4)$$
$$= - 3/4 * (-0.415) - 1/4 * (-2)$$
$$= 0.811 \text{ bits}$$

This definition formalizes many of our intuitions about the information content of messages. Information theory is widely applied in computer science and telecommunications, being used in such applications as determining the information carrying capacity of communications channels, developing data compression algorithms, and developing noise resistant communication strategies. ID3 uses information theory to select the test that gives the greatest information gain in classifying the training examples.

We may think of a decision tree as conveying information about the classification of examples in the decision table. The information content of the tree is computed from the probabilities of the different classifications. For example, if we assume that all the examples in Table 10.1 occur with equal probability, then:

$$p(\text{risk is high}) = 6/14$$
$$p(\text{risk is moderate}) = 3/14$$
$$p(\text{risk is low}) = 5/14$$

It follows that the information in the table and, consequently, any tree that covers those examples is:

$$I \text{ (Table 10.1)} = -6/14 \log_2 (6/14) -3/14 \log_2 (3/14) -5/14 \log_2 (5/14)$$
$$= -6/14 * (-1.222) - 3/14 * (-2.222) - 5/14*(-1.485)$$
$$= 1.531 \text{ bits}$$

For a given test, the information gain provided by making that test the root of the current tree is equal to the total information in the tree minus the amount of information needed to complete the classification after performing the test. The amount of information needed to complete the tree is defined as the weighted average of the information in all its subtrees. We compute the weighted average by multiplying the information content of each subtree by the percentage of the examples present in that subtree and summing these products.

Assume a set of training instances, C. If we make property P, with n values, the root of the current tree, this will partition C into subsets, $\{C_1, C_2, ... C_n\}$. The expected information needed to complete the tree after making P the root is:

$$E(P) = \sum_{i=1}^{n} (|C_i|/|C|) \, I(C_i).$$

The gain from property P is computed by subtracting the expected information to complete the tree from the total information content of the tree:

gain (P) = I (C) - E (P)

In the example of Table 10.1, we make income the property tested at the root of the tree. This partitions examples into $C_1 = \{1,4,7,11\}$, $C_2 = \{2,3,12,14\}$, and $C_3 = \{5,6,8,9,10,13\}$. The information needed to complete the tree is:

E(income)   = 4/14 * I (C_1) + 4/14 * I (C_2) + 6/14 * I (C_3)
             = 4/14 * 0.0 + 4/14 * 1.0 + 6/14 * 0.650
             = 0.564 bits

The information gain is:

gain(income)   = I (table 12.1) - E (income)
                = 1.531 - 0.564
                = 0.967 bits

Similarly, we may show that

gain(credit history) = 0.266
gain(debt) = 0.581
gain(collateral) = 0.756

Since income provides the greatest information gain, ID3 will select it as the root of the tree. The algorithm continues to apply this analysis recursively to each subtree until it has completed the tree.

10.3.3   Evaluating ID3

Although the ID3 algorithm produces simple decision trees, it is not obvious that such trees will be effective in predicting the classification of unknown examples.

Size of Training Set	Percentage of Whole Universe	Errors in 10,000 Trials	Predicted Maximum Errors
200	0.01%	199	728
1,000	0.07%	33	146
5,000	0.36%	8	29
25,000	1.79%	7	6
125,000	8.93%	2	1

TABLE 10.2 Results of the ID3 evaluation on chess end games. From Quinlan (1983)

ID3 has been evaluated in both controlled tests and applications, and has proven to work well in practice. Quinlan (1983), for example, evaluated its performance on the problem of learning to classify boards in a chess end game. The end game involved white, playing with a king and a rook, against black, playing with a king and a knight. ID3's goal was to learn to recognize boards that led to a loss for black within three moves. The attributes were different properties of boards, such as "an inability to move the king safely." The test used 23 such attributes.

Once board symmetries were taken into account, the entire problem domain consisted of 1.4 million different boards, of which 474,000 were a loss for black in three moves. ID3 was tested by giving it a randomly selected training set, and then testing it on 10,000 different boards, also randomly selected. Quinlan's tests gave the results found in Table 10.2. The predicted maximum errors were derived from a statistical model of ID3's behavior in the domain (see Quinlan 1983).

These results are impressive, and are supported by other empirical studies and anecdotal results. Variations of ID3 have been developed to deal with such problems as noise and very large training sets (see Quinlan 1986a).

10.4 KNOWLEDGE AND LEARNING

ID3 and the candidate elimination algorithm generalize on the basis of regularities in training data. Such algorithms are often referred to as *similarity based*, in that generalization is primarily a function of similarities across training examples. The biases employed by these algorithms are limited to syntactic constraints on the form of learned knowledge. They make no strong assumptions about the semantics of the domains. In this section, we examine algorithms that use prior knowledge to guide generalization.

Initially, the idea that knowledge of a domain may be necessary for learning seems contradictory. However, researchers have made a case for exactly that notion, arguing that the most effective learning occurs when the learner already has considerable knowledge of the domain. One argument for the importance of knowledge in learning is the reliance of similarity based learning techniques on relatively large amounts of training data. Humans, in contrast, can form reliable generalizations from very few or even a single training instance. Many practical applications require that a learning program do the same.

Another argument for the importance of prior knowledge recognizes that any set of training examples can support an unlimited number of generalizations, most of which are either irrelevant or nonsensical. Inductive bias is one means of making this distinction. In this section, we examine algorithms that go beyond purely syntactic biases to consider the role of knowledge in learning patterns in a problem situation.

10.4.1   Meta-DENDRAL

Meta-DENDRAL (Buchanan & Mitchell 1978) is one of the earliest and still one of the best examples of the use of knowledge in inductive learning. Meta-DEN-DRAL acquires rules to be used by the DENDRAL program for analyzing mass spectrographic data. DENDRAL infers the structure of organic molecules from their chemical formula and mass spectrographic data.

A mass spectrograph bombards molecules with electrons, causing some of the chemical bonds to break. Chemists measure the weight of the resulting pieces and interpret these results to gain insight into the structure of the compound. DENDRAL employs such knowledge in the form of rules for interpreting mass spectrographic data. The premise of a DENDRAL rule is a graph of some portion of a molecular structure. The conclusion of the rule is that graph with the location of the cleavage indicated.

Meta-DENDRAL infers these rules on the basis of mass spectrographic results on molecules of known structure. Meta-DENDRAL is given the structure of a known compound, along with the mass and relative abundance of the fragments produced by spectrography. It interprets these, constructing an account of where the breaks occurred. These explanations of breaks in specific molecules are used as examples for constructing general rules.

In determining the site of a cleavage in a training run, DENDRAL uses a "half-order theory" of organic chemistry. This theory, while not powerful enough to support the direct construction of DENDRAL rules, does support the interpretation of cleavages in known molecules. The half-order theory consists of such constraints and heuristics as:

Double and triple bonds do not break.

Only fragments larger than two carbon atoms show up in the data

Using the half-order theory, meta-DENDRAL constructs explanations of the cleavage. These explanations indicate the likely sites of cleavages along with possible migrations of atoms across the break.

These explanations become the set of positive instances for a rule induction program. This component induces the constraints in the premises of DENDRAL rules through a general to specific search. It begins with a totally general description of a cleavage: $X_1 * X_2$. This pattern means that a cleavage, indicated by "*," can occur between any two atoms. It specializes the pattern by adding atoms:

$$X_1 * X_2 \rightarrow X_3 - X_1 * X_2$$

where the "-" operator indicates a chemical bond, or instantiating atoms or attributes of atoms:

$$X_1 * X_2 \rightarrow C * X_2$$

Meta-DENDRAL learns from positive examples only and performs a hill climbing search of the concept space. It prevents overgeneralization by requiring candidate rules to cover only about half of the training instances. Subsequent components of the program evaluate and refine these rules looking for redundant rules or modifying rules that may be overly general or specific.

The strength of meta-DENDRAL is in its use of domain knowledge to change raw data into a more usable form. This gives the program noise resistance, through the use of its theory to eliminate extraneous or potentially erroneous data, and the ability to learn from relatively few training instances. The insight that training data must be so interpreted to be fully useful is the basis of explanation based learning.

10.4.2   Explanation Based Learning

Explanation based learning (EBL) uses an explicitly represented domain theory to construct an explanation of a training example, usually a proof that the example logically follows from the theory. By generalizing from the explanation of the instance, rather than from the instance itself, explanation based learning filters noise, selects relevant aspects of experience, and organizes training data into a systematic and coherent structure.

There are several alternative formulations of this idea. For example, the STRIPS program for learning general operators for planning has exerted a powerful influence on this research (Fikes et al. 1972). Meta-DENDRAL, as we have just discussed, established the power of theory based interpretation of training instances. More recently, a number of authors (DeJong & Mooney 1986, Minton 1988) have proposed alternative formulations of this idea. The *Explanation Based Generalization* algorithm of Mitchell et al. (1986) is also typical of the genre. In this section, we examine a variation of the explanation based learning algorithm developed by DeJong:

EBL begins with:

1. A *target concept*, the learner's task is to determine an effective definition of this concept. Depending upon the specific application, the target concept may be a classification, a theorem to be proven, a plan for achieving a goal, or a heuristic for a problem solver.
2. A *training example*, an instance of the target.
3. A *domain theory*, a set of rules and facts that are used to explain how the training example is an instance of the goal concept.
4. *Operationality criteria*, some means of describing the form that concept definitions may take.

To illustrate this, we present an example of learning when an object is a cup. This is a variation of a problem explored by Winston (1983) and adapted to explanation based learning by Mitchell et al (1986). The target concept is a rule that may be used to infer if an object is a cup:

$$premise(X) \rightarrow cup(X)$$

where premise is a conjunctive expression containing the variable X.

Assume a domain theory which includes the following rules about cups:

$$liftable(X) \wedge holds\_liquid(X) \rightarrow cup(X)$$
$$part(Z, W) \wedge concave(W) \wedge points\_up(W) \rightarrow holds\_liquid(Z)$$
$$light(Y) \wedge part(Y, handle) \rightarrow liftable(Y)$$
$$small(A) \rightarrow light(A)$$
$$made\_of(A, feathers) \rightarrow light(A)$$

The training example is an instance of the goal concept. Thus, we are given:

$$cup(obj1)$$
$$small(obj1)$$
$$part(obj1, handle)$$
$$owns(bob, obj1)$$

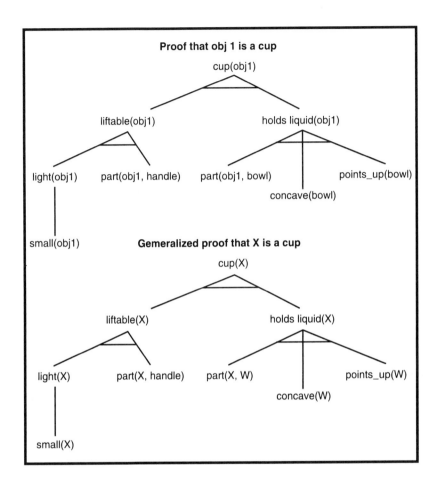

FIGURE 10.15 Specific and generalized proof that an object, X, is a cup.

part(obj1, bottom)
part(obj1, bowl)
points_up(bowl)
concave(bowl)
color(obj1, red)

Finally, assume the operationality criteria require that target concepts be defined in terms of observable, structural properties of objects, such as part and points_up. We may provide domain rules that enable the learner to infer if a description is operational or we may simple list operational predicates.

Using this theory, a theorem prover may construct an explanation of why the example is indeed an instance of the training concept; that is, a proof that the target concept logically follows from the example, as in the first tree in Figure 10.15. Note that this explanation eliminates such irrelevant concepts as color(obj1, red) from the training data and captures those aspects of the example known to be relevant to the goal.

The next stage of explanation based learning generalizes the explanation to produce a concept definition that may be used to recognize other cups. EBL accomplishes this by substituting variables for those constants in the proof tree that depend solely on the particular training instance (see Figure 10.15, bottom tree). Based on the generalized tree, EBL defines a new rule whose conclusion is the root of the tree and whose premise is the conjunction of the leaves:

$$small(X) \land part(X, handle) \land part(X, W) \land concave(W) \land points\_up(W) \to cup(X).$$

In constructing a generalized proof tree, our goal is to substitute variables for those constants that are part of the training instance while retaining those constants and constraints that are part of the domain theory. In this example, the constant "handle" originated in the domain theory rather than the training instance. We have retained it as an essential constraint in the acquired rule.

Explanation based learning clearly falls within the class of learning algorithms which can only acquire knowledge within the deductive closure of the learner's original theory. Finally, there are a number of ways in which we may construct a generalized proof tree using a training instance as a guide. See Mitchell (1986) or DeJong and Mooney (1986) for more details of this process.

10.4.3   Analogical Reasoning

Analogical reasoning assumes that if two situations are known to be similar in some respects, it is likely that they will be similar in others. For example, if two houses have similar locations, construction, and condition, then they probably have the same sales value. Unlike the proofs used in EBL, analogy is not logically sound. In this sense it is similar to induction. Russell (1989) and others have observed that analogy is a species of single instance induction. In our house example, we are inducing properties of one house from what is known about another.

Analogy allows great flexibility in applying existing knowledge to new situations. For example, assume that a student is trying to learn about the behavior of electricity, and assume that the teacher tells her that electricity is analogous to water, with voltage corresponding to pressure, amperage to the amount of flow, and resistance to the capacity of a pipe. Using analogical reasoning, the student may more easily grasp such concepts as Ohm's law.

The standard computational model of analogy defines the *source* of an analogy to be a problem solution, example, or theory that is relatively well-understood. The *target* is not completely understood. Analogy constructs a *mapping* between corresponding elements of the target and source. Analogical inferences extend this mapping to new elements of the target domain. Continuing with the "electricity is like water" analogy, if we know that this analogy maps switches onto valves, amperage onto quantity of flow, and voltage onto water pressure, we may reasonably infer that there should be some analogue to the capacity, that is, the cross sectional area, of a water pipe and this could lead to an understanding of electrical resistance.

A number of authors have proposed a unifying framework for computational models of analogical reasoning (Hall 1989, Kedar-Cabelli 1988, Wolstencroft 1989); a typical framework consists of the following stages:

1. *Retrieval*: Given a target problem, it is necessary to select a potential source analogue. Problems in analogical retrieval include selecting those features of the target and source that increase the likelihood of retrieving a useful source analogue and indexing knowledge according to those features. Generally, retrieval establishes the initial elements of an analogical mapping.

2. *Elaboration*: Once the source has been retrieved, it is often necessary to derive additional features and relations of the source. For example, it may be necessary to develop a specific problem solving trace or explanation in the source domain as a basis for analogy with the target.

3. *Mapping and inference*: Develop the mapping of source attributes into the target domain. This involves both known similarities and analogical inferences.

4. *Justification*: Determine that the mapping is indeed valid. This stage may require modification of the mapping.

5. *Learning*: Store the acquired knowledge in a form that will be useful in the future.

These stages have been developed in a number of computational models of analogical reasoning. For example, *structure mapping theory* (Falkenhainer et al. 1989, Gentner 1983, and see Example 7.8) not only addresses the problem of constructing useful analogies, but also provides a plausible model of how humans understand analogies. A central question in the use of analogy is how we may distinguish expressive deep analogies from more superficial comparisons. Gentner argues that true analogies should emphasize systematic, structural features of a domain over more superficial similarities. For example, the analogy, "the atom is like the solar system" is deeper than "the sunflower is like the sun" because the former captures a whole system of causal relations between orbiting bodies while the latter describes superficial similarities such as the fact that both sunflowers and the sun are round and yellow. This property of an analogical mapping is called *systematicity*.

Structure mapping formalizes this intuition. Consider the example of the atom/solar system analogy introduced in Chapter 7 (Figure 7.7) as explicated by Gentner (1983). The source domain includes the predicates:

yellow(sun)
blue(earth)
hotter-than(sun, earth)
causes(more-massive(sun, earth), attract(sun, earth))
causes(attract(sun, earth), revolves-around(earth, sun))

The target domain that the analogy is intended to explain includes:

more-massive(nucleus, electron)
revolves-around(electron, nucleus)

Structure mapping attempts to transfer the causal structure of the source to the target. The mapping is constrained by the following rules:

1. *Drop properties from the source.* Because analogy favors systems of relations, the first stage is to eliminate those predicates that describe superficial properties of the source. Structure mapping formalizes this by eliminating predicates of a single argument, or unary predicates, from the source. The rationale for this is that predicates of higher arity, by virtue of describing a relationship between two or more entities, are more likely to capture the systematic relations intended by the analogy. In our example, this eliminates such assertions as yellow(sun) and blue(earth). Note that the source may still contain assertions, such as hotter-than(sun, earth), that are not relevant to the analogy.
2. *Relations map unchanged from the source to the target, but the arguments to the relations may differ.* In our example, such relations as revolves-around and more-massive are the same in both the source and the target. This constraint is used by many theories of analogy and greatly reduces the number of possible mappings. It is also consistent with the heuristic of giving relations preference in the mapping.
3. *In constructing the mapping, prefer higher order relations as a focus of the mapping.* In our example, causes is a higher order relation since it takes other relations as its arguments. This is called the *systematicity principle.*

These constraints lead to the mapping:

sun -> nucleus
earth -> electron

Extending the mapping leads to the inference:

causes(more-massive(nucleus, electron), attract(nucleus, electron))
causes(attract(nucleus,electron),revolves-around(electron, nucleus)).

Structure mapping theory has been implemented and tested in a number of domains. While it remains far from a complete theory of analogy, failing to address such problems as analogue retrieval, it has proven both computationally practical and able to explain many aspects of human analogical reasoning.

Before concluding our discussion of analogy, it is useful to comment on *case based reasoning*. Case based reasoning, introduced in Chapter 6, requires some type of analogy map to identify which stored cases might be useful in a new problem situation. Unlike the learning and problem solving methods discussed in the text so far, case based reasoning de-emphasizes the use of general rules. Instead, it stores solutions to problems in their original or slightly modified form. On addressing a new problem, a case based reasoner retrieves a case it deems similar and uses it as a basis for solving the new problem (Kolodner 1988).

10.4.4   Chunking in Soar

In Chapter 9 we introduced *Soar* as part of a unified theory of cognition based on the production system architecture. Learning for Soar rests in the ability to create new production rules and add them into production memory when new regularities are discovered in its problem solving environment. An essential aspect of the "unified theory" is that knowledge is represented by production rules and the discovery of new knowledge is reflected by Soar's creation and subsequent use of new production rules.

Chunking can also be seen as learning from experience. It is a way of converting search based problem solving into knowledge rules in long term memory. Whenever production based search produces a result a new production is created whose actions are the new successful result and whose conditions are the working memory patterns used in producing the result that were present before the problem solving began. This new result is immediately added to the set of rules in production memory to be used when the problem situation is encountered again.

Figure 10.16, adapted from Newell (1990), describes what happens in chunking. The production system is trying to accomplish a particular task. Figure 10.16 does not represent the goals active in the problem solving. A, B, and C, along with the numbered items, 1, 2, ..., 9, represent the facts asserted to working memory in the normal processing of the production system. The "point of impasse" represents the situation when no further progress in the current search space can be made. Soar then dynamically creates a new search space composed of more primitive elements and operators. Typically, work at this lower level involves more brute force search. The impasse is resolved when this lower level search asserts to working memory elements that allow the productions in the original space to continue. A link is then explicitly built between the patterns in working memory that were present at the impasse point and the results of the lower level search. In Newell's Figure 10.16, A, B, and C are directly linked to D and E. Newell refers to this method as *backtracing*. This new chunk is added to the productions and becomes from then on part of normal problem solving.

Chunks are active processes, Newell (1990) refers to them as a form of *permanent goal based caching*. It can also represent what psychologists sometimes call "compiled" knowledge; solution processes that are no longer directly thought through, but rather applied in new situations without conscious search. Chunks are also generalized implicitly, by ignoring whatever detail the original problem solving eventually did not use, for example, the searched states after the impasse in Figure 10.16. Chunking learns only what the search based component of the problem solving has directly experienced. The total problem solving system is the learning mechanism, and the new chunked rules are effective as soon as they are created. Similar results are found in planning with the use of *triangle tables* to reflect generalizations of searched solutions (Fikes & Nilsson 1971).

10.5   UNSUPERVISED LEARNING

The learning algorithms discussed so far, with the exception of Soar, implement forms of *supervised learning*. They assume the existence of a teacher, fitness function, or some other external method of classifying training instances. *Unsupervised learning* eliminates the teacher and requires that the learner form and evaluate concepts on its own. Science is perhaps the best example of unsupervised learning in humans. Scientists do not have the benefit of a teacher. Instead, they propose hypotheses to explain observations, evaluate them using such criteria as simplicity, generality, and elegance, and test them through experiments.

10.5.1   Discovery and Unsupervised Learning

AM the *Automated Mathematician* (Davis & Lenat 1982, Lenat & Brown 1984),

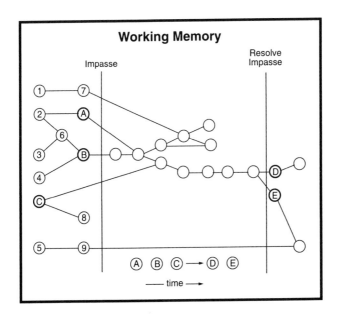

FIGURE 10.16 Diagram of behavior of Soar during chunking. From Newell (1990).

is one of the earliest and most successful discovery programs, deriving a number of interesting even if not original, concepts in mathematics. AM began with the definitions of set theory, operations for creating new knowledge by modifying and combining existing knowledge, and a set of heuristics for detecting "interesting" concepts. By searching this space of mathematical entities, AM discovered the natural numbers along with several important concepts of number theory, such as the existence of prime numbers.

For example, AM discovered the natural numbers by modifying its notion of bags. A *bag* is a generalization of a set that allows multiple occurrences of the same element. For example, {a, a, b, c, c} is a bag. By specializing the definition of bag to allow only a single type of element, AM discovered an analogy of the natural numbers, that is, the bag {1, 1, 1, 1} corresponds to the number 4. Union of bags led to the notion of addition: {1,1} $\cup$ {1,1} = {1,1,1,1}, or 2 + 2 = 4. Exploring further modifications of these concepts, AM discovered multiplication as a series of additions. Using a heuristic that defines new operators by inverting existing operators, AM discovered integer division. It found the concept of prime numbers by noting that certain numbers had exactly two divisors, themselves and 1.

On creating a new concept, AM evaluates it according to a number of heuristics, keeping those concepts that prove "interesting." AM determined that prime numbers were interesting based on the frequency with which they occur. In evaluating concepts using this heuristic, AM generates instances of the concept, testing each to see if the concept holds. If a concept is true of all instances, it is a tautology and AM gives it a low evaluation. Similarly, AM rejects concepts that are true for no instances. If a concept is true of a significant portion of the examples, as is the case with prime numbers, AM evaluates it as interesting and selects it for further modification.

Although AM discovered prime numbers and several other interesting concepts, it failed to progress much beyond elementary number theory. In a later analysis of this work, Lenat and Brown (1984) examined the reasons for the program's success and its limitations. While he originally believed that AM's heuristics were the prime source of its power, his later evaluation attributed much of the program's success to the language used to represent mathematical concepts. AM represented concepts as recursive structures in a variation of the LISP programming language. Because of its basis in a well-designed programming language, this representation defined a space that contained a high density of interesting concepts. This was particularly true in the early stages of the search. As exploration continued, the space grew combinatorially and the percentage of interesting concepts "thinned out." This observation further underscores the relationship between representation and search.

Another reason AM failed to continue the impressive pace of its early discoveries is its inability to "learn to learn." It did not acquire new heuristics as it gained mathematical knowledge; consequently, the quality of its search degraded as its mathematics grew more complex. In this sense, AM never developed a deep understanding of mathematics. Lenat (1983) addressed this problem in later work on a program called *EURISKO* that attempts to learn new heuristics.

A number of other programs have continued to explore the problems of automatic discovery. *IL* (Sims 1987) applied a variety of learning techniques to mathematical discovery, including analytical methods such as theorem proving and explanation based learning. *BACON* (Langley et al. 1987) developed computational models of the formation of quantitative scientific laws. For example, using data on the distance of the planets from the sun and the period of their orbits, BACON "re discovered" Kepler's laws of planetary motion. By providing a plausible computational model of how humans may have achieved discovery in a variety of domains, BACON has provided a useful tool and methodology for examining the process of human scientific discovery. Shrager and Langley (1990) describe a number of other discovery systems.

Although scientific discovery is an important research area, progress to date has been slight. A more basic, and perhaps more fruitful, problem in unsupervised learning concerns the discovery of categories. Lakoff (1987) suggests that categorization is fundamental to human cognition: Higher level theoretical knowledge depends upon the ability to organize the particulars of our experience into coherent taxonomies. Most of our knowledge is about categories of objects, such as cows, rather than specific individuals, such as Blossom or Ferdinand. Nordhausen and Langley (1990) have emphasized the formation of categories as the basis for a unified theory of scientific discovery. In developing explanations of why chemicals react in the way that they do, chemistry built on prior work in classifying compounds into categories such as "acid" and "alkaline." In the next section, we examine *conceptual clustering*, the problem of discovering useful categories in unclassified data.

10.5.2   Conceptual Clustering

The *clustering problem* begins with a collection of unclassified objects and some means of measuring the similarity of objects. Its goal is an organization of the objects into a hierarchy of classes that meet some standard of quality, such as maximizing the similarity of objects in the same class.

Numeric taxonomy is one of the oldest approaches to the clustering problem. Numeric methods rely upon the representation of objects as a collection of features, each of which may have some numeric value. A reasonable similarity metric treats each object, a vector of n feature values, as a point in n-dimensional space. The similarity of two objects is the euclidean distance between them in this space.

Using this similarity metric, a common clustering algorithm builds clusters in a bottom up fashion. This approach, called an *agglomerative clustering* strategy, forms categories by:

1. Examining all pairs of objects, selecting the pair with the highest degree of similarity and making them a cluster.
2. Defining the features of the cluster as some function, such as average of the features of the components, then replacing the components with this cluster definition.
3. Repeating this process on the collection of objects until all objects have been reduced to a single cluster.

The result of this algorithm is a binary tree, whose leaf nodes are instances and whose internal nodes are clusters of increasing size.

We may extend this algorithm to objects represented as sets of symbolic, rather than numeric, features. The only problem is in measuring the similarity of objects defined using symbolic, rather than numeric, values. A reasonable approach defines the similarity of two objects as the proportion of features that they have in common. Given the objects:

object1 = {small, red, rubber, ball}
object2 = {small, blue, rubber, ball}
object3 = {large, black, wooden, ball}

this metric would compute the similarity values:

similarity(object1, object2) = 3/4
similarity(object1, object3) = similarity(object2, object3) = 1/4

Similarity based clustering algorithms do not adequately capture the under-lying role of semantic knowledge in cluster formation. For example, humans did not define constellations of stars on the basis of their closeness in the sky. Instead, they were formed on the basis of existing human concepts, such as "the big dipper." In defining categories, we cannot give all features equal weight. In any given context, certain of an object's features are more important than others; simple similarity metrics treat all features equally. Human categories depend upon the goals of the categorization and prior knowledge of the domain much more than on surface similarity; consider, for example, the classification of whales as mammals instead of fish. Surface similarities cannot account for this classification. It depends upon the wider goals of biological classification and extensive physiological and evolutionary evidence.

Traditional clustering algorithms not only fail to take goals and background knowledge into account, they also fail to produce meaningful semantic explana-tions of the resulting categories. These algorithms represent clusters *extensionally*, that is, by enumerating all of their members. The algorithms pro-duce no intensional definition, no general rule that defines the semantics of the category, and may be used to classify both known and future members of the cat-egory. For example, an extensional definition of the set of people who have served as secretary general of the United Nations would simply list those individ-uals. An intensional definition, such as:

{X | X has been elected secretary general of the United Nations}

would have the added benefits of defining the class semantically and allowing us to recognize future members of the category.

Conceptual clustering addresses these problems by using machine learning techniques to produce general concept definitions and apply background knowl-edge to the formation of categories. *CLUSTER/2* (Michalski et al. 1983) is a good example of this approach. It uses background knowledge in the form of biases on the language used to represent categories.

CLUSTER/2 forms k categories by constructing individuals around k *seed* objects, where k is a parameter that may be adjusted by the user. CLUSTER/2

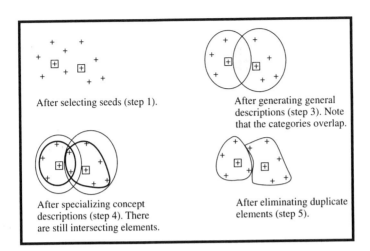

After selecting seeds (step 1).

After generating general descriptions (step 3). Note that the categories overlap.

After specializing concept descriptions (step 4). There are still intersecting elements.

After eliminating duplicate elements (step 5).

FIGURE 10.17. The steps of a CLUSTER/2 run.

evaluates the resulting clusters, selecting new seeds and repeating the process until its quality criteria are met. Figure 10.17 shows the stages of a CLUSTER/2 execution. The algorithm is defined:

1. Select k seeds from the set of observed objects. This may be done randomly or according to some selection function.
2. For each seed, using that seed as a positive instance and all other seeds as negative instances, produce a maximally general definition that covers all of the positive and none of the negative instances.
3. Classify all objects in the sample according to these descriptions. Replace each maximally general description with a maximally specific description that covers all objects in the category. This decreases likelihood that classes overlap on unseen objects.
4. Classes may still overlap on given objects. CLUSTER/2 includes an algorithm for adjusting overlapping definitions.
5. Using a distance metric, select an element closest to the center of each class. The distance metric could be similar to the similarity metric.
6. Using these central elements as new seeds, repeat 1-5. Stop when clusters are satisfactory. A typical quality metric is the complexity of the general descriptions of the classes. For instance, a variation of Occam's razor might prefer clusters that yield syntactically simple definitions, such as those with a small number of conjuncts.
7. If clusters are unsatisfactory and no improvement occurs over several iterations, select new seeds closest to the edge of the cluster.

10.5.3   COBWEB and the Structure of Taxonomic Knowledge

Many clustering algorithms, as well as many supervised learning algorithms such as ID3, define categories in terms of necessary and sufficient conditions for membership. These conditions are a set of properties possessed by all members of a category, and only by members of the category. Although many categories, such as the set of all United Nations delegates, may be so defined, human categories do not always fit this model. Indeed, human categorization is characterized by greater flexibility and a much richer structure than we have so far examined.

For example, if human categories were indeed defined by necessary and sufficient conditions for membership, we could not distinguish degrees of category membership. However, psychologists have noted a strong sense of prototypicality in human categorization (Rosch 1978, Lakoff 1987). For instance, we generally think of a robin as a better example of a bird than a chicken; an oak is a more typical example of a tree than a palm, at least in northern latitudes.

Family resemblance theory (Wittgenstein 1953) supports these notions of prototypicality by arguing that categories are defined by complex systems of similarities between members rather than necessary and sufficient conditions for membership. Such categories may not have any properties shared by all of their members. He cites the example of games: not all games require two or more players, not all games are fun for the players, not all games have well articulated rules, not all games involve competition. Nonetheless, we consider the category to be well-defined and unambiguous.

Human categories also differ from most formal inheritance hierarchies (Chapter 6) in that not all levels of human taxonomies are equally important. Psychologists (Rosch 1978) have demonstrated the existence of *base level* categories. The base level category is the classification most commonly used in describing objects, the terminology first learned by children, and the level that in some sense captures the most fundamental classification of an object. For example, the category *chair* is more basic than either its generalizations, such as *furniture*, or its specializations, such as *office chair*. *Car* is more basic than either *sedan* or *vehicle*.

Common methods of representing class membership and hierarchies, such as logic, inheritance systems, feature vectors, or decision trees, do not account for these effects. Yet doing so is not only important to cognitive scientists, whose goal is the understanding of human intelligence, it is also valuable to the engineering of useful AI applications. Users evaluate a program in terms of its flexibility, robustness, and its ability to behave in ways that seem reasonable by human standards. Although we do not require that all algorithms parallel the architecture of the human mind, any algorithm that proposes to discover categories must meet user expectations as to the structure and behavior of those categories.

COBWEB (Fisher 1987) addresses these issues. Although it is not intended as a model of human cognition, it does account for base level categorization and degrees of category membership. In addition, COBWEB learns incrementally: it does not require that all instances be present before it begins learning. In many applications, the learner acquires data over time. In these situations, it must construct usable concept descriptions from an initial collection of data and update them as more data become available. COBWEB also addresses the problem of determining the correct number of clusters. CLUSTER/2 produced a prespecified number of categories. Although the user could vary this number, or the algorithm could try different values in an effort to improve categorization, such approaches are not particularly flexible. COBWEB uses global quality metrics to determine the number of clusters, the depth of the hierarchy, and the category membership of new instances.

Unlike the algorithms we have seen so far, COBWEB represents categories probabilistically. Instead of defining category membership as a set of values that must be present for each feature of an object, COBWEB represents the probability with which each feature value is present. $p(f_i = v_{ij} | c_k)$ is the conditional probability with which feature f_i will have value v_{ij}, given that an object is in category c_k.

Figure 10.18 illustrates a COBWEB taxonomy taken from Gennari et al. (1989). In this example, the algorithm has formed a categorization of the four single cell animals at the bottom of the figure. Each animal is defined by its value for the features: number of tails, color, and number of nuclei. The members of category C3, for example, have a 1.0 probability of having two tails, a 0.5 probability of having light color, and a 1.0 probability of having two nuclei.

As the figure illustrates, each category in the hierarchy includes probabilities of occurrence for all values of all features. This is essential to both categorizing new instances and modifying the category structure to better fit new instances. Indeed, as an incremental algorithm, COBWEB does not separate these actions. When given a new instance, COBWEB considers the overall quality of either placing the instance in an existing category or modifying the hierarchy to accommodate the instance. The criterion COBWEB uses for evaluating the quality of a classification is called *category utility* (Gluck & Corter 1985). Category utility was developed in research on human categorization. It accounts for base level effects and other aspects of human category structure.

Category utility attempts to maximize both the probability that two objects in the same category have values in common, and the probability that objects in different categories will have different property values. Category utility is defined:

$$\Sigma_k \Sigma_i \Sigma_j \, p(\, f_i = v_{ij}\,) \, p\,(\, f_i = v_{ij} | c_k\,) \, p\,(c_k | f_i = v_{ij}\,)$$

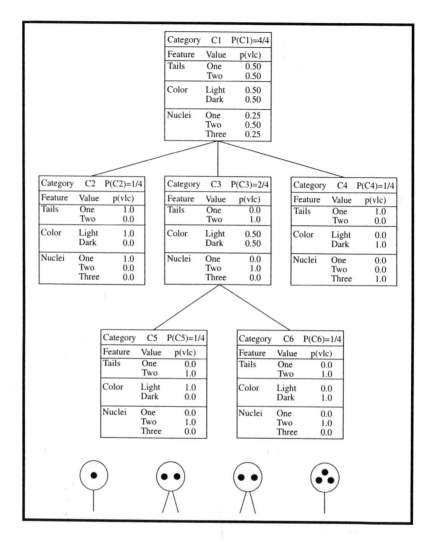

FIGURE 10.18 COBWEB clusters for one-celled organisms. From Gennari et al. (1989).

This sum is taken across all categories, c_k, all features, f_i, and all feature values, v_{ij}. $p(f_i = v_{ij} \mid c_k)$, called *predictability*, is the probability that an object has value v_{ij} for feature f_i given that the object belongs to category c_k. The higher this probability, the more likely two objects in a category share the same feature values. $p(c_k \mid f_i = v_{ij})$, called *predictiveness*, is the probability with which an object belongs to category c_k given that it has value v_{ij} for feature f_i. The greater this probability, the less likely objects not in the category will have those feature values. $p(f_i = v_{ij})$ serves as a weight, assuring that frequently occurring feature values will exert a stronger influence on the evaluation. By combining these values, high category utility measures indicate a high likelihood that objects in the same category will share properties, while decreasing the likelihood of objects in different categories having properties in common.

COBWEB performs a hill climbing search of the space of possible taxonomies using category utility to evaluate and select possible categorizations. It initializes the taxonomy to a single category whose features are those of the first instance. For each subsequent instance, the algorithm begins with the root category and moves through the tree. At each level it uses category utility to evaluate the taxonomies resulting from:

1. placing the instance in the best existing category
2. adding a new category containing only the instance
3. merging two existing categories into one and adding the instance to that category
4. splitting an existing category, and placing the instance in the best category in the resulting taxonomy.

COBWEB is efficient and produces taxonomies with a reasonable number of classes. Because it allows probabilistic membership, its categories are flexible and robust. In addition, it has demonstrated base level category effects and, through its notion of partial category matching, supports notions of prototypicality and degree of membership.

Instead of relying on two valued logic to achieve soundness and completeness in reasoning, COBWEB, like fuzzy logic and similar approaches, views the often frustrating vagueness of human cognition as a necessary component for learning and reasoning in a flexible and intelligent fashion. This point of view is partly motivated by the brittleness that plagues symbolic approaches. Systems including COBWEB, fuzzy reasoning, and certainty theory (Chapter 7) attempt to solve these problems in a symbolic context. Chapter 11 examines *connectionist* and other *subsymbolic* models of intelligence and their success in solving such problems.

10.6   EPILOGUE AND REFERENCES

Learning is one of the most exciting subfields of cognitive science, addressing a problem that is central to intelligent behavior and raising a number of important questions about knowledge representation and search based problem solving.

One of the best surveys of work in the field is found in *Machine Learning: An Artificial Intelligence Approach* (Michalski et al. 1983, 1986; Kodratoff

1990). This series consists of three volumes (to date) and includes introductory material, surveys, and papers on specific research. *Readings in Machine Learning* (Shavlik & Dietterich 1990) represents the collection of a number of important papers in the field, going back as far as 1958. *Production System Models of Learning and Development* (Klahr et al 1987) is a collection that includes work that reflects a cognitive approach. Newell's (1990) *Unified Theories of Cognition* describes learning in Soar.

Computer Systems that Learn (Weiss & Kulikowski 1991) is a survey of the whole field of machine learning, including treatments of neural networks and statistical methods in learning. It is strong for its evaluation of learning systems.

Readers interested in more discussion of analogical reasoning should examine Gentner (1983), Carbonell (1983, 1986), Holyoak (1985), Kedar-Cabelli (1988), and Thagard (1988).

For discovery and theory formation, we recommend *Scientific Discovery: Computational Explorations of the Creative Processes* (Langley et al. 1987) and *Computational Models of Scientific Discovery and Theory Formation* (Shrager & Langley 1990).

Concept Formation: Knowledge and Experience in Unsupervised Learning (Fisher et al. 1991) presents a number of papers on clustering, concept formation, and other forms of unsupervised learning.

Machine Learning is the primary journal of these fields. Other sources of current research include the yearly proceedings of the *International Conference on Machine Learning*, as well as the proceedings of the *AAAI Conference* and the *International Joint Conference on Artificial Intelligence*.

Chapter 11

CONNECTIONIST NETWORKS: HISTORY, THE PERCEPTRON, AND BACKPROPAGATION

... all inferences from experience suppose, as their foundation, that the future will resemble the past and that similar powers will be conjoined with similar sensible qualities...

David Hume

A cat that once sat on a hot stove will never again sit on a hot stove or on a cold one either...

Mark Twain

11.0 INTRODUCTION

In Chapter 10 we emphasized a symbol based approach to learning. The algorithms and representations considered there reflect the physical symbol system hypothesis: intelligence can be achieved through formal operations on symbol structures. A central aspect of this hypothesis is the use of symbols to refer to objects and relations in a domain. In the present chapter, we introduce *neurally* inspired and *biology* based approaches to learning.

Neurally inspired models, also known as *parallel distributed processing (PDP)* or *connectionist* systems, de-emphasize the explicit use of symbols in problem solving. Instead, they hold that intelligence arises in systems of simple, interacting components (neurons) through a process of learning or adaptation by which the connections between components are adjusted. Processing in these systems is distributed across collections or layers of neurons. Problem solving is parallel in the sense that all the neurons within the collection or layer process their inputs simultaneously and independently. These systems also tend to degrade gracefully because information and processing are distributed across the network's nodes and layers.

Biology based approaches, such as genetic algorithms and cellular automata, attempt to mimic the learning implicit in the evolution of life forms. Processing in these models is also parallel and distributed. In the genetic algorithm model, for example, a population of patterns represents the candidate solutions to a problem. As the algorithm cycles, this population of patterns "evolves" through operations which mimic reproduction, mutation, and natural selection.

In neurally inspired and biology based models there is a strong representational character both in the creation of input parameters as well as in the interpretation of output values. To build a neural network, for example, the designer must create a scheme for encoding patterns in the world into numerical quantities in the net. The choice of an encoding scheme can play a crucial role in the eventual success or failure of the network to learn.

Internal to connectionist systems, however, processing is parallel and distributed with no manipulation of symbols as symbols. Patterns in a domain are encoded as numerical vectors. The connections *between* components (neurons) are also represented by numerical values. Finally, the transformation of patterns is the result of a numerical operations, usually, matrix multiplications.

The computational techniques presented in this chapter are designed to model adaptive and emergent behavior. The algorithms and architectures that implement these techniques are usually trained or conditioned rather than explicitly programmed. Indeed, this is a major strength of the approach: an appropriately designed network and learning algorithm can often capture invariances in the world, even in the form of strange attractors, without being explicitly programmed to recognize them. The details of how this can happen make up the material of the chapter.

The tasks for which this approach is well suited include:

- *classification*, deciding the category or grouping to which an input value belongs;
- *pattern recognition*, or identifying structure in sometimes noisy data;
- *memory recall*, including the problem of content addressable memory;
- prediction, such as identifying disease from symptoms, causes from effects;
- *optimization*, or finding the best organization of constraints; and
- *noise filtering*, or separating signal from background, factoring out the irrelevant components of a signal

In fact, the methods of this chapter work best on those tasks which symbolic models seem to handle poorly. This typically includes tasks in which the problem domain requires perception based skills, or lacks a clearly defined syntax, or where the property of compositionality is missing.

We begin with neurally inspired learning models, and in Section 11.1 introduce them from an historical vantage. We present the basic components of neural network learning, including the "mechanical" neuron, and describe some historically important early work, including the McCulloch-Pitts (1943) neuron. Learning in these systems may be described as the problem of training them. The evolution of the network training paradigms over the past 40 years offers important insights into the present state of the discipline.

In Section 11.2, we continue the historical presentation with the introduction of *perceptron* learning, and the creation of the *delta* rule. We present an example of the perceptron used as a classifier.

In Section 11.3 we introduce nets with hidden layers, and the "backpropagation" learning rule. These innovations were introduced in the evolution of artificial neural networks to overcome problems the early systems had in learning, in particular, problems in generalizing across data points that were not linearly separable. Backpropagation is an algorithm for apportioning "blame" for incorrect responses across the nodes of a multilayered system with continuous thresholding.

In Chapter 12 we continue our presentation of connectionist networks with models for *competitive* learning developed by Kohonen (1984) and Hecht-Nielsen (1987). We also present Hebb's model of *reinforcement* learning. Then we introduce a very important family of connectionist networks, sometimes referred to as *attractor networks*, that are used for pattern retrieval. Finally, we present evolutionary or biology based models with *genetic algorithms* and *cellular automata* models which base their learning on the evolutionary paradigm of survival of the fittest.

At the end of Chapter 12, we summarize the features, as well as the potential problems, of neurally and biologically inspired approaches to learning. In Chapter 17 we have a final discussion of the crucial and interrelated issues of learning and representation.

11.1 FOUNDATIONS OF NEURAL NETWORKS

11.1.1 Early History

Although connectionist architectures are often thought of as a recent development, we can trace their origins to early work in computer science, psychology, and philosophy. John von Neumann, for example, was fascinated by both cellular automata and neurally inspired approaches to computation. Early work in neural learning was influenced by psychological theories of animal learning, especially that of Hebb (1949). In this section, we outline the basic components of neural network learning, and present historically important early work in the field.

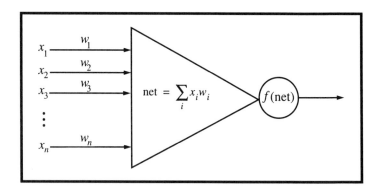

FIGURE 11.1   An artificial neuron, an input vector x_i , weights assigned to each input line, and a thresholding function f that determines the neuron's output value.

The basis of neural networks is the artificial neuron (see Figure 11.1). An artificial neuron consists of:

- Input signals, x_i. These data may come from the environment, or the activation of other neurons. Different models vary in the allowable range of the input values; typically inputs are discrete, from the set $\{0,1\}$ or $\{-1, 1\}$, or real numbers.

- A set of real valued weights, w_i, used to describe connection strengths.

- An activation level. The neuron's activation level is determined by the cumulative strength of its input signals where each input signal is scaled by the connection weight w_i along that input line. The activation level is thus computed by taking the sum of the scaled inputs, that is, $\Sigma w_i x_i$.

- A threshold function, f, that computes the neuron's final or output state by determining how far the neuron's activation level is below or above some threshold value. This is intended to model the on/off state of actual neurons.

In addition to these properties of individual neurons, a neural network is also characterized by global properties such as:

- The network topology, or the pattern of connections between the individual neurons. The topology of a network is a primary source of its inductive bias.

- The learning algorithm used.

- The encoding scheme. This includes the interpretation placed on the data to the network and the results of its processing.

The earliest example of neural computing is the McCulloch-Pitts neuron (McCulloch & Pitts, 1943). The inputs to a McCulloch-Pitts neuron are either excitatory (+1) or inhibitory (-1). The activation function multiplies each input by its corresponding weight and sums the results; if the sum is greater than or equal to zero, the neuron returns 1, otherwise, -1. McCulloch and Pitts showed how these neurons could be constructed to compute any logical function, demonstrating that systems of these neurons provide a complete computational model.

Figure 11.2 shows the McCulloch-Pitts neurons for computing logical functions. The and neuron has three inputs: X and Y are the values to be conjoined; the third, sometimes called a *bias*, has a constant value of +1. The input data and bias have weights of +1, +1, and -2, respectively. Thus, for any values of X and Y, the neuron computes the value of X + Y - 2: if this value is less than 0, it returns -1, otherwise a 1. Table 11.1 illustrates the neuron computing X *and* Y. Similarly, the weighted sum of input data for the *or* neuron (also Figure 11.2) is greater than or equal to 0 unless both X and Y equal -1.

Although McCulloch and Pitts demonstrated the power of neural computation, interest in the approach really began to flourish with the development of practical learning algorithms. Early learning models drew heavily on the work of the psychologist D. O. Hebb (1949), who speculated that learning occurred in brains through the modification of synapses. Hebb theorized that repeated firings across a synapse increase its sensitivity and the future likelihood of its firing. If a particular stimulus repeatedly caused activity in a group of cells, those cells come to be strongly associated. In the future, similar stimuli would tend to excite the same neural pathways, resulting in the recognition of the stimuli. Hebb's model worked purely on the reinforcement of used paths and ignored inhibition,

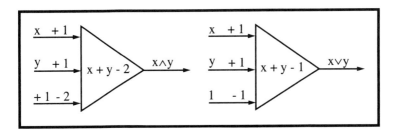

FIGURE 11.2 McCulloch-Pitts neurons for calculating the logic functions *and* and *or*.

X	Y	X+Y-2	Output
1	1	0	1
1	0	-1	-1
0	1	-1	-1
0	0	-2	-1

TABLE 11.1   The McCulloch-Pitts model for logical *and*.

punishment for error, or attrition. When more modern psychologists attempted to recreate Hebb's model they failed to produce general results without the addition of an inhibitory mechanism (Rochester et al. 1988, Quinlan 1991).

In the next section we extend our neural model to layers of connected neural mechanisms. The first version of this was called the *perceptron*.

11.2 PERCEPTRON LEARNING

11.2.1 Introduction and the Perceptron Training Algorithm

In the late 1950s, Frank Rosenblatt devised a learning algorithm for a type of single layer network called a *perceptron* (Rosenblatt 1958). In its signal propagation the perceptron was similar to the McCulloch-Pitts neuron. See, for example, the network of Figure 11.6. The input values and activation levels of the perceptron are either -1 or 1; weights are real valued. The activation level of the perceptron is given by summing the weighted input values, $\Sigma x_i w_i$. Perceptrons use a simple hard-limiting threshold function, where an activation above a threshold results in an output value of 1, and -1 otherwise. Therefore, given input values x_i, weights w_i, and a threshold, t, the perceptron computes its output value as:

1 if $\Sigma x_i w_i >= t$
-1 if $\Sigma x_i w_i < t$

The perceptron uses a simple form of supervised learning. After attempting to solve a problem instance, a teacher gives it the correct result. The perceptron then changes its weights in order to reduce the error. The following rule is used. Let c be a constant whose size determines the learning rate and d be the desired output value. The adjustment for the weight on the ith component of the input vector, Δw_i, is given by:

$$\Delta \, w_i = c(d - \text{sign}(\Sigma x_i w_i)) \, x_i$$

The $\text{sign}(\Sigma x_i w_i)$ is the perceptron output value. It is +1 or -1. The difference between the desired output and the actual output values will thus be 0, 2, or -2. Therefore for each component of the input vector:

- If the desired output and actual output values are equal, do nothing.

- If the actual output value is -1 and should be 1, increment the weights on the ith line by $2cx_i$.

- If the actual output value is 1 and should be -1, decrement weights on the ith line by $-2cx_i$.

This procedure has the effect of producing a set of weights which minimize the average error over the entire training set. If *there exists* a set of weights which give the correct output for every member of the training set, the perceptron learning procedure will learn it (Minsky & Papert 1969).

Perceptrons were initially greeted with enthusiasm. However, Nils Nilsson (1965) and others analyzed the limitations of the perceptron model. They demonstrated that perceptrons could not solve a certain difficult class of problems, namely problems in which the data points are not linearly separable. Although various enhancements of the perceptron model, including multilayered perceptrons, were envisioned at the time, Marvin Minsky and Seymour Papert, in their book *Perceptrons* (1969), argued that the linear separability problem could not be overcome by any form of the perceptron network.

An example of a nonlinearably separable classification is *exclusive-or*. As presented in Chapter 7, exclusive-or may be represented by the truth table:

x_1	x_2	Output
1	1	0
1	0	1
0	1	1
0	0	0

TABLE 11.2   The truth table for *exclusive-or*.

Consider a perceptron with two inputs, x_1, x_2, two weights, w_1, w_2, and threshold t. In order to learn this function, a network must find a weight assignment that satisfies the following inequalities:

$w_1*1 + w_2*1 < t$, from line 1 of the truth table.
$w_1*1 + 0 > t$, from line 2 of the truth table.
$0 + w_2*1 > t$, from line 3 of the truth table.
$0 + 0 < t$, or t must be positive, from the last line of the table.

This series of equations on w_1, w_2, and t has no solution, proving that a perceptron that solves *exclusive-or* is impossible. Although multilayer networks would eventually be built that could solve the exclusive-or problem (see Section 11.3.3), the perceptron learning algorithm only worked for single layer networks.

What makes exclusive-or impossible for the perceptron is that the two classes denoted by the output values of -1 and 1 are not *linearly separable*. This can be seen in Figure 11.3. It is impossible to draw a straight line in two dimensions that separates the data points having -1 from those having 1 as output.

We may think of the set of data values for a network as defining a space. Each parameter of the input data corresponds to one dimension, with each input value defining a point in the space. In the exclusive-or example, the four input values, indexed by the x_1, x_2 coordinates, make up the data points of Figure 11.3. The problem of learning a binary classification of the training instances reduces to that of separating these points into two groups. For a space of n dimensions, a classification is linearly separable if its classes can be separated by an n - 1 dimensional hyperplane. (In two dimensions an n dimensional hyperplane is a line; in three dimension it is a plane.)

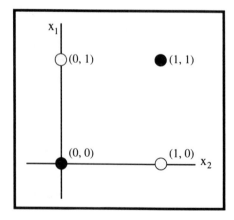

FIGURE 11.3 The exclusive-or problem. No straight line in 2-dimensional space can separate the 0, 1 and 1, 0 data points from (0, 0) and (1, 1).

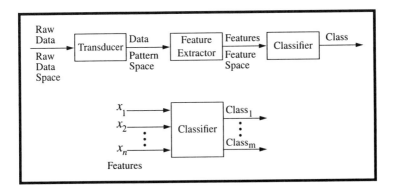

FIGURE 11.4   A full classification system.

As a result of the linear separability limitation, research shifted toward work in symbol based architectures, slowing progress in the connectionist methodology. Subsequent work in the 1970s and 1980s has shown these problems to be solvable, however. In Section 11.3 we discuss *backpropagation*, an extension of perceptron learning that works for multilayered networks. Before examining backpropagation, we offer an example of a perceptron network that performs classifications. We end Section 11.2 by defining the *delta rule*, a generalization of the perceptron learning algorithm that is used in many neural network architectures, including backpropagation.

11.2.2   An Example: Using a Perceptron Network to Classify

Figure 11.4 offers an overview of the classification problem. Raw data from a space of possible points are selected and transduced to a new data/pattern space. In this new pattern space features are identified, and finally, the entity these features represent is classified. An example would be sound waves recorded on a digital recording device. From there the acoustic signals are translated to a set of amplitude and frequency parameters. Finally, a classifier system might recognize these feature patterns as the voiced speech of a particular person. Another example would be the capture of information by medical test equipment. The features found in this pattern space would then be used to classify symptom sets into different disease categories.

For our classification example, the transducer and feature extractor of Figure 11.4 translates the problem information into parameters of a two dimensional Cartesian space. Figure 11.5 presents the two-feature perceptron analysis of the information in Table 11.3. The first two columns of the table present the data points on which the network was trained. The third column represents the classi-

x1	x2	Output
1.0	1.0	1
9.4	6.4	-1
2.5	2.1	1
8.0	7.7	-1
0.5	2.2	1
7.9	8.4	-1
7.0	7.0	-1
2.8	0.8	1
1.2	3.0	1
7.8	6.1	-1

TABLE 11.3 A data set for perceptron classification.

fication, +1 or -1, used as feedback in network training. Figure 11.5 is a graph of the actual activation levels when the trained network was run on each data point.

We discuss first the general theory of classification. Each data grouping that a classifier identifies is represented by a region in multidimensional space. Each class R_i has a discriminant function g_i measuring membership in that region. Within the region R_i, the ith discriminant function has the largest value:

$g_i(x) > g_j(x)$ for all j, $1 < j < n$.

In the simple example of Table 11.3, the two input parameters produce two obvious regions or classes in the space.

An important special case of discriminant functions is one which evaluates class membership based on distance from some central point in the region. Classification based on this discriminant function is called *minimum distance classification*. A simple argument shows that if the classes are linearly separable there exists a minimum distance classification.

If the regions of R_i and R_j are adjacent, as are the two regions in Figure 11.5, there is a boundary region where the discriminant functions are equal:

$g_i(x) = g_j(x)$ or $g_i(x) - g_j(x) = 0$.

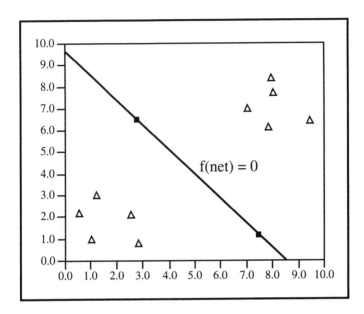

FIGURE 11.5 A two dimensional plot of the data points in Table 11.3. The perceptron of Section 11.1.2 provides a linear separation of the data sets.

If the classes are linearly separable, as those of Figure 11.5, the discriminant function separating the regions will describe a straight line, that is $g_i(x) - g_j(x)$ is a linear function. Since a line is defined as the locus of points equally distant from two fixed points, the discriminant functions, $g_i(x)$ and $g_j(x)$, can be treated as minimum distance functions, where distance is measured from the Cartesian center of each of the regions.

The perceptron of Figure 11.6 will compute precisely this linear function. We need two input parameters and will have a bias with a constant 1 output value. The perceptron computes:

$$f(net) = f(w_1 * x_1 + w_2 * x_2 + w_3 * 1), \text{ where } f(x) \text{ is the sign of x.}$$

When f(x) is +1, x is interpreted as being in one class, when it is -1, x is in the other class. This thresholding to +1 or -1 is called linear bipolar thresholding (see Figure 11.7a). The bias serves to shift the thresholding function on the horizontal axis. The extent of this shift is learned by adjusting the weight w_3 during training.

We now use the data points of Table 11.3 to train the perceptron of Figure 11.6. We assume random initialization of the weights to [.75, .5, -.6] and use the perceptron training algorithm of Section 11.1.1. The superscripts represent the

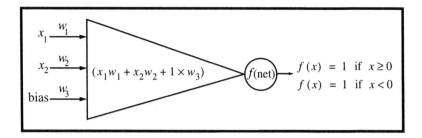

FIGURE 11.6   The perceptron net for the example data of Table 11.3. The thresholding
function is linear and bipolar (see Figure 11.7a).

iteration of the algorithm. We start by taking the first data point in the table:

$$f(net)^1 = f(.75* 1 + .5*1 - .6*1) = f(.65) = 1$$

Since $f(net^1) = 1$, the correct output value, we do not adjust the weights.
Thus $W^2 = W^1$. For our second data point:

$$f(net)^2 = f(.75* 9.4 + .5*6.4 - .6*1) = f(9.65) = 1$$

This time our result should have been - 1 so we have to apply the learning
rule, described in Section 11.1.1:

$$W^t = W^{t-1} + c(d^{t-1} - sign\ (W^{t-1}*X^{t-1}))\ X^{t-1}$$

where c is the learning constant, X and W are the input and weight vectors, and t
the iteration of the net. d^{t-1} is the desired result at time t-1, or in our situation at
t=2. The net output at t=2 is 1. Thus the difference between the desired and actual
net output, $d^2 - sign\ (W^2*X^2)$, is -2. In fact, in a hard limited bipolar perceptron,
the learning increment will always be either +2c or else -2c times the training
vector. We let the learning constant be a small positive real number, 0.2. We
update the weight vector:

$$W^3 = W^2 + 0.2\,(-1-1)\,X^2 = \begin{bmatrix} 0.75 \\ 0.50 \\ -0.60 \end{bmatrix} - 0.4 \begin{bmatrix} 9.4 \\ 6.4 \\ 1.0 \end{bmatrix} = \begin{bmatrix} -3.01 \\ -2.06 \\ -1.00 \end{bmatrix}$$

We now consider the third data point with the newly adjusted weights:

$$f(net)^3 = f(- 3.01* 2.5 - 2.06*2.1 - 1.0*1) = f(-12.84) = -1$$

Again, the net result is not the desired output. We show the W^4 adjustment:

$$W^4 = W^3 + 0.2\,(1 - (-1))\,X^3 = \begin{bmatrix} -3.01 \\ -2.06 \\ -1.00 \end{bmatrix} + 0.4 \begin{bmatrix} 2.5 \\ 2.1 \\ 1.0 \end{bmatrix} = \begin{bmatrix} -2.01 \\ -1.22 \\ -0.60 \end{bmatrix}$$

After 10 iterations of the perceptron net the linear separation of Figure 11.5 is produced. After repeated training on the data set, about 500 iterations in total, the weight vector converges to [-1.3, -1.1, 10.9]. We are interested in the line separating the two classes. In terms of the discriminant functions g_i and g_j, the line is defined as the locus of points at which $g_i(x) = g_j(x)$ or $g_i(x) - g_j(x) = 0$, that is, where the net output is 0. The equation for the net output is given in terms of the weights. It is:

output = $w_1x_1 + w_2x_2 + w_3$.

Thus, the line separating the two classes is defined by the equation:

$-1.3*x_1 + -1.1*x_2 + 10.9 = 0$.

11.2.3 The Delta Rule

A straightforward way to generalize the perceptron network is to replace its hard limiting thresholding function with other types of activation functions. For example, continuous activation functions offer the possibility of more sophisticated learning algorithms by allowing for a finer granularity in error measurement.

Figure 11.7 shows the graph of some thresholding functions: a linear bipolar threshold function (Figure 11.7a) similar to that used by the perceptron, and a number of *sigmoidal* functions. Sigmoidal functions are so called because their graph is an "S" shaped curve, as in Figure 11.7b. A common sigmoidal activation function, called the *logistic* function, is given by the equation:

$f(net) = 1/(1 + e^{-\lambda*net})$, where net $= \Sigma x_i w_i$

As with previously defined functions, x_i is the input on line i, w_i is the weight on line i, and λ a "squashing parameter" used to fine-tune the sigmoidal curve. As λ gets large, the sigmoid approaches the linear threshold function of 11.7a; as it gets closer to 1 it approaches a straight line.

These threshold graphs plot the input values, the activation level of the neuron, against the scaled activation or output of the neuron. The sigmoidal activation function is continuous, which allows a more precise measure of the error on

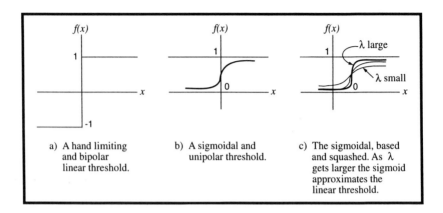

a) A hand limiting
   and bipolar
   linear threshold.

b) A sigmoidal and
   unipolar threshold.

c) The sigmoidal, based
   and squashed. As λ
   gets larger the sigmoid
   approximates the
   linear threshold.

FIGURE 11.7   Thresholding functions.

a unit. Like the hard limiting thresholding function, the sigmoidal activation
function maps most values in its domain into regions close to 0 or 1. However,
there is a region of rapid but continuous transition between 0 and 1. In a sense, it
approximates a thresholding behavior while providing a continuous output function. The use of λ in the exponent adjusts the slope of the sigmoid shape in the
transition region.

The historical emergence of networks with continuous activation functions
suggested new approaches to error reduction learning. The Widrow-Hoff (1960)
learning rule is independent of the activation function, minimizing the squared
error between the desired output value and the network activation, $net_i = WX_i$.
Perhaps the most important learning rule for continuous activation functions is
the *delta rule*, developed by Rumelhart and McClelland (1986).

Intuitively, the delta rule is based on the idea of an error surface, as illustrated in Figure 11.8. This error surface represents cumulative error over a data
set as a function of network weights. Each possible network weight configuration
is represented by a point on this surface. Given a weight configuration, we want
our learning algorithm to find the direction on this surface which most rapidly
reduces the error. This approach is called *gradient descent learning* because the
gradient is a measure of slope as a function of direction from a point on a surface.

To use the delta rule, the network must use an activation function which is
continuous and therefore differentiable. The logistic formula just presented has
this property. The delta rule learning formula for weight adjustment on the jth
input to the ith node is:

$$c \, (d_i - O_i) \, f \, ' \, (net_i) \, x_j,$$

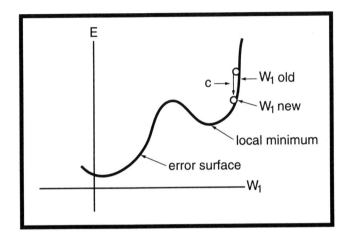

FIGURE 11.8   An error surface in two dimensions. Constant c dictates the size of the learning step.

where c is the constant controlling the learning rate, d_i and O_i are the desired and actual output values of the ith node. The derivative of the activation function for the ith node is f', and x_j is the jth input to node i. We now show the derivation of this formula.

The mean squared network error is found by summing the squared error for each node:

$$\text{Error} = (1/2) * \sum_i \left(d_i - O_i \right)^2$$

where d_i is the desired value for each output node and O_i is the actual output of the node. We square each error so that the individual errors, some, possibly, with negative and others with positive values, will not, in summation, cancel each other out.

We consider here the case where the node is in the output layer; we describe the general case when we present networks with hidden layers in Section 11.2. We want first to measure the rate of change of network error with respect to output of each node. To do this, we use the notion of a *partial derivative*, which gives us the rate of change of a multivariable function with respect to a particular variable. The partial derivative of the total error with respect to each output unit i is:

$$\frac{\delta \text{Error}}{\delta O_i} = \frac{\delta (1/2) * \Sigma \left(d_i - O_i \right)^2}{\delta O_i} = \frac{\delta (1/2) * \left(d_i - O_i \right)^2}{\delta O_i}$$

The second simplification is possible because we are considering a node on the output layer, where its error will not affect any other node. Taking the derivative of this quantity, we get:

$$\frac{\delta\,(1/2)\,*\!\left(d_i - O_i\right)^2}{\delta O_i} = -\!\left(d_i - O_i\right)$$

What we want is the rate of change of network error as a function of change in the weights at node i. To get the change in a particular weight, w_k, we rely on the use of the partial derivative, this time taking the partial derivative of the error at each node with respect to the weight, w_k, at that node. The expansion on the right side of the equal sign is given us by the chain rule for partial derivatives:

$$\frac{\delta\mathrm{Error}}{\delta w_k} = \frac{\delta\mathrm{Error}}{\delta O_i} * \frac{\delta O_i}{\delta w_k}$$

This gives us the pieces we need to solve the equation. Using our earlier result, we obtain:

$$\frac{\delta\mathrm{Error}}{\delta w_k} = -(d_i - O_i) * \frac{\delta O_i}{\delta w_k}$$

We continue by considering the right most factor, the partial derivative of the actual output at the ith node taken with respect to each weight at that node. The formula for the output of node i as a function of its weights is:

$$O_i = f(W_i X_i), \text{ where } W_i X_i = net_i.$$

Since f is a continuous function, taking the derivative we get:

$$\frac{\delta O_i}{\delta w_k} = x_k * f'(W_i X_i) = f'(net_i) * x_k$$

Substituting in the previous equation:

$$\frac{\delta\mathrm{Error}}{\delta w_k} = -(d_i - O_i)\, f'(net_i) * x_k$$

The minimization of the error requires that the weight changes be in the direction of the negative gradient component. Therefore:

$$\Delta w_k = -c\frac{\delta\mathrm{Error}}{\delta w_k} = -c\,[-(d_i - O_i)*f'(net_i)*x_k] = c\,(d_i - O_i)*f'(net_i)*x_k$$

We observe that the delta rule is like *hillclimbing* (Section 8.5.1), in that at every step, it attempts to minimize the local error measure by using the derivative to find the slope of the error space in the region local to a particular point. This makes delta learning vulnerable to the problem of distinguishing local from global minima in the error space.

The learning constant, c, exerts an important influence on the performance of the delta rule, as further analysis of Figure 11.8 illustrates. The value of c determines how much the weight values move in a single learning episode. The larger the value of c, the more quickly the weights move toward an optimal value. However, if c is too large, the algorithm may overshoot the minimum and end up oscillating around the optimal weights. Smaller values of c are less prone to this problem, but do not allow the system to learn as quickly. The optimal value of the learning rate, sometimes enhanced with a momentum factor (Zurada 1992), is a parameter that is often adjusted for a particular application through experiment.

Although the delta rule does not by itself overcome the limitations of single layer networks, its generalized form is central to the functioning of backpropagation, an algorithm for implementing learning in a multilayer network. This algorithm is presented in the next section.

11.3   BACKPROPAGATION LEARNING

11.3.1   Deriving the Backpropagation Algorithm

As we have seen, single layer perceptron networks are limited as to the classifications that they can perform. We show in Sections 11.3 and 11.4 that the addition of multiple layers can overcome many of these limitations. In Section 11.7 we observe that multilayered networks are computationally complete, that is, equivalent to the class of Turing machines. Early researchers, however, were not able to design a learning algorithm for their use. We present in this section the generalized delta rule, which offers one solution to this problem.

The neurons in a multilayer network (Figure 11.9) are connected in layers, with units in layer k passing their activations only to neurons in layer k+1. Multilayer signal processing means that errors deep in the network can spread and evolve in complex, unanticipated ways through successive layers. Thus, the analysis of the source of error at the output layer is complex. Backpropagation provides an algorithm for apportioning blame and adjusting weights accordingly.

The approach taken by the backpropagation algorithm is to start at the output layer and *propagate* error backwards through the hidden layers. When we analyzed learning with the delta rule, we saw that all the information needed to update the weights on a neuron was local to that neuron, except for the amount of error. For output nodes, this is easily computed as the difference between the

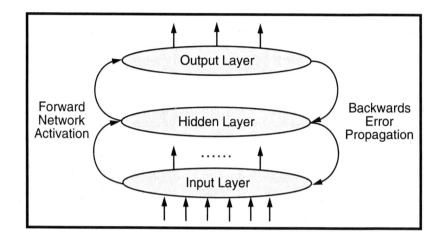

FIGURE 11.9 Backpropagation in a connectionist network having a hidden layer.

desired and actual output values. For nodes in hidden layers, it is considerably more difficult to determine the error for which a node is responsible. The activation function for backpropagation is usually the logistic function:

$$f(net) = 1/(1 + e^{-\lambda * net}), \text{ where } net = \Sigma x_i w_i.$$

This function is used for three reasons. First, it has the sigmoid shape. Second, as a continuous function, it has a derivative everywhere. Finally, the derivative is easily computed by a subtraction and multiplication:

$$f'(net) = f'(1/(1 + e^{-\lambda * net})) = f(net) * (1 - f(net)).$$

The method used in backpropagation training is the generalized delta rule. This uses the same gradient descent approach presented in Section 11.1. The primary difference is that for nodes in the hidden layer we need to look at their contribution to the total error on the layer just above.

The formulas for computing the adjustment of the kth weight of the ith node in backpropagation training are:

1) $\Delta w_{ik} = -c(d_i - O_i) * O_i (1 - O_i) x_{ik}$, for nodes on the output layer, and

2) $\Delta w_{ik} = -c * O_i (1 - O_i) \Sigma (- delta_j * w_{ij}) x_{ik}$, for nodes on hidden layers.

In 2), j is the index of the nodes in the next layer to which i's signals fan out and:

$$\text{delta}_j = -\frac{\delta \text{Error}}{\delta \text{net}_j} = (d_i - O_i) * O_i (1 - O_i).$$

We now show the derivation of these formulae. First we derive 1), the formula for weight adjustment on nodes in the output layer. As before, what we want is the rate of change of network error as a function of change in the kth weight, w_k, of node i. We treated this situation in the derivation of the delta rule in Section 11.1.3. There we showed that:

$$\frac{\delta \text{Error}}{\delta w_k} = -((d_i - O_i) * f'(\text{net}_i) * x_k)$$

Since f is now the logistic activation function, we have:

$$f'(\text{net}) = f'(1/(1 + e^{-\lambda * \text{net}})) = f(\text{net}) * (1 - f(\text{net})).$$

Recall that $f(\text{net}_i)$ is simply O_i. Substituting in the previous equation, we get:

$$\frac{\delta \text{Error}}{\delta w_k} = -(d_i - O_i) * O_i * (1 - O_i) * x_k$$

Since the minimization of the error requires that the weight changes be in the direction of the negative gradient component, we multiply by -c to get the weight adjustment for the ith node of the output layer:

$$\Delta w_k = -c(d_i - O_i) * O_i (1 - O_i) x_k.$$

We next derive the weight adjustment for hidden nodes. For the sake of clarity we initially assume a single hidden layer. We take a single node i on the hidden layer and analyze its contribution to the total network error. We do this by initially considering node i's contribution to the error at a node j on the output layer. We then sum these contributions across all nodes on the output layer. Finally, we describe the contribution of the kth input weight on node i to the network error. Figure 11.10 illustrates this situation.

We first look at the partial derivative of the network error with respect to the output of node i on the hidden layer. We get this by applying the chain rule:

$$\frac{\delta \text{Error}}{\delta O_i} = \frac{\delta \text{Error}}{\delta \text{net}_j} * \frac{\delta \text{net}_j}{\delta O_i}$$

The negative of the first term on the right hand side, $\delta \text{Error} / \delta \text{net}_j$, is called, by convention, *delta_j*.

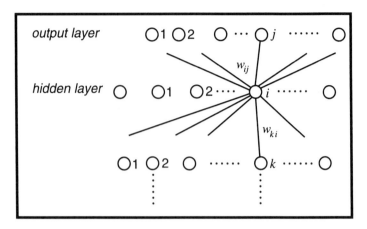

Figure 11.10 $\sum_j -delta_j * w_{ij}$ is the total contribution of node i to the error at the output layer. Our derivation gives the adjustment for w_{ki}.

Thus, we can rewrite the equation as:

$$\frac{\delta Error}{\delta O_i} = -delta_j * \frac{\delta net_j}{\delta O_i}$$

Recall that the activation of node j, net_j, on the output layer is given by the sum of the product of its weights and the output values of the nodes on the hidden layer:

$$net_j = \sum_i w_{ij} O_i$$

Since we are taking the partial derivative with respect to only one component of the sum, namely the connection between node i and node j, we get:

$$\frac{\delta net_j}{\delta O_i} = w_{ij} \,,$$

where w_{ij} is the weight on the connection from node i in the hidden layer to node j in the output layer. Substituting this result:

$$\frac{\delta Error}{\delta O_i} = -delta_j * w_{ij}$$

Now we sum over all the connections of node i to the output layer:

$$\frac{\delta Error}{\delta O_i} = \sum_j -delta_j * w_{ij}$$

This gives us the sensitivity of network error to the output of node i on the hidden layer. We next determine the value of *delta_i*, the sensitivity of network error to the net activation at hidden node i. This will allow us to determine the sensitivity of network error to the incoming weights of node i. Using the chain rule again:

$$-delta_i = \frac{\delta Error}{\delta net_i} = \frac{\delta Error}{\delta O_i} * \frac{\delta O_i}{\delta net_i}$$

Since we are using the logistic activation function,

$$\frac{\delta O_i}{\delta net_i} = O_i * (1 - O_i)$$

We now substitute this value in the equation for *delta_i* to get:

$$-delta_i = O_i * (1 - O_i) * \sum_j -delta_j * w_{ij}$$

Finally, we can evaluate the sensitivity of the network error on the output layer to the incoming weights on hidden node i. We examine the kth weight on node i, w_k. By the chain rule:

$$\frac{\delta Error}{\delta w_{ki}} = \frac{\delta Error}{\delta net_i} * \frac{\delta net_i}{\delta w_{ki}} = -delta_i * \frac{\delta net_i}{\delta w_{ki}} = -delta_i * x_k$$

where x_k is the kth input to node i. We substitute into the equation the value of *-delta_i*:

$$\frac{\delta Error}{\delta w_{ki}} = O_i (1 - O_i) \sum_j (-delta_j * w_{ij}) x_k$$

Since the minimization of the error requires that the weight changes be in the direction of the negative gradient component, we get the weight adjustment for the kth weight of i by multiplying by the negative of the learning constant:

$$\Delta w_{ki} = -c \frac{\delta Error}{\delta w_{ki}} = -c * O_i (1 - O_i) \sum_j (-delta_j * w_{ij}) x_k .$$

For networks with more than one hidden layer, the same procedure is applied recursively to propagate the error from hidden layer n to hidden layer n-1.

Although it provides a solution to the problem of learning in multilayer networks, backpropagation is not without its own difficulties. As with hillclimbing, it may converge to local minima (see Figure 11.8). Finally, backpropagation can be expensive to compute, especially when the network converges slowly.

11.3.2 Backpropagation Example 1: NETtalk

NETtalk is an interesting example of a neural net solution to a difficult learning problem (Sejnowski & Rosenberg 1987). NETtalk learned to pronounce English text. This is a difficult task for an explicit symbol based approach, since

English pronunciation is highly irregular. Although rule based programs have been written for this task, they are complex and do not perform perfectly.

NETtalk learned to read a string of text and return a phoneme and an associated stress for each letter in the string. A phoneme is the basic unit of sound in a language; the stress is the relative loudness of that sound. Because the pronunciation of a single letter depends upon the letters around it, NETtalk was given a 7 character window. As the text moves through this window, NETtalk returns a phoneme/stress pair for each letter.

Figure 11.11 shows the architecture of NETtalk. The network consists of three layers of units. The input units correspond to the 7 character window on the text. Each position in the window is represented by 29 input units, one for each letter of the alphabet, and 3 for punctuation and spaces. The letter in each position activates the corresponding unit. The output units encode phonemes using 21 different features of human articulation. The remaining 5 units encoded stress and syllable boundaries. NETtalk has 80 hidden units, 26 output values, and 18,629 connections. NETtalk is trained by giving it a 7 character window and letting it attempt to pronounce the middle character. Comparing its attempted pronunciation to the correct pronunciation, it adjusts its weights using backpropagation.

The program illustrates a number of interesting properties of neural networks, many of which reflect the nature of human learning. For example, learning, when measured as a percentage of correct responses, proceeds rapidly at first, and slows as the percent correct increases. As with humans, the more words the network learns to pronounce, the better it is at correctly pronouncing new words. Experiments in which some of the weights in a fully trained network were randomly altered showed the network to be damage resistant, degrading gracefully as weights were altered. Researchers also found that relearning in a damaged network was highly efficient.

Another interesting aspect of multilayered networks is the role of the hidden layers. Any learning algorithm must learn generalizations that apply to unseen instances in the problem domain. The hidden layers play an important role in allowing a neural network to generalize. NETtalk, like many backpropagation networks, has fewer neurons in the hidden layer than in the input layer. This means that since fewer nodes on the hidden layer are used to encode the information in the training patterns, some form of abstraction is taking place. The shorter encoding implies that different patterns on the input layer can be mapped into identical patterns at the hidden layer. This reduction serves the function of generalization.

NETtalk learns effectively, although it requires a large number of training instances, as well as repeated passes through the training data. In a series of empirical tests comparing backpropagation and ID3 on this problem, Shavlik et al. (1991) found that the algorithms performed comparably. This research evalu-

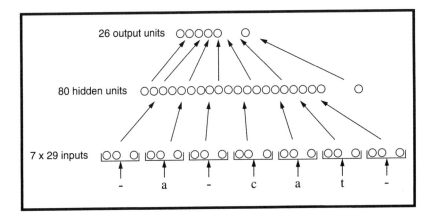

FIGURE 11.11 The network topology of NETtalk.

ated the algorithms by dividing the total set of examples into separate training sets and test sets. Both ID3 (Section 10.3) and NETtalk were able to correctly pronounce about 60% of the test data after training on 500 examples. However, where ID3 required only a single pass through the training data, NETtalk required many repetitions of the training set. In this research, NETtalk was allowed 100 passes through the training data.

As our example demonstrates, the relationship between connectionist and symbolic learning is more complicated than it might seem at first. In our next example we work through the details of a backpropagation solution to the exclusive-or problem.

11.3.3   Backpropagation Example 2: Exclusive-or

We end this section by presenting a simple hidden layer solution to the *exclusive-or* problem. Figure 11.12 shows a network with two input nodes, one hidden node and one output node. The network also has two bias nodes, the first to the hidden node and the second to the output node. The net values for the hidden and output nodes are calculated in the usual manner, as the vector product of the input values times their trained weights. The bias is added to this sum. The weights are trained by backpropagation and the activation function is sigmoidal.

It should be noted that the input nodes are also directly linked, with trained weights, to the output node. This additional linking can often let the designer get a network with fewer nodes on the hidden layer and quicker convergence. In fact there is nothing unique about the network of Figure 11.12; any number of different networks could be used to compute exclusive-or.

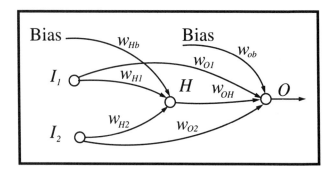

FIGURE 11.12 A backpropagation connectivist net to solve the exclusive-or problem.

We trained our randomly initialized network with multiple instances of the four patterns that represent the truth values of exclusive-or:

$$(0, 0) \rightarrow 0; (1, 0) \rightarrow 1; (0, 1) \rightarrow 1; (1, 1) \rightarrow 0$$

After about 1400 training instances we produced the following values, rounded to the nearest tenth, for the weight parameters of Figure 11.12:

$W_{h1} = -7.0$ $\quad W_{hb} = 2.6$ $\quad W_{o1} = -5.0$ $\quad W_{oh} = -11.0$
$W_{h2} = -7.0$ $\quad W_{ob} = 7.0$ $\quad W_{o2} = -4.0$

With input values $(0, 0)$, the output of the hidden node is:

$$f(0*(-7.0) + 0*(-7.0) + 1*2.6) = f(2.6) \rightarrow 1$$

The output of the output node for $(0,0)$ is:

$$f(0*(-5.0) + 0*(-4.0) + 1*(-11.0) + 1*(7.0)) = f(-4.0) \rightarrow 0$$

With input values $(1, 0)$, the output of the hidden node is:

$$f(1*(-7.0) + 0*(-7.0) + 1*2.6) = f(-4.4) \rightarrow 0$$

The output of the output node for $(0,0)$ is:

$$f(1*(-5.0) + 0*(-4.0) + 0*(-11.0) + 1*(7.0)) = f(2.0) \rightarrow 1$$

The input value of $(1,0)$ is similar. Finally, let us check our exclusive-or network with input values of $(1, 1)$. The output of the hidden node is:

$$f(1*(-7.0) + 1*(-7.0) + 1*2.6) = f(-11.4) \rightarrow 0$$

The output of the output node for (1,1) is:

$$f(1*(-5.0) + 1*(-4.0) + 0*(-11.0) + 1*(7.0)) = f(-2.0) \rightarrow 0$$

The reader can see that the backpropagation network made a nonlinear separation of these data points. The threshold function f is the usual sigmoidal of Figure 11.7b, the learned biases have translated it slightly in the positive direction.

In this chapter we offered an historical perspective on connectionist learning. We spent most of our effort deriving the mathematical support for the most commonly used architecture, backpropagation. In Chapter 12 we introduce a number of alternative connectionist architectures, including the reinforcement, attractor, and competitive learning models. We conclude Part III (Section 12.5) with a general discussion of the strengths and limitations of machine learning.

11.4 EPILOGUE AND REFERENCES

The ability to learn, along with the use of language are probably the most distinctive skills we as humans possess. They also offer the greatest challenge to us as cognitive scientists.

We present connectionist networks in two chapters. This, the first, presents them from an historical perspective. We feel it is important to review the very early research in this field, much of which was presented in Section 11.1. For further reading we recommend McCulloch and Pitts (1943), Oliver Selfridge (1959), Claude Shannon (1948), and F. Rosenblatt (1958). Early psychological models are also important, especially those of Donald Hebb (1949).

For cognitive scientists, the backpropagation network is the most commonly used connectionist architecture. Therefore we have given most of a chapter to its origins and growth. Many important issues remain concerning its design and use; we touch on a number of them in Section 12.5.

The two volumes of *Parallel Distributed Processing* (Rumelhart 1986) give an excellent introduction to neural networks both as computational and cognitive tools. *Neural Networks and Natural Intelligence* (Grossberg 1988) is another thorough treatment of the subject.

We have not addressed many important mathematical as well as computational aspects of connectionist architectures. For an overview of these issues we especially recommend Robert Hecht-Nielsen (1990), Jacek Zurada (1992), and James Freeman and David Skapura (1992).

There are many issues, both representational and computational, that the cognitive scientist must consider. These include architecture and connectivity selection for the network as well as determining what cognitive parameters of the environment are to be processed and what the results might "mean."

There are further questions for use of the backpropagation networks, including the number of hidden nodes and layers, selecting the training set, fine-tuning the learning constant, the use of bias nodes, and so on. Many of these issues come under the general heading of *inductive bias*: the role of the knowledge, expectations, and tools that the problem solver and network designer brings to problem solving. We address many of these issues in Section 12.5, after presenting alternative architectures in the early sections of Chapter 12. A number of these important issues are touched on again in our Epilogue, Chapter 17.

Chapter 12

COMPETITIVE, REINFORCEMENT, AND ATTRACTOR LEARNING MODELS

So far as the laws of mathematics refer to reality, they are not certain. And so far as they are certain, they do not refer to reality.

Albert Einstein

Everything is vague to a degree you do not realize till you have tried to make it precise.

Bertrand Russell

12.0 INTRODUCTION

In Chapter 11 we began our description of neural and biologically based models of learning. We introduced the relevant issues from an historical perspective, describing an artificial neuron, the early work by McColloch and Pitts, and the perceptron of Rosenblatt. We ended Chapter 11 with the presentation of back-propagation networks, including the mathematical support for the delta rule, gradient descent learning, and the backpropagation algorithm.

In Chapter 12 we continue our presentation, introducing competitive learning, Hebbian reinforcement learning, and attractor networks. We conclude our overview with biologically inspired learning models, including cellular automata and genetic algorithms. We end Part III with a summary discussion of issues in learning and problems in the construction of machine learning systems.

In Section 12.1 we present models for "competitive" learning developed by Kohonen (1984) and Hecht-Nielsen (1987). In these models, network weight vectors are used to represent patterns rather than connection strengths. The *winner-take-all* learning algorithm selects the node whose pattern of weights is most like the input vector and adjusts it to make it more like the input vector. It is unsupervised in that *winning* is simply identifying the node whose current weight vector most closely resembles the input vector. The combination of Kohonen and Grossberg (1982) layers in a single network offers a model for S-R learning.

In Section 12.2 we present Hebb's (1949) model of reinforcement learning. Hebb conjectured that each time one neuron contributes to the firing of another neuron, the strength of the pathway between the neurons is increased. Hebbian learning is modeled by a simple algorithm for adjusting connection weights. We discuss the adequacy of this algorithm as a model of reinforcement or "conditioning." We present both unsupervised and supervised versions of Hebbian learning. We also introduce the linear associator, a Hebbian based model for pattern retrieval from memory.

Section 12.3 introduces a very important family of networks called "attractor networks". These networks employ feedback connections to repeatedly cycle a signal within the network. The network output is considered to be the network state upon reaching equilibrium. Network weights are constructed so that a set of "attractors" is created. Input patterns within an attractor *basin* reach equilibrium at that attractor. The attractors can therefore be used to store patterns in a memory. Given an input pattern, we retrieve either the closest stored pattern in the network or a pattern associated with the closest stored pattern. The first type of memory is called *autoassociative*, the second type *heteroassociative*. John Hopfield (1982), a theoretical physicist, defined a class of attractor networks whose convergence can be represented in terms of energy minimization. Hopfield networks can be used to solve constraint problems, such as the traveling salesperson problem, by mapping the optimization function into an energy function.

In Section 12.4 we present evolutionary or biology based models. Genetic algorithms and cellular automata base their learning on the evolutionary paradigm of survival of the fittest. For example, the genetic algorithm "evolves" a population of potential problem solutions. A "fitness" function evaluates each solution to decide whether it will contribute to the next generation of solutions. Then, through operations analogous to gene transfer in sexual reproduction, the algorithm creates a new population of candidate solutions.

In Section 12.5 we summarize the features, as well as the potential problems, of neurally and biologically inspired approaches to learning. Finally, in Chapter 17, we revisit several pivotal issues in learning.

12.1   COMPETITIVE LEARNING

12.1.1   Winner-Take-All Learning for Classification

The winner-take-all algorithm (Kohonen 1984, Hecht-Nielsen 1987) works with the single node in a layer of nodes that responds most strongly to the input pattern. Winner-take-all may be viewed as a competition among a set of network nodes, as in Figure 12.1. In this figure we have a vector of input values, $X=(x_1, x_2, ..., x_m)$, passed into a layer of network nodes, A, B,..., N. The diagram shows node B the winner of the competition, with an output signal of 1.

Learning for winner-take-all is unsupervised in that the winner is determined by a "maximum activation" test. The weight vector of the winner is then rewarded by bringing its components closer to those of the input vector. For the weights, W, of the winning node and components X of the input vector, the increment is:

$$\Delta W^t = c(X^{t-1} - W^{t-1}),$$

where c is a small positive learning constant that usually decreases as the learning proceeds. The winning weight vector is then adjusted by adding ΔW^t. This amounts to incrementing each component of the winner's weight vector by a fraction of the $x_i - w_i$ difference. The effect is of course to make the winning node match more closely the input vector.

The winner-take-all algorithm does not need to directly compute activation levels to find the node with the strongest response. The activation level of a node is directly related to the closeness of its weight vector to the input vector. For a node i with a normalized weight vector W_i, the activation level, $W_i X$, is a function of the Euclidean distance between W_i and the input pattern X. This can be

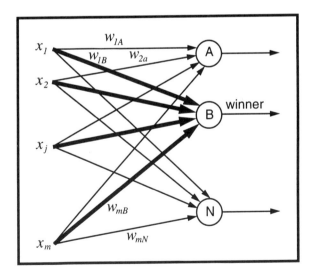

FIGURE 12.1 A layer of nodes for application of a winner-take-all algorithm. The bold input vectors support the winning node.

seen by calculating the Euclidean distance:

$$\| X - W_i \| = \text{square root } (X - W_i)^2 = \text{square root } (XX - 2WX_i - 1).$$

From this equation it can be seen that for a set of normalized weight vectors, the weight vector with the smallest Euclidean distance, $\| X - W \|$, will be the weight vector with the maximum activation value, WX. In many cases it is more efficient to determine the winner by calculating Euclidean distances rather than comparing activation levels on normalized weight vectors.

We consider the "winner-take-all" Kohonen learning rule for several reasons. First, we consider it as a classification method and compare it to perceptron classification. Second, it may be combined with other network architectures to offer more sophisticated models of learning. We look at the combination of Kohonen prototype learning with an outstar, supervised learning network. This hybrid, first proposed by Robert Hecht-Nielsen (1987, 1990), is called a *counterpropagation* network. We see, in Section 12.1.3, how we can describe conditioned learning using counterpropagation.

Before we leave this introduction, there are a number of issues important for winner-take-all algorithms. Sometimes a "conscience" parameter is set that keeps individual nodes from winning too often. This ensures that all network nodes eventually participate in representing the pattern space. In some algorithms, rather than identifying a winner that takes all, a *set* of closest nodes are selected and the weights of each are differentially incremented. Another approach is to differentially reward the neighboring nodes of the winner. Weights are typically initialized at random values and then normalized during this learning method (Zurada 1992). Hecht-Nielsen (1990) shows how "winner-take-all algorithms may be seen as equivalent to the k-means analysis of a set of data. In the next section we present Kohonen's winner-take-all unsupervised method for the learning of clusters.

12.1.2   A Kohonen Network for Learning Prototypes

Classification of data and the role of prototypes in learning are constant concerns of psychologists, linguists, computer scientists, and cognitive scientists (Wittgenstein 1953, Rosch 1978, Lakoff 1987). The role of prototypes and classification in intelligence is also a constant theme of this book. We demonstrated symbol based-classification and probabilistic clustering algorithms with COB-WEB and CLUSTER/2 in Section 10.5. In connectionist models, we demonstrated perceptron based classification in Section 11.2 and now show a Kohonen (1984) winner-take-all clustering algorithm.

Figure 12.2 presents again the data points of Table 11.3. Superimposed on these points are a series of prototypes created during network training. The perceptron training algorithm converged after a number of iterations, resulting in a network weight configuration defining a linear separation between the two classes. As we saw, the line defined by these weights was obtained by implicitly computing the Euclidean "center" of each cluster. The Euclidean center of a cluster serves in perceptron classification as an implicit prototype of the class.

Kohonen learning, on the other hand, is unsupervised, with a set of prototypes randomly created and then refined until they come to explicitly represent the clusters of data. As the algorithm continues, the learning constant is progressively reduced so that each new input vector will cause less perturbation in the prototypes.

Kohonen learning, like CLUSTER/2, has a strong inductive bias in that the number of desired prototypes is explicitly identified at the beginning of the algorithm and then continuously refined. This allows the net algorithm designer to identify a specific number of prototypes to represent the clusters of data. Counterpropagation (Section 12.1.3) allows further manipulation of this selected number of prototypes.

Figure 12.3 is a Kohonen learning network for classification of the data of Table 11.2. The data are represented in Cartesian two dimensional space, so pro-

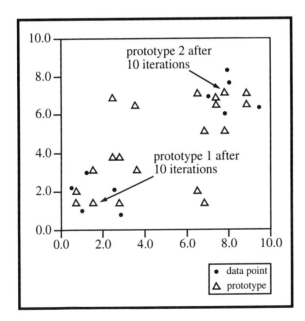

FIGURE 12.2 The use of a Kohonen layer, unsupervised, to explicitly generate a sequence of prototypes to represent the two classes of Table 11.3.

totypes to represent the data clusters will also be order pairs. We select two proto-types, one to represent each data cluster. We have randomly initialized node A to (7, 2) and node B to (2, 9). Random initialization only works in simple problems such as ours; an alternative is to set the weight vectors equal to representatives of each of the clusters.

The winning node will have a weight vector closest to that of the input vector. This weight vector for the winning node will be rewarded by being moved even closer to the input data, while the weights on the losing nodes are left unchanged. Since we are explicitly calculating the Euclidean distance of the input vector from each of the prototypes we will not need to normalize the vectors, as described in Section 12.1.1.

Kohonen learning is unsupervised, in that a simple measure of the distance between each prototype and the data point allows selection of the winner. Classification will be "discovered" in the context of this *self-organizing* network. Although Kohonen learning selects data points for analysis in random order, we take the points of Table 11.3 in top to bottom order. For point (1, 1), we measure the distance from each prototype:

$$\|(1, 1) - (7, 2)\| = (1 - 7)^2 + (1 - 2)^2 = 37, \text{ and}$$
$$\|(1, 1) - (2, 9)\| = (1 - 2)^2 + (1 - 9)^2 = 65.$$

Node A (7, 2) is the winner since it is closest to (1, 1). $\|(1, 1) - (7, 2)\|$ represents the distance between these two points; we do not need to apply the square root function in the Euclidean distance measure because the relation of magnitudes is invariant. We now reward the winning node, using the learning constant c set to 0.5. For the second iteration:

$$
\begin{aligned}
W^2 &= W^1 + c(X^1 - W^1), \text{ and} \\
&= (7, 2) + .5((1, 1) - (7, 2)) = (7, 2) + .5((1 - 7), (1 - 2)) \\
&= (7, 2) + (-3, -.5) = (4, 1.5).
\end{aligned}
$$

At the second iteration of the learning algorithm we have, for data point (9.4, 6.4):

$$\|(9.4, 6.4) - (4, 1.5)\| = (9.4 - 4)^2 + (6.4 - 1.5)^2 = 53.17, \text{ and}$$
$$\|(9.4, 6.4) - (2, 9)\| = (9.4 - 2)^2 + (6.4 - 9)^2 = 60.15.$$

Again, node A is the winner. The weight for the third iteration is:

$$
\begin{aligned}
W^3 &= W^2 + c(X^2 - W^2), \text{ and} \\
&= (4, 1.5) + .5((9.4, 6.4) - (4, 1.5)) \\
&= (4, 1.5) + (2.7, 2.5) = (6.7, 4).
\end{aligned}
$$

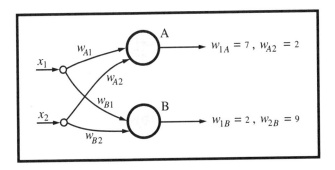

FIGURE 12.3   The architecture of the Kohonen based learning network for the data of Table 11.3 and classification of Figure 12.2.

At the third iteration we have, for data point (2.5, 2.1):

$$\|(2.5, 2.1) - (6.7, 4)\| = (2.5 - 6.7)^2 + (2.1 - 4)^2 = 21.25, \text{ and}$$
$$\|(2.5, 2.1) - (2, 9)\| = (2.5 - 2)^2 + (2.1 - 9)^2 = 47.86.$$

Node A wins again and we go on to calculate its new weight vector. Figure 12.2 shows the evolution of the prototype after 20 iterations. The algorithm used to generate the data of Figure 12.2 selected data randomly from Table 11.3, so the prototypes shown will differ from those just created. The progressive improvement of the prototypes can be seen moving toward the centers of the data clusters. Again, this is an unsupervised, winner-take-all reinforcement algorithm. It builds a set of evolving and explicit prototypes to represent the data clusters. A number of researchers, including Zurada (1992) and Hecht-Nielsen (1990), point out that Kohonen unsupervised classification of data is basically the same as k-means analysis.

We next consider, with a Grossberg, or outstar, extension of Kohonen winner-take-all analysis, an algorithm that will let us extend the power of prototype selection.

12.1.3   Grossberg Learning and Counterpropagation

To this point we considered the unsupervised clustering of input data. Learning here requires little *a priori* knowledge of a problem domain. Gradually detected characteristics of the data, as well as the training history, lead to the identification of classes and the discovery of boundaries between them. Once data points are clustered according to similarities in their vector representations, a teacher can assist in calibrating or giving names to data classes. This is done by a form of supervised training.

We wish to take the output nodes of a "winner-take-all" network layer and use them as input to a second network layer. We will then explicitly reinforce decisions at this output layer. This allows us, for example, to use the results of a Kohonen net to map the input pattern into an output pattern or class. A Grossberg (1982, 1988) layer, implementing an algorithm called *outstar*, allows us to do this. The combined network, a Kohonen layer joined to a Grossberg layer, is called *counterpropagation* and was first proposed by Robert Hecht-Nielsen (1987, 1990).

In Section 12.1.2 we considered in some detail the Kohonen layer; here we consider the Grossberg layer. Figure 12.4 shows a layer of nodes, A, B, ..., N, where one node, J, is selected as the winner. Grossberg learning is supervised in that we wish, with feedback from a teacher, represented by vector Y, to reinforce the weight connecting J to the node I in the output layer which is supposed to fire. With outstar learning, we identify and increase the weight w_{JI} on the outbound link of J to I.

To train the counterpropagation net we first train the Kohonen layer. When a winner is found, the values on all the links going out from it will be 1, while all the output values of its competitors remain 0. That node, together with all the nodes on the output layer to which it is connected, form what is called an *outstar*

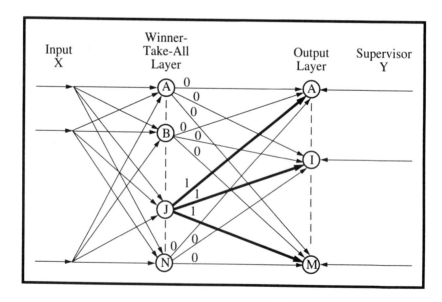

FIGURE 12.4   The "outstar" of node J, the "winner" in a winner-take-all network. The Y vector supernovas the response on the output layer in Grossberg training. The "outstar" is bold with all weights 1; all other weights are 0.

(see Figure 12.4). Training for the Grossberg layer is based on outstar components.

If each cluster of input vectors represents a single class and we want all members of a class to map onto the same value at the output layer, we do not need an iterative training. We need only determine which node in the winner-take-all layer is linked to which class and then assign weights from those nodes to output nodes based on the association between classes and desired output values. For example, if the J-th winner-take-all unit wins for all elements of the cluster for which I=1 is the desired output of the network, we set $w_{JI} = 1$ and $w_{JK} = 0$ for all other weights on the outstar of J.

If the desired output for elements of a cluster vary, then there is an iterative procedure, using the supervision vector Y, for adjusting outstar weights. The result of this training procedure is to *average* the desired output values for elements of a particular cluster. We train the weights on the outstar connections from the winning node to the output nodes according to the equation:

$$W^{t+1} = W^t + c(Y - W^t)$$

where c is a small positive learning constant, W^t is the weight vector of the outstar component, and Y is the desired output vector. Note that this learning algorithm has the effect of increasing the connection between node I on the Kohonen layer and node J on the output layer precisely when I is a winning node with an output of 1 and the desired output of J is also 1. This makes it an instance of Hebbian learning, a form of learning in which a neural pathway is strengthened every time one node contributes to the firing of another. We discuss Hebbian learning in more detail in Section 12.2.

We next apply the rule for training a counterpropagation network to recognize the data clusters of Table 11.3. We also show with this example how counterpropagation nets offer an example of conditioned learning. Suppose the x1 parameter in Table 11.3 represents engine speed in a propulsion system. x2 represents engine temperature. Both the speed and the temperature of the system are calibrated to produce data points in the range 0 .. 10. Our monitoring system samples data points at regular intervals. Whenever speed and temperature are excessively high, we want to broadcast a warning. Let us rename the output values of Table 11.3 from +1 to "safe" and from -1 to "dangerous." Our counterpropagation network will look like Figure 12.5.

Since we know exactly what values we want each winning node of the Kohonen net to map to on the output layer of the Grossberg net, we could directly set those values. To demonstrate outstar learning, however, we will train the net using the formula just given. If we make the (arbitrary) decision that node S on the output layer should signal safe situations and node D dangerous, then the outstar weights for node A on the output layer of the Kohonen net should be [1, 0] and the outstar weights for B should be [0, 1]. Because of the symmetry of the situation, we show the training of the outstar for node A only.

The Kohonen net must have stabilized before the Grossberg net can be trained. We demonstrated the Kohonen convergence of this same net in Section 12.1.2. The input vectors for training the A outstar node are of the form $[x_1, x_2, 1, 0]$. x_1 and x_2 are values from Table 11.3 that are clustered at Kohonen output node A and the last two components indicate that when A is the Kohonen winner, safe is "true" and dangerous is "false," as in Figure 12.5. We initialize the outstar weights of A to [0, 0] and use .2 as the learning constant:

$$W^1 = [0, 0] + .2[[1, 0] - [0, 0]] = [0, 0] + [.2, 0] = [.2, 0]$$
$$W^2 = [.2, 0] + .2[[1, 0] - [.2, 0]] = [.2, 0] + [.16, 0] = [.36, 0]$$
$$W^3 = [.36, 0] + .2[[1, 0] - [.36, 0]] = [.36, 0] + [.13, 0] = [.49, 0]$$
$$W^4 = [.49, 0] + .2[[1, 0] - [.49, 0]] = [.49, 0] + [.10, 0] = [.59, 0]$$
$$W^5 = [.59, 0] + .2[[1, 0] - [.59, 0]] = [.59, 0] + [.08, 0] = [.67, 0].$$

As we can see, with training these weights are moving toward [1, 0]. Of course, since in this case elements of the cluster associated with A always map

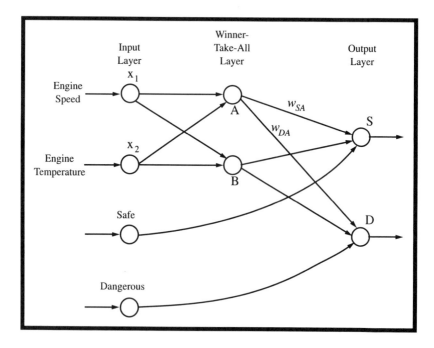

FIGURE 12.5 A counterpropagation network to recognize the classes in Table 11.3. We train the outstar weights of node A, w_{SA} and w_{DA}.

into [1,0], we could have used the simple assignment algorithm rather than the averaging algorithm for training.

We now show that this assignment gives the appropriate response from the counterpropagation net. When the first input vector from Table 11.3 is applied to the network in Figure 12.5, we get activation of [1, 1] for the outstar weights of node A and [0, 0] for the outstar of B. The dot product of activation and weights for node S of the output layer is [1, 0] * [1, 0]; this gives activation 1 to the S output node. With outstar weights of B trained to [0, 1], the activation for node D is [1, 0] * [0, 1]; these are the values that we expect. Testing the second row of data points on Table 11.3, we get activation [0, 0] from the A node and [1,1] from the B at the winner-take-all level. The dot product of these vales and the trained weights gives 0 to the S node and 1 to the D, again what is expected. The reader may continue to test other data from Table 11.3.

From a cognitive perspective, we can give an associationist interpretation to the counterpropagation net. Consider again Figure 12.5. The learning on the Kohonen layer can be seen as acquiring a conditioned stimulus, since the network is learning patterns in events. The learning on the Grossberg layer, on the other hand, is an association of data clusters to some response. The learning on the Grossberg level, on the other hand, is an association of nodes (unconditioned stimuli) to some response. In our situation the system learns to broadcast a danger warning when data fit into a certain pattern. Once the appropriate response is learned, then even without the continued coaching of a teacher, the system responds appropriately to new data.

A second cognitive interpretation of counterpropagation is in terms of the reinforcement of memory links for pattern of phenomena. This is similar to building a lookup table for responses to data patterns.

Counterpropagation has, in certain cases, a considerable advantage over backpropagation. Like backpropagation it is capable of learning nonlinearly separable classifications. It does this, however, by virtue of the preprocessing which goes on in the Kohonen layer, where the data set is partitioned into clusters of homogenous data. This partitioning can result in a significant advantage over backpropagation in learning rate since the explicit partitioning of data into separate clusters replaces the often extensive search required on the hidden layers in backpropagation networks.

12.2   HEBBIAN COINCIDENCE LEARNING

12.2.1   Introduction

Hebb's theory of learning, as first presented in Chapter 5, is based on the observation that in biological systems when one neuron contributes to the firing of another neuron, the connection or pathway between the two neurons is strengthened. Hebb (1949) stated:

> When an axon of cell A is near enough to excite a cell B
> and repeatedly or persistently takes place in firing it, some
> growth process or metabolic change takes place in one or
> both cells such that A's efficiency, as one of the cells firing
> B, is increased.

Hebbian learning is appealing because it establishes behavior based reward concepts on the neuronal level. Neural physiological research has confirmed that Hebb's idea is at least approximately correct. As we saw in Chapter 5, there were other mechanisms modifying cells at the neuron level, including chemical metabolism, cell attrition, and the production of new cells. Nonetheless in response to Hebb's pioneering contributions to neuroscience, the particular learning law presented in this section is now referred to as Hebbian learning. This learning belongs to the *coincidence* category of learning laws which cause weight changes in response to localized events in neural processing. We describe the learning laws of this category by their local time and space properties.

Hebbian learning has been used in a number of network architectures. It is used in both supervised and unsupervised learning modes. The effect of strengthening the connection between two neurons, when one contributes to the firing of another, may be simulated mathematically by adjusting the weight on their connection by a constant time the sign of the product of their output values.

Let's see how this works. Suppose neurons i and j are connected so that the output of i is an input of j. We can define the weight adjustment on the connection between them, ΔW, as $c * (o_i * o_j)$, where c is a constant controlling the learning rate. Consider Table 12.1, where O_i is the output value of i and O_j the output of j:

O_i	O_j	O_i*O_j
+	+	+
+	-	-
-	+	-
-	-	+

TABLE 12.1 The signs and product of signs of node output values.

From the first line of the table we see that when O_i and O_j are both positive, the weight adjustment, ΔW, is positive. This has the effect of strengthening the connection between i and j when i has contributed to j's "firing." In the second and third rows, i and j have opposite signs. Since their signs differ, we want to inhibit i's contribution to j's output value. Therefore we adjust the weight of the connection by a negative increment. Finally, in the fourth row, i and j again have the same sign. This means that we increase the strength of their connection. This weight adjustment mechanism has the effect of reinforcing the path between neurons when they have similar signals and inhibiting them otherwise.

In the next sections we consider two types of Hebbian learning, unsupervised and supervised. We begin by examining an unsupervised form.

12.2.2   An Example of Unsupervised Hebbian Learning

Recall that in unsupervised learning a critic is not available to provide the "correct" output value; thus the weights are modified solely as a function of the input and output values of the neuron. The training of this network has the effect of strengthening the network's responses to patterns that it has already seen. In the example to follow, we show how Hebbian learning can be used to model conditioned response learning as described in Section 2.2.

A formula for weight adjustment, ΔW, of a node i in unsupervised Hebbian learning is:

$$\Delta W = c * f(X, W) * X$$

where c is the learning constant, a small positive number, $f(X, W)$ is i's output, and X is the input vector to i.

We now show how a network can use Hebbian learning to transfer its response from a primary or unconditioned stimulus to a conditioned stimulus. This allows us to model the type of learning studied in Pavlov's experiments, where by simultaneously ringing a bell every time food was presented, a dog's salivation response to food was transferred to the bell. The network of Figure 12.6 has two layers, an input layer i with six nodes and an output layer j with one node. The jth layer returns either +1, signifying that the output neuron has fired, or a -1, signifying that it is quiescent.

We let the learning constant be the small positive real number .2. In this example we train the network on the pattern [1, -1, 1, -1, 1 -1] which is the concatenation of the two patterns, [1, -1, 1] and [-1, 1, -1]. The pattern [1, -1, 1] represents the unconditioned stimulus and [-1, 1, -1] represents the new stimulus. We assume that the network already responds positively to the unconditioned stimulus but is neutral with respect to the new stimulus. We simulate the positive response of the network to the unconditioned stimulus with the weight vector [1, -1, 1], exactly matching the input pattern, while the neutral response of the network to the new stimulus is simulated by the weight vector [0, 0, 0]. The concatenation of these two weight vectors gives us the initial weight vector for the network, [1, -1, 1, 0, 0, 0].

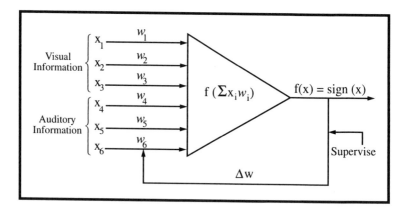

FIGURE 12.6 An example neuron for application of a Hebbian learning node. Learning is supervised.

We now train the network on the input pattern, hoping to induce a configuration of weights which will produce a positive network response to the new stimulus. The first iteration of the network gives:

$$W * X = (1 * 1) + (-1 * -1) + (1 * 1) + (0 * -1) + (0 * 1) + (0 * -1)$$
$$= (1) + (1) + (1) = 3$$
$$f(3) = \text{sign}(3) = 1.$$

We now create the new weight W^2:

$$W2 = [1, -1, 1, 0, 0, 0] + .2 * (1) * [1, -1, 1, -1, 1 -1]$$
$$= [1, -1, 1, 0, 0, 0] + [.2, -.2, .2, -.2, .2, -.2]$$
$$= [1.2, -1.2, 1.2, -.2, .2, -.2.]$$

We expose the adjusted network to the original input pattern:

$$W * X = (1.2 * 1) + (-1.2 * -1) + (1.2 * 1) + (-.2 * -1) + (.2 * 1) + (-.2 * -1)$$
$$= (1.2) + (.1.2) + (1.2) + (+.2) + (.2) + (.2) = 4.2 \text{ and}$$
$$\text{sign}(4.2) = 1.$$

We now create the new weight W^3:

$$W^3 = [1.2, -1.2, 1.2, -.2, .2, -.2] + .2 * (1) * [1, -1, 1, -1, 1 -1]$$
$$= [1.2, -1.2, 1.2, -.2, .2, -.2] + [.2, -.2, .2, -.2, .2, -.2]$$
$$= [1.4, -1.4, 1.4, -.4, .4, -.4.]$$

It can now be seen that the vector product, W * X, will continue to grow in the positive direction, with the absolute value of each element of the weight vector increasing by .2 at each training cycle. After 10 more iterations of the Hebbian training the weight vector will be:

$$W^{13} = [3.4, -3.4, 3.4, -2.4, 2.4, -2.4].$$

We now use this trained weight vector to test the network's response to the two partial patterns. We would like to see if the network continues to respond to the unconditioned stimulus positively and, more importantly, if the network has now acquired a positive response to the new, conditioned stimulus. We test the network first on the unconditioned stimulus [1, -1, 1]. We fill out the last three arguments of the input vector with random 1, -1 assignments. For example, we test the network on the vector [1, -1, 1, 1, 1, -1]:

$$
\begin{aligned}
\text{sign}(W*X) \ &= \text{sign}((3.4*1) + (-3.4*-1) + (3.4*1) \\
&\quad + (-2.4*1) + (2.4*1) + (-2.4*-1)) \\
&= \text{sign}(3.4 + 3.4 + 3.4 - 2.4 + 2.4 + 2.4) \\
&= \text{sign}(12.6) = +1.
\end{aligned}
$$

The network thus still responds positively to the original unconditioned stimulus. We now do a second test using the original unconditioned stimulus and a different random vector in the last three positions: [1, -1, 1, 1, -1, -1]:

$$
\begin{aligned}
\text{sign}(W*X) \ &= \text{sign}((3.4*1) + (-3.4*-1) + (3.4*1) \\
&\quad + (-2.4*1) + (2.4*-1) + (-2.4*-1)) \\
&= \text{sign}(3.4 + 3.4 + 3.4 - 2.4 - 2.4 + 2.4) \\
&= \text{sign}(7.8) = +1.
\end{aligned}
$$

The second vector also produces a positive network response. In fact we note in these two examples that the network's sensitivity to the original stimulus, as measured by its raw activation, has been strengthened, due to repeated exposure to that stimulus.

We now test the network's response to the new stimulus pattern, [-1, 1, -1], encoded in the last three positions of the input vector. We fill the first three vector positions with random assignments from the set {1,-1}. We first test the network on the vector [1, 1, 1, -1, 1, -1]:

$$
\begin{aligned}
\text{sign}(W*X) \ &= \text{sign}((3.4*1) + (-3.4*-1) + (3.4*1) \\
&\quad + (-2.4*1) + (2.4*1) + (-2.4*-1)) \\
&= \text{sign}(3.4 - 3.4 + 3.4 + 2.4 + 2.4 + 2.4) \\
&= \text{sign}(10.6) = +1.
\end{aligned}
$$

The pattern of the secondary stimulus is also recognized!

We do one final experiment, with the vector patterns slightly degraded. This could represent the stimulus situation where the input signals are slightly altered, perhaps because a new food and a different sounding bell are used. We test the network on the input vector [1, -1, -1, 1, 1, -1], where the first three parameters are one off the original unconditioned stimulus and the last three parameters are one off the conditioned stimulus:

$$
\begin{aligned}
\text{sign}(W*X) &= \text{sign}((3.4*1) + (-3.4*-1) + (3.4*1) \\
&\quad + (-2.4*1) + (2.4*1) + (-2.4*-1)) \\
&= \text{sign}(3.4 + 3.4 - 3.4 - 2.4 + 2.4 + 2.4) \\
&= \text{sign}(5.8) = +1.
\end{aligned}
$$

Even the partially degraded stimulus is recognized!

What has the Hebbian learning model produced? We created an association between a new stimulus and an old response by repeatedly presenting the old and new stimulus together. The network learns to transfer its response to the new stimulus without any supervision. This strengthened sensitivity also allows the network to respond in the same way to a slightly degraded version of the stimuli. This was achieved by using Hebbian coincidence learning to increase the strength of the network's response to the total pattern, an increase which has the effect of increasing the strength of the network's response to each individual component of the pattern.

12.2.3 Supervised Hebbian Learning

The Hebbian learning rule is based on the principle that the strength of the connection between neurons is increased whenever one neuron contributes to the firing of another. This principle can be adapted to a supervised learning situation by basing the weight adjustment for this connection on the desired output of the neuron rather than the actual output. For example, if the input of neuron A to neuron B is positive, and the *desired* response of neuron B is a positive output, then the weight on the connection from A to B is increased.

We examine an application of supervised Hebbian learning showing how a network can be trained to recognize a set of associations between patterns. The associations are given by a set of ordered pairs, $\{<X_1, Y_1>, <X_2, Y_2>, ..., <X_t, Y_t>\}$, where X_i and Y_i are the vector patterns to be associated. Suppose that the length of the X_i is n and the Y_i is m. Therefore, the network we use has two layers, an input layer of size n and an output layer of size m, as in Figure 12.7.

The learning formula for this network can be derived by starting with the Hebbian learning formula from the previous section:

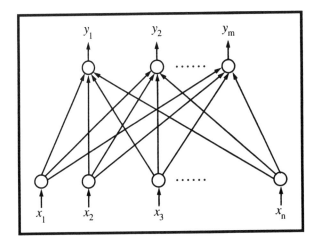

FIGURE 12.7 A supervised Hebbian network for learning pattern association.

$\Delta W = c * f(X, W) * X$

where $f(X, W)$ is the actual output of the network node. In supervised learning, we replace this actual output of a node with the desired output vector D, giving us the formula:

$\Delta W = c * D * X$

Given a vector pair, $<X,Y>$ from the set of associated pairs, we apply this learning rule to the kth node in the output layer:

$\Delta W_{ik} = c * d_k * x_i,$

where ΔW_{ik} is the weight adjustment on the ith input to the kth node in the output layer, d_k is the desired output of the kth node, and x_i is the ith element of X. We apply this formula to adjust all the weights on all the nodes in the output layer. The vector $<x_1, x_2, .., x_n>$ is just the input vector X and the vector $<d_1, d_2, .., d_m>$ is the output vector Y. Applying the formula for individual weight adjustments across the entire output layer and collecting terms, we can write the formula for the weight adjustment on the output layer as:

$\Delta W = c * Y * X,$

where the vector product $Y*X$ is the *outer vector product*. We explain how to compute outer products in the next section.

To train the network on he entire set of associated pairs, we cycle through these pairs, adjusting the weight for each pair $<X_i, Y_i>$ according to the formula:

$$W^{t+1} = W^t + c*Y_i*X_i.$$

For the entire training set we get:

$$W^1 = W^0 + c (Y_1 * X_1 + Y_2 * X_2 + ... + Y_t * X_t),$$

where W^0 is the initial weight configuration. If we initialize W^0 to the 0 vector, $<0, 0, ...,0>$, and set the learning constant c to 1, we get the following formula for assigning network weights:

$$W = Y_1 * X_1 + Y_2 * X_2 + ... + Y_t *X_t.$$

A network which maps input vectors to output vectors using this formula for weight assignment is called a *linear associator*. We have shown that linear associator networks are based on the Hebbian learning rule. In practice this formula can be applied directly to initialize network weights without explicit training.

In the next section we analyze the properties of the linear associator. This model, as we have just seen, stores multiple associations in a matrix of weight vectors. This raises the possibility of interactions between stored patterns. We analyze the problems created by these interactions in the next sections.

12.2.4   Associative Memory and the Linear Associator

The *linear associator* network was first proposed by Tuevo Kohonen (1972) and James Anderson (1976). In this section we present the linear associator network as a method for storing and recovering patterns from memory. We examine different forms of memory retrieval, including the heteroassociative, autoassociative, and interpolative models. We analyze the linear associator network as an implementation of interpolative memory based on the Hebbian learning model. We end this section by considering problems with interference or crosstalk which arise when encoding multiple patterns in memory.

We begin our examination of memory with some definitions. Patterns and memory values are represented as vectors. There is always an inductive bias in reducing the representation of a problem to a set of feature vectors. The associations which are to be stored in memory are represented as sets of vector pairs, $\{<X_1, Y_1>, <X_2, Y_2>, ..., <X_t, Y_t>\}$. For each vector $<X_i, Y_i>$ the X_i pattern is a key for retrieval of the Y_i pattern. There are three types of associative memories:

1) *Heteroassociative*: This is a mapping from X to Y such that if an arbitrary vector X is closer to X_i than any other exemplar, the associated vector Y_i is returned.

2) *Autoassociative*: This mapping is the same as the heteroassociative except that $X_i = Y_i$ for all exemplar pairs. Since every pattern X_i is related to itself, this form of memory is primarily used when a partial or degraded stimulus pattern serves to recall the full pattern.

The autoassociative and heteroassociative memories are used for retrieval of one of the original exemplars. They constitute memory in the true sense, in that the pattern that is retrieved is a literal copy of the stored pattern. We also may want to construct an output pattern that differs from the patterns stored in memory in some systematic way. This is the function of an interpolative memory.

3) *Interpolative*: This is a mapping Φ of X to Y such that when X differs from an exemplar, that is, $X = X_i + \Delta_i$, then the output of the $\Phi(X) = \Phi(X_i + \Delta_i) = Y_i + E$ where $E = \Phi(\Delta_i)$. In an interpolative mapping, if the input vector is one of the exemplars X_i the associated Y_i is retrieved. If it differs from one of the exemplars by the vector Δ then the output vector also differs by the vector difference E, where $E = \Phi(\Delta)$.

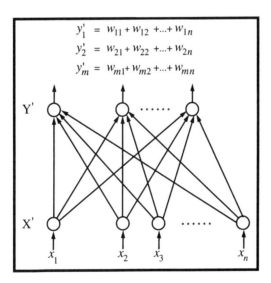

FIGURE 12.8   The linear association network. The vector X_i is entered as input and the associated vector Y' is produced as output. y'_i is a linear combination of the *x* input. In training each y'_i is supplied with its correct output signals.

The linear associator network in Figure 12.8 implements a form of interpolative memory. As shown in Section 12.2.3, it is based on the Hebbian learning model. The network weight initialization is described by the equation derived in Section 12.2.3:

$$W = Y_1 * X_1 + Y_2 * X_2 + ... + Y_t * X_t.$$

Given this weight assignment, the network will retrieve with an exact match one of the exemplars; otherwise it produces an interpolative mapping.

We next introduce some concepts and notation to help us analyze the behavior of this network. First we want to introduce a metric that allows us to define precisely distance between vectors. All our pattern vectors in the examples are *Hamming* vectors, that is vectors composed of +1 and -1 values only. We use *Hamming distance* to describe the distance between two Hamming vectors. Formally, we define a Hamming space:

$$H^n = \{X = (x_1, x_2, ..., x_n)\}, \text{ where each } x_i \, \varepsilon \, \{+1, -1\}.$$

Hamming distance is defined for any two vectors from a Hamming space as:

$\|X, Y\|$ = the number of components by which X and Y differ.

For example, the Hamming distance, in four dimensional Hamming space, between:

(1, -1, -1, 1) and (1, 1, -1, 1) is 1
(-1, -1, -1, 1) and (1, 1, 1, -1) is 4
(1, -1, 1, -1) and (1, -1, 1, -1) is 0.

We need two further definitions. First, the complement of a Hamming vector is that vector with each of its elements changed: +1 to -1 and -1 to +1. For example, the complement of (1, -1, -1, -1) is (-1, 1, 1, 1).

Second, we define the *orthonormality* of vectors. Vectors that are orthonormal are orthogonal, or perpendicular, and of unit length. Two orthonormal vectors, when multiplied together with the *dot product*, have all their cross-product terms go to zero. Thus, in an orthonormal set of vectors, when any two vectors, X_i and X_j, are multiplied the product is 0, unless they are the same vector:

$X_i X_j = \delta_{ij}$ where $d_{ij} = 1$ when $i = j$ and 0 otherwise.

We now show that the linear associator network defined above has the following two properties, with $\Phi(X)$ representing the mapping function of the network. First, for an input pattern X_i which exactly matches one of the exemplars, the network output, $\Phi(X_i)$, is Y_i, the associated exemplar. Second, for an input pattern X_k, which does not exactly match one of the exemplars, the network output, $\Phi(X_i)$, is Y_k, that is the linear interpolation of X_k. More precisely, if $X_k = X_i + \Delta_i$, where X_i is an exemplar, the network returns:

$Y_k = Y_i + E$, where $E = \Phi(\Delta_i)$.

We begin by showing that, when the network input X_i is one of the exemplars, the network returns the associated exemplar.

$\Phi(X_i) = WX_i$, by the definition of the network activation function.

Since $W = Y_1X_1 + Y_2X_2 + ... + Y_iX_i + ... + Y_nX_n$, we get:

$$\begin{aligned}\Phi(X_i) &= (Y_1X_1 + Y_2X_2 + ... + Y_iX_i + ... + Y_nX_n)X_i \\ &= Y_1X_1X_i + Y_2X_2X_i + ... + Y_iX_iX_i + ... + Y_nX_nX_i, \text{ by distributivity.}\end{aligned}$$

Since, as defined above, $X_iX_j = \delta_{ij}$:

$$\Phi(X_i) = Y_1\delta_{1i} + Y_2\delta_{2i} + ... + Y_i\delta_{ii} + ... + Y_n\delta_{ni}.$$

By the orthonormality condition, $\delta_{ij} = 1$ when $i = j$ and 0 otherwise. Thus we get:

$$\Phi(X_i) = Y_1*0 + Y_2*0 + ... + Y_i*1 + ... + Y_n*0 = Y_i.$$

It can also be shown that, for X_k not equal to any of the exemplars, the network performs an interpolative mapping. That is, for $X_k = X_i + \Delta_i$, where X_i is an exemplar,

$$\begin{aligned}\Phi(X_k) &= \Phi(X_i + \Delta_i) \\ &= Y_i + E,\end{aligned}$$

where Y_i is the vector associated with X_i and

$$E = \Phi(\Delta_i) = (Y_1X_1 + Y_2X_2 + ... + Y_nX_n)\,\Delta_i.$$

For the sake of brevity, we omit the proof.

We now give an example of linear associator processing. Figure 12.9 presents a simple linear associator network that maps a four element vector X into a three element vector Y. Since we are working in a Hamming space, the network activation function f is the *sign* function used earlier.

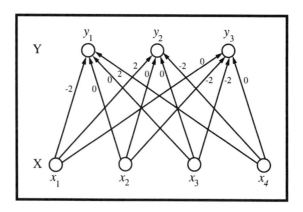

FIGURE 12.9 A linear associator network for the example in Section 12.2.4.
The weight matrix is calculated using the formula presented in the previous section:

Suppose we want to store the following two vector associations $<X_1, Y_1>$, $<X_2, Y_2>$, where:

$$X_1 = [1, -1, -1, -1] \leftrightarrow Y_1 = [-1, 1, 1],$$
$$X_2 = [-1, -1, -1, 1] \leftrightarrow Y_2 = [1, -1, 1].$$

The *outer vector product* YX is defined in general as the matrix:

$$YX = \begin{bmatrix} y_1 \bullet x_1 & y_1 \bullet x_2 & \cdots & y_1 \bullet x_m \\ y_2 \bullet x_1 & y_2 \bullet x_2 & \cdots & y_2 \bullet x_m \\ \cdots & \cdots & \cdots & \cdots \\ y_n \bullet x_1 & y_n \bullet x_2 & \cdots & y_n \bullet x_m \end{bmatrix}$$

Using the weight initialization formula for linear associators:

$$W = Y_1X_1 + Y_2X_2 + Y_3X_3 + \ldots + Y_NX_N,$$

we calculate $Y_1X_1 + Y_2X_2$, the weight matrix for the network:

$$W = \begin{bmatrix} -1 & 1 & 1 & 1 \\ 1 & -1 & -1 & -1 \\ 1 & -1 & -1 & -1 \end{bmatrix} + \begin{bmatrix} -1 & -1 & -1 & 1 \\ 1 & 1 & 1 & -1 \\ -1 & -1 & -1 & 1 \end{bmatrix} = \begin{bmatrix} -2 & 0 & 0 & 2 \\ 2 & 0 & 0 & -2 \\ 0 & -2 & -2 & 0 \end{bmatrix}$$

We now run the linear associator on one of the exemplars. We start with

X = [1, -1, -1, -1] from the first exemplar pair to get back the associated Y:

$y_1 = (-2*1) + (0*-1) + (0*-1) + (2*-1) = -4$, and sign(-4) = -1,
$y_2 = (2*1) + (0*-1) + (0*-1) + (-2*-1) = 4$, and sign(4) = 1, and
$y_3 = (0*1) + (-2*-1) + (-2*-1) + (0*-1) = 4$, and sign(4) = 1.

Thus $Y_1 = [1, 1, 1]$, the other half of the exemplar pair, is returned.

We next show an example of linear interpolation. Consider the X vector [1, -1, 1, -1]:

$y_1 = (-2*1) + (0*-1) + (0*1) + (2*-1) = -4$, and sign(-4) = -1,
$y_2 = (2*1) + (0*-1) + (0*1) + (-2*-1) = 4$, and sign(4) = 1, and
$y_3 = (0*1) + (-2*-1) + (-2*1) + (0*-1) = 0$, and sign(0) = 1.

Notice that Y = [-1, 1, 1] is not one of the original Y exemplars. Notice also that the mapping preserves the values which the two Y exemplars have in common. In fact [1, -1, 1, -1], the X vector, is Hamming distance 1 from each of the X exemplars; the output vector [-1, 1, 1] is also Hamming distance 1 from each of the Y exemplars.

We summarize with a few observations regarding linear associators. The desirable properties of the linear associator depend on the requirement that the exemplar patterns comprise an orthonormal set. This restricts its practicality in two ways. First, there may be no obvious mapping from situations in the world to orthonormal vector patterns. Second, the number of patterns which can be stored is limited by the dimensionality of the vector space. When the orthonormality requirement is violated, interference between stored patterns occurs, causing a phenomenon called *crosstalk*.

Observe also that the linear associator retrieves an associated Y exemplar only when the input vector exactly matches an X exemplar. When there is not an exact match on the input pattern, the result is an interpolative mapping. It can be argued that interpolation is not memory in the true sense. We often want to implement true memory retrieval function where an approximation to an exemplar retrieves the exact pattern associated with it. What is required is a *basin* of attraction to capture vectors in the surrounding region. In the next section we consider an *attractor* version of the linear associator.

12.3 ATTRACTOR NETWORKS OR "MEMORIES"

12.3.1 Introduction

The networks discussed to this point are *feedforward*. In feedforward networks information is presented to a set of input nodes and the signal moves forward through the nodes or layers of nodes until some result emerges. Another important class of connectionist networks are *feedback* networks. The architecture of these nets is different in that the output signal of a node can be cycled back, directly or indirectly, as input to that node.

Feedback networks differ from feedforward networks in several important ways:

   i)   the presence of feedback connections between nodes,
   ii) a time delay -- noninstantaneous signal propagation,
   iii) output of the network is the network's state upon convergence,
   iv) network usefulness depends on convergence properties.

When a feedback network reaches a time in which it no longer changes, it is said to be in a state of equilibrium. The state which a network reaches on equilibrium is considered to be the network output.

In the feedback networks of Section 12.3.2, the network state is initialized with an input pattern. The network processes this pattern, passing through a series of states until it reaches equilibrium. The network state on equilibrium is the pattern retrieved from memory. In Section 12.3.3 we consider networks that implement an heteroassociative memory, in Section 12.3.4 an autoassociative memory.

The cognitive aspects of these memories are both interesting and important. They offer us a model for content addressable memory. This type of associator can describe the retrieval of a phone number, the feeling of sadness from an old memory, or even the recognition of a person from a partial facial view. Researchers have attempted to capture many of the associative aspects of this type memory in symbol based data structures, including semantic networks, frames, and object systems, as seen in Chapter 6.

An *attractor* is defined as a state toward which states in a neighboring region evolve across time. Each attractor in a network will have a region where any network state inside that region evolves toward that attractor. That region is called its *basin*. An attractor can consist in a single network state or a series of states through which the network cycles.

Attempts to understand attractors and their basins mathematically have given rise to the notion of a network energy function (Hopfield 1985). Feedback networks with an energy function that has the property that every network transition reduces total network energy are guaranteed to converge. We describe these networks in Section 12.3.3.

Attractor networks can be used to implement content addressable memories by installing the desired patterns as attractors in memory. They can also be used to solve optimization problems, such as the traveling salesperson problem, by creating a mapping between the cost function in the optimization problem and

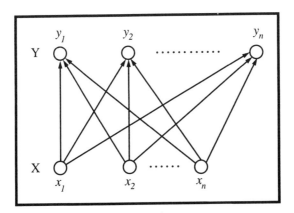

Figure 12.10   A BAM network for the examples of Section 12.3.2. Each node may also
be connected to itself.

the network energy. The solution of the problem then comes through the
reduction of total network energy. This type problem solving is done with what is
called a Hopfield network.

12.3.2   BAM, the Bidirectional Associative Memory

The BAM network, first described by Bart Kosko (1988), consists of two fully
interconnected layers of processing elements. There can also be a feedback link
connecting each node to itself. The BAM mapping of an n dimensional input vector X_n into the m dimensional output vector Y_m is presented in Figure 12.10.
Since each link from X to Y is bidirectional, there will be a weight associated
with information flow in each direction.

Like the weights of the linear associator, the weights on the BAM network
can be worked out in advance. In fact we use the same method for calculating
network weights as that used in the linear associator. The vectors for the BAM
architecture are taken from the set of Hamming vectors.

Given the N vector pairs that make up the set of exemplars we wish to store,
we build the matrix as we did in Section 12.2.4:

$$W = Y_1 * X_1 + Y_2 * X_2 + ... + Y_t * X_t.$$

This equation gives the weights on the connections from the X layer to the Y
layer, as can be seen in Figure 12.10. For example, w_{32} is the weight on the connection from the second unit on the X layer to the third unit on the Y layer. We

assume that any two nodes only have one pathway between them. Therefore, the weights connecting nodes on the X and Y layers are identical in both directions. Thus, the weight matrix from Y to X is the transpose of the weight matrix W.

The BAM network can be transformed into an autoassociative network by using the same weight initialization formula on the set of associations <X1, X1>, <X2, X2>, .. . Since the X and Y layers resulting from this procedure are identical we can eliminate the Y layer, resulting in a network which looks like Figure 12.11. We look at an example of an autoassociative network in Section 12.3.4.

The BAM network is used to retrieve patterns from memory by initializing the X layer with an input pattern. If the input pattern is a noisy or incomplete version of one of the exemplars, the BAM can often complete the pattern and retrieve the associated pattern.

To recall data with BAM, we do the following:

1. Apply an initial vector pair (X, Y) to the processing elements. X is the pattern for which we wish to retrieve an exemplar. Y is randomly initialized.
2. Propagate the information from the X layer to the Y layer and update the values at the Y layer.
3. Send the updated Y information back to the X layer, updating the X units.
4. Continue the preceding two steps until the vectors stabilize, that is until there is no further changes in the X and Y vector values.

The algorithm just presented gives BAM its feedback flow, its bidirectional movement toward equilibrium. The preceding set of instructions could have begun with a pattern at the Y level leading, upon convergence, to the selection of an X vector exemplar. It is fully bidirectional: we can take an X vector as input and can get a Y association on convergence or we can take a Y vector as input and get back a X association. We will see these issues worked through with an example in the next section.

Upon convergence, the final equilibrium state gives back one of the exemplars used to build the original weight matrix. If all goes as expected, we take a vector of known properties, either identical to or slightly different, from one of the exemplar vector pairs. We use this vector to retrieve the other vector in the exemplar pair. The distance is Hamming distance measured by component wise comparison of the vectors, counting one for each element difference. Because of the orthonormality constraints, when BAM converges for a vector, it also converges for its complement. Thus we note that the complement of the vector also becomes an attractor. We give an example of this in the next section.

There are several things that can interfere with the BAM convergence. If too many exemplars are mapped into the weight matrix, the exemplars themselves

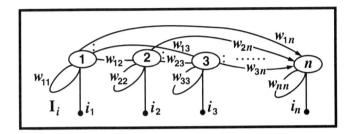

FIGURE 12.11 An autoassociative network with an input vector I_i. We assume single links between nodes with unique insights, thus $w_{ij} = w_{ji}$ and the weight matrix is symmetric.

can be too close together and produce pseudo stabilities in the network. This phenomenon is called *crosstalk,* and occurs as local minima in the network energy space.

We next consider briefly the BAM processing. The multiplication of an input vector by the weight matrix computes the sums of the pairwise vector products of the vectors for each element of the output vector. A simple thresholding function then translates the resultant vector back to a vector in the Hamming space. Thus:

net $(Y) = WX$, or for each Y_i component,
net $(Y_i) = \Sigma w_{ij}{}^* y_j$,

with similar relationships for the X layer. The thresholding function f for net at time t+1 is also straightforward:

$$f(\text{net}^{t+1}) = \begin{cases} +1 & \text{if net} > 0 \\ f(\text{net}^t) & \text{if net} = 0 \\ -1 & \text{if net} < 0 \end{cases}$$

In the next section we illustrate this *bidirectional associative memory* processing with several examples.

12.3.3 Examples of BAM Processing

Figure 12.12 presents a small BAM network, a simple variation of the linear associator presented in Section 12.2.4. This network maps a four element vector X into a three element vector Y. Suppose we want to create the following two vector pair exemplars:

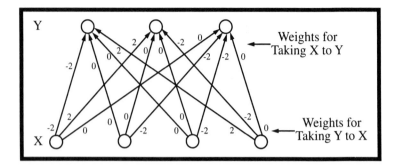

FIGURE 12.12 A BAM network for the examples of Section 12.3.3.

$x_1 = [1, -1, -1, -1] \leftrightarrow y_1 = [1, 1, 1]$, and
$x_2 = [-1, -1, -1, 1] \leftrightarrow y_2 = [1, -1, 1]$.

We now create the weight matrix according to the formula presented in the previous section

$$W = Y_1 X_1^t + Y_2 X_2^t + Y_3 X_3^t + \ldots + Y_N X_N^t$$

$$W = \begin{bmatrix} 1 & -1 & -1 & -1 \\ 1 & -1 & -1 & -1 \\ 1 & -1 & -1 & -1 \end{bmatrix} + \begin{bmatrix} -1 & -1 & -1 & 1 \\ 1 & 1 & 1 & -1 \\ -1 & -1 & -1 & 1 \end{bmatrix} = \begin{bmatrix} 0 & -2 & -2 & 0 \\ 2 & 0 & 0 & -2 \\ 0 & -2 & -2 & 0 \end{bmatrix}$$

The weight vector for the mapping from Y to X is the transpose of W, or:

$$\begin{bmatrix} 0 & 2 & 0 \\ -2 & 0 & -2 \\ -2 & 0 & -2 \\ 0 & -2 & 0 \end{bmatrix}$$

We now select several vectors and test the BAM associator. Let's start with an exemplar pair, choosing the X component and seeing if we get the Y. Let $X = [1, -1, -1, -1]$:

$Y_1 = (0*1) + (-2*-1) + (-2*-1) + (-1*0) = 4$, and $f(4) = 1$,
$Y_2 = (1*2) + (-1*0) + (-1*0) + (-1*-2) = 4$, and $f(4) = 1$, and
$Y_3 = (1*0) + (-1*-2) + (-1*-2) + (-1*0) = 4$, and $f(4) = 1$.

Thus the other half of the exemplar pair is returned. The reader can make this Y vector an input vector and verify that that the original X vector [1, -1, -1, -1] is returned.

For our next example, consider the X vector [1, 1, 1, -1], with Y randomly initialized. We map X with our BAM network:

$$Y_1 = (1*0) + (1*-2) + (1*-2) + (-1*0) = -4,$$
$$Y_2 = (1*2) + (-1*0) + (1*0) + (-1*-2) = 4,$$
$$Y_3 = (1*0) + (-1*-2) + (1*-2) + (-1*0) = -4.$$

This result, with the thresholding function applied to [-4, 4, -4], is [-1, 1, -1]. Mapping back to X gives:

$$X_1 = (-1*0) + (1*2) + (-1* 0) = 2,$$
$$X_2 = (-1*-2) + (1*0) + (-1*-2) = 4,$$
$$X_3 = (-1*-2) + (1*0) + (-1*-2) = 4,$$
$$X_4 = (-1*0) + (1*-2) + (-1*0) = -2.$$

The threshold function applied, again as above, gives the original vector [1, 1, 1, -1]. Since the starting vector produced a stable result with its first translation, we might think we have just discovered another prototype exemplar pair. In fact, the example we selected is the complement of the original $<X_2, Y_2>$ vector exemplar! It turns out that in a BAM network, when a vector pair is established as an exemplar prototype, so is its complement. Therefore, our BAM network includes two more prototypes:

$$X_3 = [-1, 1, 1, 1] \leftrightarrow Y_3 = [-1, -1, -1], \text{ and}$$
$$X_4 = [1, 1, 1, -1] \leftrightarrow Y_4 = [-1, 1, -1].$$

Let us next select a vector near an X exemplar, [1, -1, 1, -1]. Note that the Hamming distance from the closest of the four X exemplars is 1. We can randomly initialize Y to [-1, -1, -1]:

$$Y_1^{T+1} = (1*0) + (-1*-2) + (1*-2) + (-1*0) = 0,$$
$$Y_2^{T+1} = (1*2) + (-1*0) + (1*0) + (-1*-2) = 4,$$
$$Y_3^{T+1} = (1*0) + (-1*-2) + (1*-2) + (-1*0) = 0.$$

The evaluation of the net function $f(Y_i^{t+1}) = f(Y_i^t)$ when $y_i^{t+1} = 0$, from the threshold equation at the end of Section 12.2. Thus, Y is [-1, 1, -1] due to the random initialization of the first and third parameters of the Y^T to -1. We now take Y back to X:

$$X_1 = (-1*0) + (1*2) + (-1* 0) = 2,$$
$$X_2 = (-1*-2) + (1*0) + (-1*-2) = 4,$$
$$X_3 = (-1*-2) + (1*0) + (-1*-2) = 4,$$
$$X_4 = (-1*0) + (1*-2) + (-1*0) = -2.$$

The threshold function maps this result to the vector X = [1, 1, 1, -1]. We repeat the process taking this vector back to Y:

$$Y_1 = (1*0) + (1*-2) + (1*-2) + (-1*0) = -4,$$
$$Y_2 = (1*2) + (-1*0) + (1*0) + (-1*-2) = 4,$$
$$Y_3 = (1*0) + (-1*-2) + (1*-2) + (-1*0) = -4.$$

The threshold function applied to [-4, 4, -4] again gives Y = [-1, 1, -1]. This vector is identical to the most recent version of Y, so the network is stable. This demonstrates that after two passes through the BAM net, a pattern that was close to X_4 converged to the stored exemplar. This would be similar to recognizing a face or other stored image with part of the information missing or obscured. The Hamming distance of the original X vector [1, -1, 1, -1] from the X_4 prototype [1, 1, 1, -1] was 1. The vector settled into the $<X_4, Y_4>$ exemplar pair. Other examples of this convergence property can be explored by the reader.

In our BAM examples we started processing with the X element of the exemplar pair. Of course, we could have designed the examples from the Y vector, initializing X when necessary.

Hecht-Nielsen (1990, p. 82) presents an interesting analysis of the BAM network. He demonstrates that the orthonormal property for the linear associator network support for BAM is too restrictive. He gives an argument showing that the requirement for building the network is that the vectors be linearly independent, that is, that no vector can be created from a linear combination of other vectors in the space of exemplars.

12.3.4   Autoassociative Memory and Hopfield Nets

The research of John Hopfield, a physicist at California Institute of Technology, is a major reason connectionist architectures have their current credibility. He studied network convergence properties, using the concept of energy minimization. He also designed a family of networks based on these principles. As a physicist, Hopfield understood stabilities of physical phenomena as energy minimization points of the physical system. An example of this approach is the simulated annealing analysis of the cooling of metals.

Let us first review the basic characteristics of feedback associative networks. These networks begin with an initial state consisting of the input vector. The network then processes this signal through feedback pathways until it reaches a stable state. To use this architecture as an associative memory we would like the network to have two properties. First, starting from any initial state we would like a guarantee that the network will converge on some stable state. Second, we would like this stable state to be the one closest to the input state by some distance metric.

We look first at an autoassociative network built on the same principles as the BAM network. We noted in the previous section that BAM networks can be transformed into autoassociative networks by using identical vectors in the X and Y positions. The result of this transformation, as we see next, is a symmetric square weight matrix. Figure 12.11 of Section 12.3.2 offered an example.

The weight matrix for the autoassociative network that stores a set of vector exemplars $\{X_1, X_2, ..., X_n\}$ is created by:

$$W = \Sigma X_i X_i^t \qquad \text{for } i = 1, 2, ..., n.$$

When we create the autoassociative memory from the heteroassociative, the weight from node x_i to x_j will be identical to that from x_j to x_i and so the weight matrix will be symmetric. This assumption only requires that the two processing elements be connected by one path having a single weight. We may also have the special case, again with neural plausibility, that no network node is directly linked to itself, that is, there are no x_i - x_i links. In this situation the main diagonal of the weight matrix, w_{ij} where $i = j$, will be all zeros.

As with BAM, we work out the weight matrix based on the patterns to be stored in memory. We clarify this with a simple example. Consider the three vector exemplar set:

$X_1 = [1, -1, 1, -1, 1]$,
$X_2 = [-1, 1, 1, -1, -1]$,
$X_3 = [1, 1, -1, 1, 1]$.

We next calculate the weight matrix using $W = \Sigma X_i X_i^t$ for i= 1, 2, 3:

$$W = \begin{bmatrix} 1 & -1 & 1 & -1 & 1 \\ -1 & 1 & -1 & 1 & -1 \\ 1 & -1 & 1 & -1 & 1 \\ -1 & 1 & -1 & 1 & -1 \\ 1 & -1 & 1 & -1 & 1 \end{bmatrix} + \begin{bmatrix} 1 & -1 & -1 & 1 & 1 \\ -1 & 1 & 1 & -1 & -1 \\ -1 & 1 & 1 & -1 & -1 \\ 1 & -1 & -1 & 1 & 1 \\ 1 & -1 & -1 & 1 & 1 \end{bmatrix} + \begin{bmatrix} 1 & 1 & -1 & 1 & 1 \\ 1 & 1 & -1 & 1 & 1 \\ -1 & -1 & 1 & -1 & -1 \\ 1 & 1 & -1 & 1 & 1 \\ 1 & 1 & -1 & 1 & 1 \end{bmatrix}$$

$$W = \begin{bmatrix} 3 & -1 & -1 & 1 & 3 \\ -1 & 3 & -1 & 1 & -1 \\ -1 & -1 & 3 & -3 & -1 \\ 1 & 1 & -3 & 3 & 1 \\ 3 & -1 & -1 & 1 & 3 \end{bmatrix}$$

We use the thresholding function:

$$f(\mathrm{net}^{l+1}) = \begin{cases} +1 & \text{if net} > 0 \\ f(\mathrm{net}^l) & \text{if net} = 0 \\ -1 & \text{if net} < 0 \end{cases}$$

We first test the network with an exemplar, $X_3 = [1, 1, -1, 1, 1]$, and obtain:

$$X_3 * W = [7, 3, -1, 9, 7],$$

and with the threshold function, $[1, 1, -1, 1, 1]$. We see this vector stabilizes immediately on itself. This illustrates that the exemplars are themselves stable states or attractors.

We next test a vector which is Hamming distance 1 from the exemplar X_3. The network should return that exemplar. This is equivalent to retrieving a memory pattern from partially degraded data. We select $X = [1, 1, 1, 1, 1]$:

$$X * W = [5, 1, -3, 3, 5].$$

Using the threshold function gives the X_3 vector $[1, 1, -1, 1, 1]$.

We next take a third example, this time a vector whose Hamming distance is 2 away from its nearest prototype, let $X = [1, -1, -1, 1, -1]$. It can be checked that this vector is 2 away from X_3, 3 away from X_1, and 4 away from X_2. We begin:

$$X * W = [3, -1, 1, 5, 3], \text{ which with threshold yields } [1, -1, 1, 1, 1].$$

This doesn't seem to resemble anything, nor is it a stability point, since:

$$[1, -1, 1, 1, 1] * W = [7, -3, -1, 1, 7], \text{ which is } [1, -1, -1, 1, 1].$$

We still do not have one of the prototypes. We check again for stability:

$$[1, -1, -1, 1, 1] * W = [9, -3, -1, 3, 9], \text{ which is } [1, -1, -1, 1, 1].$$

The net is now stable, but not with one of the original stored memories! Have we found another energy minimum? On closer inspection we note that this new vector is the complement of the original X_2 exemplar $[-1, 1, 1, -1, -1]$. Again, as in the case of the heteroassociative BAM network, our autoassociative network creates attractors for the original exemplars as well as for their complements, in this case, six attractors in all.

To this point in our presentation, we have looked at autoassociative networks based on a linear associator model of memory. One of John Hopfield's goals was to give a more general theory of autoassociative networks which would apply to any single layer feedback network meeting a certain set of simple restrictions.

For this class of single layer feedback networks Hopfield proved that there would always exist a network energy function guaranteeing convergence.

A further Hopfield goal was to replace the discrete time updating model used previously with one that more closely resembles the continuous time processing of actual neurons. A common way to simulate continuous time asynchronous updating in Hopfield networks is to update nodes individually rather than as a layer. This is done using a random selection procedure for picking the next node to be updated, while also applying some method for ensuring that on average all the nodes in the network will be updated equally often.

The structure of a Hopfield network is identical to that of the autoassociative network above: a single layer of nodes completely connected (see Figure 12.11). The activation and thresholding also work as before. For node i,

$$x_i^{\text{new}} = \begin{cases} +1 & \text{if} \sum w_{ij} x_j^{\text{old}} > T_i, \\ x_i^{\text{old}} & \text{if} \sum w_{ij} x_j^{\text{old}} = T_i, \\ -1 & \text{if} \sum w_{ij} x_j^{\text{old}} < T_i, \end{cases}$$

Given this architecture, only one further restriction is required to characterize a Hopfield net. If w_{ij} is the weight on the connection into node i from node j, we define a Hopfield network as one which respects the weight restrictions:

$$w_{ii} = 0 \qquad \text{for all i,}$$
$$w_{ij} = w_{ji} \qquad \text{for all i, j.}$$

The Hopfield network does not typically have a learning method associated with it. Like the BAM, its weights are usually calculated in advance.

The behavior of Hopfield networks is now better understood than any other class of networks except perceptrons. This is because its behavior can be characterized in terms of a concise energy function discovered by Hopfield:

$$H(X) = -\sum_i \sum_j w_{ij} x_i x_j + 2 \sum_i T_i x_i$$

We will now show that this energy function has the property that every network transition reduces the total network energy. Given the fact that H has a predetermined minimum and that each time H decreases it decreases by at least a fixed minimum amount, we can infer that from any state the network converges.

We first show that for an arbitrary processing element k which is the most recently updated, k changes state if and only if H decreases. The change in energy ΔH is:

$$\Delta H = H(X^{\text{new}}) - H(X^{\text{old}}).$$

Expanding this equation using the definition of H, we get:

$$\Delta H = -\sum_i \sum_j w_{ij} x_i^{new} x_j^{new} + 2\sum_i T_i x_i^{new} + \sum_i \sum_j w_{ij} x_i^{old} x_j^{old} + 2\sum_i T_i x_i^{old}$$

Since only x_k has changed, $'x_i^{new} = {'x_i^{old}}$ for i not equal to k. This means that the terms of the sum that do not contain x_k cancel each other out. Rearranging and collecting terms we get:

$$= -2x_k^{new}\sum_j w_{kj} x_j^{new} + 2T_k x_k^{new} + 2x_k^{old}\sum_j w_{kj} x_j^{old} - 2T_k x_k^{old}.$$

Using the fact that $w_{ii} = 0$ and $w_{ij} = w_{ji}$ we can finally rewrite this as:

$$\Delta H = 2\,(x_k^{old} - x_k^{new})\left[\sum_j w_{kj} x_j^{old} - T_k\right].$$

To show that ΔH is negative we consider two cases. First, suppose x_k has changed from -1 to +1. Then the term in square brackets must have been positive to make $'x_k^{new}$ be +1. Since $'x_k^{old} - {'x_k^{new}}$ is equal to -2, ΔH must be negative. Suppose that x_k has changed from 1 to -1. By the same line of reasoning, ΔH must again be negative. If x_k has not changed state, $'x_k^{old} - {'x_k^{new}} = 0$ and $\Delta H = 0$.

Given this result, from any starting state the network must converge. Furthermore, the state of the network on convergence must be a local energy minimum. If it were not then there would exist a transition that would further reduce the total network energy and the update selection algorithm would eventually choose that node for updating.

We have now shown that Hopfield networks have one of the two properties which we want in a network that implements associative memory. It can be shown, however, that Hopfield networks do not, in general, have the second desired property: they do not always converge on the stable state nearest to the initial state. There is no general known method for fixing this problem.

Hopfield networks can also be applied to the solution of optimization problems, such as the travelling salesperson problem. To do this the designer needs to find a way to map the cost function of the problem to the Hopfield energy function. By moving to an energy minimum the network will then also be minimizing the cost with respect to a given problem state. Although such a mapping has been found for some interesting problems, including the travelling salesperson problem, in general, this mapping is very difficult to discover.

In this section we introduced heteroassociative and autoassociative feedback networks. We analyzed the dynamical properties of these networks and presented very simple examples showing evolution of these systems toward their attractors. We showed how the linear associator network could be modified into an attractor network called the BAM. In our discussion of continuous time Hopfield networks, we saw how network behavior could be described in terms of an energy function. The class of Hopfield networks have guaranteed convergence because every network transition can be shown to reduce total network energy.

There still remains some problems with the energy based approach to connectionist networks. First, the energy state reached need not be a global minimum of the system. Second, Hopfield networks need not converge to the attractor nearest to the input vector. This makes them unsuitable for implementing content addressable memories. Third, in using Hopfield nets for optimization, there is no general method for creating a mapping of constraints into the Hopfield energy function. Finally, there is a limit to the total number of energy minima that can be stored and retrieved from a network, and even more importantly, this number cannot be set precisely. Empirical testing of these networks shows that the number of attractors is a small fraction of the number of nodes in the net. These and other topics are ongoing issues for research (Hecht-Nielsen 1990, Zurada 1992, Freeman & Skapura 1991).

12.4 EVOLUTION AND BIOLOGY BASED LEARNING

12.4.1 Introduction

Just as connectionist networks received much of their early support and excitement from the goal of creating an artificial neuronal system, so also a number of other analogies have entered into the creation of learning algorithms. A different metaphor, evolution shaped by the survival of the fittest, supports work in learning based on cellular automata and genetic algorithms.

Cellular automata may be viewed as finite state machines, complete with sets of states and transition rules. We require that the automata be able to accept information from outside themselves, in particular, from their close neighbors. The transition rules include instructions for birth, continuing in life, and dying. When a population of such automata is set loose in a domain and are allowed to act as parallel asynchronous cooperating agents, we sometimes witness the evolution of seemingly independent "life forms." The state rules for creation and support of life are a function of the state of the machine as well as those of the machines in close proximity. From the interactions of multiple autonomous agents, life forms seem to emerge!

This type of adaptive interaction leading to survival can be seen as learning and can be found in video games such as *The Game of Life*. It may also be found in the cooperation and interactions of other finite state machines. Rodney Brooks (1986) has designed cooperative agents in the form of simple robots whose evolution and support is seen as that of autonomous agents interacting in a laboratory situation. There is no central control algorithm; rather cooperation emerges as an artifact of their distributed and autonomous interactions.

Genetic algorithms (Holland 1986, Holland et al. 1986) are another approach to learning that exploits parallelism, mutual interactions, and a bit-level representation. Like neural networks, genetic algorithms are based on a biological metaphor: they view learning as a competition among a population of evolving, alternative concepts. A genetic algorithm maintains a population of candidate problem solutions. Based on their performance, the fittest of these solutions not only survive, but, through an analogy with sexual reproduction, exchange information with other candidates to form new potential solutions.

12.4.2   The Genetic Algorithm

Let P(t) define a population of candidate solutions at time t:

$$P(t) = \{x_1^t, x_2^t, \ldots x_n^t\}$$

The genetic algorithm is defined:

```
procedure genetic algorithm;
    begin
        t:= 0;
        initialize P(t);
        while termination condition not met do
        begin
            evaluate P(t);
            select pairs of solutions according to the quality of
                their evaluation;
            produce the offspring of these pairs using genetic operators;
            replace the weakest candidates with the offspring;
            t := t+1;
        end
    end.
```

For example, suppose we want a genetic algorithm to learn to classify strings of 1s and 0s. We can represent a class of bit strings as a pattern of 1s, 0s, and #s, where # may match with either 0 or 1. For example, the pattern 1##00##1 represents all strings of eight bits that begin and end with 1 and have two 0s in the middle. We first discussed this representation, along with its strengths and weaknesses, in Section 12.4.1. The algorithm initializes P(0) to a population of candidate patterns. Typically, initial populations are selected randomly. Evaluation of candidate solutions assumes a fitness function, $\text{'f}\langle \text{'x}_i^t\rangle$ that returns a measure of the candidate's fitness at time t. A common measure of a candidate's fitness is to test each candidate on a set of training instances and return the percentage of correct classifications. Using such a fitness function, an evaluation assigns each candidate solution the value:

$$f\,(x_i^t)\,/m\,(P,\,t)$$

where m(P,t) is the average fitness over all members of the population.

After evaluating each candidate, the algorithm selects pairs for recombination. Recombination uses *genetic operators* to produce new solutions that combine components of their parents. As with natural evolution, the fitness of a candidate determines the extent to which it reproduces, with those candidates having the highest evaluations being given a greater probability of reproducing. Note that selection is probabilistic; weaker candidates are given a smaller likelihood of reproducing, but are not eliminated outright. This is important since a seemingly bad candidate may still include some essential component of a solution and reproduction may extract this component.

There are a number of genetic operators that produce offspring having features of their parents; the most common of these is *crossover*. Crossover takes two candidate solutions and divides them, swapping components to produce two new candidates. Figure 12.13 illustrates crossover on bit string patterns of length 8. The operator splits them in the middle and forms two children whose initial segment comes from one parent and whose tail comes from the other.

For example, suppose the target class is the set of all strings beginning and ending with a 1. Both the parent strings in Figure 12.13 would have performed relatively well on this task. However, the first offspring would be much better than either parent: it would not have any false positives and would fail to recognize fewer strings that were actually in the class. Note also that its sibling is worse than either parent and will probably be eliminated over the next few generations.

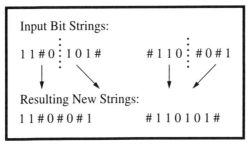

Figure 12.13   The crossover operator on two bit strings of length eight. # indicates "don't care."

Mutation is another important genetic operator. Mutation takes a single candidate and randomly changes some aspect of it. In our example, mutation may randomly select an element of a pattern and change it, switching a 1 to a 0 or #, and so forth. Mutation is important in that the initial population may exclude an essential component of a solution. In our example, if no member of the initial population has a 1 in the first position, then crossover alone will not produce any solution that does. The genetic algorithm continues until some termination requirement is met, such as having one or more candidate solutions whose fitness exceeds some threshold.

12.4.3   Evaluating the Genetic Algorithm

The power of genetic algorithms is in the parallel nature of their search. Genetic algorithms implement a powerful form of hill climbing that maintains multiple solutions, eliminates unpromising solutions, and improves good solutions. Figure 12.14, adapted from Holland (1986), shows multiple solutions converging toward optimal points in a search space. In this figure, the horizontal axis represents the possible points in a solution space, while the vertical axis measures the quality of those solutions. The dots on the curve are members of the genetic algorithm's current population of candidate solutions. Initially, the solutions are randomly scattered through the space of possible solutions. After several generations, they tend to cluster around areas of high solution quality.

Note that genetic algorithms, unlike sequential forms of hill climbing, do not immediately discard unpromising solutions. Through genetic operators, even weak solutions may continue to contribute to the makeup of future candidate solutions.

Another source of the algorithm's power is the *implicit parallelism* inherent in the evolutionary metaphor. By restricting the reproduction of weak candidates, genetic algorithms not only eliminate that solution, but all of its descendants. This tends to make the algorithm likely to converge toward high quality solutions in a few generations. For example, the string, 101#0##1, if broken at its midpoint, can parent a whole family of strings of the form 101#____. If the parent string is found to be unfit, its elimination also eliminates all of these potential descendants.

The genetic operators used are important to the success of this search. All genetic algorithms require some form of crossover, as this allows the creation of new solutions that have, by virtue of their parent's success, a high probability of exhibiting good performance. In practice, crossover is the most important of the genetic operators, while mutation is used much less frequently. Although crossover attempts to preserve the beneficial aspects of candidate solutions and eliminate undesirable components, the random nature of mutation is probably more

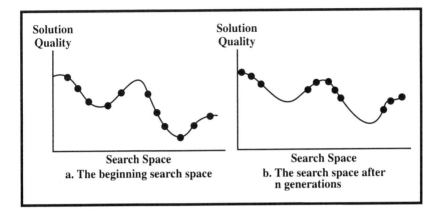

Figure 12.14 Genetic algorithms visualized as parallel hill climbing. Adapted from Holland (1986).

likely to degrade a strong candidate solution than it is to improve it.

By representing solutions as bit strings, we may apply crossover with a great deal of flexibility. This flexibility is important, giving genetic algorithms many of the advantages of other subsymbolic approaches. An important issue in genetic algorithm research is the extension of this methodology to different representations (Koza 1991).

This problem has been approached in a number of ways. One is to define analogues of crossover that may apply to higher level representations such as rules. However, it is difficult to define such operators that honor the syntactic constraints of logic. Alternatively, we may translate the logical rules into bit strings and use the standard crossover operator. Here the problem is that under many approaches to translation, most bit strings do not correspond to meaningful logical sentences. Perhaps the most promising way of applying genetic algorithms is to avoid the issues of logical representation altogether, finding ways of translating problems into bit strings or similar representations.

Research is continuing on this and other problems. Holland, for example, has developed a problem solving architecture called *classifier systems* that implements genetic learning in the context of a parallel production system (Holland 1986). Classifier systems increase the expressiveness of the representation by allowing multiple step problem solving processes.

The classifier program operates on three levels: The lowest level, the performance system, does classification with a set of if then rules much like those described in a production system (see Chapters 3 and 9). The condition part of the classification rule considers patterns in a message list of bit strings. When the conditions of the rule are met the action component alters the bit string and places it back on the message list. To this point we have a system much like the genetic algorithms just described. However, there is an added "strength" measure attached to each production rule.

The two levels higher in the classifier system are responsible for changes in the strength measure of the if then classification rules. The immediately higher level uses a credit assignment algorithm, much like that employed in backpropagation (Section 11.3). This algorithm is used to adjust the production rule's strength measure according to its success in producing useful bit strings for the message list. This reward is propagated back, again giving smaller reward increments to those rules that adjusted the bit string for its later successful match. Finally, on the top level is another genetic algorithm that produces new production rules. This is necessary because the original set of production rules may not be able to produce the full range of "interesting" bit strings. From the dynamical systems perspective it is interesting to examine the sets of classifiers that emerge and how they effect the performance of the system.

12.5   FURTHER ISSUES IN MACHINE MODELS OF LEARNING: A SUMMARY OF PART III

In Part III we have presented a broad overview of automated learning models. It is broad because we wanted to touch on many issues in this interesting and dynamic area. It is not deep because, in the context of our book, it simply couldn't be. There are a number of excellent books available now, many mentioned in Section 12.6 Epilogue and References, that can take the reader deeper into any of the domains we have introduced.

The examples we use to introduce various learning models often contain only a few nodes or one partial layer simulation. This is appropriate in that the main learning laws can be adequately explained in the context of single neurons or partial layers. It can be very misleading in that neural net applications are usually considerably larger and the problem of scale IS important. For example, for backpropagation learning, a large number of training examples with larger networks is generally required to solve problems of any significant practical interest. Many researchers comment extensively on the matter of selecting appropriate numbers of input values, the ratio between input parameters and hidden nodes, and the training trials necessary before convergence can be expected (Hecht-Nielsen 1990, Zurada 1992, Freeman & Skapura 1991). In fact, other than acknowledging that these are difficult, important, and often open issues, this type of "engineering" discussion is beyond the scope of our book.

There is now a very large literature and experience that can make entry into this exciting area easier. But be aware: the engineering tasks are important, and sometimes very difficult. In fact, in designing applications we have found that up

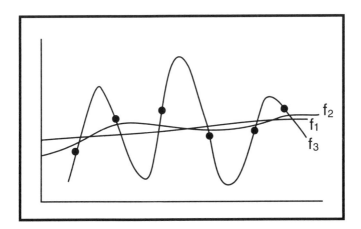

FIGURE 12.15 A set of data points and three function approximations.

to 85% of development time is spent working out the appropriate net architecture for an application and in cleaning up data sets so that networks are not "distracted" by bad data. This data cleanup issue is important because connectionist architectures, without any built-in knowledge of a domain, can be totally misled attempting to find patterns in noisy or bad data.

Let us illustrate the importance of these issues with an example using backpropagation to induce a general function from a set of data points. Figure 12.15 might represent a set of data points we are asking our algorithm to generalize across. The lines across this set of points represent functions induced by training our network. Remember that once the net is trained we want to offer new data points and have the trained network offer a good generalization for this data also.

The induced function f_1 might represent a fairly accurate least mean squares fit. With further training the system might produce f_2, which seems a fairly "good" fit to the set of data points; but still, f_2 does not exactly capture the data points. Further training can produce functions that exactly fit the data but offer terrible generalizations for further data! This phenomena is referred to as *over training* a network. One of the strengths of backpropagation learning is that in many application domains it is known to produce effective generalizations, that is, functional approximations which fit the training data well *and also* handle new data correctly. However, identifying the point where a network passes from an undertrained to an overtrained state is nontrivial. It is naive to think that one can present a neural network with raw data and then simply step aside and watch while it produces effective generalizations.

As we have intimated throughout our presentation, many aspects of network behavior are still not well understood. For instance, the limitations of perceptron networks led to the introduction of hidden nodes. We may well ask what contribution the hidden nodes make in solution generation. One way of understanding what hidden nodes do is to add dimensions to the representation space. As a simple example of this, we saw in Section 11.3.3 that the data points for the ex-or problem were not linearly separable in two dimensions. The learned weight on the hidden node, however, provides another dimension to the representation. In three-space the points are separable using a two dimensional plane. Given the two dimensions of the input space and the hidden node, the output layer of this network can then be seen as an ordinary perceptron, finding the plane which separates the points in three dimensions.

There are also a number of interesting interarchitectural relationships in automated learning. We pointed many of these out: the relationship between clustering with CLUSTER/2 in Section 10.5, the perceptron in Section 11.2, and prototype networks in Section 12.1. We noted that counterpropagation, the coupled network that uses unsupervised competitive learning on a Kohonen layer together with supervised Hebbian learning on a Grossberg layer, is in many ways similar to backpropagation learning. In counterpropagation, clustered data on the Kohonen layer play a role similar to the generalizations learned by the hidden nodes of backpropagation.

In many important ways the tools we presented are similar. In fact, even the discovery of prototypes representing clusters of data offers the complementary case to function approximation. In the first situation we are attempting to classify sets of data; in the second we are generating functions that explicitly divide data clusters from each other. We saw this when the minimum distance classification algorithm used by the perceptron also gave the parameters defining the linear separation.

Even the generalizations that produce functions can be seen from many different viewpoints. Statistical techniques have for a long time been able to discover data correlations. Iterative expansion of Taylor series can be used to approximate most functions. Polynomial approximation algorithms have been used for over a century to approximate functions from data points.

There can be great excitement in creating networks based on exemplars or energy minimization. These can be seen as fixed-point attractors or basins for complex relational invariances. We watch as data points "settle" toward these attractors and are tempted to see these new architectures as tools for modeling dynamic phenomena. These dreams can be as naive as those of the medieval alchemist trying to transmute lead into gold or the modern economists attempting to predict the future of markets.

In fact, researchers have shown (Siegelman & Sontag 1991) that recurrent networks are computationally complete, that is, equivalent to the class of Turing Machines presented in Chapter 2. This extends earlier results. Kolmogorov (1957) showed that for any continuous function there exists a neural network that computes that function. It has also been shown that a one hidden layer backprop-agation network can approximate any of a more restricted class of continuous functions (Hecht-Nielsen 1989). Thus connectionist networks appear to be but one more class of algorithms capable of computing virtually any computable function.

So what is it that the connectionist learning architectures in their various forms offer us?

1.   One of the most attractive features of connectionist learning is that most models are data or example driven. They are not explicitly programmed as are the symbol based learning architectures. They learn by example, generalizing from data in a particular problem domain.

2.   They may be viewed as instances of parallel asynchronous processing. They provide us with concrete examples of results achievable through parallel processing that we do not yet know to achieve through explicit sequential programming.

3.   Even though the neural inspiration is not important to many modern practitioners of connectionist learning, these networks do reflect many important aspects of human neural physiology. We saw several instances of this, including the error reduction learning in perceptron and backpropagation, Hebbian learning models, and the autoassociative Hopfield nets in Section 12.3.4.

4.   As we saw in Chapter 3, the expressiveness of a representational scheme was by far its most important feature. Thus for connectionist networks we need to ask how effective they are in capturing invari-ances. Connection networks are clearly effective in recognizing patterns in perceptual data, such as visual or auditory stimuli. They also show promise in recognizing predictive patterns in data where explicit rules may be hard to formulate, for example, in identifying faults in complex systems.

5.   Finally, all representational schemes are tools for empirical enquiry. After we capture the invariants of our world in a representation, we can then begin to ask further questions related to the nature of perception, understanding, and problem solving.

We end Part III by pointing out several limitations of our current generation of computational tools in cognitive science. They do not yet offer us a methodol-ogy for:

1. Addressing inductive bias. That is, they give us a medium for encoding an already interpreted world. They do not offer us mechanisms for questioning our interpretations or for backtracking and changing them when they are unsuccessful.

2. Building a unified theory of cognition. Allen Newell (1990) points out that the mutual constraints of a full cognitive architecture are essential for creating realistic models of cognition. He proposes that such models contain (at least) perception, problem solving, memory, and learning components. The constraints imposed by these interacting modules assist in understanding the full range of intelligent powers.

3. Modeling human performance. Many current symbol based and connectionist architectures arise out of model-free attempts to simulate aspects of human performance. In fact neural modeling of human performance is even more unconstrained than that of most symbolic approaches (McCloskey 1991).

4. Following from the previous point, there has been little integration of semantic or pragmatic constraints into learning models. In contrast, human learning is generally both knowledge driven and goal oriented.

5. Finally, the current state of our computational learning models still fails to provide productivity, systematicity, and compositionality. Without productivity, systematicity, and compositionality, our models will fail to capture the creativity and subtlety of human cognition.

We address many of these issues again in Chapter 17.

12.6   EPILOGUE AND REFERENCES

Along with understanding human language skills (Part IV) learning is probably the most difficult challenge for cognitive scientists. In Part III we laid out the parameters and approaches researchers are taking to this most important task. We presented an explicit symbol based approach, a connectionist approach, and several architectures in the middle. We remind our readers of references at the end of Chapters 10 and 11.

The two volumes of *Parallel Distributed Processing* (Rumelhart et al. 1986) give an excellent presentation of neural networks both as computational and as cognitive tools. *Neural Networks and Natural Intelligence* (Grossberg 1988) is another thorough treatment of the subject. Genetic algorithms are discussed by Michalski (1986), as well as by John Holland (1986, Holland et al. 1986), and Stephanie Forrest (1993).

Many of the original connectionist network architecture designers are still actively working in the field and we refer the reader directly to their publications. These include John Anderson et al. (1977, 1989), Stephan Grossberg (1976, 1988), Geoffrey Hinton and Terrance Sejnowski (1986), Robert Hecht-Nielsen (1989, 1990), John Hopfield (1982, 1984), Tuevo Kohonen (1972, 1984), Bart Kosko (1988), and Carver Mead (1989).

We have chosen not to address many important mathematical as well as computational aspects of connectionist architectures. For a modern overview of these issues we especially recommend Robert Hecht-Nielsen (1990), Jacek Zurada (1992), and James Freeman and David Skapura (1991).

LIMITATIONS OF TECHNOLOGY

Part IV

LANGUAGE

The ability to produce and understand language is arguably the greatest achievement of humans. Without language, we would not have a means to pass on knowledge across generations; would not be able to represent future and past actions to other members of the species; and, quite conceivably, would not have been able to form the complex social structures that we now have. The study of language, and its relation to cognition, must therefore be a central focus within the discipline of cognitive science.

We are concerned with the contributions of two important groups of cognitive scientists: those who study the properties of languages in general, *linguists*, and those who study the representation, processing, and acquisition of language, *psycholinguists*. While it has traditionally been the case that linguistics was concerned with theoretical descriptions of language and psycholinguistics with experimental tests of linguistic theory, the distinction between the disciplines is becoming fuzzier as the fields increase their collaboration.

The great challenge for psycholinguistics is to explain how speakers formulate thoughts into words which listeners can then comprehend almost as soon as they are uttered. When we consider that humans typically play both roles in a conversation, the complexity of language processing is even more impressive. Listeners and speakers both have an incredible task of simultaneously coordinating a vast number of cognitively significant units. These units are hierarchically arranged such that on their own they have little significance, but when combined with others they take on meaning. Thus individual speech sounds, or *phonemes*, convey little or no meaning independently, but when changed can completely alter the meaning of a word. For example, consider the sound "s," written as $/s/$, which on its own has no meaning. When the first sound of the word "mad" is changed to $/s/$, however, the meaning changes completely ("sad").

Speech perception is not a simple matter of recognizing a series of invariant sounds and combining them to make words. Each sound is affected by its environment and will be produced differently depending on the preceding or following sound. Word boundaries are not obvious in speech, in contrast to writing, but instead their determination often requires knowledge of permissible sound sequences, or *phonological* rules, in the language as well as the recognition of the preceding words (Cole & Jakimik 1980).

Thus the same sequence of sounds can support two different interpretations, depending on the context and knowledge available to the listener. If this were not the case, how could we explain the listener who heard "I hope you never have enough air" when the speaker said "I hope you never have an affair." (Say them to yourself and you will realize that there is really no difference in the sound of these two utterances, although there is a world of difference in their meanings!) You can imagine the speaker's surprise on hearing in reply "Why not? Why don't you want me to breathe?" This reply still does not solve the problem as its metaphorical interpretation fits with the intended meaning. With two very different contexts in mind, the two participants in this conversation arrived at two very different interpretations of the utterance. The location of the word boundaries was thus not given by the speech stream, but was instead a product of the perceiver's mind. [Cole and Jakimik (1980) offer a discussion of similar evidence from experimental studies].

Even if one ignores difficulties imposed by the medium, there is still an amazing amount of cognitive activity that must take place during production and comprehension. The importance of cognitive processes in perception is not restricted to the spoken modality, however, as you will realize when considering reading or the understanding of signed languages. For example, the speaker must not only select the correct *lexical* items, or words, to express her thought, but must arrange these thoughts into strings of words that follow the *syntax*, or rules for arranging words into acceptable sequences in the language.

Utterances should also be produced with an *intonation contour* that is appropriate to the sentence type, such as a question or statement and that, at least for English, marks the important and/or new elements (Halliday 1967, Prince 1981a). The individual sentences must do more than merely make sense locally but must also fit with the ongoing topic of the discourse (Clark & Haviland 1977, Grice 1975) and obey linguistic and cultural conventions for structuring conversation (Schegloff 1968).

The listener's task is equally complex. She must comprehend the utterance almost as soon as it is produced or else run the risk of being left hopelessly behind. Much psycholinguistic research has centered on the immediate processing of linguistic input, addressing such questions as what is the nature of the perceptual unit (Garrett et al. 1966), how short is the lag between perception and comprehension (Marslen-Wilson & Welsh 1978), how is context used during lexical access (Swinney 1979), and what is the role of syntax in sentence processing (Garrett 1990)? Because of the speeded nature of the task, there is considerable evidence that listeners engage in *top-down* or *expectation driven* processing during sentence comprehension (Dell & Newman 1980, Marslen-Wilson & Tyler 1987, Tyler & Marslen-Wilson 1977). However, a number of researchers argue that the components of language are modular (Fodor 1983, Forster 1990) and therefore do not affect one another during processing.

The classic problem facing the listener, as well as the psycholinguist who hopes to build a theory of language processing, is that of *productivity*, which is probably the most important feature of human language. Productivity, first introduced as a constraint on representational models of intelligence in Section 3.1, means that each human language is essentially an open-ended system in which speakers can combine words into a potentially infinite number of novel utterances. Most of what we hear, except perhaps idioms and other formulaic phrases such as "How are you?" are utterances that the listener will not have heard before and that the speaker may never utter again. Listeners therefore have to be equally productive in their comprehension and cannot simply rely on a pattern-matching strategy for decoding the input directed to them.

Once the sounds have been identified, the listener's task is not finished. The word may have more than one meaning; which one was intended must be determined from the context (Swinney 1979, but see Tabossi 1988). If the listener is incorrect in her interpretation, then time will be lost as retracing occurs. The grammatical structure itself may be ambiguous or complex and also requires additional processing (Rayner et al. 1983). The speaker must also attend to the *intonation contour* and *prosodic* aspects, the rhythm and timing, of the utterance in order to determine the information focus, or what the speaker intends to mark as most important (Cutler 1976, Bock & Mazzella 1983, Newman 1985).

Even after the words have been decoded, the syntax parsed, and the intonation contour noted, the listener may still arrive at the wrong interpretation if she ignores the *pragmatics* of the situation. Suppose one parent of an infant says to the other, "Nina needs changing." The second parent *could* thank the first parent for the useful piece of information just conveyed to her, but at her peril. One doesn't need much experience with infants and dirty diapers to realize that what was stated was a request, however indirect, that the listener take the necessary action to remedy the situation.

Thus the utterance meaning does not always equal the speaker's meaning; this observation is a critical component of speech act theory (Austin 1962, Searle 1969) and is crucial for our understanding of language comprehension in context. Consider too the fact that conventions as to how to convey speaker's meaning vary across cultures; the requirements for "communicative competence" (Hymes 1971) among the Subanun in the Philippines are quite different from those in North America, where one must be aware of the four stages of discourse involved in asking for a drink during a "drinking encounter." Knowing how to produce a grammatical utterance of content equivalent to an English request will not work. Frake notes that "it may elicit praise for one's fluency in Subanun, but it will not get you a drink" (Frake 1964, pg. 260). More generally, speaking appropriately requires knowledge of what to say, how to say it, to which people, and in which situations.

Chapter 13, *Language Representation and Processing*, is concerned with the cognitive representation and processing required in order to produce and comprehend language. Chapter 14, *Pragmatics and Discourse*, addresses the pragmatic and sociolinguistic aspects of language in use. Our goal is to introduce major issues and approaches in linguistics, psycholinguistics, and sociolinguistics. Readers interested in greater detail are referred to the in-text references and to the epilogue at the end of each chapter.

Chapter 13

LANGUAGE REPRESENTATION AND PROCESSING

From a psychological point of view, the sentence is both a simultaneous and a sequential structure. It is simultaneous because at each moment it is present in consciousness as a totality even though individual subordinate elements may occasionally disappear from it. It is sequential because the configuration changes from moment to moment in its cognitive condition as individual constituents move into the focus of attention and out again one after another..

Wilhelm Wundt (1912)

"When I use a word," Humpty Dumpty said in a rather scornful tone, "It means just what I choose it to mean--neither more nor less."

Lewis Carroll, *Alice through the Looking Glass*

13.0   INTRODUCTION

Scholars from many disciplines are concerned with the study of language but differ in their approaches and the questions they address. For example, anthropologists are interested in the interaction of language and culture, asking such questions as does language affect or reflect the way in which members of the culture see the world? (Berlin & Kay 1969, Rosch 1973, Whorf 1956). Their primary research methods are descriptive in nature, involving ethnographic research in a field setting rather than laboratory studies.

Research on language can also be found in schools of education, where there are interests in language development, the relation between language and thought, the development of literacy, second language learning and testing, and increasingly, in bilingual education. The techniques used cover the continuum from observational studies in the classroom to experimental studies in the laboratory.

The study of language can also be found in fields that specialize in a particular language, as for example in departments of English, where English grammar is often taught and where there is also considerable interest in applying linguistic theory to literary criticism (see, for example, Pratt 1977). Philosophers, too, have long been interested in the relation between language and mind and research on the logic of conversation (Grice 1975). Pragmatics, and speech act theory (Austin 1962, Searle 1969), has had a large impact on the study of language in context. As might be expected, the approach taken by philosophers is formal and analytic rather than empirical or experimental in nature.

An understanding of language is also central to the work of therapists and clinicians working with unusual populations such as aphasics. The field that studies the relationship between brain and language, known as *neurolinguistics*, has a long and highly respected tradition dating back to the last century. With the advent of new technology that allows us to observe brain functions in real time such as MRI and PET (Section 5.4), it is now possible to get a closer look at the brain/language relation (Damasio & Damasio 1992). The interpretation of such data, however, is still controversial as it is not clear whether there is a one-to-one correspondence between location and function in a network with the complexity of the human brain (see Section 5.3 for more detailed analysis of this point).

Computer scientists, primarily researchers in artificial intelligence, are also concerned with natural language understanding (Allen 1987, Grosz & Sidner 1990). Their goal is usually to build a system that can comprehend, that is respond or act appropriately to the linguistic input, but not necessarily to model the human's processing of the same input. Thus the techniques are very similar in spirit to those of the formal linguists, being rather deductive. Increasingly, however, AI research has been influenced by research in psycholinguistics, discourse analysis, and sociolinguistics (Sidner 1983).

Without question, however, the two most influential disciplines that study human language are linguistics and psycholinguistics. In the next section we introduce and contrast these two approaches. In Section 13.2 we consider the origins and most important features of human languages. In Section 13.3 we present the levels of analysis we use in the study of language. We present pragmatics and the analysis of discourse in Chapter 14.

13.1 GOALS AND CRITERIA FOR EXPLANATION

13.1.1 Linguistics

The goal of linguistics is to provide an account of human language. The primary emphasis is on language as an interrelated system which is described in terms of the different levels that comprise it. Linguists, by and large, do not emphasize "performance," that is how an individual speaker might produce or comprehend their language. Instead their efforts are directed toward providing an explanation of the workings of language as a whole, as it would be used by an idealized native speaker. For many theoretical linguists the goal is to discover a set of rules that generate all possible utterances in a language but that would not also generate any impossible or "ungrammatical" utterances.

As in other fields, there is a difference in focus and approach between theoreticians and empiricists. Linguists who are in the more formal disciplines of syntax, semantics, morphology, and phonology use deductive and introspective approaches, the direct and indirect methods of Chapter 4, in the study of linguistic phenomena. They often rely on their own knowledge as native speakers of a language. On the other hand, many, particularly sociolinguists, have a descriptive focus, collecting data in field settings much like anthropologists, and using techniques of data collection and analysis similar to sociologists and psychologists. In addition, linguists are relying increasingly on sophisticated analytical and statistical tools to analyze large bodies of data collected from the grammars of many different languages in order to discover *universals* or properties that are common to many languages (Bybee et al. 1994, Comrie 1989, Croft 1990). These empirically determined universals are then used as the basis for new ideas about the structure and evolution of human language, complementing introspection and deduction as the primary tools for linguistic analysis.

13.1.2   Psycholinguistics

The field of language study that is most central to cognitive science is psycholinguistics. As the name implies, this field was formed as a combination of cognitive psychology and linguistics. While its ancestry can be traced to Wundt, one of the founding fathers of experimental psychology (Blumenthal 1980), most psycholinguists claim the origin to be in the early 1950s. This "hybrid" discipline was reputedly created at an interdisciplinary conference in 1951 of "three psychologists and three linguists" (Brown 1970, pg. vii; Tanenhaus 1988) sponsored by the Social Science Research Council. The term itself has analogies in other disciplines concerned with language, such as sociolinguistics and neurolinguistics, and implies an equal partnership between both fields.

A fundamental distinction between linguistics and psycholinguistics is that the former is concerned with describing and accounting for regularities in the tacit knowledge of language possessed by each native speaker. This tacit knowledge is termed *competence* and is typically described as representing the knowledge of an ideal speaker. Psycholinguists are interested in describing how this knowledge is represented but are also concerned with describing language processing, that is, how linguistic knowledge is accessed and used during comprehension and production. In order to do this, they must rely on overt linguistic behavior, or what a linguist would term *performance*. Psycholinguists are not able to look directly at mental processes but must make inferences about representation and processing based on patterns of responses to overt tasks, such as timed responses to sentences and words. Although it is becoming easier to look at brain functions in normal individuals, for various philosophical reasons it is inappropriate to equate mind and brain (see Chapter 2). Thus psycholinguists continue to use performance data to make inferences about underlying processes and types of representation.

Psycholinguistics in its formative years was primarily concerned with testing the then dominant linguistic theory of transformational grammar (Chomsky 1957, 1965). This emphasis included both adult studies of comprehension and studies of language development. One important issue studied by psycholinguists of this period was the "psychological reality" of transformational grammar. A typical question might be: Does it take longer to understand a sentence with two transformations, such as a negative question, than it does to understand a sentence with one transformation, such as an affirmative question (Mehler 1963, Miller & McKean 1964)? The goal of child language research in this period was to demonstrate, following the theoretical orientation of transformational grammar, that language is innate and develops in a consistent order across children, regardless, within reasonable limits, of the input conditions.

Thus psycholinguistics in its early period can be seen as a testing ground for linguistic theories rather than as a source of theories about language. The primary unit of experimentation in this era, as in linguistic theory, was the sentence, and the primary focus of research was syntax (both comprehension and acquisition). That focus has broadened, as we shall see, such that psycholinguists now propose and test their own theories of language representation and processing. The research questions are still constrained by the knowledge about, and analyses of, language contributed by linguists. The study of human language is approached from a number of different, but interrelated, levels of analysis. Each of these levels of linguistic analysis and theorizing have their counterparts in psycholinguistic theory and research.

In the remainder of this chapter we shall look both at the different levels of language that have traditionally been studied by linguists and at representative examples of psycholinguistic approaches to processes implied by each of the levels. Our examination of psycholinguistics will focus on four levels of language and corresponding research questions in psycholinguistics. The levels that we shall address are: *sound* (phonetics and phonology), *meaning* (morphology and semantics), *syntax* (the arrangement of words into acceptable sentences), and, in the next chapter, *pragmatics* (language in context). Chapter 14 also discusses issues in *sociolinguistics* (social aspects of language use). We do not discuss the fascinating and important topic of language acquisition in other than a cursory fashion. See Pinker (1994) for one view of this field.

13.2 THE ORIGINS OF HUMAN LANGUAGES

Linguists and psycholinguists are unsure about the actual origins of human language--after all no one was around with a tape recorder to record the first human utterance. There are, however, a number of interesting speculations that merit consideration. Philip Lieberman (1984) has proposed that early humans needed to evolve the necessary vocal apparatus, primarily the lengthening of a cavity known as the *pharynx*, above the larynx, before they were capable of uttering the full range of speech sounds that we now use. Lieberman claims the lack of this apparatus contributed to the demise of some early hominids, in particular Neanderthals, who "specialized for chewing" rather than for speech (pg. 276). Others suggest that language may have a gestural origin, much as deaf children of hearing parents (who do not use a signed language) have been shown to spontaneously generate *home signs* (Goldin-Meadow 1982).

One controversial proposal, advocated by Derek Bickerton (1990), is that language appeared in humans abruptly after the development of *protolanguage* which can also be observed in the early stages of child language. Bickerton draws his research from the formation of *Creoles* as evidence for his position (Bickerton 1983). These languages are found primarily in the tropics where speakers of two different languages came into contact as a result of trade or slavery during colonial times. The adults in these language groups spoke a *pidgin*, which has very reduced syntax and vocabulary, to speakers of other languages but retained their first languages. Children raised in this linguistic environment received a pidgin as their input but produced a Creole, which none of the adults used. The resulting Creoles are full-blown languages, not reduced like the pidgins, and could only have come from the children themselves. Not all linguists agree with Bickerton's theory concerning the evolution of Creoles; fewer still with his view on protolanguage (see, for example, Pinker 1992), but it is a thought-provoking idea nonetheless.

Although speculations about the origins of human language are very interesting, they are ultimately controversial and unresolvable. There is agreement, however, on the common features of human languages that set them apart from other communication systems. The best-known list of such features is Hockett's (1960). We summarize the four most important features: *semanticity, arbitrariness, displacement,* and *productivity.*

The first important feature of human languages is that they convey meaning or, in other terms, possess *semanticity.* This feature seems trivial when you first consider it because we take it for granted, but it is crucial. Hockett pointed out that many other species perform actions that communicate information but these are by-products of some other acts. Hockett's example is that of a dog panting; the action is performed as a way to cool off, but it often conveys to the owner the information that the dog is hot. Humans, in contrast, use a specialized system to convey meaning, it has no other function than to communicate. Human language is not a by-product of some other activity but is an end in itself.

Furthermore, the sounds (or, in the case of signed languages, the gestures) that we use to convey these meanings are arbitrarily related to the ideas that we are trying to convey. When we, as English speakers, choose to refer to a very young human as a "baby," there is no sense in which the string of sounds, or phonemes, chosen could possibly tell us what is intended. You simply have to know the meaning of the word; if we all agreed, we could, with no loss of meaning, suddenly decide to refer to the same entity as a "pig" (with apologies to Lewis Carroll). This feature, known as *arbitrariness*, has significant implications for theories of cognition as it means that humans must master an enormously complex symbol system in order to use their language.

Efforts to investigate the capacity of other species to acquire language have also stressed the importance of manipulating semanticity and arbitrariness in order to ensure that the animal under study is not merely decoding the meaning by reading the cues in the situation. Some investigators, such the Rumbaughs (Savage-Rumbaugh et al. 1980), have invented artificial languages with representational systems that are totally arbitrary in order to study the capacity of apes to acquire language. Without the property of arbitrariness, critics could argue that apes are merely memorizing the relation between a form and the outcome, if for example, they were taught to associate a plastic shape that looks like a banana with the piece of fruit itself. Even with the insurance of using an arbitrary symbol system, there is great disagreement as to whether apes are able to use language, primarily because they do not appear to exhibit evidence for *displacement* and *productivity*, the next properties of language that we shall discuss [see de Luce and Wilder (1983), especially the article by Terrace; see Savage-Rumbaugh et al. (1993); and Wallman (1992) for further discussion of these issues].

Although most aspects of the form-referent relation are arbitrary, not all are. There are some ways in which words in a language can be *iconic*, that is, resemble the things that they stand for. *Onomatopoeia* is a classic example; these are words whose sounds resemble their referents or a sound that the referent makes. Some well-known examples in English are "cuckoo," "buzz," and "meow." All of these words are transparent in meaning and are therefore not arbitrarily related to their referents. This class of words is very small, however.

There are also other more subtle ways in which a language can be iconic. One linguistic device that has been proposed is *phonetic symbolism* in which the phonemes used in the word provide some analogy to the concept being expressed; compare the vowels in "tiny" and "huge," for example. It appears that the choice of sounds used in both phonetic symbolism and onomatopoeia are language-specific, however, as the sounds made by dogs in Japan and the United States are probably the same, but are represented differently in their respective languages: "wang-wang" and "bow-wow" (Taylor 1990).

Many people who are unfamiliar with the signed languages of the deaf mistakenly believe that these languages are transparent, like pantomime, or at least largely iconic. This would imply that a monolingual English speaker could understand a conversation between two people signing *American Sign Language* (ASL) merely through observation. Nothing could be further from the truth. Signed languages are as complex as spoken languages and are described with equivalent linguistic categories and levels (Stokoe 1978). The relation between form and meaning is as arbitrary in signed languages as it is in spoken languages. If the relation was nonarbitrary then signers of ASL would be able to understand signers of *British Sign Language* (BSL), but they cannot. ASL and BSL are different languages for historical reasons, and despite their common medium are mutually unintelligible (Deuchar 1984, Chap. 6).

It should be quite obvious that there is another reason that human languages need to have the feature of arbitrariness. Many of the ideas we express are abstract or without a concrete, physical, referent. It is hard to know, for example, how one might pick a sound that instantly conveys the meaning of the word "intelligence." Once a language learner progresses beyond the first 100 or so words of early childhood which refer to objects and events in the immediate environment (toy, food, dirty, etc.; Nelson 1973), it becomes necessary to learn the meanings of new concepts through previously acquired words. The child's understanding of semanticity and arbitrariness is related to the realization that words are not properties of objects but are labels for them. These two features are crucial not only for the acquisition of more complex linguistic skills but also for the acquisition of more advanced knowledge. There is evidence (Bialystok 1991, Diaz & Klingler 1991) that bilingual children develop *metalinguistic awareness*, that is, the insight that language is an arbitrary symbolic system, earlier than monolingual children because they have learned early in life that one referent can be referred to in two very different ways.

As we noted above, a very useful result of the invention of human languages is that we as a species can pass on our accumulated wisdom and mistakes to later generations. Part of our knowledge, of course, is language itself. Thus language is *culturally transmitted*. Over time, languages change as the result of many different pressures and influences. Some change results from contact with other languages and other speakers, either through conquest or trade, as in the "borrowing" of Spanish terms into English, for example, rodeo, canyon, etc. Other reasons for change are linguistic innovations introduced by younger speakers (see the discussion of Creoles, above).

Diachronic changes, changes over time, influence the state of a language at any given point. For example, over time lexical items can become "grammaticalized" and lose their independent identity. One such case is the use of the contraction "gonna" in informal English (Bybee 1985, pg. 138). *Gonna* has lost its original meaning, derived from "going to," as physical movement toward a goal but instead has become a future tense marker, as in "I'm gonna read that book next week." One can see from this diachronic evidence that the minds of many speakers across the ages come to determine the form of a language. It is therefore useless, despite many protestations to the contrary by self-appointed guardians of linguistic "purity," to resist the force of linguistic change by holding fast to obsolete forms and meanings. A language that is static is a language, that, if it isn't already dead, is rapidly losing speakers!

The ability to convey information across time is, as we've seen, a critical cultural benefit of the development of human language. Just as important, on the individual level, is the ability to convey information about events occurring at different points in time. The feature of *displacement* means that we can talk about events that are removed in time and/or space. We can describe what we did upon awakening in the morning, what we plan to do upon returning home, and, especially in academic circles, describe ideas and events that are hypothetical and may never occur.

The capacity to make use of displacement does not appear in early child language. Most early language is about the "here and now" and adults tailor the input directed to young children in recognition of this fact (Ferguson 1977, Snow 1977). When, for instance, was the last time you discussed the possible outcomes of an election campaign with a 3 year old? or for that matter, discussed your plans for next weekend? Studies of language in other species consistently fail to show strong evidence of displacement. Most of the ape language studies demonstrate credible language use with respect to events and objects in the current environment but only anecdotal evidence of references to past or future events.

Finally, and most importantly, human languages are, as we noted above, *productive*. This feature means that speakers use their language to produce novel utterances that have never been said before. Theoretical linguists claim that the number of possible acceptable utterances in a language is infinite and therefore language must be described by a rule-based system. Since one couldn't possibly have stored all the possible utterances of a language without having heard them, so the argument goes, native speakers must have a grammar consisting of a finite set of rules that can generate all possible utterances and, equally importantly, fails to produce unacceptable utterances.

The fact of productivity was used by Noam Chomsky (1959) as the main argument against the operant learning theory model proposed by B.F. Skinner in his book *Verbal Behavior* (1957). Language could not be learned, Chomsky said, through simple S-R connections and principles of learning such as generalization. The fact that novel utterances can be produced, and understood, suggests to many people, including Chomsky, that language is special, unique to humans, and, contrary to the position taken in this book, separate from other cognitive processes (see Pinker 1994).

The human ability to generate novel utterances is also what confounds current computer models of speech recognition. It is not enough to match a pattern of sounds as one can never predict what sounds the human is going to produce! The most successful systems to date are those which are restricted to a limited domain such as commands for word processing or making travel arrangements. Language comprehension is much more than simply looking up sounds and their referents in memory--it is an immensely complex problem-solving task that must be performed almost instantaneously. The comprehender makes use of every available scrap of information, including, as we will see in the next chapter, features of the setting and knowledge of the speaker and his or her social relationship to the listener.

13.3 LEVELS OF ANALYSIS IN LANGUAGE

13.3.1 Sound: Phonetics and Phonology

The logical place to start the study of human language is to examine the properties of the medium and the input. For most of us, the primary experience with language is in the spoken form. Although literate individuals spend considerable time with the written word, most of the time we use speech. Deaf individuals, however, use signed languages, and these differ between countries. Interestingly, signed languages have been shown to have basic organizing principles that mirror those of spoken languages (Stokoe 1978), without the acoustic properties of course. The similarities in organization between language in two such distinct modalities argue strongly for the universality of the levels of analysis used by linguists.

We can analyze the stimulus itself from two perspectives: production and perception. The study of speech sounds is known as *phonetics*, and is concerned with descriptions of the physical properties of the stimulus and the apparatus used to produce (articulatory phonetics) and perceive (acoustic phonetics) them. Phoneticians describe regularities in the production of sounds and study the involvement of the different articulators, the tongue, lip, palate, etc., in making those sounds. Acoustic phonetics analyzes the properties of the sounds themselves by examining the waveforms of speech. In its focus and techniques it shares much with the study of acoustics in physics. (We will use [ ] notation to indicate phonetic transcriptions.)

Phonology is the field of linguistics concerned with describing the rules used to combine sounds into permissible sequences in a language. For example, while the consonant sequence [mg] is certainly physically possible for English speakers to produce, it is not a possible word initial string in English. Thus when we hear the sequence of sounds [aymb] we know that there must be a word boundary between [m] and [b] as in "I'm bored." (The English pronoun "I" is actually a combination of two sounds known as a *dipthong*.)

Our knowledge of the *phonological* rules of English can help us segment spoken input. Often, though, a sequence of sounds can be ambiguous as to segmentation as in [ayme] which could support either "I'm a" or "I may" as possible segmentations. The only way to resolve the ambiguity is to (a) consult the preceding context or, if that proves to be uninformative, (b) decode more of the subsequent input. Sometimes, though, we choose one interpretation only to discover that it is incorrect and are then forced to reprocess what we thought had already been decoded. This process of changing interpretations is referred to in the literature as "garden-pathing," because the listener has been led astray down the garden path!

The basic unit for the study of phonology is the *phoneme*. Phonemes are abstract entities that are realized by physical sounds, or *phones*, in the language. Different notation is used to distinguish the abstract phonemes (e.g., /p/) from phones (e.g., [p]), which represent the sounds themselves. Linguists discover the inventory of phonemes in a language by constructing *minimal pairs*, which are pairs of words in which all of the sounds are identical except for one sound in one position. For example, the words "pin" and "bin" are identical except for the initial sound. Changing the [p] in *pin* to a [b], however, completely changes the meaning of the word, allowing us to infer the existence of the two phonemes, /p/ and /b/, in English. Thus phonemes are defined by their effects on the meaning of a sequence of sounds.

A given phoneme can be realized in more than one way, depending on the surrounding phonetic environment. For example, /p/ is typically said with aspiration (a release of air) in the word "pin" but without aspiration in the word "spin." Hold your hand two inches from your mouth as you say the two words and you will feel the difference in air flow. The two variants of /p/ are referred to as *allophones*, meaning that they represent the same, abstract, phoneme but are two, different, phones ([pʰ] and [p], respectively). English speakers hearing these two sounds will treat them as instances of the same phoneme. Thus we do not distinguish a meaning difference between the sequences [pɪt] and [pʰɪt], hearing them both as instances of the word "pit," although the second, aspirated, version is the way most speakers would produce the word.

Interestingly, the sounds [p] and [b] are articulated in exactly the same way except that the onset of *voicing*--referring to the point at which the vocal cords start vibrating relative to the release of the sound--is earlier in the case of [b] than in the case of [p]). This slight change in *voice onset time* (VOT) has a large effect on the English speaker's decoding of the intended word. Thus, once again, small differences in sound can result in differences in meaning.

Differences that are not *phonemic* in one language, such as our example of aspiration in English, may be phonemic in another. Although aspiration contrasts do not change the meaning of English words, they do affect the meaning of words in Urdu, a language spoken in Pakistan and northern India. For example, the following two sequences constitute a minimal pair in Urdu because of aspiration on the initial sound /pʰəl/ (fruit) vs. /pəl/ (moment). /ə/ is an unstressed vowel, such as the first vowel in the English word "above." The range of possible human speech sounds is thus assigned to different meanings, depending on the language being used. The existence of this incredible flexibility points, once again, to the central role of cognition in the production and processing of human language. Clearly the relationship between the acoustic input and its eventual comprehension is a complex one and must be affected by higher-level cognitive processes. We explore some of the processes involved in speech perception in the next section.

13.3.2   Speech Perception

In order to determine how humans decode and understand sound waves, we turn to the field of speech perception. This highly technical discipline has produced a wealth of data in the past few decades. In discussing research on speech perception we concentrate on two major findings as illustrative of the theoretical debates and research in the field.

Many researchers in speech perception have long been interested in the issue of what and how much variation humans attend to when perceiving speech. A basic finding, termed *categorical perception*, indicates that we ignore variation among the different allophones of a phoneme provided they occur within a particular range (Liberman et al. 1957). Thus, we can ignore differences in the VOT for English [b]s provided they occur within the range of VOT that we, as English speakers, define as /b/. Once the VOT crosses the (implicit) category boundary into the range for English /p/, about +30 msec VOT, then English speakers will label the sound as /p/.

Interestingly, it is not the absolute discrepancy in VOT that is relevant. We can discriminate two sounds that are separated by 20-msec steps when they come from opposite sides of the category boundary, a +20-msec [b] and a +40-msec [p], for example. We cannot, however, discriminate two speech sounds, also separated by 20 msec, if they are from the same side of the boundary, one [b] at +0 msec and another [b] at +20 msec, for example. The phenomenon of categorical perception has been found for many other phonemes and for dimensions other than voicing (e.g., place of articulation) and other languages (Eimas 1985). Categorical perception does not appear to apply to vowels (Fry et al. 1962) which are continuous sounds. This finding, plus research on hemispheric differences in speech perception, suggests that different mechanisms may be required for vowel perception (Shankweiler & Studdert-Kennedy 1967).

Much of the research on speech perception has centered on whether humans are able to process speech in a way that is different from other acoustic input, a question for which the phenomenon of categorical perception is clearly important. The debate has often been summed up by the question "Is speech special?" The answer, for many researchers, appears to be yes. They point to evidence that infants can make discriminations between phonemes shortly after birth.

This ability to discriminate appears to apply to phonemic distinctions in any language in the first few months of life, but then is restricted to phonemic contrasts within the language that the child hears in the linguistic environment. For example, young English-learning children can discriminate between Hindi phonemes up to the age of 8 months or so, but after 10 months, the ability to discriminate phonemic contrasts in a language that they are not being exposed to disappears. Conversely, Hindi-learning children can make those same discriminations at the age of 11 months, although presumably at that age they also could not discriminate phonemes in a language they were not being exposed to, such as English (Eimas 1985). These results suggest that humans are equipped to perceive phonemic contrasts in any language, while ignoring differences in speech sounds that have no linguistic significance but rapidly lose their overall sensitivity as they are exposed to, and acquire, one language.

The finding of categorical perception suggests that we impose some stage of processing on speech sounds that allows us to ignore irrelevant variation and focus on the meaningful elements of the signal. Thus it appears that speech is an acoustic signal that is treated specially. However, the finding of categorical perception in another species, chinchillas (Kuhl & Miller 1978), who presumably have no biological predisposition to perceive human speech, undermines the logical argument that categorical perception shows that humans are unique in having processing systems devoted solely to perceiving speech.

Perhaps we do have specialized systems that perceive speech differently from other acoustic input, but that does not necessarily imply that we are the only species that is capable of perceiving human speech. Nor is speech the only means of linguistic interaction. Must we claim, by analogy, that because of the existence of signed languages, that humans are born with specialized visual perceptual systems that are designed only to perceive contrasts in signed languages? If so, this capacity goes unused by the vast majority of the population! Furthermore, the existence of specialized systems to decode the sounds of human speech does not imply that language is isolated from other cognitive functions, as we shall see when we look at speech understanding.

13.3.3 Top-Down Effects in Speech Understanding

Our understanding of the processes involved in decoding spoken input changes when we look beyond the recognition of individual phonemes to the comprehension of words in connected speech. The human comprehender is faced with a number of problems that are unique to speech, and not found in written discourse (Cole & Jakimik 1980). For example, it is a logical precondition that the listener must be able to recognize where words begin and end in order to then access their meanings in the mental lexicon. With printed words, the boundaries are clear--they are those white spaces on the page that allow us to segment the stream of letters into words. Although one might naively assume that pausing serves the same function in speech, this is not the case. Pauses of any significant length occur infrequently and usually for planning purposes (Boomer 1965). Segmentation also requires the application of phonological rules, as we saw in the "I'm/ I may" vs. "I'm bored" example (Section 13.3.1) and the use of context, as we shall see in Section 13.3.4.

Consider the example, in the Introduction to Part IV, "I hope you never have an affair," produced in casual conversation. As you recall, the listener perceived the original utterance as "I hope you never have enough air." The speech stream supports both interpretations; it is only with the appropriate context, which apparently existed in the speaker's, but not the listener's, mind that the intended segmentation could be made. The listener heard the word boundary as occurring after the [f] so that the result was "enough air" rather than "an affair." (Don't be fooled by the spelling; English orthography is notoriously unreliable, as is obvious when one realizes that there are only 26 letters to represent 24 consonants, 13 vowels, and 3 dipthongs. Furthermore, the specific inventory of vowels and dipthongs varies across dialects of English!)

Additional complications arise when we consider that phonemes are not invariant--which means that the same intended phoneme can be produced in more than one way, because of the influence of surrounding speech sounds. These *coarticulation* effects, while predictable, result in the need to recognize many more sounds than the 40 mentioned above. Each phoneme must be recognized in the context of other sounds, with the result that a simple template matching procedure will not work for connected speech. Some psycholinguistically inclined researchers in speech perception have argued that we must incorporate top-down or contextual, knowledge-driven processing in models of the perception of connected speech (Morton & Long 1976, Warren 1970) rather than the bottom-up, or stimulus, data-driven processing advocated by those who study isolated phonemes and syllables (Liberman & Mattingly 1985). The position we advocate is that speech understanding is probably interactive (Cole & Jakimik 1980, Dell & Newman 1980), relying on both processes. Bottom-up processing is particularly useful in the absence of context, as with isolated phonemes and syllables and at the beginning of an utterance, but in the presence of strong contextual constraints, as is typically found in connected discourse, top-down processing helps constrain the possible interpretations of the input.

Finally, and perhaps obviously but not trivially, speech is temporary and the signal fades rapidly. Unlike the written form, the medium does not afford a look back at the actual stimulus in cases of difficulty, but rather listeners must rely on memory. There is evidence to suggest that there is a greater advantage for the most recent input in auditory, rather than in visual, short term memory (Crowder 1972). This may be a means of compensating for differences in the permanence of the two types of input.

In addition, there are some linguistic differences that may largely be consequences of the modality differences. For example, spontaneous English speech allows for some "marked" word orders such as topicalization as in "Bagels, I really enjoy" that would not be found in written discourse (Prince 1981b). Constructions such as these show that the "information flow" in an utterance reflects the thought processes of the speaker (Chafe 1979). In turn, the listener's comprehension of an utterance is directed by the order, and manner, in which information is presented or "staged" (MacWhinney 1977). Unfortunately most psycholinguistic research makes use of written materials, which have been shown in studies comparing spoken and written discourse to have rather different properties, particularly with respect to the ordering and density of information. There is still much left to be learned about the processing of language in the most frequently used modality (Chafe & Danielewicz 1987).

13.3.4   Meaning: Morphology and Semantics

Perhaps the most intuitively appealing area of psycholinguistic research is the study of meaning. Most speakers assume that the purpose of language is to convey meaning and that words are the means for doing so. Philosophers and linguists have long been interested in *semantics*, which is the field concerned with meaning. Semantics is a broad term that can encompass a large range of topics that refer to the sense, or meaning, of language. It includes both *denotative* meaning, which is the thing, event, or thought being referred to by the word or sentence, and *connotative* meaning which refers to the emotional and subjective effect that is conveyed by the word or sentence.

Theories of semantics are typically concerned with denotative rather than connotative meaning because the latter is a property of individuals rather than the language. Most semantic theories are concerned with *lexical* semantics, or the relationship between meanings in the lexicon. (The lexicon is the inventory of words in a language.) In addition, one can study semantics at the sentence level. The goal for sentence semantics is to describe the meaning relations expressed in the entire sentence by studying the relationships between its words.

Linguists also study the structure of words, which is known as *morphology*. The study of morphology gives psycholinguists important insights into the representation of word meanings and is used to formulate hypotheses about *lexical access* or how we find the meanings of words in our "mental" lexicon. We start our discussion of meaning with an examination of morphology, as it is logically prior to lexical and sentence semantics.

Units of Meaning: Morphology

The goal of morphology is to describe the structure of words: the elements of words, their meanings, and the relationships of those elements to each other. In order to study the elements of words, linguists posit the existence of theoretical units known as *morphemes*. Like phonemes, morphemes are abstract units that are realized overtly in words. Morphemes are the smallest units of meaning. For example, linguists posit the existence of a plural morpheme, which is realized in English through a number of different *allomorphs*. (The reader should notice the parallel to the phoneme/allophone distinction.)

Thus we can indicate the plural of a word by adding different allomorphs: $/s/$, as in *cat + plural → cats*; $/z/$, as in *dog + plural → dogs*; or $/\partial z/$, as in *house + plural → houses*. Notice that in all cases the written forms add the letter "s," but the spoken forms use different phonemes. In addition, there are irregular forms, which are also allomorphs of the plural, as in *mouse + plural → mice*, where the plural is realized as an internal change in the stem. Finally, a very few cases where the plural is formed by using the "zero" allomorph as in *sheep + plural → sheep.*

In our last example we posit the existence of a morpheme to explain why "sheep" can be used in plural contexts even though its realization is "zero." Thus we can describe a child who says "Mummy I see a black sheep and a white sheep. I see two sheeps" as *overregularizing* the plural form "add $/s/$" to inappropriate contexts. The child clearly understands that a plural morpheme is needed, but does not yet have control over the various forms that the morpheme takes.

It should be clear from this discussion that morphemes are not equal to syllables. Our example word *cat* is one syllable in length and consists of one morpheme. However, the word *cats*, which is also one syllable long, consists, as we have seen, of two morphemes. The plural morph in *cats* is clearly a different kind of morpheme than the word to which it was attached. A morpheme which can stand on its own is referred to as a *free* morpheme. Morphemes which must be attached to other morphemes to have any meaning are known as *bound* morphemes. Note that $/s/$ by itself is meaningless and cannot be used as a word. One class of morphemes that should come readily to mind is the set known as *inflections*. These bound morphemes indicate grammatical role, and include, for English, the plural markers discussed above, markers of tenses such as progressive +*ing* and past +*ed*, possessives such as John's, and comparatives such as small*er*, small*est*. In English the inflections are all *suffixes* since they appear after the stem. In other languages they may be *prefixes*, before the stem, or even *infixes*, occurring in the middle of words.

The second major class of bound morphemes is particularly interesting to psycholinguists interested in lexical access and representation. These are the set of *derivational* morphemes which can be used to produce new words. These morphemes are very productive and are used to expand the vocabulary of a language. They also can occur as prefixes, suffixes, or infixes, although the latter are very rare in English, occurring in expressions such as "absobloominglutely." Derivational morphemes can turn nouns into adjectives, such as *truth* into *truthful*, verbs into nouns, such as *sing* into *singer*, *develop* into *development*, and adjectives into adverbs, *slow* into *slowly*. They can be combined with other derivational morphemes to express ever more complex ideas, such as, *truthful*, *untruthful*, and *untruthfully*. There are clearly tacit rules governing the possible combinations of morphemes, as there are for phonology, which is a closely related field. These tacit rules help explain why *unslowly* sounds possible even though it does not (yet) exist.

An interesting question for psycholinguistic research is whether the derivational history of a word is represented in the individual speaker's lexicon. Do we, on hearing or reading *unfairly* decompose the word into its stem, *fair*, plus the derivational morphemes? That is, do we perform the derivational process in reverse? According to some psycholinguists, the answer is yes (Forster 1990, Taft & Forster 1976).

MacKay (1978) argues that a similar process occurs in production, where the speaker first finds the stem then attaches the appropriate derivational morpheme. Advocates of this position also point to evidence from speech errors in which speakers appear to find the wrong derivational morpheme when producing the word. How else could speech errors such as (1) occur?

(1)   *grouping → groupment*
         intended   error   (Fromkin 1973)

This and other experimental evidence leads, they argue, to the conclusion that humans must have a mental lexicon in which stems plus a list of possible bound morphemes are stored together to be combined as needed. A similar process appears to be used by children when first acquiring the morphology of their language as shown by such common *overregularization* errors as *go → goed*, rather than the irregular past tense form *went*.

An alternative proposal might be that this system is too cumbersome to be true for all words. Instead high frequency words are stored as complete units, particularly in the case of irregular high frequency words, such as *ate*. Low frequency words may be derived on the those few occasions when they are needed.

Theories of Meaning: Semantics

It is traditional to discuss the field of lexical semantics in terms of the types of theories that have been proposed to account for meaning. As one might imagine, there have been many theories but little consensus. Proposals concerning the correct representation of meaning include the so-called *referential* theory where the word in some sense stands for the object it refers to, for example, the meaning of the word *flower*, is that which can be pointed to, such as a rose. This class of theories has obvious limitations as it cannot begin to account for abstract words or in fact any word that depends for its definition on other words. That most of our lexicon consists of such words becomes very apparent when one becomes the parent of a curious 6 year old. How else can one answer the question "What does *criticize* mean, Mummy?" except by making reference to other concepts and words. Pointing to criticism does not work!

More successful approaches to semantics incorporate some aspect of *featural* representations, in which word meanings are thought to be sets of basic elements, or features. This approach of course raises the question of where such features come from: are they innate? is there some set of pre-existing primitives? if so, shouldn't they be universal? Which features are criterial and which are merely characteristic of the entity referred to by the word (Smith et al. 1974)? Features also do not account for those aspects of meaning which involve experience or knowledge of the world. For example, while we can analyze bachelor as (human, adult, not female, not married), we have somehow failed to capture the true meaning of *spinster* by describing its meaning as (adult, human, female, not married). If spinsters were merely female bachelors, then there would have been no need for the Dating Game to invent the new word *bachelorette*. (And one wishes that they hadn't!)

Featural representations can be incorporated within a network representation, in which semantic relatedness and category membership, for example, *chair* is an instance of the category of *furniture*, are coded through links between words. At each node in the network, one can include the features which are criterial, or strongly associated, features of that word (Collins & Quillian 1969, Collins & Loftus 1975). This approach was taken by the semantic net representation we considered in Chapter 6. Similarly, one can incorporate aspects of the referential theory by suggesting that the representation of some word meaning, notably concrete nouns, relies on images or pictorial information (Paivio 1971), although this leads to problems of who, or what mechanism, is doing the perceiving of the image (Kosslyn 1981, Pylyshyn 1973)!

One of the more interesting proposals concerning the representation of meaning is that we rely on *prototypes* in order to form mental categories and judge membership by similarity to the mental prototype (Rosch 1973, 1975, Rosch & Mervis 1975). For example, the explanation of why North Americans can judge the statement *A robin is a bird* faster than *A chicken is a bird* is that presumably the robin is closer to the North American prototype of birds than chickens are. Prototypes rely on the concept of "family resemblances" in order to determine similarity, and thus do away with the idea of a criterial set of features.

The concept of prototypes has had some influence on research in semantics, particularly for studies of cross-cultural categorization of color terms (Berlin & Kay 1969, Heider 1972) and the acquisition of word meaning in children (Mervis & Mervis 1982, Rosch et al. 1976) but current psycholinguistic theories of meaning are more strongly affected by featural and network representations. Within the linguistic field of cognitive grammar, however, prototypes have experienced a resurgence of interest; for example, one current theory of the formation of syntactic categories relies heavily on the idea of prototypes (Croft 1991). Prototypes are an intuitively appealing concept and may yet deliver on their original promise as a cognitive basis for a theory of meaning.

Lexical Ambiguity

Because of the overwhelming and ever-increasing amount of psycholinguistic research on lexical access, it is impossible to review all of the major issues and findings. Instead, we present a long-standing, but contemporary problem in lexical access and examine how the theories and studies of this issue have evolved since the 1960s. The issue is lexical ambiguity, and the history of research and theorizing on this topic provides a microcosm of the evolution of experimental psycholinguistics.

The central question in the study of lexical ambiguity is: How do we represent the meanings of words that have two or more meanings? Are the two meanings stored together such that every time we hear or read a word with more than one meaning we access both, even if one meaning is inappropriate in the context? Common sense tells us that although *polysemous words*, words with many meanings, are relatively frequent, listeners seldom consciously encounter difficulties with them. As an example of our ability to ignore potential ambiguity, consider the high frequency *homophone* set *to*, *too*, and *two*; we hear the members of this set very often but very seldom misinterpret their intended meaning.

Exceptions occur, of course, in puns and jokes, but it is precisely because they point out the ambiguity that they are funny. Most of the time ambiguities are resolved through the use of context, without the listener or reader being consciously aware that an ambiguity has been presented. An explanation at the level of conscious awareness, however, does not satisfy a psycholinguist, no matter how much it may suit the native speaker's intuitions. Thus the original question about ambiguity resolution remains, intuitions notwithstanding, and has been the focus of considerable research over the years.

There are two basic theoretical positions concerning the processing of lexical ambiguities: (1) The meanings of ambiguous words are represented and accessed in exactly the same way as words with single meanings, which is to say that ambiguity has no additional effect on processing. This approach assumes that the meanings are stored separately. (2) Both meanings are represented and accessed together. The first hypothesis is essentially the null hypothesis, which says that there is no difference, and is impossible to prove directly. The second hypothesis, also known as the "two-meaning hypothesis," is rather simplistic as it fails to account for the common observation that listeners and readers are usually not aware of ambiguity. If they must process both meanings, why isn't comprehension constantly disrupted? In addition, the relative importance of the two meanings can differ (Hogaboam & Perfetti 1975). Differences in meaning dominance can influence the automaticity, and necessity, of accessing both meanings.

Current research takes the assumption of the two-meaning hypothesis as a given in the absence of context, that is, with isolated words or in "neutral" sentential contexts which support both meanings. The theoretical and experimental debate centers instead on determining the locus of context effects: Are they pre- or post-lexical access? In other words, do we use context in advance to guide lexical access so that only the contextually appropriate meaning is activated? This is also known as the *selective-access* hypothesis. Alternatively, is lexical access automatic and insulated from contextual effects such that all meanings are accessed and context is only consulted afterwards in order to choose between the alternatives? This latter position is advocated by proponents of *modularity* in language processing (Fodor 1983, Garfield 1987, Garrett 1990).

Many of the studies conducted during the 1960s and 1970s supported the two-meaning hypothesis. The usual logic of the experiments was that ambiguity, because of the hypothesized automatic access of both meanings, would slow down processing in some way. For example, in a well-known study by Foss and Jenkins (1973), listeners performed a "phoneme monitoring task" in which they had to respond to a target phoneme that immediately followed an ambiguous word, as in the following example (the target is $/b/$):

(2)   a. *Neutral context, ambiguous word:*
        The merchant put the *straw* beside the machine.

    b. *Neutral context, unambiguous word:*
        The merchant put the *hay* beside the machine.

    c. *Biased context, ambiguous word:*
        The farmer put the *straw* beside the machine.

    d. *Biased context, unambiguous word:*
        The farmer put the *hay* beside the machine.

In this example, *straw* is intended to be ambiguous, although the two meanings, bedding for animals and implement for drinking, are obviously related in origin. Responses were measured from the onset of the target phoneme until the subject pushed a button.

Response times were longer following ambiguous rather than unambiguous control words, even with a biasing context. Thus (2a) led to longer reaction times than (2b), and contrary to the "selective access" hypothesis, (2c) also led to longer reaction times than (2d). The selective access hypothesis, of course, has to predict that there would be no difference in response times between (2c) and (2d) because the context of *farmer* should automatically activate the 'bedding" interpretation of *straw*. These results were therefore interpreted as supporting the two-meaning hypothesis. However, there were some problems with this result. The paradigm was found to be sensitive to other, phonological, variables (Newman & Dell 1978) and additionally does not actually provide positive evidence that both meanings are activated. That was shown in an important study by Swinney (1979).

Swinney (1979) had listeners perform a "cross-modal lexical decision" task in which they listened to a pair of sentences and at some point during the second sentence, a letter string appeared on a computer monitor in front of them. The subjects' task was to decide, as quickly as possible, whether the visual stimulus was a word. Their "lexical" decision was indicated by a button press which stopped a reaction time clock. The point at which the letter string was presented appeared to be random from the subjects' point of view, but of course it was not. Some of the sentences contained ambiguous words, such as *bugs* in example (3),

(3)   *The man was not surprised when he found several spiders, roaches, and other bugs* Δ *in the corner of his roo*m.

The Δ marks the point at which the stimulus letter string or word appeared. Unambiguous control sentences were constructed by substituting an unambiguous word, such as *insects*, in the same location as the ambiguous word.

There were three different types of target stimuli. The target was an *unrelated* word, such as *sew*, on some trials, but on others it was related to the contextually *appropriate* meaning, as in *spy* (see example 4), and on still others, it was related to the other, contextually *inappropriate*, meaning, as in *ant*. Of course, some of the trials consisted of non-words to ensure that subjects had to make real decisions and, in order to determine whether there was an ambiguity effect at all in the absence of context, an equal number of trials consisted of unambiguous control sentences. Finally, Swinney manipulated the type of context that preceded the ambiguous word or its unambiguous control, such that it was either neutral and supported both meanings or was biased toward one of the meanings:

(4)   *No context (neutral)*:

Rumor had it that, for years, the government building had been plagued with problems. The man was not surprised when he found several *bugs* Δ in the corner of his room.
          insects Δ

(5)   *Biasing context*:
Rumor had it that, for years, the government building had been plagued with problems. The man was not surprised when he found several spiders, roaches, and other *bugs* Δ in the corner of his room.
                              insects Δ

The rather impressive result of this clever experiment is that both meanings of the ambiguous word were found to be active immediately after the ambiguity, regardless of the type of preceding context. The evidence for this conclusion is the finding that both *spy* <u>and</u> *ant* were "primed" following *bugs*. This means that both the appropriate and the inappropriate words were judged to be words in less time than that taken to decide that the unrelated target, *sew*, was in fact a word. Furthermore, there was no statistical difference between the decision times for *spy* and *ant*.

Context is not irrelevant, however; it just takes time to have an effect. Swinney showed that by three syllables later only the contextually appropriate meaning remained activated. Subjects in a second experiment performed exactly the same task except that the lexical decision occurred three syllables after the ambiguous word or its control. Thus since *spy* had been primed by *bugs* and was consistent with the contextually appropriate meaning, it could be judged as a word rapidly. On the other hand, *ant* was now, because of the post-lexical effects of context, eliminated from consideration as the intended meaning and had effectively become an unrelated word. The lexical decision time for *ant* was thus equivalent in decision time to *sew*, the unrelated word.

Swinney's results have been interpreted as strong evidence for two claims: that we represent and access both (all) meanings of an ambiguous word and that the lexicon is a separate "module" which is not affected by sentence context and top-down processes (Forster 1990). Recently this strong interpretation of Swinney's results has been criticized, as Tabossi (1988) has shown that the type of relation between the context and target word is critical. Tabossi's research indicates that Swinney's original result depended on whether the target was a semantic associate or a property of the ambiguous word. Thus the strong position that lexical access is automatic and insulated from other processing must be qualified, but it does appear, given the current state of research, that comprehenders store the meanings of an ambiguous word together and access them automatically.

Given the appropriate type of relation between the ambiguous word and the sentence context, however, they may be able to selectively access only one of those meanings (Tabossi 1988, Tabossi & Zardon 1993).

Although a satisfactory theory of word meanings is clearly a desirable goal, and probably a very long way off, it is obviously not sufficient for a theory of language processing. Native speakers produce words according to implicit rules, not as strings of random words. Listeners use their knowledge of these tacit rules in order to recognize sequences of words as "grammatical" or acceptable. These rules operate independently of the meaning of those words, as shown by Chomsky's now famous example *Colorless green ideas sleep furiously.* This string is recognizable as a grammatical sentence in English although it is clearly semantically *anomalous* (unless you happen to have seen it used many times as an example of grammaticality without meaning!). The linguistic field that describes the set of implicit rules for arranging words into sentences is known as *syntax* and will be discussed in the next section.

13.3.5   Syntax

The central concern in the study of syntax is to develop a theory that adequately explains the structure of acceptable or *grammatical* sentences in a language. Such a theory should ultimately be capable of generating all possible grammatical sentences and not generate any ungrammatical ones. One could conceivably, given infinite time, generate a very large number of possible sentences by randomly combining words of different parts of speech. However, this approach would also generate a staggering number of impossible sentences. We would not want to allow such a system to pass as a theory of syntax.

Linguists believe that all native speakers of a language have tacit knowledge or *competence* concerning which sequences of words are or are not grammatical, although they may not be overtly aware of this knowledge. This reliance on native speaker intuitions for grammaticality judgments, most often those of the linguist presenting the particular syntactic analysis, runs counter to the commonly perceived view of grammar as *prescriptive*. A prescriptive approach is one which strives to lay down laws and criteria for "good" sentences such as the often-cited prescription to avoid split infinitives, as in "to boldly go." Grammaticality is a matter of consensus and tacit knowledge, and not the province of grammar teachers or self-appointed pundits.

It is customary to introduce the study of syntax by differentiating it from the study of traditional grammar. The latter, as most lay persons mean the term, is concerned with specifying the "parts of speech" and the "rules" for combining them into acceptable sentences. Linguists often construe grammar more broadly to mean an overall description of a language that includes phonology, morphology, and semantics, as well as the description of sentence structure. Our discussion of syntax is concerned with parts of speech and grammatical categories but also encompasses the structure and ordering of units within sentences.

Phrases and Phrase Structure

All sentences have words that refer to objects or entities in the world, *nouns*, and *predicates*, which make statements about those nouns. Thus, in the sentence *Skunk Woman tricked Coyote*, Skunk Woman is a proper noun and *tricked Coyote* is a predicate that describes an action that she performed. We can make the referring expression more complex by using an adjective as in *Clever Skunk Woman tricked Coyote*. We have provided more information by modifying Skunk Woman; the syntactic function is the same as the proper noun, however, as after all, it is the same entity that is being referred to, albeit with more information provided. The process of "embellishment" we are engaging in allows us to expand *phrases* into larger units.

The realization that we are still referring to the same individual when we include the adjective *clever* can be captured by the grammatical unit *noun phrase*. A noun phrase minimally consists of a noun, such as a proper name or pronoun, but can be expanded through the application of *phrase structure rules*. Thus we can indicate the possible options for noun phrases in English by the following rule. Parentheses indicate optionality, Det = determiner, such as an article; Adj = adjective, N = noun, including proper names. The arrow indicates "is rewritten as"; the asterisk indicates "ungrammatical." We took a similar approach with our introduction of parse trees with graphs in Chapter 6.

(6)   NP → (Det) (Adj) N

Thus, with the addition of *lexical insertion rules*, which provide constraints on which words can be put into each of these possible positions, we could generate a number of different noun phrases. Thus we can use

N →	Coyote
	Skunk Woman
	rabbit
	rock
Det →	A
	The
Adj →	clever
	big

to generate noun phrases, such as *clever Coyote*, *a big rabbit*, and *the rock*.

Of course this is a minuscule portion of the possible words in English that could fit each of these roles. Note that there are obviously semantic restrictions on some potential noun phrases, such as *A/The clever rock*. *Clever* applies to, at least some, animate beings. Furthermore, we don't use determiners with proper names, as in *A Skunk Woman*.

We can replace a NP with a pronoun. Thus we could substitute *She* for *Clever Skunk Woman*, as in *She tricked Coyote*. The fact that we can replace an entire phrase with one word is evidence that the noun phrase functions as a single unit. Notice, however, that we have to replace the entire NP, since *Clever she tricked Coyote* would sound odd indeed!

Sentences do more than refer to entities, however; they also describe events. We have all been taught in English class that each sentence must minimally consist of a subject and a predicate. The subject of a sentence is a NP, and linguists refer to the predicate as the *verb phrase* or *VP*. Thus we can produce a rule for generating sentences (where S = sentence):

(7)   S → NP VP

In a fashion similar to the expansion of NPs above, we can expand the VP in our original example, *Skunk Woman tricked Coyote*, without changing its grammatical function. The VP that we have used is a simple one, containing only a verb and a proper noun. We could expand this sentence to provide more information about the action by using a *prepositional phrase*, consisting of a preposition followed by a NP, to indicate where the action took place: *Skunk Woman tricked Coyote under the tree*. Notice that we could also provide more information about Coyote, using our rules for NPs, as in *Skunk Woman tricked foolish Coyote under the tree*. Our VP to this point actually has a number of components:

(8)   VP → V (NP) (PP)

Minimally, of course, we can have simple *intransitive* sentences that consist only of a NP and V, as in *She slept*. *Sleep* is an intransitive verb, which means that it does not take an object (you can't "sleep" someone or something). Transitive verbs, such as *trick*, require an object, someone has to be tricked, and thus minimally would require a NP following the verb. Prepositional phrases are optional, as we have seen.

Verb phrases can become more complex, with the addition of embedded clauses, as in: *Clever Skunk Woman told Coyote that he was foolish*. The new addition is itself a sentence, *he was foolish*. We can capture this option by adding another component to the VP rule (notice that it precedes the optional PP):

(9)   VP → V (NP) (S) (PP)

This particular rule shows the power of *recursion*, in which the product of one application of a rule can serve as the input to the reapplication of that same rule. We can capture the generalization that VPs can contain sentences within them by using the (S) notation to refer to them. In order to find out what (S) refers to, we consult our original rule, S → NP VP, which of course itself can have an (S) embedded within it, and so on, indefinitely. Although recursion can allow for the generation of an infinite number of sentences by making each progressively more complex, research indicates that humans cannot comprehend sentences that are embedded more than two clauses deep (Reich & Dell 1978).

Order is particularly important in English, where there are no inflections to indicate the roles of sentence participants, except on pronouns (as in *he vs. him*). Consider the difference between (10) and (11):

(10)   Mary ate the fish.
(11)   The fish ate Mary.

Who ate whom is indicated solely by the relative sentence position with respect to the verb. In English active sentences we take the first noun to be the grammatical subject and the second to be the object.

Our knowledge of the world affects the likelihood of one interpretation over another, however. In (10), we imagine the fish to be small, say the size of a trout, and in (11) we can only imagine that the fish was a member of the shark family, and a large one at that! Had the two nouns been *Mary* and a *tomato*, there would have been no ambiguity as in

(12)   ?*The tomato ate Mary.*

This is a very unlikely event, unless it's the *Attack of the Killer Tomatoes*! (Linguists use "?" to indicate a *semantic anomaly* which is an instance of a grammatical sentence whose meaning does not make sense. Thus we can analyze the syntactic structure of a sentence independently of its meaning as Chomsky made clear by popularizing the sentence *Colorless green ideas sleep furiously*.)

With sentences such as (13) and (14),

(13)   Mary liked John.
(14)   John liked Mary.

there are no cues, other than sentence position, to subject and object roles in the sentence. Sentence pairs such as (13) and (14) are *reversible*, in that each participant can appear in either position; sentences such as (12),

(12)   Mary ate the tomato.

are *nonreversible* because the two participants have unequal status with respect to the action being performed. *Mary,* because she satisfies the *selectional restrictions* on the verb, that is, she is animate, can be the *agent* of the action, *eat,* but *tomato,* since it is inanimate, cannot. Here we see that semantic relations play a role in sentence structure, thus indicating that linguistic levels are not independent of one another.

Interestingly Caramazza and Zurif (1976) showed that Broca's aphasics can comprehend nonreversible sentences but have difficulties with reversible sentences. Broca's aphasics are individuals who have suffered trauma to a region of the brain known as Broca's area (in the left frontal lobe, next to the motor cortex) that results in difficulty processing and producing syntactically correct utterances. They generally produce content words, such as nouns, verbs, and adjectives, but lack function words (articles, prepositions, etc.) and do not use much syntax. The result is that their language sounds like a series of words rather than fluent sentences. Their speech production is effortful and has atypical intonation, however, it is meaningful. Caramazza and Zurif's finding that Broca's aphasics can comprehend nonreversible sentences indicates that they can use semantics and world knowledge, such as the fact that tomatoes can't eat humans, to compensate for difficulties in processing syntax. This finding once again shows that language processing involves the interaction of multiple linguistic levels.

Transformations

Over the past three decades the study of syntax has been dominated by a framework that is largely attributed to one, very influential, linguist. Noam Chomsky revolutionized the study of syntax in 1957 with the publication of his book, *Syntactic Structures.* This book broke with a largely descriptive tradition and instead proposed that sentences could be reduced to an abstract *deep structure,* the meaning, plus a set of rules that could be applied to derive the actual *surface structures,* the sequences of words that speakers produce.

For each sentence, the grammar first produces a *phrase structure* of the type we have discussed above, then *lexical insertion* rules are used to provide the words. The deep structure, also known as *underlying structure,* is the next stage in the syntactic component but it is not what speakers actually say. The surface structure refers to the actual form of the sentence that is produced. In order to produce the surface structure speakers apply a *transformational rule* that changes the order of phrases in the deep structure, known as *constituents,* into a surface order. In some instances, however, such as active declaratives, the surface word order may be the same as the underlying word order and so no transformation is necessary.

Through the process of recursion (also see VPs, above) it is possible to account for the crucial linguistic feature of productivity. According to this account, the reason that humans can produce and comprehend an infinite number of sentences is that they generate each sentence anew by applying rules. This approach does away with the logical problem of how it is that one can reproduce from memory a sentence that one has never heard, as would be required by a simple memory model of human language.

Furthermore, the generative approach provided an insight into the semantic relations that hold between sentences of two different surface structures, such as the active and passive in

(15) *The squirrels emptied the bags of nuts.*
(16) *The bags of nuts were emptied by the squirrels.*

These two sentences share the same deep structure, as they describe the same event. The relationship between them can be captured by the application of the *passive transformation*, which allows us to produce a passive sentence structure from the same underlying structure as the active. The transformation is (we use $\Rightarrow$ as the symbol for a transformation, rather than a phrase structure rule):

(17) NP_1 V NP_2 $\Rightarrow$ NP_2 *be* V *en by* NP_1.

Note that NP refers to a noun phrase, V to the main verb, *be* to the use of the auxiliary verb *to be*, and *en* to indicate the past participle. Thus in our example,

(18) NP_1	V	NP_2	$\Rightarrow$
The squirrels	*emptied*	*the bags of nuts.*	
(19) NP_2	*be V en by*	NP_1	
The bags of nuts	*were emptied by*	*the squirrels.*	

Of course, the passive is only one of many syntactic phenomena which can be captured by transformational rules; indeed the theory was intended to capture all of the possible grammatical syntactic structures, not just of English, but of all human languages. The theoretical position that one could posit a distinction between an underlying meaning and the surface form of its realization was particularly intriguing to cognitive psychologists in the infant discipline of psycholinguistics in the 1960s.

Psycholinguists designed experiments to test the psychological reality of one aspect of transformational grammar, using a theory that became known as the derivational theory of complexity (Mehler 1963, Miller & McKean 1964). This theory proposed that human syntactic processing behaved in a way analogous to the derivation of surface forms in transformational theory. Thus, in order to understand a passive sentence, listeners or readers applied their knowledge of transformations in reverse to arrive at the "kernel" or deep structure. The more transformations that had to be removed, the longer the sentence should take to process. A passive should therefore take longer to understand than the corresponding active, and in turn a passive question should take longer to understand than a passive statement.

Transformational grammar in the early 1960s served as a source of experimental hypotheses which were often nothing more than literal tests of linguistic theory. The experiments, and their methodology, seem rather naive from our current perspective, particularly with the advent of neuropsychological technology, but they were seminal to the field.

Although there was initially some empirical evidence to support the derivational theory, it rapidly became apparent that the theory was too cumbersome, and there was too much contradictory evidence for it to serve as a useful theory of language processing. Furthermore, the standard transformational theory came under some theoretical fire within linguistics and has since been altered many times. The currently dominant syntactic framework is Chomsky's theory of government and binding, which is beyond the scope of this chapter (Chomsky 1981, Lasnik & Uriagereka 1988).

Current Psycholinguistic Approaches to Sentence Processing

The importance of transformational grammar to psycholinguistics is of historical interest, as attempts to validate it spawned a close collaboration between the disciplines. Psycholinguists are now more likely to propose their own theories rather than merely serving as field testers for linguists, but there is still a close relationship between the disciplines, particularly in syntax. For example, most, though by no means all, current psycholinguistic theories of sentence processing take a *modular* view of the relationship between syntax and semantics. The basic premise, advocated by syntacticians in the generative tradition, is that syntactic processing operates independently of semantic processing. Parsing is believed to be an autonomous process that consults the semantic system only after the parse of the sentence has been determined (Clifton & Ferreira 1987, Garrett 1990).

The modularity position is at odds with the *interactive* view of sentence processing in which both syntax and semantics are believed to be available simultaneously and consulted during sentence processing (Tyler & Marslen-Wilson 1977, Marslen-Wilson & Tyler 1987). Furthermore, modular theories are, for the most part, incompatible with connectionist approaches to language processing [but see Reilly and Sharkey (1992)].

Although predictions from the two opposing camps result in very small processing time differences, the significance of the debate is far greater. If modular theorists are correct, then considerably more processing of language is automatic than had been popularly believed. Instead of worrying about how to build intelligent systems that can make predictions about the likely interpretation of the input based on knowledge of the world, a modular system would perform the first available parse, even if, in a particular semantic context, it results in an unlikely interpretation. Any difficulties would be resolved afterwards by consulting the semantic content. This automatic processing of the first available option is held to be more cognitively economical than hypothesis generation and testing, as the first available parse is usually the most frequent. Thus the effort needed to interpret unusual syntactic constructions arises after the parse, not before or during.

A well-known example of this parsing strategy is provided by an experiment demonstrating the *minimal attachment strategy* (Rayner et al. 1983). Thus in sentence (20), the prepositional phrase *with binoculars* describes how the action is performed, and is part of the VP at the same level as the NP, *the cop*. The PP is "minimally" attached to the noun phrase, *the cop*, that preceded it.

(20)   The spy saw the cop with binoculars, but the cop didn't see him.

In contrast, the PP, *with a revolver*, in (21) is nonminimally attached to the NP, as it provides further description of *the cop*. In order to correctly interpret this sentence, the comprehender must realize that both *the cop* and *with a revolver* are parts of a larger noun phrase, and must construct a more complex parse.

(21)   The spy saw the cop with a revolver, but the cop didn't see him.

According to the results of Rayner et al.'s study, readers initially interpret sentences such as (21) as if they are minimally attached. By using sophisticated eye-tracking equipment, Rayner and colleagues showed that readers spent more time looking at the critical PP in (21) than in (20). They interpreted this eye movement pattern as showing that readers had initially committed to the first possible parse (presumably because it is easier than constructing a more complex NP) and then had to reprocess the PP when subsequent context indicated that the parse was incorrect.

While this cognitive "parsimony" argument is attractive, it fails to account for some common phenomena in on-line processing, such as the speech perception error cited earlier in this chapter (recall "an affair" and "enough air"). Since both parses are plausible (determiner + noun vs. adjective + noun) it is hard to see how selecting the structurally most likely parse could explain the phenomenon. If, like Swinney's (1979) subjects, the processor computes both meanings, how is it that only one interpretation was available to the listener? Although one could argue that context selected only one alternative after both interpretations had been considered, it seems surprising that the other alternative would have disappeared so completely from consciousness. However, without appropriate psycholinguistic experimentation it is impossible to conclude that the other meaning was not momentarily accessed. Unfortunately -- or fortunately, perhaps -- in real life you never have the proper control condition when you need it!

Furthermore, there is considerable evidence from speech production errors that more than one level of linguistic processing operates at a time. Speech errors often have multiple causes. Consider, for example, the following:

(22)   STUDENT   Will you have the grades tested by then?

The speaker had just taken a test and was trying to ask how soon he could expect to learn his grade. He probably intended to say "the tests graded" rather than "the grades tested." Obviously both *test* and *grade* were very salient in the setting; both can be used in either noun or verb form, and the speaker failed to determine their syntactic roles before posing his question. Thus the stems, *test* and *grade,* may have transposed positions and then acquired the appropriate morphs for the noun and verb roles (+*s* and +*ed*).

Because it is also common to ask "when will you have *the grades posted*," it is possible that there was competition from this similar phrase such that *grade* had an additional influence that helped determine its use as a noun rather than a verb. Fortunately the intent was very clear from the context and the addressee's considerable prior experience with, and expectation of, this type of question.

While anecdotal, such examples illustrate the predictive importance of context in language processing. Unfortunately, anecdotes are not acceptable evidence for scientific debates and more empirical support is needed for the interactive position. Although it is ultimately impossible to prove that any one theoretical perspective is the only true account of language processing, the debate is useful in that it serves as a focus for research. In that respect, both positions are valuable.

13.4   EPILOGUE AND REFERENCES

In the last decade psycholinguistics has seen an increase in research on lexical access and representation and there has been a rekindling of interest in syntax. The study of speech production, which had previously been rather marginal and consigned mainly to the study of speech errors, has also received more attention thanks to new models, for example, Dell (1986) and Levelt (1989). A major motivation for the current interest in these areas is the lively debate concerning modularity in language processing (Fodor 1983, Garfield 1987). Modularity proponents argue that lexical access is automatic and autonomous and is not affected by "top-down" or expectation-driven processing. Garrett (1990) provides an extensive review of sentence processing from a modular perspective.

Interactive models of word recognition and lexical access, in contrast, argue that top-down and bottom-up processing are both used in order to comprehend the input. Logically prior processes, for example, speech perception, can be influenced by the output of logically higher-level processes such as word recognition [see Dell and Newman (1980), Marslen-Wilson (1984), Marslen-Wilson and Tyler (1987)]. For interesting overviews of cognitive approaches to speech perception see the collections in Cole and Jakimik (1980) and Altmann (1990).

The role of morphology in lexical representation has become a rather lively field of enquiry and the interested reader is referred to the sources listed in the chapter plus Bybee (1985) and Matthews (1991) for linguistic introductions to the field.

The currently dominant syntactic framework is Chomsky's theory of government and binding, which is beyond the scope of this chapter. The reader is referred to Cowper (1992) and Lasnik and Uriagereka (1988) for a linguistic introduction. In addition, there are a number of theoretical alternatives to the generative approach to syntax, notably cognitive and functional approaches [see Croft (1991), Givon (1984), and Langacker (1987)] that focus on communicative and cognitive, rather than formal rule-based motivations for grammatical phenomena.

This discussion of language representation and processing has barely mentioned research on child language. The interested reader is referred to Berko Gleason's (1993) introductory book for an overview, and the collection in Slobin (1985) for a fascinating look at cross-linguistic studies of language acquisition.

Much current psycholinguistic research has been fueled by a shift in methodology that enables the study of "on-line" processing. As measurement techniques become more precise, stronger claims can be made concerning the time course of processing and the degree to which various subcomponents are autonomous. Reaction time is now the dependent variable of choice in psycholinguistics and much time is devoted to studies of the nature of the tasks used to look at processing. The explosion in laboratory computers has led to a corresponding explosion of studies; where articles in the seventies would present a series of two or three experiments to explore parametric manipulations in a task, it is now not uncommon to see as more than 10 experiments in one article!

New technology has also affected psycholinguistic theories. The widespread availability of increasingly powerful computers has heavily influenced theorizing and model-building in psycholinguistics. Connectionist models of language, for example, Dell's (1986) model of speech production and Rumelhart and McClelland's (1986) parallel distributed processing model of verb learning, require computer simulation to both generate and test predictions.

The development of PET and MRI technology (see Section 5.4) is having a strong impact on neurolinguistic research and, increasingly, on predictions concerning lexical access and representation in normal individuals (Damasio & Damasio 1992). Even in the short time that psycholinguistics has been a recognized discipline, we have seen great increases in our knowledge about language representation and processing. With the increased collaboration brought about through the development of cognitive science, the next decade of research on language representation and processing promises to be very exciting indeed!

Chapter 14

PRAGMATICS AND DISCOURSE

I don't want to talk grammar, I want to talk like a lady.

George Bernard Shaw, *Pygmalion*

...I understand a fury in your words,
But not the words.

William Shakespeare, *Othello*

14.0   INTRODUCTION

The 1970s saw the discovery by psycholinguists of connected discourse and the study of texts longer than a single sentence. The interest in discourse resulted from an extension of work on the role of *propositions* in memory that had shown that people remember the meaning, or gist, of an utterance in a text, but not the form in which it appeared (Sachs 1967). Propositions (Section 7.2) are theoretical entities that represent the semantic content in the underlying structure. They typically consist of a relation (a verb, adjective, or adverb) and one or more arguments (nouns).

Subsequent research showed that comprehenders not only recall gist rather than the exact form, but use their world knowledge and inferential processes when processing sentences and texts. Memory for linguistic material is often "reconstructive" in nature. Comprehenders go beyond the information given and draw inferences from the input. They make use of all sources of information available, as shown by a classic study demonstrating that the amount and type of information recalled can be dramatically influenced by the presence of a biasing title (Bransford et al. 1972, Bransford & Johnson 1973). Obviously comprehenders are more than parsing machines; syntax is at the service of meaning, the determination of which is the comprehenders' primary goal.

Research on memory for discourse, usually in the form of short written texts such as stories, demonstrated that propositions were arranged in a hierarchy, rather analogous to sentence tree structures, with those that were "higher" in the tree being remembered better (Kintsch et al. 1975). Furthermore, propositional density, not number of words, affects processing time; increasing the number of propositions in a text results in increased reading time (Kintsch & Keenan 1973).

Psycholinguists' fascination with grammar and formalisms did not end with the demise of the derivational theory of complexity. The 1970s brought the development of *text grammars*, complete with rewrite rules, to represent knowledge of the underlying structure of a text (Kintsch 1974, Mandler & Johnson 1977, Rumelhart 1977, Thorndyke 1977). Debates concerning the psychological reality of these grammars and their role in processing (Mandler 1982, Mandler & Goodman 1982) were reminiscent of the central issue in the study of syntax during the sixties.

The 1970s also saw the introduction of *pragmatics* and *speech act* theory into the study of connected discourse. While most psycholinguists continued to be interested in the representation of "utterance meaning," some attempted to study "speaker's meaning" (Searle 1969) and the listener/reader's understanding of the speaker/writer's intent. Concerns with intangible issues such as the speaker's intent and tacit knowledge are obviously central to comprehension but notoriously difficult to study. There is considerable recent progress in linguistics and related disciplines in the area of pragmatics and discourse. We discuss these topics in this chapter: *pragmatics* in Section 14.1, *discourse analysis* in Section 14.2, *conversation and turn-taking* in Section 14.3, and *social influences on language use* in Section 14.4.

14.1 PRAGMATICS

14.1.1 An Example

We begin this section with an anecdote that demonstrates the importance of pragmatics in everyday language comprehension.

> One day in mid-autumn, shortly after the start of flu season, I came down with a bad cold. Showing great dedication, I came to campus and gave a lecture in my morning class, using copious amounts of tissue throughout. Later in the day, just before the start of my laboratory class, there was a knock on the office door, and the receptionist walked in. "Is your class canceled?" she enquired. "No. Why did you think so?" I asked. She replied that there was a note on the blackboard saying that the afternoon class was canceled because of my illness. I quickly went to the classroom, whereupon seeing the announcement, I intercepted the remaining students (it was a small class) and told them

that, obviously, I was here and class was not canceled. It was not until going back into the room that I took a second look at the "cancellation announcement" which stated the following (true) assertion and nothing more: "Dr. Newman is ill today." The students, and I at first, had read the announcement as if it said that class was canceled, although nowhere was that actually written. What caused us to automatically arrive at that conclusion while ignoring what the note actually said? And who had written the announcement in the first place? (That mystery was never solved.)

The explanation of the incorrect interpretation of "Dr. Newman is ill today" is that the people who read the statement understood it in terms of conveyed, or intended, meaning. As the reader is no doubt aware, in academic settings the statement that a teacher or professor is ill is very often given as a reason for a class cancellation. In this case, there was no accompanying statement of class cancellation, but that did not stop the students from interpreting the statement as saying that it was canceled. Otherwise, why write the information that the professor is ill on the board? This example nicely demonstrates the extent to which we rely on intended meaning for a large part of our language understanding.

It doesn't much matter what kind of theory of syntactic processing we propose to account for the parsing of a sentence (Chapter 13), if in fact the literal meaning of the sentence is irrelevant to the interpretation arrived at by the comprehender. We may, in some cases of isolated statements, actually interpret the literal meaning first, but in context, we go directly to the intended, or *speaker's*, meaning (Clark & Lucy 1975, Gibbs 1979). When the cashier at McDonald's fast food restaurant asks whether the two Happy Meals ordered are for boys or girls and I reply that I want two trucks, even though I have a child of each sex, I am obviously responding to the intention that, at McDonald's, boys get trucks and girls get dolls with their Happy Meals rather than to the literal meaning of the question. (I have to answer the question twice, however, as the McDonald's employees have formed a rather tight association between gender and toy type.)

14.1.2 The Importance of Pragmatics

The realization that there may be a distinction between what the words say and what the speaker meant is central to the field of language study known as *pragmatics*. Pragmatics is the study of language use in context and is concerned with the function, and purpose, of language. One way to interpret our class cancellation example is to say that there is conflict between the *utterance meaning* and the *speaker's meaning.* Clearly, it is ultimately the latter that we, as social beings, really care about. The words are a means of conveying the speaker's meaning, but in conversational settings certainly are not an end in themselves.

The insight that there is a distinction between these two aspects of an utterance is usually credited to J.L. Austin, a philosopher, who in 1955 gave a series of lectures at Harvard that were subsequently published in a little book entitled *How to Do Things with Words* (Austin 1962). The title of Austin's book nicely summarizes the pragmatic approach to the study of language. The theory sketched in his book started the field that has come to be known as *speech act theory.* The fundamental assumption is that each utterance can be thought of as an action: something that the speaker is trying to accomplish. There are a number of different types of speech acts that have been defined and studied; we discuss a few of the most important ones here.

Searle (1969, pg. 24-25), following and expanding upon Austin's (1962) work, suggests that one can describe each utterance on a number of different levels: (1) as uttering words, known as *utterance acts*; (2) referring and making predicates, known as *propositional acts*; (3) stating, questioning, etc., known as *illocutionary acts;* and (4) the effects of these illocutionary acts upon the listener, known as *perlocutionary acts.* The first level corresponds to the perception and decoding of the input. What are the sounds, letters, and words that are produced? The second level concerns most of the research discussed in the last chapter: What do the words refer to? What are the meanings of the words and sentences? How are they accessed?

The third level provides the most important insight, namely the idea that the speaker is attempting to accomplish something by "uttering words." Illocutionary acts do not stand in one-to-one correspondence with a specific set of words or a given propositional act, although there may be conventional means for expressing a particular wish. For example, one can make a request, a type of speech act known as a "directive" in many systems, by using a formal utterance with an imperative, as in "Close the window." This form should be transparent to any native speaker of the language as a request for an action and should have the perlocutionary effect on the listener of causing them to close the window.

By adding "Please" the imposition on the addressee can be softened so as to increase the likelihood that the speaker's request will be carried out. On the other hand, the statement "It's cold in here" said to a listener standing next to an open window, while propositionally being an assertion about the temperature of the room, should, if the speaker is sensitive to the conveyed, or indirect meaning, have the same effect of getting the window closed (Gibbs 1979). Of course the form of the request is quite different, but its function is the same. The ability to recognize the functional equivalence of different forms, such as the indirect and direct requests, is affected by the context and the listener's knowledge of the speaker.

Sociolinguists have argued that differences in the forms of speech acts are also determined by social variables such as gender. Clark and Schunk (1980) have proposed that one reason that indirect forms are used is so that the speaker can avoid imposing directly on the listener, giving the listener the apparent opportunity to construe the request as a mere statement of fact. Notice, of course, that saying "Yes, it is cold" as a response to the indirect request above can, quite rightly, be construed as "smart-alecky" in context, although it is clearly relevant to the propositional content of the utterance. One can easily imagine how differences between conversational partners in their responses to indirect forms can lead to miscommunication, although superficially the responses may seem quite appropriate!

14.2 LANGUAGE COOPERATION: DISCOURSE

14.2.1 Grice's Conversational Maxims

The development of speech act theory was important for psycholinguistics as it provided a way of looking at language that went beyond the words themselves to a consideration of the purpose of the utterance. Implicit in speech act theory is the assumption that language is ultimately a cooperative act whose primary purpose, formalist analyses aside, is for interaction between human beings. While there are clearly cases in which language can be used for purely informational purposes, such as conveying the facts of a recent event in a newspaper story, or for purely aesthetic reasons, as in poetry and fiction, most language is produced in a setting with other speakers present. When speaking with other users of the language, we, as skilled conversationalists, make a number of important assumptions about the interaction. These have been termed *conversational maxims* by the philosopher H.P. Grice (1975).

Perhaps the most crucial assumption made by listeners is that speakers will be telling the truth. This assumption is known as the maxim of *quality*. Thus we expect that speakers will, to the best of their knowledge, be referring to things, events, and ideas that they believe to be true. That we place a high premium on truthfulness can be seen by the fact that in our culture one can go to jail for slander, libel, fraud, and perjury, all of which are cases of lying, in one form or another. It is critical, from a processing perspective, that speakers tell the truth so that the conversational partner can be sure that they share the background and context for the discourse. One of the disturbing aspects of discourse with many mentally ill individuals is that they often do not adhere to this maxim, and as quickly becomes apparent, nor do they adhere to another very important maxim, that of *relation* (Rochester & Martin 1979).

The maxim of *relation* is a crucial requirement for conversational interaction. Simply, it is the rather basic assumption that the speaker's utterance is relevant to the current topic of the discourse. If there is no obvious relation between the current utterance and the previous topic, then rational listeners either wait for such a relation to become apparent or assume that a topic shift has taken place. Listeners are fully prepared to give the speaker the benefit of the doubt, although if after a few sentences it appears that the new utterance is not relevant, then they may quite legitimately feel that the conversational "floor" has been snatched away, or that the speaker is thought-disordered!

Typically topic shifts are signaled in some way, often overtly with markers such as "by the way," "speaking of X" (which often the speaker was not in fact speaking of), or "not to change the subject but...." Merely starting a new topic "out of the blue" would be considered rude in our culture. We should bear in mind, however, that topic markers and conversational conventions differ between societies, and therefore across languages, and what may be rude in one culture may be perfectly acceptable in another. The notion of relevance is also closely linked to that of *coherence*, which we discuss in Section 14.2.2.

Two other maxims were proposed by Grice, those of *quantity* and *manner*. These maxims are less critical to the meaning of a conversation but do have implications for processing. Quantity, as might be supposed, refers to the amount of information provided by the speaker; the speaker is enjoined to provide neither too much nor too little information in a given exchange. For example, if I tell you that "Mary is at New Mexico State" without any context or background information, that is, Mary is unknown to you, then you can quite rightly say that I have violated the maxim of quantity by not providing enough information.

If on the other hand, I say "Mary, who is an old friend from my undergraduate days, was born in England, and received her undergraduate degree at McGill University, her graduate degree at Yale, and is now a professor at New Mexico State University where she studies obesity in mice," you might, quite legitimately, feel overwhelmed by the excessive amount of information that I am conveying to you: more than a total stranger would want to know about my friends! Instead, I could satisfy the maxim of quantity by stating "My friend Mary is a physiological psychologist at New Mexico State University," and then, if you were interested in more details, you could ask about relative birth order, education, field of specialization, and so on.

How one presents information is also very critical. Grice admonished speakers to "avoid prolixity" as one of the components of the maxim of *manner*. This of course is not helpful unless one knows that *prolixity* refers to excessive wordiness. At the same time one should avoid "ambiguity" and "obfuscation" (confusion and bewilderment). Thus one should be clear, using words and topics that have known referents to the listener, and be as concise as necessary to convey the information. How one copes with the maxims of quantity and manner can be explored through the study of information structure (Halliday 1970, Prince 1981b), "packaging" (Chafe 1979, 1982), and cohesion (Halliday & Hasan 1976). We examine these topics, and coherence, in the next section.

14.2.2   Coherence and Cohesion

When we speak to one another, we assume that what is being communicated makes sense, or is semantically *coherent*. That is, the speaker, or author, in the case of written texts, has ideas that he or she wants to express and these ideas are related to one another in some way. The speaker then formulates these ideas into words which the listener, as we saw in the last chapter, attempts to comprehend. If the ideas are incoherent, as in the case of schizophrenic language (Rochester & Martin 1979) or Wernicke's aphasics (see, for example, Christiansen 1993), then the input becomes very difficult to understand.

There is a distinction between the coherence of the ideas themselves and the way in which they are expressed. The expression of the ideas is often referred to in formal linguistics as the "surface structure" and the ideas themselves as "propositions," or in syntactic analyses as "deep structure." There are a number of linguistic devices in each language that contribute to the "texture" of a discourse by providing *cohesive* links between utterances and sentences. For example, we can use the pronominal reference system to refer to entities that have previously been introduced in the discourse without having to repeat the name, or noun, that it refers to. Thus in (1) below, we see that the possessive pronoun *its* refers to the *Caterpillar*; if Lewis Carroll had instead written "Caterpillar's mouth," the reader might justifiably suppose that a second caterpillar had appeared on the scene. The use of *its* in this context is the only appropriate choice.

(1)   The Caterpillar and Alice looked at each other for some
       time in silence: at last the Caterpillar took the hookah out
       of its mouth, and addressed her in a languid sleepy voice
       (Carroll 1865/1989, p. 73).

Notice, too, that *Alice* is referred to as *her*, the grammatical object, on second mention. Although pronominalization is the most common way to refer to subsequent mentions of an entity in a discourse, repetition is a possible form of cohesion in written texts if it is used judiciously, as in the second instance of *Caterpillar* in example (1). There is no possibility here of ambiguity as to which caterpillar is being referred to, as it is marked by the definite article *the*. In English, the use of *the* almost always indicates information that has been previously mentioned in the discourse, is salient in the listener/reader's consciousness, or is inferable (Prince 1981b). This information is said to be *given* and is distinct from *new information*, which the listener/reader is not presumed to already know. We shall return to a discussion of types of information and their "flow" in our presentation of discourse analysis in Section 14.3.

Types of Cohesion: Repetition and Pronominalization

Repetition may be more common in spoken discourse than written text (Tannen 1989). Writers are often encouraged to increase the lexical variety in their texts by using synonyms or pronominalization rather than repetition. Repetition is also a common form of cohesion in young children's speech, partly because they have not yet mastered the pronominal system. Young children have particular troubles with pronouns because of their *deictic* nature. Deictic terms are those that are dependent on context for their interpretation because they "point" to their referents. A well-studied example (2) of this confusion is provided by *Nigel*, approximately 22 months old, who consistently refers to himself as "you" (Halliday 1975, pg. 70-71):

> (2)   "... on being given a present by his uncle, he turned to his mother who was present and said <u>Uncle gave you some marbles</u>, that is, 'you saw that Uncle gave me some marbles; <u>you</u> = 'me' regularly throughout this stage. He then ran out to show his father who had not been present, and said <u>Daddy, did Uncle give you some marbles?</u>, (i.e., 'you didn't see, but Uncle gave me some marbles')."

The reason for this error is quite obvious when you think about it. Nigel, like all of us, constantly heard others addressing him as "you" and others referring to themselves as "I." Nigel had not learned yet that these referring expressions require a computation based on the current identity of the speaker in order to be interpreted. This pronominal confusion can persist until quite late; one of the author's children continued to make this error until shortly after their fourth birthday.

There is also a good processing reason why repetition is used more frequently in speech than in writing. Authors have the luxury of revision because the intended audience is not present and often spend hours laboring over a single paragraph or searching for the right word. Speakers are under constraints to produce coherent discourse in "real time." It may be easier from a speaker's perspective to repeat a noun phrase that has recently been activated rather than search for a synonym or compute the appropriate pronoun and risk interrupting the flow of discourse.

Repetition may also serve a social function in conversation as it serves to echo and provide "solidarity" with the previous speaker's utterance. As an example of such social functions, Tannen proposes that listeners often repeat the speaker's last utterance as a means of indicating participation in the conversation. In turn, speakers "ratify" the listener's role by incorporating small contributions made by the listener into the current discourse, as in example (3) from (Tannen 1989, p. 62):

(3)	1	CHAD	they all want to touch this ... silly little mouse
	2	STEVE	At five o'clock in the MORNING on the TRAIN station?
	3	CHAD	Yeah.
	4	DAVID	In New Mexico?
	5	CHAD	In New Mexico.
			With ice on the...ICE hanging down from things.

It should be apparent from this example that informal spoken discourse differs from formal written discourse, such as this book, in the complexity and completeness of its sentence structures. Differences between conversation and written text cause many to say that spoken discourse is "ungrammatical." This generalization results from the assumption that the sentence is the basic unit of linguistic analysis and from the (mis)application of formalisms intended for the analysis of written texts to spoken discourse.

Furthermore, such generalizations about spoken discourse confound the dimensions of *genre*, referring to the type of discourse--narrative, conversation, expository, etc.--and *formality* with *modality*. Sociolinguists (Biber 1988) and functional linguists (Chafe 1982, Chafe & Danielewicz 1987) have shown that informal spoken discourse contains many linguistic properties that are different from those of formal written discourse. Many of these differences reflect the genre and not the modality. For example, a greater number of low-frequency words and more varied vocabulary are found in formal academic spoken discourse than in informal conversation. There are analogous differences in the distribution of lexical items found in expository written text and personal letters (Chafe & Danielewicz 1987).

Obviously the vocabulary differences found in the different genres of text reflect differences in the intended audiences and subject matter. However, some of the differences, such as the reduction in lexical variation, may be due, as we just noted, to cognitive constraints that differ across the modalities. One way to examine the cognitive constraints imposed on processing in the two modalities is to explore the "information flow" in spoken discourse. The importance of information structure and flow (Chafe 1979) has been pursued vigorously in the past decade by functional linguists who have analyzed examples of naturally occurring spoken discourse in great depth. Unfortunately there has not been a corresponding psycholinguistic interest in the processing consequences of these linguistic variables on the comprehension of spoken discourse. Rather, most psycholinguistic research has focused on the comprehension of written materials.

14.2.3 Information Structure and Flow in Discourse

We have seen that speakers are expected to produce coherent discourse and that they rely on various linguistic devices to promote cohesion. There are also other ways that the speaker can structure the discourse to lessen the processing load on the comprehender. In particular, speakers indicate what is important or the "point" of the current utterance so that comprehenders can focus their processing. H.O. Coleman, writing in 1914, eloquently and aptly described *intonational emphasis*, one such device used for "prominent" information, as marking "the last word one would sacrifice to save a half penny on a telegram" (1914, pg. 9).

Given and New Information

A number of the linguistic devices used to indicate the structure and importance of information in discourse are common to all modalities, but others, such as intonational emphasis, are unique to speech. Languages have means of marking lexical items, and indeed whole phrases or clauses, with respect to their informational status in the discourse. It is common to divide the information structure of an utterance into (1) "given" information, also referred to as "old" or "background," and (2) "new" information. The definitions seem intuitively straightforward but have been the subject of considerable discussion in the linguistic literature (Chafe 1976, Prince 1981b). Usage of the terms *given* and *new* is closely related to, but not identical with, the theoretical notions of *presupposed* and *focused* information and *topic* and *comment*.

We follow a simple definition recently provided by Prince (1992), who uses the terms "old" and "new" where we use "given" and "new." Using her taxonomy, we can regard information from either the perspective of the hearer or that of the developing discourse. Prince describes information as "hearer-old" if the speaker can reasonably assume that the hearer is already aware of the information being conveyed, and "hearer-new" if not. Speakers are expected to introduce new information appropriately if they believe that the speaker is not already aware of the information being discussed.

Thus if I say to a friend, "I think a terrorist group was responsible for the bombing," I am assuming, by my use of the definite article *the,* that she is aware of the recent bombing and that I am referring to it as "given" information. I am asserting as "new" my, not very surprising, theory that "a terrorist group" performed the act. As a speaker I have a model of the hearer's knowledge that I refer to in constructing my utterances. The same remark directed at my 7-year-old son would require my providing the background information. In fact, much of our interaction with young children requires providing background information in order that they will have an appropriate frame of reference to engage in discourse with us.

Notice that in the example above, given information is marked with *the* and new information with *a.* The sense of the sentence would change considerably if it were phrased "I think a terrorist group was responsible for a bombing." The hearer cannot reasonably be expected to know which bombing is referred to, Bosnia? the Middle East? or the World Trade Center? Additionally, we don't know who did it! The sentence is surely vacuous as it stands.

Changing it slightly yet again we get "I think the terrorist group was responsible for a bombing." This means that we have a particular terrorist group in mind and have reason to believe that they must have engaged in incendiary acts but we are not aware which specific acts they were responsible for. Thus the use of definite and indefinite articles in English is quite informative. English articles are, not surprisingly, often difficult for non-native speakers to master.

We can also consider information to be *given* if it was previously introduced in the discourse. Thus by definition, it is both discourse-old and hearer-old, unless the hearer has had a lapse in attention and failed to hear what the speaker said! Similar linguistic devices are used for discourse-old given information: On the first mention of a noun in a discourse, the speaker typically uses the indefinite article and on later mentions the speaker employs the definite article or pronouns.

Discourse-new items, in Prince's terms, are those that have not previously been mentioned in the discourse, though of course they could already be known to the hearer. A discourse that is maximally informative and "cooperative" would be one that does not redundantly introduce as *new* information what is already known to the hearer. While an ideal, this is not always possible to accomplish. There are many occasions on which one must negotiate with the conversational partner in order to determine how much background knowledge is shared. Presuming too much can cause the hearer to become hopelessly lost; presuming too little, on the other hand, can be perceived as patronizing.

A mismatch in perceptions concerning shared knowledge may lead to some misunderstandings. One can readily imagine situations in which a speaker might refer to an entity as *the* when it has not previously been mentioned in the discourse, nor, contrary to the speaker's belief, is it known to the hearer, as in (4):

> (4) JOHN   Have you felt any effects of the new
>   gasoline tax?
>
>   BILL   What tax?

John might, at this point, incorrectly surmise that Bill has answered his question by using a conventional expression that indicates that the new tax hasn't affected him at all. In fact, Bill may be unaware of the reason for the sudden rise in gas prices and may be genuinely asking for more information.

There are some nouns that are almost always referred to using the definite article, since they are presumed to be shared by speakers. The referents for these nouns are often unique, and thus unambiguous. For example, such noun phrases as *the moon*, *the sun*, and *the President* have a single referent in most everyday speech and can therefore be referred to with the definite article on first mention. Notice how odd it would be to say "A moon shone on a canyon. The moon was full." This sequence gives the impression that two moons were involved; appropriate for Jupiter perhaps, but not for Earth!

Through intonational cues, speech affords means of indicating given and new information that are not available in writing. Linguists generally agree that English speakers indicate new information with intonational "prominence" or "focus" and given information by "deaccentuation" or the lack of focus. The intonation contour of English declaratives typically falls across the duration of the utterance. New information, except in "marked" syntactic constructions and topicalizations, discussed below, usually follows given information and receives the highest pitch or the greatest change in pitch. Cutler (1976) has demonstrated that hearers have internalized this knowledge and make use of the contour to predict where the most important word will be located. This prediction leads to faster lexical access of the prominent word. The speaker's effective, and cooperative, use of intonational emphasis can thus provide the listener with important clues on how, and where, to allocate attention during discourse processing.

Word Order

Although the unmarked order of information in English sentences is for *given* to precede *new* information in an active sentence, alternate sentence constructions can be used to rearrange the distribution of information. For example the passive, as seen in Chapter 13, maintains the order of given followed by new, but reassigns the roles of given and new to the logical object and subject, respectively.

Note the difference in information structure in the following pair:

(5)   John broke the window.
(6)   The window was broken by John.

Sentence (5) focuses on John's actions and is probably the culmination of a description of a series of events initiated by John. Clearly in the second instance we are aware that the fate of the window is known, and is probably the current topic of discussion. What we don't know, until this sentence, is that John is the culprit. Compare two possible contexts for these sentences:

Context A. John was playing baseball in the garden. Mary pitched a slow curve ball. He hit a long fly ball toward the house. *John broke the window.*

Context B. John's house needed some minor repairs before it could be sold. The dog had chewed the front door. The children had ripped the back door screen. *The window was broken by John.*

Other syntactic constructions can be used to affect the flow of information. For example, one can use cleft constructions to keep the subject in initial position but mark it as new, as in "It was John who broke the window." This construction would be particularly useful if one were trying to determine the culprit from a set of possible window breakers. Also possible, but very rare, is the pseudo-cleft: "The one who broke the window was John." Most of these constructions -- passives, clefts, and pseudo-clefts -- are used in written discourse rather than spoken (Chafe 1982).

As we have seen, speakers can use intonational cues which are nonexistent in writing. Speakers also occasionally use structural devices to alter word order and mark important information. These constructions, which would often be considered ungrammatical in written discourse, simply move the to-be-focused element into a new position, either at the beginning or end of the utterance. An example, collected by the author in a Toronto bakery, illustrates what has been called *Yiddish movement* (Prince 1981a): "A can opener you want? A can opener I got." Here the object *can opener* was moved to the beginning of the utterance.

Other types of focusing devices can be heard in casual conversation. A good source is the speech of sportscasters, as in "Up to the plate steps Darryl Strawberry." Here the subject noun phrase is moved after the verb, in this case to the end of the utterance. This is sometimes referred to as "inversion" (Birner 1993). Clearly the fact that someone was "stepping up to the plate" was known, presumably it was time for the next batter. The new information was the identity of the batter.

This discussion has shown that speakers, and writers, perform a delicate juggling act, structuring words in such a way that they accurately portray the flow, and relative importance, of the ideas that they are trying to communicate. Writers have the luxury of revision, speakers do not. Speakers must take the hearer's processing demands and background knowledge into account when producing an utterance. Success in a conversation depends crucially on the ability to indicate the importance of, and relation between, pieces of information in the discourse.

14.3   LANGUAGE SKILLS IN ACTION: CONVERSATIONAL ANALYSIS

How do speakers coordinate conversations so that each person receives their fair share of speaking time? What makes us judge one individual as "rude" and another as a "good" conversationalist? Why are we sometimes unable to extricate ourselves gracefully from a conversation? All of these questions can be addressed by studying the tacit rules and conventions for determining "turns" and for holding the "floor" in conversation.

The field of *conversational analysis* was originally dominated by anthropologists interested in the "ethnography of speaking" rather than by psycholinguists or linguists, although the situation has changed in recent years, particularly in language acquisition (Warren-Leubecker & Bohannon 1989). Seminal work by Schegloff (1968) and his colleagues caused considerable excitement by demonstrating that, like other aspects of human language, conversations are rule governed, albeit tacitly, and that these rules can be discovered and described.

14.3.1   Conversational Conventions

Native speakers of English generally agree that in a smooth conversation only one person speaks at a time. If this were not the case, then interruptions would not be viewed as negatively as they are by most speakers nor would overlaps between speakers cause so many apologies. Who gets to speak, and when, is worked out through a complex set of conventions that depends on the language and culture. Our examples apply to most varieties of English. How does one start a conversation? Certainly not with this technique employed by a phone solicitor.

(7)   A: Hello. This is Armstrong Carpet
                  Cleaners calling? [rising intonation]

         B: I'm not interested, thank you. [Click]

Speaker A undoubtedly intended to provide a conversational *opening*. That is, she meant to identify herself, and the purpose of the call. Openings are a form of negotiation in which greetings are usually exchanged and the initiator then provides a reason, or topic, for the proposed conversation. The solicitor thought she was merely opening, and meant to keep control of the floor in order to make her sales pitch.

However, because she used a question intonation on her opening, she unwittingly passed the floor to the addressee. Questions are used by speakers to select the next speaker. In fact, the addressee is under an obligation to respond, and then has the right, in most instances, teacher-pupil questions being a notable exception, to retain the floor or return it to the questioner. The addressee no doubt knew that the speaker wasn't really intending to pose a question, but instead took advantage of tacit knowledge about the role of questions in discourse in order to end the conversation early.

The original speaker can also give up the floor by providing a series of cues that they have finished speaking. These include a change in intonation, such as a final fall in pitch, or the rise signifying a question that we have already discussed, a pause at the end of a grammatical unit, and/or making eye contact with another potential speaker. Conversely, the speaker can indicate an unwillingness to give up the floor by maintaining level pitch, pausing in the middle of a grammatical constituent, and/or avoiding eye contact. The reader probably knows a number of individuals who are very skilled at monopolizing the conversational floor. It would be interesting to determine how many of these techniques they employ.

How does one get out of a conversation when one feels that it's time to end? All of us have undoubtedly experienced the feeling of being trapped in a conversation when we'd really rather be elsewhere. Simply stating that you're leaving and saying good-bye would be considered rude by most addressees. The act of ending a conversation involves a complex ritual of negotiation that must be agreed upon by both parties. It is somewhat easier to extricate oneself from a multiparty conversation as presumably one's presence is not crucial. In fact, it is often entertaining to observe how quickly one interlocutor will remove himself from a conversation when a new participant comes upon the scene!

Consider the fate of Speaker B in the following exchange, based loosely on real conversations that the author has had with talkative friends and colleagues.

(8)   A: Well, I think it must be time to pick up the kids from preschool. [This is intended as a *preclosing* to signal the desire to bring the conversation to an end. An astute and polite conversational partner would recognize it and agree that yes the hour was late and, regretfully, it must be time to go.]

B: Your son goes to Montessori, doesn't he? Did you know that Mary was a Montessori teacher? [Note the skillful use of a question to obligate the hapless Speaker A to respond to the, tangentially related, new topic.]

A: No, I didn't. [Stopping at this point would be perceived as rude so Speaker A makes another contribution to the conversation, staring nervously at her watch all the while.]

        Is she still at the Montessori school?

B: No, that was years ago. She was only there for a year. Now of course she's in the public schools. She's had quite a year with the new science curriculum... [This is the beginning of a long story about how the books didn't arrive on time, the students were ill-prepared, how tough it is being a teacher these days. Speaker A is quite desperate at this point because the preschool is about to lock up and her children are still there.]

A: [Speaker A finally breaks in, feeling very rude.] I don't envy her job. Look, I really must be at the school in the next five minutes. Bye.

B: Bye. [Speaker B turns around and walks off quickly, leaving Speaker A to wonder if B is mad at her.]

It is of course Speaker A who should be annoyed since Speaker B resolutely ignored A's preclosing attempts. Speaker A had made it clear that she wanted to end the conversation but it was, according to our internalized conventions about conversational sequencing (Sacks et al. 1974), Speaker B who had to indicate that she had accepted the overture. Speaker B is either conversationally unskilled or, more likely, aware of the convention and exploiting it for her own purposes, that is, to keep the conversation going. Unfortunately this strategy will backfire in the long run as others catch on and begin avoiding her. It's no fun having a conversation with someone when you can't get out of it gracefully.

As competent speakers of a language we rely on our knowledge of the turn-taking conventions to ensure that our exchanges run smoothly and cooperatively.

It is quite remarkable to realize how finely tuned the system is, and the degree to which we rely on others to follow the same conventions. Conversing with an individual who has never learned these conventions, or worse yet, flaunts them, can cause a tremendous drain on our processing resources, leading us to realize how much we take turn-taking skills for granted.

14.3.2 The Challenge of Conversational Analysis: An Example

The following short excerpt from an hour-long conversation among four friends illustrates many of the challenges faced by discourse analysts studying conversation. Often the biggest challenge is transcribing the conversation! Depending on the "narrowness" or detail of the transcription, a single minute of speech may take more than an hour to transcribe. Each speaker is indicated by a letter (A-D); each utterance, defined by a single intonation contour, occupies a single line. A single speaker's "turn" may consist of a number of utterances. A hockey game was playing on the TV in the background.

(9) A: Complete with his surgical room slippers....
          You called him the Frank Zappa of business.

     B: Did you punch your dough?

     C: No.
          It isn't rising as fast.

     B: Uh oh....Maybe.

     A: [Interruption] Well, maybe it's because the
          weather's gotten colder.

     B: [Continuing] It's not warm enough.
          Why don't you turn on the stove or....

     D: Does he not do it in the stove?
          My mother normally does it in the oven.

     B: What?

     C: I've had it in the oven.
          I turned the oven to about three hundred.
          Kept it on the top for a while.
          Opened...turned the oven off.
          Opened the oven door.

Put it on the door til the oven cooled down a lot.
Then I put it in the oven.

D: It's cooking without rising? [Laugh]

C: We'll just let it rise some more.
I think I just....
Alright, now it has to rise again.
And I think I can knead it and make it rise again.

B: Do you really have to do it twice?
I thought you just....

A: [Interruption] To get bubbles in it.

B: hmmmm.

D: Yeah.
If you imagine bread without the bubbles it'd be a
bit like eating a brick.

B: hmmmm.
Is the game over or something?

There are clearly three distinct topics under discussion, although this excerpt includes only the second in its entirety. The first topic, which Speaker A finishes, is a discussion of a mutual acquaintance and his actions at a party. The second, and major topic concerning baking bread, appears to be introduced by Speaker B in the third line. In fact, just prior to that utterance Speaker C had returned to the living room from the kitchen where he had been checking on some bread dough. Thus the topic was situationally determined, triggered by the reappearance of Speaker C. However, since Speaker A had the floor prior to Speaker C's appearance, we might ask how Speaker B knew that she could take the conversational floor at that point. Cues that are not apparent from the transcript, such as eye contact and gaze direction, a terminal fall in intonation, and the additional participant, probably all contributed to Speaker B's taking of the floor.

Speaker C is obligated, by Speaker B's question, the first half of an "adjacency pair" (Sacks et al. 1974), to take the floor, if only for as long as is necessary to answer the question. Speaker B maintains the right to reassert ownership but Speaker A interrupts, in what may be an unsuccessful attempt to regain the floor after losing it two turns previously. Speaker B persists in her questioning and a new participant, Speaker D, joins in, rather oddly referring to Speaker C in the third person, "Does he not do it in the stove?"

After an exclamation by Speaker A in response to hearing that Speaker D's mother "does it in the oven," poor Speaker C finally gets a chance to speak for himself. He proceeds to recount the history of his bread baking in considerable detail. This turn is remarkable for its extensive use of lexical repetition as a cohesive device. We first notice this repetition when Speaker B asks about turning on "the stove" and Speaker D uses "the stove" in his contribution. Speaker D then offers "the oven" as a contrast to the stove. Speaker C counters by insisting that he is already using the oven and not the stove. From that point on, Speaker D refers to the "oven" in almost every utterance.

The reason for this referential pattern is obvious given knowledge of the English pronominal system and the conversational context. The dough, or would-be bread, is the undisputed topic of this segment of the conversation. The dough is referred to on second mention, in the second utterance of Speaker C's first turn, and all subsequent references as "it." Because "it" is the only English pronoun for inanimate entities, referring to the oven as "it" as well would lead to ambiguity. Speaker C has chosen to resolve this problem by reserving the pronoun for the major topic, bread dough, and the definite noun phrase for what might be considered a secondary topic, the oven. Thus, although both entities are *given*, and central to the discussion, only one can be pronominalized. As a consequence, we can use the information about what is pronominalized as a means of determining the hierarchy of topics in this short exchange.

An interesting question to consider is whether the two means of referring, pronominalization and repetition, differ in processing difficulty. For example, do the addressees have to compute the meaning of *it* on each occurrence by searching for the referent in memory? This hardly seems likely as "it" is the primary discourse topic, yet according to one well-known theory of pronoun comprehension, a pronoun whose referent is in the immediately preceding clause is processed much more rapidly than one whose referent is two or more clauses back in the discourse (Clark & Sengul 1979). Thus we would have to predict that the first instance of "it," Speaker C, Turn 1, would be easier to comprehend than the multiple uses of "it" in Speaker C's second turn. Given the prominence of the dough in the discourse, this seems unlikely.

Some experimental evidence suggests that sentences are interpreted from the perspective of the first noun phrase (Gernsbacher & Hargreaves 1992), which would make the first NP a likely referent for an ambiguous pronoun. It is difficult, however, to generalize the results of experimental studies using sentence pairs or miniature texts to natural discourse processing. Furthermore, even though it is tempting to equate the first noun phrase with the sentence "topic" there are some difficult theoretical issues involved in the intuitive concept of *topic* (Reinhart 1981). Ideally one would want to study natural discourse processing "on-line," as it actually happens, but any intervention during the conversation, particularly measuring reaction times or brain functions, would distort the subject under study.

Our final remark about this short segment of conversation, though we could make many more, concerns the finality with which Speaker D closes the topic of bread baking. His comparison of a bubbleless loaf of a bread to a brick has the effect of summing up the premise behind, and indeed the justification for, the discussion of kneading and rising the dough that has preoccupied Speaker C. There is not much more that other participants could contribute to this conversational topic following that remark!

Instead, Speaker B again turns to an external event, the closing chords of the theme song for the sports show, as an inspiration for a new conversational topic. While the four participants were enraptured with the topic of flat dough, the game that they were watching came to an end. We would suggest that it is the finality of Speaker D's remark about the brick, plus the environmental stimulus, that has led to the topic shift. Speaker D clearly closed the bread topic, without proposing anything in its place, and Speaker B taking the path of least resistance, seized on the external event as a potential new discourse topic. The conversation then progressed to a discussion of the prevalence of fixed games in hockey, supposedly the result of a collaboration between crooked players and the gambling industry. This new topic, which was introduced as an elaboration on the previously established topic of the final score, was broached, not surprisingly, by Speaker D.

14.4 SOCIAL INFLUENCES ON LANGUAGE USE

14.4.1 Variation in Language

Our discussion has centered on only a few of the possible indicators of conversational turns and those that we have examined are not necessarily assigned universal values across languages and cultures, or even across speakers, dialects, and situations within a language. In fact, there is considerable variation within languages with respect to most aspects of discourse, a fact well-recognized by linguists. *Sociolinguistics* is the branch of linguistics concerned with variation in language use as a function of social variables.

Because discourse always occurs in a social setting, even if that setting is a psycholinguistic laboratory, it is important for us to be familiar with some of the major social factors affecting language use. In our discussion we make considerable use of the term *dialect* to refer to a variety of a language, used by a particular group of speakers. It should be noted that linguists use the term *accent* to refer only to pronunciation and *dialect* to include lexical, syntactic, and pragmatic variants in addition to pronunciation differences.

14.4.2 Genre, Style, and Register

All of us are masters of many varieties of our native language. We use different varieties of our language for different purposes, with different addressees, and in different situations. Thus the structure and form of a lecture are quite different than that of an informal conversation. So, too, a political speech is quite a different form than a novel, though both may share fictional aspects! Each of these *genres* has a particular structure and a specific purpose. Competent native speakers of a language are able to produce and comprehend discourse in a number of genres. An obvious part of acquiring the use of a native language as a child is that of learning the forms of different genres. The number of available genres also becomes considerably larger once one acquires maturity.

We use different *styles* of speaking in different contexts, often without being consciously aware of what we are doing. Speakers change styles depending on the audience and the level of formality required. A language variety that is characteristic of a particular situation, rather than of a speaker, is referred to as a *register* by sociolinguists. Thus the language of the courtroom is referred to as the *legal register*. Similarly, the speech used to address a child of two is, one hopes, quite different from that used to address adult friends, even though both may be instances of the genre of casual conversation. When talking to a young child we alter the discourse by using simple sentence structures, a small range of vocabulary, clear pronunciation, and, typically, a more exaggerated intonation than with adults. This variety has been termed the *baby talk* register by Ferguson (1977).

Many of us use a similar way of speaking to our pets, and, unfortunately, to foreigners whom we perceive to have limited knowledge of our language. This would be completely inappropriate in a university setting, where the academic register is required. Interestingly, the same professor who produces a propositionally and syntactically dense lecture, full of low-frequency words, is probably perfectly capable of engaging in conversation consisting of short simple utterances with high-frequency words outside of class! It is important to know when, and if, it is necessary to switch style when changing situations. Not knowing the appropriate speech style for a particular situation can lead one to be deemed a social incompetent. (Sadly, many of us know such individuals.)

Speaking style can vary because of regional differences, even between individuals of similar ages and social backgrounds. For example, Tannen (1984) has pointed out that there is a large "Coast" effect in the expected duration of turn-final pauses, depending on the regional and social origin of the speaker. She performed a microanalysis of a multispeaker conversation among friends recorded at a Thanksgiving dinner and found striking differences in "conversational style" among speakers of different origins. New Yorkers, for example, were perceived as rude and constantly trying to monopolize the conversation because they would not let their Californian friends finish their turns. Conversely, Californians were perceived as somewhat too slow and "laid-back."

The major difference between speakers from the two geographic regions was in speaking rate; furthermore, what was merely a pause to collect one's thoughts in California was considered by the more rapidly speaking New Yorkers to be a signal that the speaker had given up the floor. Had a new speaker waited the same interval in New York, they would not have been judged rude at all. Unfortunately, linguistic differences such as these often become the basis of regional stereotypes. These can be particularly damaging when they are also correlated with ethnicity and can lead to misunderstanding and confrontation.

14.4.3 Speaker Characteristics: Gender, Age, and Ethnicity

Personal characteristics of the speaker can also be the source of variation in language use. If the speaker and addressee use different variants of the language, this can lead to miscommunication. An obvious personal characteristic, and one that has been shown to be correlated with differences in language use, is gender. Tannen (1990), Lakoff (1973), and others have argued convincingly that conversational conventions differ between the genders. Tannen, in fact, claims that "male-female conversation is cross-cultural communication" (p. 42). Women are said to have as their primary communicative goal the desire to further interaction rather than impart information, which is said to be the male conversational norm.

Fishman (1983) reported evidence that the female partners in couples suggest more topics than their male partners, but a far greater number of men's topics are actually taken up in the conversation. Thus the impression is one of women working hard to initiate conversations in order to facilitate interaction, and being more willing to respond to their male partner's suggestions than the reverse. Not surprisingly, female speakers are claimed to monitor the conversation closely for signs of feedback from the addressee. One linguistic device, the tag question, was suggested by Lakoff (1973) as a means of checking on the reaction of the addressee. Thus the speaker who says "It's hot today, *isn't it?*" is not unsure of the temperature but is instead looking for confirmation of her observation.

From the perspective of the male *genderlect*, however, tag questions may be viewed as a sign of insecurity, which of course is not their intended function. Additionally, women also use more varied intonation and a greater amount of rising "question" intonation (Lakoff 1973), which could be interpreted within the conventions of North American conversations as cues that signal completion of a turn. Recall that holding one's pitch level is one way of monopolizing the conversational floor. Since there is strong evidence that women are interrupted more often than men in mixed-sex conversations it may be that male conversational participants incorrectly interpret female "feedback checks" as cues that they are willing to give up the conversational floor (West & Zimmerman 1983, Zimmerman & West 1975).

It is not clear whether gender differences in language use are biologically or socially determined, although most linguists would argue in favor of the latter. Furthermore, it is important to stress that these are generalizations and not necessarily true of any one individual. Finally, as in most linguistic research, there is no value judgment associated with either the so-called feminine or masculine speech styles.

Another personal characteristic that has a large effect on language use is *age*. It is generally the case that older speakers of a language are more conservative than younger speakers and less likely to accept innovations in language. Most language change occurs through young speakers. Linguists interested in recording and studying an endangered dialect or language seek out older, rural, and typically male speakers. The younger generation is not only crucial for linguistic innovation, it is critical for language preservation. A culture that loses the younger generation as native speakers is in danger of losing its first language, as many Native American peoples and immigrant groups in this country are only too painfully aware.

Sociolinguists have also documented the effects of *ethnicity* on language use. The most well-known, and ground-breaking, example of such research is that of Labov (1972). This study used careful linguistic analysis to demonstrate that the grammar of an urban African-American dialect, at that time referred to as Black English, or BE, is internally consistent and therefore rule governed and not random, as was mistakenly thought by many.

Speakers who believe they speak so-called Standard English often assume that their dialect is superior and "correct" and that other forms, in particular BE, are full of errors and "substandard." In reality, English consists of a large number of dialects which have been shaped by different historical, regional, and social influences. Henry Higgins (and his attempts to transform Eliza Doolittle's Cockney speech) to the contrary, there is nothing inherently superior about one form of the language over another. It is the fact that we have come to associate social status, and indeed our own ethnic prejudices, with particular ways of speaking that has led to the value judgments that are imposed on different dialects.

Our brief discussion of sociolinguistics makes it clear that fluent language use involves more than simply knowing the grammatical rules of a language. Social variables exert considerable influence over our everyday use of language, even though we are seldom consciously aware of them. The ability to tailor our speech to appropriately respond to these social pressures is a critical feature of acquiring *communicative competence* (Hymes 1971).

A complete theory of language would necessarily include these social features as an important set of factors. Experimental studies of language processing should ideally locate the particular discourse, subjects, and situation under study, in its social "coordinates." This "situatedness" is one reason computers have great difficulty understanding human languages and conversing with them. For humans, each situation brings out a set of expectations and reliance on a particular set of linguistic skills that are based on experience.

As it is, the experimental psycholinguistic literature is built primarily on one genre, experimental texts; one register, formal, primarily written, English; and one type of speaker-addressee interaction, experimenter and college student. It is quite possible that in the interests of experimental control, psycholinguists have built a body of research that does not have much generalizabilty to the larger range of possible human social situations.

14.5   EPILOGUE AND REFERENCES

The study of pragmatics is intuitively much closer to our everyday experiences with language than is the study of isolated "decontextualized" sentences in the laboratory. However, this does not invalidate the approach to language processing taken in Chapter 13. A complete theory of language processing must encompass both types of research. An intelligent hearer requires both types of knowledge: the ability to access and comprehend the "utterance" meaning as well as the ability to discern what the speaker intended by the words that she uttered. In order to arrive at even an approximation of the speaker's intention, the listener must rely on knowledge from a large range of sources.

Conversational participants need to know the appropriate turn-taking conventions for their culture and how they are modified by the particular situation. For example, the rules for who gets to speak next are very rigid in a classroom setting where one "super" speaker has absolute control over the conversational floor. It is often quite difficult for children, used to the linguistic free-for-all of the preschool setting, to make the transition to the conversational conventions of the elementary school classroom.

The listener also must possess adequate, and appropriate, background knowledge for the discourse topic under discussion. The speaker, too, must be sensitive to the listener's level of knowledge and mark the information structure of the discourse accordingly. Listeners must be cognizant of speech act conventions, being able to recognize indirect forms from the context when appropriate. In addition, the appropriate interpretation of a particular utterance may also be affected by knowledge of speaker characteristics such as age, gender, and ethnicity. Understanding how humans coordinate this incredible, interconnected system of language is the challenge for cognitive scientists.

Good introductions to the field of discourse analysis can be found in Brown and Yule (1983) and Stubbs (1983). Blakemore (1992) and Levinson (1983) provide basic introductions to the field of pragmatics. Searle's (1969) book on speech acts is a classic in the field. The concept of *relevance* has been recognized as a very important pragmatic principle and is explored in considerable detail by Sperber and Wilson (1986). Rochester and Martin (1979) provide an interesting application of discourse analysis to schizophrenic language. For more on politeness, see Brown and Levinson (1987) and Clark and Schunk (1980). Tannen's (1984) work on conversational style and Goodwin's (1981) study of conversational organization provide interesting microanalyses of conversational interaction.

The field of gender and language is currently very active; see Tannen (1990) for a popular discussion of the topic. An interesting collection of research papers on gender and language can be found in Phillips, Steele and Tanz (1987). For a fascinating study of the effects of ethnicity on language, see Gumperz's research on the perception of "Indian English" by native speakers of "British English" (Gumperz 1982, Gumperz et al. 1982). Bates' (1976) work on the acquisition of pragmatics is a classic in child language research. See Warren-Leubecker and Bohannon (1989) for a review of research on the acquisition of pragmatics.

THEORETICAL CONSTRUCTS

Part V

BUILDING COGNITIVE REPRESENTATIONS IN PROLOG

PROLOG, for PROgramming in LOGic, is an implementation of predicate logic as a programming language. It is a robust, general purpose language used for problem solving by both the research and application oriented computing communities. We present it here as a representational medium, as a concrete language, and as a scientific tool for cognitive science. PROLOG is a highly interactive language and a medium for both representation and interpretation.

PROLOG is first of all a language in that it is a sign system that is intended to be interpreted. The PROLOG interpreter is interactive, in that we can give it a descriptive specification of what is true in some situation, and then ask questions about that situation. PROLOG takes a query and returns an interpretation of this query in the context of our descriptions. Although PROLOG is based on logic and its action can produce mathematically sound results, it is a general purpose programming tool, able to represent and interpret imprecise and uncertain situations, for example, with data structures such as frames and schemas that are not mathematically sound.

As we noted in Part I, a computational environment is an essential tool for the cognitive scientist. This is true for a number of reasons: First, as computational, it allows the researcher to "cash out" all homunculi from an information processing or any other model of cognition. Simply put, this means that rather than saying, "Subsystem *foo* takes care of that part of the cognitive process," we can write and run subsystem *foo* and determine whether or not it actually does compute the process. The computational environment gives us the tools to be both precise in our design as well as to produce models that are sufficient for accomplishing the task.

Second, we use our computer based specifications to understand the limits of both formalism and mechanism. We make bold claims as cognitive scientists. Most importantly, that intelligence is mechanistic, and as a mechanism may be specified. In our research we build and test these mechanistic models of intelligence.

A computational specification allows us to be experimental scientists. We can design processes and structures, we can encode information from a problem situation, and we can run our experiments and interpret the adequacy of there results. We can deconstruct our experimental scenario and generalize its strengths and repair its inadequacies for further experiment. The computational environment allows our research to become science.

Chapter 15 introduces PROLOG, gets the user comfortable with its interactive environment, and builds a number of simple representational structures. These include simple depth-first and recursive search strategies and the production system architecture. We demonstrate these on a number of simple problems. The production system is one of the tools that allows us to create "knowledge level" representations, as described by Newell (1982) and presented in Chapter 9.

Chapter 16 introduces *meta-interpreters*. A meta-interpreter is an important tool for the cognitive scientist in that it allows the creation of an interpreter within a high level language specification. With the meta-interpreter technology we can design semantic nets, frame and schema systems, as well as other complex interpretative environments. For example, in Section 16.4 we design a *recursive descent semantic net parser* for interpreting a subset of English sentences. In Section 16.5 we implement the *version space search* learning algorithm from Chapter 10. The chapter epilogues give further information on PROLOG and its application for research in cognitive science and artificial intelligence.

Chapter 15

PROLOG AS REPRESENTATION
AND LANGUAGE

I contend that each science is a real science insofar as it is mathematics...

Immanuel Kant

"Contrariwise," continued Tweedledee, "if it was so, it might be; and if it were so, it would be; but as it isn't, it aint; that's logic..."

Lewis Carroll, *Alice's through the Looking Glass.*

15.0 INTRODUCTION

In Section 15.1 we present PROLOG syntax and several simple programs. These programs begin to build the representational schemes and algorithms introduced in Part II and demonstrate the power of the predicate calculus as a representation language. In Section 15.2 we introduce the PROLOG problem solving environment. We show how to interact with the interpreter and how to monitor PROLOG's built-in depth-first, left-to-right, backtracking control.

Section 15.3 introduces the design of search algorithms in PROLOG. We begin with depth-first search; breadth-first search and best-first search are added in Chapter 16. In Section 15.3 we use recursion as a mechanism for implementing graph search; we do this with simple list handling examples. In Section 15.4 we build a production system in PROLOG, and show how the predicate cut, !, can be used to alter the PROLOG search process. In Section 15.5 we end the chapter with some comments on PROLOG as a representational language for cognitive scientists. We consider its pattern driven semantics and that it can be seen from both a procedural and a declarative viewpoint.

In Chapter 16 we design meta-interpreters in PROLOG. A meta-interpreter is an interpreter built in or on top of, thus "meta," a language. Meta-interpreters offer a methodology for the interpretation of other structures also written in the language. We will use this approach to create interpreters for semantic nets, frames, schemas, natural language utterances, and version space learning.

Our introduction to PROLOG is not intended to be exhaustive, but rather to assist the new user in understanding predicate calculus based representations and an interpretative environment. We recommend the beginner obtain a users' manual containing, at least, PROLOG'S built-in predicates. A number of excellent books on PROLOG are now available and are mentioned in the epilogue and references (Section 15.6).

15.1   WORDS AND SENTENCES IN THE LANGUAGE

15.1.1   PROLOG Predicates and Connectives

A PROLOG program is a set of specifications in the first order predicate calculus (Section 7.3) describing the objects and relations in a problem domain. We often refer to the set of specifications, or what is true about a particular problem situation, as the *data base* for that problem. The PROLOG interpreter responds to questions about this set of specifications.

Queries to the data base are patterns in the same logical syntax as the data base entries. The PROLOG interpreter uses pattern directed search, to be described in detail in Section 15.2, to find if these queries logically follow from the specifications of the data base. PROLOG is an interactive language; the user enters queries in response to the PROLOG prompt: ?-. This prompt will precede all PROLOG example queries in the chapter.

The data base, as well as the query, are constructed in a form of the first order predicate calculus. Although there are a number of dialects of PROLOG, the syntax used throughout this text is the original Warren and Periera C-PROLOG (Clocksin and Mellish 1984). To simplify presentation of both logic and the PROLOG language, our introduction of the syntax for predicate calculus presented in Chapter 7 used many PROLOG conventions. There are, however, a number of differences between PROLOG and predicate calculus syntax. In C-PROLOG, for example, the symbol :- replaces the implies sign of first order predicate calculus.

Several other symbols differ from those presented in Chapter 7:

English	**Predicate Calculus**	**PROLOG**
and	$\wedge$	,
or	$\vee$	;
implies	<-	:-
not	$\neg$	not

TABLE 15.1 Predicate calculus and related PROLOG symbols

15.1.2 PROLOG Facts and Rules

We now create some descriptions in PROLOG. These will be in the form of logic statements describing a situation. As in Chapter 7, predicate names and bound variables are expressed as a sequence of alphabetic or numeric characters beginning with an alphabetic. Variables are also represented as a string of characters beginning (at least) with an uppercase alphabetic. Thus:

> major(sarah, psychology).

could represent the fact that "Sarah is a psychology major." Note that in this specification sarah begins with a lowercase s, indicating it is a bound value. Variables, again as in Chapter 7, have their first character uppercase. Thus:

> major(Student, psychology).

would indicate that in our application, all members of the domain of Student are psychology majors.

Our program, or the set of all specifications true for this domain of interpretation, is a set of similar specifications. Thus, to describe the situation of four university students, we might say:

> major(sarah, psychology).
> major(david, psychology).
> major(peter, linguistics).
> major(george, psychology).
> major(george, computer_science).

Note that a period "." ends each description and the "_" is used because spaces are not acceptable characters within a word. Thus, we have one word here, computer_science. As in Chapter 7, the predicate name, major, precedes the two arguments. In this example the first argument is a student name, the second that student's major area of study. We have now created a set of descriptions or a program containing five facts, and no rule relationships. We can now query these specifications:

?- major(sarah, psychology).

and the system responds:

yes

PROLOG then gives another request, ?-. Similarly we can ask:

?- major(sarah, X).

and PROLOG would respond:

X = psychology
?-

When there are multiple answers possible we may request more with the ";" or "or" query placed after the PROLOG prompt. (In some PROLOGs the user gives the ";" query after the interpreter answers and then a "return" to get a new prompt):

?- major(Students, psychology).
Students = sarah
?- ;
Students = david
?- ;
Students = george
?- ;
no
?-

where the no indicates that there are no more true interpretations of this query in the set of specifications.

If a query to the interpreter contains a variable, as just shown, then the action of the interpreter is to find an instance where the specification query is true. This corresponds loosely to the existential quantification of variables, that is, to finding an instance under which the variable based specification is true. The use of a variable in a data base specification, on the other hand, indicates that the relation is true for all members of its domain of definition, that is, the variable is universally quantified. The domain is also implicit in the specifications. For example, the domain includes all the students that are explicitly listed as psychology majors. The method of reasoning based on defining a domain by the explicit listing of all, and only those elements in it, is referred to as the *closed world assumption* and is discussed in Section 15.1.3.

We now add a rule relationship to our specifications. Suppose we wish to describe the fact that some students may have two majors:

double_major(Student) :-
    major(Student, X), major(Student, Y), X \== Y.

This rule relationship states that a student has a double_major if he or she is a major in two different departments. Note that the <- or "if" is represented by the :-. Note also that a comma "," separates each of the three conditions that makes the double_major predicate true; thus the "and" in the table of connectives above. The symbol \== stands for the "unequal" or "are not identical" relationship; thus the student must be a major in two different departments. Finally, Student is a variable, first character uppercase, and global to the entire expression. That is, it may have only one binding, or tied to one student's name, for each interpretation of double_major.

Now if we make the query:

?- double_major(X).

PROLOG responds:

X = george
?- ;
no
?-

The response of no to our ; indicated there are no other double majors in our specifications.

We could now use the ; to state that a student will graduate in arts and sciences if he or she is either a major in psychology or a major in linguistics:

```
graduate(Student, arts_and_sciences) :-
    major(Student, psychology); major(Student, linguistics).
```

Finally, we can use the not to say that a computer science major cannot be an arts and sciences graduate:

```
graduate(Student, arts_and_sciences) :-
    not(major(Student, computer_science)).
```

These examples show how the predicate calculus connectives ^ , v , not, and <- are expressed in PROLOG. The predicate names such as major, the number or order of parameters, or even whether one predicate always has the same number of parameters is determined by the design requirements, the implicit "semantics," of the problem. There are no expressive limitations other than the predicate calculus syntax. Actually, PROLOG uses a form of the predicate calculus called the *Horn clause logic*, where at most one positive predicate can be left of the :- sign, as we see in Section 15.1.3.

PROLOG is almost always used interactively: the user enters a query or goal using the problem's specifications. The interpreter processes the query, searching the data base to find out if the query is a logical consequence of the data base of specifications. Some versions of PROLOG run in interpretive mode only, while others allow compilation of part or all of the set of specifications for faster execution.

15.1.3   The *Closed World Assumption* and *Negation as Failure*

The previous example of students and their majors illustrates the *closed world assumption* or notion of *negation as failure*. PROLOG assumes that anything is false whose opposite is not provably true. In the query:

?- major(kate, psychology).

The interpreter looks to the specifications for the predicate major(kate, psychology) or some rule that could establish that major(kate, psychology) is true. Failing in this task, it asserts that the request is false. Thus, PROLOG assumes that all necessary knowledge of the world is present and placed in the data base of specifications.

The closed world assumption introduces a number of practical and philosophical difficulties with the language. For example, failure to include a fact in the data base means that it is not true: the closed world assumption treats it as false. If a predicate is omitted or even if there is a misspelling, e.g., major(kate, psichology), the PROLOG response remains no.

The negation as failure issue is currently a very important research topic. Both its advantages, such as how it can be used to represent aspects of the world, as well as its disadvantages, such as how we can possibly interpret specifications that are missing, open up important research questions. These include the design of nonmonotonic logics and truth maintenance systems, as discussed in Section 7.4. It is also an important issue in the design of more advanced representations, such as *networks* and *frames*, as we saw in Chapter 6.

In creating a PROLOG rule, only one predicate is permitted on the left hand side of the if symbol, :-. All predicate calculus expressions which contain implication or equivalence relationships (->, and <->) must be reduced to this form. This form for predicate calculus statements is referred to as part of *Horn clause logic* specifications.

In Horn clause form, the left hand side or conclusion of a rule or implication must be a single positive predicate expression, i.e., not can't be used left of the :- in any expression. The Horn clause calculus is equivalent to the full first order predicate calculus for proofs by refutation. That is, for proof procedures such as that used by the PROLOG interpreter, anything that can be expressed in full predicate calculus can be written using Horn clauses, although the number of clauses required may differ. Techniques for demonstrating equivalency of expressions in the predicate calculus were presented in Chapter 7, with more detail available in Luger and Stubblefield (1993, Chap. 13).

15.2 THE ENVIRONMENT: MONITORING PROLOG PROCESSING

15.2.1 Interacting with the PROLOG Data Base

When we create a PROLOG program we must build a set of specifications. We can do this directly in the interactive PROLOG environment using the built-in PROLOG predicate **assert**. This predicate enters new specifications directly into our current programming environment. Thus:

?- assert(major(david, computer_science)).

adds this predicate to our current set of specifications. The query:

?- major(david, X).

will return:

X = computer_science

as a possible interpretation of the data base.

We can also use **assert** within our rules to augment the specifications set as the program runs. For example, we can add the following rule to the data base describing majors that we created in Section 15.1:

> college(Student, arts_and_sciences) :-
>   (major(Student,linguistics); major(Student,psychology)),
>   assert(graduate(Student,arts_and_sciences)).

Now, whenever the **college** predicate finds an interpretation for **Student,** a new **graduate** predicate will be added to the specifications in the data base. Thus **assert** allows the program to all new facts and rules while it is running. This might be used to reflect the results of a learning program.

Because the PROLOG interpreter considers the predicates in the order they appear in the data base, we can change the order of interpretation with the asserta(foo) and assertz(foo) predicates. The predicate asserta puts the new clause foo first in the order of all the clauses with the same name. Similarly, assertz puts the predicate foo at the end of the list, to be tried only after all the others.

The predicate retract removes predicates from the set of specifications. Suppose that when a student drops out of the university we want to remove that student from our records. We might create the specification:

drops(Student) :- retract(major(Student, Area)).

This would allow us to remove one major area for each student that drops out. If some students have more than one major, as in our example, we would prefer to use the predicate retractall. (retractall is not standard to all PROLOG environments). This predicate continues to call the retract predicate until there are no more matches on major for that student in the specifications:

drops(Student) :- retractall(major(Student, Area)).

It very quickly becomes tedious to build interactively a set of specifications using assert and retract. The programmer usually takes her favorite editor and builds a file containing the set of specifications. Once the file is created, call it myfile, and PROLOG is called, the predicate consult may be used to build the data base using the specifications contained in myfile:

?- consult(myfile).
yes
?-

an abbreviated form of consult is to enclose the file name in square brackets:

?- [myfile].
yes
?-

The predicate list can be used to present to the user the set of all specifications in the data base at any time. The predicates read and write are also important for getting information from and placing information in external files.

The predicate read(X) takes the next term from the current input stream and binds it to X. The symbol "." is used to delimit any term that is read. The predicate write(X) puts X in the output stream. If X is unbound, then an integer preceded by an underline, e.g., _69, is printed. This integer comes from the internal bookkeeping necessary for the interpreter to separate and keep track of all variables, and can be very useful in debugging.

15.2.2   Monitoring PROLOG's Interpretations

A number of PROLOG predicates help us keep track of the state of the data base as well as the state of the computing about the data base. The most important of these are listing, trace, and spy. If, from the prompt ?-, we use listing(predicate) where predicate is the name of a predicate, such as major, or graduate, all the clauses in the data base with name predicate will be returned by the interpreter. Note that the number of arguments of predicate is not indicated; in fact all specifications using that predicate name, regardless of the number of arguments, will be returned.

The predicates trace and spy allow us to monitor the progress of the PROLOG interpreter. The predicate trace tells the interpreter to put to the output file every goal it attempts to satisfy. The tracing facilities in many PROLOG environments are a bit cryptic and often take some study to understand. The trace information usually includes the following:

1. The depth level of the recursive calls (marked left to right at the beginning of the line).
2. When a goal is tried for the first time (sometimes call is used).
3. When a goal is satisfied (with an exit).
4. When a goal is failed and further matches remain (retry).
5. When a goal fails all attempts (the term fail is often used).
6. The variable bindings for each state of the computation are usually given by the interpreter when tracing.

trace can give the user too much information and some PROLOG environments provide better trace control facilities than others. The top level goal notrace will stop the exhaustive tracing.

When a more selective tracing is required, the goal spy is useful. The predicate spy takes a predicate name as argument, as in spy(graduate); although in some environments spy can be an operator applied to a predicate, as in spy graduate. In either format, spy causes the interpreter to print out each use of the predicate graduate, along with its current variable bindings. Of course spy can be used on more than one predicate at a time. The goal nospy(predicate) removes the spy points set up for predicate. Some interpreters use the predicate trace with arguments to perform spying. More details on monitoring the PROLOG environment can be obtained from any user's manual.

15.2.3   Prolog Search: Left-to-Right and Depth-First

We conclude Section 15.2 with a demonstration of PROLOG's left-to-right and depth-first search. We present a set of specifications, limited in this case to the propositional calculus, to demonstrate how the built-in interpreter considers them in problem solving. In Section 15.3, with the full predicate calculus, we describe the backtracking nature of PROLOG's search and how the predicate cut, !, can be used to control backtracking.

Example 15.1: **A PROLOG Search Space**

Consider a set of propositional specifications. Suppose the following descriptions make up the PROLOG data base:

        a :- b, c, d.
        b :- e, f.
        b :- g.
        c :- h; i.
        e :- j.
        d.
        g.
        i.
        j.

The top five specifications are, of course, rules. The bottom four are facts that are true in the domain. Suppose we make the query:

?- a.

This asks the interpreter to determine if there is an interpretation of the data base under which a is true. There are no facts in the data base that give a directly, so the first rule is matched: a is true if b and c and d are all true, or:

        a :- b, c, d.

The interpreter works left to right on b, c, and d, first attempting to see if there is an interpretation for b. Again, there are no facts demonstrating b directly, so the interpreter considers the first of the two rules for b: b :- e, f. Consider what has happened this way: when the interpreter looked to solve a, it found it needed b; when it looked to solve b, it found it needed e and f. The top level goal at this point of interpretation, with appropriate substitutions is:

a :- e, f, c, d.

In the attempt to solve e no facts are found to confirm it directly, so the rule e :- j further reduces the top level goal to:

a :- j, f, c, d.

The reader should note that what the interpreter has done is solve for the goal using a depth-first search, as in Section 8.4.2 (this usually is done with a last-in-first-out, or stack, data structure).

Let's continue the evaluation. We now consider j and find it is true in the data base. Our proof is now:

a :- f, c, d.

Since we have no fact or rule to prove f, it fails. By the closed world assumption (Section 15.1) anything that can't be proven true is assumed false. Since e and f had to be proven for b, the entire rule is seen as false in this situation. At this point the interpreter backs up to look for another possible proof of b and finds the third rule b :- g. The goal stack is now:

a :- g, c, d.

When g is seen as true the goal b is marked true and then c is replaced by its first proof, since c is true if either h or i are true:

a :- h, d.

Now h is considered and determined false. The goal reduces to:

a :- i, d.

both of which are determined true; therefore a, the top level goal, is true.

The full proof tree for our example is presented in the and-or search space of Figure 15.1, where the order of evaluation is represented by the numbers to the left of each node, where the leaves of the tree are marked either true or false and the subtree proof of a is marked in bold.

It should be noted that we only asked the interpreter to prove one goal, namely a. We could have made other queries about the specifications, such as to prove b or to prove c. These would have produced other and-or search spaces. The reader should try these, and ask further questions such as what would happen if the goal f :- a were added to the specifications.

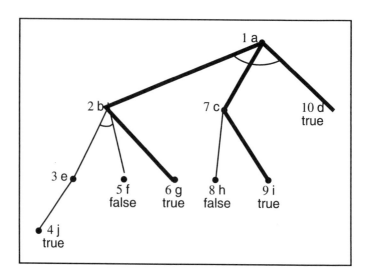

FIGURE 15.1 The and-or proof of goal a in Example 15.1. The number near each state
is the order in which it is considered. Leaf nodes are marked true or
false. The final proof is in bold.

Finally, there is backtracking in this example when the interpreter went back,
on failure, to find alternate interpretations for b and c. A more complete example
of backtrack is presented when variables are introduced in the next section.

15.3   RECURSION BASED SEARCH IN PROLOG

15.3.1   Introduction

The previous subsection presented PROLOG syntax and search with several
examples. These examples introduced PROLOG as an engine for computing with
predicate calculus expressions in Horn clause form. This is consistent with all the
principles of predicate calculus representation presented in Chapter 7. The notion
of computing by pattern matching on a data base of expressions is especially
important. In the full predicate calculus PROLOG uses pattern matching on the
problem's specifications and returns the bindings that make an expression true.

Our first look at recursion was in Chapter 8 when we described control
regimes for search. The top level control of a search algorithm in Chapter 8,
whether it be depth-first, breadth-first, or best-first, can be described as "if you
haven't found the goal and there are states left to search then apply the search
algorithm again." This control, stated as a loop that refers back to itself, is an
example of *recursion*.

We will see recursion described again in this and the next chapter as we create list and graph search algorithms. There it will be seen as the primary control mechanism for PROLOG programming. We will demonstrate this in Section 15.4, with the knight's tour problem with the design of a PROLOG based production system to search its graph. But first, in the present section, we consider some simpler examples, including the knight's moves on a 3 x 3 board.

15.3.2 Pattern Matching and Recursive Processing of Lists

Recursion is the "natural" way to process the list or graph structures. Pattern matching and recursion come together in list processing in PROLOG. But before we discuss these issues further, let us introduce the syntax of PROLOG lists: list elements are enclosed by brackets [ ] and separated by commas. Examples of PROLOG lists include:

[1, 2, 3, 4]
[[george, kate], [peder, debbie], [carl, ann]]
[sarah, nina, david, peter]
[ ]

The last example is the empty list. The first elements of a list may be separated from the tail of the list by the bar operator: I. The *tail* of a list is that list with its first element removed. For instance, when the list is [sarah, nina, david, peter], the first element is sarah and the tail is the list: [nina, david, peter]. Using the vertical bar operator, we can break a list into its components:

If [sarah, nina, david, peter] is matched to [X|Y] then
    X = sarah and Y = [nina, david, peter].
If [sarah, nina, david, peter] is matched to [X,Y|Z] then
    X = sarah, Y = nina and Z = [david, peter].
If [sarah, nina, david, peter] is matched to [X,Y,Z|W] then
    X = sarah, Y = nina, Z = david and W = [peter].
If [sarah, nina, david, peter] matches [W,X,Y,Z|V] then
    W = sarah, X = nina, Y = david, Z = peter, and V = [ ].
[sarah, nina, david, peter] will not match [V,W,X,Y,Z|U].
[sarah, nina, david, peter] matches [sarah,X|[david, peter]]
    to give X = nina, and so on.

The last example demonstrates that besides "tearing lists apart" to get at particular elements, PROLOG pattern matching can also be used to "build" the list structure. For example if X = sarah, Y = [nina], and L unifies with [X|Y], then L will be bound to [sarah, nina].

To summarize, the variables separated by commas before the | are all elements of the list, while the structure after the | is always a list, often referred to as the tail of the list. We now take a simple example of recursive processing of lists: the list member check. We define a predicate to determine if an item, represented by X, is in a list. The predicate member takes two arguments, an element and a list, and is true if the element is a member of the list. For example, we want member to respond:

```
? - member(a, [a, b, c, d, e]).
yes
? - member(a, [1,2,3,4]).
no
? - member(X, [a, b, c]).
X = a
? - ;
X = b
?- ;
X = c
? - ;
no
```

To define member, we first test if the element X is the first item in the list. We describe this check in the following manner:

```
    member(X,[X|T]).
```

This tests if X and the first element of the list are identical. If they are not then it is natural to check if X is an element of the rest, T, of the list. This is defined by:

```
    member(X,[Y|T]) :- member(X,T).
```

The two lines of PROLOG for checking list membership are then:

```
    member(X,[X|T]).
    member(X,[Y|T]) :- member(X,T).
```

The first line asks if X and the head of the list are identical. If this fails and X isn't the head of the list, member checks if X is a member of the tail of the list. The reader should convince herself why the order of the member predicates is as above (Section 15.3). To partially answer this question we show a trace of the call, member(c,[a,b,c]), follows:

For this example,   1.   is member(X,[X|T]). and
                       2.   is member(X,[Y|T]) :- member(X,T).

?- member(c,[a,b,c]).

call 1.   fail, since c \== (is not equal to) a
call 2.   X = c, Y = a, T = [b,c], member(c,[b,c])?
          call 1. fail, since c \== b
          call 2. X = c, Y = b, T = [c], member(c,[c])?
                  call 1. success, c = c yes (to second call 2.)
          yes (to first call 2.)
yes

We next move from recursive list processing to the design of a recursive graph search algorithm.

15.3.3   A Recursive Graph Search Algorithm

Example 15.2: **Knight Moves on a 3 x 3 Board**

We now present the 3 x 3 version of the knight's tour problem in the predicate calculus. Figure 15.2 is a 3 x 3 chess board, with the squares numbered 1 through 9. A legal move of a knight chess piece may be represented in PROLOG using a move predicate with two arguments, the first the location at the beginning of the knight move and the second the location after the move.

move(1,6).	move(3,4).	move(6,7).	move(8,3).
move(1,8).	move(3,8).	move(6,1).	move(8,1).
move(2,7).	move(4,3).	move(7,6).	move(9,4).
move(2,9).	move(4,9).	move(7,2).	move(9,2).

We now design a simple predicate path to find a path through this set of move specifications. A one move path between two points may be defined:

path1(X,Y) :- move(X,Y).

We can query our specifications with the PROLOG calls:

?- path1(4,9).
yes

1	2	3
4	5	6
7	8	9

FIGURE 15.2 The 3x3 knight's tour board.

```
?- path1(4,X).
X = 3
?- ;
X = 9
?- ;
no
?- path1(X,5).
no
```

Similarly, a two move path may be defined by finding a location, here Z, that can be reached in one move and then finding a second move from that location to the desired square:

```
path2(X,Y) :- move(X,Z), move(Z,Y).
```

Running this predicate can find all possible two move paths on the 3 x 3 board, as well as answer questions such as where can we get from a location in exactly two moves.

We can now define a three move path in this problem by locating two intermediate squares, Y and Z, that we can go to in our attempt to find the three move path:

```
path3(X,W) :- move(X,Y), move(Y,Z), move(Z,W).
```

We can demonstrate backtracking in this search space by calling:

```
?- path3(3,6).
yes
```

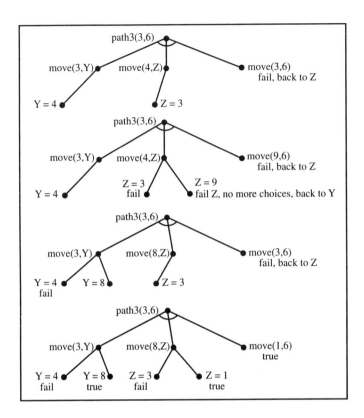

FIGURE 15.3 The evolving search space for path3(3,6) in Example 15.2. The tree is generated left to right and depth-first. As possible bindings are found the intermediate variable Y and Z are bound.

The trace of the search is presented in Figure 15.3. Note that Y and Z take on two different variable bindings before the path, with Y = 8 and Z = 1 is found. Further examples are to consider all the three move paths from some square or to try to find three moves to get to square 5 (from any location).

Note that our progressively longer path predicate continues to perform the same procedure: look for one more move predicate. Thus, we could have described path3 using path2:

path3(X,Y) :- move(X,Z), path2(Z,Y).

Even better might be a definition of path in terms of itself:

path(X,Y) :- move(X,Z), path(Z,Y).

This is an interesting recursive definition and the reader should experiment with it. Quickly we see that path always calls itself, even when it has found a solution! Thus we must tell path when to stop by creating another predicate that says there is always a path from a square to itself. These two path predicates together make up our recursive path call:

> path(Z,Z).
> path(X,Y) :- move(X,Z), path(Z,Y).

Again, we try this algorithm on the 3 x 3 knight tour of Example 15.2. There are still problems. For instance if we call:

?- path(6,1).

we are quickly into an infinite loop, going from square 6 to 7 and then back to 6, and so on. We never find the one move solution! The reason for this is that the knight puzzle we are searching is a graph that is not a tree, as defined in Section 6.1. That is, all the states have more than one, in fact, exactly two parents in the search space.

We next create a path predicate that describes a nonlooping algorithm for finding a sequence of moves between its arguments:

> path(Z,Z).
> path(X,Y) :-
>   move(X,W), not(been(W)), assert(been(W)), path(W,Y).

This recursive definition path uses assert, described in Section 15.2, the built-in PROLOG predicate which always succeeds by placing its argument in the data base of specifications. The been predicate is used to record previously visited states to avoid loops in the search space. Every time we come to a state in the search, we first check whether or not we have been there before. If we have, we backtrack and find another move. If we haven't, we assert(been(W)) and continue on in our search. We create as the search progresses new markers for every state visited.

This use of the been predicate violates the program designer's goal of building predicate calculus specifications that do not use the creation of global predicates to control search. Thus, been(3), asserted into the data base when the knight lands on square 3, is indeed a fact available to any other procedure in the data base and, as such, has global extension.

Even more importantly, creating global structures to alter program control violates the basic tenet of the production system model (Sections 9.3 and 15.4) where the logic of a problem's specifications should be kept separate from the control of the program. Here been structures were created as global specifications to modify the program execution.

A much cleaner search algorithm uses a list, *closed*, to keep track of visited states, and so prevent the path call from looping. The member predicate is used to detect duplicate states or loops. The following PROLOG clauses implement the depth-first graph search with backtracking algorithm of Section 8.4.2. The third argument of path is the *closed* list, and member is as given:

```
path(Z,Z,L).
path(X,Y,L) :- move(X,Z), not(member(Z,L)), path(Z,Y,[Z|L]).

(X,[X|T]).
member(X,[Y|T]) :- member(X,Y).
```

The third parameter of path is a local variable representing the list of states that have already been visited. When a new state Z is generated, using the move predicate, and this state is not already on the list of visited states, not(member(Z,L)), it is placed on the front of the state list, [Z|L], for the next path call.

It should be noted that all the parameters of path are now local and get their current values depending on where they are called in the graph search. Each recursive call adds a state to this list. If all continuations from a certain state fail, then that particular path call fails. When the interpreter backs up to the parent call, the third parameter, representing the list of states visited, still contains its previous values. Thus, states are added to and deleted from this list as the backtracking search moves through the graph.

The path call finally succeeds when the first two parameters are identical. At that time the third parameter is the list of states visited on the path from the start state to the goal state, in reverse order. Thus, we can print out the solution path. The search is depth-first with backtracking. To call the PROLOG interpreter use:

```
?- path(X,Y,[X]).
```

where X and Y are replaced by numbers between 1 and 9. The result will be a path from state X to state Y, the third parameter is the path list (starting at X).

Thus, path is a general depth-first search algorithm that may be used with any graph. In Section 15.4, we use this to implement a goal-driven production system solution to the full 8 x 8 knight tour problem, with problem state descriptions replacing the numbers of the squares in the call to path.

We now present the trace of a solution for the knight tour (Example 15.2):

```
1.   is path(Z,Z,L).
2.   is path(X,Y,L) :- move(X,Z), not(member(Z,L)), path(Z,Y,[Z|L])).
```

?- path(1,3,[1]).

path(1,3,[1]) attempts to match 1. fail 1 \== (does not equal) 3.
path(1,3,[1]) attempts to match 2. X is 1, Y is 3, L is [1]
    move(1,Z) gives Z as 6, not(member(6,[1])) is true,
    call path(6,3,[6,1])

      path(6,3,[6,1]) attempts to match 1. fail 6 \== 3.
      path(6,3,[6,1]) matches 2. X is 6, Y is 3, L is [6,1]
         move(6,Z) matches Z = 7, not(member(7,[6,1]) true,
         call path(7,3,[7,6,1])

            path(7,3,[7,6,1]) attempts 1. fail 7 \== 3
            path(7,3,[7,6,1]) matches 2. X is 7,Y is 3, L is [7,6,1].
               move(7,Z) has Z = 6, not(member(6,[7,6,1])) fails,
               backtrack! In move(7,Z), Z = 2,not(member(2,[7,6,1]))
               is true, call path(2,3,[2,7,6,1]))

                  path call attempts 1, fail, 2 \== 3.
                  path matches 2, X is 2, Y is 3, L is [2,7,6,1]
                     move Z = 7, not member fails, backtrack!
                     move makes Z be 9, not member is true,
                     call path(9,3,[9,2,7,6,1])

                        path fails 1, 9 \== 3.
                        path 2 has X 9, Y 3, L is [9,2,7,6,1]
                           Z = 4, not member is true, call
                           call path(4,3,[4,9,2,7,6,1])

                             path fails 1. 4 \== 3.
                           path matches 2, X is 4, Y is 3
                             L is [4,9,2,7,6,1], Z = 3,
                             not member true, call
                             path(3,3,[3,4,9,2,7,6,1])

                                  path tries 1, 3 = 3, yes
                          yes
                    yes
              yes
         yes
    yes
yes

We next, with the creation of the production system, demonstrate the recursive path call as a shell or general control structure for search in a graph. All the checks are made for a graph search algorithm: in path(X,Y,L), X is the present state, Y is the goal state. When X and Y are identical the recursion terminates. L is the list of states on the current path to state Y, and as each new state, Z, is found with the call move(X,Z), it is placed on the list [Z|L]. The state list is checked, using not(member(Z,L)), so that path does not loop.

The difference between the state list L in the path call above and closed list used in graph search in Chapter 8 is that closed records all states visited, while the state list L only keeps track of states on the present path. It is quite straightforward to expand the record keeping in the path call along the lines presented in Chapter 8, and we do this in Section 16.3.

15.4   A PRODUCTION SYSTEM IN PROLOG

15.4.1   The 8 x 8 Knight Tour

In this section we write a production system solution to the full 8 x 8 knight tour problem. This problem is stated as follows: *Place a knight piece on a square of the chess board. Determine a set of legal moves to take it to any other square on the board.*

Figure 8.4 presented the legal moves of a knight on the chess board, two rows and one column or one row and two columns in any direction. This creates a total of eight different moves when the knight is near the center of the board. Figure 8.5 presents the first few steps in the search space for the knight problem.

In the next several paragraphs we present a goal-driven production system solution to this problem. First, as we have just noted, the problem may be represented as a search through a graph. To do this we consider the possible moves that might be available at any time in the solution process. Some of these moves are eventually ruled out because they produce states that are illegal in that they move off the board.

For the moment, suppose that we only produce legal moves and simply consider the graph of states that can be generated. The knight can be moved in eight ways: A new state of the world is created by applying any one of these moves.

States of the world may be represented using a predicate, square(Row, Column), with the row location as first parameter, and column location as second parameter. Thus, square(1,1) has the knight in the upper left corner square, the start square of Figure 8.5.

It must be pointed out that these choices are conventions that have been arbitrarily chosen by the authors. Indeed, as researchers continually point out, the selection of an appropriate representation is the most critical aspect of problem solving. These conventions were selected to fit the predicate calculus representation in PROLOG. Different states of the world are created by legal moves generating different positions of the board; these in turn are represented by changes in the values of the parameters of the square predicate. Other representations are certainly possible.

To create move rules we briefly consider arithmetic in PROLOG.

15.4.2   Arithmetic in PROLOG

Since we want to add and subtract row and column values we need to introduce arithmetic operators in PROLOG. First, we describe the PROLOG operator is. This operator evaluates the arithmetic functions +, -, *, div, or mod and assigns the result to a local variable. Suppose we create a PROLOG specification for addition, where the first two arguments are added together to give the third:

add(X, Y, Z) :- Z is X + Y.

The interpreter responds to the queries:

?- add(3,4,X).
X = 7
?- add(3,X,7).
error in arithemetic expression: not a number.

or gives some such error message. This reminds us that all variables to the right of the is operator must be bound when is is processed or we get an error. We can use the basic operators to create new operators, for example, absolute value:

abs(X,X) :- X > 0.
abs(X,Y) :- Y is - X.

These predicates state that the absolute value of X is X, if X is positive; otherwise the absolute value of X is the negative of X.

We can also introduce the comparison operators. These, >, <, =, \==, and so on, compare two expressions to see how they are related. The reader may test these operators directly in the PROLOG environment:

?- 7 < 9.
yes
?- 7 > 8.
no

```
?- 7 \== 8.
yes
?- 7 is 3 + 4.
yes
?- 7 = 3 + 4.
no
```

It is very important to understand what happened with this last example. The comparison operator = compares two patterns by seeing if they are identical, and the pattern 3 + 4 is not the same pattern as 7. Note again that is evaluates 3 + 4 and assigns that result to the symbol at its left, which in this case had the value 7; so this was fine. Since evaluation is not the same as direct comparison, there are different operators for each in the logic language PROLOG. If we want to compare 3 + 4 and 7, we first must evaluate 3 + 4 and only then compare the result. Be careful!

15.4.3   The 8 x 8 Knight Tour as a Production System

In Section 3.3.5, and again in Section 9.3 we presented the production system. There are three separate modules in a production system, as shown in Figure 9.4:

1. The set of production rules stated as if.. then.. rule pairs.
2. The working memory that monitors the state of the processing by retaining information such as the present state, the goal state, and the progress to any point of the problem solving.
3. The control regime.

The recursive path predicate described in Section 15.3 can provide a control mechanism for the production system search. The three parameters of the path call, the present state, the goal state, and the list of states visited so far, represent the working memory. The production rules are the rules for changing state in the search. Our example will be goal-driven since each rule application attempts to reduce the difference between the present state and a fixed goal, the second parameter of the path call. We now define these as move rules in PROLOG form.

Since PROLOG uses Horn clauses, a production system designed in PROLOG must either represent production rules directly in Horn clause form, or translate rules to this format. We take the former option here, the latter in Section 16.4 when we describe a parser. Horn clauses require the pattern for the present state and the pattern for the next state both be placed to the left of the :-.

We create a predicate called move with two arguments. These arguments of the move predicate are the present state and the new state. The conditions that the production rule requires to "fire" and return the next state are placed to the right of :-. As is seen in the following example, these conditions are also expressed with pattern matching constraints.

Recall again that each location on our 8 x 8 board is represented by a predicate square(Row,Column). Our first move rule advances the Row by 1 and the Column by 2:

> move(square(Row, Column), square(New_row, New_Column)) :-
>   New_row is Row + 1, New_column is Column + 2.

This is clear, but we should note that we are not sure the new state, square(New_row, New_column), is on the 8 x 8 board.

Next, we create a predicate called safe to test whether each new state is safe or not, that is whether the square is on the board:

> safe(square(X,Y)) :- X > 0, X < 9, Y > 0, Y < 9.

We have a choice here: we can add the safe check to each production rule, or we can check that each new state is safe within the recursive path controller for the production system. We choose the second option, for one thing, it keeps our code simple by not repeating the check with each of the eight rules.

In a similar fashion, we can now create the seven other production rules to represent the other legal knight moves. We have added a print predicate to each production rule to write out a trace of the rules being tried. This is purely to help the program designer watch each rule fire during the problem solving.

Finally, we add a ninth "pseudo rule" that always succeeds, since no conditions are placed on it. This rule only fires when all previous rules have failed, it indicates that there are no legal moves left from the present square: either the children are off the board or they are already on the list of visited states. The pseudo rule tells us that path is backtracking from the current state and then the rule itself fails. As with the print predicate with each rule, the pseudo rule is only added to assist the user in seeing what is going on as the production system is running.

We now present the full production system program in PROLOG to solve the 8 x 8 knight tour problem. The interpreter may be called by requesting:

?- path(square(1,1), square(4,4), [square(1,1)]).

It should be noted that this is a general call that may be used to try to find a path from any square on the board to any other square. The third argument, the list of visited states, is initialized by placing the start square in square brackets, thus creating a list that starts with one element in it.

The full code follows:

```
move(square(R,C), square(NR,NC)) :-
    NR is R + 1, NC is C + 2,
    tab(4), write('move to square'), write(NR), write(NC), nl.

move(square(R,C), square(NR,NC)) :-
    NR is R + 2, NC is C + 1,
    tab(4), write('move to square'), write(NR), write(NC), nl.

move(square(R,C), square(NR,NC)) :-
    NR is R + 1, NC is C - 2,
    tab(4), write('move to square'), write(NR), write(NC), nl.

move(square(R,C), square(NR,NC)) :-
    NR is R - 2, NC is C + 1,
    tab(4), write('move to square'), write(NR), write(NC), nl.

move(square(R,C), square(NR,NC)) :-
    NR is R - 1, NC is C + 2,
    tab(4), write('move to square'), write(NR), write(NC), nl.

move(square(R,C), square(NR,NC)) :-
    NR is R + 2, NC is C - 1,
    tab(4), write('move to square'), write(NR), write(NC), nl.

move(square(R,C), square(NR,NC)) :-
    NR is R - 1, NC is C - 2,
    tab(4), write('move to square'), write(NR), write(NC), nl.

move(square(R,C), square(NR,NC)) :-
    NR is R - 2, NC is C - 1,
    tab(4), write('move to square'), write(NR), write(NC), nl.

move(square(R,C), square(R,C)) :-
    tab(8), write('BACKTRACK from square'),
    write(NR), write(NC), nl, fail.
```

These nine rules make up the set of productions for the knight tour problem. We now bring in the recursive path predicate, created and explained in the preceding section, to control the search of the productions:

```
path(Z,Z,L) :- print('Solution found. The path is:' ), nl, rpt(L).
path(X,Y,L) :-
    move(X,Z),
    safe(Z),
    not(member(Z,L)),
    print('Use this square as next state in the search'),
        path(Z,Y,[Z|L]).
```

Finally, we need several utility predicates to check for legal moves, to check if a new square is on the list of already visited squares, and to print out the solution path.

```
safe(square(R,C)) :- R > 0, R < 9, C > 0, C < 9.

member(X,[X|T]).
member(X,[Y|T]) :- member(X,T).

rpt([]).
rpt([H|T]) :- rpt(T), write(H), nl.
```

Recall again that the three parameters of the path predicate make up the contents of working memory. The first argument gives us the present state, the second the goal state, and the third the list of all states on the path up to the present state. The search is a goal-driven and depth-first weak method approach (Chapter 8) since it exhaustively tries to generate a path between the current state and a fixed goal. When the path predicate terminates with success, the third argument represents the list of all states on the path from the start to the goal. This list is printed out with the rpt predicate, which the reader should explore. Finally, the order of generation of children from each state (conflict resolution) is determined by the order in which the rules are placed in the production memory.

15.4.4   Cut: Altering PROLOG's Built-in Search

As the previous subsection demonstrated, PROLOG uses depth-first search with backtracking. This search strategy is a result of PROLOG's implementation as a resolution theorem prover with a fixed search strategy (Luger and Stubblefield 1993, Chap. 13). We now show how this strategy can be altered using the predicate cut. In Section 16.3 we use cut to design search strategies for breadth-first and best-first search.

The cut is an predicate designed to control backtracking, and is represented by an explanation point: !. The syntax for interpreting cut is that of a goal with no arguments. It has several side effects: First, it always succeeds, and second, if it is "failed back to" in the normal course of backtracking, it causes the entire clause in which it is contained to fail.

For a simple example of the effect of the cut, recall the two move path call from the knight's example of Section 15.3.3. The predicate path2 was created:

path2(X,Y) :- move(X,Z), move(Z,Y).

As in Example 15.2, this predicate says that there is a two move path between X and Y if there exists an intermediate square Z between them. Z must be reachable in one move from and X and in turn lead on to Y in one move. For this example, assume part of the knight move's data base:

move(1,6).   move(1,8).   move(6,7).
move(6,1).   move(8,3).   move(8,1).

When the interpreter is asked to find all the two move paths from 1, there are four answers:

```
?-
path2(1,W).
W = 7
?- ;
W = 1
?- ;
W = 3
?- ;
W = 1
?- ;
no
```

When path2 is altered to contain the cut, and the same goal is presented:

path2(X,Y) :- move(X,Z), !, move(Z,Y).

?- path2(1,W).

Only two answers result:

```
W = 7
?- ;
W = 1
```

?- ;

no

This happens because variable Z only takes on one value, the first value it is bound to, namely 6. Once the first subgoal succeeds, and Z is bound to 6, the cut is encountered. This prohibits further backtracking to the first subgoal; no further bindings for the Z parameter are allowed.

There are several uses for the cut in programming: First, as this example demonstrates, it allows the programmer to explicitly control the shape of the search tree. When further exhaustive search is not required, the tree can be explicitly pruned at that point. This allows PROLOG code to have the flavor of function calling: when one set of values or bindings is found in an interpretation and the cut is encountered, the interpreter does not search for other variable binding interpretations. If that set of values does not lead on to a solution then no further values are attempted.

A second use of cut is to control recursion. In the path call of Section 15.3, cut may be added after the recursion:

```
path(Z,Z,L).
path(X,Z,L) :- move(X,Y), not(member(Y,L)), path(Y,Z,[Y|L]), !.
```

This addition of cut means that (at most) one solution to the graph search is produced. Only one solution is produced because further solutions occur after the clause path(Z,Z,L) is satisfied. When PROLOG finds one solution path and the user asks for more solutions, path(Z,Z,L) is then failed, and the second path call is reinvoked to continue the search of the graph. When the cut is placed after the recursive path call, the call can't be reentered for further search.

An important side effect of the cut is to make the program run faster and conserve memory locations. When cut is used within a predicate, the pointers in memory needed for backtracking to predicates to the left of the cut are not created. This is, of course, because they will never be needed. Thus, cut can produce the desired solution, and only the desired solution, with more efficient use of memory.

The cut can also be used with recursion to reinitialize the path predicate. We saw in Chapter 8 that backtracking on failure was an essential part of depth-first search. There we had an explicit *open* and *closed* list that was changed with each call of the algorithm. In Chapter 16 we will use cut within the recursive call so that we don't backtrack to previous versions of open and closed.

We end the present chapter with a discussion of PROLOG and its flexibility as either a declarative or a procedural representation language.

15.5   PROLOG AS A DECLARATIVE AND PROCEDURAL SPECIFICATION LANGUAGE

In Chapter 15, the emphasis on PROLOG has been that of a procedural language: we have shown how to create interpreters of rule sets or other representational specifications, including a production system. This interpretation of a specification as a set of things to do is the traditional procedural understanding of an interpreter. We now want to consider briefly the power of a language that offers a declarative as well as a procedural representation of problem solving.

In traditional computer languages such as FORTRAN and 'C,' the logic for the problem's specification and the control for executing the solution algorithm are inextricably mixed together. A program in these languages is simply a sequence of things to be done to get an answer. An important goal of the designers of PROLOG has been to separate the logic or specification of a problem from the execution of that specification. There are several reasons for this separation, not the least of which is the ability to determine after the specifications are created what might be the best control for executing them.

Another goal of this separation of logic from control is that each aspect of the problem may be analyzed separately. The specifications may themselves be translated to other specifications before execution. Specifications may be checked for correctness or otherwise evaluated independently of their interpretation. And, as we will demonstrate with our parser and sentence generator in Section 16.4, the same code specifications can be used in response to different queries. The interpreter uses different patterns in the queries to evoke very different, yet appropriate, responses.

We now show how the PROLOG language exhibits some of the benefits of a nonprocedural or declarative semantics. Consider the predicate append that is defined:

```
append([], L, L).
append([X|T], L, [X|NL]) :- append(T, L, NL).
```

We can understand append by tracing its execution while it joins two lists together. If the following call is made:

```
?- append([a,b,c], [d,e], Y).
```

The response is:

```
Y = [a,b,c,d,e,f]
```

The execution of **append** requires that the local variable values are accessed after the recursive call has succeeded. In this case, X is placed on the head of the list, [X|NL], after the recursive call has finished. We now present the trace of **append** on the problem above. For purposes of reference in this trace:

1.   append([ ], L, L)
2.   append([X|T], L, [X|NL]) :- append(T, L, NL)

?- append([a,b,c], [d,e], Y).
　　try to match 1, fail [a,b,c] \== [ ]
　　match 2, X = a, T = [b,c], L = [d,e],
　　call append([b,c], [d,e], NL)

　　　　try to match 1, fail [b,c] \== [ ]
　　　　match 2, X = b, T = [c], L = [d,e],
　　　　call append([c], [d,e], NL)

　　　　　　try to match 1, fail [c] \== [ ]
　　　　　　match 2, X = c, T = [ ], L = [d,e],
　　　　　　call append([ ], [d,e], NL)

　　　　　　　　match 1, L = [d,e], for BOTH Ls, yes

　　　　　　yes, NL = [d,e], [X|NL] = [c,d,e]

　　　　yes, NL = [c,d,e], [X|NL] = [b,c,d,e]

　　yes, NL = [b,c,d,e], [X|NL] = [a,b,c,d,e]

Y = [a,b,c,d,e]
yes

In the PROLOG algorithms shown in this chapter, the parameters of the predicates are intended as either "input" or "output" parameters; most definitions assumed that certain parameters would be bound in the call and others would be unbound. This need not be so. In fact there is no commitment at all to parameters being input or output in PROLOG!

PROLOG code is intended to be simply a set of specifications of what is true, a statement of the logic of the situation. Thus, **append** specifies the relationship among three lists, such that the third list is the catenation of the first onto the front of the second.

To demonstrate this fact we can give **append** a different set of goals:

```
?- append([a,b], [c], [a,b,c]).
yes ?-
append([a], [c], [a,b,c]).
no
```

We can also use an unbound variable for different parameters of the call to append:

```
?- append(X, [b,c], [a,b,c]).
X = [a]
?- append(X, Y, [a,b,c]).
X = [ ] Y = [a, b, c]
?- ;
X = [a] Y = [b, c]
?- ;
X = [a, b] Y = [c]
?- ;
X = [a, b, c] Y = [ ]
?- ;
no
```

In the last query, PROLOG returns all the lists X and Y which appended together will produce the original list [a,b,c], four pairs of lists in all. Thus, append is a statement of the logic of a relationship among three lists. What the interpreter produces depends on the specific query pattern it is given. In this sense it interprets a set of declarative specifications. It is a pattern driven query whose response is a procedure for accomplishing the task. The representational medium is the predicate calculus, the interactive interpreter is a theorem prover acting on predicate based specifications (Luger & Stubblefield 1993, Chap. 13).

15.6   EPILOGUE AND REFERENCES

PROLOG is a general purpose computing language. We ignored a great number of its important concepts because of the space limitations of our book. We recommended that the interested reader pursue some of the available texts, such as *Programming in PROLOG* (Clocksin & Mellish 1984), *Computing with Logic* (Maier & Warren 1988), *The Art of PROLOG* (Sterling & Shapiro 1986), and *The Craft of PROLOG* (O'Keefe 1990).

We focused our introduction to PROLOG on developing the representation and search topics introduced in Chapters 7, 8, and 9 of this text. The most important topic of this chapter, however, is the introduction of the language itself. The notion of solving a problem based on a set of specifications for correct relation-ships in a domain area, coupled with the action of a theorem prover, is exciting and important. The move that PROLOG offers towards a fully declarative specifi-cation language is also important.

Indeed, a strength of PROLOG interpreters is that they are open to a proce-dural as well as a declarative conceptualization. Thus a clause such as:

A :- B, C, D.

might in one instance be a specification logic: A is true if B and C and D are true, and in another instance be a procedure for doing something: To accomplish A go out and first do B and then do C and finally do D. This procedural interpretation allowed us to construct the production system and lends representational flexibil-ity to the PROLOG language.

How the PROLOG interpreter works can not be properly understood without the concepts of resolution theorem proving, especially the Horn clause refutation process (Luger and Stubblefield 1993, Chap. 13). The intellectual roots of PRO-LOG reside in the theoretical concepts of using logic for problem specification and solution. An excellent commentator on these issues is Robert Kowalski. Especially recommended is *Logic for Problem Solving* (Kowalski 1979b) and *Algorithm = Logic + Control* (Kowalski 1979a).

In Chapter 16 we design meta-interpreters in PROLOG to build more advanced representational media, including semantic nets, frames, and schemas. We also create models for language understanding and learning.

Chapter 16

CREATING META-INTERPRETERS IN PROLOG

The whole of mathematics consists in the organization of a series of aids to the imagination in the process of reasoning...

Alfred North Whitehead

Everything is vague to a degree you do not realize till you have tried to make it precise...

Bertrand Russell

16.0 INTRODUCTION TO META-INTERPRETERS

In Chapter 15 we introduced PROLOG as a representational medium as well as an interactive communication language. PROLOG interpreted our queries in the context of the specifications we created to describe a problem domain. In Chapter 15 most of our representations were based directly on the predicate calculus. In Chapter 16 we use PROLOG to create more expressive and flexible representational schemes, those symbol based representations introduced in Chapters 3, 6, and 10.

The Chapter 16 representations are intended to give a richer context for interpretation of a problem and semantic nets, frames, scripts, and schemas can help us create this context. To accomplish this task we create interpretative environments on top of a computing language. One of the important properties of very high level languages is the ease with which they allow the creation of such meta-interpreters. A *meta-interpreter* is a new language built in or on top of another language to interpret structures also built in that language.

In one sense, building a meta-interpreter is analogous to English speakers learning Italian so they can interpret Dante's poetry, or a person learning the language of astrophysics so she can better interpret the universe. So we will also create interpreters in PROLOG to assist the computer in interpreting our world. We do this as cognitive scientists: building a computational representation that we can use as a model to better understand intelligence.

We begin this chapter by describing the tools necessary for building such an interpreter. These include the use of *meta-predicates* as well as the typing and pattern matching powers of PROLOG. We finish by demonstrating interpreters for a number of application areas, including natural language understanding and version space learning.

In Section 16.1, we introduce meta-predicates. These are called meta-predicates in the sense that the objects they test or manipulate are PROLOG expressions themselves. For example, atom(X) succeeds if X is bound to an atom. This can help us decide how to manipulate X. Section 16.1 also discusses *typing* in PROLOG and the use of pattern matching in equality testing and structure creation.

In Section 16.2, we design our first meta-interpreters. We create an interpreter for PROLOG in PROLOG. This can be seen as a production system like rule interpreter that we expand slightly to query the user when it can't determine an answer from its original specifications. Next we create an interpreter for inheritance evaluation in semantic nets. We also design frames and schemas in PROLOG and consider their interpretation.

In Section 16.3 we expand on the depth-first search algorithm we designed in Section 15.4 by building breadth-first and best-first interpreters for production rules. In Section 16.4 we build interpreters for a subset of English expressions. We begin with a context-free grammar and simple language expressions. We next add context sensitivity to our grammar specifications to interpret a broader subset of English. Finally, we bring together our grammar rules and the richer interpretative context of semantic nets with the design of a recursive descent semantic net parser. In Section 16.5 we build the version space search learning algorithm in PROLOG.

All our software, including a C-PROLOG interpreter, is available (see the Preface) and open to further development by the interested reader.

16.1   PROLOG TOOLS: META-PREDICATES, TYPING, AND PATTERN MATCHING

16.1.1   Meta-Predicates

Metalogical constructs offer an important extension to the expressive power of any programming environment. In PROLOG these predicates are outside the scope of first order predicate calculus as they query the status of the computational environment as well as create and manipulate predicates within the solution procedure. We refer to these predicates as *meta* because they query and manipulate other predicates rather than the terms or objects these other predicates denote.

We need meta-predicates in PROLOG for at least five reasons:

1. To build, take apart, and evaluate PROLOG structures.
2. To compare values of expressions.
3. To convert predicates passed as data to executable code.
4. To determine the type of a structure, i.e., whether it is an integer, a list, or some other structure.
5. To add typing and other restrictions to PROLOG specifications.

In Chapter 15 we introduced our first meta-predicates when we described how global structures, that is, those that can be accessed by the entire predicate set, are entered into a PROLOG program. The command assert(C), adds the clause *C* to the current set of clauses. We can also add an entire list of clauses to the data base by the command assert ([C1, C2,...]). Similarly we can remove clauses using the command retract ([C1, C2,...]).

There are many dangers associated with programming with assert and retract. Since they create and remove global structures, these commands introduce side effects and other problems associated with poorly structured programs. We discussed this issue when designing a loop check for graph search in Chapter 15. However, it is sometimes necessary to create and delete global structures. We do this when creating semantic nets and frames in a PROLOG environment, and it is important in natural language understanding and learning.

We may also use global structures to describe new results as they are found with our production system interpreter. We want this information to be global so that other predicates (rules) may access it when appropriate. Meta-predicates that are useful for manipulating representations include:

var (X) succeeds only when X is an unbound variable.

nonvar (X) succeeds only when X is bound to a nonvariable term.

=.. creates a list from a predicate term. For example, foo(a,b,c) =.. Y unifies Y with [foo,a,b,c]. The head of the list Y is the function name, and its tail the function's arguments. =.. can be used "backwards," of course. Thus if X =.. [foo,a,b,c] succeeds, then X has the value foo(a,b,c).

functor (A, B, C) succeeds with A a term whose principal functor has name B and arity C. For example, functor(foo(a,b), X, Y). will succeed with X = foo and Y = 2. functor(A, B, C) can also be used with any of its arguments bound in order to produce the others, for example, all the terms with a certain name and/or arity.

clause(A, B) unifies B with the body of a clause whose head unifies
with A. If p(X) :- q(X) exists in the data base, then
clause(p(a),X) succeeds with X = q(a).

any_predicate(...,X,...) :- X. executes predicate X, the argument of an
arbitrary predicate. Thus a predicate, here X, may be passed for a
time as a parameter and then interpreted at a later time in
the computation.

call(X), where X is a clause, also succeeds with the interpretation of
predicate X.

This short list of meta logical predicates will be very important in building
and interpreting the data structures in the remainder of Chapter 16. Because
PROLOG can manipulate its own structures in this straightforward fashion, it is
easy to implement interpreters which modify the PROLOG semantics.

16.1.2   Types in PROLOG

The *type* of a computational structure, say X, is a description of the nature of the
structure X. For example, X might be of type *integer*, of type *list*, or of type *predicate*. Some languages, such as Pascal, "C," ML, and most object-oriented languages, are very restrictive on type declaration and use. Other languages, such as
PROLOG, are untyped, and up to a certain point are very permissive in their type
based constraints. For example, when we worked with list membership in Section 15.3.2, we created queries such as:

?- member(a, [c,b,a]).

PROLOG did not check first to see if the first argument of member was an
element and the second argument a list. In fact, the first argument could have
been a list and the second a list of lists. Or the first argument could have been a
list and the second an atom. Only when PROLOG tries to decompose a structure
into its head and tail would there be a potential problem, and the response
wouldn't be an error message; rather PROLOG would just fail to take the structure apart and respond no to the membership query. We also saw in Section
15.4.2 how variables to the right of the is operator had to be bound at the time is
was interpreted. This too is a type constraint.

For a number of problem solving applications the unconstrained use of unification can introduce unintended error. Pattern matching simply binds variables,
without restricting them according to type. In many cases related to the design of

meta-interpreters we want PROLOG to do limited type checking. For example, we may want our interpreter to find a production rule whose head, the predicate left of :-, is a particular predicate. This requires finding a structure of a certain name and type, or telling us that none exists.

There are a number of ways that we can more strongly type structures in PROLOG. First, and most powerful, is the use of unification to constrain variable assignment. That is, as program designers, we can add constraints to the patterns themselves that eliminate undesirable matches. An example would be the explicit assignment of integer values, with checks that they are within range, to the square(Row, Column) predicate in the knight tour example.

Second, PROLOG itself provides predicates to do limited type checking. We saw this with meta-predicates such as var(X), clause(X,Y), and integer(X) in the previous section. A third constraint based on typing occurs when PROLOG predicates explicitly check lists for legitimate variable bindings or other properties of predicates. A fourth, and more radical approach, is the complete predicate and data type check proposed by certain PROLOG interpreters such as Turbo-PROLOG. In this situation programming with PROLOG becomes more like designing a code in Pascal or "C" where all predicate names are typed and given a fixed arity.

Rather than providing built-in type checking as a default, PROLOG allows run-time type checking under complete programmer control. This approach offers a number of benefits, including:

1. The programmer is not forced to adhere to strong type checking at all times. This allows creation of predicates that work across any type of object. For example, the member predicate performs general member checking, regardless of the type of elements in the list.

2. Flexibility in typing helps exploratory programming. Programmers can relax type checking in the early stages of program development and introduce it to detect errors as they come to better understand the problem.

3. AI representations seldom conform to the built-in data types of languages like Pascal. PROLOG allows types to be defined with the full power of predicate calculus.

4. Because type checking is done at run-time rather than compile time, the programmer determines when the program should perform a check. This allows programmers the delay of type checking until it is necessary, or until certain variables have become bound.

5. Programmer control of type checking at run-time also allows the building of programs that create and enforce new type constraints during execution. This is of use in many learning programs.

After our discussion of pattern matching with restricted type checking and the use of meta-predicates we can proceed to the design of meta-interpreters.

16.2   META-INTERPRETERS IN PROLOG

16.2.1   Introduction: PROLOG in PROLOG

A meta-interpreter is an interpreter written in a language for the processing of a class of structures also built in that language. For example, a meta-interpreter acting as a production rule interpreter interprets a knowledge base of knowledge about a particular problem. Although the rules may be written in the syntax of the underlying language, in our example, PROLOG, the meta-interpreter defines a different meaning or semantics for these structures.

As a simple example of a meta-interpreter, we now define the semantics of pure PROLOG using PROLOG itself. We use a predicate called solve.

```
solve(true).
solve(not A) :- not(solve(A)).
solve((A,B)) :- solve(A), solve(B).
solve(A) :- clause(A,B), solve(B).
```

The first predicate says that a structure determined to be true, for example, a fact, is true. The second says that to check that a predicate is false, check that the predicate itself is not true. (This is an example of the closed world assumption.) The third solve predicate says that if you wish to solve for the conjunction of two or more predicates, here A and B, check if the and of them individually is true. Finally, if a structure to be solved is neither a fact nor the negation or conjunction of structures, see if there is a rule, clause, whose head matches the structure. If there is, go out and solve the tail, or left hand side of that structure.

This meta-interpreter defines the semantics of PROLOG using PROLOG; it implements the same left to right, depth-first goal-directed search as the built-in interpreter. In its conciseness and elegance, it illustrates the power of both unification and PROLOG's built-in meta-predicates, clause in this example. It would be much more difficult and require many more lines of code to create a similar definition of Pascal in Pascal.

The ability to easily write meta-interpreters for a language has certain theoretical advantages. For example, we may wish to modify the standard PROLOG semantics so that it will ask the user about the truth value of any goal that PROLOG cannot directly prove. We do this by adding to the solve definition:

```
solve(A) :- askuser(A).
```

> askuser(A) :- writelist([A, '? Enter true if the goal
> is true, false otherwise']), read(true).

We add this extension of solve to the end of the other solve predicates. It is called if all of these fail and invokes askuser to query the user for the truth value of the goal A. askuser prints the goal and instructions for answering. The read(true) goal attempts to match the user's input with the term true, failing if the user enters anything other than true. In this way, we have changed the semantics of solve to extend the behavior of PROLOG.

Our solve predicates are already very close to an interpreter for a rule based expert system. Simple additions would include a parameter to solve to keep track of the rules used, the matches of clause. This is called a *rule stack*. We would also add an algebra for uncertain reasoning (Section 7.5.3) and some nicer input/output routines. The basics are already here! [These extensions are made in Section 13.2 of Luger and Stubblefield (1993)].

In the following sections, we use this methodology to implement semantic net and frame interpreters.

16.2.2   Semantic Nets in PROLOG

The semantic net, as introduced in Sections 3.3 and 6.2, is composed of a collection of nodes and links. The nodes are connected by links that specify relationships between the nodes. In this section, we discuss the implementation of inheritance for a simple semantic network language. Our language allows us to demonstrate the implementation of properties, such as inheritance and default assignments, in a network representation.

In the semantic net of Figure 6.3, nodes represent individuals such as the canary *tweety*; classes such as *ostrich, crow,* and *robin*; and superclasses such as *bird* and *vertebrate*. The most common links are *isa*, to represent the class hierarchy relationship, and *hasproperty*, to indicate properties of an individual or a class.

For representational clarity and consistency as well as for ease in building search procedures, we adopt canonical forms for the data relationships within the semantic net. We use an isa(Type, Supertype) predicate to indicate that Type is a member of the Supertype class, for instance isa(canary,bird). We use a hasprop(Entity, Property, Value) predicate to indicate that Entity has a Property of some Value. Entity and Value are nodes in the network, Property is the name of the link that joins them, for instance, hasprop(tweety,color,white).

A partial list of the predicates necessary to describe the semantic network of Figure 6.1 includes:

```
isa(canary,bird).                    isa(robin,bird).
isa(ostrich,bird).                   isa(penguin,bird).
isa(bird,animal).                    isa(fish,animal).
isa(opus,penguin).                   isa(tweety,canary).
hasprop(tweety,color,white).         hasprop(robin,color,red).
hasprop(canary,color,yellow).        hasprop(penguin,color,brown).
hasprop(bird,travel,fly).            hasprop(fish,travel,swim).
hasprop(ostrich,travel,walk).        hasprop(penguin,travel,walk).
hasprop(robin,sound,sing).           hasprop(canary,sound,sing).
hasprop(bird,cover,feathers).        hasprop(animal,cover,skin).
etc.
```

We next create a recursive search algorithm to find whether an entity in our semantic net has a particular property. As we noted in Section 6.2, properties are located in the net at the most general level at which they are true. Through inheritance, an individual or subclass acquires the properties of its superclasses. Thus the property fly holds for bird and all its subclasses. Exceptions are located at the most general level at which the exception is true. Thus ostrich and penguin travel by walking instead of flying. The hasproperty predicate begins search at a particular object, Entity. If the information is not directly attached to that object, hasproperty follows isa links to its superclasses, Supentity. If no more superclasses exist, and hasproperty has not located property, it fails.

```
hasproperty(Entity, Property, Value) :-
    hasprop( Entity, Property, Value), !.
hasproperty(Entity, Property, Value) :-
    isa( Entity, Supentity),
    hasproperty( Supentity, Property, Value), !.
```

hasproperty searches the inheritance hierarchy in a depth-first fashion. This definition only implements tree inheritance, each node has only a single parent. The cut, !, guarentees that the search terminates once the lowest value in the inheritance hierarchy is found. We next show inheritance for a frame based representation and then implement both tree and multiple inheritance search algorithms.

16.2.3   Frames and Schemas in PROLOG

Semantic nets can be partitioned, with information added to node descriptions, to give them a *frame* or *schema* structure (Section 6.3). We redefine the bird example of the previous subsection using frames, where each frame represents a collection of relationships of the semantic net, and the isa slots of the frame define the frame hierarchy, as seen in Figure 16.1.

The first slot of each frame names the node, for example, name(tweety), or name(vertebrate). The second slot gives the inheritance links between the node and its parents. Since our example has a tree structure, each node will have only one link, the isa predicate with one argument. The third slot in the frame is a list of features that describe it. We use any PROLOG predicate, such as flies, feathers, or color(brown). The final slot is the list of exceptions and default values for the node, again either a single word or a predicate indicating a property.

Each frame organizes its slot names into lists of properties and default values. This allows us to distinguish these different types of knowledge and give them different behaviors in the inheritance hierarchy. Although our implementation allows subclasses to inherit properties from both lists, other representations are possible and may be useful in certain applications. We may wish to specify that only default values are inherited. Or we may wish to build a third list containing the properties specific to the class itself and not able to be inherited by its members. These are sometimes called *class values*. For example, we may wish to state that the class canary names a species of songbird. This should not be inherited by subclasses or instances: tweety does not name a species of songbird.

We now represent the relationships in Figure 16.1 with the PROLOG fact predicate frame with four arguments. We may use the methods suggested in Section 16.1.2 to check the parameters of the frame predicate for appropriate type, for instance to ensure that the third frame slot is a list that contains only values from a fixed list of properties. For simplicity, we have not represented procedures that may be attached to frames and interpreted by messages sent to the frame system. We will have examples of this in the pulley schemas of our next example:

```
frame(name(bird),
    isa(animal),
    [flies, feathers],
    [color(brown)] ).

frame(name(penguin),
    isa(bird),
    [color(brown)],
    [travel(walk)] ).

frame(name(canary),
    isa(bird),
    [color(yellow),call(sing)],
    [size(small)] ).
```

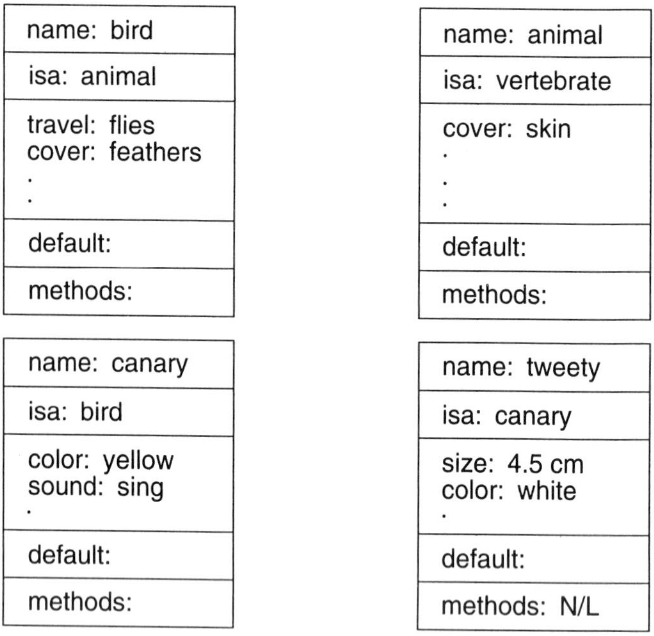

name: bird
isa: animal
travel: flies cover: feathers . . .
default:
methods:

name: animal
isa: vertebrate
cover: skin . . .
default:
methods:

name: canary
isa: bird
color: yellow sound: sing .
default:
methods:

name: tweety
isa: canary
size: 4.5 cm color: white .
default:
methods: N/L

FIGURE 16.1   Part of a frame system to represent the bird semantic net of Figure 6.1.

```
frame(name(tweety),
    isa(canary),
    [ ],
    [color(white)] ).
```

Once the full set of frame descriptions and inheritance relationships are defined for Figure 16.1, we create procedures to infer properties from this representation. The first get predicate considers the Object directly for the Property. The second get predicate looks for the Property in the set of default values of the Object. If both of these attempts fail the third get predicate calls all the get predicates recursively on the Parent of the Object.

```
get(Property, Object) :-
    frame(name(Object), _, List_of_properties,_),
    member(Property, List_of_properties).

get(Property, Object) :-
    frame(name(Object), _, _,List_of_defaults),
    member(Property, List_of_defaults).
```

```
get(Property, Object) :-
    frame(name(Object), isa(Parent), _, _),
    get(Property, Parent).
```

The variables indicated by "_" are necessary for the pattern matching, but their values are not used later in the computation. These are sometimes called *don't care* variables.

We now create a frame structure with multiple inheritance of properties, as in, for example, Figure 6.23. We must make this change both in our representation and in our search strategy. First, in the frame representation we make the argument of the isa predicate a list of the superclasses of the Object. Thus, each superclass in the list is a parent of the entity named in the first argument of frame.

If opus is a penguin and a cartoon_char, as in Figure 6.23, we can represent this situation by:

```
frame(name(opus), isa([penguin, cartoon_char]),
    [color(black)], [ ]).
```

We test for properties of opus by recurring up the isa hierarchy for both penguin and cartoon_char. We add this additional definition between the third and fourth get predicates of the previous example:

```
get(Property, Object) :-
    frame(name(Object),
    isa(List),_,_),
    get_multiple(Property, List).
```

We define get_multiple by:

```
get_multiple(Property, [Parent|_]) :-
    get(Property, Parent).
get_multiple(Prop, [_|Rest]) :-
    get_multiple(Prop, Rest).
```

With this depth-first and left-to-right inheritance preference, properties of penguin and its superclasses will be examined before those of cartoon_char. We get all potential answers in the search of the inheritance hierarchy. We must still add cut at the appropriate places in the search (see code in Section 16.2.2) if we only wish the first answer in the search.

Finally, any PROLOG procedure may be attached to a frame slot. As we designed the frame representation in our examples, this would entail making a PROLOG rule, or list of PROLOG rules, one of the arguments of the frame predicate. To do this we put the rule in parentheses, as we see in the next example.

***Example 16.1:* A PROLOG Schema for Pulley Problems**

In Section 5.3.2 we described the solutions for a set of applied mathematics problems and discussed how researchers built schema structures to model the understanding and solution strategies of human experts in these tasks. We restate one problem here, a pulley problem We then describe the schema that represents the problem solver's knowledge. We then show this schema in PROLOG:

> A man of 15 stone and a weight of 10 stone are connected
> by a light rope passing over a pulley. Find the acceleration
> of the man (one *stone* is 14 pounds).

The schema information is in three parts: declaration information, to initialize the needed entities; facts and inferences, to create the needed reasoning procedures; and default values to give the knowledge assumed in this domain. The schema in PROLOG with four arguments:

1. The first argument is the name with its own argument list of principle components. The schema is part of a hierarchy of schemas.
2. The second argument is a list of calls to other related schemas.
3. The third is a list of entities to be created and rules used to relate these entities. A rule, because it contains an :-, must be enclosed in ( ).
4. The fourth parameter is a list of default assumptions about the situation.

We now present a PROLOG description of this schema. The reader should note that a number of the decisions that went into creating this data structure were arbitrary with alternative approaches possible. Further details of this project are available in Section 6.3.2 and the references (Bundy et al. 1979, Luger 1981).

```
schema(pulley_sys_min(Sys,Pulley,String,Dir1,Dir2,Time),
    [call(string_sys(String,Leftbit,Pulleypt,Rightbit, Time))],
    [problemtype(pulley, Time),
        isa(particle, Pulley),
        contact(Pulley, Pulleypt, Time),
        tangent(Leftbit, Time),
        tangent(Rightbit, Time),
        (tension(Leftbit, T1, Time) :-
            coef_friction(Pulley, 0),tension(Rightbit,T1,Time)),
        (tension(Rightbit, T2, Time) :-
            coef_friction(Pulley, 0),tension(Leftbit,T2,Time))],
```

[coef_friction(Pulley, 0),
mass(Pulley, 0, Time)]).

Researchers over the past twenty years have created a number of other schema based models of human performance. These often include production rules describing knowledge. Among these are models of the development of skills in young children, including seriation (Young 1976); object permanence (Luger et al. 1984); and algebra problem solving (Hinsley et al. 1977). Other applications include problem solving in thermodynamics (Bhaskar & Simon 1977), the comparison of novice and expert students (Simon & Simon 1978; Larkin et al. 1980), and the analysis of programming skills (Anderson 1983b, Soloway et al. 1983). The foundation for much of this analysis rests in the Newell and Simon research tradition described in Section 9.2.

16.3   META-INTERPRETERS FOR SEARCH

16.3.1   Refining Depth-First Search Using Open and Closed Lists

It is quite natural to think of designing a meta-interpreter for control of graph search. In this spirit we first described graph search using *open* and *closed* lists in Chapter 8. In fact, as we saw with the production system that the search control for a graph may be considered independent of its application; that is, independent of the particular rules or knowledge used to change state within the graph.

In Chapter 15 we created our first meta-interpreter for graph search. This was the simple path predicate used in Section 15.3 for depth-first search and used in Section 15.4 to give us a control algorithm for problem solving with the production system. Because the production rules are independent of their controller, this is the ideal situation for creation of a meta-interpreter.

Since the values of variables were preserved with each backtrack, the list of visited states in the depth-first path algorithm of Section 15.4 only records states on the current path to the goal. Although the test for membership in this list prevents loops, it still allows branches of the space to be re-examined if they are reached along different paths. Another implementation keeps track of all the states ever encountered. This makes up the list called *closed* in Section 8.4.

Closed holds all states on the current path plus the states that were rejected when we backtracked out of them. A simple method for creating closed, without relinquishing a current ordered list of states on the path to the present state, is to record rejected states in the data base. This record must be global since these states have been exhaustively examined and rejected, and the search should not consider them again.

This global structure can be created by adding assert(dead(S)) to the algorithm. All the states on the present path list L plus the dead states make up closed. (An even better method is offered in Section 15.3.2 where closed is again a local variable but backtracking is controlled by the cut.) The proper time for recording a state as dead is after all the production rules have failed using it and before the recursive path call fails back to its preceding success. This situation was captured in the ninth move rule of the 8 x 8 knight tour example (Section 15.4) when all other rules had been applied and failed. Then the current state, having no further children, is dead. When a new state is discovered in the search, we must check whether it was ever seen, not just whether it is a member of the current path.

We now present a meta-interpreter for depth-first search in PROLOG that keeps track of closed list information on a list called Path_list. It then checks each new state to be sure it has not been previously visited. path_df (depth-first) has three arguments and is called:

?- path_df(Start, Goal,[Start]).

Start and Goal are variables that assume the values of the start and goal states. The third parameter, Path_list, is a list that represents the current path. The move predicates are as before and will change for each problem, the final move rule records the present state as dead before failing:

```
path_df(Goal,Goal,Path_list) :-
    write('Solution Found. The path is:'), write(Path_list), nl.
path_df(Current, Goal, Path_list) :-
    move(Current, New),
    not(member(New,Path_list)),
    not(dead(New)),
        path_df(New,Goal,[New|Path_list]).

move(Current, New) :- ... %test first rule.
move(Current, New) :- ... %test second rule.
.... ....
move(Current, New) :- assert(dead(Current)), print('Backtrack'),
                        fail.
```

An alternative program for depth-first search can keep track of states on both *open* and *closed* lists, as the searches in Section 8.4. This implementation collects all used states in a closed list, which would be a local variable to the path call, not global as was the dead predicate used above. This choice makes creating the solution path list more difficult. This meta-interpreter will be analogous to those developed in the next two sections, and is left as an exercise.

16.3.2 Breadth-First Search in PROLOG

The cut, Section 15.5, can be used with recursion to reinitialize the path predicate for further search within the graph. Our implementations of breadth-first and best-first search use open and closed lists to record states in the search. The records of local variables such as we created in Section 15.4, are not used for this purpose. If search fails at any point we do not go back to the preceding values of open and closed. Instead, we update open and closed within the path call and the search continues with these new values. The cut predicate is used in these implementations to keep PROLOG from using old versions of open and closed.

We now present a meta-interpreter for breadth-first search using explicit open and closed lists. This code exactly implements the algorithm of Section 8.4.1, and is called by:

?- path_brf([Start], [ ], Goal).

Start and Goal have their obvious meanings. The first parameter of path_brf is the open list, initialized above with Start; the second is the closed list, initially empty; and the third argument is the Goal state.

The algorithm for path_brf has no production rules, predicates move, given. These must be supplied to fit the problem domain. The termination condition in the first path_brf call describes the situation where its first argument, the open list, is empty. This only happens when there are no more states in the graph remaining to be searched and there is no solution. A solution is found in the second termination condition if the head of open and the goal state are the same.

The third situation for path_brf is when search continues with the head, or first element, of the open list as the next state in the search. Open and closed are then printed to watch the progress of the search. Next, get_new_children is called to generate all the children of the current state. These are then appended to the end of the open list, forming a queue, to continue the search. Don't care variables, whose values must be matched but are not used, are written as _.

```
path_brf([ ], _, _) :-
    print('graph searched, no solution found').
path_brf([Goal|_], _, Goal) :- print('solution found').
path_brf([CS|Rest_open], Closed, Goal) :-
    write('open:'), printlist([CS|Rest_open]),
    write('closed:'), printlist(Closed),
    write('current state:'), write(CS),
    get_new_children(CS, Rest_open, Closed, Children),
    append(Rest_open, Children, New_open), !,
        path_brf(New_open,[CS|Closed], Goal).
```

Notice that most of the code above is to inform the user of the state of the search. There are a number of utilities, described next, that support the breadth-first path predicate. move rules are supplied according to the application.

get_new_children uses bagof, a PROLOG predicate standard to most interpreters. bagof lets us gather all the matches of a pattern into a single list. The second parameter of bagof is the pattern to be matched in the data base, namely, the full set of moves possible in this problem situation. Thus, bagof collects the states reached by firing ALL of the enabled move production rules. The first parameter of bagof specifies the components of the second parameter that we wish to collect. The collected list is the third argument, in this case, Children. Some implementations of PROLOG fail if bagof returns the empty list. We do not want bagof to fail so we add the *or* clasue for Children, as in the example.

```
get_new_children(CS, Rest_open, Closed, Children) :-
    (bagof(X, moves(CS, Rest_open, Closed, X), Children);
    Children = [ ]).

moves(S, T, C, X) :- move(S, X), X \== S,
    not(member(X,T)), not(member(X,C)).

member(X,[X|_]).
member(X,[_|T]) :- member(X,T).

append([],L,L).
append([H|T],L,[H|NT]) :- append(T,L,NT).

printlist([]).
printlist([H|T]) :- printlist(T), print(H).
```

To fire all the enabled production rules, the second argument of bagof, contains a predicate named moves, which calls the move predicate to generate all the states that may be reached using the production rules. The arguments to moves are the present state, the open list, the closed list, and a variable bound to the state reached by a good move. Before returning this state, moves checks that it is not a member of either open or closed. bagof calls moves and collects all the states that meet these conditions.

The third argument of bagof represents the new states that are placed in their proper position on open. This is done using the append predicate, discussed in detail in Section 15.6, to join two lists together. The list passed back from bagof is the second argument of append and thus is placed on the right end of open, forming a queue, according to the breadth-first search algorithm of Section 8.4.1. This open list then becomes the first argument of the next call to path_brf where its head is taken as the new state for evaluation. The head of open, once it has been used by bagof for generation of descendants, is added to closed.

Finally, the predicate printlist will print out, in reverse order, the elements of a list. Can you trace it's execution?

16.3.3   Best-First Search in PROLOG

Our meta-interpreter for best-first search is a modification of the breadth-first algorithm in which open is ordered by heuristic merit before calling path each new time. It exactly implements the algorithm of Section 8.5.1.

In our path_bestf algorithm, we attach a heuristic measure permanently to each new state generated by get_new_children and use these measures for ordering states on open. Each new child is then merged into the already sorted open list. Other versions of the algorithm retain the parent of the state. This information can be used to build the solution path once the goal is found.

In our algorithm, each state is represented as a list of four elements: the first the state description, the second an integer giving the depth in the graph of its discovery, the third element an integer giving the heuristic measure of the state, and fourth, the integer sum of the second and third elements. The first element is found in the usual way, the second is determined by adding one to the depth of its parent, the third element is determined by the heuristic measure of the particular problem. The fourth element, used for ordering the states on open, is f = g + h, as presented in Section 8.5. The algorithm is called by:

?- path_bestf([[Start,0,H,H]|[ ]], [ ], [Goal,_,_,_]).

H is the heuristic evaluation of the Start state and we don't care about the second, third, and fourth parameters of the Goal. The code for best first search is:

```
path_bestf([ ], _, _) :-
    write('Search over, no solution found.').
path_bestf([[Goal, _, _, _]| _], _, [Goal, _, _, _]) :-
    write('Solution found.').
path_bestf([[CS,D,H,T]|Rest_open],Closed,[Goal,_, _, _]) :-
    print('present state:', CS),
    print('open:'), printlist(Rest_open),
    print('closed:'), printlist(Closed),
    get_new_children([CS,D,H,T],Rest_open,Closed, Children),
    merge(Children, Rest_open, New_open), !,
        path_bestf(New_open,[[CS,D,H,T]|Closed],[Goal,_,_, _]).
```

The meta-interpreter for best-first search contains a number of print and printlist statements to monitor the solution. A set of move rules will be called by the get_new_children predicate and these must be added according to the application. We also add a number of utility predicates such as bagof (described in Section 16.3.2), printlist, append, and member to support the algorithm.

calculate, which depends on the problem domain, is a measure applied to each state to determine its heuristic weight, the third element of its description list. The algorithm, as breadth-first above, has two termination conditions, the first when there are no states left to search (open is empty) and the second when the head of open matches the goal and we end with success. member, merge, and insert must be written for states that are described by a four element list.

```
get_new_children([CS, D, H, T],Rest_open, Closed, Children) :-
    bagof(X,moves([CS,D,H,T],Rest_open,Closed,X), Children).

moves([S, D, H, T], R, C, [A, B, E, F]) :-
    move(S, A), S \== A,
    not(member([A, _, _, _], R)),
    not(member([A, _, _, _], C)),
    B is D + 1, calculate(A, E), F is E + B.

member([X, _, _, _], [[X, _, _, _]| _]).
member([X, _, _, _], [[ _, _, _, _]|T]) :- member([X, _, _, _], T).

merge([], X, X).
merge([H|T], X, New_open) :- insert(H, X, NX),
    merge(T, NX, New_open).

insert([State, D, H, T], [ ], [State, D, H, T]).
insert([State, D, H, T], [[HS, HD, HH, HT]|T],
    [[State, D, H, T], [HS, HD, HH, HT]|T]) :- T =< HT.
insert([State, D, H, T], [H|T], [H|New_tail]) :-
    insert([State, D, H, T], T, New_tail).

move(S, NS) to be added by the reader
calculate(NS, V) to be added by the reader
```

The predicate calculate determines the heuristic value of the state that is its first argument. This calculation will depend on the current problem. If the goal changes in the context of a problem (for example, the knight going to any square on the chess board), then that goal state must be passed as a parameter from the path predicate, through bagof to calculate.

16.4 NATURAL LANGUAGE UNDERSTANDING IN PROLOG

16.4.1 Introduction

Because of its built-in search and pattern matching, PROLOG offers a powerful tool for representing and processing language structures. We can write natural language grammars directly in PROLOG, as we see with the *context free* and *context sensitive* grammars of Sections 16.4.2 and 16.4.3.

Semantic representations are also easy to create in PROLOG. Semantic relationships can either be built directly using the first order predicate calculus or by constructing meta-interpreters for other representation languages, as we did for the semantic net and frame system interpreters of Section 16.2. Finally, semantic inference, for instance, *join* and *restrict* operations on graphs or inheritance structures, can be done directly in PROLOG; we see this in Section 16.4.4.

Type information can be added to parameters as indicated in Section 16.1.2. We can also define the type hierarchy through a variation of isa predicates (Section 16.2.2) or directly in a predicate:

> noun(fred, [man(fred)]).
> noun(fido, [dog(fido)]).
> noun(dog, [dog(X), animal(dog)]).

The second argument is the list of parents for inheritance. dog(X) indicates the dog is unnamed, but in parsing can be assigned a variable name, to be identified as the agent of some action, for example.

Case frames (Fillmore 1968, Simmons 1973) are also easily defined in PRO-LOG. The case frame of the verb bites, for example, describes an action requiring an agent and an object:

> verb(bites, [action([biting(Y)]),agent([dog(X)]),
>   object([animate(Y)])]).

In the English sentence "Fido bites Fred," this structure takes the obvious assignments. We define *default values* in a case frame by binding the appropriate values in the case frame. For example, we can give bite a default instrument of teeth:

> verb(bites, [action..., agent..., object..., instrument(teeth)]).

Again, type constraints (Section 16.1.2) may be used to enforce variable bindings that match semantic constraints. Logic programming offers a powerful medium for building grammars as well as representations for semantic meanings.

We now use PROLOG to build several of these structures: context free and context sensitive grammars as well as a recursive descent parser that links and joins pieces of semantic nets to the parsed fragments of a sentence.

16.4.2   A Context Free Parser

In Section 13.3.5 we presented the syntactic analysis of language. We identified the main components of language and showed how grammar rules could to determine whether or not these language pieces were well-formed. For example, with the small subset of English grammar rules below, we can account for the syntactic correctness of a large number of simple sentences. The <=> symbol indicates that one language structure *may be replaced by* another. For instance, a sentence may be described as a noun phrase followed by a verb phrase: the dog bites; or a noun phrase may be described as an article followed by a noun: the man. This set of grammar rules is context free since there is no global constraint, or context, that both the noun phrase and the verb phrase have to satisfy. In particular, there is no requirement for noun verb agreement.

> sentence <=> nounphrase verbphrase
> nounphrase <=> noun
> nounphrase <=> article noun
> verbphrase <=> verb
> verbphrase <=> verb nounphrase

When we add to these rules a set of dictionary items, say a set of nouns, verbs, and articles, then we can begin to generate and parse sentences:

> article(a).
> article(the).
> noun(man).
> noun(dog).
> noun(fido).
> verb(likes).
> verb(bites).

The parse tree of a simple sentence, the dog bites the man, follows as Figure 16.2. The general and/or graph of Figure 6.4 shows the full set of sentences that may be built with this set of grammar rules and the dictionary.

The specification rules of the grammar are transcribed into PROLOG rules in a natural fashion. For example, consider the rule that a sentence is a noun phrase followed by a verb phrase. This may be represented in PROLOG:

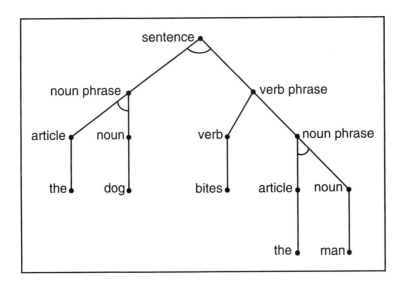

FIGURE 16.2 Parse tree for the sentence "the dog bites the man."

sentence(Start, End) :- nounphrase(Start, Rest), verbphrase(Rest, End).

The sentence itself, for our representation, is cast as a list: [the,man,likes, the,dog]. The sentence predicate attempts to determine if some initial part of the list is a nounphrase. Any remaining suffix of the list that has not been parsed as a noun phrase will match the second parameter, Rest and passed over as the first argument of verbphrase. What is left after the identification of a verb phrase is bound to End. If the sentence predicate succeeds, the second parameter of sentence will have what remains after the nounphrase and verbphrase parse; if the list is a correct sentence then nothing is left over and End = [ ].

The two alternatives for nounphrase and verbphrase are next defined. As the parse proceeds the sentence list is broken up and passed to the various grammar components to be examined for syntactic correctness. Note how the pattern matching works on the list in question: pulling off the head, or the head and second element, passing on what is left over, and so on.

The utterance predicate takes the list to be parsed and calls the sentence rule. It initializes the second parameter of sentence to [ ], indicating that nothing should remain in the list after a successful parse. The complete grammar:

utterance(X) :- sentence(X,[]).

sentence(Start, End) :- nounphrase(Start, Rest), verbphrase(Rest, End).

```
nounphrase([Noun|End],End) :- noun(Noun).
nounphrase([Article, Noun|End], End) :- article(Article), noun(Noun).

verbphrase([Verb|End], End) :- verb(Verb).
verbphrase([Verb|Rest], End) :- verb(Verb), nounphrase(Rest, End).

article(a).
article(the).
noun(man).
noun(dog).
verb(likes).
verb(bites).
```

Example sentences may be tested to see if they are formed correctly according to the dictionary and grammar rules:

```
?- utterance([the,man,bites,the,dog]).
yes
?- utterance([the,man,bites,the]).
no
```

New partial sentences may be proposed and the interpreter asked to fill in potential remaining words, so that the resulting sentence is syntactically correct:

```
?- utterance([the,man,likes,X]).
X = man
?- ;
X = dog
?- ;
no
```

PROLOG finds all legitimate ways the sentence may be concluded! Finally, the same code may be used to generate the set of all well-formed sentences using this limited dictionary and set of grammar rules:

```
?- utterance(X).
X = [man, likes]
?- ;
X = [man, bites]
?- ;
X = [man, likes, man]
?- ;
```

X = [man, likes, dog]
etc.

If the user continues asking for more solutions, eventually all possible sentences that can be generated from our grammar rules and limited vocabulary are returned as values for X.

The grammar rules and vocabulary provide the sets of constraints for well-formed expressions in this subset of legitimate English sentences. The interpreter is asked questions about this set of specifications. The answer to the query is a function of the constraints and the question asked. This is a major benefit of computing with a language that is itself a theorem prover able to act on sets of specifications! (We introduced this issue in discussing declarative and procedural computing in Section 15.6.)

16.4.3 A Context Sensitive Parser

We now add context sensitivity to our set of grammar rules. We do this by creating a context for interpreting the specifications for each rule. Suppose we desire to have noun-verb agreement in sentences. We include in the dictionary entry for each word its singular or plural form. Then in the grammar specifications a further parameter is used to signify the number constraint for each component of the parse. Thus a sentence has to associate a singular noun with a singular verb. Our example retains the contextual information needed to check number agreement.

These additions are made to the previous code. Note that the nounphrase that is part of the verbphrase does not have to agree in number with anything:

```
utterance(X) :- sentence(X, [ ]).

sentence(Start, End) :-
    nounphrase(Start,Rest,Number), verbphrase(Rest,End,Number).

nounphrase([Noun|End], End, Number) :- noun(Noun, Number).
nounphrase([Article, Noun|End], End, Number) :-
    noun(Noun, Number), article(Article, Number).

verbphrase([Verb|End], End, Number) :- verb(Verb, Number).
verbphrase([Verb|Rest], End, Number) :-
    verb(Verb, Number), nounphrase(Rest, End, _).

article(a, singular).
article(these, plural).
```

```
article(the, singular).
article(the, plural).
noun(man, singular).
noun(men, plural).
noun(dog, singular).
noun(dogs, plural).
verb(likes, singular).
verb(like, plural).
verb(bites, singular).
verb(bite, plural).
```

New sentences may now be tested:

```
?- utterance([the,men,like,the,dog]).
yes
?- utterance([the,men,likes,the,dog]).
no
```

The answer to the second query is no since the subject, men, and the verb, likes, do not agree in number. If we enter the goal:

```
?- utterance([the,men|X]).
```

X will return all possible verb phrases for completing the sentence "the men ..." with noun-verb number agreement! As before, we may request all legitimate sentences, according to the constraints of this grammar and the elements in the dictionary:

```
?- utterance(X).
```

The present example uses the parameters on dictionary entries to introduce more information on the meanings in the sentence. This approach may be generalized to a powerful parser for natural language. More and more information may be included in the dictionary about the items described in the sentences, implementing a knowledge base of the meaning of English words. For example, men are animate and human. Similarly, dogs may be described as animate and nonhuman. With these descriptions new rules may be added for parsing sentences such as "humans do not bite animate nonhumans" to eliminate sentences such as [the,man,bites,the,dog]. If the nonhuman is no longer animate, of course, it might be eaten in a restaurant!

Semantic networks and other representational formalisms of this sort have played an important role in capturing semantic meaning. We now add more semantic analysis to our parser by attaching pieces of semantic nets to the leaves of the parse tree and constraining these meanings as they are brought together in the parse of a sentence.

16.4.4 A Recursive Descent Semantic Net Parser

The action of our meta-interpreter is very much as it was in the previous two sections. When the parse descends to the leaves of the tree, however, it matches on pieces of semantic nets. As these pieces are brought back up the parse tree they are "joined" with the pieces from the other branches of the tree. The finished parse produces a Sentence_graph representing the meaning of the sentence.

The grammar rules are presented next. Notice that at the places where two structures come together, the verb and the nounphrase in the verbphrase description, for instance, an appropriate graph join operation is called.

```
utterance(X, Sentence_graph) :-
    sentence(X, [ ], Sentence_graph).

sentence(Start, End, Sentence_graph) :-
    nounphrase(Start, Rest, Subject_graph),
    verbphrase(Rest, End, Predicate_graph),
    join([agent(Subject_graph)],Predicate_graph, Sentence_graph).

nounphrase([Noun|End], End, Noun_phrase_graph) :-
    noun(Noun, Noun_phrase_graph).
nounphrase([Article, Noun| End], End, Noun_phrase_graph) :-
    article(Article), noun(Noun, Noun_phrase_graph).

verbphrase([Verb| End], End, Verb_phrase_graph) :-
    verb(Verb, Verb_phrase_graph).
verbphrase([Verb|Rest], End, Verb_phrase_graph) :-
    verb(Verb, Verb_graph),
    nounphrase(Rest, End, Noun_phrase_graph),
    join([object(Noun_phrase_graph)],Verb_graph,
        Verb_phrase_graph).
```

Next we describe some graph join operators that merge the pieces of graphs as the parse continues. These are best seen as utilities that propagate constraints between the pieces of semantic nets that are joined. This approach of semantic graph constraint is similar to that proposed by Quillian (1967) in Section 6.2.1.

```
join_frames([A|B], C, D, OK) :-
    join_slot_to_frame(A, C, E), !,
    join_frames(B, E, D, ok).

join_frames([A|B], C, [A|D], OK) :-
    join_frames(B, C, D, OK), !.

join_frames([], A, A, ok).
join_slot_to_frame(A, [B|C], [D|C]) :-
    join_slots(A, B, D).

join_slot_to_frame(A, [B|C], [B|D]) :-
    join_slot_to_frame(A, C, D).
join_slots(A, B, D) :-
    functor(A, FA, _),
    functor(B, FB, _),
    match_with_inheritance(FA, FB, FN),
    arg(1, A, Value_a),
    arg(1, B, Value_b),
    join(Value_a, Value_b, New_value),
    D =..[FN|[New_value]].

join(X, X, X).
join(A, B, C) :- isframe(A), isframe(B), !,
    join_frames(A, B, C, not_joined).
join(A, B, C) :- isframe(A), is_slot(B), !,
    join_slot_to_frame(B, A, C).

join(A, B, C) :- isframe(B), is_slot(A), !,
    join_slot_to_frame(A, B, C).

join(A, B, C) :- is_slot(A), is_slot(B), !,
    join_slots(A, B, C).

isframe([_|_]).
isframe([ ]).

is_slot(A) :- functor(A, _, 1).
```

Finally, we have the dictionary, inheritance hierarchy, and the case frames for the verbs:

```
match_with_inheritance(X, X, X).
match_with_inheritance(dog, animate, dog).
match_with_inheritance(animate, dog, dog).
match_with_inheritance(man, animate, man).
match_with_inheritance(animate, man, man).
match_with_inheritance(animate, man, john).

article(a).
article(the).

noun(fido, [dog(fido)]).
noun(man, [man(X)]).
noun(john, [man(john)]).
noun(dog, [dog(X)]).

verb(likes,[action([liking(X)]),agent([animate(X)]),
    object([animate(Y)])]).
verb(bites,[action([biting(Y)]),agent([dog(X)]),
    object([animate(Z)])]).
```

We end with the parse of several sentences:

```
?- utterance([the, man, likes, the, dog], X).
X = [action([liking(_27)]), agent([man(_17)]), object([dog(_30)])]
?- utterance([fido, likes, the, man], W).
W = [action([liking(fido)]), agent([dog(fido)]), object([man(_72)])]
?- utterance([john, bites, fido], Z).
no
```

The first result states that some man, name unknown, likes some unknown dog. In the second example a particular dog, fido, likes the unnamed man. The third sentence, although syntactically correct, does not meet the semantic criteria determined through an inheritance check, where a dog has to be the agent of the verb bites. In a final example we reverse the situation and the dog bites the man:

```
?- utterance([the, dog, bites, the, man], Z).
Z = [action([biting( _22)]), agent([dog(_15)]), object([man(_35)])]
```

This parser may be extended in a number of ways, adding adjectives and adverbs, for instance. The semantic graph for each piece of the sentence must be bound, constrained, and passed back up the tree to be part of the final sentence graph.

In the last section of Chapter 16 we design a meta-interpreter in PROLOG for *version space* search.

16.5   VERSION SPACE SEARCH IN PROLOG

In Chapter 10, we presented a number of machine learning algorithms. In this section we build one of them: *version space* search. PROLOG is widely used in machine learning research because, as this implementation illustrates, its meta-level reasoning capabilities simplify the construction and manipulation of new representations. We will not discuss the version space search algorithms in the present chapter so the reader might consult the related material in Section 10.2.

Section 10.2.2 we offered three algorithms for searching concept spaces:

1.   Searching in a *specific to general* direction.
2.   Searching in a *general to specific* direction.
3.   A bidirectional search, the *candidate elimination* algorithm.

In this section we implement the *specific to general* search, and give hints on how the reader may construct the *general to specific* version space search. The complete form of this and a number of other machine learning algorithms may be found in Luger and Stubblefield (1993).

16.5.1   The Feature Vector Representation of Concepts and Instances

These algorithms are independent of the representation used for concepts, as long as the chosen representation supports appropriate generalization and specialization operations. We choose to describe objects as lists of features. For example, a small, red, ball is the list:

[small, red, ball]

Similarly, we describe the concept of all small, red things by making the third list element a variable:

[small, red, X]

This representation, called a *feature vector*, is less expressive than full logic. For example, it cannot represent the class "all red or green balls." However, it simplifies generalization and provides a strong inductive bias (Chapter 10). We generalize a feature vector by substituting a variable for a constant, for example, the most specific common generalization of [small, red, ball] and [small, green, ball] is [small, X, ball]. This vector will cover both of the specializations and is the most specific vector to do so.

We define a feature vector as covering another if the first is either identical to or more general than the second. Note that unlike unification, covers is asymmetrical: values exist for which X covers Y, but Y does not cover X. For example, [X, red, ball] covers [large, red, ball], but the reverse is not true. We define covers for feature vectors:

```
covers([ ],[ ]).
covers([H1|T1], [H2|T2]) :-
     var(H1), var(H2), covers(T1, T2).    % variables cover each other
covers([H1|T1], [H2|T2]) :-
     var(h1), atom(H2), covers(T1, T2).    % variable covers a constant
covers([H1|T1], [H2|T2]) :-
     atom(H1), atom(H2), H1=H2,covers(T1, T2).% constants match
```

In the algorithm, we determine if one feature vector is strictly more general than another. The strictness property requires that the vectors not be identical. We define the more_general predicate as:

```
more_general(X, Y) :- not(covers(Y, X)), covers(X, Y).
```

We implement generalization of feature vectors as a predicate, generalize, where the first argument is a feature vector representing a hypothesis that may contain variables, the second argument is an instance, containing no variables. generalize binds its third argument to the most specific generalization of the hypothesis that covers the instance. generalize recursively scans the feature vectors, comparing corresponding elements. If two elements match, the result contains the value of the hypotheses vector in that position. If two elements do not match, it places a variable in the corresponding position of the generalized feature vector. Note the use of the expression, not(Feature \= Inst_prop), in the second definition of generalize. This double negative enables us to test if two atoms will unify without actually performing the unification and forming any unwanted variable bindings. We define generalize:

```
generalize([ ],[ ],[ ]).
generalize([Feature|Rest], [Inst_prop|Rest_inst], [Feature|Rest_gen]) :-
     not(Feature \== Inst_prop),
          generalize(Rest, Rest_inst, Rest_gen).
generalize([Feature|Rest], [Inst_prop|Rest_inst], [_|Rest_gen]) :-
     Feature \== Inst_prop,
          generalize(Rest, Rest_inst, Rest_gen).
```

These predicates define the essential operations on feature vectors. The remainder of the implementation in Section 16.5.2 is independent of any specific representation, and may be adapted to a variety of generalization operators (see Section 10.2).

16.5.2   Specific to General Search

As we discussed in Section 10.2, we search a concept space in a specific to general direction by maintaining a list H of candidate hypotheses. The hypotheses in H are the most specific concepts that cover all the positive examples and none of the negative examples seen so far.

The heart of the algorithm is the predicate process with three arguments. The first argument is a training instance, positive(X) or negative(X), indicating that X is a positive or negative example. The second and third arguments are the current list of hypotheses and the list of negative instances. On completion, process binds its fourth and fifth arguments to the updated lists of hypotheses and negative examples, respectively.

The first clause in the definition initializes an empty hypothesis set to the first positive instance. The second handles positive training instances by generalizing candidate hypotheses to cover the instance. It then deletes all over generalizations by removing those that are more general than some other hypothesis and eliminating any hypothesis that covers some negative instance. The third clause in the definition handles negative examples by deleting any hypothesis that covers those instances.

```
process(positive(Instance), [ ], N, [Instance], N).
process(positive(Instance), H, N, Updated_H, N) :-
    generalize_set(H,Gen_H, Instance),
    delete(X, Gen_H, (member(Y, Gen_H),
        more_general(X, Y)), Pruned_H),
    delete(X, Pruned_H, (member(Y, N), covers(X, Y)),
        Updated_H).
process(negative(Instance), H, N, Updated_H, [Instance|N]) :-
    delete(X, H, covers(X, Instance), Updated_H).
process(Input, H, N, H, N):-    % Catches mistyped input
    Input \== positive(_),
    Input \== negative(_),
    write('Enter positive(Instance) or negative(Instance)'), nl.
```

An interesting aspect of this implementation is the delete predicate, a generalization of the usual process of deleting all matches of an element from a list.

One of the arguments to delete is a test that determines which elements to remove from the list. Using bagof, delete matches its first argument, usually a variable, with each element of its second argument, this must be a list. For each such binding, it then executes the test specified in argument three. This test is any sequence of callable PROLOG goals. If a list element causes this test to fail, delete includes that element in the resulting list. It returns the result in its final argument. The delete predicate is an excellent example of the power of meta reasoning in PROLOG: by letting us pass in a specification of the elements we want to delete from a list, delete gives us a general tool for implementing a range of list operations. Thus, delete lets us define the various filters used for the processing in an extremely compact fashion. We define delete:

```
delete(X, L, Goal, New_L) :-
    (bagof(X, (member(X, L), not(Goal)), New_L); New_L = [ ]).
```

Generalize_set is a straightforward predicate that recursively scans a list of hypotheses and generalizes each one against a training instance. Note that this assumes that we may have multiple candidate generalizations at one time. In fact, the feature vector representation of Section 16.5.1 only allows a single most specific generalization. However, this is not true in general and we have defined the algorithm for the general case:

```
generalize_set([ ], [ ], _).
generalize_set([Hypothesis|Rest],Updated_H,Instance):-
    not(covers(Hypothesis, Instance)),
    (bagof(X,generalize(Hypothesis,Instance,X),Updated_head);
        Updated_head = [ ]),
    generalize_set(Rest,Updated_rest, Instance),
    append(Updated_head, Updated_rest, Updated_H).
generalize_set([Hypothesis|Rest],[Hypothesis|Updated_rest],
        Instance) :-
    covers(Hypothesis, Instance),
    generalize_set(Rest,Updated_rest, Instance).
```

specifiᶜ_to_general implements a straightforward loop that reads and processes training ᵔstances:

```
specific_to_general(H, N) :-
    write('H ='), write(H),nl,
    write('N ='), write(N),nl,
    write('Enter Instance'),
    read(Instance),
```

```
process(Instance, H, N, Updated_H, Updated_N),
specific_to_general(Updated_H, Updated_N).
```

The following transcript illustrates the execution of the algorithm. (Recall that PROLOG creates variable symbols by using _X, where X is 0 or a positive integer.)

```
?- specific_to_general([ ], [ ]).
"H ="[ ]
"N ="[ ]
"Enter Instance"positive([small, red, ball]).
"H ="[[small,red,ball]]
"N ="[ ]
"Enter Instance"negative([large, green, cube]).
"H ="[[small,red,ball]]
"N ="[[large,green,cube]]
"Enter Instance"negative([small, blue, brick]).
"H ="[[small,red,ball]]
"N ="[[small,blue,brick],[large,green,cube]]
"Enter Instance"positive([small, green, ball]).
"H ="[[small,_66,ball]]
"N ="[[small,blue,brick],[large,green,cube]]
"Enter Instance"positive([large, blue, ball]).
"H ="[[_116,_66,ball]]
"N ="[[small,blue,brick],[large,green,cube]]
```

The second version of the algorithm searches in a general to specific direction (Section 10.2.2). In the general to specific search, the set of candidate hypotheses are initialized to the most general possible concept. In the case of the feature vector representation, this is a list of variables. It specializes candidate concepts to prevent them from covering negative instances. In the feature vector representation, this involves replacing variables with constants. When given a new positive instance, it eliminates any candidate hypothesis that fails to cover that instance.

We may implement this algorithm in a way that closely parallels the specific to general search described above, including the use of the general delete predicate to define the various filters of the list of candidate concepts. Each predicate in the specific to general search has its counterpart in the general to specific version.

In defining a *general to specific* search, process takes six arguments. The first five reflect the specific to general version: the first is a training instance, of the form positive(Instance) or negative(Instance) The second argument is a list of candidate hypotheses, these are the most general hypotheses that cover no negative instances. The third argument is the list of positive examples; the algorithm uses this to delete any overly specialized candidate hypothesis. The fourth and fifth arguments are the updated lists of hypotheses and positive examples respectively. The sixth argument is a list of allowable variable substitutions for specializing concepts.

Specialization, by substituting a constant for a variable requires the algorithm to know the allowable constant values for each field of the feature vector. These values will have to be passed in as the sixth argument to process. In our example of [Size, Color, Shape] vectors, a sample list of types might be: [[small, medium, large], [red, white, blue], [ball, brick, cube]]. Note that the position of each sublist determines the position in a feature vector where those values may be used. Thus, the first sublist defines allowable values for the first position of a feature vector, the second sublist defines values for the second feature, and so on.

```
process(negative(Instance), H, P, Updated_H, P, Types) :-
    specialize_set(H,Spec_H, Instance, Types),
    delete(X, Spec_H, (member(Y, Spec_H),
        more_general(Y, X)), Pruned_H),
    delete(X, Pruned_H, (member(Y, P), not(covers(X, Y)))),
    Updated_H).

process(positive(Instance), H, P, Updated_H, [Instance|P], _) :-
    delete(X, H, not(covers(X, Instance))), Updated_H).
process(Input, H, P, H, P,_):-          %traps bad input
    Input \== positive(_),
    Input \== negative(_),
    write("Enter either positive(Instance) or negative(Instance)"), nl.
```

We leave construction of the rest of the algorithm to the reader. For further guidance, we include a run of our implementation:

```
?- general_to_specific([[_,_,_]], [ ],
        [[small, medium, large], [red, blue, green], [ball, brick, cube]]).
"H ="[[_0,_1,_2]]
"P ="[ ]
"Enter Instance"positive([small, red, ball]).
"H ="[[_0,_1,_2]]
"P = "[[small,red,ball]]
"Enter Instance"negative([large, green,cube]).
"H ="[[small,_89,_90],[_79,red,_80],[_69,_70,ball]]
```

"P ="[[small,red,ball]]
"Enter Instance"negative([small, blue, brick]).
"H ="[[_79,red,_80],[_69,_70,ball]]
"P ="[[small,red,ball]]
"Enter Instance"positive([small, green, ball]).
"H ="[[_69,_70,ball]]
"P ="[[small,green,ball],[small,red,ball]]

The full candidate elimination algorithm, as described in Section 10.2, is a combination of the two single direction searches. As before, the heart of the algorithm is the definition of the predicate **process**. As before, the first argument to **process** is a training instance. Arguments two and three are **G** and **S**, the sets of maximally general and maximally specific hypotheses respectively. The fourth and fifth arguments are bound to the updated versions of these sets. The sixth argument lists allowable variable substitutions for specializing feature vectors.

We conclude this section with a trace of the *candidate elimination* algorithm. More details, and code for this and other learning algorithms, may be found in Luger and Stubblefield (1993, Chap. 13).

?- run_candidate_elim.
"G="[[_0,_1,_2]]
"S="[ ]
"Enter Instance"positive([small, red, ball]).
"G="[[_0,_1,_2]]
"S="[[small,red,ball]]
"Enter Instance"negative([large, green, cube]).
"G="[[small,_96,_97],[_86,red,_87],[_76,_77,ball]]
"S="[[small,red,ball]]
"Enter Instance"negative([small, blue, brick]).
"G="[[_86,red,_87],[_76,_77,ball]]
"S="[[small,red,ball]]
"Enter Instance"positive([small, green, ball]).
"G="[[_76,_77,ball]]
"S="[[small,_351,ball]]
"Enter Instance"positive([large, red, ball]).
"target concept is"[_76,_77,ball]
yes

16.6 EPILOGUE AND REFERENCES

The references after the first PROLOG chapter are also appropriate here. The semantics of logic programming and declarative specifications is addressed by Maarten van Emden and Robert Kowalski (1976) and Kowalski (1979a, 1979b).

Most PROLOG texts (Sterling & Shapiro 1986, O'Keefe 1990) treat the meta-predicates and type constraints presented in Section 16.1. A number of researchers have proposed the introduction of types to PROLOG (Mycroft & O'Keefe 1984). Typed data can be appropriate for design and control of relational data bases (Neves et al. 1986, Malpas 1987). The rules of logic can be used as constraints on the data and the data itself typed to enforce consistent and meaningful interpretation of the queries. A discussion of types is presented in *A Polymophic Type System for Prolog* by Alan Mycroft and Richard O'Keefe (1984).

Building AI representations such as semantic nets, frames, and objects is discussed in a number of books, especially *Knowledge Systems and PROLOG* by Adrian Walker, Michael McCord, John Sowa, and Walter Wilson (Walker et al. 1987); *PROLOG, a Relational Language and Its Applications* by John Malpas (1987); and *Advanced Prolog* by Peter Ross (1989).

The PROLOG representation medium is so applicable for natural language understanding that many projects use PROLOG to model language. The first PROLOG interpreter was designed to analyze French using metamorphosis grammars (Colmerauer et al. 1973, Colmerauer 1975). Fernando Pereira and David Warren (1980) created definite clause grammars. Veronica Dahl (1977, 1983), Michael McCord (1982, 1986), and John Sowa (1984) have all contributed to this research.

The full set of version space learning algorithms plus more detailed analysis of this approach may be found in Section 10.2.2. All machine learning references may be found at the end of the chapters of Part III. Full specification and running code for the meta-interpreters of this chapter may be found in Luger and Stubblefield (1993).

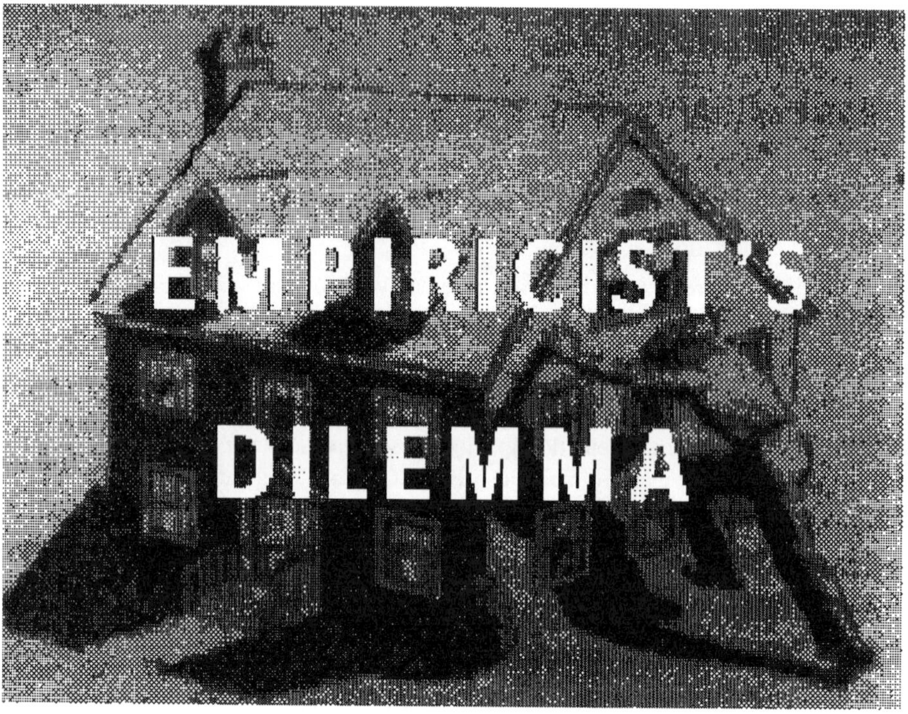
EMPIRICIST'S
DILEMMA

Part VI

EPILOGUE

In the first 16 chapters of this book we proposed a foundation for a science of intelligent systems. Cognitive science, along with cognitive psychology, psycholinguistics, and artificial intelligence, must be seen as empirical disciplines. We design experiments where many of the theory based conjectures are brought to life in the computational abstractions of a connectionist network or with the data structures and associated search algorithms of an explicit symbol system. We run experiments where computational mechanisms are asked to replicate and explain aspects of human performance. If we are beginning to understand the phenomena, and our models are appropriate, the experimental results support some of our expectations and disconfirm others. We then can ask even more questions.

As cognitive scientists we take a constructivist approach. The explicit link of a running program that embodies a theory is crucial to our endeavor. The program forces us to be explicit in our theoretical constructs and "cash out" the homunculi and other imprecise constructs of folk psychology. Most importantly, our program forces us to be precise enough for a failure that can open us to new insights and theoretical growth.

Part I of the book brought these issues forward. There we considered intelligence as a natural category and prepared a vocabulary for its description. Our vocabulary emerged from the work philosophers, psychologists, and linguists brought to this endeavor. Above all, the presence of the computational environment allowed us, as empirical scientists, to address issues of intelligence. To capture the invariants of intelligence in a computational model we proposed a number of representational schemes, both explicit symbol based and connectionist. We also proposed in Part I a number of constraints on our models, both from the psychological as well as a physiological perspective.

To clarify our epistemological basis, we described a viewpoint called *constructivism*. This epistemology is an alternative to naive realism, where reality is simply "out there," and to idealism, where there is no systematic link possible between our ideas and an external world.

Part II, with chapters on representation, logic, and weak and strong method problem solving, presented the techniques of the explicit symbol system

585

approach to representation. We saw in Chapter 6 the many representational techniques brought forward by this approach, including semantic nets, frames or schemas, scripts, and object systems with inheritance. In Chapter 7 we saw the logicist approach. Besides the primary approaches of propositional and predicate logic, we saw alternative logic extensions, including nonmonotonic, default logic, and truth maintenance systems. In Chapter 8 we saw *weak method* problem solvers. This approach began with the general problem solver, and continues with general exhaustive search techniques, including depth-first, breadth-first, and best-first search.

In Chapter 9 we saw *strong method* problem solvers, those based on the problem specific knowledge built into the solver rather than the generality of the search methods used. In particular we considered in detail the Newell Simon tradition, including the use of protocol analysis, problem behavior graphs, and the production system. We looked at a short session where a subject solved a cryptarithmetic problem and showed how that protocol could be transformed into a rule set in a production system. This served as the prototype of the physical symbol system method for analyzing human problem solving.

Part III presented models of learning. Chapter 10, based on the *explicit symbol system approach,* began with a general framework for learning. It continued by covering version space search and ID3, both examples of similarity learning. The chapter concluded with explanation based learning, analogical learning, and several algorithms for conceptual clustering. Chapters 11 and 12 presented learning from the connectionist viewpoint. We took an historical approach beginning with early models including McColloch-Pitts networks and the perceptron. We continued with gradient descent search and the backpropagation network. We then considered competitive learning with the winner-take-all and genetic models. We continued with Hebb's model of reinforcement learning, and Hopfield's attractor networks, sometimes called "memories.' We finished Part III with comments on the limitations of our current models of learning.

Part IV described our understanding of language. Learning and language are central to our understanding of the nature of intelligence. Our ability to model these powers offers a measure of our success in the discipline of cognitive science.

Part V introduced PROLOG as a language and a modeling tool. Many of the representations and search algorithms of Part II were built in PROLOG. We build a recursive descent parser for analysis and interpretation of English sentences. We also designed an algorithm for version space search in PROLOG.

In this final chapter we review many of the pieces of the presentation and bring them together in a final, more unified picture. We also present a number of the open issues in cognitive science, indicative of the challenging work that lies ahead.

Chapter 17

COGNITIVE SCIENCE: PROBLEMS AND PROMISE

... connectionism offers cognitive science a number of excellent opportunities for turning methodological, theoretical, and meta-theoretical schisms into powerful integrations - opportunities for forging constructive synergy out of the destructive interference that plagues the field.... We argue that...it is...possible for connectionism to play a central role in a unification of cognitive science....

Paul Smolensky et al. (1992)

Psychology has arrived at the possibility of unified theories of cognition - theories that gain their power by positing a single system of mechanisms that operate together to produce the full range of human cognition....

Allen Newell (1990)

Each new program that is built is an experiment. It poses a question to nature, and its behavior offers clues to an answer. Neither machines or programs are black boxes; they are artifacts that have been designed, both hardware and software, and we can open them up and look inside. We can relate their structure to their behavior and draw many lessons from a single experiment.

Allen Newell & Herbert Simon (1976)

17.0 INTRODUCTION

The questions cognitive scientists address are not new; rather they are as old as recorded thought. The many pieces that fit together to make our current understanding come from the disciplines of philosophy, mathematics, linguistics, psychology, neurophysiology, and computing. It wasn't until rather recently, however, that these issues came together for systematic study in a *science of intelligent systems*.

Section 17.1 reviews progress through the early chapters of the book and offers answers where, as scientists, we have discovered them. In Section 17.2 we consider once again the representation issue that has dominated the discipline. In

Section 17.3 we present attempts at developing a unified theory of cognition. Finally, in Section 17.4 we end with a number of open issues that must be addressed if progress is to continue.

17.1 A SCIENCE OF INTELLIGENT SYSTEMS

17.1.1 The Object of Cognitive Science

The fate of a science is ultimately determined by the way in which it defines its *object of study*. The choice of an object of study represents the commitment to an abstraction, the belief that the object will exhibit invariance across situations and contexts. Only if such invariance exists will the science be successful in discovering context independent laws describing the object's characteristics and behavior.

The rise of modern physics, for example, was made possible by the pioneering work of Galileo and Kepler. Their work laid the foundation for a new kind of scientific study of *bodies in motion*. They insisted that universal laws of motion could be discovered, laws that were invariant across space and time as well as independent of the particular constitution of the object. This challenged the prevailing neo-Aristotelian view that the motion of a body was determined primarily by its inherent nature or essence with different laws governing the motion of astronomical and terrestrial bodies.

By the same token, cognitive science has arisen from the assumption that the laws governing cognitive processes are invariant across subjects and modes of embodiment. The practice of studying these processes in groups of subjects and in computer simulations is premised on the belief that we can discover a universal structure or law in these processes that is independent of the constitution of the particular subject. To varying degrees we also hope to find universal laws that are independent of the particular characteristics of cultures and even biological species.

These assumptions challenge some deeply felt intuitions. They appear to contradict a cherished belief in the individuality and spontaneity of inner mental life. These intuitions have been expressed in a variety of forms by artists and philosophers. Existentialists such as Camus, Sartre, and Heidegger, for example, emphasize the role of individual will and creativity in constructing the meaning of the subject's experience. Philosophers such as John Searle argue that intentionality plays an essential role in mental life, a role without which cognitive processes would not have their semantic character. Philosophers in the hermeneutic school emphasize the role of cultural-historical tradition in shaping the subject's understanding of experience. What all of these views have in common is the denial that consciousness and cognition can be treated as abstract objects independent of their embodiment in particular biological and historical subjects.

This goal of studying cognitive processes in abstraction from their particular embodiment has also been challenged by a methodological perspective within cognitive science called *situated cognition*. Proponents of the situated cognition view argue that the notion of a cognitive process as an internal or intra-agent process is too narrow and abstract, that cognitive processes can only be understood as a component in the structure of interaction between an intelligent agent and its environment.

By defining its object of study as *cognitive processes* and by assuming that these processes can fruitfully be studied apart from their connection to individual subjects, cultures, or even biological species, cognitive science has based itself on a distinct and defeasible methodological commitment. In the sections that follow we discuss and analyze various challenges to this methodological commitment.

17.1.2   Cognitive Modeling

A powerful reason for defining the object of a science abstractly is that it often assists the construction of mathematical models. In cognitive science, computational models play a key role. It is the use of computational models that unify the approaches of linguists, psychologists, computer scientists, and philosophers in the study of cognitive phenomena.

In what sense do our computational models allow us to study cognitive phenomena? A number of different answers have been given to this question. As we have seen in our discussion of the physical symbol system hypothesis, Newell and Simon believe that physical symbol systems, as embodied in running computer programs, are themselves cognitive processes. Given the fact that the hardware and software are the product of our own designs, computational models give us cognitive processes which are particularly easy to study. Thus, "We can relate their structure to their behavior and draw many lessons from a single experiment" (Newell & Simon 1976).

On this view a computational model is itself a miniature cleaned up version or instance of the object under study. It is like the experiment that a biologist might conduct by constructing a terrarium or miniature ecosystem to study the relationships between a set of organisms in a natural ecosystem.

There are two important objections to this view of model building in cognitive science. First, it is highly doubtful that our current generation of computer programs are capable of intelligent performance in any but the most superficial sense. This means that the justification for labeling those computations *cognitive* processes is very weak. Second, the observation of the behavior of a running program cannot be called an empirical experiment in the strict sense. The computer's behavior is a mathematical consequence of the statements that make up the program, in the same way that a theorem in group theory is a consequence of the axioms of group theory. Current techniques in program analysis can be used to mathematically deduce virtually every aspect of program behavior. Only practical limitations of time prevent us from using these analytical techniques rather than running the program. This view of modeling in cognitive science would thus make cognitive science primarily a mathematical discipline, validating the rationalist assertions of Plato and Leibniz.

Another and more plausible view is that cognitive science builds computational models as a means for simulating and predicting cognitive phenomena. This would make the method and purpose of computational modeling more like that used in the physical sciences, where it is clear that the physical phenomenon being modeled does not actually exist inside the computer simulation. The purpose of computational models in cognitive science, on this view, is to give a more precise specification to our theories and to exhibit for us the precise consequences of those theories. What makes cognitive science an empirical science, however, is the comparison of those theoretical consequences or predictions with the observed behavior of cognitive systems in nature.

There is a third view of model building activity in cognitive science, a view falling somewhere between the two previous views. On this view, also advocated by Newell and Simon, we build computational models to determine whether a given theory can account for a certain range of behaviors characteristic of cognitive systems. In this sense, computational model building provides an empirical test of the *viability* of a cognitive theory. The question asked in this type of *experiment* is whether one can build a computational model based on a certain set of design principles, for example, a knowledge level specification of a cognitive process, which exhibits a desired range of behavior.

Observe that whether or not we use a particular type of design in building a computational system to achieve a certain behavior is, in itself, an engineering issue. Generally it is difficult to establish that such a system *cannot in principle* be constructed from a given design except by some form of logical or mathematical argument. Once one such system is constructed, the construction counts as an interesting and perhaps significant existence proof. However, the construction of computational models in accordance with a set of design principles would not, by itself, make cognitive science an empirical science. Model construction, taken in isolation, must be regarded as an engineering task, falling properly within the scope of an engineering discipline such as *artificial intelligence*. What is required to make this model building activity a integral component of an empirical science is the use of these computational models to explain and predict the behavior of natural cognitive systems.

17.1.3 The Constructivist Methodology

Constructivists hypothesize that all understanding is the result of an interaction between energy patterns in the world and mental categories imposed on the world by the intelligent subject (Piaget 1954, 1970; von Glasersfeld 1978). Using Piaget's descriptions, we *assimilate* external phenomena according to current understanding and *accommodate* our understanding to the "demands" of the phenomena.

Constructivists often use the term *schemata* to describe the *a priori* structure used to organize experience of the external world. This term is taken from the British psychologist Bartlett (1932) and its philosophical roots go back to Kant (1781/1964). From this viewpoint, observation is not passive or neutral but active and interpretive (Section 1.3).

Perceived information, Kant's *a posteriori* knowledge, never fits precisely into our preconceived, and *a priori*, schemata. From this tension, the schema based biases the subject uses to organize experience are either modified or replaced. The need for accommodation in the face of unsuccessful interactions with the environment drives a process of cognitive equilibration. Thus, the constructivist epistemology is fundamentally one of cognitive evolution and refinement. An important consequence of constructivism is that the interpretation of any situation involves the imposition of the observer's concepts or categories on reality.

When Piaget (1954, 1970) proposed a constructivist approach to understanding, he named it *genetic epistemology*. The lack of a comfortable fit of schemata to the world "as it is" creates a cognitive tension. This tension drives a process of schema revision. Schema revision, Piaget's *accommodation*, explains the continued evolution of understanding towards *equilibration*.

Schema revision and movement toward equilibration is a genetic predisposition and an accommodation to the structures of the society and the external world. It combines both these forces and represents an embodied predisposition for survival. Schema modification is both an *a priori* of our genetics as well as an *a posteriori* function of society and the world; it is a product of our being in space and time, of our embodiment.

There is a blending here of the empiricist and rationalist traditions. As embodied, we can comprehend nothing except what first passes through the senses. As accommodating, we survive through learning the general patterns of an external world. What we perceive is mediated by what we expect; what we expect is influenced by what is perceived: that is, these two functions can only be understood in terms of each other.

Finally, we are seldom consciously aware of the schemata that support our interaction with the world. As the sources of bias and prejudice both in science and society we are more often than not unaware of their content. These are constitutive of our equilibration with the world and not a perceptible element of our conscious mental life.

Why is a constructivist epistemology particularly useful in addressing the problems of cognitive science? We believe that constructivism helps address the *epistemological access* problem in psychology. For more than a century there has been a struggle in psychology between two factions, a positivist faction which proposes to infer mental phenomena from observable physical behavior, and a more phenomenological approach which allows the use of first person reporting to access psychological phenomena. This factionalism exists because both modes of access to psychological phenomena require some form of inference or construction. In comparison to physical objects which seem to be directly observable, the mental states and dispositions of a subject seem particularly difficult to characterize with certainty. We believe that the dichotomy between direct access to physical phenomena and indirect access to mental phenomena is illusory. The constructivist analysis shows that no experience of things is possible without the use of some schema for organizing the experience. In scientific inquiry this implies that *all* access to phenomena in the world is through model building, approximation, and refinement.

17.1.4   The Intentional Stance

If we want to build systems or models that function at the level of humans in complex environments, these systems must function at a level of knowledge, meaning, and intention. That is, they must be *semantic* engines (Haugheland 1981). At the same time, any model must be realized as a physical-material entity. If its functioning can be characterized totally by physical descriptions, it may be the case that we do not need a knowledge level description.

On the basis of our discussions of behavioral and brain reductions in Chapter 2, we saw that it is difficult if not impossible to capture the significant regularities in cognitive processes with purely physical level descriptions. Thus, an intelligent system's functioning must be understood at an *intentional* and *goal oriented* level. We therefore claim that our computational models of intelligence are only as good as our models of intentional actions.

Our vocabulary is that of *representational theory* (Fodor 1981). This theory adopts the vocabulary of intentional concepts, including *desire* and *belief*, from folk psychology and then embeds it in a global theoretical perspective.

Some philosophers, including Searle (1980), have argued that the semantic aspect of cognitive processes cannot be modeled by computational processes. The reason is that computational processes are in some sense purely formal: the behavior of a computer program is determined purely by the syntactical structure of the symbols and not by the semantic content or representational character of those symbols. This can be verified, Searle argues, by a type of thought experiment. We can imagine putting ourselves in the place of the computational machinery executing program instructions. For example, as someone ignorant of the Chinese language, I can nonetheless conceive myself executing the instructions of a program for conversing in Chinese. I respond to the appearance of a particular sequence of Chinese characters by taking an action specified in the program instructions. The fact that I do not understand Chinese will not affect how I execute program instructions since these are triggered by purely syntactic rules matching characters to instructions. Hence it can be seen that to explain the program behavior I do not need to attribute to the running program any understanding of the meaning of the symbols which it manipulates.

Against Searle, Daniel Dennett (1978, 1987) develops an argument for describing the behavior of computer programs in intentional terms. He proposes a set of criteria for choosing an intentional level of description rather than a physical or syntactic level. The criterion is one of usefulness: how good and economical a job does the intentional description do in allowing us to understand and predict the behavior of a system. By this proposed criterion, it is sometimes justifiable to use intentional attribution in understanding and describing the behavior of computational processes.

In this spirit, Dennett proposes to describe systems in terms of their beliefs and desires. He refers to this class of systems as *intentional* and suggests that we move to this level of description only when a physical level explanation fails. As an example, we might explain the functioning of a thermostat in terms of its belief about the temperature of a room. This is unnecessary, however, since all relevant generalizations of the thermostat's functioning can be described without appealing to mental or intentional constructs.

Dennett notes that some systems, including humans and properly programmed computers, can only be completely described using intentional constructs. To make this point, suppose we were attempting to predict the drug therapy selection of a good computer based medical care delivery system such as MYCIN. We have a choice of three types of descriptions: We could know the electrical state of all the components of the computer, we could see the program that runs the medical advisor, or, alternatively, we could describe the medical knowledge which we think the program will use in making its decision. We contend that it would be impossible to accurately predict the choices of the computer on the basis of physical or programming information since aspects of the implementation are too complex. Our best option is to anticipate program behavior by considering the knowledge which it will use to make its decision.

We have multiple levels of description in most sciences. The physicist, for example, has Heisenberg's, Einstein's, and Newton's laws; atomic and molecular relationships; and subatomic particles with indeterminacy. For each science, different phenomena are best understood at certain levels of abstraction. In sports, a bat hitting a baseball is covered by Newton's laws. The particle accelerator requires Einstein's physics; subatomic interactions need Heisenberg's indeterminacy. Heisenberg's principles are operative when a baseball player hits the ball; it is just that Newton's force, acceleration, and gravity equations offer a sufficient physical description. For the sports' broadcaster, the intentional descriptions of hits, outs, runs, and winning offer more coherent and economical explanatory constructs than do the principles of indeterminacy or even Newton's laws.

Dennett justifies the intentional stance by claiming that it can best capture the generalizations of intelligent systems, including properly programmed computers. His position makes no assumptions about the causal role of representational states. Intentional description offers the only way to account for behavior in terms of represented knowledge.

When asked if a computer is "really an intentional system," Dennett replies that we don't know the answer to this any more than whether a person is "an intentional system." We cannot know whether anyone acts because he or she has a certain belief. We simply observe a correlation between evidence of a belief and certain actions. In fact, there is absolutely no method by which we could demonstrate that some belief caused a person to behave in a particular manner!

What is unconvincing about Dennett's argument is that it appears to sidestep the hard question of whether a system is, in fact, intentional. Dennett reinterprets the question as one of how we should describe or talk about a system. On the other hand, Pylyshyn's (1984) analysis of type-type and type-token identity presented in Section 2.3 provides an even stronger criterion for deciding whether a system's behavior is semantically determined. We believe this analysis establishes that the significant regularities in cognitive systems cannot be characterized in terms of any reduction to physical processes and events. Unfortunately, the same criterion does not establish the need to characterize computational processes in intentional or semantic terms, since as we noted in Section 17.1.2, program behavior can be completely understood in terms of a physical execution sequence. We feel that to evaluate the semantic character of computational processes requires another kind of analysis.

To properly judge whether computational systems are capable of effectively modeling the semantic aspect of cognitive processes we need to have a clear and precise concept of what meaning and intention are. Although some interesting and suggestive theories of semantics have been proposed in the last century, including those of Tarski and Montague, these theories are epistemologically naive. It appears that a more complete resolution of this issue must await the development of a more sophisticated theory of semantics.

17.1.5   The Mind-Body Problem and Symbol Instantiation

Dennett's intentional stance sidesteps the mind-body problem. He claims that representational models are descriptive of behavior and do not entail any causal relationships between mental and physical states. In fact, as we just noted, John Searle claims that computers can never be intentional systems (Searle 1980).

Representational theory is left with an obvious problem. If, with Dennett, we argue for the need of intentional accounts, but leave open the issue of what actually causes the consistencies of behavior, there is a missing piece. We agreed that mental states cannot produce anything physical and that only physical things can cause anything to happen. At this point representational theory's marriage with computation spares us the fate of folk psychology.

We think of computational theory as the implementation of a cognitive or intention based model in a program that is run on a computer. When as cognitive scientists we do this, we say that the semantic model is instantiated in a physical symbol system; the computer code is in turn instantiated and interpreted by the physical computing device. This is the *symbol instantiation hypothesis*, the conjecture that semantic states can be realized in terms of a computational system, which in the case of a computer program, can be realized in a particular physical system.

We must recognize the difference between instantiation and reduction. The instantiation hypothesis does not suggest that mental states are reduced to physical states; that is, we are not implying a type-type relationship. We say that a semantic type can be realized and interpreted as part of a set of symbol tokens. There are a potentially infinite number of ways that any particular mental state can be realized by a set of symbol states, and similarly an infinite number of ways symbol states can be realized in the physical states of a computer. The instantiation hypothesis and computational theory provide a means by which semantic states can be mechanistically and physically realized.

Symbol instantiation as a response to the mind-body problem is strongly associated with the physical symbol system hypothesis. In Searle's caricature of this position, brains are seen as computers and cognitive processes as programs. We have, in Chapter 4, discussed why certain aspects of the physical symbol system hypothesis must be questioned, especially the notion of a running program as a *valid* model of intelligence. In fact, current connectionist architectures have also suggested how the brain can function as an interpreter of its inputs, obviating the need for homunculi.

A more modern response to the mind-body problem is to question the radical distinction between mental stuff and physical stuff which is the premise of the problem. Mind-body dualism goes back to Pythagoras, Plato, and, more recently, Descartes. It has played a crucial role in shaping the classical Christian worldview. This view associates mental and emotional processes with a distinct kind of *thinking substance*, the *res cogitans*.

Modern advances in science, including the biological theory of evolution, give us reason to question this radical dualism. From an evolutionary point of view, it is no longer necessary to appeal to a "life force" to explain living systems. We can now understand living systems in terms of complex processes and modes of organization, where what is essential is not the presence of a particular kind of matter but rather the way which that matter is *organized*, the genetic codes which control its development and processing. Cognitive systems also constitute a complex organization of material existence. A nondualistic theory views intelligence as a by-product of complex modes of organization. The functionality of the cognitive system thus derives from the *form of organization* of a material substrate rather than from the uniqueness of the *stuff* that is organized.

17.2   REPRESENTATIONS AND COGNITIVE SCIENCE

17.2.1   Introduction

What is a representation? We begin by observing that we must talk about representations from two different perspectives. First, as we established in Part I of our book, representation is a part of virtually every aspect of intelligence, from remembering past events, to generating speech, and acting in a goal oriented fashion. Representation is inherent in information preservation (memory) as well as encoding invariants in tokens that can be used as a medium for communication and reflection. As scientists, we are faced with the task of modeling the representational structures used by intelligent agents.

Chapter 3 and Parts II and III presented a number of structures used to model various aspects of human performance. These included the explicit symbol systems of logic, semantic nets, frames and objects, as well as connectionist networks. Even though historically there has been a schism between proponents of symbol based and connectionist models in cognitive science, we see all representational schemes as simply tools for modeling the representational capabilities of intelligent agents. Given the range of representational mechanisms used by cognitive agents, it is obvious that we need a wide range of models to capture this diversity.

The traditional view of representations in cognitive science is that associated with the physical symbol system hypothesis. Newell and Simon hypothesize that the physical symbol system and its potential for representation and search are necessary and sufficient for the production of intelligent behavior. Many researchers in cognitive science take this hypothesis quite literally. In what sense may it be demonstrated? Or is it simply a conjecture necessary to support much of the research in the area? Are the successes of the neural or subsymbolic models of intelligence refutations of the physical symbol system hypothesis?

Even a weak interpretation of this hypothesis--that a physical symbol system is *sufficient* to produce intelligent behavior--has yielded many useful results in the field of cognitive psychology. This *sufficiency hypothesis* has supported the construction and testing of symbol based models for many aspects of human performance (Pylyshyn 1984, Posner 1989). But the strong interpretation--that physical symbol systems and search are *necessary* for intelligent activity--remains open to question.

As NETtalk and many other connectionist applications presented in Part III illustrate, neural networks are proving themselves as both practical and theoretically interesting models of learning. Consequently, there has been a renewed debate over the relative merits of connectionist and symbolic cognitive science. Although there is clearly a difference between connectionist and classical symbol system architectures, it is unclear whether this constitutes a difference between symbolic and subsymbolic approaches, as it is usually described.

We believe that this debate is misguided for a number of reasons. Each approach models intelligence using a different set of primitives, and is therefore capable of raising different questions. Although researchers may someday show how symbols from a language of symbols reduce to patterns in a network or how symbol structures can indeed equal the behavior of neural nets, such reductions will certainly not eliminate one model or the other. To take an example from another field, while the laws governing chemical structures may in principle be derived from quantum mechanics, many of the questions asked by chemists can be better formulated and answered at a chemical rather than at a quantum mechanical level.

In machine learning, for example, an important question concerns the role of prior knowledge. Can effective learning occur on a *tabula rasa*, or "blank slate," starting with no initial knowledge and then learn entirely from experience? Or must it start out with some prior inductive bias? What about the role of knowledge in more sophisticated forms of learning, such as scientific discovery? This problem of inducing structure from "raw" phenomena is referred to as the *empiricist's dilemma*.

Connectionist networks are not very good at answering these questions. Although the design of the network, the number of nodes at each layer, and the patterns of connections all constitute a form of bias, it is difficult to describe this bias as "knowledge about a domain." Instead, neural network researchers characterize nets in terms of their statistical properties, number of nodes in a hidden layer, connectivity, number of elements in the training set, and so on. No matter how developed a connectionist theory of learning may become, questions about the knowledge used by a learner may inherently require a symbolic answer.

Suppose we are developing a computational model of scientific discovery, and want to theorize about how Copernicus shifted from a geocentric to heliocentric view of the universe. This requires that we represent both the Copernican and Ptolemaic views in a computer program. While we could represent them as patterns of activation in a neural network, this tells us nothing about their behavior *as theories*. Instead, we prefer explanations such as "Copernicus was troubled by the complexity of the Ptolemaic system and preferred the simpler model of letting the planets revolve around the sun." This explanation requires symbols.

Similarly, neural nets can answer a number of questions that are outside the expressive abilities of symbol based models. An important class of such questions concerns perceptual pattern recognition. Nature is not so generous as to deliver our perceptions to a sound inferencing system in the form of neat bundles of predicate calculus expressions. Connectionist networks are better at learning to recognize patterns in the rich flux of visual, auditory, and tactile sensations.

A theory of how symbols reduce to patterns in a network would be an extraordinary contribution, allowing the integration of network based pattern recognition and knowledge based reasoning facilities in a single agent. In the meantime, however, both approaches have considerable work to do in refining their own models. In the next section we consider more closely the relationship and differences between symbol based and connectionist approaches.

17.2.2   How are "Symbol" and "Connectionist" Systems Differentiated?

It is useful to understand the difference between symbol based and connectionist models in terms of language. In a language, symbols are combined to form a meaningful expression. Meaning is constructed through the rule governed juxtaposition of tokens. In a language, syntactical rules determine which symbols can be combined, and in what order. Semantic rules determine how the particular choice of symbol at a certain position in a sentence systematically determines the meaning of the sentence as a whole. (We addressed many of these issues in the sections on logic, Chapter 7, and language, Part IV.)

The physical symbol system hypothesis (Newell & Simon 1976) and symbol based architectures in general are concerned with representation in this sense. They study the laws governing the manipulation and permutation of symbol structures. Symbol based approaches, insofar as they engage in the construction of formal languages, implement the same principles of systematicity, compositionality, and productivity that are characteristic of languages in general.

Fodor's (1975) famous phrase, "the language of thought," illustrates how deeply the phenomena of language influences the way symbol based researchers think about cognitive phenomena. When carried to its logical extreme, this linkage between thought and language leads to strange consequences, suggesting for instance, that thoughts are formulated in an *inner* language to which *outer* language gives expression. Another example is the attempt to perform perceptual tasks with physical symbol systems. Vera and Simon (1993), for instance, have argued that the connectionist architectures used to perform tasks, such as the guidance of autonomous vehicles down a highway, can be replaced without loss of functionality by conventional symbol based systems.

Representation for the connectionist, in contrast, is rooted in a different paradigm. *Natural* representation, such as that found in a photograph, mirror, or painting, is not based on the combination of conventionally defined symbols. It is rather based on loose forms of similarity or isomorphism between the representation and the objects represented. Significantly, in painting, sculpture, and acting this natural or isomorphism based representation is sometimes able to capture the essential structure or invariances in objects.

Another significant feature of connectionist representation is its distributed character. Much like a pixelated image which functions as a representation through the configuration of dots, the individual nodes in a network need have no inherent content or association with any aspect of the environment. The distributed processing of connectionist systems is thus much like perceptual processing in humans in that it is highly parallel.

Memory structure also has much in common with natural representation. In its most primitive form, memory might be thought to store a literal copy of a previous experience. More sophisticated forms of memory however, encode abstract features and relationships of experienced objects, thereby capturing useful invariances. We saw low level memory models in the linear associator network of Section 12.2. We saw higher level memory models in the perceptron classification network of Section 11.2 and the prototype based networks of Section 12.1.

We can visualize representational schemes as a continuum spanning between the two extremes, the passive trapping of perceptual invariance and the active composition of symbol structures in a language. As research in cognitive science evolves we may find more links fashioned between these extremes, such as in David Marr's (1982) model of vision where patterns from a retina are mapped into organized concepts. We may expect to find other intermediate points along this continuum, such as prototypal and iconic representations which play an important role in artistic creation and mathematical discovery. For example, when Socrates drew a right triangle in the sand, Meno saw not only a particular triangle, nor merely an icon standing for all right triangles, but also an invariant relationship holding between the lengths of the sides of all such triangles!

17.3 TOWARD A UNIFIED THEORY OF COGNITION

Allen Newell (1973) offers a challenge to the field of cognitive psychology. In a paper aptly titled *You Can't Play Twenty Questions with Nature and Win*, Newell makes the point that discrete minimum constraint theories of the phenomena of intelligence are doomed to failure. His position in the paper is that even if we have definitive answers to a large number of microlevel questions about intelligence, the sum total of the results might not give us sufficient information to address macrolevel issues.

Newell's criticism of the then current state of psychology was that no clear candidates for macrotheories of intelligence yet existed; rather, psychologists spent their energies focusing on ever smaller questions. Is a process massed or distributed? What is attention? Is some aspect of intelligence serial or parallel? What is happening in single and multichannel signal processing?

Newell calls for the creation of larger cognitive architectures, ones that capture phenomena on a number of levels and offer mutual constraints. He observes:

> Psychology has arrived at the possibility of unified theories of cognition - theories that gain their power by positing a single system of mechanisms that operate together to produce the full range of human cognition.

We find ourselves in full agreement with Newell's challenge. In fact we would broaden it, conjecturing that only in the context of systems of mutually constraining mechanisms can the functionality of intelligence be fully operational. As we noted in Section 17.1, intelligence is a product of complex forms of organization rather than simply a matter of the "right stuff." There are now a number of promising research ventures that begin to build on this approach. This work is motivated by the hope of combining the strengths of different paradigms. For example, Holland (1986) develops a multilevel model of learning based on natural selection and evolution. Other researchers are working on the integration of connectionist and symbolic approaches, an integration which would allow network learning to exploit existing symbolic knowledge.

Across the history of cognitive science, a number of more complex cognitive architectures and unified theories have appeared. We briefly summarize several of the most important:

- Allen Newell and Herbert Simon (1972) offered the first serious unified theory with their production system accounting of human behavior. This is described quite extensively in Section 9.2 and has been applied to the analysis human solutions of logic puzzles, simple game playing, and chess (Ernst & Newell 1969). This early research served as a paradigm for a large number of cognitive science research projects of the subsequent 20 years, including ACT* and Soar described below.

- John Anderson (1983b, 1990) created the ACT and ACT* architectures (see Section 9.5). This approach was used to provide the memory and processing structures for a wide range of tasks, including geometry problem solving, language learning, and the acquisition of other skills. These programs contain models of their own processing and are able to learn.

- John Holland (1986, Holland et al. 1986) with several of his colleagues created *classifier systems*. These systems are based on the insights of genetic algorithms (see Section 11.6). They are multilayered. At the low end, sets of classification rules process bit strings. These classifiers are rewarded by an algorithm, much like backpropagation, according to their ability to produce "good" results. On the highest level is a genetic algorithm that constantly produces new genetic operators to complement the classification task.

- Soar, created by Allen Newell and his colleagues (Newell 1990, Laird et al. 1986), is based on the extension of the production system model to include dynamic creation of new search spaces that handle *impasses*. The psychological support for this model of problem solving was presented in Section 9.3, while its learning component, producing new production rules through chunking patterns found in data, was presented in Section 10.4.4. Soar is currently the most generally defined as well as extensively tested unified model of cognition.

The examples of unified theories just presented are impressive for their extensibility and attempt to capture a wide range of intelligent behavior. A number of less ambitious attempts at integrating the phenomena of intelligence are also important:

- Marr (1982) proposed an integrated three level analysis of vision. His general thesis was that visual perception is a process of subconscious inference from the structure of a perceived image to a mental model of that structure. On the hardware level there is an interaction between light focused on retinal cells and their sensitivity. This interaction builds and links through a "two and a half dimensional" sketch of the image that makes explicit relative distances and orientations. To this point image processing is data driven. The two and a half dimensional sketch then triggers a mental model or a viewer independent representation of the observed situation. This mental model could be described by a frame or object-oriented structure of a chair, or table, or whatever. Marr's research offers one of the few cognitively plausible descriptions of vision.

- The Hearsay research (Reddy 1976, Erman et al. 1980) presents a model of speech perception. In the context of a blackboard (Section 9.4), various levels of speech patterns are analyzed, from the wave form of the acoustic signal, through the possible phonemes and syllables, to the words and word sequences that make up the utterance. Natural language understanding programs are also quite important as integrated systems of constraints.

- Rodney Brooks (1986) has proposed that intelligence and other sociological phenomena emerge from the interactions of agents within an environment. In his article *Intelligence without Representations*, he proposes that goals, processes, and other phenomena of intelligence are not constituent of an individual nor need they be directly represented within an individual; rather they emerge as an artifact of the individual's interactions.

- Smolensky (Smolensky et al. 1992), in work on modeling language production, presents a research basis for unifying symbol and connectionist architectures. We feel research of this nature will prove important in understanding not only the artifacts of language but the nature of representation as well.

In all these example we see movement toward more general models of intelligence. Certainly intelligence operating in a rich environment must integrate many different forms of cognitive processing, including perception, memory, learning, and planning. It is important that, as cognitive science researchers, we develop architectures modeling the interaction and constraints across these multiple dimensions.

17.4   OPEN ISSUES

Several major unresolved issues remain for cognitive science. These include both theoretical and methodological problems. We close by summarizing several of these pivotal questions.

17.4.1   What Does the Turing Characterization of Computation Tell Us about Cognitive Processes?

In Section 2.5 we presented two important issues. First, with the universal Turing machine, we offered an abstract specification for what is computable. Second, we offered a method for determining the equivalence of different formal systems. Extending these ideas, we discussed the functional equivalence of several computational paradigms, including Turing machines, post production systems, and partial recursive functions and examined the Church-Turing speculation that this class constitutes the most powerful model of computation possible. More recently it has been shown that a class of recurrent connectionist networks is also Turing complete.

One conclusion that might be drawn from this presentation is that human intelligence is just another data point in this family of computationally equivalent systems. This speculation misses a crucial point. These computational models are not resource bounded. Turing machines, for example, have an infinite tape and thus an infinite memory. Their computations as a class are also without time bounds. Human intelligence, on the other hand, is essentially and necessarily resource limited. It may be that the need to adapt to time and memory resource bounds is precisely what has constrained human cognition to assume the particular form which it has.

Brachman and Levesque (1985), Doyle (1979), and others have suggested that human intelligence may depend upon more computationally efficient, and less expressive representations including the use of Horn clauses, a restricted form of predicate relationships, for reasoning. Levesque suggests the limiting of factual representations to ground clauses and the use of computationally tractable inference procedures. Doyle proposes that we use economic models for the management of limited resources as a way of understanding an essential aspect of human rationality.

In fact, the disciplined use of limited resources may be exactly where many of the important issues in the analysis of cognitive systems lie. Good representational schemes make appropriate information accessible in a timely fashion. On the other hand, many current models of reasoning are based on the assumption that agents can compute the logical closure of their beliefs. In most cases this would require an infinite amount of time. Cognitive scientists must be more careful in accounting for the practical aspects of resource limited cognitive processing.

17.4.2 Can We Model the Processes by Which Agents Construct Interpretations?

In the physical symbol system model, computational symbol structures simulate the symbol processing used by cognitive agents in problem solving. What is not modeled in this methodology is the relationship between the cognitive agent's symbol structures and the world that is represented in those structures. This means that the computational systems do not replicate the processes by which the problem solving situation was originally encoded or interpreted. Only those aspects of problem solving are modeled which occur after a basic representation is selected.

This problem is not unique to the physical symbol system methodology. Most computational models, both symbol based and connectionist, work within an already interpreted domain. In these models, there is an implicit *a priori* commitment of the system's designers to an interpretive encoding. Under this commitment there is little ability to shift contexts, goals, or representations as the problem solving evolves.

The Tarskian and Montague views (see Chapter 7) of a semantic commitment as a set of mappings between symbols and objects is plainly weak and doesn't explain, for example, the fact that one domain may have different interpretations in the light of different practical goals. Linguists generally try to remedy the limitations of semantic theories by adding a level of pragmatics.

Speech act theorists (Austin 1962, Searle 1969, Grice 1975) observe that language is generally used by a speaker to accomplish some purpose in a specific context: to request, command, question, commit, reassure, invite, etc. Even sentences which have an indicative form are frequently used to accomplish some contextual goal. To understand how individual words are used we must attend, therefore, to the speaker's goals, as well as his or her model of the listener's background knowledge and intentions. Building on the insights of speech act theory, discourse analysis holds that the meanings of individual sentences must be analyzed in terms of larger structures, structures at the paragraph and discourse levels. This approach is taken even further by those who argue that language use must be understood in terms of situations and goals (Lave 1988, Grosz & Sidner 1990). We discussed the pragmatic issues of language use at some length in Chapter 14.

The semiotic approach proposed by C.S. Peirce (1958) and developed by Eco, Seboek, and others (Eco 1976, Seboek 1985) takes a more radical approach to language. It places language use within the wider context of signs and signification. To demystify language use we must see it as the development of a more primitive phenomenon, the ability of humans and other animals to take an object, for example, smoke or dark clouds, as a sign or indication of something else. The semiotic analysis shows how the process of interpreting a set of signs or symbolic expressions is mediated by an *interpretant*, a structure for mapping signs into significations. The mapping pattern encoded by an interpretant reflects a particular set of activities and goals. This means that the same set of signs can allow different interpretations in different contexts.

Although cognitive science has made much progress since Newell and Simon originally proposed the physical symbol system hypothesis, it is not clear that progress has been made in modeling the process of interpretation. An important question is whether we can, in principle, advance beyond the construction of computational models that work in an already interpreted domain. We might expect the research in machine learning on category formation and classification to contribute to our understanding of interpretation. However, as we noted in Part III, most learning models also presuppose an interpreted domain.

17.4.3 Can Cognitive Science Escape Its Rationalist Origins?

A number of researchers (Winograd & Flores 1986, Dreyfus & Dreyfus 1985, Weizenbaum 1976) claim that the most important aspects of intelligence are not and, in principle, cannot be modeled. These areas include natural language understanding, learning, and certain aspects of practical problem solving. Many of the arguments against cognitive modeling have deep roots in certain philosophical traditions. Winograd and Flores's criticisms, for example, are based on issues raised in phenomenology (Husserl 1970, Heidegger 1962).

We consider, as an example, the line of argument developed by Winograd and Flores (1986) in their book *Understanding Computers and Cognition*. They argue that our modeling of cognitive processes is based on a number of incorrect rationalist premises. Cognitive scientists, particularly those in the symbol based tradition, implicitly presuppose a world of objects whose properties exist independently of any act of interpretation. Our symbolic representations stand for those objects and encode their properties and relationships. Perception is thought to be the mechanism by which representations enter the cognitive arena, directly registering the properties of independent objects. Action is understood as the result of a causal relation between our thoughts and volitions and the motion of our bodies. Problem solving in this context is merely a matter of manipulating our internal representations in a way that brings them into agreement with the objects that they represent or using them to connect actions to goals.

Winograd and Flores appeal to a variety of intellectual traditions, including phenomenology, speech act theory, and neurobiology, to contest these rationalist assumptions. They argue that the view of a completely objective "real world," a world independent of the work of the subject in constructing and interpreting objects, is, at best, naive. A proper understanding of cognitive processes must thus begin with a recognition of these interpretive activities.

Winograd and Flores argue that interpretation takes place within a definite milieu, including a particular cultural historical framework inherited by the individual, as well as a practical context defined by the subject's goals in the specific situation. This framework is at least partially opaque because the subject's reflection on his or her own interpretive framework is itself conditioned and biased by that framework. Winograd and Flores agree with Heidegger that our experience of the world is originally and fundamentally practical, with things identified for us with respect to our needs and activities, for example, as food, families, toys, or tools. Only when there is some kind of breakdown or impasse in our practical life does the subject emerge from this everyday "life-world" to reflect on "objective" properties and relations.

A number of perspectives in linguistics, philosophy, and psychology recognize the role of practical context in shaping representation. If this view is correct we must ask: how can cognitive science computationally model the practical contexts and conditions which determine cognitive activity? Will we eventually be able to model what happens in critical situations of breakdown where the accepted or conventional interpretation of a situation no longer works and an intelligent problem solver discovers a new interpretation that resolves the impasse?

Some research has already begun to address these issues. Soar, for example, attempts to model the process of impasse resolution. Some work in linguistics is focusing on the construction of formal models of pragmatics. Perhaps the most interesting and relevant development is a variety of research taking place under what has been loosely called the *situated cognition* perspective. We discuss this next.

17.4.4. In What Sense Do We Need a "Situated" Theory of Intelligence?

In Section 17.1 we noted that the fate of a science is often sealed by its definition of the object of study. In the case of cognitive science, a group of researchers has recently argued that cognitive science has defined its object too narrowly. Still influenced by Cartesian dualism, cognitive science has attempted to study the internal cognitive processes of an agent in isolation from the agent's embodied interaction with its environment. To correct this problem, researchers have proposed a shift in attention to relationships between representation and embodiment, representation and social practice, and representation and the technological environment.

The situated cognition perspective has led to exploration in a variety of directions. Researchers studying *expertise in context* have noted that an expert's problem solving knowledge is not adequately represented by the declarative knowledge encoded in, for example, a set of production rules. Frequently this knowledge also includes sensory and motor skills upon which the successful application of the rules depends. A medical student in training must learn how to read an x-ray or to palpate a liver to determine whether and how it is enlarged before he or she is able to function as an effective diagnostician. The meaning of many medical terms, such as *enlarged* or *inflamed liver*, is thus defined relative to a set of sensory motor skills and practices.

Studies of expertise in context have also shown that expert action, in many cases, must be analyzed relative to the organizational context or structure in which the expert functions. The expert's actions will be valuable to an organization only to the degree to which they interact with a larger organizational system to result in desirable outcomes. The expert, however, does not need to work from an explicit representation of these larger organizational structures and processes. In a healthy organization, desirable outcomes are achieved through structural integration of actions, where individual agents and subgroups act within a *local* context of goals, resources, and strategies.

Another area where the situated cognition perspective holds promise is in the analysis of meaning. The predominant model of meaning in cognitive science has been the one which Tarski formalized: meaning as a mapping between representations "inside" the agent and objects, properties, and relations "in the world." Note again the Cartesian flavor of this account. The situated cognition view is that meaning must be analyzed in terms of types of interaction between agents and the world. Different types of interactions, different practices, give rise to different vocabularies and modes of description. In the context of a baseball game, certain objects are described as a bat, a ball, a first baseman, a second baseman, and so on. In other contexts these same things have altogether different descriptions. Wittgenstein (1953) argued in his *Philosophical Investigations* that the proper method for semantic analysis is to study the contexts or practices, the *language games* in which words are used, to observe the role and function of particular words in those practices.

A third area in which the situated cognition perspective may be useful is in studying the role which a physical environment plays in supporting various types of cognitive function. A somewhat simple but often neglected example is the use of the environment to support information storage and retrieval. Studies of the function of memory in problem solving sometimes forget to account for the way in which memory cues are stored in the environment, on a piece of paper, a calendar, a package left by the door.

Less obvious is the way in which our technology, our tools for acting on and observing the world, affects our representations. Pliers, blowtorches, cranes, and lasers extend our bodies and hence our representations of the properties of objects that we manipulate. Microscopes, telescopes, oscilloscopes, and other measuring instruments extend our physical senses and hence our notions of what sorts of things exist in the world around us. To accurately model how an agent represents and responds to a domain of objects we must thus also analyze the role of the tools which support those interactions.

The unifying theme in these various approaches is the claim that cognitive science needs to study not internal or intra-agent representation and symbol manipulation but rather embodied interaction. This appears to be the call for something like a computational anthropology, that is, a study of intelligence in the setting of concrete social historical practices. Such a study would also allow us to understand cognitive processes from an evolutionary point of view, as a consequence of adaptation of practices and representational structures to the evolving requirements of historical conditions.

It is too soon to judge whether situated cognition research will fulfill any of these promises or produce interesting and useful results.

17.4.5 What Are the Limitations of the Scientific Method?

Throughout our book we have emphasized the important distinction between research in artificial intelligence and that in cognitive science. As noted in Part I, these differences include practical goals, solution tools, and research methodologies. At the extreme, AI can be seen as an engineering discipline whereas cognitive science must maintain its credibility as a theoretical science.

In closing, we want to emphasize the symbiosis of these two disciplines. When searching for elucidation of intellectual processes, the AI practitioner often looks to the cognitive scientist for help. After all, when our only goal is to create intelligent artifacts, the human processing system is our primary data point as a model of intelligence in action. Arguably, this is how cognitive science began in Newell and Simon's (1972, p. 885) attempt to build intelligence into the *logic theorist*.

From the viewpoint of the cognitive scientist, the architectures developed in artificial intelligence laboratories, both symbol based and connectionist, are an important resource. This works in two ways. First, as scientists we need precise, testable models for human intelligence. We argued for this need in our sufficiency discussions of Chapter 4, especially as it offers a methodology for "cashing out" the often vague constructs and processes of the psychological tradition. With their transformation to code, these constructs can be made precise.

The second benefit for the cognitive scientist is that constructs and theories can be evaluated in terms of realistic *computability* constraints. We can ask questions about memory sufficiency or the space/time requirements for computing a particular algorithm. For example, since the infinite tape of the universal Turing machine has no human analog, we come to see human intelligence as a disciplined use of scarce processing resources.

To appreciate the symbiotic relationship of these two disciplines we cannot be epistemological naive. We have espoused a constructivist approach and the use of the scientific method for three reasons. First, scientists must not confuse the model with the phenomenon being modeled. Although the model allows us to progressively approximate the phenomenon, there will, of necessity, always be a "residue" that is not empirically explained. A model is used to explore, explain, and predict; and if it allows scientists to accomplish this, it is successful. Indeed, different models may successfully explain different aspects of a single phenomenon as, for instance, the wave and particle theories of light.

Second, many see a radical distinction between "hard" sciences such as physics, chemistry, and molecular biology and the "soft" sciences including psychology, linguistics, and sociology. We refer to this attitude as *physics envy*. It is both a vestige of "common sense" realism and a misinterpretation of the methods of the "hard" sciences. Every view of the world is constructive. Even physicists in attempting to understand the nature of matter or the origins of the universe couch their theories in terms of constructs that are not directly observable, including elementary particles, field strengths, and singularities. The so-called "soft" sciences must deal with higher levels of organizational complexity. Evolution has blessed us with ever more intricate biological systems, each better able to cope with the rigors of survival. The methods of science must differ according to the level of this organizational complexity. Thus, understanding intelligence will require theoretical constructs appropriate for expressing the patterns and regularities of cognitive processes, processes characterized by properties such as systematicity, compositionality, and productivity.

Finally, when critics claim that aspects of cognitive phenomena lie outside the scope of the scientific method, this claim must be evaluated by comparing the theoretical fruitfulness of alternative methodologies. Every theory, even philosophical theories, if they are to have any interest, must in some way illuminate our experience and beliefs. Theories which claim that certain things such as consciousness and intentionality cannot be empirically studied or computationally modeled must give an account of precisely those qualities that make consciousness and intentionality impervious to scientific scrutiny. Such theories must provide their own account of consciousness and intentionality, an account whose fruitfulness and power of illumination can then be compared to the results of cognitive science.

Questions of this sort generate much of the excitement that infuses cognitive science. We have a powerful and growing repertoire of tools for addressing them. The answers, as they emerge, bring richness, not just to the practice of empirical science, but more importantly to the understanding of activities which are foundationally human, including perceptual pattern recognition, tractable reasoning, deliberation, and action, as well as to intellectual discovery and growth. As we have seen, analyses of the limitations of current symbol based and connectionist approaches point us out of our Cartesian cave toward an understanding of intelligence as a concretely embodied physical, social, and historical phenomenon.

REFERENCES

Allen, J. 1987. *Natural Language Understanding.* Menlo Park, CA: The Benjamin/Cummings Publishing Company, Inc.

Altmann, G.T.M. (ed.), 1990. *Cognitive Models of Speech Processing: Psycholinguistic and Computational Perspectives.* Cambridge, MA: MIT Press (Bradford).

Anderson, J.A., Silverstein, J.W., Ritz, S.A., & Jones, R.S. 1977. Distinctive features, categorical perception, and probability learning: Some applications of a neural model. *Psychological Review,* 84, 413-451.

Anderson, J.R. 1976. *Language, Memory, and Thought.* Hillsdale, NJ: Erlbaum.

Anderson, J.R. 1978. Arguments concerning representations for mental imagery. *Psychological Review,* 85; 249-277.

Anderson, J.R. 1983a. Acquisition of proof skills in geometry. In Michalski et al. (1983).

Anderson, J.R. 1983b. *The Architecture of Cognition.* Cambridge, MA: Harvard University Press.

Anderson, J.R. 1990. *Cognitive Psychology and Its Implications.* New York: W.H. Freeman.

Anderson, J.R., & Bower, G.H. 1973. Human Associative Memory. Washinton, DC: Winston.

Anderson, J.R., & Thompson, R. 1989. Use of analogy in a production system architecture. In S. Vosniadou & A. Ortony (eds.), *Similarity and Analogy.* New York: Cambridge University Press.

Anderson, R.A., & Rosenfeld, E. (eds.), 1988. *Neurocomputing: Foundations of Research,* Cambridge, MA: MIT Press.

Arbas, E.A., Meinertzhagen, I.A., & Shaw, S.R. 1991. Evolution in nervous systems. *Annual Review of Neurosciences,* 14, 9-38.

Austin, J.L. 1962. *How To Do Things with Words*. New York: Oxford University Press. Reprinted (1975) by the Harvard University Press, Cambridge, MA.

Averbach, E., & Coriel, A.S. 1961. Short-term memory in vision. *Bell System Technical Journal*, 40, 309-328.

Ayer, A.J. 1936. *Language, Truth, and Logic*. New York: Oxford University Press.

Azari, N.P., Rapoport, S.I., Grady, C.L., DeCarli, C., Haxby, J.V., Schapiro, M.B., & Horwitz, B. 1992. Gender differences in correlations of cerebral glucose metabolic rates in young normal adults. *Brain Research,* 574, 198-208.

Bachant, J., & McDermott, J. 1984. R1 revisited: Four years in the trenches. *AI Magazine* 5(3).

Baddeley, A.D., Grant, S., Wight, E., & Thomson, N. 1975. Imagery and visual working memory. In P.M.A. Rabbitt & S. Dornic (eds.), *Attention and Performance V* (pp. 205-217). London: Academic Press.

Balzer, R., Erman, L.D., London, P.E., & Williams, C. 1980. HEARSAY III: A domain independent framework for expert systems. *Proceedings AAAI* 1980.

Barkow, J.H., Cosmides, L., & Tooby, J. 1992. *The Adapted Mind*. New York: Oxford Press.

Barr, A., & Feigenbaum, E.A. 1986. *The Handbook of Artificial Intelligence*, Vol. I-IV. Reading, MA: Addison Wesley.

Bartlett, F. 1932. *Remembering*. London: Cambridge University Press.

Bates, E. 1976. *Language and Context: Studies in the Acquisition of Pragmatics*. New York: Academic Press.

Bateson, G. 1979. *Mind and Nature: A Necessary Unity*. New York: Dutton.

Belliveau, J.W., Kennedy, O.N., McKinstry, R.C. et al. (1991). Functional mapping of the human visual cortex by magnetic reconance imaging. *Science*, 254, 716-719.

Belmont, J.M., & Butterfield, E.C. 1971. The development of short-term memory, in *Human Development*, 14, 236-248.

Berko, G.J. (ed.), 1993. *The Development of Language*, 3rd Ed. New York: Macmillan.

Berlin, B., & Kay, P. 1969. *Basic Color Terms: Their Universality and Evolution.* Berkeley, CA: University of California Press.

Bhaskar, R., & Simon, H.A. 1977. Problem solving in semantically rich domains. *Cognitive Science,* 1, 193-215.

Bialystok, E. 1991. Metalinguistic dimensions of language proficiency. In E. Bialystok (ed.), *Language Processing in Bilingual Children* (pp. 113-140). Cambridge, U.K.: Cambridge University Press.

Biber, D. 1988. *Variation Across Speech and Writing.* Cambridge, U.K.: Cambridge University Press.

Bickerton, D. 1990. *Language and Species.* Chicago: The University of Chicago Press.

Bickerton, D. 1983, July. Creole languages. *Scientific American.* Reprinted in W. S-Y. Wang (ed.), *Language, Writing, and the Computer* (pp. 24-30). New York: W. H. Freeman.

Binet, A., & Simon, T. 1905. Methodes nouvelles pour le diagnostic du niveau intellectuel des anormaux. *L'Ann'ee Psychological Measurement,* 11, 191-204.

Birner, B. 1993. Information status and English inversion. Paper presented at the 67th Annual Meeting of the Linguistic Society of America, Los Angeles, CA, January 7-10, 1993.

Blakemore, D. 1992. *Understanding Utterances: An Introduction to Pragmatics.* Oxford, U.K.: Blackwell.

Block, N. 1978. Troubles with functionalism. In C.W. Savage (ed.), *Perception and Cognition: Issues in the Foundations of Psychology,* Minnesota Studies in the Philosophy of Science., Vol 9. Minneapolis: University of Minnesota Press.

Blumenthal, A.L. 1980. *Language and Psychology: Historical Aspects of Psycholinguistics.* New York: Robert E. Krieger.

Bobrow, D.G. 1975. Dimensions of representation. In Bobrow & Collins (1975).

Bobrow, D.G., & Collins, A. (eds.), 1975. *Representation and Understanding.* New York: Academic Press.

Bock, J.K., & Mazzella, J.R. 1983. Intonational marking of given and new information: Some consequences for comprehension. *Memory & Cognition*, 11, 64-86.

Boomer, D.S. 1965. Hesitation and grammatical encoding. *Language and Speech*, 8, 148-158.

Bower, G.H., Black, J.B., & Turner, T.J. 1979. Scripts in text comprehension and memory. *Cognitive Psychology*, 11, 177-220.

Brachman, R.J. 1979. On the epistemological status of semantic networks. In Brachman & Levesque (1985).

Brachman, R.J. 1985a. I lied about the trees. *AI Magazine* 6(3).

Brachman, R.J. 1985b. On the epistemological status of semantic networks. In Brachman & Levesque (1985).

Brachman, R.J., & Levesque, H. J. 1985. *Readings in Knowledge Representation.* Los Altos, CA: Morgan Kaufmann.

Bransford, J.D., & Johnson, M.K. 1973. Considerations of some problems of comprehension. In W.G. Chase (ed.), *Visual Information Processing* (pp. 383-438). New York: Academic Press.

Bransford, J.D., Barclay, J.R., & Franks, J.J. 1972. Sentence memory: A constructive versus interpretive approach. *Cognitive Psychology*, 3, 193-209.

Brooks, L.R. 1968. Spatial and verbal components in the act of recall. *Canadian Journal of Psychology*, 22, 349-368.

Brooks, R.A. 1986. A robust layered control systemfor a mobile robot, IEEE. *Journal of Robotics and Automation*, 4, 14-23.

Brown, R. 1970. *Psycholinguistics: Selected Papers by Roger Brown.* New York: The Free Press.

Brown, G., & Yule, G. 1983. *Discourse Analysis.* Bath, U.K.: Cambridge University Press.

Brown, J.S., & Burton, R.R. 1978. Dianostic models for procedural bugs in basic mathematical skills. *Cognitive Science, 2,* 155-192.

Brown, J.W., & Jaffe, J. 1975. Hypothesis on cerebral dominance. *Neuropsychologia,* 13, 107-110.

Brown, J.S., & VanLehn, K. 1980. Repair theory: A generative theory of bugs in procedural skills. *Cognitive Science, 4,* 379-426.

Brown, P., & Levinson, S.C. 1987. *Politeness: Some Universals in Language Usage.* Cambridge, U.K.: Cambridge University Press.

Bruner, J.S., Goodnow, J.J., & Austin, G.A. 1956. *A Study of Thinking.* New York: John Wiley and Sons.

Buchanan, B.G., & Mitchell, T.M. 1978. Model-directed learning of production rules. In Waterman & Hayes-Roth (1978).

Buchanan, B.G. & Shortliff, E.H. (eds.), 1984. *Rule-Based Expert Systems: The MYCIN Experiments of the Stanford Heuristic Programming Project.* Reading, MA: Addison-Wesley.

Bundy, A., Byrd, L., Luger, G., Mellish, C., Milne, R., & Palmer, M. 1979. Solving mechanics problems using meta-level inference. *Proceedings of IJCAI-1979,* 1017-1027.

Bybee, J.L. 1985. *Morphology: A Study of the Relation between Meaning and Form.* Amsterdam/Philadelphia: John Benjamins Publishing Company.

Bybee, J.L., Perkins, R., & Pagliuca, W. 1994. *The Evolution of Grammar: Tense, Aspect, and Modality in the Languages of the World.* Chicago: University of Chicago Press.

Caramazza, A., & Zurif, E.B. 1976. Dissociation of algorithmic and heuristic processes in language comprehension: Evidence from ephasia. *Brain and Language,* 3, 572-582.

Carbonell, J.G. 1983. Learning by analogy: Formulating and generalizing plans from past experience. In Michalski et al. (1983).

Carbonell, J.G. 1986. Derivational analogy: A theory of reconstructive problem solving and expertise acquisition. In Michalski et al. (1986).

Carnap, R. 1967. *The Logical Structure of the World; PseudoProblems in Philosophy.* Berkeley, CA: University of California Press.

Carroll, L. 1989. *Alice's Adventures in Wonderland: The Ultimate Illustrated Edition.* New York: Bantam Books. (Originally published in 1865.)

Ceccato, S. 1961. *Linguistic Analysis and Programming for Mechanical Translation.* New York: Gordon and Breach.

Chafe, W.L. 1976. Givenness, contrastiveness, definiteness, subjects, topics, and point of view. In C.N. Li (ed.), *Subject and Topic* (pp. 25-55). New York: Academic Press.

Chafe, W.L. 1979. The flow of thought and the flow of language. In T. Givon (ed.), *Syntax and Semantics: Vol. 12, Discourse and Syntax* (pp. 159-181). New York: Academic Press.

Chafe, W.L. 1982. Integration and involvement in speaking, writing, and oral literature. In D. Tannen (ed.), *Spoken and Written Language: Exploring Orality and Literacy* (pp. 35-53). Norwood, NJ: Ablex.

Chafe, W.L., & Danielewicz, J. 1987. Properties of spoken and written language. In R. Horowitz & S.J. Samuel (eds.), *Comprehending Oral and Written Language* (pp. 83-113). San Diego, CA: Academic Press.

Chaitin, G.J. 1990a. Information, Randomness, and Incompleteness. London, U.K.: World Scientific.

Chairtin, G.J. 1990b. Algebraic Information Theory. Cambridge, U.K.: Cambridge University Press.

Chang, C.L., & Lee, R.C.T. 1973. *Symbolic Logic and Mechanical Theorem Proving.* New York: Academic Press.

Charniak, E. 1972. Toward a model of children's story comprehension. Rep No. TR-266, AI Laboratory, MIT.

Charniak, E., & McDermott, D. 1985. *Introduction to Artificial Intelligence.* Reading, MA: Addison Wesley.

Chase, W.G., & Simon, H.A. 1973. The mind's eye in chess. In W.G. Chase (ed.), *Visual Information Processing.* New York: Academic Press.

Cherniak, C. 1990. The bounded brain: Toward quantitative neuroanatomy. *Journal of Cognitive Neuroscience*, 2, 58-68.

Chi, M.T.H., Glaser, R., & Farr, M. 1982. *The Nature of Expertise.* Hillsdale, NJ: Erlbaum.

Chi, M.T.H., Glaser, R., & Rees E. 1988. Expertise in problem solving. In R.J. Sternberg (ed.), 1982. *Advances in the Psychology of Human Intelligence (I).* Hillsdale, NJ: Erlbaum.

Chomsky, N. 1957. *Syntactic Structures.* The Hague: Mouton

Chomsky, N. 1959. A review of B.F. Skinner's verbal behavior. *Language*, 35, 26-58.

Chomsky, N. 1965. *Aspects of the Theory of Syntax.* Cambridge, MA: MIT Press.

Chomsky, N. 1981. *Lectures on Government and Binding: The Pisa Lectures.* Dordrecht Holland: Foris Publications.

Christiansen, J.A. 1993. Coherence disturbance in Wernicke's aphasia. Paper presented at the 67th Annual Meeting of the Linguistic Society of America, Los Angeles, CA, January 7-10.

Church, A. 1941. The calculi of lambda-conversion. *Annals of Mathematical Studies,* Vol 6. Princeton: Princeton University Press.

Churchland, P.M. 1979. *Scientific Realism and the Plasticity of Mind.* Cambridge, U.K.: Cambridge University Press.

Churchland, P.M. 1984. *Matter and Consciousness.* Cambridge, MA: MIT Press.

Churchland, P.M. 1985. Some reductive strategies in cognitive neurobiology. *Mind*, 95, 279-309.

Churchland, P.S. 1986. *Neurophilosophy: Toward a Unified Science of the Mind/ Brain*. Cambridge, MA: MIT Press.

Churchland, P.S., & Sejnowski, T.J. 1992. *The Computational Brain*. Cambridge, MA: MIT Press.

Clark, A. 1989. *Microcognition: Philosophy, Cognitive Science, and Parallel Distributed Processing*. Cambridge, MA: MIT Press (Bradford Books).

Clark, H.H., & Haviland, S.E. 1977. Comprehension and the given-new contract. In R.O. Freedle (ed.), *Discourse Production and Comprehension* (pp. 1-40). Norwood, NJ: Ablex Publishing Company.

Clark, H.H., & Lucy, P. 1975. Understanding what is meant from what is said: A study of conversationally conveyed requests. *Journal of Verbal Learning and Verbal Behavior,* 14, 56-72.

Clark, H.H., & Schunk, D.H. 1980. Polite responses to polite requests. *Cognition*, 8, 111-143.

Clark, H.H., & Sengul, C.J. 1979. In search of referents for nouns and pronouns. *Memory & Cognition*, 7, 35-41.

Clifton, C, & Ferreira, F. 1987. Modularity in sentence comprehension. In Garfield, J.L. (Ed.) (1987).

Clifton, C., & Task, J. 1973. Effect of syllable word length on memory-search rate. *Journal of Experimental Psychology*, 99, 231-235.

Clocksin, W.F., & Mellish, C.S. 1984. *Programming in PROLOG,* 2nd Ed. New York: Springer Verlag.

Cohen, N.J., & Squire, L.R. 1980. Preserved learning and retention of pattern analyzing skill in amnesics: Dissociation of knowing how and knowing that. *Science*, 207-210.

Cole, R.A., & Jakimik, J. 1980. A model of speech perception. In R.A. Cole (ed.), *Perception and Production of Fluent Speech* (pp. 133-163). Hillsdale, NJ: Lawrence Erlbaum.

Coleman, H.O. 1914. Intonation and emphasis. *Miscellanea Phonetica*. Association Phonetique.

Collins, A.M., & Loftus, E.F. 1975. A spreading-activation theory of semantic processing. *Psychological Review*, 82, 407-428.

Collins, A.M., & Quillian, M.R. 1969. Retrieval time from semantic memory. *Journal of Verbal Learning and Verbal Behavior,* 8, 240-247.

Collins, A.M., & Smith, E.E. (eds.), 1988. *Readings in Cognitive Science.* Palo Alto, CA: Morgan Kaufman.

Colmerauer, A. 1975. *Les Grammaires de Metamorphose,* Groupe Intelligence Artifi cielle, Universite Aix-Marseille II.

Colmerauer, A., Kanoui, H., Pasero, R., & Roussel, P. 1973. *Un Systeme de Communication Homme-Machine en Francais.* Research Report, Groupe Intelligence Artifi cielle, Universite Aix-Marseille II.

Comrie, B., 1989. *Language Universals and Linguistic Typology.* (2nd edition). Chicago: Chicago University P{ress.

Comtex 1985. *The Scientific Datalink Index to AI Research*, 1954-1984. New York: Comtex Scientific Corporation.

Conati, C., & Lehman, J.F. 1993. Towards a model of student education in microworlds. In *Proceedings of the Fifteenth Annual Conference of the Cognitive Science Society.* Hillsdale, NJ: Lawrence Erlbaum.

Conners, B.W., & Gutnick, M.J. 1990. Intrinsic firing patterns of neocortical neurons. *Trends in The Neurosciences*, 13, 99-104.

Conrad, R. 1964. Acoustical confusions in immediate memory. *British Journal of Psychology*, 55, 75-84.

Conrad, C. 1972. Cognitive economy in semantic memory. *Journal of Experimental Psychology*, 92, 149-154.

Cosmides, L., & Tooby, J. 1992. Cognitive adaptations for social change. In J.H. Barkow, L. Cosmides, & J. Tooby (eds.), *The Adapted Mind.* NewYork: Oxford Press.

Cowper, E. 1992. *A Concise Introduction to Syntactic Theory: The Government-Binding Approach..* Chicago: University of Chicago Press.

Crick, F.H., & Asanuma, C. 1986. Certain aspects of the anatomy and physiology of the cerebral cortex. In McClelland et al. (1986).

Croft, W. 1990. *Typology and Universals.* Cambridge, UK: Cambridge University Press.

Croft, W. 1991. *Syntactic Categories and Grammatical Rrelations: The Cognitive Organization of Information.* Chicago: University of Chicago Press.

Crowder, R.G. 1972. Visual and auditory memory. In J.F. Kavanagh & I.G. Mattingly (eds.), *Language by Ear and by Eye* (pp. 251-275). Cambridge, MA: MIT Press.

Crowder, R.G. 1976. *Principles of Learning and Memory.* Hillsdale, NJ: Erlbaum.

Crowder, R.G. 1982. *The Psychology of Reading: An Introduction.* New York: Oxford University Press.

Cutler, A. 1976. Phoneme-monitoring reaction time as a function preceding intonation contour. *Perception & Psychophysics,* 20, 55-60.

Dahl, V. 1977. *Un Systeme Deductif d'Interrogation de Banques de Donnes en Espagnol.* PhD. Thesis. Universite Aix-Marseille.

Dahl, V., & McCord, M.C. 1983. Treating coordination in logic grammars. *American Journal of Computational Linguistics,* 9, 69-91.

Damasio, A.R., & Damasio, H. 1992. Brain and language. *Scientific American,* September, 89-95.

Davis, E. 1990. *Representations of Common Sense Knowledge.* Los Altos, CA: Morgan Kaufmann.

Davis, R. 1982. Applications of meta level knowledge to the construction, maintenance, and use of large knowledge bases. In Davis & Lenat (1982).

Davis, R., & Lenat, D.B. 1982. *Knowledge-Based Systems in Artificial Intelligence.* New York: McGraw-Hill.

de Chardin, T. 1959. *The Phenomenon of Man.* New York: Harper Row.

de Luce, J., & Wilder, H.T. (eds.), 1983. *Language in Primates: Perspectives and Implications.* New York: Springer-Verlag.

de Groot, A. 1965. *Thought and Choice and Chess.* The Hague: Mouton.

de Groot, J. 1991. *Correlative Neuroanatomy,* 21st Ed. Norwalk, CT: Appleton & Lange.

DeJong, G., & Mooney, R. 1986. Explanation-based learning: An alternative view. *Machine Learning,* 1(2), 145-176.

de Kleer, J. 1986. An assumption based truth maintenance system. *Artificial Intelligence,* 28.

Dell, G.S. 1986. A spreading activation theory of retrieval in sentence production. *Psychological Review,* 93, 283-321.

Dell, G.S., & Newman, J.E. 1980. Detecting phonemes in fluent speech. *Journal of Verbal Learning and Verbal Behavior,* 19, 608-623.

Dennett, D. 1981. *Brainstorms.* Sussex: Harvester Press.

Dennett, D. 1987. *The Intentional Stance.* Cambridge, MA: MIT Press.

Dennett, D. 1991. *Consciousness Explained.* Boston: Little, Brown.

Dennett, D.C. 1978. *Brainstorms: Philosophical Essays on Mind and Psychology.* Montgomery, AL: Bradford.

Dennett, D.C. 1984. *Elbow Room: The Varieties of Free Will Worth Wanting.* London: Cambridge University Press.

Descartes, R. 1637/1969. *Discourse on Method: Meditations on the First Philosophy.* New York: Dutton.

Deuchar, M. 1984. *British Sign Language.* London, U.K.: Routledge & K. Paul.

Diaz, R.M., & Klingler, C. 1991. Towards an explanatory model of the interaction between bilingualism and cognitive development. In E. Bialystok (ed.), *Language Processing in Bilingual Children* (pp. 167-192). Cambridge, U.K.: Cambridge University Press.

Doyle, J. 1979. A truth maintenance system. *Artificial Intelligence*, 12.

Dreyfus, H.L., & Dreyfus, S.E. 1985. *Mind Over Machine*. New York: Macmillan/The Free Press.

Duda, R.O., Gaschnig, J., & Hart, P.E. 1979. Model design in the PROSPECTOR consultant system for mineral exploration. In Michie (1979).

Eco, U. 1976. *A Theory of Semiotics*. Bloomington, IN: University of Indiana Press.

Eimas, P.D. 1985, January. The perception of speech in early infancy. *Scientific American*. Reprinted in W. S-Y. Wang (ed.), *Language, Writing, and the Computer* (pp. 17-23). New York: W.H. Freeman.

Ellison, M.L., & Degerton, H.A. 1941. The Thurstone Primary Mental Abilities tests and college marks. *Educational and Psychological Measurement*, 1, 399-406.

Epstein, R. 1992. The quest for the thinking computer. In *AI Magazine*, Vol. 13, No. 2, Summer 1992.

Erman, L.D., Hayes-Roth, F., Lesser, V., & Reddy, D. 1980. The HEARSAY II speech understanding system: Integrating knowledge to resolve uncertainty. *Computing Surveys*, 12(2), 213-253.

Erman, L.D., London, P.E., & Fickas, S.F. 1981. The design and an example use of HEARSAY III. In *Proceedings IJCAI-7*.

Ernst, G.W., & Newell, A. 1969. *GPS: A Case Study in Generality and Problem Solving*. New York: Academic Press.

Estes, W.K. 1963. *Learning Theory and Mental Development*. New York: Academic Press.

Fahlman, S.E. 1981. Representing duplicit knowledge, In *Parallel Models of Associative Memory*, G.E. Kinter & J.A. Anderson (eds.), Hillsdale, NJ: Erlbaum.

Falkenhainer, B.K., Forbus, D., & Gentner D. 1989. The structure mapping engine: Algorithm and examples. *Artificial Intelligence*, 41(1), 1-64.

Feigenbaum, E.A. 1963. The simulation of verbal learning behavior. In Feigenbaum & Feldman (1963).

Feigenbaum, E.A. & Feldman, J. (eds.), 1963. *Computers and Thought.* New York: McGraw-Hill.

Feigenbaum, E.A., & Simon, H.A. 1984. EPAM-like models of recognition and learning, *Cognitive Science*, 8, 305-336.

Feigenbaum, E.A., Barr, A., & Cohen, P.R. 1989. *The Handbook of Artificial Intelligence,* Vols. I - IV. New York: Addison-Wesley.

Ferguson, C.A. 1977. Baby talk as a simplified register. In C.E. Snow & C.A. Ferguson (eds.), *Talking to Children: Language Input and Acquisition* (pp. 209-235). Cambridge, U.K.: Cambridge University Press.

Fikes, R.E., Hart, P.E., & Nilsson, N.J. 1972. Learning and executing generalized robot plans. *Artificial Intelligence,* 3(4), 251-88.

Fikes, R.E., & Nilsson, N.J. 1971. STRIPS: A new approach to the application of theorem proving to artificial intelligence. *Artificial Intelligence*, 1(2).

Fillmore, C.J. 1968. The case for case. In Bach & Harms (1968).

Fisher, D. 1987. Knowledge acquisition via incremental conceptual clustering. *Machine Learning*, 2, 139-172.

Fisher, D.H., Jr., Pazzani, M.J., & Langley, P. 1991. *Concept Formation: Knowledge and Experience in Unsupervised Learning.* San Mateo, CA: Morgan Kaufmann Publishing.

Fishman, P.M. 1983. Interaction: The work women do. In B. Thorne, C. Kramarae & N. Henley (eds.), *Language, Gender and Society* (pp. 89-101). Rowley, MA: Newbury House Publishers.

Flanagan, O.J. 1984. Cognitive psychology and artifical intelligence: Philosophical assumptions and implications. In *The Science of Mind.* Boston, MA: Bradford Books (MIT Press).

Fodor, J.A. 1975. *The Language of Thought.* Cambridge, MA: Harvard University Press.

Fodor, J.A. 1980. Methodological solipsism considered as a research strategy in cognitive psychology. *Behavioral and Brain Sciences*, 3, 63-73.

Fodor, J.A. 1981. *Representations*. Cambridge, MA: The MIT Press.

Fodor, J.A. 1983. *The Modularity of Mind*. Cambridge, MA: The MIT Press.

Fodor, J.A., & Pylyshyn, Z.W. 1988. Connectionism and cognitive architecture: A critical analysis. *Cognition*, 28, 3-71.

Forrest, S. 1993. Genetic algorithms: Principles of natural, selection applied to computation. *Science*, 261, 872-878.

Forster, K.I. 1990. Lexical processing. In D.N. Osherson & H. Lasnik (eds.), *Language: An Invitation to Cognitive Science,* Vol. 1 (pp. 95-131). Cambridge, MA: The MIT Press.

Foss, D.J., & Jenkins, C.M. 1973. Some effects of context on the comprehension of ambiguous sentences. *Journal of Verbal Learning and Verbal Behavior*, 12, 577-589.

Frake, C.O. 1964. How to ask for a drink in Subanun. *American Anthropologist*, 66, 127-132.

Freeman, J.A., & Skapura, D.M. 1991. *Neural Networks: Algorithms, Applications, and Programming Techniques*. New York: Addison-Wesley.

Frege, G. 1884. *De Grundlagen der Arithmetic*. Breslau: W. Koeber.

Freud, S. 1920/1966. *A General Introduction to Psychoanalysis*, authorized English translation of the revised edition by J. Riviere. New York: Washington Square Press.

Fromkin, V.A. 1973, December. Slips of the tongue. *Scientific American*. Reprinted in W. S-Y. Wang (ed.), *Language, Writing, and the Computer* (pp. 151-157). New York: W.H. Freeman.

Fry, D.B., Abramson, A.S., Eimas, P.D., & Liberman, A.M. 1962. The identification and discrimination of synthetic vowels. *Language and Speech*, 5, 171-189.

Galilei, G. 1638/1914. *Dialogues Concerning Two New Sciences*. (A reprint and translation.) New York: MacMillan.

Garfield, J.L. (ed.), 1987. *Modularity in Knowledge Representation and Natural Language Understanding*. Cambridge, MA: Bradford Books, MIT Press.

Garrett, M.F. 1990. Sentence processing. In D.N. Osherson & H. Lasnik (eds.), *Language: An Invitation to Cognitive Science*, Vol. 1. Cambridge, MA: The MIT Press.

Garrett, M.F., Bever, T.G., & Fodor, J.A. 1966. The active use of grammar in speech perception. *Perception & Psychophysics*, 1, 30-32.

Gennari, J.H., Langley, P., & Fisher, D. 1989. Models of incremental concept formation. *Artificial Intelligence*, 40(1-3), 11-62.

Gentner, D. 1983. Structure-mapping: A theoretical framework for analogy. *Cognitive Science* 7, 155-170.

Gernsbacher, M.A., & Hargreaves, D. 1992. The privilege of primacy: Experimental data and cognitive explanations. In D.L. Payne (ed.), *Pragmatics of Wordorder Flexibility* (pp. 83-116). Amsterdam.

Geschwind, N., & Levitsky, W. 1968. Left-right asymmetries in temporal speech region. *Science*, 161, 186-187.

Gibbs, R.W. 1979. Contextual effects in understanding indirect requests. *Discourse Processes*, 2, 1-10.

Gibson, E.J. 1940. A systematic application of the concepts of generalization and differentiation to verbal learning. *Psychological Review*, 47, 196-229.

Givon, T. 1984. *Syntax: A Functional-Typological Introduction*. Amsterdam:John Benjamins.

Glick, M.L., & Holyoak, K.J. 1980. Analogical problem solving. *Cognitive Psychology*, 12, 306-355.

Gluck, M., & Corter, J. 1985. Information, uncertainty and the utility of categories. *Seventh Annual Conference of the Cognitive Science Society* in Irvine, CA.

Godel, K. 1931. Uber formal unentscheidbare Satze der Principia Mathematica und verwandter Systeme I. *Monatatshefte fur Mathematik und Physik*, 38, 173-198.

Goldberg, E., & Costa, L.D. 1981. Hemisphere differences in the acquisition and use of descriptive systems. *Brain and Language,* 14, 144-173.

Goldin-Meadow, S. 1982. The resilience of recursion: A study of a communication system developed without a conventional language model. In E. Wanner & L. Gleitman (eds.), *Language Acquisition: The State of the Art.* Cambridge University Press.

Goodwin, C. 1981. *Conversational Organization: Interaction Between Speakers and Hearers.* New York: Academic Press.

Gould, S.J. 1977. *Ontogeny and Phylogeny.* Cambridge, MA: Belknap Press.

Gould, S.J. 1979. Panselectionist pitfalls in Parker and Gibson's model of the evolution of intelligence. *The Behavioral and Brain Sciences*, 2, 385-386.

Graesser, A.C. 1981. *Prose Comprehension Beyond the Word.* New York: Springer.

Graf, P., & Schacter, D.L. 1985. Implicit and Explicit Memory for New Associations in Normal and Amnesic Subjects. In *Journal of Experimental Psychology: Learning, Memory and Cognition*, Vol. II, 511-518.

Grice, H.P. 1975. Logic and conversation. In P. Cole & J.L. Morgan (eds.), *Syntax and Semantics 3: Speech Acts.* New York: Academic Press.

Griggs, R.A., & Cox, J.R. 1982. The elusive thematic materials effect in Wason's selection task. *British Journal of Psychology*, 73, 407-420.

Grossberg, S. 1976. Adaptive pattern classification and universal recoding. I. Parallel development and coding of neural feature detectors, *Biological Cybernetics*, 23, 121-134.

Grossberg, S. 1982. *Studies of Mind and Brain: Neural Principles of Learning, Perception, Development, Cognition, and Motor Control.* Boston: Reidel Press.

Grossberg, S. (ed.), 1988. *Neural Networks and Natural Intelligence*. Cambridge, MA: MIT Press.

Grosz, B.J., & Sidner, C.L. 1990. Plans for discourse, 417-444. In P.R. Cohen & M.E. Pollack (eds.), *Intentions in Communication*. Cambridge: MIT Press.

Guilford, J.P. 1956. The structure of intellect. *Psychological Bulletin*, 53, 267-293.

Gumperz, J.J. 1982. Interethnic communication. Chapter 8 of Discourse Strategies (pp. 171-186). Cambridge, U.K.: Cambridge University Press.

Gumperz, J.J., Aulakh, G., & Kaltman, H. 1982. Thematic structure and progression in discourse. In J.J. Gumperz (ed.), *Language and Social Identity*, (pp. 22-56). Cambridge, UK: Cambridge University Press.

Gur, R.C., Gur, R.E., Obrist, W., Hungerbuhler, D., Younkin, D., Rosen, A., Skolnick, B., & Reivich, M. 1982. Sex and handedness differences in cerebral blood flow during rest and cognitive activity. *Science*, 217, 659-660.

Hall, R.P. 1989. Computational approaches to analogical reasoning: A comparitive analysis. *Artificial Intelligence*, 39(1): 39-120.

Halliday, M.A.K., 1967. Theme and information in the English clause. Extract from some aspects of the thematic organisation of the English clause. Santa Monica, CA: The Rand Corporation (R.M. 5224 P-R).

Halliday, M.A.K. 1970. Language structure and language function. In J. Lyons (ed.), *New Horizons in Linguistics* (pp. 140-165). Harmondsworth, England: Penguin Books.

Halliday, M.A.K. 1975. *Learning How to Mean: Explorations in the Development of Language*. London, U.K.: Edward Arnold.

Halliday, M.A.K., 1976. *Halliday: System and function in language; Selected papers*. London, U.K.: Oxford University Press.

Halliday, M.A.K., & Hasan, R. 1976. *Cohesion in English*. London, U.K.: Longman.

Harlow, H.F. 1949. The formation of learning sets. *Psychological Review*, 56, 51-65.

Harmon, P., & King, D. 1985. Expert Systems: Artificial Intelligence in Business. New York: Wiley.

Haugeland, J. (ed.), 1981. *Mind Design: Philosophy, Psychology, Artificial Intelligence.* Cambridge, MA: MIT.

Hayes, P. J. 1979. The logic of frames. In Metzing (1979).

Hayes, J.R., & Simon, H.A. 1974. Understanding written problem instructions. In L.W. Gregg (ed.), *Knowledge and Cognition.* Potomac, MD: Erlbaum.

Hebb, D.O. 1949. *Organization of Behavior.* NewYork: John Wiley.

Hecht-Nielsen, R. 1982. Neural analog processing. *Proc. SPIE*, 360, 180-89, Bellingham, WA.

Hecht-Nielsen, R. 1987. Counterpropagation networks. *Applied Optics*, 26, 4979-4984, December 1987.

Hecht-Nielsen, R. 1989. Theory of the backpropagation neural network. *Proc. of the Int. Joint Conf. on Neural Networks, I*, 593-611. New York: IEEE Press.

Hecht-Nielsen, R. 1990. *Neurocomputing.* New York: Addison-Wesley.

Heidegger, M. 1962. *Being and Time.* Translated by J. Masquarrie and E. Robinson. New York: Harper and Row.

Heider, E.R. 1972. Universals in color naming and memory. *Journal of Experimental Psychology*, 93, 10-20.

Hillis, D.W. 1985. *The Connection Machine.* Cambridge: MIT Press.

Hinsley, D., Hayes, J., & Simon, H. 1977. From words to equations: Meaning and representation in algebra word problems. In Carpenter & Just (1977).

Hinton, G.E., & Sejnowski, T.E. 1986. Learning and relearning in Boltzmann machines. In McClelland et al. (1986).

Hintzman, D.L. 1986. "Schema abstraction" in a multiple-trace memory model. *Psychological Review*, 93, 411-428.

Hobbes, T. 1651/1965. *Leviathan* (reprint). New York: Dutton.

Hockett, C.F. 1960. The origin of speech. *Scientific American.* Reprinted in W.S-Y. Wang (ed.), *Human Communication: Language and Its psychobiological Bases.* (pp. 4-18). New York: W.H. Freeman.

Hogaboam, T.W., & Perfetti, C.A. 1975. Lexical ambiguity and sentence comprehension. *Journal of Verbal Learning and Verbal Behavior,* 14, 265-274.

Holland, J.H. 1986. Escaping brittleness: The possibilities of general purpose learning algorithms applied to parallel rule-based systems. In Michalski, Carbonell, & Mitchell (1986).

Holland, J.H., Holyoak, K.J., Nisbett, R.E., & Thagard, P.R. 1986. *Induction: Processes of Inference, Learning and Discovery.* Cambridge, MA: MIT Press.

Holyoak, K.J. 1985. The pragmatics of analogical transfer. *The Psychology of Learning and Motivation,* 19, 59-87.

Hopcroft, J.E., & Ullman, J.D. 1979. *Introduction to Automata Theory, Languages and Computation.* Reading, MA: Addison-Wesley.

Hopfield, J.J. 1982. Neural networks and physical systems with emergent collective computational abilities. *Proceedings of the National Academy of Sciences,* 79.

Hopfield, J.J. 1984. Neural networks and physical systems with emergent collective computational abilities. *Proceedings of the National Academy of Sciences,* 79, 2554-2558.

Horowitz, E., & Sahni, S. 1978. *Fundamentals of Computer Algorithms.* Rockville, MD: Computer Science Press.

Hume, D. 1748. *An Inquiry Concerning Human Understanding.* New York: Bobbs-Merril.

Husserl, E. 1970. *The Crisis of European Sciences and Transcendental Phenomenology,* translated by D. Carr. Evanston, IL: Northwestern University Press.

Hymes, D.H. 1971. On communicative competence. Philadelphia: University of Pennsylvania Press. Excerpts reprinted in J.B. Pride & J. Holmes (eds.), 1972. *Sociolinguistics* (pp. 269-293). Harmondsworth, U.K.: Penguin Books.

Jacobs, B., Schall, M., & Scheibel, A.B. 1993. A quantitative dendritic analysis of Wernicke's area in humans. II. Gender, hemispheric, and environmental factors. *Journal of Comparative Neurology*, 327, 97-111.

Jerison, H.J. 1975. *The Evolution of the Brain and Intelligence*. New York: Academic Press.

Jessor, R., & Hammond, K.R. 1957. Construct validity and the Taylor anxiety scale. *Psychological Bulletin*, 54(3), 161-170.

Johnson, P.J., & Bailey, D.E. 1966. Some determinants of the use of relationships in discrimination learning. *Journal of Experimental Psychology*, 71, 365-372.

Johnson-Laird, P.N. 1983. *Mental Models: Towards a Cognitive Science of Language, Inference, and Consciousness*. Cambridge, MA: Harvard Univesity Press.

Johnson-Laird, P.N., & Wason, P.C. (eds.), 1977. *Thinking: Readings in Cognitive Science*. Cambridge, U.K.: Cambridge University Press.

Kandel, E.R., & Jessell, T.M. 1991. Touch. In E.R. Kandel, J.H. Schwartz, & T.M. Jessel (eds.), *Principles of Neural Science*, 3rd Ed., 367-384.

Kandel, E.R., Schwartz, A.L., & Jessell, T.M. 1991. *Principles of Neural Science*, 3rd Ed. Norwalk, CT: Appleton & Lange.

Kant, I. 1781/1964. *Immanuel Kant's Critique of Pure Reason.*. Smith, N.K (translator). New York: St. Martin's press.

Karmiloff-Smith, A. 1992. *Beyond Modularity: A Developmental Perspective on Cognitive Science*. Cambridge, MA: MIT Press.

Kedar-Cabelli, S. 1988. Analogy - From a unified perspective. In Helman (1988).

Kimura, D. 1983. Sex differences in cerebral organization for speech and praxic functions, *Canadian Journal of Psychology*, 37, 19-35.

Kintsch, W. 1974. *The Representation of Meaning in Memory*. Hillsdale, NJ: Erlbaum.

Kintsch, W., & Keenan, J.M. 1973. Reading rate and retention as a function of the number of propositions in the base structure of sentences. *Cognitive Psychology*, 5, 257-274.

Kintsch, W., Kozminsky, E., Streby, W.J., McKoon, G., & Keenan, J. 1975. Comprehension and recall of text as a function of content variables. *Journal of Verbal Learning and Verbal Behavior*, 14, 196-214.

Klahr, D., Langley, P., & Neches, R. (eds.), 1987. *Production System Models of Learning and Development*. Cambridge, MA: MIT Press.

Kodratoff, Y., & Michalski, R.S. (eds.), 1990. *Machine Learning: An Artificial Intellience Approach,* Vol. 3. Los Altos, CA: Morgan Kaufmann Publishing.

Kohonen, T. 1972. Correlation matrix memories, IEEE Trans. *Computers*, 4, 353-359.

Kohonen, T. 1984. *Self-Organization and Associative Memory.* Berlin: Springer-Verlag.

Kolb, B., & Whishaw, I.Q. 1990. *Fundamentals of Human Neuropsychology.* New York: W.H. Freeman.

Kolmogorov, A.N. 1957. On the representation of continuous functions of many variables by superposition of continuous functions of one variable and addition, in Russian. *Dokl. Akad. Nauk USSR*, 114, 953-956.

Kolodner, J.L. 1984. *Retrieval and Organization Strategies in Conceptual Memory: A Computer Model.* Northvale, NJ: Erlbaum.

Kolodner, J.L. 1988. Retrieving events from a case memory: A parallel implementation. J.L. Kolodner (ed.), *Proceedings of the Case-Based Reasoning Workshop.* Los Altos, CA: Morgan Kaufmann.

Kolodner, J.L. 1993. *Case-Based Reasoning.* San Mateo, CA: Morgan Kaufmann.

Kosko, B. 1988. Bidirectional associative memories. *IEEE Transactions Systems, Man & Cybernetics*, 18, 49-60.

Kosslyn, S.M. 1981. The medium and the message in mental imagery: A theory. *Psychological Review*, 88, 46-65.

Kowalski, R. 1979a. Algorithm = Logic + Control. *Communications of the ACM*, 22, 42, 4-436.

Kowalski, R. 1979b. *Logic for Problem Solving*. Amsterdam: North Holland.

Koza, J.R. 1991. Genetic evolution and co-evolution of computer programs. In Langton et al. (1991).

Kuhl, P.K., & Miller, J.D. 1978. Speech perception by the chinchilla: Identification functions for synthetic VOT stimuli. *Journal of the Acoustical Society of America*, 63, 905-917.

Kuhn, T.S. 1962. *The Structure of Scientific Revolutions*. Chicago: Universtiy of Chicago Press.

Labov, W. 1972. *Language in the Inner City*. Philadelphia: University of Pennsylvania Press.

Lachman, R., Lachman, J.L., & Butterfield, E.C. 1979. *Cognitive Psychology and Information Processing*. Hillsdale, NJ: Erlbaum.

Laird, J., Lehman, J.F., Rosenbloom, P., & Simon, T. 1993. Symposium in memory of Allen Newell. In *Proceedings of the Fifteenth Annual Conference of the Cognitive Science Society*. Hillsdale, NJ: Lawrence Erlbaum.

Laird, J., Rosenbloom, P., & Newell, A. 1986. *Universal Subgoaling and Chunking: The Automatic Generation and Learning of Goal Hierarchies*. Dordrecht: Kluwer.

Lakoff, G. 1987. *Women, Fire, and Dangerous Things*. Chicago: University of Chicago Press.

Lakoff, R. 1973. Language and woman's place. *Language in Society*, 2, 45-79.

Langacker, R.W., 1987. *Foundations of Cognitive Grammar*. Stanford, CA: Stanford University Press.

Langley, P., Simon, H.A., Bradshaw, G.L., & Zytkow, J.M. 1987. *Scientific Discovery: Computational Explorations of the Creative Processes*. Cambridge, MA: MIT Press.

Larkin, J.H., McDermott, J., Simon, D.P., & Simon, H.A. 1980. Models of competence in solving physics problems. *Cognitive Science*, 4.

Larkin, J.H., & Simon, H.A. 1987. Why a diagram is sometimes worth ten thousand words. *Cognitive Science*, 11, 65-99.

Lasnik, H., & Uriagereka, J. 1988. *A Course in GB Syntax*. Cambridge, MA: MIT Press.

Lave, J. 1988. *Cognition in Practice*. Cambridge, MA: Cambridge University Press.

Lawrence, D.H., & DeRivera, J. 1954. Evidence for relational discrimination. *Journal of Comparative Physiological Psychology*, 47, 465-471.

Lazlow, E. 1972. *The Systems View of the World*. New York: George Braziller.

Lebowitz, M. 1986. Integrated learning: Controlling explanation. *Cognitive Science*, 10, 219-240.

Lenat, D.B. 1983. EURISKO: A program that learns new heuristics. *Artificial Intelligence*, 21 (1 & 2), 61-98.

Lenat, D.B., & Brown, J.S. 1984. Why AM and Eurisko appear to work. *Artificial Intelligence*, 23(3).

Lesser, V.R., & Corkill, D.D. 1983, The distributed vehicle monitoring testbed. *AI Magazine*, 4, 3.

Levelt, W.J.M. 1989. *Speaking: From Intention to Articulation*. Cambridge, MA: MIT Press (Bradford Books).

Levesque, H. 1984. Foundations of a functional approach to knowledge representation. *Artificial Intelligence*, 23(2).

Levinson, S. 1983. *Pragmatics*. Cambridge, U.K.: Cambridge University Press.

Lewicki, P., Czyzewaska, M., & Hoffman, H. 1987. Unconscious acquisition of complex procedural knowledge. *Journal of Experimental Psychology: Learning, Memory, and Cognition*, 13, 523-530.

Lewis, D.J. 1979. Psychobiology of active and inactive memory. *Psychological Bulletin*, 86, 1054-1083.

Lewis, R.L. 1992. *Recent Developments in the NL-Soar Garden Path Theory.* Pittsburgh: Carnegie Mellon University, School of Computer Science Technical report, CS-92-141.

Liberman, A.M., Harris, K.S., Hoffman, H.S., & Griffith, B.C. 1957. The discrimination of speech sounds within and across phoneme boundaries. *Journal of Experimental Psychology*, 54, 358-368.

Liberman, A.M., & Mattingly, I.G. 1985. The motor theory of speech perception revisited. *Cognition*, 21, 1-36.

Lieberman, P. 1984. *The Biology and Evolution of Language.* Cambridge, MA: Harvard University Press.

Lindsay, R.K., Buchanan, E.A., Feigenbaum, E.A., & Lederberg, J. 1980. *Applications of Artificial Intelligence for Organic Chemistry: The DENDRAL project.* New York: McGraw-Hill.

Locke, J. 1690/1970. *An Essay Concerning Human Understanding.* Cambridge, U.K.: The University Press.

Luger, G.F. 1976. The use of the state-space to record the behavioral effects of subproblems and symmetries in the Tower of Hanoi problem. *International Journal Man-Machine Studies*, 8.

Luger, G.F. 1981. Mathematical model building in the solution of mechanics problems: Human protocols and the MECHO trace. *Cognitive Science, 5,* 55-77.

Luger, G.F., & Bauer, M.A. 1978. Transfer effects in isomorphic problem solving. *Acta Psychologia, 42,* 121-131.

Luger, G.F., & Stern, C. 1993. Expert systems and the abductive circle. In R.J. Jorna, van Heusden, & R. Posner (eds.), *Signs, Search and Communication.* Berlin: Walter D. Gruyter.

Luger, G.F., & Stubblefield, W.A. 1993. *Artificial Intelligence: Structures and Strategies for Complex Problem Solving.* Redwood City, CA: Benjamin/ Cummings.

Luger, G.F., Wishart, J.G., & Bower, T.G.R. 1984. Modelling the stages of the identity theory of object-concept development in infancy. *Perception*, 13, 97-115.

MacKay, D.G. 1978. Derivational rules and the internal lexicon. *Journal of Verbal Learning and Verbal Behavior*, 17, 61-71.

MacWhinney, B. 1977. Starting points. *Language*, 152-168.

Maier, D., & Warren, D. S. 1988. *Computing with Logic*. Menlo Park, CA: Benjamin Cummings.

Maier, N.R.F. 1931. Reasoning in humans, II. The solution of a problem and its appearance in consciousness. *Journal of Comparative Psychology*, 12, 181-194.

Malpas, J. 1987. *PROLOG: A Relational Language and Its Applications*. Englewood Cliffs, NJ: Prentice Hall.

Mandler, J.M. 1982. Some uses and abuses of a story grammar. *Discourse Processes*, 5, 305-318.

Mandler, J.M., & Goodman M. 1982. On the psychological validity of story structure. *Journal of Verbal Learning and Verbal Behavior*, 21, 507-523.

Mandler, J.M., & Johnson, N.S. 1977. Remembrance of things parsed: Story structure and recall. *Cognitive Psychology*, 9, 111-151.

Marcel, A.J. 1983. Concious and unconscious perception: An approach to the relations between phenomenal experience and perceptual process. *Cognitive Psychology*, 15, 238-300.

Markov, A. 1954. *A Theory of Algorithms*. Moscow: National Academy of Sciences.

Marr, D. 1982. *Vision: A Computational Investigation into the Human Representation and Processing of Visual Information*. San Francisco, CA: Freeman.

Marslen-Wilson, W.D. 1984. Function and process in spoken work recognition: A tutorial review. In H. Bouman & D.G. Bouwhuis (eds.), *Attention and Performance X: Control of Language Processes* (pp. 125-150), Hillsdale, NJ: Lawrence Erlbaum.

Marslen-Wilson, W.D., & Tyler, L.K. 1987. Against modularity. In J.L. Garfield (ed.), *Modularity in Knowledge Representation and Natural Language Understanding* (pp. 37-62). Cambridge, MA: MIT Press (Bradford Books).

Marslen-Wilson, W., & Welsh, A. 1978. Processing interactions and lexical access during word recognition in continuous speech. *Cognitive Psychology*, 10, 29-63.

Mason, C., & Kandel, E.R. 1991. Central visual pathways. In *Principles of Neural Science*, 3rd Ed., 420-437

Masterman, M. 1961. Semantic message detection for machine translation, using Interlingua. *Proceedings of the 1961 International Conference on Machine Translation.*

Matthews, P.H. 1991. *Morphology: An Introduction to the Theory of Word Structure,* 2nd Ed. Cambridge, U.K.: Cambridge University Press.

McCarthy, J. 1968. Programs with common sense. In Minsky (1968), 403-418.

McCarthy, J. 1980. Circumscription - A form of non-monotonic reasoning. *Artificial Intelligence,* 13.

McCarthy, J., & Hayes, P. J. 1969. Some philosophical problems from the standpoint of artificial intellience. In Meltzer & J. McCarthy (1977). Epistemological problems in artificial intelligence. *Proceedings IJCAI-77*, 1038-1044.

McCloskey, M. 1991. Networks and theories: A place of connectionism in cognitive science. *Psychological Science*, Vol. 2, No. 6 (pp. 387-395).

McCord, M.C. 1982. Using slots and modifiers in logic grammars for natural lang uage. *Artificial Intelligence,* 18, 327-367.

McCord, M.C. 1986. Design of a PROLOG based machine translation system. In *Proceedings of the Third International Logic Programming Conference.* London.

McCulloch, W.S., & Pitts, W. 1943. A logical calculus of the ideas immanent in nervous activity. *Bulletin of Mathematical Biophysics,* 5, 115-133.

Mead, C. 1989. *Analog VLSI and Neural Systems*. Reading, MA: Addison-Wesley.

Mecacci, L. 1993. On spatial frequencies and cerebral hemispheres: Some remarks from the electrophysiological and neuropsychological points of view. *Brain and Cognition*, 22, 199-212.

Mehler, J. 1963. Some effects of grammatical transformations on the recall of English sentences. *Journal of Verbal Learning and Verbal Behavior*, 2, 250-262.

Mervis, C.B., & Mervis, C.A. 1982. Leopards are kitty-cats: Object labelling by mothers for their thirteen-month-olds. *Child Development*, 53, 267-273.

Meyer, D.E., & Schvaneveldt, R.W. 1971. Facilitation in recognizing pairs of words: Evidence of a dependence between retrieval operations. *Journal of Experimental Psychology*, 90, 227-234.

Michalski, R.S., Carbonell, J.G., & Mitchell, T.M. (eds.), 1983. *Machine Learning: An Artificial Intelligence Approach,* Vol. 1. Palo Alto, CA: Tioga.

Michalski, Ryszard S., Carbonell J.G., & Mitchell, T.M. (eds.), 1986. *Machine Learning: An Artificial Intelligence Approach*, Vol. 2. Los Altos, CA: Morgan Kaufmann.

Michalski, Ryszard, S., & Stepp, R.E. 1983. Learning from observation: conceptual clustering. In Michalski, Carbonell, & Mitchell (1983).

Miller, G.A., & McKean, K.O. 1964. A chronometric study of some relations between sentences. *Quarterly Journal of Experimental Psychology*, 16, 297-308.

Miller, J.L. 1990. Speech perception. In D.N. Osherson & H. Lasnik (eds.), *Language: An Invitation to Cognitive Science*, Vol. 1 (pp. 69-93). Cambridge, MA: The MIT Press.

Minsky, M. 1975. A framework for representing knowledge. In Brachman & Levesque (1985).

Minsky, M., & Papert, S. 1969. *Perceptrons: An Introduction to Computational Geometry.* Cambridge, MA: MIT Press.

Minton, S. 1988. *Learning Search Control Knowledge.* Dordrecht: Kluwer Academic Publishers.

Mitchell, T.M. 1982. Generalization as search. *Artificial Intelligence*, 18(2), 203-226.

Mitchell, T.M, Keller, R.M., & Kedar-Cabelli, S.T. 1986. Explanation-based generalization: A unifying view. *Machine Learning*, 1, 47-80.

Moore, G.E. 1986. *G.E. Moore: The Early Essays*. Philadelphia, PA: Temple University Press.

Moore, R.C. 1982. The role of logic in knowledge representation and common-sense reasoning. *Proceedings AAAI-82*.

Moore, O.K., & Anderson, S.B. 1954. Modern logic and tasks for experiments on problem solving behavior. *Journal of Psychology*, 38, 151-160.

Morton, J., & Long, J. 1976. Effect of word transition probability on phoneme identificaton. *Journal of Verbal Learning and Verbal Behavior*, 15, 43-52.

Mycroft, A., & O'Keefe, R.A. 1984. A polymorphic type system for PROLOG. *Artificial Intelligence,* 23, 295-307.

Mylopoulos, J., & Levesque, H.J. 1984. An overview of knowledge representation. In M.L. Brodie, J. Mylopoulos, & J.W. Schmidt (eds.), *On Conceptual Modeling*. New York: Springer Verlag.

Nauta, W.J.H., & Feirtag, M. 1979. The organization of the brain. *Scientific American*.

Neisser, U. 1982. *Memory Observed*. San Francisco, CA: Freeman.

Nelson, K. 1973. Structure and strategy in learning to talk. *Monographs of the Society for Research in Child Development*, 38.

Nelson, M.E., & Bower, J.M. 1990. Brain maps and parallel computers. *Trends in Neurosciences*, 13, 403-408.

Neves, J.C.F.M, Luger, G.F., & Carvalho, J.M. 1986. A formalism for views in a logic data base. In *Proceedings of the ACM Computer Science Concerence*, Cincinatti, OH (1986).

Newell, A. 1955. The chess machine: An example of dealing with a complex task by adaptation. *Proceedings of the Western Joint Computer Conference*, 7.

Newell, A. 1962. Some problems of the basic organization in problem solving programs. In M.C. Yovits (ed.), *Proceedings of the Second Conference on Self-Organizing Systems.*

Newell, A. 1969. Heuristic programming: Ill-structured problems, In J. Aronsky (ed.), *Progress in Operations Research.* New York: John Wiley.

Newell, A. 1973. You can't play 20 questions with nature and win: Projective comments on the papers of this symposium. In W.G. Chase (ed.), *Visual Information Processing.* New York: Academic Press.

Newell, A. 1982. The knowledge level. *Artificial Intelligence,* 18(1), 87-127.

Newell, A. 1990. *Unified Theories of Cognition.* Cambridge, MA: Harvard University Press.

Newell, A., & Simon, H. 1956. The logic theory machine. *IRE Transactions of Information Theory,* 2, 61-79.

Newell, A., & Simon, H. 1963a. GPS: A program that simulates human thought. In Feigenbaum & Feldman (1963).

Newell, A., & Simon, H. 1963b. Empirical explorations with the logic theory machine: a case study in heuristics. In Feigenbaum & Feldman (1963).

Newell, A., & Simon, H. 1972. *Human Problem Solving.* Engelwood Cliffs, NJ: Prentice Hall.

Newell, A., & Simon, H. 1976. Computer science as empirical inquiry: symbols and search. *Communications of the ACM,* 19(3), 113-126.

Newman, J.E. 1985. Processing spoken discourse: Effects of position and emphasis on judgments of textual coherence. *Discourse Processes,* 8, 205-227.

Newman, J.E., & Dell, G.S. 1978. The phonological nature of phoneme monitoring: A critique of some ambiguity studies. *Journal of Verbal Learning and Verbal Behavior,* 17, 359-374.

Nii, H.P. 1986. Blackboard Systems, I. *AI Magazine,* 7, 2, 38-53.

Nii, H.P., & Aiello, N. 1979. AGE: A knowledge based program for building knowledge based programs. *Proceedings IJCAI-6.*

Nilsson, N. 1965. *Learning Machines*, New York: McGraw-Hill.

Nilsson, N.J. 1980. *Principles of Artificial Intelligence*. Palo Alto, CA: Tioga.

Nisbett, R.E., & Wilson, T.D. 1977. Telling more than we know: Verbal reports on mental processes. *Psychological Review*, 84, 231-259.

Nordhausen, B., & Langley, P. 1990. An integrated approach to empirical discovery. In Shrager & Langley (1990).

Norman, D.A. 1972. Memory, knowledge and the answering of questions. *CHIP Technical Report 25*, Center for Human Information Processing, University of California, San Diego.

Norman, D.A. 1981. *Perspectives on Cognitive Science*. Hillsdale, NJ: Erlbaum.

Norman, D.A., Rumelhart, D.E., & The LNR Research Group. 1975. *Explorations in Cognition*. San Francisco, CA: Freeman.

Ojemann, G.A. 1983. Brain organization from the perspective of electrical stimulation mapping. *The Behavioral and Brain Sciences*, 6, 189-230.

O'Keefe, R. 1990. *The Craft of PROLOG*. Cambridge, MA: MIT Press.

Oliphant, G.W. 1983. Repetition and recency effects in word recognition. *Austrailian Journal of Psychology*, 35, 393-403.

Paivio, A. 1971. *Imagery and Verbal Processes*. New York: Holt, Rinehart, & Winston.

Palmer, S.E. 1978. Fndamental aspects of cognitive representation. In E. Rosch & B.B. Lloyd (eds.), *Cognition and Categorization*.

Pasqual-Leone, A., & Torres, F. 1993. Plasticity of the sensori-motor cortex representation of the reading finger in Braille readers. *Brain*, 116, 39-52.

Pearl, J. 1984. *Heuristics: Intelligent Strategies for Computer Problem Solving*. Reading, MA: Addison-Wesley.

Pearl, J. 1988. *Probabilistic Reasoning in Intelligent Systems: Networks of Plausible Inference*. Los Altos, CA: Morgan Kaufman.

Peirce, C.S. 1958. *Collected Papers 1931-1958.* Cambridge, MA: Harvard University Press.

Penfield, W. & Rasmussen, T. 1950. *The Cereberal Cortex of Man: A Clinical Study of Localization of Function.* New York: Macmillan.

Penrose, R. 1989. *The Emperor's New Mind.* New York: Oxford University Press.

Periera, F., & Warren, D.H.D. 1980. Definite clause grammars for language analysis: A survey of the formalism and a comparison with augmented transition networks. *Artificial Intelligence,* 13, 231-278.

Petersen, S.E., & Fiez, J.A. 1993. The processing of single words studied with position emission tomography. *Annual Review of Neuroscience,* 16, 509-530.

Peterson, L.R., & Peterson, M.J. 1959. Short term retention of individual verbal items. *Journal of Experimental Psychology,* 58, 193-198.

Phillips, S.U., Steele, S., & Tanz, C. (eds.), 1987. *Language, Gender, and Sex in Comparative Perspective.* Cambridge, U.K., University Press.

Piaget, J. 1931. Children's Philosophies. In C. Murchison (ed.), *Handbook of Child Psychology.* Worcester, MA: Clark University Press.

Piaget, J. 1954. *The Construction of Reality in The Child.* New York: Basic Books .

Piaget, J. 1970. *Structuralism.* New York: Basic Books.

Pinker, S. 1992. Review of Bickerton's *Language and Species. Language,* 68, 375-382.

Pinker, S. 1994. *The Language Instinct.* New York: William Monroe & Company.

Pinker, S., & Bloom, P. 1990. Natural language and natural selection. *Behavioral and Brain Sciences,* 13, 707-784

Pinker, S., & Bloom, P. 1992. Natural language and natural selection. In J.H. Barkow, L. Cosmides, & J. Tooby (eds.), *The Adapted Mind.* New York: Oxford Press.

Platt, R.D., & Griggs, R.A. 1993. Darwinian algorithms and the Wason selection task: A factorial analysis of social contract selection. *Cognition,* 48, 163-192.

Polk, T.A. 1992. *Verbal Reasoning.* Pittsburgh: Carnegie Mellon University, School of Computer Science, Doctoral Dissertation.

Popper, K.R. 1959. *The Logic of Scientific Discovery.* London, U.K.: Hutchinson.

Posner, M.I. 1978. *Chronometric Explorations of Mind.* Hillsdale, N.J.: Erlbaum.

Posner, M.I. (ed.), 1989. *Foundations of Cognitive Science.* Cambridge, MA: MIT Press.

Posner, M.I., & Boies, S.J. 1971. Components of attention. *Psychological Review,* 78, 391-408.

Posner M.I., & Keele, S.W. 1968. On the genesis of abstract ideas. *Journal of Experimental Psychology,* 77, 393-403.

Post, E. 1943. Formal reductions of the general combinatorial problem. *American Journal of Mathematics,* 65, 197-268.

Pratt, M.L. 1977. *Towards a Speech Act Theory of Literary Discourse.* Bloomingon, IN: Indiana University Press.

Prince, E.F. 1981a. Topicalization, focus-movement, and Yiddish-movement: A pragmatic differentiation. In D.K. Alford, K.A. Hunold, M.A. Macaulay, J. Walter, C. Brugman, P. Chertok, I. Civikulis, & M. Tobey (eds.), *Proceedings of the 7th Annual Meeting of the Berkeley Linguisitcs Society* (pp. 249-264). Berkeley, CA: Berkeley Linguistics Society.

Prince, E.F. 1981b. Toward a taxonomy of given-new information. In P. Cole (ed.), *Radical Pragmatics* (pp. 223-255). New York: Academic Press.

Prince, E.F. 1992. The ZPG letter: Subjects, definiteness, and information-status. In W.C. Mann & S. Thompson (eds.), *Discourse Description: Diverse Linguistic Analyses of a Fund-Raising Text* (pp. 295-325). Philadelphia, PA: John Benjamins Publishing Co.

Putnam, H. 1988. *Representation and Reality.* Cambridge, MA: MIT Press.

Pylyshyn, Z.W. 1973. What the mind's eye tells the mind's brain: A critique of mental imagery. *Psychological Bulletin*, 80, 1-24.

Pylyshyn, Z.W. 1980. The causal power of machines. *Behavioral and Brain Sciences*, 3, 442-444.

Pylyshyn, Z.W. 1981. The imagery debate: Analogue media versus tacit knowledge. *Psychological Review*, 88, 16-45.

Pylyshyn, Z.W. 1984. Computation and Cognition: Toward a Foundation for *Cognitive Science*. Cambridge, MA: MIT.

Quillian, M.R. 1967. Word concepts: A theory and simulation of some basic semantic capabilities. In Brachman & Levesque (1985).

Quine, W.V.O. 1963. *From a Logical Point of View*, 2nd Ed. New York: Harper Torchbooks.

Quinlan, J.R. 1983. Learning efficient classification procedures and their application to chess endgames. In Michalski, Carbonell, & Mitchell (1983).

Quinlan, J.R. 1986a. Induction of decision trees. *Machine Learning*, 1(1), 81-106.

Quinlan, J.R. 1986b. The effect of noise on concept learning. In Michalski et al. (1986).

Quinlan, P. 1991. *Connectionism and Psychology*. Chicago, IL: University of Chicago Press.

Rayner, K., Carlson, M., & Frazier, L. 1983. The interaction of syntax and semantics during sentence processing: Eye movements in the analysis of semantically biased sentences. *Journal of Verbal Learning and Verbal Behavior*, 22, 358-374.

Reddy, D.R. 1976. Speech recognition by machine: A review. *Proceedings of the IEEE 64* (May).

Reed, J., & Johnson P. 1994. Assessing implicit learning with indirect tests: Determining what is learned about sequence structure. *Journal of Experimental Psychology: Learning, Memory, and Cognition*.

Reed, S.K., Ernst, G., & Banerji, R.B. 1974. The role of analogy in transfer between similar problem states. *Cognitive Psychology*, 6, 436.

Reich, P.A., & Dell, G.S. 1977. Finiteness and embedding. In R.J. DiPietro, & E.L. Blansitt (eds.), *The Third LACUS Forum*. Columbia, SC: Hornbeam Press.

Reilly, R.G., & Sharkey, N.E. (eds.), 1992. *Connectionist Approaches to Natural Language Processing*. Hillside, NJ: L. Erlbaum.

Reinhart, T. 1981. Pragmatics and linguistics: An analysis of sentence topics. *Philosophica*, 27, 53-94.

Reiter, R. 1980. A logic for default reasoning, *Artificial Intelligence*, 13, 81-132.

Reitman, W.R. 1965. *Cognition and Thought*. New York: Wiley.

Rochester, N., Holland, J.H., Haibit, L.H., & Duda, W.L. 1988. Test on a cell assembly theory of the actuation of the brain, using a large digital computer. In J.A. Anderson & E. Rosenfeld (eds.), *Neurocomputing: Foundations of research*, 68079. Cambridge, MA: MIT Press.

Rochester, S., & Martin, J.R. 1979. *Crazy Talk: A Study of the Discourse of Schizophrenic Speakers*. New York: Plenum Press.

Rosch, E. 1973. On the internal structure of perceptual and semantic categories. In T.E. Moore (ed.), *Cognitive Development and the Acquisition of Language* (pp. 111-444). New York: Academic Press.

Rosch, E. 1975. Cognitive representations of semantic categories. *Journal of Experimental Psychology: General*, 104, 192-233.

Rosch, E. 1978. Principles of categorization. In Rosch & Lloyd (1978).

Rosch, E., & Lloyd, B.B. (eds.), 1978. *Cognition and Categorization*. Hillsdale, NJ: Erlbaum.

Rosch, E., & Mervis, C.B. 1975. Family resemblances: Studies in the internal structure of categories. *Cognitive Psychology*, 8, 382-439.

Rosch, E., Mervis, C.B., Gray, W.D., Johnson, D.M., & Boyes-Braem, P. 1976. Basic objects in natural categories. *Cognitive Psychology*, 8, 382-439.

Rosenblatt, F. 1958. The perceptron: A probablistic model for information storage and organization in the brain. *Psychological Review*, 65, 386-408.

Rosenblatt, F. 1962. *Principles of Neurodynamics*. New York: Spartan.

Rosenbloom, P.S., Lehman, J.F., & Laird, J.E. 1993. Overview of Soar as a unified theory of cognition: Spring 1993. In *Proceedings of the Fifteenth Annual Conference of the Cognitive Science Society*. Hillsdale, NJ: L. Erlbaum.

Rosenbloom, P.S., & Newell, A. 1987. Learning by chunking, a production system model of practice. In Klahr et al. (1987).

Ross, P. 1989. *Advanced PROLOG*. Reading, MA: Addison-Wesley.

Rumelhart, D.E. 1977. Understanding and summarizing brief stories. In D. LaBerge & S.J. Samuels (eds.), *Basic Processes in Reading: Perception and comprehension*. Hillsdale, NJ: L. Erlbaum Associates.

Rumelhart, D.E., Lindsay, P.H., & Norman, D.A. 1972. A process model for long-term memory. In Tulving & Donaldson (1972).

Rumelhart, D.E., & McClelland, J.L. 1986. PDP models and general issues in cognitive science. In D.E. Rummelhart & J.L. McClelland (eds.), *Parallel Distributed Processing. Explorations in the Microstructure of Cognition*. Cambridge, MA:MIT Press.

Rumelhart, D.E., & McClelland, J.L. 1986. On learning the past tenses of English verbs. In Rumelhart, D.E., & McClelland, J.L. (eds.), *Parallel Distributed Processing. Explorations in the Microstructure of Cognition*. Cambridge, MA:MIT Press(1986).

Rumelhart, D.E., McClelland, J.L., & The PDP Research Group. 1986. *Parallel Distributed Processing*, Vol. 1. Cambridge, MA: MIT Press.

Rumelhart, D.E., & Norman, D.A. 1973. Active semantic networks as a model of human memory. *Proceedings IJCAI-3*.

Russell, B. 1956. *Logic and Knowledge; Essays, 1901-1950*. London, U.K.: G. Allen & Unwin.

Russell, S.J. 1989. *The Use of Knowledge in Analogy and Induction*. San Mateo, CA: Morgan Kaufmann.

Ryle, G. 1949. *The Concept of Mind*. Chicago, IL: University of Chicago Press.

Sachs, J.S. 1967. Recognition memory for syntactic and semantic aspects of connected discourse. *Perception & Psychophysics*, 2, 437-442.

Sacks, H., Schegloff, E.A., & Jefferson, G.A. 1974. A simplest systematics for the organization of turn-taking for conversation. *Language*, 50, 696-735.

Savage-Rumbaugh, E.S., Rumbaugh, D.M., & Boysen, S. 1980. Do apes use language? *American Scientist*, 68, 49-61.

Savage-Rumbaugh, E.S., Murphy, J., Sevcik, R.A., Brakke, K.E., Williams, S.L., & Rumbaugh, D.M. 1993. Language comprehension in ape and child, *Momographs of the Society for Research in Child Development*, Serial No 233, V. 58, 3-4.

Schank, R.C. 1982. *Dynamic Memory: A Theory of Reminding and Learning in Computers and People*. London, U.K.: Cambridge University Press.

Schank, R.C. 1986. *Explanation Patterns: Understanding Mechanically and Creatively*. Northvale, NJ: Erlbaum.

Schank, R.C., & Abelson, R. 1977. *Scripts, Plans, Goals and Understanding*. Hillsdale, NJ: Erlbaum.

Schank, R.C., & Colby, K.M. (eds.), 1973. *Computer Models of Thought and Language*. San Francisco, CA: Freeman.

Schank, R.C., & Nash-Webber, B.L. (eds.), 1975. *Theoretical Issues in Natural Language Processing*. Association for Computational Linguistics.

Schank, R.C., & Reiger, C.J. 1974. Inference and the computer understanding of natural language. *Artificial Intelligence,* 5(4), 373-412.

Schank, R.C., & Riesbeck, C.K. (eds.), 1981. *Inside Computer Understanding: Five Programs Plus Miniatures*. Hillsdale, NJ: Erlbaum.

Schegloff, E.A. 1968. Sequencing in conversational openings. *American Anthropologist*, 70, 1075-1095.

Scherbel, A.B. 1990. Dendritic correlate of higher cognitive function. In A.B. Scherbel & A.-F. Wechsler (eds.), *Neurobiology of Higher Cognitive Function* (pp. 239-270). New York: Guilford Press.

Scheibel, A.B. 1990. Dendritic correlates of higher cognitive function. In A.B. Scheibel & A.W. Wechsler (Eds.), *Neurobiology of Higher Cognitive Function*, New York: Guilford Press, Pg. 239-270.

Searle, J.R. 1969. *Speech Acts*. London, U.K.: Cambridge University Press.

Searle, J.R. 1980. Minds, brains and programs. *The Behavioral and Brain Sciences*, 3, 417-424.

Searle, J.R. 1992. *The Rediscovery of the Mind*. Cambridge, MA: MIT Press.

Seboek, T.A. 1985. *Contributions to the Doctrine of Signs*. Lanham, MD: University Press of America.

Sejnowski, T.J., & Churchland, P.S. 1989. *Brain and Cognition*. In M. Posner (1989).

Sejnowski, T.J., & Rosenberg C.R. 1987. Parallel networks that learn to pronounce english text. *Complex Systems,* 1, 145-168.

Selfridge, O. 1959. Pandemonium: A paradigm for learning. *Symposium on the Mechanization of Thought*. London: HM Stationery Office.

Seltz, O. 1913. *Uber die Gesetze des Geordneten Denkverlaufs*. Stuttgart: Spemann.

Seltz, O. 1922. *Zur Psychologie des Produktiven Denkens und des Irrtums*. Bonn: Friedrich Cohen.

Semmes, J. 1968. Hemisphere specialization: A possible clue to mechanism. *Neuropsychologia*, 6, 11-26.

Sergent, J. 1982. The cerebral balance of power: Confrontation or cooperation? *Journal of Experimental Psychology: Human Perception and Performance*, 8, 253-272.

Sergent, J. 1983. Role of input in visual hemispheric asymmetries. *Psychological Bulletin*, 93, 481-512.

Shafer, G., & Pearl, J. (eds.), 1990. *Readings in Uncertain Reasoning.* Los Altos, CA: Morgan Kaufmann.

Shallice, T. 1988. *From Neuropsychology to Mental Structures.* New York: Cambridge University Press.

Shankweiler, D.P., & Studdert-Kennedy, M. 1967. Identification of consonants and vowels presented to left and right ears. *Quarterly Journal of Experimental Psychology,* 19, 59-63.

Shannon, C. 1948. *A Mathematical Theory of Communication.* Bell System Technical Journal.

Shapiro, S.C. (ed.), 1992. *Encyclopedia of Artificial Intelligence.* New York: Wiley.

Shavlik, J.W., & Dietterich, T.G. (eds.), 1990. *Readings in Machine Learning.* San Mateo, CA: Morgan Kaufmann.

Shavlik, J.W., Mooney, R.J., & Towell, G.G. 1991. Symbolic and neural learning algorithms: An experimental comparison. *Machine Learning,* 6(1), 111-143.

Shepherd, G.M. 1979. *The Synaptic Organization of the Brain.* New York: Oxford University Press.

Shepherd, G.M. 1991. The significance of real neuron architectures for neural network simulations. In E. Schwartz (ed.), *Computational Neuroscience.*

Shepard, R.N., & Metzler, J. 1971. Mental rotation of three-dimensional objects. *Science,* 171, 701-703.

Shrager, J., & Langley, P. (eds.), 1990. *Computational Models of Scientific Discovery and Theory Formation.* San Mateo, CA: Morgan Kaufmann.

Sidner, C.L. 1983. Focusing and discourse. *Discourse Processes,* 6, 107-130.

Siegelman, H. & Sontag, E.D. 1991. Neural networks are universal computing devices. *Technical Report SYCON 91-08.* New Jersey: Rutgers Center for Systems and Control.

Simmons, R.F. 1973. Semantic networks: Their computation and use for understanding english sentences. In Schank (1972).

Simon, D.P., & Simon, H.A. 1978. Individual differences in solving physics problems. In Siegler (1978).

Simon, H.A. 1981. *The Sciences of the Artificial,* 2nd Ed. Cambridge, MA: MIT Press.

Simon, H.A. 1983. Why should machines learn? In Michalski, Carbonell & Mitchell (1983).

Simon, H.A. 1991. *Models of My Life.* New York: Basic Books.

Simon, H.A., & Ericsson, 1984. *Protocol Analysis.* Cambridge, MA: MIT Press.

Sims, M.H. 1987. Empirical and analytic discovery in IL. *Proceedings of the Fourth International Workshop on Machine Learning.* Los Altos, CA: Morgan Kaufmann.

Singley, M.K., & Anderson, J.R. 1989. *The Transfer of Cognitive Skill.* Cambridge, MA: Harvard University Press.

Skinner, B.F. 1953. *Science and Human Behavior.* New York: MacMillan.

Skinner, B.F. 1957. *Verbal Behavior.* New York: Appleton-Century-Crofts.

Sleeman, D. 1982. Assessing aspects of competence in basic algebra. In Sleeman & Brown (1982).

Slobin, D.I. (ed.), 1985. *The Cross-Linguistic Study of Language Acquistion: Volume 1: The Data.* Hillsdale, NJ: L. Erlbaum.

Smith, E.E., Shoben, E.J., & Rips, L.J. 1974. Structure and process in semantic memory: A featural model for semantic decisions. *Psychological Review,* 81, 214-241.

Smolensky, P. 1988. On the proper treatment of connectionism. *Behavioral and Brain Sciences,* 11, 1-74.

Smolensky, P., Legendre, G., & Miyata, Y. 1992. *Principles for an Integrated Connectionist/Symbolic Theory of Higher Cognition.* Boulder, CO: University of Colorado Computer Sceince Technical Report, CU-CS-600-92.

Snow, C.E. 1977. Mother's speech research: From input to interaction. In C.E. Snow & C.A. Ferguson (eds.), *Talking to Children: Language Input and Acquisition* (pp. 31-49). Cambridge, U.K.: Cambridge University Press.

Soloway, E., Rubin, E., Woolf, B., Bonar, J., & Johnson, W.L. 1983. MENO-II: an AI-based programming tutor. *Journal of Computer Based Instruction,* 10(1,2).

Solso, R.L. 1991. *Cognitive Psychology.* Boston: Allyn & Bacon.

Sowa, J.F. 1984. *Conceptual Structures: Information Processing In Mind and Machine.* Reading, MA: Addison-Wesley.

Spence, K.W. 1956. *Behavior Theory and Conditioning.* New Haven, CT: Yale University Press.

Spencer, H. 1885. *The Principles of Psychology.* New York: Appleton.

Sperber, D., & Wilson, D. 1986. *Relevance: Communication and Cognition.* Cambridge, MA: Harvard University Press.

Sperling, G. 1960. The information available in brief visual presentations. *Psychological Monographs,* 74 (Entire No. 498).

Squire, L.R. 1987. *Memory and Brain.* Oxford: Oxford University Press.

Squire, L.R. 1992. Memory and the hippocampus: A synthesis from findings with rats, monkeys, and humans. *Psychological Review,* 99, 195-231.

Squire, L.R., & Zola-Morgan, S. 1991. The medial temporal lobe memory system. *Science,* 253, 1380-1386.

Staudenmayer, H. 1975. Understanding conditional reasoning with meaningful propositions. In R.C. Falmagne (ed.), *Reasoning: Representation and Process.* Hillside, NJ: Erlbaum.

Steele, G.L. 1989. *Common LISP: The Language,* 2nd Ed. Bedford, MA: Digital Press.

Sterling, L., & Shapiro, E. 1986. *The Art of PROLOG: Advanced Programming Techniques.* Cambridge, MA: MIT Press.

Stern, C., & Luger, G.F. 1992. A model for abductive problem solving based on explanation templates and lazy evaluation. *International Journal of Expert Systems*, 5, 3.

Sternberg, R.J. (ed.), 1982. *Advances in the Psychology of Human Intelligence (I-X)*. Hillsdale, NJ: Erlbaum.

Sternberg, S. 1966. High speed scanning in human memory. *Science*, 153, 652-654.

Sternberg, S. 1969a. The discover of processing stages: Extensions of Donder's method. *Acta Psychologica*, 30, 276-315.

Sternberg, S. 1969b. Memory scanning: Mental processes revealed by reaction time experiments. *American Scientist*, 57, 421-457

Stitch, S.P. 1983. *From Folk Psychology to Cognitive Science*. Cambridge, MA: MIT Press (Bradford Books).

Stokoe, W.C. 1978. *Sign Language Structure*. Silver Spring, MD: Linstok Press.

Stubbs, M. 1983. *Discourse Analysis: The Sociolinguistic Analysis of Natural Language*. Chicago, IL: University of Chicago Press.

Stytz, M.P., & Frieder, O. 1990. Three-dimensional medical imagery modalities: An Overview. *Critical Review of Biomedical Engineering*, 18, 11-25.

Swinney, D.A. 1979. Lexical access during sentence comprehension: (Re)consideration of context effects. *Journal of Verbal Learning and Verbal Behavior*, 18, 645-660.

Symons, D. 1992. On the use and misuse of darwinism in the study of human behavior. In J.H. Barkow, L. Cosmides, & J. Tooby (eds.), *The Adapted Mind*. New York: Oxford Press.

Tabossi, P. 1988. Accessing lexical ambiguity in different types of sentential contexts. *Journal of Memory and Language*, 27, 324-340.

Tabossi, P., & Zardon, Z 1993. Processing ambiguous words in context. *Journal of Memory and Language*, 32, 359-372.

Taft, M., & Forster, K.I. 1976. Lexical storage and retrieval of polymorphemic and polysyllabic words. *Journal of Verbal Learning and Verbal Behavior*, 15, 607-620.

Tanenhaus, M.K. 1988. Psycholinguistics: An overview. In F.J. Newmeyer (ed.), *Linguistics: The Cambridge Survey III, Language: Psychological and Biological Aspects* (pp. 1-37). Cambridge, U.K.: Cambridge University Press.

Tannen, D. 1984. *Conversational Style: Analyzing Talk Among Friends*. Norwood, NJ: Ablex Publishing Company.

Tannen, D. 1989. *Talking Voices: Repetition, Dialogue, and Imagery in Conversational Discourse*. Cambridge, U.K.: Cambridge University Press.

Tannen, D. 1990. *You Just Don't Understand: Women and Men in Conversation*. New York: William Morrow and Company.

Tarski, A. 1944. The semantic conception of truth and the foundations of semantics. *Philos. and Phenom. Res.* 4, 341-376.

Taylor, I. 1990. *Psycholinguistics: Learning and Using Language* (with M.M. Taylor). Englewood Cliffs, NJ: Prentice-Hall.

Terrace, H.S. 1983. Apes who "talk": Language or projection of language by their teachers? In J. de Luce & H.T. Wilder (eds.), *Language in Primates: Perspectives and Implications* (pp. 19-42). New York: Springer-Verlag.

Thagard, P. 1988. Dimensions of analogy. In Helman (1988).

Thorndyke, P.W. 1977. Cognitive structures in comprehension and memory of narrative discourse. *Cognitive Psychology,* 9, 77-110.

Thurstone, L.L. 1938. Primary mental abilities. *Psychometric Monographs, I.* (a).

Touretzky, D.S. 1986. *The Mathematics of Inheritance Systems*. Los Altos, CA: Morgan Kaufmann.

Tulving, E., & Donaldson, W. 1972. *Organization of Memory*. New York: Academic Press.

Turner, R. 1984. *Logics for Artificial Intelligence*. Chichester: Ellis Horwood Ltd.

Tyler, L.K., & Marslen-Wilson, W. 1977. The on line effects of semantic context on syntactic processing. *Journal of Verbal Learning and Verbal Behavior*, 16, 683-692.

van Emden, M., & Kowalski, R. 1976. The semantics of predicate logic as a programming language. *Journal of the ACM*, 23, 733-742,

Vera, A.H., & Simon, H.A. 1993. Situated action: A symbolic interpretation. *Cognitive Science*, 17, 7-48.

von Glasersfeld, E. 1978. An introduction to radical constructivism. In P. Watzlawick (ed.), *The Invented Reality* (pp. 17-40). New York: Norton.

Walker, A., McCord, M., Sowa, J., & Wilson, W. 1987. *Knowledge Systems and PROLOG: A Logical Approach to Expert Systems and Natural Language Processing*. Reading, MA: Addison-Wesley.

Wall, J.T., & Kaas, J.H. 1985. Critical reorganization and sensory recovery following nerve damage and regeneration. In C.W. Catman (ed.), Synoptic Plasticity (pp. 231-260). New York: Guilford Press.

Wallman, J. 1992. *Aping Language*. Cambridge, U.K.: Cambridge University Press.

Ward, B. 1991. *ET-Soar: Towards an ITS for Theory Based Representations*. Pittsburgh: Carnegie Mellon University, School of Computer Science, Doctoral Dissertation.

Warren, R.M. 1970. Perceptual restoration of missing speech sounds. *Science*, 167, 392-395,

Warren-Leubecker, A., & Bohannon, J.N., III. 1989. Pragmatics: Language in social contexts. In J.B. Gleason (ed.), The development of language, 2nd Ed. (pp. 327-368). Columbus, OH: Merrill Publishing.

Wason, P.C. 1966. Reasoning. In B. Foss (ed.), *New Horizons in Psychology*. Harmondsworth Middlesex: Penguin.

Watson, J.B. 1930. *Behaviorism* (rev. ed.). New York: Norton.

Weismeyer, M., & Laird, J. 1993. NOVA, covert attention explored through unified theories of cognition. In *Proceedings of the Fifteenth Annual Conference of the Cognitive Science Society*. Hillsdale, NJ: Lawrence Erlbaum.

Weiss, S.M., & Kulikowski, C.A. 1991. *Computer Systems that Learn*. San Mateo, CA: Morgan Kaufmann.

Weizenbaum, J. 1976. *Computer Power and Human Reason*. San Francisco, CA: W. H. Freeman.

Werner, H. 1957. *Comparative Psychology of Mental Development*. New York: International University Press.

West, C., & Zimmerman, D.H. (1983). Small insults: A study of interruptions in cross-sex conversations between unacquainted persons. In B. Thorne, C. Kramarae, & N. Henley (eds.), *Language, Gender and Society* (pp. 103-117). Rowley, MA: Newbury House Publishers.

Weyrauch, R.W. 1980. Prolegomena to a theory of mechanized formal reasoning. *Artificial Intelligence,* 13(1,2), 133-170.

Whitehead, A.N., & Russell, B. 1950. *Principia Mathematica,* 2nd Ed. London, U.K.: Cambridge University Press.

Whorf, B.L. 1956. *Language, Thought and Reality: Selected Writings of Benjamin L. Whorf*, J.B. Carroll (ed.). Cambridge, MA: MIT Press.

Wickelgren, W.A. 1965. Acoustic similarity and intrusion errors in short-term memory. *Journal of Experimental Psychology*, 70, 102-108.

Wickelgren, W.A. 1975. The long and the short of memory. *Psychological Bulletin*, (80), 425-438.

Widrow, B., & Hoff, M.E. 1960. Adaptive switching circuits. *1960 IRE WESTCON Convention Record,* 96-104, New York.

Wilks, Y.A. 1972. *Grammar, Meaning and the Machine Analysis of Language*. London, U.K.: Routledge & K. Paul.

Winograd, T., & Flores, F. 1986. *Understanding Computers and Cognition*. Norwood, NJ: Ablex.

Winston, P.H. 1975a. Learning structural descriptions from examples. In Winston (1975b).

Winston, P.H. (ed.), 1975b. *The Psychology of Computer Vision*. New York: McGraw-Hill.

Witelson, S.F. 1991. Structural correlates of cognition in the human brain. In A.B. Scheibel & A. Wechsler (eds.), *Neurobiology of Higher Cognitive Function*. New York: Guilford Press.

Wittgenstein, L. 1933. Tractatus Logico-Philosophicus, 2nd Ed., London, U.K.: K. Paul, Trench, Trubner; New York: Harcourt Brace.

Wittgenstein, L. 1953. *Philosophical Investigations*. New York: Macmillan.

Wolstencroft, J. 1989. Restructuring, reminding and repair: What's missing from models of analogy. *AICOM* 2(2), 58-71.

Woods, W. 1985. What's in a link: Foundations for semantic networks. In Brachman & Levesque (1985).

Wundt, W. 1910. *Principles of Philosophical Psychology*. Translated by E.B. Kitchner. New York: MacMillan

Wundt, W. 1912. The psychology of the sentence. From *Die Sprache*, sections from Chap. 7, *Die Satzfugng*, Book 2, Vol I of the *Volkerpsychologie* series. in Blumenthal (1980).

Yeo, R.A. 1989. Individual differences. In E.D. Bigler, R.A. Yeo, & E. Turkheimer. *Neuropsychological Function and Brain Imaging*. New York: Plenum.

Young, R.M. 1976. *Seriation by Children: An Artificial Intelligence Analysis of a Piagetian Task*. Basel: Birkhauser.

Young, R.M., & O'Shea, T. 1981. Errors in children's subtraction. *Cognitive Science*, 5, 153-177.

Zadeh, L.A. 1983. Common sense knowledge representation based on fuzzy logic. *Computer*, 16, 61-65.

Zeaman, D., & House, B.J. 1963. The role of attention in retardate discrimination learning. In N.R. Ellis (ed.), *Handbook of Mental Deficiency.* New York: McGraw-Hill.

Ziff, P. 1972. *Understanding Understanding.* Ithaca, NY: Cornell University-Press.

Zimmerman, D.H. & West, C. 1975. Sex roles, interruptons and silences in conversation. In B. Thorne & N. Henley (eds.), *Language and Sex: Difference and Dominance* (pp. 105-129). Rowley, MA: Newbury House Publishers.

Zurada, J.M. 1992. *Introduction to Artificial Neural Systems.* New York: West Publishing.

INDEX